Lecture Notes in Computer Science 10168

Commenced Publication in 1973
Founding and Former Series Editors:
Gerhard Goos, Juris Hartmanis, and Jan van Leeuwen

More information about this series at http://www.springer.com/series/7407

Frank Drewes · Carlos Martín-Vide
Bianca Truthe (Eds.)

Language and Automata Theory and Applications

11th International Conference, LATA 2017
Umeå, Sweden, March 6–9, 2017
Proceedings

Springer

Editors
Frank Drewes
Umeå University
Umeå
Sweden

Bianca Truthe
University of Giessen
Giessen
Germany

Carlos Martín-Vide
Rovira i Virgili University
Tarragona
Spain

ISSN 0302-9743 ISSN 1611-3349 (electronic)
Lecture Notes in Computer Science
ISBN 978-3-319-53732-0 ISBN 978-3-319-53733-7 (eBook)
DOI 10.1007/978-3-319-53733-7

Library of Congress Control Number: 2017931058

LNCS Sublibrary: SL1 – Theoretical Computer Science and General Issues

Printed on acid-free paper

This Springer imprint is published by Springer Nature
The registered company is Springer International Publishing AG
The registered company address is: Gewerbestrasse 11, 6330 Cham, Switzerland

Preface

These proceedings contain the papers that were presented at the 11th International Conference on Language and Automata Theory and Applications (LATA 2017), held in Umeå, Sweden, during March 6–9, 2017.

The scope of LATA is rather broad, including: algebraic language theory, algorithms for semi structured data mining, algorithms on automata and words, automata and logic, automata for system analysis and program verification, automata networks, automatic structures, codes, combinatorics on words, computational complexity, concurrency and Petri nets, data and image compression, descriptional complexity, foundations of finite-state technology, foundations of XML, grammars (Chomsky hierarchy, contextual, unification, categorial, etc.), grammatical inference and algorithmic learning, graphs and graph transformation, language varieties and semigroups, language-based cryptography, mathematical and logical foundations of programming methodologies, parallel and regulated rewriting, parsing, patterns, power series, string processing algorithms, symbolic dynamics, term rewriting, transducers, trees, tree languages and tree automata, weighted automata.

LATA 2017 received 73 submissions. Every paper was reviewed by three Program Committee members. There were also a few external experts consulted. After a thorough and vivid discussion phase, the committee decided to accept 31 papers (which represents an acceptance rate of about 42%). The conference program included four invited talks.

The excellent facilities provided by the EasyChair conference management system allowed us to deal with the submissions successfully and handle the preparation of these proceedings in time.

We would like to thank all invited speakers and authors for their contributions, the Program Committee and the external reviewers for their cooperation, and Springer for its very professional publishing work.

December 2016

Frank Drewes
Carlos Martín-Vide
Bianca Truthe

Preface

Organization

LATA 2017 was organized by the Department of Computing Science at the University of Umeå, Sweden, and the Research Group on Mathematical Linguistics (GRLMC) at the Rovira i Virgili University in Tarragona, Spain.

Program Committee

Eric Allender	Rutgers University, Piscataway, USA
Amihood Amir	Bar-Ilan University, Ramat Gan, Israel
Christel Baier	Technical University of Dresden, Germany
Armin Biere	Johannes Kepler University Linz, Austria
Avrim Blum	Carnegie Mellon University, Pittsburgh, USA
Ondřej Bojar	Charles University in Prague, Czech Republic
Jin-Yi Cai	University of Wisconsin, Madison, USA
Liming Cai	University of Georgia, Athens, USA
Alessandro Cimatti	Bruno Kessler Foundation, Trento, Italy
Rocco De Nicola	IMT School for Advanced Studies Lucca, Italy
Rod Downey	Victoria University of Wellington, New Zealand
Frank Drewes	Umeå University, Sweden
Zoltan Fülöp	University of Szeged, Hungary
Gregory Gutin	Royal Holloway, University of London, UK
Lane A. Hemaspaandra	University of Rochester, USA
Dorit S. Hochbaum	University of California, Berkeley, USA
Deepak Kapur	University of New Mexico, Albuquerque, USA
Marek Karpinski	University of Bonn, Germany
Joost-Pieter Katoen	RWTH Aachen University, Germany
Evangelos Kranakis	Carleton University, Ottawa, Canada
Lars Kristensen	Bergen University College, Norway
Kim G. Larsen	Aalborg University, Denmark
Axel Legay	Inria, Rennes, France
Leonid Libkin	University of Edinburgh, UK
Carsten Lutz	University of Bremen, Germany
João Marques-Silva	University of Lisbon, Portugal
Carlos Martín-Vide (Chair)	Rovira i Virgili University, Tarragona, Spain
Mitsunori Ogihara	University of Miami, Coral Gables, USA
Arlindo Oliveira	Instituto Superior Técnico, Lisbon, Portugal
David Parker	University of Birmingham, UK
Madhusudan Parthasarathy	University of Illinois, Urbana-Champaign, USA
Doron A. Peled	Bar Ilan University, Ramat Gan, Israel
Dominique Perrin	Paris-Est Marne-la-Vallée University, France
Jean-Eric Pin	Paris Diderot University, France
Sanguthevar Rajasekaran	University of Connecticut, Storrs, USA

Bruce Reed	McGill University, Montréal, Canada
Wojciech Rytter	University of Warsaw, Poland
Kunihiko Sadakane	University of Tokyo, Japan
Davide Sangiorgi	University of Bologna, Italy
Helmut Seidl	Technical University of Munich, Germany
Jens Stoye	Bielefeld University, Germany
Wing-Kin Sung	National University of Singapore, Singapore
Dimitrios M. Thilikos	CNRS, LIRMM, France and National and Kapodistrian University of Athens, Greece
Ioannis G. Tollis	University of Crete, Heraklion, Greece
Bianca Truthe	University of Giessen, Germany
Frits Vaandrager	Radboud University, Nijmegen, The Netherlands
Rob Van Glabbeek	CSIRO, Sydney, Australia

Organizing Committee

Yonas Demeke	University of Umeå, Sweden
Frank Drewes (Co-chair)	University of Umeå, Sweden
Petter Ericson	University of Umeå, Sweden
Anna Jonsson	University of Umeå, Sweden
Carlos Martín-Vide (Co-chair)	Rovira i Virgili University, Tarragona, Spain
Manuel Jesús Parra Royón	University of Granada, Spain
Bianca Truthe	University of Giessen, Germany
Niklas Zechner	University of Umeå, Sweden

Additional Reviewers

Aceto, Luca
Allauzen, Cyril
Asín Achá, Roberto Javier
Bangalore, Srinivas
Bès, Alexis
Biondi, Fabrizio
Björklund, Henrik
Chen, Yijia
Choffrut, Christian
D'Alessandro, Flavio
Demri, Stéphane
Doerr, Daniel
Droste, Manfred
Dubslaff, Clemens
Fahrenberg, Uli
Forys, Wit
Gasarch, William
Gulan, Stefan
Han, Yo-Sub
Hermelin, Danny
Holzer, Markus
Iván, Szabolcs
Kamiyama, Naoyuki
Kutrib, Martin
Lanese, Ivan
Leiß, Hans
Lhoussaine, Cédric
Lombardy, Sylvain
López, Damián
Maletti, Andreas
Matheja, Christoph
Mezzina, Claudio Antares
Mikulski, Łukasz
Moerman, Joshua
Mossakowski, Till
Nagano, Kiyohito
Nayak, Ashwin
Nederhof, Mark-Jan
Ng, Timothy
Noll, Thomas
Pearce, David
Rabbi, Fazle
Reger, Giles
Reischuk, Rüdiger
Rogojin, Vladimir
Smetsers, Rick
Sokol, Dina
Strozecki, Yann

Subramanian, K.G.
Tewari, Raghunath
Torres Vieira, Hugo
Traonouez, Louis-Marie
Tribastone, Mirco
Van Der Merwe, Brink
Varacca, Daniele
Volk, Matthias
Watrous, John
Weil, Pascal
Wendlandt, Matthias
Yakaryılmaz, Abuzer

Invited Talks

Approximation in Description Logics: How Weighted Tree Automata Can Help to Define the Required Concept Comparison Measures in $\mathcal{FL}_0$

Franz Baader, Oliver Fernández Gil, and Pavlos Marantidis

Theoretical Computer Science, TU Dresden, Dresden, Germany
{franz.baader,oliverfernandez.gil,
pavlos.marantidis}@tu-dresden.de

Abstract. Recently introduced approaches for relaxed query answering, approximately defining concepts, and approximately solving unification problems in Description Logics have in common that they are based on the use of concept comparison measures together with a threshold construction. In this paper, we will briefly review these approaches, and then show how weighted automata working on infinite trees can be used to construct computable concept comparison measures for $\mathcal{FL}_0$ that are equivalence invariant w.r.t. general TBoxes. This is a first step towards employing such measures in the mentioned approximation approaches.

Pavlos Marantidis—Supported by DFG Graduiertenkolleg 1763 (QuantLA).

LARS Stream Reasoning and Temporal Logic

Harald Beck, Minh Dao-Tran, and Thomas Eiter

TU Wien, Vienna, Austria
{fbeck,dao,eiterg}@kr.tuwien.ac.at

Abstract. In this talk, we revisit the LARS framework for logic-based reasoning on streams and contrast it with temporal logic. While there are commonalities between LARS and LTL resp. TEL (temporal equilibrium logic), respectively, there are yet differences which are discussed. Furthermore, bridging between the formalisms is explored.

1 Introduction

Stream Reasoning is a recent field of computation with broad interest[1] in which streams of data over time are considered. These streams may origin in different ways and at different velocities, ranging from low frequency updates in the realm of minutes, days, or even months, to high frequency changes such as sensor data produced in real-time environment (e.g., in transport and traffic scenarios), to very high speed changes such as of bonds at the stock market. Typically, a large amount of data is produced, and processing these large data streams requires special methods and techniques in order to cope with it.

In the database and data processing area, stream processing addresses this issue by limiting the available memory, such that only a snapshot of the data, a *window*, is kept and other data is dropped. In practice, the latter is guided by the underlying infrastructure: if data arrives in buffers, then the size of the buffer may regulate the contents that can be handled, and only the latest data is kept (tuple-based windows); alternatively, data within a certain time of arrival are kept (time-based window). In addition, arrival times of data might be dropped. The way in which windows are changed over time (continuously, periodically, etc) is another aspect of low-level data management. An important note is that ideally, dropping data does not result in a loss of information, but it may be voluntarily accepted in order to cope with the data.

This work was partially supported by the Austrian Science Fund (FWF) under projects P26471 and W1255-N23.

[1] Several workshops on this subject have been held in the recent years, e.g. in Vienna 2015 and in Berlin 2016 apart from further workshops at conferences.

2 Lars

As many of the stream processing systems have an operational semantics, LARS [1] has been proposed as a logic-based framework that provides a means to express semantics of stream processing formally, and in a declarative way. Furthermore, LARS has been conceived in order to model more expressive reasoning than plain filtering, joining and aggregation of data. To this end, a language has been proposed in which besides Boolean connectives windows are native elements, where the latter are unary operators $\boxplus^w$. Within a stream resp. window, truth of a formula ϕ everywhere ($\Box\phi$) or somewhere ($\Diamond\phi$) is expressible (the latter corresponds to *detemporalizing* data, i.e., remove time information); furthermore, an operator $@_t\phi$ enables on to evaluate the formula ϕ at the time point t.

For example, a formula $\boxplus^{60}\ \Box(tram \rightarrow \boxplus^{+5}\ \Diamond bus)$ may informally express that within the last 60 time points (say minutes), there whenever a tram arrived at a stop, within five minutes also a bus was arriving.

The semantics of the LARS language is based on streams, which are pairs $S = (T, \upsilon)$ of a closed interval $T \subseteq \mathbb{N}$ of natural numbers and an assignment $\upsilon : T \rightarrow 2^{\mathcal{A}}$ of interpretations (sets of atoms) of an underlying propositional alphabet $\mathcal{A}$. Window functions $w(S, t)$ map a stream S at a time point t of evaluation to a substream, i.e., a stream $S' = (T', \upsilon)$ such that $T' \subseteq T$ and $\upsilon' \subseteq \upsilon$.

LARS structures consist, in simplified form, of a pair $M = \langle S^{\star}, W\rangle$ of stream $S^{\star}$ and an interpretation W of the window operators, i.e., each $\boxplus^w$ is associated with a window function $w \in W$. Given a substream $S = (T, u)$ of $S^{\star}$ and a time point $t \in \mathbb{N}$, entailment $M, S, t \Vdash \phi$ of formulas ϕ is inductively defined as follows:

$$
\begin{aligned}
\phi \in \mathcal{A} &\Leftrightarrow a \in v(t), & \Diamond\phi_1 &\Leftrightarrow M, S, t' \Vdash \phi_1 \text{ for some } t' \in T,\\
\neg\phi_1 &\Leftrightarrow M, S, t \nVdash \phi_1, & \Box\phi_1 &\Leftrightarrow M, S, t' \Vdash \phi_1 \text{ for all } t' \in T,\\
\phi_1 \wedge \phi_2 &\Leftrightarrow M, S, t \Vdash \phi_1 \text{ and } M, S, t \Vdash \phi_2, & @_{t'}\phi_1 &\Leftrightarrow M, S, t' \Vdash \phi_1 \text{ and } t' \in T,\\
\phi_1 \vee \phi_2 &\Leftrightarrow M, S, t \Vdash \phi_1 \text{ or } M, S, t \Vdash \phi_2, & \boxplus^w\phi_1 &\Leftrightarrow M, S', t \Vdash \phi_1, \text{ where } S' = w(S, t),\\
\phi_1 \rightarrow \phi_2 &\Leftrightarrow M, S, t \nVdash \phi_1 \text{ or } M, S, t \Vdash \phi_2, & \triangleright\phi_1 &\Leftrightarrow M, S^{\star}, t \Vdash \phi_1.
\end{aligned}
$$

Here $\triangleright$ is a further operator that allows one to access the original input stream inside a formula (this replaces the more complicated original mechanism of stream choice). Besides the monotone semantics of LARS, also an answer set (i.e., stable model) semantics has been introduced for a rule language with nonmonotonic negation, which properly generalizes the stable model semantics of logic programs.

Deciding $M, S, t \Vdash \phi$, i.e., formula evaluation, is PSPACE-complete in general, under the assumption that window functions are evaluable in polynomial time; likewise is satisfiability, where we require $S = S^{\star}$ and that for $S^{\star} = (T, \upsilon)$ a suitable assignment υ is found. The stable semantics has the same complexity, but is lower for relevant fragments of the language.

3 Temporal Logic

LARS is apparently related to temporal logic, most prominently to LTL but also to MTL (metric temporal logic) [5]; as for the rule language, it is related to the recent formalism of temporal equilibrium logic (TEL) [4], which extends logic programs under Pearce's logical characterization of stable model semantics [6] to temporal sequences of models.

While from a complexity perspective, LTL has like LARS PSPACE complexity, these results can not be simply compared. This is not only because the formalisms have different operators, but also as the underlying problem definitions are different: in temporal logic, reasoning centers around possible future states of the system, while in stream reasoning as in LARS, it is concerned with a history of data that is considered to be input (like sensor readings) up to a query evaluation time; future evolutions would regard *predictions* of evaluation results. Furthermore, in stream reasoning repeated evaluation, possibly in an incremental manner, is regarded as important.

In this talk, we shall look more in detail into this issue, and we shall highlight commonalities and differences between LARS and temporal logic. Furthermore, we shall consider the possibility to express fragments of LARS in temporal logic, and to provide in this way alternative characterizations of LARS semantics via temporal logic. Besides monotonic LARS, we shall also consider its nonmonotonic version and discuss its relation to temporal equilibrium logic. The latter has much higher complexity than LTL and is EXPSPACE-complete [2, 3]. As arbitrary window operators in LARS are incompatible with the intuitionistic model structures for TEL, restrictions are necessary to obtain a reformulation of LARS in TEL; on the other hand, via TEL also alternative nonmonotonic semantics of LARS can be given.

This investigation aims at a better understanding of stream reasoning versus temporal logic, and to bridge between these subjects such that results and techniques developed for temporal logic can be exploited for stream reasoning.

References

1. Beck, H., Dao-Tran, M., Eiter, T., Fink, M.: LARS: A logic-based framework for analyzing reasoning over streams. In: Bonet, B., Koenig, S. (eds.) Proceedings 29th Conference on Artificial Intelligence (AAAI '15), 25–30 January 2015, Austin, Texas, USA. pp. 1431–1438. AAAI Press (2015)
2. Bozzelli, L., Pearce, D.: On the complexity of temporal equilibrium logic. In: 30th Annual ACM/IEEE Symposium on Logic in Computer Science, LICS 2015, Kyoto, Japan, 6–10 July 2015, pp. 645–656. IEEE (2015). http://dx.doi.org/10.1109/LICS.2015.65
3. Cabalar, P., Demri, S.: Automata-based computation of temporal equilibrium models. In: Vidal, G. (ed.) LOPSTR 2011, LNCS, vol. 7225, pp. 57–72. Springer, Heidelberg (2011). http://dx.doi.org/10.1007/978-3-642-32211-2_5
4. Cabalar, P., Vega, G.P.: Temporal equilibrium logic: a first approach. In: EUROCAST 2007. LNCS, vol. 4739, pp. 241–248. Springer, Heidelberg (2007). http://dx.doi.org/10.1007/978-3-540-75867-9_31

5. Koymans, R.: Specifying real-time properties with metric temporal logic. Real-Time Syst. **2** (4), 255–299 (1990)
6. Pearce, D.: Equilibrium logic. Ann. Math. Artif. Intell. **47**(1–2), 3–41 (2006)

Logic, Languages, and Rules for Web Data Extraction and Reasoning over Data

Georg Gottlob[1], Christoph Koch[2], Andreas Pieris[3]

[1]University of Oxford, Oxford, USA
georg.gottlob@cs.ox.ac.uk
[2]École Polytechnique Fédérale de Lausanne, Lausanne, Switzerland
christoph.koch@epfl.ch
[3]University of Edinburgh, Edinburgh, UK
apieris@inf.ed.ac.uk

Abstract. This paper gives a short overview of specific logical approaches to data extraction, data management, and reasoning about data. In particular, we survey theoretical results and formalisms that have been obtained and used in the context of the Lixto Project at TU Wien, the DIADEM project at the University of Oxford, and the VADA project, which is currently being carried out jointly by the universities of Edinburgh, Manchester, and Oxford. We start with a formal approach to web data extraction rooted in monadic second order logic and monadic Datalog, which gave rise to the Lixto data extraction system. We then present some complexity results for monadic Datalog over trees and for XPath query evaluation. We further argue that for value creation and for ontological reasoning over data, we need existential quantifiers (or Skolem terms) in rule heads, and introduce the Datalog$^{\pm}$ family. We give an overview of important members of this family and discuss related complexity issues.

Finite Backward Deterministic Automata on Infinite Words

Thomas Wilke

Kiel University, Kiel, Germany
thomas.wilke@email.uni-kiel.de

Around the turn of the millennium, Olivier Carton and Max Michel [1] introduced a model of automata for infinite words which here is referred to as finite *backward deterministic ω-automata*. Their main result was that their new model is equivalent with respect to expressive power to all the models studied before, be it Büchi, Muller or parity automata.

Since their introduction by Carton and Michel, backward deterministic ω-automata have been studied intensively.

In my presentation, I explain what backward deterministic ω-automata are and what they can be used for. In particular, I present the following:

- transformations between traditional ω-automata models and backward deterministic ω-automata,
- characterization of fragments of temporal logic using backward deterministic ω-automata,
- counter-free backward deterministic ω-automata and bi-machines,
- the connection between the alternation-free modal μ-calculus (and alternation in general) and backward deterministic ω-automata.

Reference

1. Carton, O., Michel, M.: Unambiguous Büchi automata. In: Gonnet, G.H., Panario, D., Viola, A. (eds.) LATIN 2000. LNCS, vol. 1776, pp. 407–416. Springer, Heidelberg (2000)

Contents

* The abstracts of all four invited talks can be found on pp. XIII–XIX.

Graphs and Petri Nets

Non-classical Automata

Pushdown Automata and Systems

Invited Talks

Approximation in Description Logics: How Weighted Tree Automata Can Help to Define the Required Concept Comparison Measures in $\mathcal{FL}_0$

Franz Baader(✉), Oliver Fernández Gil, and Pavlos Marantidis

Theoretical Computer Science, TU Dresden, Dresden, Germany
{franz.baader,oliver.fernandez,pavlos.marantidis}@tu-dresden.de

Abstract. Recently introduced approaches for relaxed query answering, approximately defining concepts, and approximately solving unification problems in Description Logics have in common that they are based on the use of concept comparison measures together with a threshold construction. In this paper, we will briefly review these approaches, and then show how weighted automata working on infinite trees can be used to construct computable concept comparison measures for $\mathcal{FL}_0$ that are equivalence invariant w.r.t. general TBoxes. This is a first step towards employing such measures in the mentioned approximation approaches.

1 Introduction

Description Logics (DLs) [5] are a well-investigated family of logic-based knowledge representation languages, which are frequently used to formalize ontologies for application domains such as biology and medicine [22]. To define the important notions of such an application domain as formal concepts, DLs state necessary and sufficient conditions for an individual to belong to a concept. These conditions can be atomic properties required for the individual (expressed by concept names) or properties that refer to relationships with other individuals and their properties (expressed as role restrictions). The expressivity of a particular DL $\mathfrak{L}$ is determined on the one hand by what sort of properties can be required and how they can be combined. On the other hand, DLs provide their users with ways of stating terminological axioms in a so-called TBox. The simplest kind of TBoxes are called acyclic TBoxes, which consist of concept definitions without cyclic dependencies among the defined concepts. Basically, such a TBox introduces abbreviations for complex concept descriptions. General TBoxes use so-called general concept inclusions (GCIs) to state subconcept-superconcept constraints between concepts. Once the relevant concepts of an application domain are formalized in a TBox, they can be employed to state information about specific entities (individuals, objects) and their relationships in a so-called ABox. Given a TBox and an ABox, queries can then be used to retrieve new information from the data formalized this way. We will introduce

P. Marantidis—Supported by DFG Graduiertenkolleg 1763 (QuantLA).

F. Drewes et al. (Eds.): LATA 2017, LNCS 10168, pp. 3–26, 2017.
DOI: 10.1007/978-3-319-53733-7_1

the basic notions of DLs in Sect. 2, and define three DLs of different expressive power, namely the DLs $\mathcal{ALC}$, $\mathcal{EL}$, and $\mathcal{FL}_0$.

Since the semantics of traditional DLs is based on classical first-order logic, the interpretation of the properties required for a concept is strict in the sense that all these properties need to be satisfied for an individual to belong to a concept, and the same is true for answers to queries. In applications where exact definitions are hard to come by, it would be useful to relax this strict requirement and allow for approximate definitions of concepts, where most, but not all, of the stated properties are required to hold. Similarly, if a query has no exact answer, approximate answers that satisfy most of the features the query is looking for could be useful. For example, in clinical diagnosis, diseases are often linked to a long list of medical signs and symptoms, but patients that have a certain disease rarely show all these signs and symptoms. Instead, one looks for the occurrence of sufficiently many of them. Similarly, people looking for a flat to rent or a bicycle to buy may have a long list of desired properties, but will also be satisfied if many, but not all, of them are met.

In order to allow for approximate definitions of concepts, we have introduced the notion of a graded membership function in [4]. Instead of a Boolean membership value 0 or 1 such a graded function yields a membership degree from the interval [0,1]. Threshold concepts can then, for example, require that an individual belongs to a concept C with degree at least 0.8. A different approach, which is based on the use of similarity measures on concepts [25], was used by Ecke et al. [19,20] to relax instance queries (i.e., queries that consist of a single concept). Given a query concept C, they are looking for answers to queries D whose similarity to C is higher than a certain threshold. While these two approaches were originally developed independently of each other, it has turned out that there are close connections. Similarity measures can be used to define graded membership functions, and threshold concepts w.r.t. these functions provide a more natural semantics for relaxed instance queries [4,6]. Thus, in both approximation approaches mentioned until now, the availability of appropriate measures for comparing concepts is crucial. The same is true for the approximate unification of concepts introduced in [8]. Basically, unification in DLs tries to make two concepts equivalent by replacing some of the concept names occurring in their descriptions by complex concepts [9,10]. In the approximate case, one requires that concepts are made "almost" equivalent, where the meaning of "almost" is formalized using distance measures between concepts. Strictly speaking, these distance measures are not similarity measures in the sense of [25] since they need not map into [0,1]. In the following, we will call functions that compare pairs of concepts by mapping them into a (usually numerical) domain equipped with a partial order *concept comparison measures.*

An indispensable requirement for the concept comparison measures used in the three approximation approaches mentioned above is that they respect the semantics of concepts in the sense that they are invariant under equivalence of concepts w.r.t. their definitions in the TBox. For the DL $\mathcal{EL}$, a framework for defining concept similarity measures that are equivalence invariant w.r.t.

acyclic TBoxes has been introduced in [25]. This was extended in [20] to general TBoxes. For $\mathcal{FL}_0$, concept similarity measures that are equivalence invariant for acyclic TBoxes were introduced in [30]. The main technical contribution of this paper is to introduce a framework for defining *computable* concept comparison measures for $\mathcal{FL}_0$ that are *equivalence invariant w.r.t. general TBoxes.* Basically, this is achieved by leveraging a new formal language-based characterization of equivalence in $\mathcal{FL}_0$ w.r.t. general TBoxes [28], where the semantics of a concept is characterized using a tuple of (possibly infinite) formal languages. Following the ideas in [10,11,28], such tuples can be represented by (infinite) trees. These trees (or more precisely, appropriate finite representations of them) can in turn be used as inputs for weighted tree automata [31], which then yield the output of the measure. We will show that, under certain conditions on the weighted tree automata, this approach indeed yields computable concept comparison measures.

2 Description Logics, Concept Comparison Measures, and Approximation

We start by recalling basic notions of Description Logics, and in particular the DLs $\mathcal{ALC}$, $\mathcal{EL}$, and $\mathcal{FL}_0$. Then, we introduce concept comparison measures, which generalize concept similarity measures, and finally we show how such measures can be used to relax query answering, approximately define concepts, and approximately solve unification problems.

2.1 Description Logics

In Description Logics, *concept constructors* are used to build complex *concept descriptions* out of *concept names* (unary predicates) and *role names* (binary predicates). A particular DL $\mathfrak{L}$ is determined by the available constructors. Given finite, disjoint sets $\mathsf{N_C}$ and $\mathsf{N_R}$ of concept names and role names, respectively, we denote the set of all concept descriptions that can be built from $\mathsf{N_C}$ and $\mathsf{N_R}$ using the constructors of $\mathfrak{L}$ with $\mathcal{C}_{\mathfrak{L}}(\mathsf{N_C}, \mathsf{N_R})$.

As an example, consider the constructors top concept ($\top$), bottom concept ($\bot$), conjunction ($C \sqcap D$), disjunction ($C \sqcup D$), negation ($\neg C$), value restriction ($\forall r.C$), and existential restriction ($\exists r.C$), which determine the DL $\mathcal{ALC}$. Then, $\mathcal{C}_{\mathcal{ALC}}(\mathsf{N_C}, \mathsf{N_R})$ is inductively defined as follows:

- $\{\top, \bot\} \cup \mathsf{N_C} \subseteq \mathcal{C}_{\mathcal{ALC}}$,
- if $C, D \in \mathcal{C}_{\mathcal{ALC}}$ and $r \in \mathsf{N_R}$, then $\{C \sqcap D, C \sqcup D, \neg C, \forall r.C, \exists r.C\} \subseteq \mathcal{C}_{\mathcal{ALC}}$.

We will also consider the following two sub-logics $\mathcal{EL}$ and $\mathcal{FL}_0$ of $\mathcal{ALC}$:

- $\mathcal{EL}$ has the constructors top concept, conjunction, *existential* restriction;
- $\mathcal{FL}_0$ has the constructors top concept, conjunction, *value* restriction.

The *semantics* of a DL $\mathfrak{L}$ is defined using first-order interpretations $\mathcal{I} = (\Delta^{\mathcal{I}}, \cdot^{\mathcal{I}})$ consisting of a non-empty domain $\Delta^{\mathcal{I}}$ and an interpretation function $\cdot^{\mathcal{I}}$

that assigns a set $A^{\mathcal{I}} \subseteq \Delta^{\mathcal{I}}$ to each concept name $A \in \mathsf{N_C}$ and a binary relation $r^{\mathcal{I}} \subseteq \Delta^{\mathcal{I}} \times \Delta^{\mathcal{I}}$ to each role name $r \in \mathsf{N_R}$. This function is extended to complex concept descriptions by assigning a set $C^{\mathcal{I}} \subseteq \Delta^{\mathcal{I}}$ to each $C \in \mathcal{C}_{\mathfrak{L}}(\mathsf{N_C}, \mathsf{N_R})$ according to the semantics of the constructors of $\mathfrak{L}$. The semantics of the constructors is defined by equations that enable the inductive definition of $C^{\mathcal{I}}$ for any interpretation $\mathcal{I}$.

For the above constructors, the equations fixing their semantics are as follows:

$$\begin{aligned}
&\top^{\mathcal{I}} = \Delta^{\mathcal{I}} \text{ and } \bot^{\mathcal{I}} = \emptyset,\\
&(C \sqcap D)^{\mathcal{I}} = C^{\mathcal{I}} \cap D^{\mathcal{I}}, (C \sqcup D)^{\mathcal{I}} = C^{\mathcal{I}} \cup D^{\mathcal{I}}, \text{ and } (\neg C)^{\mathcal{I}} = \Delta^{\mathcal{I}} \setminus C^{\mathcal{I}},\\
&(\forall r.C)^{\mathcal{I}} = \{x \in \Delta^{\mathcal{I}} \mid \forall y \in \Delta^{\mathcal{I}} : (x, y) \in r^{\mathcal{I}} \Rightarrow y \in C^{\mathcal{I}}\},\\
&(\exists r.C)^{\mathcal{I}} = \{x \in \Delta^{\mathcal{I}} \mid \exists y \in \Delta^{\mathcal{I}} : (x, y) \in r^{\mathcal{I}} \wedge y \in C^{\mathcal{I}}\}.
\end{aligned}$$

An $\mathfrak{L}$ *terminology (TBox)* $\mathcal{T}$ is a finite set of *general concept inclusions (GCIs)*, which are expressions of the form $C \sqsubseteq D$ for $C, D \in \mathcal{C}_{\mathfrak{L}}(\mathsf{N_C}, \mathsf{N_R})$. The interpretation $\mathcal{I}$ is a *model* of $\mathcal{T}$ if it satisfies all its GCIs, i.e., $C^{\mathcal{I}} \subseteq D^{\mathcal{I}}$ holds for all GCIs $C \sqsubseteq D$ in $\mathcal{T}$. An $\mathfrak{L}$ *ABox* $\mathcal{A}$ is a finite set of *assertions*, which are expressions of the form $C(a)$ or $r(a, b)$, where $C \in \mathcal{C}_{\mathfrak{L}}(\mathsf{N_C}, \mathsf{N_R}), r \in \mathsf{N_R}$ and a, b are elements of an additional set $\mathsf{N_I}$ of individual names, which is disjoint with $\mathsf{N_C}$ and $\mathsf{N_R}$. An interpretation then additionally assigns elements $a^{\mathcal{I}} \in \Delta^{\mathcal{I}}$ to individual names $a \in \mathsf{N_I}$. The interpretation $\mathcal{I}$ is a *model* of $\mathcal{A}$ if it satisfies all its assertions, i.e., $a^{\mathcal{I}} \in C^{\mathcal{I}}$ (resp. $(a^{\mathcal{I}}, b^{\mathcal{I}}) \in r^{\mathcal{I}}$) holds for all assertions $C(a)$ (resp. $r(a, b)$) in $\mathcal{A}$.

Given an $\mathfrak{L}$ TBox $\mathcal{T}$ and two $\mathfrak{L}$ concept descriptions C, D, we say that C *is subsumed by* D (denoted as $C \sqsubseteq_{\mathcal{T}} D$) if $C^{\mathcal{I}} \subseteq D^{\mathcal{I}}$ for all models $\mathcal{I}$ of $\mathcal{T}$. These two concept descriptions are *equivalent* (denoted as $C \equiv_{\mathcal{T}} D$) if $C \sqsubseteq_{\mathcal{T}} D$ and $D \sqsubseteq_{\mathcal{T}} C$. Equivalent concept descriptions have the same meaning w.r.t. $\mathcal{T}$ in the sense that they always (i.e., in every model of $\mathcal{T}$) yield the same set. In the presence of an $\mathfrak{L}$ ABox $\mathcal{A}$, we can also consider the *instance problem*: given an individual name a and an $\mathfrak{L}$ concept description C we say that *a is an instance of C in $\mathcal{A}$ w.r.t. $\mathcal{T}$* (written $\mathcal{A} \models_{\mathcal{T}} C(a)$) if $a^{\mathcal{I}} \in C^{\mathcal{I}}$ for all models $\mathcal{I}$ of $\mathcal{T}$ that are also models of $\mathcal{A}$. For the DL $\mathcal{EL}$, the subsumption, equivalence, and instance problem are polynomial [15] whereas they are ExpTime-complete for $\mathcal{FL}_0$ [3] and for $\mathcal{ALC}$ [32].

2.2 Concept Comparison Measures

Subsumption and equivalence can be seen as operations that compare concept descriptions, and yield the comparison value 1 if the relation holds and 0 otherwise, i.e.,

$$\sqsubseteq_{\mathcal{T}}(C, D) = 1 \text{ if } C \sqsubseteq_{\mathcal{T}} D \quad \text{and} \quad \sqsubseteq_{\mathcal{T}}(C, D) = 0 \text{ if } C \not\sqsubseteq_{\mathcal{T}} D,$$

and accordingly for equivalence. Intuitively, concept comparison measures generalize such operations by yielding a degree to which the comparison relation is satisfied. More formally, they return a value in a partially ordered set.

Definition 1. *Let $\mathfrak{L}$ be a DL. A* concept comparison measure (CCM) *for $\mathfrak{L}$ is a family of functions $\mathfrak{c}$ that contains, for every $\mathfrak{L}$ TBox $\mathcal{T}$, an equivalence invariant function $\mathfrak{c}_{\mathcal{T}} : \mathcal{C}_{\mathfrak{L}}(\mathsf{N_C}, \mathsf{N_R}) \times \mathcal{C}_{\mathfrak{L}}(\mathsf{N_C}, \mathsf{N_R}) \to S$, where*

- *S is a non-empty set equipped with a partial order $\leq_S$,*
- *and* equivalence invariant *means that $\mathfrak{c}_{\mathcal{T}}(C, D) = \mathfrak{c}_{\mathcal{T}}(C', D')$ whenever $C \equiv_{\mathcal{T}} C'$ and $D \equiv_{\mathcal{T}} D'$.*

The reason we require equivalence invariance is that we do not view concept descriptions as syntactic objects, but rather as semantic ones that, for every interpretation, yield a subset of the interpretation domain. Since equivalent concept descriptions always yield the same sets, they are the same objects from a semantic point of view, and thus should also be treated the same way by the comparison function. The partial order on S allows us to compare different comparison degrees. We will later use the natural numbers and the non-negative real numbers, possibly extended with infinity $+\infty$, as well as the closed real interval $[0, 1]$ with the obvious orders as sets S.

Well-investigated examples of CCMs are *concept similarity measures (CSMs)*, for which $S = [0, 1]$ (see e.g., [25]). Intuitively, a CSM $\bowtie_{\mathcal{T}}$ is a graded variant of equivalence, where two concept descriptions C, D are equivalent iff $\bowtie_{\mathcal{T}}(C, D) = 1$, and they become less and less similar with decreasing value $\bowtie_{\mathcal{T}}(C, D)$. Usually, one also requires CSMs to be symmetric in the sense that $\bowtie_{\mathcal{T}}(C, D) = \bowtie_{\mathcal{T}}(D, C)$. For the DL $\mathcal{EL}$, a framework for defining CSMs satisfying certain additional properties has been introduced in [25], but equivalence invariance was only achieved for so-called acyclic TBoxes. This was extended in [20] to general TBoxes. For $\mathcal{FL}_0$, CSMs that are equivalence invariant for acyclic TBoxes were introduced in [30]. We will show later how CCMs for $\mathcal{FL}_0$ that are equivalence invariant for general TBoxes can be obtained by using weighted tree automata. CSMs for $\mathcal{ALC}$ are, for instance, investigated in [16].

Our definition of CCMs encompasses CSMs, but also covers other measures such as concept distance measures, which are mappings into $[0, +\infty)$ for which a larger value indicates that the concept descriptions are less similar (see e.g., [8]). In addition, it covers graded variants of subsumption, which map into $[0, 1]$, but in contrast to CSMs are not supposed to be symmetric. For example, the CSMs for $\mathcal{EL}$ and $\mathcal{FL}_0$ in [34] and [30], respectively, are based on asymmetric concept subsumption measures, which are then turned into symmetric CSMs by combining the results of the comparisons in both directions by computing the average.

2.3 Approximation

In contrast to approaches that try to speed up reasoning by employing approximate inference techniques [27], we use approximation as a way to extend the range of admissible answers to queries or admissible elements of concept descriptions. In this context, CCMs can be used together with a threshold construction to define which answers or individuals are admissible.

Relaxing Instance Queries. Ecke et al. [19,20] use CSMs to *relax instance queries* in $\mathcal{EL}$, i.e., instead of requiring that an individual is an instance of the query concept, they only require that it is an instance of a concept description that is "similar enough" to the query concept.

Definition 2. *Let $\bowtie$ be a CSM for $\mathcal{EL}$, $\mathcal{T}$ an $\mathcal{EL}$ TBox, $\mathcal{A}$ an $\mathcal{EL}$ ABox, and $t \in [0,1)$. The individual $a \in \mathsf{N_I}$ is a* relaxed instance *of the $\mathcal{EL}$ concept description Q w.r.t. $\mathcal{T}$, $\mathcal{A}$, $\bowtie$, and the threshold t if there exists an $\mathcal{EL}$ concept description X such that $\bowtie_{\mathcal{T}}(Q,X) > t$ and $\mathcal{A} \models_{\mathcal{T}} X(a)$.*

Ecke et al. [19,20] show that, under certain conditions on the CSMs used, the relaxed instance problem for $\mathcal{EL}$ is decidable. They also introduce a class of polynomially computable CSMs on $\mathcal{EL}$ concept descriptions for which the relaxed instance problem is in NP.

Adding Threshold Concepts to $\mathcal{EL}$. In [4], a similar construction is used to *relax membership in $\mathcal{EL}$ concept descriptions.* To be more precise, the authors introduce the notion of a graded membership function m to generalize elementhood in concept descriptions, and then use a threshold construction to obtain new concept constructors.

Definition 3. *A* graded membership function *m is a family of functions that contains for every interpretation $\mathcal{I}$ a function $m^{\mathcal{I}} : \Delta^{\mathcal{I}} \times \mathcal{C}_{\mathcal{EL}}(\mathsf{N_C}, \mathsf{N_R}) \rightarrow [0,1]$ satisfying the following conditions (for $C, D \in \mathcal{C}_{\mathcal{EL}}(\mathsf{N_C}, \mathsf{N_R})$):*

$$M1{:}\forall \mathcal{I}\ \forall d \in \Delta^{\mathcal{I}} : d \in C^{\mathcal{I}} \Leftrightarrow m^{\mathcal{I}}(d,C) = 1,$$
$$M2{:}C \equiv D \Leftrightarrow \forall \mathcal{I}\ \forall d \in \Delta^{\mathcal{I}} : m^{\mathcal{I}}(d,C) = m^{\mathcal{I}}(d,D).$$

Intuitively, given an interpretation $\mathcal{I}$ and $d \in \Delta^{\mathcal{I}}$, $m^{\mathcal{I}}(d,C) \in [0,1]$ represents the degree to which d belongs to C in $\mathcal{I}$. The threshold concept $C_{\sim t}$ for $\sim \in \{<, \leq, >, \geq\}$ then collects all the elements of $\Delta^{\mathcal{I}}$ that belong to C with degree $\sim t$, as measured by m. To be more precise, the formal semantics of threshold concepts is then defined as follows: $(C_{\sim t})^{\mathcal{I}} := \{d \in \Delta^{\mathcal{I}} \mid m^{\mathcal{I}}(d,C) \sim t\}$. The DL $\tau\mathcal{EL}(m)$ extends $\mathcal{EL}$ with such threshold concepts.

In [4] a specific such graded membership function called *deg* is introduced and the complexity of reasoning in $\tau\mathcal{EL}(deg)$ w.r.t. empty TBoxes (NP-complete or coNP-complete, depending on the reasoning problem) is investigated in detail. In addition, it is shown that, using a construction similar to the one in Definition 2, a CSM $\bowtie$ satisfying certain properties can be used to define a graded membership function:

$$m^{\mathcal{I}}_{\bowtie}(d,C) := \max\{\bowtie_{\emptyset}(C,D) \mid D \in \mathcal{C}_{\mathcal{EL}}(\mathsf{N_C}, \mathsf{N_R}) \text{ and } d \in D^{\mathcal{I}}\}.$$

To ensure that this construction yields a well-defined graded membership function, the CSM must be equivalence invariant, role-depth bounded, and equivalence closed (see [4,25] for definitions of the latter two properties). Finally, the authors of [4] prove that answering relaxed instance queries w.r.t. $\bowtie$ is the same as answering instance queries for threshold concepts $C_{>t}$ in $\tau\mathcal{EL}(m_{\bowtie})$.

In [6] it is shown that, for *computable* CSMs $\bowtie$ satisfying these properties, reasoning in $\tau\mathcal{EL}(m_{\bowtie})$ can effectively be reduced to reasoning in the DL $\mathcal{ALC}$, but the reduction is in general non-elementary. The authors then introduce a class of CSMs $\bowtie$ such that reasoning in $\tau\mathcal{EL}(m_{\bowtie})$ has the same complexity as reasoning in $\tau\mathcal{EL}(deg)$.

2.4 Approximate Unification

Unification has been introduced as a novel inference service that can be used to detect redundancies in ontologies. Basically, in unification one views some of the concept names in concept descriptions as variables, which can be replaced by concept descriptions using a *substitution*. The goal is then to make two concept descriptions equivalent by applying the same substitution to both. For example, consider the $\mathcal{FL}_0$ concept descriptions

$$C = A \sqcap \forall r.(X \sqcap \forall s.B) \quad \text{and} \quad D = Y \sqcap \forall r.(Z \sqcap A \sqcap \forall r.B).$$

Obviously, the substitution σ that replaces X by $A \sqcap \forall r.B$, Y by A, and Z by $\forall s.B$ makes C, D equivalent (w.r.t. the empty TBox):

$$\sigma(C) = A \sqcap \forall r.(A \sqcap \forall r.B \sqcap \forall s.B) \equiv_{\emptyset} A \sqcap \forall r.(\forall s.B \sqcap A \sqcap \forall r.B) = \sigma(D).$$

Such substitutions are called *unifiers*.

Unification was first investigated in detail for the DL $\mathcal{FL}_0$ [10], and later on for the DL $\mathcal{EL}$ [9]. The unification problem, i.e., deciding whether two concept descriptions with variables have a unifier or not, is ExpTime-complete in $\mathcal{FL}_0$ and NP-complete in $\mathcal{EL}$. Both works basically restrict their attention to the case of an empty TBox. For $\mathcal{EL}$, some attempts have been made to extend the results to unification w.r.t. GCIs [2], but these approaches can at the moment only deal with TBoxes that satisfy a certain restriction on cyclic dependencies between concept names. For $\mathcal{ALC}$, decidability of the unification problem (even w.r.t. the empty TBox) is a longstanding open problem, though it is known that undecidability holds for extensions of $\mathcal{ALC}$ by so-called nominals or the universal role [36].

Approximate unification relaxes the requirement that the two concept descriptions must be made equivalent. Instead, it requires that they are made "almost" equivalent, where the meaning of "almost" is formalized using distance measures between concept descriptions. Such measures are CCMs that map into $[0, +\infty)$ and satisfy some additional properties. Basically, given such a measure and a threshold value, one then asks whether one can lower the distance between two concept descriptions below the threshold value by applying a substitution. This is called the decision problem for approximate unification. For the computation problem, one wants to calculate the lowest achievable distance.

In [8], approximate unification is introduced and then investigated for the DL $\mathcal{FL}_0$ and two concept distance measures that are induced by distance measures between formal languages (see the next section). It is shown that (w.r.t. the empty TBox and these two measures), approximate unification has the same complexity (ExpTime) as unification.

3 Concept Comparison Measures for $\mathcal{FL}_0$

Until recently, the research on concept comparison measures in DLs was mostly concerned with $\mathcal{EL}$ [20,25,34] and more expressive DLs [16]. To achieve equivalence invariance, concept descriptions are usually first translated into an appropriate normal form, and then the structure of the normalized descriptions is compared. For instance, measures that achieve equivalence invariance only for the empty TBox or for acyclic TBoxes in $\mathcal{EL}$ [25,34] make use of the reduced form of $\mathcal{EL}$ concept descriptions introduced in [24]. Extensions to general TBoxes [20] use the so-called canonical model, which is generated by the polynomial-time subsumption algorithm for $\mathcal{EL}$ [3].

Two recent approaches for defining concept comparison measures for $\mathcal{FL}_0$ [8,30] were restricted to the case of the empty TBox. Both approaches employ a formal language-based characterization of equivalence between $\mathcal{FL}_0$ concept descriptions. In the remainder of this paper, we will develop a general approach for defining concept comparison measures for $\mathcal{FL}_0$ concept descriptions that are equivalence invariant also w.r.t. general TBoxes. This is achieved by using a new formal language-based characterization of equivalence in $\mathcal{FL}_0$ w.r.t. general TBoxes [28], where the semantics of a concept description is characterized using a tuple of (possibly infinite) formal languages. Basically, this tuple serves as a normal form for the concept description. In order to define equivalence invariant measures on $\mathcal{FL}_0$ concept descriptions, it is thus sufficient to define measures that compare such tuples. We will show how tuples of languages can be represented by infinite trees, and then use appropriate weighted tree automata to compute the comparison value.

3.1 From $\mathcal{FL}_0$ Concept Descriptions to Tuples of Formal Languages

In $\mathcal{FL}_0$, subsumption and equivalence can be nicely characterized using language inclusion. This characterization relies on transforming $\mathcal{FL}_0$ concept descriptions into an appropriate normal form as follows. First, the semantics given to concept constructors in $\mathcal{FL}_0$ implies that value restrictions distribute over conjunction, i.e., for all $C, D \in \mathcal{C}_{\mathcal{FL}_0}(\mathsf{N_C}, \mathsf{N_R})$ and $r \in \mathsf{N_R}$ it holds that

$$\forall r.(C \sqcap D) \equiv_{\emptyset} \forall r.C \sqcap \forall r.D.$$

Using this equivalence as a rewrite rule from left to right, each $\mathcal{FL}_0$ concept description can be translated into an equivalent concept description that is either $\top$ or a conjunction of concept descriptions of the form $\forall r_1 \dots \forall r_n.A$, where $\{r_1, \dots, r_n\} \subseteq \mathsf{N_R}$ and $A \in \mathsf{N_C}$. Such concept descriptions can be abbreviated as $\forall w.A$, where w represents the word $r_1 \dots r_n$. Note that $n = 0$ means that w is the empty word ε, and thus $\forall\varepsilon.A$ corresponds to A. Furthermore, a conjunction of the form $\forall w_1.A\sqcap\ldots\sqcap\forall w_m.A$ can be written as $\forall L.A$ where $L \subseteq \mathsf{N_R}^*$ is the finite language $\{w_1,\ldots,w_m\}$. We use the convention that $\forall\emptyset.A$ corresponds to the top concept $\top$. Thus, if we fix the set of concept names as $\mathsf{N_C} := \{A_1,\ldots,A_\ell\}$, then any two concept descriptions $C, D \in \mathcal{C}_{\mathcal{FL}_0}(\mathsf{N_C},\mathsf{N_R})$ can be represented as

$$\begin{aligned} C &\equiv_\emptyset \forall K_1.A_1 \sqcap \ldots \sqcap \forall K_\ell.A_\ell, \\ D &\equiv_\emptyset \forall L_1.A_1 \sqcap \ldots \sqcap \forall L_\ell.A_\ell, \end{aligned} \tag{1}$$

where $K_1, L_1, \ldots, K_\ell, L_\ell$ are finite languages over the alphabet of role names $\mathsf{N_R}$, i.e., finite subsets of $\mathsf{N_R}^*$. Using this representation, it was shown in [10] that $C \sqsubseteq_\emptyset D$ iff $L_i \subseteq K_i$ for all $i, 1 \leq i \leq \ell$. Since equivalence corresponds to subsumption in both directions, the $\mathcal{FL}_0$ concept descriptions C, D in (1) are equivalent w.r.t. the empty TBox iff $L_i = K_i$ for all $i, 1 \leq i \leq \ell$.

In the presence of a non-empty TBox $\mathcal{T}$, a similar characterization of subsumption and equivalence can be obtained [28], but now the definition of the languages needs to take the GCIs in $\mathcal{T}$ into account. Given an $\mathcal{FL}_0$ concept description C and a TBox $\mathcal{T}$, we define for all $A \in \mathsf{N_C}$ the following language

$$\mathcal{L}_\mathcal{T}(C, A) := \{w \in \mathsf{N_R}^* \mid C \sqsubseteq_\mathcal{T} \forall w.A\},$$

and call this language the value restriction set of C with respect to $\mathcal{T}$ and A. It can easily be verified that, for all concept names $A_i \in \mathsf{N_C}$, the sets K_i in (1) are actually equal to $\mathcal{L}_\emptyset(C, A_i)$. However, while in the case of the empty TBox these languages are finite, they may be infinite for non-trivial TBoxes. This is illustrated by the following example.

Example 1. Let C be the $\mathcal{FL}_0$ concept description $C := A \sqcap \forall s.(A \sqcap B)$ and $\mathcal{T}$ the TBox $\mathcal{T} := \{A \sqsubseteq \forall r.A, B \sqsubseteq \forall s.B\}$. It is easy to see that the value restriction sets for A and B are

$$\mathcal{L}_\mathcal{T}(C, A) = r^* \cup sr^* \quad \text{and} \quad \mathcal{L}_\mathcal{T}(C, B) = ss^*,$$

where we have used standard notation for writing regular expressions to describe these infinite languages.

Just as in the case of the empty TBox, the value restriction sets can be used to characterize equivalence and subsumption w.r.t. general TBoxes (see [28]):

$$C \sqsubseteq_\mathcal{T} D \quad \text{iff} \quad \mathcal{L}_\mathcal{T}(D, A_i) \subseteq \mathcal{L}_\mathcal{T}(C, A_i) \quad (1 \leq i \leq \ell), \tag{2}$$

$$C \equiv_\mathcal{T} D \quad \text{iff} \quad \mathcal{L}_\mathcal{T}(C, A_i) = \mathcal{L}_\mathcal{T}(D, A_i) \quad (1 \leq i \leq \ell). \tag{3}$$

The equivalence (3) shows that, in $\mathcal{FL}_0$, formal languages can be used to represent the semantic content of concept descriptions: up to equivalence, every $\mathcal{FL}_0$ concept description $C \in \mathcal{C}_{\mathcal{FL}_0}(\mathsf{N_C},\mathsf{N_R})$ is uniquely represented by the tuple of languages

$$\mathcal{L}_\mathcal{T}(C) := (\mathcal{L}_\mathcal{T}(C, A_1), \ldots, \mathcal{L}_\mathcal{T}(C, A_\ell)).$$

We will use this fact to reduce the definition of concept comparison measures between $\mathcal{FL}_0$ concept descriptions w.r.t. a TBox to the definition of measures comparing tuples of languages: given two $\mathcal{FL}_0$ concept descriptions C, D, we define $\mathfrak{c}_\mathcal{T}(C, D)$ by comparing the tuples $\mathcal{L}_\mathcal{T}(C)$ and $\mathcal{L}_\mathcal{T}(D)$. One advantage of this approach is that equivalence invariance comes "for free" since equivalent concept descriptions are indistinguishable from the language point of view.

3.2 Using Tuples of Languages to Define CCMs

The idea of using tuples of languages to compare $\mathcal{FL}_0$ concept descriptions has already been employed in [8,30], but restricted to the empty TBox. In both works, the general approach used to define such measures consists of the following three steps:

1. Translate the $\mathcal{FL}_0$ concept descriptions C and D into their corresponding tuples of languages $\mathcal{L}_\emptyset(C) = (K_1, \ldots, K_\ell)$ and $\mathcal{L}_\emptyset(D) = (L_1, \ldots, L_\ell)$. For the sake of readability, we will denote these tuples as $\mathbf{K}$ and $\mathbf{L}$, respectively.
2. To compare the tuples $\mathbf{K}$ and $\mathbf{L}$, their components K_i and L_i are compared pairwise, and the values obtained this way are then appropriately combined into a value $s(\mathbf{K}, \mathbf{L})$.
3. Finally, the value $s(\mathbf{K}, \mathbf{L})$ is used to define $\mathfrak{c}_\emptyset(C, D)$.

In the following, we recall the exact definitions of the measures introduced in [8,30].

Example 2. In [30], the authors' goal is to define concept similarity measures. To this end, given $\mathbf{K}$ and $\mathbf{L}$, they first define an asymmetric measure s, which they apply to $(\mathbf{K}, \mathbf{L})$ and $(\mathbf{L}, \mathbf{K})$. The obtained values are then combined using average. For the definition of the asymmetric measure, they propose two possible functions e_1 and e_2 to compare every pair (K_i, L_i):

- the function e_1 checks inclusion: $e_1(K_i, L_i) = 1$ if $L_i \subseteq K_i$, and 0 otherwise;
- the function e_2 returns the fraction of the words in L_i that also belong to K_i, and thus yields 1 if $L_i \subseteq K_i$, but 0 only if the two languages are disjoint:[1]

$$e_2(K_i, L_i) = \frac{|K_i \cap L_i|}{|L_i|}$$

The asymmetric measure s is then defined as $s(\mathbf{K}, \mathbf{L}) = f(e_j(K_1, L_1), \ldots, e_j(K_\ell, L_\ell))$, where f is the average operator and $j \in \{1, 2\}$. Finally, the CSM $\bowtie_\emptyset$ for $\mathcal{FL}_0$ concept descriptions is defined as

$$\bowtie_\emptyset(C, D) := \frac{s(\mathcal{L}_\emptyset(C), \mathcal{L}_\emptyset(D)) + s(\mathcal{L}_\emptyset(D), \mathcal{L}_\emptyset(C))}{2}.$$

[1] Note that this function is well-defined only for finite languages. Thus, e_2 cannot be used in the presence of general TBoxes, where the languages may be infinite.

Example 3. In [8], the authors introduce the notion of concept distance measures for $\mathcal{FL}_0$. They obtain such measures by applying a language distance (which is assumed to be a topological metric) to the pairs of languages (K_i, L_i), and then combining these values using a function f. In particular, they define two language distances d_1 and d_2, which we introduce below.

Let M_1 and M_2 be two languages over an alphabet Σ. We denote the symmetric difference of M_1 and M_2 as $M_1 \mathbin{\Delta} M_2$, i.e.,

$$M_1 \mathbin{\Delta} M_2 := (M_1 \setminus M_2) \cup (M_2 \setminus M_1). \tag{4}$$

The language distances d_1 and d_2 are now defined as

$$\begin{aligned} d_1(M_1, M_2) &:= 2^{-n} && \text{where } n = \min\{|w| \mid w \in M_1 \mathbin{\Delta} M_2\}, \\ d_2(M_1, M_2) &:= \mu(M_1 \mathbin{\Delta} M_2) && \text{where } \mu(M) = \tfrac{1}{2} \sum_{w \in M} (2|\Sigma|)^{-|w|}. \end{aligned}$$

Intuitively, the symmetric difference captures all the discrepancies between two concept descriptions C and D with respect to a concept name A. More precisely, if for instance, $w \in \mathcal{L}_\emptyset(C, A) \setminus \mathcal{L}_\emptyset(D, A)$ for some $w \in \mathsf{N_R}^*$, then $C \sqsubseteq_\emptyset \forall w.A$ and $D \not\sqsubseteq_\emptyset \forall w.A$, which amounts to a semantically relevant difference between C and D. Based on this intuition, the first distance looks for the shortest such discrepancy, while the second one takes all differences into account, but differences for longer words count less than differences for shorter ones (see [8] for a more detailed explanation).

As already mentioned, these language distances are then used to define a measure s on tuples by setting $s(\mathbf{K}, \mathbf{L}) := f(d_j(K_1, L_1), \ldots, d_j(K_\ell, L_\ell))$ where $j \in \{1, 2\}$. For functions f satisfying certain properties (called *combining* functions in [8]), this yields a concept distance $m_{d,f}$ for $\mathcal{FL}_0$ concept descriptions:

$$m_{d,f}(C, D) := s(\mathcal{L}_\emptyset(C), \mathcal{L}_\emptyset(D))$$

In the two examples above, the definition of a CCM for $\mathcal{FL}_0$ was in the end reduced to define a distance function that compares two languages. Thus, the input for this function is a pair of languages. In general, one may also want to allow for definitions of distance functions on language tuples that do not resort to binary comparisons of the components of the tuples. The inputs for the function are then 2ℓ-tuples of languages. For this reason we now develop means for defining functions that receive tuples of languages as input, which covers both the binary and the general case.

Though developed for the case of the empty TBox, and thus with finite languages in mind, the functions e_1, d_1, d_2 of our examples are also well-defined for infinite languages, and thus can also be employed in the more general setting of non-empty TBoxes. However, if we are not only interested in defining, but also in computing the functions, we need to find ways of representing their input (i.e., tuples of possibly infinite languages) in a finite way. In the next section, we show that finite automata working on infinite trees can be used for this purpose.

3.3 Finitely Representing Tuples of Languages

Following the ideas in [10,11,28], we will represent tuples of (possibly infinite) languages using infinite trees.

Definition 4. *Let $\Sigma = \{\sigma_1, \ldots, \sigma_k\}$ be a non-empty, finite set of symbols. Given a set of labels L, an L-labeled Σ-tree is a mapping $t : \Sigma^* \to L$ that assigns a label $t(w) \in L$ to every node $w \in \Sigma^*$. The set of all L-labeled Σ-trees is denoted as $T^{\omega}_{\Sigma,L}$.*

Intuitively, the nodes of a Σ-tree t correspond to finite words in Σ^*, where the empty word ε represents the root of t and every node w has k children corresponding to the words $w\sigma_1, \ldots, w\sigma_k$. Since for a non-empty alphabet Σ the set Σ^* of all words over Σ is infinite, Σ-trees are by definition infinite. We use tuples over $\{0, 1\}$ as labels to represent tuples of languages over Σ.

Definition 5. *Let Σ be a finite set of symbols and $\ell \in \mathbb{N}$. We define the mapping $\gamma_\ell : \left(2^{\Sigma^*}\right)^\ell \to T^{\omega}_{\Sigma,\{0,1\}^\ell}$ as follows. Given a tuple of languages $\mathbf{L} = (L_1, \ldots, L_\ell)$ over Σ, $\gamma_\ell(\mathbf{L}) := t_{\mathbf{L}}$ where $t_{\mathbf{L}} : \Sigma^* \to \{0,1\}^\ell$ is the Σ-tree such that*

$$t_{\mathbf{L}}(w) := (x_1, \ldots, x_\ell), \text{ where } x_i = 1 \text{ iff } w \in L_i \quad (\text{for all } w \in \Sigma^*).$$

It is easy to see that γ_ℓ is a *bijection* between tuples of languages over the alphabet Σ and $\{0,1\}^\ell$-labeled Σ-trees. Given a tree $t \in T^{\omega}_{\Sigma,\{0,1\}^\ell}$, the inverse function yields the tuple $\gamma_\ell^{-1}(t) = (L_1, \ldots, L_\ell)$ where L_i consists of the words w for which the ith component of $t(w)$ is equal to 1.

Basically, this translation of tuples of languages into trees is used in [28] to represent the tuple of value restriction sets $\mathcal{L}_\mathcal{T}(C)$ of an $\mathcal{FL}_0$ concept description C as an $\mathsf{N_R}$-tree t_C. Strictly speaking, the label set employed in [28] is $2^{\mathsf{N_C}}$ for $\mathsf{N_C} = \{A_1, \ldots, A_\ell\}$ rather than $\{0,1\}^\ell$, but it should be clear that, by fixing a linear order $A_1 < A_2 < \ldots < A_\ell$ on $\mathsf{N_C}$, these two representations can be translated into each other. Obviously, a single value restriction set $\mathcal{L}_\mathcal{T}(C, A_i)$ can be represented as a $\{0,1\}$-labeled $\mathsf{N_R}$-tree t_{C,A_i}, where the words belonging to this language receive label 1 and the others label 0.

The following example illustrates this representation of value restriction sets by trees using the concept description C and the TBox $\mathcal{T}$ of Example 1.

Example 4. Recall from Example 1 that $\mathcal{L}_\mathcal{T}(C, A) = r^* \cup sr^*$ and $\mathcal{L}_\mathcal{T}(C, B) = ss^*$. To express the tuple of these languages as a tree, we assume that r is the first symbol of the alphabet and s is the second, and that $A < B$. Then $\mathcal{L}_\mathcal{T}(C) = (r^* \cup sr^*, ss^*)$, and this tuple is represented by the tree sketched on the left-hand side of Fig. 1. For better readability, we have labeled the edges with the symbols r and s. As an example for the labeling, consider the node corresponding to the word sr. It has label $(1, 0)$ since this word belongs to $r^* \cup sr^*$, but not to ss^*. The extension of this tree to infinity is obtained as follows. On the one hand, the outgoing *dotted* edges tell us that all the nodes below are labeled with the tuple $(0, 0)$. Notice, for example, that there are no

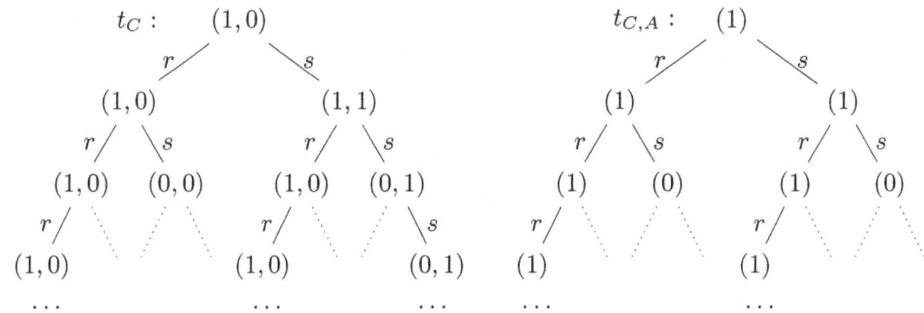

Fig. 1. Tuples of languages as infinite trees.

words starting with rs or srs in any of the two languages. On the other hand, the nodes rrr, srr and sss are the roots of infinite trees representing the tuples of languages $(r^*, \emptyset)$, $(r^*, \emptyset)$ and $(\emptyset, s^*)$, respectively.

The tree on the right-hand side of the figure represents the language $\mathcal{L}_{\mathcal{T}}(C, A)$, which is obtained from t_C by projecting the label-tuples to the first component.

Using the same approach, given two concept descriptions C, D, the pair of tuples $(\mathcal{L}_{\mathcal{T}}(C), \mathcal{L}_{\mathcal{T}}(D))$ can obviously be represented as an infinite $\mathsf{N_R}$-tree $t_{(C,D)} : \mathsf{N_R}^* \rightarrow \{0,1\}^\ell \times \{0,1\}^\ell$.

As mentioned before, our goal is to represent such input tuples in a finite way. Using infinite trees obviously does not solve this problem. Thus, we need to develop an approach for representing such trees in a finite way. For general tuples of infinite languages and thus arbitrary Σ-trees this is clearly not possible. However, a closer look at the trees t_C constructed in [28] shows that they are actually *regular* trees, which admit a finite representation. Therefore, we restrict our attention to the class of regular trees. We start by formally defining the notion of a regular tree, and then show that regular trees can always be represented using certain kinds of tree automata.

Definition 6 (Regular tree). *Let t be a tree in $T^\omega_{\Sigma,L}$. Given a node $w \in \Sigma^*$, the* subtree *$t_w : \Sigma^* \rightarrow L$ of t is defined as $t_w(v) := t(wv)$ for all $v \in \Sigma^*$. We say that t contains the subtree t_w. Then, t is a* regular *tree if it contains finitely many distinct subtrees.*

There are different ways to represent regular trees in a finite way [35]. Here, we use *looping tree automata* for this purpose.

Definition 7 (Looping Tree Automaton (LTA)). *A* looping tree automaton *is a tuple $\mathcal{A} = (\Sigma, Q, L, \Delta, I)$ where $\Sigma = \{\sigma_1, \ldots, \sigma_k\}$ is a finite set of symbols, Q is a finite set of states, L is a finite set of labels, $\Delta \subseteq Q \times L \times Q^k$ is the transition relation and $I \subseteq Q$ is a set of initial states. A run of this automaton on a tree $t \in T^\omega_{\Sigma,L}$ is a Q-labeled Σ-tree $r : \Sigma^* \rightarrow Q$ such that $r(\varepsilon) \in I$ and*

$$(r(w), t(w), r(w\sigma_1), \ldots, r(w\sigma_k)) \in \Delta$$

for all $w \in \Sigma^*$. *The tree language* $\mathcal{L}(\mathcal{A})$ *recognized by* $\mathcal{A}$ *is the set of all trees* $t \in T^{\omega}_{\Sigma,L}$ *such that* $\mathcal{A}$ *accepts* t, *i.e.,* $\mathcal{A}$ *has a run on* t.

In general, LTAs recognize *sets* of trees. Therefore, to uniquely represent a tree we only consider those recognizing singleton sets.

Definition 8. *Let* $\mathcal{A} = (\Sigma, Q, L, \Delta, I)$ *be a looping tree automaton. We say that* $\mathcal{A}$ represents the infinite tree $t \in T^{\omega}_{\Sigma,L}$ *if* $\mathcal{L}(\mathcal{A}) = \{t\}$.

It is easy to see that trees that can be represented by looping tree automata are indeed regular. In fact, LTAs are Rabin tree automata [29,35] with trivial acceptance conditions, and it is well-known that non-empty tree languages recognized by Rabin tree automata always contain a regular tree. Thus, if such an automaton recognizes the singleton set $\{t\}$, then t must be regular. Conversely, we can show that any regular tree can be represented in this way.

Proposition 1. *Let* $t \in T^{\omega}_{\Sigma,L}$ *be an* L*-labeled* Σ*-tree. Then,* t *is regular iff it can be represented by an LTA.*

Proof. We have already seen that the if-direction holds. To show the only-if direction, assume that t is a regular tree. By Definition 6 it thus contains only finitely many distinct subtrees, say $t^0, t^1, \dots, t^m$ where we assume without loss of generality that $t^0 = t$. For all $1 \leq i \leq m$, we denote the direct subtrees of t^i as $t^i_{\sigma_1}, \dots, t^i_{\sigma_k}$. Note that these are also subtrees of t, and thus belong to the set $\{t^0, t^1, \dots, t^m\}$. We build the looping tree automaton $\mathcal{A}_t = (\Sigma, Q_t, L, \Delta_t, \{t^0\})$ as follows: $Q_t := \{t^0, t^1, \dots, t^m\}$ and $\Delta_t := \{(t^i, t^i(\varepsilon), t^i_{\sigma_1}, \dots, t^i_{\sigma_k}) \mid 1 \leq i \leq m\}$. It is easy to see that $t = t^0$ is the only tree accepted by $\mathcal{A}_t$. □

The automaton $\mathcal{A}_t$ constructed in the above proof actually has a very specific syntactic shape (see Definition 9 below), which ensures that it accepts only one tree.

Definition 9 (Representing Looping Tree Automaton (rLTA)). *A* representing *looping tree automaton is a looping tree automaton* $\mathcal{A} = (\Sigma, P, L, \Delta, \{p_s\})$ *such that* Δ *satisfies the following condition:*

- *for every* $p \in P$, *there exists a unique symbol* $l_p \in L$ *and a unique tuple* $(p_1, \dots, p_{|\Sigma|}) \in P^{|\Sigma|}$ *such that* $(p, l_p, p_1, \dots, p_{|\Sigma|}) \in \Delta$.

The following proposition states some obvious consequences of this definition and the proof of Proposition 1.

Proposition 2. *Let* $\mathcal{A}$ *be an rLTA and* t *a regular tree. Then*

1. t *can be represented by some rLTA* $\mathcal{A}_t$.
2. $L(\mathcal{A})$ *is a singleton set consisting of a regular tree* $t_{\mathcal{A}}$ *and* $\mathcal{A}$ *has a unique run* $r_{\mathcal{A}}$ *on* $t_{\mathcal{A}}$.

In [28] it is shown that, given an $\mathcal{FL}_0$ concept description C and a TBox $\mathcal{T}$, the tree t_C encoding the tuple $\mathcal{L}_{\mathcal{T}}(C)$ can be represented by an rLTA.

Theorem 1 [28]. *Let C be an $\mathcal{FL}_0$ concept description and $\mathcal{T}$ a TBox. Then one can construct a representing looping tree automaton that represents t_C in time exponential in the size of C and $\mathcal{T}$.*

In case we are given a general LTA $\mathcal{A}$, we should like to know whether it actually represents a tree (i.e., recognizes a singleton set), and if the answer is affirmative construct an rLTA that represents the same tree. Basically, this can be achieved as follows. Given $\mathcal{A}$, we apply the emptiness test for looping automata [13] to check whether $\mathcal{L}(\mathcal{A}) = \emptyset$. If this is the case, $\mathcal{A}$ does not represent a tree. Otherwise, we reduce $\mathcal{A}$ to an automaton $\mathcal{A}^r$ by removing superfluous states and then removing all but one transition for every state. If $\mathcal{A}$ represents a tree, $\mathcal{A}^r$ is the rLTA we are looking for. To check whether this is the case, we check whether $\mathcal{A}$ accepts a tree that is different from the unique tree accepted by $\mathcal{A}^r$ (see [7] for details).

Lemma 1. *Let $\mathcal{A}$ be an LTA. We can decide in polynomial time whether $\mathcal{A}$ represents a tree. If $\mathcal{A}$ represents a tree $t \in T^{\omega}_{\Sigma,L}$, then we can construct an rLTA representing t in polynomial time.*

The results of this section show that we can restrict the attention to rLTAs when representing regular trees.

4 Using Weighted Looping Tree Automata to Assign a Value to a Tuple of Languages

Our goal is now to assign values from a (numerical or other) domain to tuples of (possibly infinite) languages that can be represented by regular trees. Consequently, we need a device that takes as input such a tree and returns a value. Weighted looping tree automata are such devices: they assign values (from a so-called semiring) to infinite trees. In the next subsection, we introduce the special type of weighted tree automata that we will use together with the necessary notions (semirings, discounting, etc.). We show how the language distances d_1, d_2 introduced in the previous section can be realized using such automata. Then, we turn to the problem of how to actually compute the value assigned by such an automaton to a regular tree that is represented by an rLTA.

4.1 Weighted Looping Tree Automata

In order to assign a value to a tree, weighted tree automata make use of transitions that are equipped with weights. These weights are usually elements of a semiring such that one can add and multiply weights. An extensive survey of weighted tree automata can be found in [21]. In a setting where the automata are required to work on infinite trees, the underlying semiring should admit suitable infinite sums and products [31]. In the context of infinite trees, it is also useful to employ discounting. This has been used for modeling systems with non-terminating behavior [1] in order to assign different degrees of importance to incidents that happen later in time. In our setting, discounting can be used to assign less importance to differences that occur for longer words, i.e., further down in the tree.

Semirings. The weight structures underlying our weighted tree automata are totally complete commutative semirings [31].

Definition 10. *A* semiring $\mathcal{S} = (S, \oplus, \otimes, \mathbb{0}, \mathbb{1})$ *consists of a set* S, *two binary operations* $\oplus$ *and* $\otimes$, *and two constant elements* $\mathbb{0}$ *and* $\mathbb{1}$ *such that:*

1. $(S, \oplus, \mathbb{0})$ *is a commutative monoid,*
2. $(S, \otimes, \mathbb{1})$ *is a monoid,*
3. *multiplication distributes over addition from left and right,*
4. $\mathbb{0} \otimes a = a \otimes \mathbb{0} = \mathbb{0}$ *for all* $a \in S$.

A semiring is called commutative *if* $a \otimes b = b \otimes a$ *for all* $a, b \in S$.

In *totally complete commutative semirings*, addition and multiplication can be extended to infinite sums $\bigoplus_{i \in I} a_i$ and countably infinite products $\bigotimes_{i \geq 0} a_i$ satisfying properties that suitably extend the properties of binary addition and multiplication in semirings to the infinite case (see [31] for formal definitions).

Examples. The following semirings are commutative and totally complete [31]:

- the semiring $(\mathbb{N} \cup \{+\infty\}, +, \cdot, 0, 1)$ of natural numbers extended with positive infinity $+\infty$,
- the *tropical semiring* $Trop = (\mathbb{N} \cup \{+\infty\}, \min, +, +\infty, 0)$ and the *arctic semiring* $Arc = (\mathbf{N} \cup \{+\infty, -\infty\}, \sup, +, -\infty, 0)$ with the binary operations extended in the natural way to infinitary operations,
- their real counterparts $\mathbb{R}_{\text{inf}} = (\mathbb{R}_{\geq 0} \cup \{+\infty\}, \inf, +, +\infty, 0)$, $\mathbb{R}_{\text{sup}} = (\mathbb{R}_{\geq 0} \cup \{+\infty, -\infty\}, \sup, +, -\infty, 0)$,
- the *Viterbi* semiring $([0, 1], \sup, \cdot, 0, 1)$,
- every complete distributive lattice.

Discounting. In the setting of semirings, discounting is defined by using semiring endomorphisms. This approach was originally used for weighted automata on infinite words by Droste and Kuske in [17], and extended to weighted automata on infinite trees by Mandrali and Rahonis [26].

Definition 11. *Let* $\mathcal{S} = (S, \oplus, \otimes, \mathbb{0}, \mathbb{1})$ *be a semiring. A mapping* $f : S \to S$ *is called an* endomorphism *if* $f(a \oplus b) = f(a) \oplus f(b)$ *and* $f(a \otimes b) = f(a) \otimes f(b)$ *for all* $a, b \in S$, *and* $f(\mathbb{0}) = \mathbb{0}$, $f(\mathbb{1}) = \mathbb{1}$. *The set* $End(\mathcal{S})$ *of all endomorphisms of* $\mathcal{S}$ *is a monoid with composition* $\circ$ *as binary operation and the identity mapping* id *as unit.*

For $\mathbb{R}_{\text{sup}}$, it was proved in [17] that every endomorphism is of the form $\overline{p}(a) = p \cdot a$ for some $p \in [0, +\infty)$, and conversely, every $p \in [0, +\infty)$ defines an endomorphism of $\mathbb{R}_{\text{sup}}$ in this way. The same result can be shown for $\mathbb{R}_{\text{inf}}$ as well [18]. Finally, it is not difficult to see that, for the Viterbi semiring, every endomorphism is of the form $\tilde{p}(a) = a^p$ for some $p \in [0, +\infty)$, and conversely every $p \in [0, +\infty)$ defines an endomorphism of Viterbi.

Definition 12. *Let $\Sigma = \{\sigma_1, \ldots, \sigma_k\}$ be a finite set of symbols and $\mathcal{S}$ a semiring. A* discounting *for Σ and $\mathcal{S}$ is a tuple $\Phi \in (End(\mathcal{S}))^k$.*[2]

For a discounting $\Phi = (\phi_1, \ldots, \phi_k)$ and for every word $w = \sigma_{i_1}\sigma_{i_2}\ldots\sigma_{i_n} \in \Sigma^*$, we define the endomorphism ϕ_w of $\mathcal{S}$ induced by Φ and w as $\phi_w = \phi_{i_1} \circ \phi_{i_2} \circ \cdots \circ \phi_{i_n}$, where for $w = \varepsilon$ the empty composition is *id*.

Weighted Looping Tree Automata. In the following, $\mathcal{S}$ is assumed to be a totally complete commutative semiring. An *infinitary tree series h* over L and $\mathcal{S}$ is a mapping $h : T^{\omega}_{\Sigma,L} \to \mathcal{S}$. The class of all infinitary tree series over L and $\mathcal{S}$ is denoted by $\mathcal{S}\langle\langle T^{\omega}_{\Sigma,L}\rangle\rangle$.

Definition 13 (Weigthed looping tree automaton with discounting Φ). *A weighted looping tree automaton with discounting Φ (Φ-wLTA) over $\mathcal{S}$ is a tuple $\mathcal{M} = (\Sigma, Q, L, in, wt)$ where Q is a finite state set, L is a finite set of labels, $\Sigma = \{\sigma_1, \ldots, \sigma_k\}$ is a finite set of symbols, $in : Q \to \mathcal{S}$ is the initial distribution, and $wt : Q \times L \times Q^k \to \mathcal{S}$ is a mapping assigning weights to the transitions of the automaton.*

Given a Φ-wLTA $\mathcal{M} = (\Sigma, Q, L, in, wt)$ over $\mathcal{S}$, a *run* of $\mathcal{M}$ on a tree $t \in T^{\omega}_{\Sigma,L}$ is a mapping $r : \Sigma^* \to Q$. We denote the set of all runs of $\mathcal{M}$ on t by $R_{\mathcal{M}}(t)$. Given a run r, we denote the transition $(r(w), t(w), r(w\sigma_1), \ldots, r(w\sigma_k))$ by $\overrightarrow{r}(w)$. The *weight* of the run r at $w \in \Sigma^*$ is defined as $wt(r, w) := wt(\overrightarrow{r}(w))$. The *$\Phi$-weight* (or simply weight) of r is defined as

$$weight(r) := in(r(\varepsilon)) \otimes \bigotimes_{w \in \Sigma^*} \phi_w(wt(r, w)).$$

Finally, the Φ-behavior (or simply behavior) of $\mathcal{M}$ is the infinitary tree series $||\mathcal{M}|| \in \mathcal{S}\langle\langle T^{\omega}_{\Sigma,L}\rangle\rangle$ whose coefficients are determined for every $t \in T^{\omega}_{\Sigma,L}$ by

$$(||\mathcal{M}||, t) := \bigoplus_{r \in R_{\mathcal{M}}(t)} weight(r).$$

If we take $\phi_i = id$ for every $i = 1, \ldots, k$, then we are left with a "normal" wLTA over $\mathcal{S}$ in the sense of [31], and thus dispense with the prefix Φ- in the notation.

If $|L| = 1$, then $T^{\omega}_{\Sigma,L}$ consists of a single tree t_{ul}, which we will call the *unlabeled tree* since the labels are then irrelevant. In this case, we omit the label from the transitions of a Φ-wLTA $\mathcal{M}$ and write $R_{\mathcal{M}}$ for its runs, omitting t_{ul}. Also note that then $\|\mathcal{M}\|$ is a single element of S rather than a tree series.

[2] In the literature, more general forms of discounting have been introduced, where the tuple of endomorphisms to be used depends also on the label of a node, but here we restrict our attention to the simpler form of discounting introduced above.

Expressing Language Distance Functions. The functions d_1, d_2 introduced in Example 3 take a pair of languages over an alphabet Σ as input. Thus, to represent this kind of input in a tree, we use the label set $L_2 := \{0,1\}^2$. We show that d_2 as well as a vital component of d_1 can be expressed by weighted looping automata with discounting over $\mathbb{R}_{\text{inf}}$. The function d_1 itself and the function e_1 of Example 2 can be expressed using the Viterbi semiring (see [7]).

Example 5. The first language distance described in [8] is $d_1(K,N) = 2^{-n}$ where $n = \min\{|w| \mid w \in K \mathbin{\Delta} N\}$. We introduce a wLTA (without discounting) that, given a tree t representing the tuple of languages (K,N), computes the minimum n rather than 2^{-n} itself. Given n, the exponentiation can be done by external computation. Consider the wLTA $\mathcal{M}_1 = (\Sigma, Q, L_2, in_1, wt_1)$ over $\mathbb{R}_{\text{inf}} = (\mathbb{R}_{\geq 0} \cup \{+\infty\}, \inf, +, +\infty, 0)$, where $Q = \{q_0, q_1\}$, $in_1(q_0) = +\infty$, $in_1(q_1) = 0$ and

$$wt_1(q,l,p_1,\ldots,p_k) = \begin{cases} 1 & \text{if } q = q_1,\ l \in \{(0,0),(1,1)\},\ p_i = q_1 \text{ for some } 1 \leq i \leq k \\ & \qquad \text{and } p_j = q_0 \text{ for } j \neq i \\ 0 & \text{if } q = q_1,\ l \in \{(1,0),(0,1)\},\ p_i = q_0 \text{ for all } 1 \leq i \leq k \\ 0 & \text{if } q = q_0,\ l \in \{0,1\}^2,\ p_i = q_0 \text{ for all } 1 \leq i \leq k \\ +\infty & \text{otherwise} \end{cases}$$

Intuitively, each run using only transitions with non-infinite weights selects one path in the tree, which it labels with q_1 until an element in the symmetric difference is found. The transitions up to this point in the selected path receive weight 1, and all other transitions have weight 0. Thus, adding up the weights (with the multiplication $\otimes = +$ of $\mathbb{R}_{\text{inf}}$) gives us the distance from the root to the node where the difference was detected, i.e., the length of the word in the symmetric difference (or $+\infty$ in case no difference is found on the chosen path). By building the infimum over all runs, the length of the shortest word in the symmetric difference is found.

Example 6. The second distance described in [8] is $d_2(K,N) = \mu(K \mathbin{\Delta} N)$, where $\mu(M) = \frac{1}{2}\sum_{w \in M}(2|\Sigma|)^{-|w|}$. We introduce a Φ-wLTA that, given a tree t representing the tuple of languages (K,N), computes $\mu(K \mathbin{\Delta} N)$. Consider the Φ-wLTA $\mathcal{M}_2 = (\Sigma, Q, L_2, in_2, wt_2)$ over $\mathbb{R}_{\text{inf}}$ where $Q = \{q_0, q_1\}$, $in_2(q_0) = in_2(q_1) = 0$ and

$$wt_2(q,l,p_1,\ldots,p_k) = \begin{cases} 0 & \text{if } q = q_0,\ l \in \{(0,0),(1,1)\} \\ \frac{1}{2} & \text{if } q = q_1,\ l \in \{(1,0),(0,1)\} \\ +\infty & \text{otherwise} \end{cases}$$

Finally, the discounting $\Phi = (\phi_1,\ldots,\phi_k)$ is defined as $\phi_i = \overline{\frac{1}{2|\Sigma|}}$ for every $i = 1,\ldots,k$, where $\overline{\frac{1}{2|\Sigma|}}(a) = \frac{1}{2|\Sigma|} \cdot a$ for $a \in \mathbb{R}_{\geq 0}$ and $\overline{\frac{1}{2|\Sigma|}}(+\infty) = +\infty$.

It is easy to see that there is a unique run r_0 with non-infinite weight, the one that assigns q_0 to the nodes labeled with $(0,0)$ or $(1,1)$, i.e., words that do not belong to $K \mathbin{\Delta} N$, and q_1 to the ones labeled with $(1,0)$ or $(0,1)$, i.e., words that belong to $K \mathbin{\Delta} N$. The discounting multiplies the weight of every word $w \in \Sigma^*$

with $(\frac{1}{2|\Sigma|})^{|w|}$. If the word does not belong to $K \,\Delta\, N$ it gets a zero weight. If it does belong to $K \,\Delta\, N$, it gets weight $\frac{1}{2}$. "Multiplying" in $\mathbb{R}_{\text{inf}}$ (i.e., summing over all words in Σ^*), we obtain exactly $\mu(K \,\Delta\, N)$ as weight for this run.

4.2 Computing the Behavior on Regular Trees

Given a Φ-wLTA $\mathcal{M}$ over a semiring $\mathcal{S}$ and an rLTA $\mathcal{A}$ representing a regular tree t, we want to compute the behavior of $\mathcal{M}$ on t, i.e., $(||\mathcal{M}||, t)$. In a first step, we reduce this problem to the problem of computing the behavior of a Φ-wLTA on the unlabeled tree. To be more precise, we combine the two automata $\mathcal{M}$ and $\mathcal{A}$ into a single Φ-wLTA $\mathcal{M}_\mathcal{A}$ that works on the unlabeled tree t_{ul} such that $(||\mathcal{M}||, t) = (||\mathcal{M}_\mathcal{A}||, t_{ul})$.

Theorem 2. *Given a Φ-wLTA $\mathcal{M} = (\Sigma, Q, L, in, wt)$ over $\mathcal{S}$ and an rLTA $\mathcal{A} = (\Sigma, P, L, \Delta, \{p_s\})$ representing a regular tree t, one can construct in polynomial time a Φ-wLTA $\mathcal{M}_\mathcal{A}$ over $\mathcal{S}$ working on the unlabeled tree t_{ul} such that $(||\mathcal{M}||, t) = (||\mathcal{M}_\mathcal{A}||, t_{ul})$.*

Proof. Let $\mathcal{S} = (S, \oplus, \otimes, \mathbb{0}, \mathbb{1})$. By the definition of rLTAs, for every state $p \in P$ there exists a unique letter $l_p \in L$ such that $(p, l_p, \ldots) \in \Delta$.

We define the Φ-wLTA $\mathcal{M}_\mathcal{A} = (Q \times P \times L, \Sigma, in', wt')$ over $\mathcal{S}$ as follows:

$$in'(q,p,l) := \begin{cases} in(q) & \text{if } p = p_s \text{ and } l = l_{p_s} \\ \mathbb{0} & \text{otherwise} \end{cases}$$

$$\begin{aligned} & wt'\big((q_0,p_0,l_0),(q_1,p_1,l_1),\ldots,(q_k,p_k,l_k)\big) \\ & \qquad := \begin{cases} wt(q_0,l_0,q_1,\ldots,q_k) & \text{if } (p_0,l_0,p_1,\ldots,p_k) \in \Delta \\ \mathbb{0} & \text{otherwise} \end{cases} \end{aligned}$$

To prove that $(||\mathcal{M}||, t) = (||\mathcal{M}_\mathcal{A}||, t_{ul})$, it is sufficient to show that there exists an injection $\tau : R_\mathcal{M}(t) \to R_{\mathcal{M}_\mathcal{A}}$ such that $weight(r) = weight(\tau(r))$ for every $r \in R_\mathcal{M}(t)$ and $weight(r') = \mathbb{0}$ for every $r' \in R_{\mathcal{M}_\mathcal{A}} \setminus im(\tau)$, where $im(\tau)$ stands for the *image* set of the mapping τ. The definition of the injection τ and a proof that it has the required properties can be found in [7]. □

Thus, it remains to show how the behavior of a Φ-wLTA working on the unlabeled tree can be computed. For wLTAs (without discounting) over complete distributive lattices this was done in [12]. In the next section, we show how the behavior of a Φ-wLTA over the semiring $\mathbb{R}_{\text{inf}}$ can be computed.

5 Computing the Behavior on the Unlabeled Tree in $\mathbb{R}_{\text{inf}}$

Concentrating on $\mathbb{R}_{\text{inf}}$ is motivated, on the one hand, by the fact that our motivating examples (the distance functions d_1 and d_2) can be expressed using wLTA with discounting over this semiring. On the other hand, discounting for this semiring is well-understood [17] and nicely behaved. Note, however, that our results can be extended to the Viterbi semiring (see [7]).

Recall that, for $\mathbb{R}_{\text{inf}}$, all endomorphisms are of the form $\overline{p}(a) = p \cdot a$ for $p \in \mathbb{R}_{\geq 0}$, and thus the discounting is of the form $\Phi = (\overline{p_1}, \dots, \overline{p_k})$. Given $w = \sigma_{i_1} \dots \sigma_{i_m} \in \Sigma^*$, we set $p_w = p_{i_1} \cdot \dots \cdot p_{i_m}$ where the empty product (case $w = \varepsilon$) is 1. Then $\phi_w(a) = \phi_{i_1} \circ \dots \circ \phi_{i_m}(a) = p_{i_1} \cdot \dots \cdot p_{i_m} \cdot a = \overline{p_w}(a)$, and thus $\phi_w = \overline{p_w}$. It is easy to see that, for $p > 0$, $\overline{p}$ distributes over inf and $\sum$. In the following, we assume that $p_i \neq 0$ for $i = 1, \dots, k$, and we will write $p_w \cdot a$ instead of $\phi_w(a)$.

A *q-run* r of $\mathcal{M}$ is a run with $r(\varepsilon) = q$. We denote the set of all q-runs of $\mathcal{M}$ as $R(q)$. The *running weight* of a q-run is defined like its weight, but without taking the initial distribution into account, i.e., $rweight(r) := \sum_{w \in \Sigma^*} p_w \cdot wt(r, w)$, and thus $weight(r) = in(q) + rweight(r)$. Consequently, if we define

$$\mu(q) := \inf_{r \in R(q)} rweight(r) \quad \text{(for every } q \in Q)$$

then $(\|\mathcal{M}\|, t_{ul}) = \min_{q \in Q} \{in(q) + \mu(q)\}$. Hence, in order to compute the behavior of $\mathcal{M}$ on t_{ul}, it suffices to calculate the values $\mu(q)$ for all $q \in Q$. These values satisfy the following system of recursive equations (see [7] for a proof):

$$\mu(q) - \min_{(q_1, \dots, q_k) \in Q^k} \left\{ wt(q, q_1, \dots, q_k) + \sum_{i=1}^{k} p_i \cdot \mu(q_i) \right\}. \tag{5}$$

Our approach for computing the values $\mu(q)$ depends on the kind of discounting used.

5.1 Behavior for Nondecreasing Discounting

In this section we assume that the discounting is *nondecreasing*, i.e., $p_i \geq 1$ for all $i = 1, \dots, k$. Note that absence of discounting corresponds to the special case where $p_i = 1$ for all $i = 1, \dots, k$.

If the discounting is nondecreasing, then we have for every run $r \in R_{\mathcal{M}}$ that

$$rweight(r) = \sum_{w \in \Sigma^*} p_w \cdot wt(r, w) \geq \sum_{w \in \Sigma^*} wt(r, w),$$

where in the latter infinite sum only finitely many distinct non-negative real numbers occur. Consequently, this sum is a finite number iff only 0 is used infinitely often in the sum. Therefore, a run r has finite weight iff from a certain depth on it has only zero-weight transitions. Consequently, we can restrict our attention to deciding for each state q whether such a (finite weight) q-run exists, and compute the smallest weight among all of them.

The first step consists of computing the set of states in Q that admit a run with only zero-weight transitions. Clearly, these are exactly the states q for which $\mu(q) = 0$. By keeping only transitions with weight 0 and then applying the emptiness test for LTAs [13] to the resulting automaton, these states can easily be computed (see [7] for details).

Lemma 2. *The set of states* $Q_{\mu=0} := \{q \in Q \mid \mu(q) = 0\}$ *can be computed in polynomial time.*

A run with finite weight does not use a transition with weight $+\infty$ and below a certain depth in the tree it contains only states that belong to $Q_{\mu=0}$. Thus, the states used in the run must have access to states in $Q_{\mu=0}$ through transitions with finite weight. To be more precise, define the set Q_{acc} of states that *have access to* $Q_{\mu=0}$ to be the least subset of Q such that (i) $Q_{\mu=0} \subseteq Q_{acc}$ and (ii) if $q_i \in Q_{acc}$ for every $i = 1, \ldots, k$ and $wt(q, q_1, \ldots, q_k) \neq +\infty$ then $q \in Q_{acc}$. States q that have access to $Q_{\mu=0}$ have a q-run with finite running weight, and hence $\mu(q) < +\infty$. If q does not have access to $Q_{\mu=0}$, then $\mu(q) = +\infty$. By using an approach inspired by Dijkstra's shortest path algorithm, we can compute the states that have access to $Q_{\mu=0}$ together with their μ-value in polynomial time (see [7] for details). Since the behavior of $\mathcal{M}$ on t_{ul} can easily be computed from the values $\mu(q)$ for $q \in Q$, this yields the following theorem.

Theorem 3. *The behavior of a* Φ*-wLTA with nondecreasing discounting* Φ *over* $\mathbb{R}_{\text{inf}}$ *on the unlabeled tree can be computed in polynomial time.*

5.2 Behavior for Contracting Discounting

In this section, we assume a *contracting* discounting, i.e., $p_i < \frac{1}{k}$ for all $i = 1, \ldots, k$, where $k = |\Sigma|$.

Recall that it suffices to compute the value $\mu(q)$ for every $q \in Q$. To achieve this, we generalize the approach used in [8] for the special case of d_2. Let $Q = \{q_1, \ldots, q_n\}$. For each $q_i \in Q$, the unknown value $\mu(q_i)$ is associated to a variable x_i. Additionally, let $I = \{1, \ldots, n\}$. Then, (5) states that $(\mu(q_1), \ldots, \mu(q_n))$ is a solution of the following system of equations:

$$x_i = \min_{(i_1,\ldots,i_k)\in I^k} \left\{ wt(q_i, q_{i_1}, \ldots, q_{i_k}) + \sum_{j=1}^{k} p_j \cdot x_{i_j} \right\} \tag{6}$$

Since we use contracting discounting, Banach's fixed point theorem [14,23] can be used to show that the system (6) has a *unique* solution in $\mathbb{R}$ (see [7] for details). Thus, to compute the values $\mu(q)$ for $q \in Q$ it is sufficient to compute a solution of (6). This can be realized using Linear Programming [33], basically by the same approach used in [8]. Since solutions of Linear Programming problems can be computed in polynomial time, this is also the case for the values $\mu(q)$, and thus for the behavior.

Theorem 4. *The behavior of a* Φ*-wLTA with contracting discounting* Φ *over* $\mathbb{R}_{\text{inf}}$ *on the unlabeled tree can be computed in polynomial time.*

6 Conclusion

We have seen that concept comparison measures are important components of several approaches for approximation in DLs. Given two concepts C, D, such a measure assigns to them a value that expresses how well they compare. In general, these values come from a partially ordered set, but in most approaches to approximation considered so far, measures that map into the real numbers, and often only into the real interval $[0, 1]$, are used. An important requirement for such measures is that they respect the semantics of concepts, i.e., are invariant under equivalence in the sense that, if we replace C, D by equivalent concepts C', D', then the returned similarity comparison value is the same. To be useful in practice, another important requirement on the measures is that they are computable.

The main technical contribution of this paper is the development of a general framework for defining concept comparison measures for the DL $\mathcal{FL}_0$ that are computable and invariant under equivalence w.r.t. general TBoxes. Our framework is based on a characterization of equivalence w.r.t. general $\mathcal{FL}_0$ TBoxes that uses tuples of formal languages. These tuples can be expressed by infinite trees, which in turn are represented by looping tree automata. Assigning a comparison value to a pair of $\mathcal{FL}_0$ concepts in an equivalence invariant way thus boils down to assigning a value to a tree that is represented by a looping tree automaton. We use weighted tree automata with discounting for this purpose, and reduce the problem of computing the comparison value to the problem of computing the behavior of such an automaton on the unlabeled infinite tree. If the weights of the automaton come from the semiring $\mathbb{R}_{\text{inf}}$, then this behavior can be computed in polynomial time provided that the employed discounting is nondecreasing or contracting. An obvious topic for future research is thus to extend these results to discounting that is neither contracting nor nondecreasing, or to other semirings as weight structures.

While the use of our framework guarantees that the obtained concept comparison measures are equivalence invariant and computable, the user of the framework needs to ensure (by appropriately defining the weighted automaton) that the obtained values make sense in the intended application. Nevertheless, it might be helpful to provide the user with automated tools for checking whether the defined measure satisfies certain properties, such as the properties often required for concept similarity measures [25]. In our framework, this boils down to deciding certain properties of weighted tree automata with discounting.

Finally, if concept comparison measures defined using our framework are employed within one of the approximation approaches sketched in Sect. 2.3, one can investigate whether the important inference problems in this approach are guaranteed to be decidable. For example, assume that a concept similarity measure defined using our approach is employed to relax instance queries in $\mathcal{FL}_0$. Can we extend our computability result for the measure to a decidability result for the relaxed instance problem? If the answer is affirmative, what is the exact complexity of the relaxed instance problem in this setting?

References

1. de Alfaro, L., Henzinger, T.A., Majumdar, R.: Discounting the future in systems theory. In: Baeten, J.C.M., Lenstra, J.K., Parrow, J., Woeginger, G.J. (eds.) ICALP 2003. LNCS, vol. 2719, pp. 1022–1037. Springer, Heidelberg (2003). doi:10.1007/3-540-45061-0_79

2. Baader, F., Borgwardt, S., Morawska, B.: Extending unification in $\mathcal{EL}$ towards general TBoxes. In: Proceedings of the 13th International Conference on Principles of Knowledge Representation and Reasoning (KR 2012), pp. 568–572. AAAI Press/The MIT Press (2012)
3. Baader, F., Brandt, S., Lutz, C.: Pushing the $\mathcal{EL}$ envelope. In: Proceedings of the 19th International Joint Conference on Artificial Intelligence (IJCAI 2005), pp. 364–369. Morgan Kaufmann, Los Altos (2005)
4. Baader, F., Brewka, G., Fernández Gil, O.: Adding threshold concepts to the description logic $\mathcal{EL}$. In: Lutz, C., Ranise, S. (eds.) FroCoS 2015. LNCS (LNAI), vol. 9322, pp. 33–48. Springer, Heidelberg (2015). doi:10.1007/978-3-319-24246-0_3
5. Baader, F., Calvanese, D., McGuinness, D., Nardi, D., Patel-Schneider, P.F. (eds.): The Description Logic Handbook: Theory, Implementation, and Applications. Cambridge University Press, Cambridge (2003)
6. Baader, F., Fernández Gil, O.: Decidability and complexity of threshold description logics induced by concept similarity measures. In: Proceedings of the 32nd Annual ACM Symposium on Applied Computing (SAC 2017). ACM (2017, to appear)
7. Baader, F., Fernández Gil, O., Marantidis, P.: Approximation in description logics: how weighted tree automata can help to define the required concept comparison measures in $\mathcal{FL}_0$. LTCS-report LTCS-16-08, Chair for Automata Theory, Institute for Theoretical Computer Science, TU Dresden, Germany (2016). http://lat.inf.tu-dresden.de/research/reports.html
8. Baader, F., Marantidis, P., Okhotin, A.: Approximate unification in the description logic $\mathcal{FL}_0$. In: Michael, L., Kakas, A. (eds.) JELIA 2016. LNCS (LNAI), vol. 10021, pp. 49–63. Springer, Heidelberg (2016). doi:10.1007/978-3-319-48758-8_4
9. Baader, F., Morawska, B.: Unification in the description logic $\mathcal{EL}$. Log. Methods Comput. Sci. **6**(3), 1–31 (2010)
10. Baader, F., Narendran, P.: Unification of concept terms in description logics. J. Symb. Comput. **31**(3), 277–305 (2001)
11. Baader, F., Okhotin, A.: On language equations with one-sided concatenation. Fundam. Inf. **126**(1), 1–35 (2013)
12. Baader, F., Peñaloza, R.: Automata-based axiom pinpointing. J. Autom. Reason. **45**(2), 91–129 (2010)
13. Baader, F., Tobies, S.: The inverse method implements the automata approach for modal satisfiability. In: Goré, R., Leitsch, A., Nipkow, T. (eds.) IJCAR 2001. LNCS, vol. 2083, pp. 92–106. Springer, Heidelberg (2001). doi:10.1007/3-540-45744-5_8
14. Banach, S.: Sur les opérations dans les ensembles abstraits et leur application aux équations intégrales. Fund. Math. **3**(1), 133–181 (1922)
15. Brandt, S.: Polynomial time reasoning in a description logic with existential restrictions, GCI axioms, and–what else? In: Proceedings of the 16th European Conference on Artificial Intelligence (ECAI 2004), pp. 298–302. IOS Press (2004)
16. d'Amato, C., Fanizzi, N., Esposito, F.: A semantic similarity measure for expressive description logics. In: Pettorossi, A. (ed.) Proceedings of Convegno Italiano di Logica Computazionale (CILC05) (2005)
17. Droste, M., Kuske, D.: Skew and infinitary formal power series. Theoret. Comput. Sci. **366**(3), 199–227 (2006)
18. Droste, M., Rahonis, G.: Weighted automata and weighted logics with discounting. Theoret. Comput. Sci. **410**(37), 3481–3494 (2009)

19. Ecke, A., Peñaloza, R., Turhan, A.Y.: Answering instance queries relaxed by concept similarity. In: Proceedings of the 14th International Conference on Principles of Knowledge Representation and Reasoning (KR 2014), pp. 248–257. AAAI Press (2014)
20. Ecke, A., Peñaloza, R., Turhan, A.Y.: Similarity-based relaxed instance queries. J. Appl. Logic **13**(4, Part 1), 480–508 (2015). Special Issue for the Workshop on Weighted Logics for AI 2013
21. Fülöp, Z., Vogler, H.: Weighted tree automata and tree transducers. In: Droste, M., Kuich, W., Vogler, H. (eds.) Handbook of Weighted Automata, pp. 313–403. Springer, Heidelberg (2009)
22. Hoehndorf, R., Schofield, P.N., Gkoutos, G.V.: The role of ontologies in biological and biomedical research: a functional perspective. Brief. Bioinform. **16**(6), 1069–1080 (2015)
23. Kreyszig, E.: Introductory Functional Analysis with Applications. Wiley Classics Library. Wiley, Hoboken (1978)
24. Küsters, R.: Non-Standard Inferences in Description Logics. LNCS (LNAI), vol. 2100. Springer, Heidelberg (2001). doi:10.1007/3-540-44613-3_3
25. Lehmann, K., Turhan, A.-Y.: A framework for semantic-based similarity measures for $\mathcal{ELH}$-concepts. In: Cerro, L.F., Herzig, A., Mengin, J. (eds.) JELIA 2012. LNCS (LNAI), vol. 7519, pp. 307–319. Springer, Heidelberg (2012). doi:10.1007/978-3-642-33353-8_24
26. Mandrali, E., Rahonis, G.: Recognizable tree series with discounting. Acta Cybern. **19**(2), 411–439 (2009)
27. Pan, J.Z., Ren, Y., Zhao, Y.: Tractable approximate deduction for OWL. Artif. Intell. **235**, 95–155 (2016)
28. Pensel, M.: An automata based approach for subsumption w.r.t. general concept inclusions in the description logic $\mathcal{FL}_0$. Master's thesis, Chair for Automata Theory, TU Dresden, Germany (2015). http://lat.inf.tu-dresden.de/research/mas
29. Rabin, M.O.: Automata on Infinite Objects and Church's Problem. American Mathematical Society, Boston (1972)
30. Racharak, T., Suntisrivaraporn, B.: Similarity measures for $\mathcal{FL}_0$ concept descriptions from an automata-theoretic point of view. In: 6th International Conference of Information and Communication Technology for Embedded Systems (IC-ICTES), pp. 1–6 (2015)
31. Rahonis, G.: Weighted muller tree automata and weighted logics. J. Autom. Lang. Comb. **12**(4), 455–483 (2007)
32. Schild, K.: A correspondence theory for terminological logics: preliminary report. In: Proceedings of the 12th International Joint Conference on Artificial Intelligence (IJCAI 1991), pp. 466–471. Morgan Kaufmann, Los Altos (1991)
33. Schrijver, A.: Theory of Linear and Integer Programming. Wiley-Interscience Series in Discrete Mathematics and Optimization. Wiley, Hoboken (1999)
34. Suntisrivaraporn, B.: A similarity measure for the description logic $\mathcal{EL}$ with unfoldable terminologies. In: 5th International Conference on Intelligent Networking and Collaborative Systems, pp. 408–413. IEEE (2013)
35. Thomas, W.: Automata on infinite objects. In: Handbook of Theoretical Computer Science, Volume B: Formal Models and Sematics (B), pp. 133–192. The MIT Press (1990)
36. Wolter, F., Zakharyaschev, M.: Undecidability of the unification and admissibility problems for modal and description logics. ACM Trans. Comput. Logic **9**(4), 25:1–25:20 (2008)

Logic, Languages, and Rules for Web Data Extraction and Reasoning over Data

Georg Gottlob[1], Christoph Koch[2], and Andreas Pieris[3](✉)

[1] University of Oxford, Oxford, UK
georg.gottlob@cs.ox.ac.uk
[2] École Polytechnique Fédérale de Lausanne, Lausanne, Switzerland
christoph.koch@epfl.ch
[3] University of Edinburgh, Edinburgh, Scotland
apieris@inf.ed.ac.uk

Abstract. This paper gives a short overview of specific logical approaches to data extraction, data management, and reasoning about data. In particular, we survey theoretical results and formalisms that have been obtained and used in the context of the Lixto Project at TU Wien, the DIADEM project at the University of Oxford, and the VADA project, which is currently being carried out jointly by the universities of Edinburgh, Manchester, and Oxford. We start with a formal approach to web data extraction rooted in monadic second order logic and monadic Datalog, which gave rise to the Lixto data extraction system. We then present some complexity results for monadic Datalog over trees and for XPath query evaluation. We further argue that for value creation and for ontological reasoning over data, we need existential quantifiers (or Skolem terms) in rule heads, and introduce the Datalog$^{\pm}$ family. We give an overview of important members of this family and discuss related complexity issues.

1 Introduction

"The web is the largest database" is a sentence one nowadays can hear quite frequently. However, this statement is not really true. The web, including the deep web, is certainly the largest data repository, but not a *database*. In a database, data is homogeneously formatted, and can be retrieved efficiently and uniformly via query languages. Web data, even when it is about the same type of items (say, used cars or any other consumer good) appears in a different format on many different websites. There is, moreover, no uniform query or retrieval mechanism. In order to be able to query such data, we thus have to extract it from the different web sources, recast it into a single format, and, if appropriate, store it in a single database. This process is called *web data extraction*, and the programs that extract data from the web are called *wrappers*.

The wrapping problem is often seen as a software and web-engineering task, but has also been addressed by a substantial amount of systems-oriented research work, see e.g. TSIMMIS [55], FLORID [46], DEByE [44], W4F [56], XWrap [45],

F. Drewes et al. (Eds.): LATA 2017, LNCS 10168, pp. 27–47, 2017.
DOI: 10.1007/978-3-319-53733-7_2

Lixto [4,6,29] and Diadem [22], some of which led to commercial spin-outs. Moreover, in [27], a logical theory of data extraction has been developed that has led people to consider monadic Datalog as a logical language for data extraction, which has, in turn, been the basis of a more practical logical language implemented in the Lixto system. In Sect. 2, which is a slightly shortened exposition of material from [29] (which in turn summarizes [27]), we will give a short survey of the logical approach to web data extraction.

Web documents in HTML are essentially labeled trees, where many labels correspond to formatting instructions for data presentation (such as <table>, <td>, or <header1>, and so on) and where the actual data items reside at the leaf level. Thus, rather than imposing a logical structure on the data, the labels in HTML take care of the display format and make sure that a web page displayed in a browser meets the eye of the beholder. However, XML[1], a well-known language quite similar to HTML, allows one to impose a tree-shaped logical structure on data. From a conceptual point of view, this generalizes the "flat" relational data format. Special query language such as XPath[2], XQuery[3], and XSLT[4] have been designed for XML databases. With some minor additions, monadic Datalog can be used to simulate the core fragment of XPath [26], which indicates that core XPath is not more expressive than monadic Datalog. This observation gave rise to complexity studies of XPath evaluation whose basic results will be summarized in Sect. 3.

Once data is extracted, one usually wants to combine it with other extracted data and corporate data from local databases. In addition, some cleaning, reasoning and further provisioning tasks have to be performed. All this together is called *data wrangling* [23]. Apparently, languages for data wrangling purposes should be able to perform complex data transformation, data exchange, data integration and ontological reasoning tasks. However, Datalog, let alone monadic Datalog, is not powerful enough for performing such tasks. In Sect. 4, which is based on the longer survey [10], we argue that the crucial limitation of Datalog is the fact that is not able to infer the existence of new objects, which are not already in the extensional database. We then proceed to introduce Datalog$^\pm$, a family of logical languages that extend Datalog with key modeling features such as existential quantifiers in rule heads, which allow to infer the existence of new objects. We give an overview of important members of this family and discuss related complexity issues.

2 Logical Foundations of Web Data Extraction

2.1 Desiderata for Wrapping Languages

To allow for a foundational study of wrapping languages, we first need to establish criteria that allow us to compare such languages. In [27], four desiderata

[1] https://www.w3.org/TR/1998/REC-xml-19980210.
[2] http://www.w3c.org/TR/xpath/.
[3] https://www.w3.org/XML/Query/.
[4] http://www.w3.org/TR/xslt.

were proposed that a good wrapping language should satisfy. In particular, such a language should

(i) have a solid and well-understood theoretical foundation,
(ii) provide a good trade-off between complexity and the number of practical wrappers that can be expressed,
(iii) be easy to use as a wrapper programming language, and
(iv) be suitable for incorporation into visual tools.

The core notion that we base our wrapping approach on is that of an *information extraction function*, which takes a labeled unranked tree (representing a Web document) and returns a subset of its nodes. A wrapper is a program which implements one or several such functions, and thereby assigns unary predicates to document tree nodes. Based on these predicate assignments and the structure of the input tree, a new data tree can be computed as the result of the information extraction process in a natural way, along the lines of the input tree, but using the new labels and omitting nodes that have not been relabeled (by some form of tree minor computation).

Given a set of information extraction functions, one natural way to wrap an input tree t is to compute a new label for each node n (or filter out n) as a function of the predicates assigned using the information extraction functions. The output tree is computed by connecting the resulting labeled nodes using the (transitive closure of) the edge relation of t, preserving the document order of t. In other words, the output tree contains a node if a predicate corresponding to an information extraction function was computed for it, and contains an edge from node v to node w if there is a directed path from v to w in the input tree, both v and w were assigned information extraction predicates, and there is no node on the path from v to w (other than v and w) that was assigned information extraction predicates. We do not formalize this operation here; the natural way of doing this is obvious.

That way, we can take a tree, re-label its nodes, and declare some of them as irrelevant, but we cannot significantly transform its original structure. This coincides with the intuition that a wrapper may change the presentation of relevant information, its packaging or data model (which does not apply in the case of *Web wrapping*), but does not handle substantial data transformation tasks. We believe that this captures the essence of wrapping.

We assume unary queries in monadic second-order logic (MSO) over trees as the expressiveness yardstick for information extraction functions. MSO over trees is well-understood theory-wise [15,18,20,58] (see also [59]) and is quite expressive. In fact, it is considered by many as the language of choice for defining expressive node-selecting queries on trees (see e.g. [27,43,53,54]; [57] acknowledges the role of MSO but argues for *even stronger* languages). In our experience, when considering a wrapping system that lacks this expressive power, it is usually quite easy to find real-life wrapping problems that cannot be handled (see also the related discussion on MSO expressiveness and node-selecting queries in [43]).

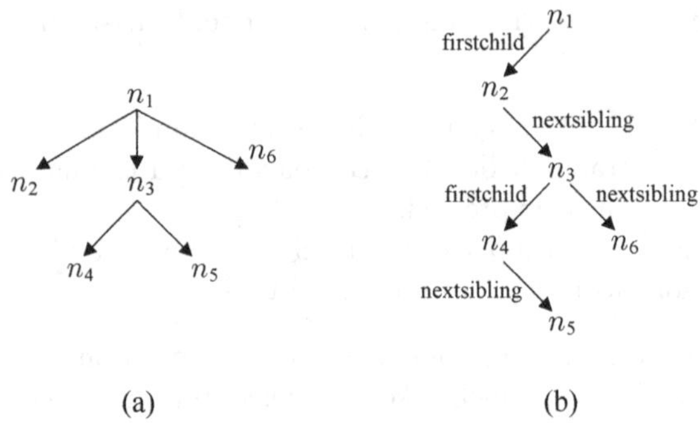

Fig. 1. (a) An unranked tree and (b) its representation using the binary relations "firstchild" (↙) and "nextsibling" (↘).

In this section, we discuss *monadic Datalog* over trees, a simple form of the logic-based language Datalog, as a wrapper programming language. Monadic Datalog satisfies desiderata (i) to (iv) raised above. Monadic Datalog is the logical core of Elog [5], which is the internal language of the Lixto system. Elog extends monadic Datalog by features for handling the most common tasks of web navigation and visual wrapper-definition. Elog it strictly more expressive than MSO. For a detailed description of Elog, which we will not further discuss here, see [5]. For a formal study of Elog and a comparison to other wrapping languages, see [27,28].

A monadic Datalog program can compute a *set* of unary queries ("information extraction functions") at once. Each intensional predicate of a program selects a subset of dom and can be considered to define one information extraction function. However, in general, not all intensional predicates define information extraction functions. Some have to be declared as auxiliary.

2.2 Tree Structures

Trees are defined in the normal way and have at least one node. We assume that the children of each node are in some fixed order. Each node has a label taken from a finite nonempty set of symbols Σ, the alphabet[5]. We consider only *unranked* finite trees, which correspond closely to parsed HTML or XML documents. In an unranked tree, each node may have an arbitrary number of children. An unranked ordered tree can be considered as a structure

$$t_{ur} = \langle \text{dom, root, leaf, } (\text{label}_a)_{a \in \Sigma}, \text{firstchild, nextsibling, lastsibling} \rangle$$

where "dom" is the set of nodes in the tree, "root", "leaf", "lastsibling", and the "label_a" relations are unary, while "firstchild" and "nextsibling" are binary.

[5] In this simple model, unrestricted sets of tags as well as string and attribute values are assumed to be encoded as lists of character symbols modeled as subtrees in our document tree.

All relations are defined according to their intuitive meanings. "root" contains exactly one node, the root node. "leaf" consists of the set of all leaves. "firstchild(n_1, n_2)" is true iff n_2 is the leftmost child of n_1; "nextsibling(n_1, n_2)" is true iff, for some i, n_1 and n_2 are the i-th and $(i+1)$-th children of a common parent node, respectively, counting from the left (see also Fig. 1). $\text{label}_a(n)$ is true iff n is labeled a in the tree. Finally, "lastsibling" contains the set of rightmost children of nodes. (The root node is not a last sibling, as it has no parent.) Whenever the structure t may not be clear from the context, we state it as a subscript of the relation names (as e.g. in dom_t, root_t, ...). By default, we will always assume trees to be represented using the schema (signature) outlined above, and will refer to them as τ_{ur}.

The *document order* relation $\prec$ is a natural total ordering of dom used in several XML-related standards. It is defined as the order in which the opening tags of document tree nodes are first reached when reading an HTML or XML document (as a flat text file) from left to right.

2.3 Monadic Datalog

We assume the function-free logic programming syntax and semantics of the *Datalog* language and refer to [1] for a detailed survey of Datalog. *Monadic Datalog* [14, 27] is obtained from full Datalog by requiring all intensional predicates to be unary. By unary query, we denote a function that assigns a predicate to some elements of dom (or, in other words, selects a subset of dom). For monadic Datalog, one obtains a unary query by distinguishing one intensional predicate as the *query predicate*. By *signature*, we denote the (finite) set of all extensional predicates (with fixed arities) available to a Datalog program. By default, we use the signature τ_{ur} for unranked trees.[6]

Example 1. The monadic Datalog program over τ_{ur}

$$\mathit{Italic}(x) \leftarrow \text{label}_i(x) \tag{1}$$

$$\mathit{Italic}(x) \leftarrow \mathit{Italic}(x_0),\ \text{firstchild}(x_0, x) \tag{2}$$

$$\mathit{Italic}(x) \leftarrow \mathit{Italic}(x_0),\ \text{nextsibling}(x_0, x) \tag{3}$$

computes, given an unranked tree (representing an HTML parse tree), all nodes whose contents are displayed in italic font (i.e., for which an ancestor node in the parse tree corresponds to a well-formed piece of HTML of the form $\langle i \rangle \ldots \langle /i \rangle$ and is thus labeled "i"). The program uses the intentional predicate, *Italic*, as the query predicate.

Monadic second-order logic (MSO) extends first-order logic by quantification over set variables, i.e., variables ranging over sets of nodes, which coexist with

[6] Note that our tree structures contain some redundancy (e.g., a leaf is a node x such that $\neg(\exists y)\text{firstchild}(x, y))$, by which (monadic) Datalog becomes as expressive as its *semipositive* generalization. Semipositive Datalog allows to use the complements of extensional relations in rule bodies.

first-order quantification of variables ranging over single nodes. A unary MSO *query* is defined by an MSO formula φ with one free first-order variable. Given a tree t, it evaluates to the set of nodes $\{x \in \text{dom} \mid t \models \varphi(x)\}$. The following holds for arbitrary finite structures:

Proposition 2 (Folklore). *Each monadic Datalog query is MSO-definable.*

Here, our main measure of query evaluation cost is *combined complexity*, i.e. where both the database and the query (or program) are considered variable. Later, we will also be interested in *data complexity*, where the query (or program) is fixed and only the database is considered variable.

Proposition 3. (see e.g. [27]) *Monadic Datalog (over arbitrary finite structures) is NP-complete w.r.t. combined complexity.*

2.4 Monadic Datalog over Trees

By restricting our structures to trees, monadic Datalog acquires a number of additional nice properties. First,

Theorem 4 [27]. *Over τ_{ur}, monadic Datalog has $O(|\mathcal{P}| \cdot |dom|)$ combined complexity (where $|\mathcal{P}|$ is the size of the program and $|dom|$ the size of the tree).*

This follows from the fact that all binary relations in τ_{ur} have bidirectional functional dependencies; for instance, each node has at most one first child and is the first child of at most one other node. Thus, given a program $\mathcal{P}$, an equivalent ground program can be computed in time $O(|\mathcal{P}| \cdot |\text{dom}|)$, while ground programs can be evaluated in linear time [52].

A unary query over trees is MSO-definable exactly if it is definable in monadic Datalog.

Theorem 5 [27]. *Each unary MSO-definable query over τ_{ur} is definable in monadic Datalog over τ_{ur}.*

(The other direction follows from Proposition 2.) Judging from our experience with the Lixto system, real-world wrappers written in monadic Datalog are small. Thus, in practice, we do not trade the complexity compared to MSO (for which query evaluation is known to be PSPACE-complete) for considerably expanded program sizes.

Each monadic Datalog program over trees can be efficiently rewritten into an equivalent program using only very restricted syntax. This motivates a normal form for monadic Datalog over trees.

Definition 6. A monadic Datalog program $\mathcal{P}$ over τ_{ur} is in *Tree-Marking Normal Form* (TMNF) if each rule of $\mathcal{P}$ is of one of the following three forms:

$$(1)\ p(x) \leftarrow p_0(x),$$
$$(2)\ p(x) \leftarrow p_0(x_0),\ B(x_0, x).$$
$$(3)\ p(x) \leftarrow p_0(x),\ p_1(x).$$

where the unary predicates p_0 and p_1 are either intensional or of τ_{ur} and B is either R or R^{-1}, where R is a binary predicate from τ_{ur}. □

In the next result, the signature for unranked trees may extend τ_{ur} to include the "child" relation – likely to be the most common form of navigation in trees.

Theorem 7 [27]. *For each monadic Datalog program $\mathcal{P}$ over $\tau_{ur} \cup \{child\}$, there is an equivalent TMNF program over τ_{ur} which can be computed in time $O(|\mathcal{P}|)$.*

From the above discussion, we conclude that monadic Datalog has the expressive power of our yardstick MSO (on trees), can be evaluated efficiently, and is a *good* (easy to use) wrapper programming language. Indeed, with respect to the desiderata listed in Subsect. 2.1, we point out that:

1. The existence of the normal form TMNF demonstrates that rules in monadic Datalog never have to be long or intricate.
2. The monotone semantics makes the wrapper programming task quite modular and intuitive. Differently from an automaton definition that usually has to be understood entirely to be certain of its correctness, adding a rule to a monadic Datalog program usually does not change its meaning completely, but *adds* to the functionality.
3. Wrappers defined in monadic Datalog are implemented as queries, whose definitions can be local and only need to consider as much context as required by the query conditions. This distinguishes them from tree automata, which, even in flavors able to define monadic queries, always recognise a language of trees and conceptually traverse the entire input tree. This makes tree automata more brittle in real-world wrapping scenarios, and causes them to require a greater effort from the programmer, much of which is directed towards accepting a large enough tree language, rather than the essence of the wrapping task at hand.

Thus, monadic Datalog over trees as a framework for Web information extraction satisfies the first three of our desiderata stated in Subsect. 2.1: efficient evaluation, appropriate expressiveness, and suitability as a practical wrapper programming language. Only the fourth desideratum – the visual specification of wrappers – is not addressed here; we refer the interested reader to [6,29], where it is clearly explained that monadic Datalog paradigm is ideally suited for representing wrappers generated by a visual wrapper definition process using successive restriction and generalization steps.

3 The Complexity of XPath Query Evaluation

We have seen in Theorem 4 that monadic Datalog over trees defined by unary relations and the binary relations "firstchild", "nextsibling", and "lastsibling" can be solved in time linear in the size of the program and linear in the size of the tree. Relations such as "child" play an important role in various query languages on trees, such as XPath (and thus, XQuery and XSLT); there, they are called *axes*.

There are two main modes of navigation in trees, horizontal and vertical. For horizontal navigation, one can distinguish between navigating among sibling nodes and among nodes – intuitively – further left or right in the tree (the "following" axis in XPath). The most natural axis relations are thus *Child*, $Child^*$, $Child^+$, *Nextsibling*, $Nextsibling^*$, $Nextsibling^+$, and *Following*, where

$$Following(x, y) := \exists z_1, z_2\ Child^*(z_1, x) \wedge Nextsibling^+(z_1, z_2) \wedge Child^*(z_2, y).$$

Note that if we consider complexity rather than expressiveness, we do not need to deal with relations such as *Firstchild* in addition; we may assume a unary predicate *Firstsibling* such that

$$Firstchild(x, y) \Leftrightarrow Child(x, y) \wedge Firstsibling(y).$$

A natural question is to ask for the complexity of monadic Datalog programs over these axes, or, to start with a more basic problem, conjunctive queries (which can be seen as Datalog programs containing only a single nonrecursive rule). Note that conjunctive queries over trees also have natural applications in computational linguistics, term rewriting, and data integration [32].

In the case that all individual rule-bodies are acyclic (conjunctive queries), it is known from [27] that monadic Datalog over arbitrary axes can be evaluated in linear time. However, in data extraction, as well as in many other practical contexts, programs with cyclic rule bodies naturally arise.

As already observed in Proposition 3, while full Datalog is EXPTIME-complete (see, e.g., [16]), monadic Datalog over arbitrary finite structures is in NP (actually, NP-complete). For a lower bound on trees, it is known [49] that already Boolean conjunctive queries over structures of the form $\langle (P_i)_i, \text{child}, \text{child}^* \rangle$ are NP-hard w.r.t. combined complexity.

A detailed study of the tractability frontier of conjunctive queries over trees is presented in [32]. As observed, the subset-maximal polynomial cases of axis sets are

- $\{\text{child}^+, \text{child}^*\}$,
- $\{\text{child}, \text{nextsibling}, \text{nextsibling}^+, \text{nextsibling}^*\}$, and
- $\{\text{following}\}$.

That is, for each class of conjunctive queries over a subset of one of these three sets and over unary relations, the query evaluation problem is polynomial (with respect to combined complexity). We have the dichotomy that for all other cases of conjunctive queries using our axis relations (e.g. *Child* and $Child^+$), the problem is NP-complete. Obviously, the complexity of monadic Datalog over a given set of axes is always the same as that of conjunctive queries over the same axes.

The special case that queries are acyclic is also worth studying, since the probably most important node-selecting query language on trees, XPath, is naturally tree-shaped. All XPath engines available in 2002 took exponential time in the worst case to process XPath [30]. However,

Theorem 8 [30]. *XPath 1 is in PTIME w.r.t. combined complexity.*

This result is based on a dynamic programming algorithm which, in an improved form [30], yielded the first XPath engine guaranteed to run in polynomial time.

Most people use only the most common features of XPath, so it is worthwhile to study restrictive fragments of this language. In [30], the *Core XPath* has been introduced, the navigational fragment of XPath, which includes both horizontal and vertical tree navigation with axes, node tests, and boolean combinations of condition predicates. As shown there, Core XPath can be evaluated in time linear in the size of the database and linear in the size of the query. However,

Theorem 9 [31]. *Core XPath is P-hard w.r.t. combined complexity.*

This property – shared by XPath, of which Core XPath is a strict fragment – renders it highly unlikely that query evaluation is massively parallelizable (= in the complexity class *NC*, c.f. [40]) or that algorithms exist that take less than a polynomial amount of space for query processing. Interestingly, if we remove negation in condition predicates, the complexity of Core XPath is reduced to LOGCFL, a parallel complexity class in NC_2 [31].

Theorem 10 [31]. *Positive Core XPath is LOGCFL-complete w.r.t. combined complexity.*

This generalizes to a very large fragment of full XPath (called pXPath), from which besides negation only few very minor features have to be removed to obtain that

Theorem 11 [31]. *pXPath is LOGCFL-complete w.r.t. combined complexity.*

Further results on the complexity of various fragments of XPath 1 can be found in [31]. Positive Core XPath queries correspond to acyclic positive queries over axis relations. Interestingly, each conjunctive query over axis relations can be mapped to an equivalent acyclic positive query, however there are no polynomial translations for doing this [32]. Thus,

Corollary 12. *For ever conjunctive query over trees, there is an equivalent positive Core XPath query.*

Of course, when talking about conjunctive queries over trees, we assume that all binary relations in the signature are relations from our set of axes.

Finally, Core XPath queries can be mapped to monadic Datalog in linear time. The slightly curious fact here is that this remains true in the presence of negation in Core XPath (for which no analogous language feature exists in Datalog.)

Theorem 13 [21]. *Each Core XPath query can be translated into an equivalent TMNF query in linear time.*

4 Datalog$^{\pm}$: A Family of Logical Languages

It is generally agreed that Datalog is a powerful language with several different applications. We have already discussed that the monadic fragment of Datalog gives rise to a good wrapping language that can be used for web data extraction purposes. Moreover, Datalog has been used as an inference engine for knowledge processing within several software tools, and has gained popularity in the context of, e.g., source code querying and program analysis, and modeling distributed systems.

Although Datalog is a powerful rule-based formalism, it is not able to infer the existence of new objects that are not already in the extensional database. For a number of applications, however, it would be desirable that a Datalog extension could be able to express the existence of certain values that are not necessarily from the domain of the extensional database. This can be achieved by allowing existentially quantified variables in rule heads. Let us give a couple of brief examples of such applications.

Data Exchange. When data needs to be transposed or copied from one relational database to another one, the problem of heterogeneous schemas often arises. Imagine, for example, company ACME stores data about their employees in a relation EmpACME with schema $(\mathsf{Emp\#}, \mathsf{Name}, \mathsf{Address}, \mathsf{Salary})$, while the FOO corporation does not store employees' addresses, but only phone numbers, keeping their employee data in a relation EmpFOO having schema $(\mathsf{Emp\#}, \mathsf{Name}, \mathsf{Phone}, \mathsf{Salary})$. Imagine ACME is acquired by FOO and the ACME employee data ought to be transferred into the FOO database, although the phone numbers of the ACME employees are not (currently) known. This could be achieved by a rule of the form:

$$\mathrm{EmpACME}(e, n, a, s) \rightarrow \exists p\ \mathrm{EmpFOO}(e, n, p, s),$$

where phone numbers are simply existentially quantified. In practice, each phone number is stored by a different (labeled) *null value*, representing a globally existentially quantified variable (i.e., a kind of Skolem constant). Advanced data management systems such as Clio [51] have been developed, that effectively manage data-exchange mappings, handle existential nulls, and allow one to query relations with nulls. In database theory, a rule of the above form is actually called a *tuple-generating dependency (TGD)*, while in the KR community is known as *existential rule*; henceforth, we adopt the term TGD. In addition to TGDs, *equality-generating dependencies (EGDs)* are often used. They cover the well-known key constraints and functional dependencies that have been studied for a long time [1]. For example, we may impose that every ACME employee has only one phone number stored. This may be expressed as a Datalog rule with an equality in the head:

$$\mathrm{EmpFOO}(e, n, p, s), \mathrm{EmpFOO}(e, n', p', s') \rightarrow p = p'.$$

The data exchange literature insists on *finite target relations* because it is assumed that these relations are actually stored. It is thus important in this context to restrict our syntax to make sure that only a *finite number of different null values* will be invented.

Ontology Querying. Description logics (DLs) [3] are used to formalize so-called ontological knowledge about relationships between objects, entities, and classes in a certain application domain. For example, we could express that every person has exactly one father who, moreover, is himself a person, by the following DL clauses, where Person is a set of objects whose initial value is specified in the form of an extensional relation, called *concept*, and where HasFather is a binary relation, a so-called *role* in DL terminology: *(i)* Person $\sqsubseteq \exists$HasFather, *(ii)* $\exists$HasFather$^{-} \sqsubseteq$ Person, *(iii)* (funct HasFather). In an appropriate extension of Datalog, the same can be expressed as:

$$\begin{aligned} \text{Person}(x) &\rightarrow \exists y\, \text{HasFather}(x, y), \\ \text{HasFather}(x, y) &\rightarrow \text{Person}(y), \\ \text{HasFather}(x, y), \text{HasFather}(x, y') &\rightarrow y = y'. \end{aligned}$$

Note that here the relation Person, which is supplied in the input with an initial value, is actually modified. Therefore, we no longer require (as in standard Datalog) that extensional relation symbols cannot occur in rule heads.

DLs usually rely on classical first-order (FO) semantics, and so arbitrary models (finite or infinite) are considered. In the above example, models with infinite chains of ancestors are perfectly legal. Rather than "materializing" such models, i.e., computing and storing them, we are interested in reasoning and query answering. For example, whenever the initial value of Person is nonempty, then the Boolean conjunctive query

$$\exists x \exists y \exists z\, (\text{HasFather}(x, y) \wedge \text{HasFather}(y, z))$$

will evaluate to *true*, while the query

$$\exists x \exists y\, (\text{HasFather}(x, y) \wedge \text{HasFather}(y, x))$$

will evaluate to *false*, because it is false in some models.

To sum up, as we have briefly tried to sketch, some applications as the ones discussed above could possibly profit from appropriate forms of Datalog extended by the possibility of using rules with existential quantifiers in their heads (TGDs), and by several additional features (such as, for example, equality, negation, disjunction, etc.).

Unfortunately, already for sets Σ of TGDs alone, most basic reasoning and query answering problems are undecidable. In particular, checking whether a Boolean conjunctive query evaluates to true w.r.t. a database D and a set Σ of TGDs is undecidable [7]. Worse than that, undecidability holds even in case both Σ and q are *fixed*, and only D is given as input [8]. It is thus important to single out large classes of formalisms for rule sets Σ that

(i) are based on Datalog, and thus enable a modular rule-based style of knowledge representation,

(ii) are syntactical fragments of first-order logic so that answering a Boolean query q under Σ for an input database D is equivalent to the classical entailment check $D \wedge \Sigma \models q$,
(iii) are expressive enough for being useful in real applications in the above mentioned areas,
(iv) have decidable query answering, and
(v) have good query answering complexity properties in case Σ and q are fixed. This type of complexity is called *data complexity*, and is an important measure, because we can realistically assume that the extensional database D is the only really large object in the input.

In what follows we report on languages that fulfill these criteria. We dubbed the family of such languages Datalog$^{\pm}$, because, as already explained, they add features to Datalog, and on the other hand make some syntactic restrictions in order to fulfill desiderata (iv) and (v). In the rest of the paper, we focus on the key feature of existential quantification, or, in other words, on languages that are based on TGDs.

4.1 Acyclicity

Recall that for data exchange purposes, it is important to ensure that the target instance is finite since it is actually stored. However, executing an arbitrary set of TGDs on an input database, in general, we are forced to build an infinite instance due to the presence of the existentially quantified variables. Consider, for example, the set Σ of TGDs:

$$\text{Person}(x) \rightarrow \exists y\, \text{HasFather}(x,y) \qquad \text{HasFather}(x,y) \rightarrow \text{Person}(y),$$

which states that each person has a father who is also a person. Assuming now that the input database is $D = \{\text{Person}(Bob)\}$, stating that Bob is a person, after executing Σ on D we obtain an infinite instance. Indeed, from the first TGD we conclude that the atom $\text{HasFather}(Bob, z_1)$ holds, where z_1 is a (labeled) null value, while from the second TGD we obtain that $\text{Person}(z_1)$ holds. But then we can infer that also the atoms $\text{HasFather}(z_1, z_2)$ and $\text{Person}(z_2)$ hold, where z_2 is a fresh labeled null value, and it is apparent that this inference process is infinite. The inference algorithm that we have just described is known in the literature as the *chase procedure* (or simply chase) [1].

It is clear that a TGD-based language is suitable for data exchange purposes if, in addition to the desiderata (i)–(v) discussed above, ensures the termination of the chase. Several languages with this property have been proposed; see, e.g., [17,19,39,48]. The general idea underlying all these languages is to pose an acyclicity condition on a graph that encodes how terms are propagated during the execution of the chase procedure. The two most basic formalisms in this family of languages are the classes of *acyclic* (a.k.a. non-recursive) and *weakly-acyclic* sets of TGDs.

Acyclic Sets of TGDs. The definition of this class relies on the notion of the predicate (dependency) graph, which encodes how predicates depend to each other. More precisely, the *predicate graph* of a set Σ of TGDs is a directed graph $G = (V, E)$, where V consists of all the relation symbols in Σ, and E is defined as follows: for each $\sigma \in \Sigma$, for each relation R in the body of σ, and for each relation P in the head of σ,[7] $(R, P) \in E$; no other edges occur in E. We say that Σ is acyclic if G is acyclic.

It is not difficult to see that the chase always terminates under acyclic sets of TGDs. This immediately implies the decidability of our main reasoning task, that is, query answering. Given a Boolean conjunctive query q, to decide whether a database D and an acyclic set Σ of TGDs entails q, we simply need to compute the chase instance C w.r.t. D and Σ, and then check whether C satisfies q. We know that:

Theorem 14 [47]. *Query answering under acyclic sets of TGDs is in AC_0 w.r.t. data complexity, and NEXPTIME-complete w.r.t. combined complexity.*[8]

Notice that to explicitly compute the chase under acyclic sets of TGDs takes polynomial time in the size of the database. Thus, to obtain the AC_0 upper bound w.r.t. the data complexity, we need a more refined approach. This is done by unfolding the given set of TGDs (using a resolution-based procedure [34]) in order to construct a (finite) union of conjunctive queries, which is then evaluated over the input database. This allows us to conclude the AC_0 upper bound stated in the above theorem.

Weakly-Acyclic Sets of TGDs. It is clear that acyclic sets of TGDs do not capture plain Datalog. Nevertheless, an acyclicity-based class exists, called weakly-acyclic sets of TGDs, that captures both acyclic sets of TGDs and Datalog. This formalism has been proposed as the main language for data exchange purposes [19]. Weak-acyclicity relies on a slightly more involved graph notion, called position (dependency) graph, which encodes how terms are propagated from one position to another during the chase. Instead of giving the rather long definition, let us explain the key idea via a simple example.

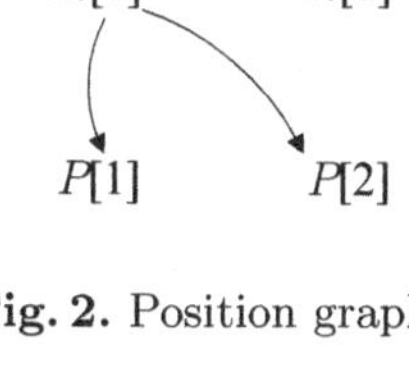

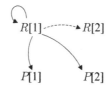

Fig. 2. Position graph.

[7] For a TGD of the form $b \rightarrow h$, b is called the body, while h is called the head.

[8] Here, the data complexity is calculated by fixing the set of TGDs and the query, while in the combined complexity we assume that everything is part of the input.

Example 15. Consider the set Σ consisting of the TGDs

$$R(x,y) \rightarrow \exists z\, R(x,z) \qquad R(x,y) \rightarrow P(x,y).$$

The position graph of Σ is shown in Fig. 2. We have an edge from $R[1]$ to itself since in the first TGD the variable x is propagated from the first position of the relation R in the body to the first position of the relation R in the head. Now, observe that at the same time, during the execution of the chase, a null value will be generated at the second position of R; this is encoded by the dashed edge, called *special*, from $R[1]$ to $R[2]$. The other two (normal) edges are present due to the second TGD.

A normal edge (π, π') keeps track of the fact that a term may propagate from π to π' during the chase. A special edge (π, π'') keeps track of the fact that propagation of a value from π to π' also creates a new value at position π''. Thus, if there is a cycle in the dependency graph that goes via a special edge, then it is likely that the generation of a null value at certain position will cause the generation of some other null value at the same position, and thus the chase is infinite. A set Σ of TGDs is weakly-acyclic if there is no cycle in its position graph that involves a special edge. We know that:

Theorem 16 [12,47]. *Query answering under weakly-acyclic sets of TGDs is PTIME-complete w.r.t. data complexity, and 2EXPTIME-complete w.r.t. combined complexity.*

The upper bounds are shown by simply constructing the chase instance C, and then evaluate the input query over C. Notice that the PTIME-hardness is immediately inherited from the fact that weakly-acyclic sets of TGDs capture plain Datalog.

4.2 Guardedness

Although (weakly-)acyclic sets of TGDs are good languages for data exchange, they are not suitable for modeling ontological knowledge. Even the very simple knowledge that each person has a father who is also a person goes beyond weakly-acyclic sets of TGDs. Thus, we need classes of TGDs that do not guarantee the termination of the chase, but still query answering is decidable. In other words, we need languages that allow us to develop methods for reasoning about infinite models without explicitly building them.

Guarded TGDs. A prime example of such a formalism is the class of *guarded* TGDs, inspired by the guarded-fragment of first-order logic. A TGD is called guarded it has an atom in its body that contains all the body-variables [8]. The reason why we can answer queries under guarded TGDs, even if the chase procedure is infinite, is because the chase instance is tree-like, or, in more formal terms, has bounded tree-width. We know that:

Theorem 17 [8]. *Query answering under guarded TGDs is PTIME-complete w.r.t. data complexity, and 2EXPTIME-complete w.r.t. combined complexity.*

A core fragment of guarded TGDs, which, despite its simplicity, captures features of the most widespread tractable description logics such as DL-Lite, is the class of *linear* TGDs. A TGD is called linear if it has only one atom in its body [9]. As expected, this allows us to show that the complexity of query answering is lower:

Theorem 18 [9,41]. *Query answering under linear TGDs is in AC_0 w.r.t. data complexity, and PSPACE-complete w.r.t. combined complexity.*

Interestingly, under some fairly weak assumptions, queries to be evaluated under linear TGDs (or corresponding DLs) can be translated into polynomially-sized Datalog programs, or even polynomially-sized first-order formulas to be evaluated directly over input databases. This is discussed in detail in [25,33,38].

Weakly-Guarded Sets of TGDs. As for acyclic sets of TGDs, we can define a weak version of guarded TGDs, called *weakly-guarded*, that captures both guarded TGDs and plain Datalog [8]. The key idea is to relax guardedness in such a way that a variable x in the body can be unguarded as long as, during the construction of the chase, x is unified only by constants that already appear in the input database. This seemingly mild relaxation gives rise to a highly expressive language. We know that:

Theorem 19 [8]. *Query answering under weakly-guarded sets of TGDs is EXPTIME-complete w.r.t. data complexity, and 2EXPTIME-complete w.r.t. combined complexity.*

It is interesting, and somehow surprising, that query answering under this class of TGDs is provably intractable even w.r.t. the data complexity. What is even more interesting is the fact that by allowing negation of a very mild form, in particular, stratified negation, weakly-guarded sets of TGDs are powerful enough to capture every database property that can be checked in exponential time, even without assuming an order in the input database. In other words, every Boolean query Q that can be evaluated in exponential time in data complexity, it can be expressed as a pair (Σ, Ans), where Σ is a weakly-guarded set of TGDs and Ans a 0-ary relation, such that the following holds: D satisfies Q iff D and Σ entails the atomic query Ans, for every database D.

Theorem 20 [37]. *Weakly-guarded sets of TGDs with stratified negation capture EXPTIME, even without assuming ordered databases.*

4.3 Stickiness

Although guardedness is a well-accepted decidability paradigm, with desirable model-theoretic and complexity properties, it is not powerful enough for cap-

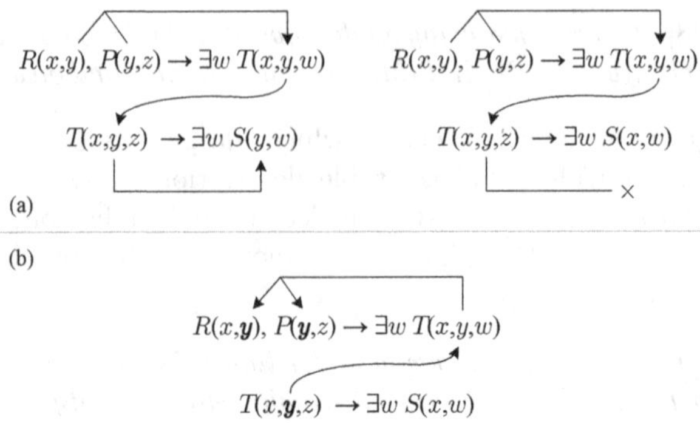

Fig. 3. Stickiness and marking.

turing knowledge that is inherently non-tree-like. Consider, for example, the following TGDs:

$$\begin{aligned} \text{Elephant}(x) &\rightarrow \exists y\, \text{HasAncestor}(x,y), \text{Elephant}(y), \\ \text{Mouse}(x) &\rightarrow \exists y\, \text{HasAncestor}(x,y), \text{Mouse}(y), \\ \text{Elephant}(x), \text{Mouse}(y) &\rightarrow \text{BiggerThan}(x,y), \end{aligned}$$

which essentially state that elephants are bigger than mice. It is clear that the first two TGDs are guarded (in fact, linear). However, the third TGD, although it looks simple and harmless, destroys the tree-likeness of the chase instance. Indeed, due to the first two TGDs, the chase will invent infinitely many null values that represent elephants and mice; let E and M be the sets of null values that represent elephants and mice, respectively. Then, the third TGD, will force the chase to compute the cartesian product of E and M, and store it in the binary relation BiggerThan. Therefore, the extension of BiggerThan in the chase instance C stores an infinite bipartite graph, which in turn implies that the tree-width of C is infinite. This immediately implies that the above set of TGDs cannot be rewritten as a set of guarded TGDs.

Sticky Sets of TGDs. The class of *sticky* sets of TGDs, introduced in [12], is a formalism that allows us to capture non-tree-like knowledge as the one captured by the above example. The key property of stickiness can be described as follows: during the chase, terms that are unified with variables that appear more than once in the body of a TGD (i.e., join variables) are always propagated (or "stick") to the inferred atoms. This is illustrated in Fig. 3(a); the first set of TGDs is sticky, while the second is not. The formal definition is based on an inductive marking procedure that marks the variables that may violate the semantic property of the chase described above. Roughly, during the base step of this procedure, a variable that appears in the body of a TGD σ but not in the head-atom of σ is marked. Then, the marking is inductively propagated from head to body as shown in Fig. 3(b). Finally, a finite set of TGDs Σ is *sticky* if no TGD in Σ contains two occurrences of a marked variable. We know that:

Theorem 21 [12]. *Query answering under sticky sets of TGDs is in AC_0 w.r.t. data complexity, and EXPTIME-complete w.r.t. combined complexity.*

Weakly-Sticky Sets of TGDs. As one might expect, a weak version of stickiness, which captures both sticky sets of TGDs and plain Datalog, can be defined. The principle under this more expressive language is the same as for weakly-acyclic and weakly-guarded sets of TGDs. Intuitively, we can relax the stickiness condition in such a way that variables that can be unified with finitely many null values during the construction of the chase are not taken into account. It is known that:

Theorem 22 [12]. *Query answering under weakly-sticky sets of TGDs is PTIME- complete w.r.t. data complexity, and 2EXPTIME-complete w.r.t. combined complexity.*

4.4 Further Applications

As already discussed at the beginning of the section, data exchange and ontological reasoning, are applications that could possibly profit from Datalog$^{\pm}$ languages that extend Datalog with existential quantifiers in rule heads. Let us conclude by briefly describing other applications that could profit from languages as the ones discussed above.

RDF and Semantic Web. Various "classical" query languages for RDF and the semantic Web are discussed in [24]. One of the distinctive features of Semantic Web data is the existence of vocabularies with predefined semantics: the *RDF Schema (RDFS)*[9] and the *Ontology Web Language (OWL)*[10], which can be used to derive logical conclusions from RDF graphs. Thus, it would be desirable to have an RDF query language equipped with reasoning capabilities to deal with these vocabularies. Besides, it has also been recognised that navigational capabilities are of fundamental importance for data models with an explicit graph structure such as RDF, and, more generally, it is also agreed that a general form of recursion is a central feature for a graph query language. Thus, it would also be desirable to have an RDF query language with such functionalities. We strongly believe that Datalog$^{\pm}$ languages are well-suited for this purpose. In fact, steps towards this direction have been already made in the recent works [2,36].

Conceptual Modeling. It has been observed that graphical conceptual modeling formalisms, and in particular UML and ER diagrams, can be faithfully translated into TGDs and EGDs. In fact, core fragments of the above formalisms can be captured via guarded TGDs (with some additional features such as equality) [11,35]. This is quite beneficial since it provides logical semantics to the above formalism, which in turn allows us to formally study relevant problems such as consistency, i.e., whether a given diagram admits at least one model.

[9] http://www.w3.org/TR/rdf-schema.
[10] http://www.w3.org/TR/owl-features/.

Object-Oriented Deductive Databases. It has been shown that formalisms introduced for object-oriented databases can be embedded into Datalog$^{\pm}$, which in turn allows us to exploit existing query answering algorithms. For example, F-Logic Lite, introduced in [13], is a small but expressive subset of F-Logic [42] that can be captured by weakly-guarded sets of TGDs [8].

Ontology-Based Multidimensional Contexts. Data quality assessment and data cleaning are context dependent activities, and thus, context models for the assessment of the quality of a database have been proposed. A context takes the form of a possibly virtual database or a data integration system into which the database under assessment is mapped, for additional analysis, processing, and quality data extraction. The work [50] extends contexts with dimensions, and hence, multidimensional data quality assessment becomes possible. At the core of multidimensional contexts we have ontologies that are modeled using Datalog$^{\pm}$, and, in particular, weakly-sticky sets of TGDs.

Acknowledgements. This work has been supported by the EPSRC Programme Grant EP/M025268/ "VADA: Value Added Data Systems – Principles and Architecture".

References

1. Abiteboul, S., Hull, R., Vianu, V.: Foundations of Databases. Addison-Wesley, Boston (1995)
2. Arenas, M., Gottlob, G., Pieris, A.: Expressive languages for querying the semantic web. In: PODS, pp. 14–26 (2014)
3. Baader, F., Calvanese, D., McGuinness, D.L., Nardi, D., Patel-Schneider, P.F.: The Description Logic Handbook: Theory, Implementation, and Applications. Cambridge University Press, Cambridge (2003)
4. Baumgartner, R., Flesca, S., Gottlob, G.: Declarative information extraction, web crawling, and recursive wrapping with *Lixto*. In: Eiter, T., Faber, W., Truszczyński, M. (eds.) LPNMR 2001. LNCS (LNAI), vol. 2173, pp. 21–41. Springer, Heidelberg (2001). doi:10.1007/3-540-45402-0_2
5. Baumgartner, R., Flesca, S., Gottlob, G.: The elog web extraction language. In: Nieuwenhuis, R., Voronkov, A. (eds.) LPAR 2001. LNCS (LNAI), vol. 2250, pp. 548–560. Springer, Heidelberg (2001). doi:10.1007/3-540-45653-8_38
6. Baumgartner, R., Flesca, S., Gottlob, G.: Visual web information extraction with lixto. In: VLDB, pp. 119–128 (2001)
7. Beeri, C., Vardi, M.Y.: The implication problem for data dependencies. In: Even, S., Kariv, O. (eds.) ICALP 1981. LNCS, vol. 115, pp. 73–85. Springer, Heidelberg (1981). doi:10.1007/3-540-10843-2_7
8. Calì, A., Gottlob, G., Kifer, M.: Taming the infinite chase: query answering under expressive relational constraints. J. Artif. Intell. Res. **48**, 115–174 (2013)
9. Calì, A., Gottlob, G., Lukasiewicz, T.: A general datalog-based framework for tractable query answering over ontologies. J. Web Sem. **14**, 57–83 (2012)
10. Cali, A., Gottlob, G., Lukasiewicz, T., Marnette, B., Pieris, A.: Datalog+/-: a family of logical knowledge representation and query languages for new applications. In: LICS, pp. 228–242 (2010)

11. Calì, A., Gottlob, G., Pieris, A.: Ontological query answering under expressive entity-relationship schemata. Inf. Syst. **37**(4), 320–335 (2012)
12. Calì, A., Gottlob, G., Pieris, A.: Towards more expressive ontology languages: the query answering problem. Artif. Intell. **193**, 87–128 (2012)
13. Calì, A., Kifer, M.: Containment of conjunctive object meta-queries. In: VLDB, pp. 942–952 (2006)
14. Cosmadakis, S.S., Gaifman, H., Kanellakis, P.C., Vardi, M.Y.: Decidable optimization problems for database logic programs (preliminary report). In: STOC, pp. 477–490 (1988)
15. Courcelle, B.: Graph rewriting: an algebraic and logic approach. In: van Leeuwen, J. (ed.) Handbook of Theoretical Computer Science, vol. 2, chap. 5, pp. 193–242. Elsevier Science Publishers B.V. (1990)
16. Dantsin, E., Eiter, T., Gottlob, G., Voronkov, A.: Complexity and expressive power of logic programming. ACM Comput. Surv. **33**(3), 374–425 (2001)
17. Deutsch, A., Tannen, V.: Reformulation of XML queries and constraints. In: Calvanese, D., Lenzerini, M., Motwani, R. (eds.) ICDT 2003. LNCS, vol. 2572, pp. 225–241. Springer, Heidelberg (2003). doi:10.1007/3-540-36285-1_15
18. Doner, J.: Tree acceptors and some of their applications. J. Comput. Syst. Sci. **4**(5), 406–451 (1970)
19. Fagin, R., Kolaitis, P.G., Miller, R.J., Popa, L.: Data exchange: semantics and query answering. Theor. Comput. Sci. **336**(1), 89–124 (2005)
20. Flum, J., Frick, M., Grohe, M.: Query evaluation via tree-decompositions. In: Bussche, J., Vianu, V. (eds.) ICDT 2001. LNCS, vol. 1973, pp. 22–38. Springer, Heidelberg (2001). doi:10.1007/3-540-44503-X_2
21. Frick, M., Grohe, M., Koch, C.: Query evaluation on compressed trees. In: LICS, pp. 22–25 (2003)
22. Furche, T., Gottlob, G., Grasso, G., Guo, X., Orsi, G., Schallhart, C., Wang, C.: DIADEM: thousands of websites to a single database. PVLDB **7**(14), 1845–1856 (2014)
23. Furche, T., Gottlob, G., Libkin, L., Orsi, G., Paton, N.W.: Data wrangling for big data: challenges and opportunities. In: EDBT, pp. 473–478 (2016)
24. Furche, T., Linse, B., Bry, F., Plexousakis, D., Gottlob, G.: RDF querying: language constructs and evaluation methods compared. In: Barahona, P., Bry, F., Franconi, E., Henze, N., Sattler, U. (eds.) Reasoning Web 2006. LNCS, vol. 4126, pp. 1–52. Springer, Heidelberg (2006). doi:10.1007/11837787_1
25. Gottlob, G., Kikot, S., Kontchakov, R., Podolskii, V.V., Schwentick, T., Zakharyaschev, M.: The price of query rewriting in ontology-based data access. Artif. Intell. **213**, 42–59 (2014)
26. Gottlob, G., Koch, C.: Monadic queries over tree-structured data. In: LICS, pp. 189–202 (2002)
27. Gottlob, G., Koch, C.: Monadic datalog and the expressive power of languages for web information extraction. J. ACM **51**(1), 74–113 (2004)
28. Gottlob, G., Koch, C.: A formal comparison of visual web wrapper generators. In: Wiedermann, J., Tel, G., Pokorný, J., Bieliková, M., Štuller, J. (eds.) SOFSEM 2006. LNCS, vol. 3831, pp. 30–48. Springer, Heidelberg (2006). doi:10.1007/11611257_3
29. Gottlob, G., Koch, C., Baumgartner, R., Herzog, M., Flesca, S.: The Lixto data extraction project: back and forth between theory and practice. In: PODS, pp. 1–12 (2004)
30. Gottlob, G., Koch, C., Pichler, R.: Efficient algorithms for processing XPath queries. In: VLDB, pp. 95–106 (2002)

31. Gottlob, G., Koch, C., Pichler, R.: The complexity of XPath query evaluation. In: PODS, pp. 179–190 (2003)
32. Gottlob, G., Koch, C., Schulz, K.U.: Conjunctive queries over trees. In: PODS, pp. 189–200 (2004)
33. Gottlob, G., Manna, M., Pieris, A.: Polynomial rewritings for linear existential rules. In: IJCAI, pp. 2992–2998 (2015)
34. Gottlob, G., Orsi, G., Pieris, A.: Query rewriting and optimization for ontological databases. ACM Trans. Database Syst. **39**(3), 25:1–25:46 (2014)
35. Gottlob, G., Orsi, G., Pieris, A.: Consistency checking of re-engineered UML class diagrams via Datalog+/-. In: RuleML, pp. 35–53 (2015)
36. Gottlob, G., Pieris, A.: Beyond SPARQL under OWL 2 QL entailment regime: rules to the rescue. In: IJCAI, pp. 2999–3007 (2015)
37. Gottlob, G., Rudolph, S., Simkus, M.: Expressiveness of guarded existential rule languages. In: PODS, pp. 27–38 (2014)
38. Gottlob, G., Schwentick, T.: Rewriting ontological queries into small nonrecursive datalog programs. In: KR (2012)
39. Grau, B.C., Horrocks, I., Krötzsch, M., Kupke, C., Magka, D., Motik, B., Wang, Z.: Acyclicity conditions and their application to query answering in description logics. In: KR (2012)
40. Greenlaw, R., Hoover, H.J., Ruzzo, W.L.: Limits to Parallel Computation: P-Completeness Theory. Oxford University Press, Oxford (1995)
41. Johnson, D.S., Klug, A.C.: Testing containment of conjunctive queries under functional and inclusion dependencies. J. Comput. Syst. Sci. **28**(1), 167–189 (1984)
42. Kifer, M., Lausen, G., Wu, J.: Logical foundations of object-oriented and frame-based languages. J. ACM **42**, 741–843 (1995)
43. Koch, C.: Efficient processing of expressive node-selecting queries on XML data in secondary storage: a tree automata-based approach. In: VLDB, pp. 249–260 (2003)
44. Laender, A.H.F., Ribeiro-Neto, B.A., da Silva, A.S.: Debye - data extraction by example. Data Knowl. Eng. **40**(2), 121–154 (2002)
45. Liu, L., Pu, C., Han, W.: XWRAP: An XML-enabled wrapper construction system for web information sources. In: ICDE, pp. 611–621 (2000)
46. Ludäscher, B., Himmeröder, R., Lausen, G., May, W., Schlepphorst, C.: Managing semistructured data with FLORID: a deductive object-oriented perspective. Inf. Syst. **23**(8), 589–613 (1998)
47. Lukasiewicz, T., Martinez, M.V., Pieris, A., Simari, G.I.: From classical to consistent query answering under existential rules. In: AAAI, pp. 1546–1552 (2015)
48. Marnette, B.: Generalized schema-mappings: from termination to tractability. In: PODS, pp. 13–22 (2009)
49. Meuss, H., Schulz, K.U., Bry, F.: Towards aggregated answers for semistructured data. In: Bussche, J., Vianu, V. (eds.) ICDT 2001. LNCS, vol. 1973, pp. 346–360. Springer, Heidelberg (2001). doi:10.1007/3-540-44503-X_22
50. Milani, M., Bertossi, L.: Ontology-based multidimensional contexts with applications to quality data specification and extraction. In: Bassiliades, N., Gottlob, G., Sadri, F., Paschke, A., Roman, D. (eds.) RuleML 2015. LNCS, vol. 9202, pp. 277–293. Springer, Heidelberg (2015). doi:10.1007/978-3-319-21542-6_18
51. Miller, R.J., Hernández, M.A., Haas, L.M., Yan, L., Ho, C.T.H., Fagin, R., Popa, L.: The clio project: managing heterogeneity. SIGMOD Rec. **30**(1), 78–83 (2001)
52. Minoux, M.: LTUR: a simplified linear-time unit resolution algorithm for horn formulae and computer implementation. Inf. Process. Lett. **29**(1), 1–12 (1988)
53. Neven, F., den Bussche, J.V.: Expressiveness of structured document query languages based on attribute grammars. J. ACM **49**(1), 56–100 (2002)

54. Neven, F., Schwentick, T.: Query automata over finite trees. Theor. Comput. Sci. **275**(1–2), 633–674 (2002)
55. Papakonstantinou, Y., Gupta, A., Garcia-Molina, H., Ullman, J.: A query translation scheme for rapid implementation of wrappers. In: Ling, T.W., Mendelzon, A.O., Vieille, L. (eds.) DOOD 1995. LNCS, vol. 1013, pp. 161–186. Springer, Heidelberg (1995). doi:10.1007/3-540-60608-4_40
56. Sahuguet, A., Azavant, F.: Building intelligent web applications using lightweight wrappers. Data Knowl. Eng. **36**(3), 283–316 (2001)
57. Seidl, H., Schwentick, T., Muscholl, A.: Numerical document queries. In: PODS, pp. 155–166 (2003)
58. Thatcher, J.W., Wright, J.B.: Generalized finite automata theory with an application to a decision problem of second-order logic. Math. Syst. Theory **2**(1), 57–81 (1968)
59. Thomas, W.: Languages, automata, and logic. In: Rozenberg, G., Salomaa, A. (eds.) Handbook of Formal Languages, vol. 3, pp. 389–455. Springer, Heidelberg (1997). Chapter 7

Algorithmic Learning and Semantics

A Stable Non-interleaving Early Operational Semantics for the Pi-Calculus

Thomas Troels Hildebrandt[1], Christian Johansen[2(✉)], and Håkon Normann[1]

[1] Department of Computer Science, IT University of Copenhagen, Rued Langgaardsvej 7, 2300 Copenhagen, Denmark
{hilde,hnor}@itu.dk

[2] Department of Informatics, University of Oslo, P.O. Box 1080 Blindern, 0316 Oslo, Norway
cristi@ifi.uio.no

Abstract. We give the first non-interleaving early operational semantics for the pi-calculus which generalizes the standard interleaving semantics and unfolds to the stable model of prime event structures. Our starting point is the non-interleaving semantics given for CCS by Mukund and Nielsen, where the so-called *structural* (prefixing or subject) causality and events are defined from a notion of locations derived from the syntactic structure of the process terms. The semantics is conservatively extended with a notion of *extruder histories*, from which we infer the so-called *link* (name or object) causality and events introduced by the dynamic communication topology of the pi-calculus. We prove that the semantics generalises both the standard interleaving early semantics for the pi-calculus and the non-interleaving semantics for CCS. In particular, it gives rise to a labelled asynchronous transition system unfolding to prime event structures.

Keywords: Concurrency · Non-interleaving · Pi-calculus · Early operational semantics · Asynchronous transition systems · Stability

1 Introduction

The pi-calculus [19] is the seminal model for concurrent mobile processes, representing mobility by the fresh creation and communication of channel names. The standard operational semantics adopt an *interleaving* approach to concurrency, that represent concurrent execution of actions as their arbitrary sequential interleaving and employ basic transition systems or automata as semantic models.

T.T. Hildebrandt—Authors ordered alphabetically. The first and last authors are supported by the Computational Artefacts (CompArt) project, funded by the Velux Foundation, grant nr. 33295.

C. Johansen—The second author (with previous name Cristian Prisacariu) was partially supported by the project IoTSec – Security in IoT for Smart Grids, with number 248113/O70 part of the IKTPLUSS program funded by the Norwegian Research Council.

F. Drewes et al. (Eds.): LATA 2017, LNCS 10168, pp. 51–63, 2017.
DOI: 10.1007/978-3-319-53733-7_3

However, the ability to distinguish concurrency from interleaving has several practical applications, including dealing with state-space explosion in model-checking [9], supporting action refinement [14] and reversibility (e.g. [17,28]).

To give a non-interleaving semantics one needs to identify the underlying events and their concurrency and causality relationships, and from that define a notion of non-interleaving observations, e.g. in terms of a bisimulation or testing equivalence [14,25] or employ a non-interleaving model (e.g. [1,6,22,27,29]), in which the concurrency can be represented explicitly. The dynamic communication topology of the pi-calculus makes it non-trivial to identify what accounts for causality, and indeed several possible approaches have been proposed. As described in [4], the source of the complexity is that the causal dependencies fall in two categories: The *structural* (prefixing or subject) dependencies, coming from the static process structure, i.e. action prefixing and parallel composition, and the *link* (name or object) dependencies, which come from the dynamic creation of communication links by scope extrusion of local names.

There has been quite some work on providing non-interleaving semantics for pi-calculus [4,6,8,10–12,16,20,25] and process algebras in general (e.g. [5,7]).

Among the most recent work, a stable operational semantics for reversible, deterministic and finite pi-calculus processes is provided in [12]. Stability means that every event depends on a unique history of past events, which supports reversibility of computations. A denotational semantics for the pi-calculus is provided in [10] as extended event structures. The semantics discards the property of stability to avoid the complexity and increase in number of events arising from achieving unique dependency histories. Both papers consider the late style pi-calculus semantics, where names received from the environment are kept abstract and thus distinct from any previously extruded names. We found no prior work providing a stable, non-interleaving, *early* style structural operational semantics generalising the standard early operational semantics of the pi-calculus. In the early style semantics, names received from the environment are concrete, and thus may be identical to a previously extruded name. Consequently, the choice between late and early style semantics influences the link causality.

Our key contribution is to provide the first stable, non-interleaving operational *early* semantics for the pi-calculus that generalises the standard, non-interleaving early operational semantics for the pi-calculus [26] and supports standard non-interleaving bisimulations [13,15,24]. Our starting point is the work of Mukund and Nielsen [21], which defines a structural operational non-interleaving semantics for Milner's CCS [18] as (labelled) asynchronous transition systems using locations to identify the structural causality, which is the only type of causality in CCS. We generalize the approach of [21] to the pi-calculus by employing also a notion of *extruder histories*, recording the location of both name extrusions and name inputs. Together, the locations and extruder histories allow to identify the underlying events of transitions and both their structural and link causal dependencies.

Overview of Paper: In Sect. 2 we generalise the structural operational early semantics for the pi-calculus with locations for transitions, extrusion histories and link dependencies. In Sect. 3 we show that the semantics yields a standard labelled asynchronous transitions system, which is known to unfold to labelled prime event structures. We conclude and comment on future work in Sect. 4. Proof details can be found in the companion technical report [23].

2 Causal Early Operational Semantics

In this section we give an early operational semantics of the pi-calculus recording both the structural and link causal dependencies between events.

We first recall the syntax for the pi-calculus with guarded choice.

Definition 1. *The set of* pi-calculus processes **Proc**, *ranged over by* P, Q, *are defined using an infinite set of names* $\mathcal{N}$, *ranged over by* n, m, *by the grammar:*

$$P ::= \Sigma\varphi_i.P_i \mid (\nu n)P \mid P \| Q \mid !P \mid \mathbf{0}, \qquad \varphi ::= \overline{a}\langle n\rangle \mid \underline{a}(n)$$

For a process P *we denote by* $n(P)$ *the set of* all names *appearing in* P, *by* $bn(P)$ *the* bound *names, i.e. those* n *that are restricted by* (νn) *or by the input action* $\underline{a}(n)$, *and by* $fn(P) = n(P) \backslash bn(P)$ *the* free *names. We assume all bound names are unique in a process and identify processes up to* α*-conversion.*

In Fig. 1 we give the causal early semantics for pi-processes with transitions of the form $(\overline{H}, \underline{H}) \vdash P \xrightarrow[u]{\alpha} (\overline{H}', \underline{H}') \vdash P'$. Following the approach in [21] we have added *location labels* u under the transitions, identifying the location of the prefixes in the term contributing to a transition and allowing to infer structural (CCS-like) events and causalities. To capture the finer notion of events and link causalities of the pi-calculus, we enrich the semantics with *extrusion histories* $(\overline{H}, \underline{H})$ to the left of the turnstile, which record the location in the parallel process of the prefixes extruding respectively receiving some name.

Formally, we define the set of prefix locations as follows.

Definition 2. *Let* $\mathcal{L} = \{0,1\}^* \times \mathbf{Proc} \times \mathbf{Proc}$ *be the set of* prefix locations *and write* $s[P][P']$ *for elements in* $\mathcal{L}$.

The location labels u of transitions in Fig. 1 are then of the following forms:

1. $s[P][P'] \in \mathcal{L}$, if α is an input or output action,
2. $s\langle 0s_0[P_0][P_0'], 1s_1[P_1][P_1']\rangle$, for $sis_i[P_i][P_i'] \in \mathcal{L}$ and $i \in \{0,1\}$, if $\alpha = \tau$.

In words, a prefix location $s[P][P']$ provides a path $s \in \{0,1\}^*$ to an input/output prefixed subterm P through the abstract syntax tree, with 0 and 1 referring to the left respectively right branch of a parallel composition, and P' being the residual sub-term after the transition. The location labels of the second form provide two prefix locations, $sis_i[P_i][P_i'] \in \mathcal{L}$ for $i \in \{0,1\}$, identifying the output and input prefix in a communication.

$$\frac{u = [\underline{a}(m).P][P'] \quad P' = P[m := n]}{(\overline{H}, \underline{H}) \vdash \underline{a}(m).P \xrightarrow[u]{\underline{a}(n)} (\overline{H}, \underline{H} \cup \{(n,u)\}) \vdash P'} \ (\text{IN})$$

$$\frac{\text{u=}[\overline{a}\langle n\rangle.\text{P}][\text{P}]}{(\overline{H}, \underline{H}) \vdash \overline{a}\langle n\rangle.P \xrightarrow[u]{\overline{a}\langle n\rangle} (\overline{H}, \underline{H}) \vdash P} \ (\text{OUT})$$

$$\frac{(\overline{H}, \underline{H}) \vdash P \xrightarrow[u]{\overline{a}\langle n\rangle} (\overline{H}', \underline{H}') \vdash P' \qquad n \neq a}{(\overline{H}, \underline{H}) \vdash (\nu n)P \xrightarrow[u]{\overline{a}\langle n\rangle} (\overline{H}' \cup \{(n,u)\}, \underline{H}') \vdash P'} \ (\text{OPEN})$$

$$\frac{(\overline{H}, \underline{H}) \vdash P \xrightarrow[u]{\alpha} (\overline{H}', \underline{H}') \vdash P' \qquad b \notin n(\alpha)}{(\overline{H}, \underline{H}) \vdash (\nu b)P \xrightarrow[u]{\alpha} (\overline{H}', \underline{H}') \vdash (\nu b)P'} \ (\text{SCOPE})$$

$$\frac{(\overline{H}, \underline{H}) \vdash P \,||\, !P \xrightarrow[u]{\alpha} (\overline{H}', \underline{H}') \vdash P'}{(\overline{H}, \underline{H}) \vdash !P \xrightarrow[u]{\alpha} (\overline{H}', \underline{H}') \vdash P'} \ (\text{REP})$$

$$\frac{(\overline{H}, \underline{H}) \vdash \varphi_i.P_i \xrightarrow[u]{\alpha} (\overline{H}', \underline{H}') \vdash P'}{(\overline{H}, \underline{H}) \vdash \Sigma_{i \in I} : \varphi_i.P_i \xrightarrow[u]{\alpha} (\overline{H}', \underline{H}') \vdash P'} \ (\text{SUM})$$

$$\frac{\begin{array}{ll} \overline{H}'' = \{(n,u) \mid \alpha = \overline{a}\langle n\rangle, n \in \mathsf{dom}([j]\overline{H}), & P_j = P_j' \\ \quad \forall l.l|_{\{0,1\}} \prec iu : (n,l) \notin \overline{H} \cup \underline{H}\} & j = 1 - i \\ \quad ([\check{i}]\overline{H}, [\check{i}]\underline{H}) \vdash P_i \xrightarrow[u]{\alpha} (\overline{H}_i', \underline{H}_i') \vdash P_i' & \tilde{b} \cap n(P_j) = \emptyset \end{array}}{(\overline{H}, \underline{H}) \vdash P_0 \,||\, P_1 \xrightarrow[iu]{\alpha} ((\overline{H} \backslash [i]\overline{H}) \cup i(\overline{H}_i' \cup \overline{H}''), (\underline{H} \backslash [i]\underline{H}) \cup i\underline{H}_i') \vdash P_0' \,||\, P_1'} \ (\text{PAR}_i)$$

$$\frac{\begin{array}{ll} \quad \underline{H}'' = \{(n,v) \mid & \\ \exists (n,l) \in [i](\overline{H} \cup \underline{H}) : l|_{\{0,1\}} \prec u\} & \tilde{b} \cap n(P_j) = \emptyset, \quad j = 1 - i \\ ([\check{i}]\overline{H}, [\check{i}]\underline{H}) \vdash P_i \xrightarrow[u]{\overline{a}\langle n\rangle} (\overline{H}_i', \underline{H}_i') \vdash P_i' & ([\check{j}]\overline{H}, [\check{j}]\underline{H}) \vdash P_j \xrightarrow[v]{\underline{a}(n)} (\overline{H}_j', \underline{H}_j') \vdash P_j' \end{array}}{(\overline{H}, \underline{H}) \vdash P_0 \,||\, P_1 \xrightarrow[\langle 0u, 1v\rangle]{\tau} (\overline{H}, \underline{H} \cup j\underline{H}'') \vdash (\nu\tilde{b})(P_0' \,||\, P_1')} \ (\text{COM}_i)$$

Fig. 1. Early operational semantics enriched with *action labels* $\alpha ::= \tau \mid \overline{a}\langle n\rangle \mid \underline{a}(x)$, *locations* u (under the arrows) and *extruder histories* $(\overline{H}, \underline{H})$ (to the left of the turnstile). We identify processes up-to α-equivalence, assume unique bound names and that for all rules, if $(\overline{H}, \underline{H}) \vdash P \xrightarrow[u]{\alpha} (\overline{H}', \underline{H}') \vdash P'$ is the conclusion, we require $\mathsf{dom}(\overline{H} \cup \underline{H}) \cap bn(P) = \emptyset$. For rules (COM$_i$) and (PAR$_i$), consider $i \in \{0,1\}$, and let $\tilde{b} = \mathsf{dom}(\overline{H}_i') \backslash \mathsf{dom}([\check{i}]\overline{H})$ and allow writing $(\nu\emptyset)P$ and $(\nu\{n\})P$ for P and $(\nu n)P$ respectively. The blue text shows what is added to the standard semantics. (Color figure online)

Note that to keep locations of action prefixes fixed, we cannot assume the usual structural congruence making parallel composition commutative. Therefore we must use two rules ($\textsc{par}_i$), $i \in \{0,1\}$ for parallel composition and two rules ($\textsc{com}_i$), $i \in \{0,1\}$ for communication.

From the locations we define our first notion of structural events and independence, which correspond to the events and independence defined for CCS in [21]. We will later show how to take into account the additional link causal relationships of the pi-calculus.

Definition 3. *Let* $Ev = \{(\alpha, u) \mid (\overline{H}, \underline{H}) \vdash P \xrightarrow[u]{\alpha} (\overline{H}', \underline{H}') \vdash P'\}$ *be the* structural events. *For* $e = (\alpha, u) \in Ev$ *define* $Loc(e) \subseteq \{0,1\}^*$, *the* locations *where* e *occurs, by*

$$Loc(e) = \begin{cases} \{s\} & \mathit{if} u = s[P][P'] \\ \{ss_0, ss_1\} & \mathit{if} u = s\langle s_0[P_0][P_0'], s_1[P_1][P_1']\rangle. \end{cases}$$

Define an independence relation on locations $I_l \subseteq \{0,1\}^* \times \{0,1\}^*$ *by*

$$(s_0, s_1) \in I_l \quad \mathit{iff} \quad s_i = sis_i',$$

where $i \in \{0,1\}$ *and* $s, s_0, s_1, s_0', s_1' \in \{0,1\}^*$. *Define the structural independence relation on events* $I_s \subseteq Ev \times Ev$ *by:*

$$(e, e') \in I_s \quad \mathit{iff} \quad \forall s \in Loc(e), \forall s' \in Loc(e') : (s, s') \in I_l.$$

As the following example shows, I_s misses the link dependencies.

Example 4. Consider the process $(\nu n)(\overline{a}\langle n\rangle \,||\, \underline{n}(x))$. According to I_s the two events $e = (\overline{a}\langle n\rangle, 0[\overline{a}\langle n\rangle][\mathbf{0}])$ and $e_m = (\underline{n}(m), 1[\underline{n}(x)][\mathbf{0}])$ are independent, for any $m \neq n$, but the semantics does not allow the input event to happen until after the name n has been extruded, i.e. there is an objective dependency between the extruding output and the input.

The next example illustrates that both names in an input action $\underline{m}(n)$ may have been previously extruded, giving rise to a conjunctive causality.

Example 5. Consider the process $P = (\nu n)(\nu m)(\overline{a}\langle n\rangle \,||\, (\overline{b}\langle m\rangle \,||\, \underline{m}(x)))$. From $(\emptyset, \emptyset) \vdash P$ we can have two extruding outputs on channels a and b of the names n respectively m, after which the output history would contain two pairs $\overline{H} = \{(n, 0[\overline{a}\langle n\rangle][\mathbf{0}]), (m, 10[\overline{b}\langle m\rangle][\mathbf{0}])\}$. We now may have an input action with label $\underline{m}(n)$ that depends on both extruders.

The final example shows that a name may have several parallel extruders, giving rise to a *disjunctive* causality.

Example 6. Consider the process $(\nu n)(\overline{a}\langle n\rangle \,||\, (\overline{b}\langle n\rangle \,||\, \underline{n}(x)))$, which has two *parallel extruders* $\overline{a}\langle n\rangle$ and $\overline{b}\langle n\rangle$. We have the three events $e_a = (\overline{a}\langle n\rangle, 0[\overline{a}\langle n\rangle][\mathbf{0}])$, $e_b = (\overline{b}\langle n\rangle, 10[\overline{b}\langle n\rangle][\mathbf{0}])$, and $e_n = (\underline{n}(m), 11[\underline{n}(x)][\mathbf{0}])$. The event e_n for the input action is independent of both output events, but it cannot happen before at least one has happened.

The extrusion histories to the left of the turnstile helps us take into account the link causalites.

Definition 7. *A* history $H \subseteq \mathcal{H} = \mathcal{N} \times \mathcal{L}$ *is a relation between names and prefix locations, and an* extrusion history $(\overline{H}, \underline{H})$ *is a pair of histories, referred to as the* output history *and* input history *respectively. For a history H and $i \in \{0,1\}$ let iH denote the history $\{(n, iu) | (n, u) \in H\}$. Let $[\check{i}]H = \{(n, u) \mid (n, iu) \in H\}$ and $[i]H = \{(n, iu) \mid (n, iu) \in H\}$ and $[\check{\epsilon}]H = H$. Finally, let* $\mathsf{dom}(H) = \{n \mid (n, u) \in H\}$, *i.e. the set of names recorded in the history.*

Based on the examples above, we refine our transitions and events to also capture link dependencies by enriching the transitions with (deterministic) histories D recording the link dependencies for each non-output name in α, i.e. the past extruding events it depends on, if it was extruded in the past.

Definition 8. *Define the* causal *early semantics as the transitions* $(\overline{H}, \underline{H}) \vdash P \xrightarrow[u,D]{\alpha} (\overline{H}', \underline{H}') \vdash P'$ *if* $(\overline{H}, \underline{H}) \vdash P \xrightarrow[u]{\alpha} (\overline{H}', \underline{H}') \vdash P'$ *and*

1. $D \subseteq \overline{H}$,
2. $(n, l), (n, l') \in D$ *implies* $l = l'$
3. $\mathsf{dom}(D) = \mathsf{dom}(\overline{H}) \cap no(\alpha)$,

where $no(\alpha)$ is the non output names *of α, defined by $no(\overline{n}\langle m \rangle) = \{n\} \backslash \{m\}$, $no(\underline{n}(m)) = \{n, m\}$ and $no(\tau) = \emptyset$.*

The link dependencies D allow us to define our final notion of events and independence relation for the causal semantics.

Definition 9. *Let the set of* events **Ev** *be defined by:*

$$\mathbf{Ev} = \{((\alpha, u), D) \in Ev \times \mathcal{H} \mid (\overline{H}, \underline{H}) \vdash P \xrightarrow[u,D]{\alpha} (\overline{H}', \underline{H}') \vdash P'\}$$

*Two events $e_i = (e_i', D_i) \in$ **Ev** for $e_i' = (\alpha_i, u_i)$ and $i \in \{0,1\}$ are independent, written $e_0 I e_1$, iff*

$$e_0' I_s e_1' \ \wedge \ \nexists n : D_i(n) = u_{1-i} \quad \textit{for } i \in \{0,1\}.$$

Returning to Example 6, the event $e_n = (\underline{n}(m), 11[\underline{n}(x)][\mathbf{0}])$ will be split in two events $(e_n, (n, 0[\overline{a}\langle n \rangle][\mathbf{0}]))$ and $(e_n, (n, 10[\overline{b}\langle n \rangle][\mathbf{0}]))$ corresponding to transitions between the same two states.

We now briefly explain the rules in Fig. 1.

The (IN) rule is the standard early input rule, substituting a received name n for the parameter m in P, yielding $P' = P[m := n]$, and enriched by recording the prefix location $u = [\underline{a}(m).P][P']$ on the transition. Moreover, the rule takes care to add the name n to the input history $\underline{H}$.

The (OUT) rule is the standard output rule, except the prefix location $u = [\overline{a}\langle n \rangle.P][P']$ is added to the transition.

The (OPEN) is the standard open rule, except the prefix location is recorded for the extruded name n in the output history and not in the label, as is custom for the standard pi-semantics. Avoiding name extrusions in the labels ensures unique labels for events in Sect. 3, and only one (COM) rule.

The (SCOPE), (REP) and (SUM) rules are the standard rules, just extended to retain locations and histories.

If we do not consider the locations and histories, the (PAR_i) rules, for $i \in \{0,1\}$ are the standard left and right parallel rules, except that we extract a possibly extruded name from the histories by the set $\tilde{b} = \mathsf{dom}(\overline{H}'_i) \backslash \mathsf{dom}([\check{i}]\overline{H})$ and not from the action label α. In the location, we record in which branch of the parallel composition the action happened by prefixing with $i \in \{0,1\}$. The extruders recorded in the set $\overline{H}''$ in the rules $(\text{PAR})_i$ captures exactly the parallel extrusion illustrated in Example 6. Specifically, an output prefix is added to the output extruder history, if the name has been extruded in the other parallel component and not previously extruded (recorded in the output history) nor received (recorded in the input history) by the current component. We illustrate the use of the input history in the example below.

Example 10. Consider the process $P = (\nu n)(\overline{a}\langle n\rangle \,||\, \underline{b}(x).\overline{c}\langle n\rangle)$. Starting with empty histories, we have the two transitions

1. $(\emptyset,\emptyset) \vdash P \xrightarrow[0[\overline{a}\langle n\rangle][\mathbf{0}]]{\overline{a}\langle n\rangle} (\{(n, 0[\overline{a}\langle n\rangle][\mathbf{0}])\},\emptyset) \vdash P_1$, for $P_1 = \mathbf{0} \,||\, \underline{b}(x).\overline{c}\langle n\rangle$
2. $(\emptyset,\emptyset) \vdash P \xrightarrow[1[\underline{b}(x).\overline{c}\langle n\rangle][\overline{c}\langle n\rangle]]{\underline{b}(m)} (\emptyset, \{(m,1)\}) \vdash (\nu n)(\overline{a}\langle n\rangle \,||\, \overline{c}\langle n\rangle)$, with $m \neq n$.

After the first transition we may both be receiving n or a name $m \neq n$:

$$(\{(n, 0[\overline{a}\langle n\rangle][\mathbf{0}])\},\emptyset) \vdash P_1 \xrightarrow[1[\underline{b}(x).\overline{c}\langle n\rangle][\overline{c}\langle n\rangle]]{\underline{b}(n)} (\{(n, 0[\overline{a}\langle n\rangle][\mathbf{0}])\}, \{(n,1)\}) \vdash (\mathbf{0} \,||\, \overline{c}\langle n\rangle).$$

$$(\{(n, 0[\overline{a}\langle n\rangle][\mathbf{0}])\},\emptyset) \vdash P_1 \xrightarrow[1[\underline{b}(x).\overline{c}\langle n\rangle][\overline{c}\langle n\rangle]]{\underline{b}(m)} (\{(n, 0[\overline{a}\langle n\rangle][\mathbf{0}])\}, \{(m,1)\}) \vdash (\mathbf{0} \,||\, \overline{c}\langle n\rangle).$$

In the first case, a subsequent output of n on channel c will not be an extrusion, since it happens after the input of n from the environment. In the second case it will, since this output is independent of the extrusion in transition 1.

Finally, if we again ignore histories and locations, the (COM_i) rules are the usual communication rules combined with the close rule, closing a scope previously opened by an (OPEN) rule. We combine the communication and close rules by abuse of notation, writing $(\nu\emptyset)P$ for P in the (COM_i) rules, thereby combining the standard (CLOSE) rule for communication of a bound name with that of communication of a free name. The location label is made into a pair, recording the two prefixes taking part in the communication. Looking at the histories, we discard any changes to histories formed in each component and only forwards input histories from the sender to the receiver via the set $\underline{H}''$.

We end by stating the result that the standard interleaving, early operational semantics can be obtained from the rules in Fig. 1 by ignoring the locations and extract only the scope extrusion from the histories.

Proposition 11. *For a pi-process P, the transition system reachable from P using the standard interleaving, early operational semantics is bisimilar to the transition system* $(\mathbf{Proc}_P, (\emptyset,\emptyset) \vdash P, \Lambda, \rightarrow_\pi)$, *where*

- $\mathbf{Proc}_P = \{(\overline{H},\underline{H}) \vdash P' \mid (\emptyset,\emptyset) \vdash P \rightarrow^* (\overline{H},\underline{H}) \vdash P'\}$, *and* $\rightarrow^*$ *is the transitive closure of the transition relation in Fig. 1*
- $\lambda \in \Lambda$ *is defined by the grammar* $\lambda ::= (\nu n)\overline{m}\langle n\rangle \mid \overline{m}\langle n\rangle \mid \underline{m}(n) \mid \tau$
- $(\overline{H},\underline{H}) \vdash P \xrightarrow{\alpha'}_\pi (\overline{H}',\underline{H}') \vdash P'$ *if* $(\overline{H},\underline{H}) \vdash P \xrightarrow[u]{\alpha} (\overline{H}',\underline{H}') \vdash P'$ *for some* $\overline{H}$, $\underline{H}$, $\overline{H}'$, $\underline{H}'$, u, *and* $\alpha' = (\nu n)\alpha$ *if* $\mathsf{dom}(\overline{H}')\backslash\mathsf{dom}(\overline{H}) = \{n\}$ *and* $\alpha' = \alpha$ *otherwise.*

3 A Stable Non-interleaving Early Operational Semantics

In this section we show that the operational semantics, events and independence relation given for the pi-calculus in the previous section yields a labelled asynchronous[1] transition system (LATS) [1,15,27,29] as recalled below.

Definition 12. *A* labelled asynchronous transition system *(LATS) is a tuple* $(S, i, E, I, \mathcal{T}, lab, \mathcal{A})$ *such that*

- $(S, i, E, \mathcal{T})$ *is a transition system with S the set of states and i an* initial state, *E a set of* events, *and* $\mathcal{T} \subseteq S \times E \times S$ *the* transition relation*;*
- $lab : E \rightarrow \mathcal{A}$ *is a* labelling *map from the set of events to the* action set $\mathcal{A}$*;*
- $I \subseteq E \times E$ *is an irreflexive, symmetric independence relation, satisfying:*
  1. $e \in E \Rightarrow \exists s, s' \in S : (s, e, s') \in \mathcal{T}$;
  2. $(s, e, s') \in \mathcal{T} \wedge (s, e, s'') \in \mathcal{T} \Rightarrow s' = s''$;
  3. $e_1 I e_2 \wedge \{(s, e_1, s_1), (s, e_2, s_2)\} \subseteq \mathcal{T} \Rightarrow \exists s_3 : \{(s_1, e_2, s_3), (s_2, e_1, s_3)\} \subseteq \mathcal{T}$;
  4. $e_1 I e_2 \wedge \{(s, e_1, s_1), (s_1, e_2, s_3)\} \subseteq \mathcal{T} \Rightarrow \exists s_2 : \{(s, e_2, s_2), (s_2, e_1, s_3)\} \subseteq \mathcal{T}$.

LATS are known to satisfy the stability property, that is, every event depends on a unique set of events, and unfold to standard labelled prime event structures [29, Ch.7]. This also implies, that LATS admits standard non-interleaving bisimulations, notably the (hereditary) history-preserving bisimulation [15].

Recalling the standard semantics derived in Proposition 11 we define the non-interleaving semantics as a labelled asynchronous transition system.

Definition 13. *The semantic rules for the pi-calculus that we gave in Fig. 1 generate a labelled asynchronous transition system* $TS_\pi(P) = (\mathbf{Proc}_P, (\emptyset,\emptyset) \vdash P, \mathbf{Ev}_P, I, \mathcal{T}, lab, \mathcal{A})$ *for a pi-process P where*

- $((\overline{H},\underline{H}) \vdash P, e, (\overline{H}',\underline{H}') \vdash P') \in \mathcal{T}$ *iff* $(\overline{H},\underline{H}) \vdash P \xrightarrow[u,D]{\alpha} (\overline{H}',\underline{H}') \vdash P'$ *and* $e = ((\alpha, u), D) \in \mathbf{Ev}$,
- $\mathbf{Ev}_P = \{e \mid (q, e, q') \in \mathcal{T}\}$
- $lab\big((\alpha, u), D\big) = \alpha$,
- $\alpha \in \mathcal{A}$ *is the set of labels generated by the grammar* $\alpha ::= \overline{a}\langle n\rangle \mid \underline{a}(n) \mid \tau$

[1] Asynchronous here refers to non-interleaving, not the style of communication.

Theorem 14. *The transition system given in Definition 13 is a labelled asynchronous transition system.*

That the semantics in 13 satisfy the first property of Definition 12 follows trivially from the definition. The following lemma states that the transition system is event deterministic, i.e. that it satisfies property 2 of Definition 12.

Lemma 15. *For any two transitions* $(\overline{H}, \underline{H}) \vdash P \xrightarrow[u,D]{\alpha} (\overline{H}', \underline{H}') \vdash P'$ *and* $(\overline{H}, \underline{H}) \vdash P \xrightarrow[u,D]{\alpha} (\overline{H}'', \underline{H}'') \vdash P''$ *then* $(\overline{H}', \underline{H}') = (\overline{H}'', \underline{H}'')$ *and* $P' = P''$.

To prove that the transition system given in Definition 13 satisfies the last two (diamond) properties of a labelled asynchronous transition system we need some intermediate results, following the approach in [21]. The following partial function makes precise how a sequence $s \in \{0,1\}^*$ identifies a subprocess, called the component, in a process.

Definition 16 (components). *Define inductively the partial function*

$$Comp : \{0,1\}^* \times \mathbf{Proc} \rightharpoonup \mathbf{Proc}$$

1. $Comp(\epsilon, P) = P$, *when* $P \neq !P_1$ *and* $P \neq (\nu n)P_1$ *(and* ϵ *is the empty string)*
2. $Comp(0s, P_0 \,||\, P_1) = Comp(s, P_0)$
3. $Comp(1s, P_0 \,||\, P_1) = Comp(s, P_1)$
4. $Comp(s, (\nu n)P) = Comp(s, P)$
5. $Comp(s, !P) = Comp(s, P \,||\, !P)$

Corollary 17. *For any* $s, s' \in \{0,1\}^*$ *and any process* P*, whenever* $Comp$ *is defined, we have* $Comp(s, Comp(s', P)) = Comp(s's, P)$.

From any transition we can recover the transition in the immediate component.

Lemma 18. *For* $s \in \{\varepsilon, 0, 1\}$ *and* $s' \in \{\varepsilon, 0, 1\}^*$ *we have* $(\overline{H}, \underline{H}) \vdash P \xrightarrow[ss'u_\varepsilon]{\alpha} (\overline{H}', \underline{H}') \vdash P'$ *if*

$$([\check{s}]\overline{H}, [\check{s}]\underline{H}) \vdash Comp(s, P) \xrightarrow[s'u_\varepsilon]{\alpha'} (\overline{H}'', \underline{H}'') \vdash Comp(s, P'),$$

where u_ε *is either* $[P''][P''']$ *or* $\langle 0s_0s_0'[P_0][P_0'], 1s_1s_1'[P_1][P_1'] \rangle$*, and depending on the case we have the following extra properties:*

1. *when* $s = 0$ *we have* $\alpha' = \alpha$ *and* $bn(\alpha) \in fn(Comp(1, P))$;
2. *when* $s = 1$ *we have* $\alpha' = \alpha$ *and* $bn(\alpha) \in fn(Comp(0, P))$;
3. *when* $s = \varepsilon$ *and* $P = (\nu\tilde{n})P_1$ *and* $P_1 \neq (\nu\tilde{m})P_2$ *for* $\tilde{n}$ *and* $\tilde{m}$ *non-empty, we either have* $(\tilde{n} \cap n(\alpha) = \emptyset$ *and* $\alpha' = \alpha)$ *or* $(\exists b \in \tilde{n} : \alpha = \overline{a}\langle b \rangle$ *and* $\alpha' = \overline{a}\langle b \rangle$ *with* $a \notin \tilde{n})$;
4. *when* $s = \varepsilon$ *and* $P = !P_1$ *we have* $\alpha' = \alpha$.

Applying several times Lemma 18, we can extend s to be a string of location components: $s \in \{0,1\}^*$. From any communication transition we can then recover the transitions in the components identified by the location labels.

Lemma 19. *For location strings $s, s_0, s_1, s'_0, s'_1 \in \{0,1\}^*$ we have*

$$(\overline{H}, \underline{H}) \vdash P \xrightarrow[s\langle 0s_0s'_0[P_0][P'_0], 1s_1s'_1[P_1][P'_1]\rangle]{\tau} (\overline{H}', \underline{H}') \vdash P'$$

if

$$([\check{s}_l]\overline{H}, [\check{s}_l]\underline{H}) \vdash Comp(s0s_0, P) \xrightarrow[s'_0[P_0][P'_0]]{\alpha} (\overline{H}'', \underline{H}'') \vdash Comp(s0s_0, P')$$

and

$$([\check{s}_r]\overline{H}, [\check{s}_r]\underline{H}) \vdash Comp(s1s_1, P) \xrightarrow[s'_1[P_1][P'_1]]{\overline{\alpha}} (\overline{H}''', \underline{H}''') \vdash Comp(s1s_1, P')$$

where $s_l = s0s_0$, $s_r = s1s_1$, and $\overline{\overline{a}\langle n\rangle} = \underline{a}(n)$ and $\overline{\underline{a}(n)} = \overline{a}\langle n\rangle$.

Conversely, we can lift a transition from a component.

Lemma 20. *For $s \in \{\varepsilon, 0, 1\}$ we have that*

$$\text{if} \quad ([\check{s}]\overline{H}, [\check{s}]\underline{H}) \vdash Comp(s, P) \xrightarrow[s'[P_0][P'_0]]{\alpha} P'_1$$

then

$$(\overline{H}, \underline{H}) \vdash P \xrightarrow[ss'[P_0][P'_0]]{\alpha'} P' \text{ with } Comp(s, P') = P'_1$$

and α' defined in terms of α, under the following restrictions:

1. *for $s = 0$ if $bn(\alpha) \in fn(Comp(1, P))$ and $\alpha' = \alpha$;*
2. *for $s = 1$ if $bn(\alpha) \in fn(Comp(0, P))$ and $\alpha' = \alpha$;*
3. *for $s = \varepsilon$ and $P = (\nu n)P_1$ if ($n \in fn(\alpha)$ and $\alpha' = \alpha$) or ($\alpha = \overline{a}\langle n\rangle$ and $\alpha' = \overline{a}\langle n\rangle$ and $n \neq a$).*

Applying several times Lemma 20, when the needed restrictions exist, we can extend s to be a string of location components: $s \in \{0,1\}^*$.

Lemma 21. *Whenever we have*

$$([\check{0}]\overline{H}, [\check{0}]\underline{H}) \vdash Comp(0, P) \xrightarrow[s_0[P_0][P'_0]]{\overline{a}\langle n\rangle} (\overline{H}'_0, \underline{H}'_0) \vdash P''_0$$

and

$$([\check{1}]\overline{H}, [\check{1}]\underline{H}) \vdash Comp(1, P) \xrightarrow[s_1[P_1][P'_1]]{\underline{a}(n)} (\overline{H}'_1, \underline{H}'_1) \vdash P''_1,$$

for $a \notin \mathsf{dom}(\overline{H}_0 \backslash \overline{H}'_0)$, then we have the communication

$$(\overline{H}, \underline{H}) \vdash P \xrightarrow[\langle 0s_0[P_0][P'_0], 1s_1[P_1][P'_1]\rangle]{\tau} (\overline{H}', \underline{H}') \vdash P'$$

with $Comp(0, P') = P''_0$ and $Comp(1, P') = P''_1$. A symmetric case was elided.

Lemma 22. *For any process P and a location string s then*

1. *if* $(\overline{H},\underline{H}) \vdash P \xrightarrow[s[P_1][P_1']]{\alpha} (\overline{H}',\underline{H}') \vdash P'$ *and* $(s,s') \in I_l$ *then* $Comp(s',P) = Comp(s',P')$,
2. *if* $(\overline{H},\underline{H}) \vdash P \xrightarrow[s\langle s_0[P_0][P_0'],s_1[P_1][P_1']\rangle]{\tau} (\overline{H}',\underline{H}') \vdash P'$ *and* $(ss_0,s') \in I_l$ *and* $(ss_1,s') \in I_l$ *then* $Comp(s',P) = Comp(s',P')$.

We end by noting that the non-interleaving semantics is a conservative extension of the one for CCS given in [21]. To this end, we let the CCS subset refer to the sub calculus of the pi-calculus obtained by allowing only input and output prefixes in which the subject and object are the same, i.e. of the form $\underline{n}(n)$ and $\overline{n}\langle n\rangle$. In this case it is easy to see that the output histories and link dependencies D are always empty and thus the independence relation and events coincide with the structural independence and events.

Proposition 23. *For the CCS subset of the pi-calculus, the non-interleaving semantics of Fig. 1 is bisimilar to the non-interleaving semantics for CCS in [21].*

4 Conclusion and Related Work

We provided the first stable, non-interleaving operational semantics for the pi-calculus conservatively generalising the interleaving early operational semantics. The semantics is given as labelled asynchronous transition systems admitting standard non-interleaving bisimulations such as (hereditary) history-preserving bisimulation [3,13,15,24]. We followed and conservatively generalised the approach for CCS in [21] by capturing the link causalities introduced in the pi-calculus processes by employing a notion of extrusion histories. In the companion technical report [23] we have worked out the generalisation to unguarded choice, which makes the notion of location more complex, as also described in [7]. We are currently working on a more thorough comparison with the related work [4,6,8,10–12,16,17,20,25], in particular we aim to explore reversibility, non-interleaving bisimulations and the differences betwen early and late style non-interleaving semantics. Finally, we work on extending this work to the psi-calculus [2].

References

1. Bednarczyk, M.A.: Categories of asynchronous systems. Ph.D. thesis, University of Sussex (1988)
2. Bengtson, J., Johansson, M., Parrow, J., Victor, B.: Psi-calculi: a framework for mobile processes with nominal data and logic. Log. Methods Comput. Sci. **7**(1), 1–44 (2011). http://dx.doi.org/10.2168/LMCS-7(1:11)2011
3. Best, E., Devillers, R., Kiehn, A., Pomello, L.: Concurrent bisimulations in petri nets. Acta Inform. **3**(28), 231–264 (1991)

4. Boreale, M., Sangiorgi, D.: A fully abstract semantics for causality in the π-calculus. In: Mayr, E.W., Puech, C. (eds.) STACS 1995. LNCS, vol. 900, pp. 243–254. Springer, Heidelberg (1995). doi:10.1007/3-540-59042-0_77
5. Boudol, G., Castellani, I., Hennessy, M., Kiehn, A.: A theory of processes with localities. Formal Asp. Comput. **6**(2), 165–200 (1994)
6. Busi, N., Gorrieri, R.: A Petri net semantics for π-calculus. In: Lee, I., Smolka, S.A. (eds.) CONCUR 1995. LNCS, vol. 962, pp. 145–159. Springer, Heidelberg (1995). doi:10.1007/3-540-60218-6_11
7. Castellani, I.: Process algebras with localities. In: Bergstra, J.A., Ponse, A., Smolka, S.A. (eds.) Handbook of Process Algebra, pp. 945–1045. Elsevier, Amsterdam (2001). Chap. 15
8. Cattani, G.L., Sewell, P.: Models for name-passing processes: interleaving and causal. In: LICS, pp. 322–333. IEEE Computer Society (2000). http://dx.doi.org/10.1109/LICS.2000.855781
9. Clarke, E., Grumberg, O., Minea, M., Peled, D.: State space reduction using partial order techniques. Int. J. Softw. Tools Technol. Transf. **2**(3), 279–287 (1999). http://dx.doi.org/10.1007/s100090050035
10. Crafa, S., Varacca, D., Yoshida, N.: Event structure semantics of parallel extrusion in the pi-calculus. In: Birkedal, L. (ed.) FoSSaCS 2012. LNCS, vol. 7213, pp. 225–239. Springer, Heidelberg (2012). doi:10.1007/978-3-642-28729-9_15
11. Cristescu, I.: Operational and denotational semantics for the reversible π- calculus. Ph.D. thesis, Université Paris Diderot - Paris 7 - Sorbonne Paris Cité (2015). http://www.pps.univ-paris-diderot.fr/~ioana/these.pdf
12. Cristescu, I., Krivine, J., Varacca, D.: A compositional semantics for the reversible pi-calculus. In: ACM/IEEE Symposium on Logic in Computer Science, LICS. pp. 388–397. IEEE Computer Society (2013). http://dx.doi.org/10.1109/LICS.2013.45
13. Degano, P., Nicola, R., Montanari, U.: Partial orderings descriptions and observations of nondeterministic concurrent processes. In: Bakker, J.W., Roever, W.-P., Rozenberg, G. (eds.) REX 1988. LNCS, vol. 354, pp. 438–466. Springer, Heidelberg (1989). doi:10.1007/BFb0013030
14. van Glabbeek, R., Goltz, U.: Refinement of actions and equivalence notions for concurrent systems. Acta Inform. **37**(4/5), 229–327 (2001). http://link.springer.de/link/service/journals/00236/bibs/1037004/10370229.htm
15. Hildebrandt, T.T.: Categorical models for concurrency: independence, fairness and dataflow. Ph.D. thesis, University of Aarhus, Denmark (1999)
16. Jategaonkar Jagadeesan, L., Jagadeesan, R.: Causality and true concurrency: a data-flow analysis of the pi-calculus. In: Alagar, V.S., Nivat, M. (eds.) AMAST 1995. LNCS, vol. 936, pp. 277–291. Springer, Heidelberg (1995). doi:10.1007/3-540-60043-4_59
17. Lanese, I., Mezzina, C.A., Stefani, J.B.: Reversibility in the higher-order pi-calculus. Theoret. Comput. Sci. **625**, 25–84 (2016)
18. Milner, R.: A Calculus of Communicating Systems, vol. 92. Springer, Berlin (1980)
19. Milner, R., Parrow, J., Walker, D.: A Calculus of Mobile Processes, I-II. Inf. Comput. **100**(1), 1–77 (1992)
20. Montanari, U., Pistore, M.: Concurrent semantics for the pi-calculus. Electron. Notes Theoret. Comput. Sci. **1**, 411–429 (1995). http://dx.doi.org/10.1016/S1571-0661(04)00024-6
21. Mukund, M., Nielsen, M.: CCS, locations and asynchronous transition systems. In: Shyamasundar, R. (ed.) FSTTCS 1992. LNCS, vol. 652, pp. 328–341. Springer, Heidelberg (1992). doi:10.1007/3-540-56287-7_116

22. Nielsen, M., Plotkin, G., Winskel, G.: Petri nets, event structures and domains. In: Kahn, G. (ed.) Semantics of Concurrent Computation. LNCS, vol. 70, pp. 266–284. Springer, Heidelberg (1979). doi:10.1007/BFb0022474
23. Normann, H., Johansen, C., Hildebrandt, T.: Non-interleaving operational semantics for the pi-calculus (long version). Technical report 453, Department of Informatics, University of Oslo (2016). http://heim.ifi.uio.no/~cristi/papers/TR453.pdf
24. Rabinovich, A., Trakhtenbrot, B.: Behaviour structures and nets. Fundamenta Informaticae **4**(XI), 357–404 (1988)
25. Sangiorgi, D.: Locality and interleaving semantics in calculi for mobile processes. Theoret. Comput. Sci. **155**(1), 39–83 (1996)
26. Sangiorgi, D., Walker, D.: The π-Calculus: A Theory of Mobile Processes. Cambridge University Press, Cambridge (2001)
27. Shields, M.W.: Concurrent machines. Comput. J. **28**(5), 449–465 (1985)
28. Ulidowski, I., Phillips, I., Yuen, S.: Concurrency and reversibility. In: Yamashita, S., Minato, S. (eds.) RC 2014. LNCS, vol. 8507, pp. 1–14. Springer, Heidelberg (2014). doi:10.1007/978-3-319-08494-7_1
29. Winskel, G., Nielsen, M.: Models for concurrency. In: Abramski, S., Gabbay, D., Maibaum, T. (eds.) Handbook of Logic in Computer Science, pp. 1–148. Oxford Universtiy Press, New York (1995)

Efficient Learning of Tier-Based Strictly k-Local Languages

Adam Jardine[1(✉)] and Kevin McMullin[2]

[1] Department of Linguistics, Rutgers University, New Brunswick, NJ, USA
adam.jardine@rutgers.edu
[2] Department of Linguistics, University of Ottawa, Ottawa, Canada
kevin.mcmullin@uottawa.ca

Abstract. We introduce an algorithm that learns the class of Tier-based Strictly k-Local (TSL_k) formal languages in polynomial time on a sample of positive data whose size is bounded by a constant. The TSL_k languages are useful in modeling the cognition of sound patterns in natural language [6,11], and it is known that they can be efficiently learned from positive data in the case that $k = 2$ [9]. We extend this result to any k and improve on its time efficiency. We also refine the definition of a canonical TSL_k grammar and prove several properties about these grammars that aid in their learning.

Keywords: Grammatical inference · Algorithmic learning

1 Introduction

This paper introduces an algorithm that provably and efficiently learns a grammar for any Tier-based Strictly k-Local (TSL) formal language [6]. In brief, this subclass of the regular languages encompasses those languages that prohibit certain sequences of adjacent symbols, where adjacency is assessed with respect to a subset of the alphabet (the tier) while ignoring all intervening non-tier symbols. A TSL_k grammar therefore comprises a tier, labeled T, and a set of k-factors (length-k sequences) that are forbidden on the tier, labeled R.

The TSL languages have been motivated from linguistic and cognitive perspectives [6,8,11,12], drawing from patterns in natural language phonology in which co-occurrence restrictions apply to a subset of the sounds, ignoring all sounds not in that subset. For example, Finnish words only contain vowels from the set $\{ü, ö, ä\}$ or the set $\{u, o, a\}$, and not both, regardless of any intervening consonants or vowels $\{i, e\}$. For example, words *pöütänä* 'the table (essive)' and *pappina* 'priest (essive)' are attested in Finnish, but words like *poütäna* and *päppina*, which contain vowels from both sets, are not attested [14,15]. This can be modeled by a TSL_2 grammar which bans, e.g., *äa* and *aä* sequences once all

We thank Jane Chandlee, Gunnar Hansson, Jeff Heinz, and three reviewers.

F. Drewes et al. (Eds.): LATA 2017, LNCS 10168, pp. 64–76, 2017.
DOI: 10.1007/978-3-319-53733-7_4

sounds not in the set $\{\ddot{u}, \ddot{o}, \ddot{a}, u, o, a\}$ (i.e., all consonants and the vowels $\{i, e\}$) have been deleted [6]. Such patterns are common in natural language, ranging over a variety of tiers [11,15]. As such, it is of interest to understand how such grammars can be learned from positive evidence.

While the learning problem is trivial when the contents of the tier are provided *a priori* [6], it has not yet been established that an efficient, non-enumerative algorithm exists which can induce both the tier and the k-factor components of the grammar for TSL_k languages of any k. For $k = 2$, the Tier-based Strictly 2-Local Inference Algorithm (2TSLIA) of [9] exactly identifies a TSL_2 tier and permitted 2-factors given positive data in $\mathcal{O}(n^4)$ time, where n is the size of the data sample. The present work generalizes and improves on this result, introducing an algorithm we call the Tier-based Strictly k-Local Inference Algorithm (kTSLIA) that learns the class of TSL_k languages for any value of k in quadratic time, with the amount of data requisite for learning bounded by a constant. A secondary result is that we refine the notion of canonical TSL_k grammars, distinct from the notion introduced for TSL_k grammars in [9], and prove properties of these grammars that the kTSLIA can use to induce a TSL grammar exactly from positive examples.

The paper is structured as follows. Section 2 summarizes the relevant notation, concepts, and definitions used throughout this paper. Section 3 defines the TSL class of formal languages and proves some properties of this class that can be exploited in learning. Section 4 presents the kTSLIA and Sect. 5 proves that the algorithm learns the TSL_k class of languages in polynomial time and data for any value of k. Section 6 summarizes the contributions of the paper, discusses future work, and concludes.

2 Preliminaries

We use standard set notation. For a set S, $|S|$ denotes its cardinality and $\mathcal{P}_{fin}(S)$ the set of finite subsets of S. For sets S and R, $S - R$ denotes $\{s \in S | s \notin R\}$.

An *alphabet* Σ is a finite set of symbols. A *string* $w = \sigma_1\sigma_2\ldots\sigma_n$ over Σ is a finite sequence of n symbols $\sigma_i \in \Sigma$; let $|w|$ denote its length (i.e., n). Let λ denote the *empty string*, the unique string of length 0. We write wv for the concatenation of strings w and v; note that $w\lambda = \lambda w = w$. By Σ^* we denote the set of all strings over Σ, including λ. A set L of strings or *language* is a subset of Σ^*. The *size* $||L||$ of a language L is the sum of the lengths of its composite strings; i.e. $||L|| = \sum_{w \in L} |w|$. A *grammar* G is some finite representation of a language; we write $L(G)$ for the language represented by G (concrete examples of how to interpret $L(G)$ for specific types of grammars are given in Sect. 3).

We often make use of special boundary symbols $\rtimes$ and $\ltimes$, assumed not to be members of Σ, to mark the beginning and end of a strings, respectively. We abuse the concatenation notation somewhat and write wL (Lw) for the concatenation of w to the beginning (and/or end) of each string in L. Thus, $\rtimes\Sigma^*\ltimes$ denotes the set of strings over Σ marked with beginning and end boundaries.

A string u is a *substring* of w if there are two strings v_1, v_2 such that $w = v_1uv_2$. Let $|w|$ be the length of w. We say u is a *k-factor* of w if u is a substring of $\rtimes w \ltimes$ and $|u| = k$. Note that λ is the single 0-factor for any string. Define a function $\texttt{fac}_k$ which returns the k-factors of $\rtimes w \ltimes$ (or $\rtimes w \ltimes$ if $| \rtimes w \ltimes | \leq k$): $\texttt{fac}_k(w) = \{u \mid u \text{ is a } k\text{-factor of } w\}$ if $|\rtimes w \ltimes| > k$, $\{\rtimes w \ltimes\}$ otherwise. Finally, we extend $\texttt{fac}_k$ to languages such that $\texttt{fac}_k(L) = \bigcup_{w \in L} \texttt{fac}_k(w)$.

2.1 Learning Paradigm

The learning paradigm considered here is exact identification in the limit [2] in polynomial time and data [7]. Under this paradigm, a learning algorithm is assumed to be given sufficient examples to identify the learning target. However, the size of these examples must be polynomial with respect to the size of the representation (grammar) for this target, and the algorithm must run in polynomial time complexity with respect to the size of the input data.

A class $\mathcal{C}$ of languages is said to be generated by a class $\mathcal{G}$ of grammars if each $G \in \mathcal{G}$ is finite and there is a total, surjective naming function $f : \mathcal{G} \to \mathcal{C}$ from any grammar to a language in $\mathcal{C}$. The goal is an algorithm A which, given a finite set of examples from any $L \in \mathcal{C}$, returns a grammar $G \in \mathcal{G}$ for L.

Definition 1 (($\mathcal{C}$, $\mathcal{G}$)-learning algorithm). *Let $\mathcal{C}$ be a class of languages over an alphabet Σ generated by a class $\mathcal{G}$ of grammars. An input* sample *I of some $L \in \mathcal{C}$ is a finite set of strings in L; that is, $I \subseteq L$. A $(\mathcal{C}, \mathcal{G})$*-learning algorithm *is a function $A : \mathcal{P}_{fin}(\Sigma^*) \to \mathcal{G}$ that takes a finite sample of strings as an input and outputs a grammar in $\mathcal{G}$.*

Given a particular $(\mathcal{C}, \mathcal{G})$-learning algorithm, a *characteristic sample* of a language in $\mathcal{C}$ is a sample of that language such that the algorithm is guaranteed to identify a grammar which exactly generates the language.

Definition 2 (Characteristic sample). *Given a $(\mathcal{C}, \mathcal{G})$-learning algorithm A, a* characteristic sample *I_C for A for a language L is a sample of L such that for all samples $I \supseteq I_C$ of L, $L = L(A(I))$.*

A further goal is that the algorithm learns any language in the class in polynomial time complexity with respect to the input data, and that the characteristic sample for any language is polynomial in size with respect to the size of any grammar G (denoted $|G|$) for the language.

Definition 3 (Identification in polynomial time and data). *A $(\mathcal{C}, \mathcal{G})$-learning algorithm A* identifies $\mathcal{C}$ in polynomial time and data *when there are two polynomial functions f and g such that, for any language $L \in \mathcal{C}$, given a sample I containing a characteristic sample of L, $L(A(I)) = L$, and (1) the size I_C of the characteristic sample of L is, for any grammar $G \in \mathcal{G}$ that represents L, at most $f(n)$, where $n = |G|$; and (2) A returns a grammar for L in $\mathcal{O}(g(||I||))$ time.*

3 Tier-Based Strictly Local Languages

3.1 Strictly Local Languages

The Tier-based Strictly Local (TSL) class of formal languages [6] is a generalization of the Strictly Local (SL) (otherwise known as Locally Testable in the Strict Sense) class of languages first studied in [13]. It will be useful to understand some concepts with respect to the SL languages, so we review these languages first.

Given an alphabet Σ, define a *SL_k grammar* as a set $R \subseteq \texttt{fac}_k(\Sigma^*)$. The language of this grammar is thus $L(R) = \{w \in \Sigma^* \mid \texttt{fac}_k(w) \cap R = \emptyset\}$. In other words, R defines a set of *forbidden k-factors* that do not appear as substrings of any string in $L(R)$. For example, for the alphabet $\Sigma = \{a, b\}$, $R = \{\rtimes a, a\ltimes\}$ describes the set of strings $L(R) = \{\lambda, b, bb, bab, bbb, \ldots\}$; i.e., exactly the strings in Σ^* that do not begin or end with an a. This $L(R)$ is a Strictly 2-Local (SL_2) language, as R consists of 2-factors of Σ^*.

The SL languages lie at the bottom of the *Sub-Regular Hierarchy* of subclasses of the Regular languages [13,16,17]. Though simple in computational complexity, SL languages are formally similar to n-gram models [10], and have been shown to model local co-occurrence restrictions in natural language phonology [4,16]. Furthermore, given k, any SL_k class is efficiently identifiable in the limit from positive data using a very simple procedure [1,3]. For a sample I of strings from a target SL_k language L, we can return a grammar R where $R = \texttt{fac}_k(\Sigma^*) - \bigcup_{w \in I} \texttt{fac}_k(w)$ such that $L(R) = L$. Remark 4 notes the efficiency of this procedure (which bears on the results of Sect. 5).

Remark 4. Calculating $\texttt{fac}_k(I)$ is linear in $||I||$.

Proof. Returning the k-factors of a string w takes $|\rtimes w \ltimes| - k - 1$ steps, which is effectively $\mathcal{O}(|w|)$. For a set of strings I the complexity is thus $\mathcal{O}(||I||)$. □

3.2 TSL Languages, Grammars, and Known Properties

The Tier-based Strictly Local (TSL) languages generalize the SL languages in that forbidden k-factors are interpreted to only apply to some subset or *tier* T of the alphabet Σ. Following [6], we define a function $\texttt{erase}_T$ that returns a string with all non-members of T removed: $\texttt{erase}_T(\sigma_1\sigma_2\ldots\sigma_n) = u_1u_2\ldots u_n$ where each $u_i = \sigma_i$ if $\sigma_i \in T$; $u_i = \lambda$ otherwise. For example, for $\Sigma = \{a, b\}$ and $T = \{b\}$, then $\texttt{erase}_T(abbaaabab) = bbbb$. We then can define the *tier k-factors* of a string as $\texttt{fac}_k(\texttt{erase}_T(w))$. A TSL grammar is thus a pair $\langle T, R\rangle$ where T is a tier and $R \subseteq \texttt{fac}_k(T^*)$ is a set of *forbidden tier k-factors*. The language of such a grammar is thus $L(\langle T, R\rangle) = \{w \in \Sigma^* \mid \texttt{fac}_k(\texttt{erase}_T(w)) \cap R = \emptyset\}$.

For example, for $\Sigma = \{a, b\}$, $L(\langle\{b\}_T, \{bbb\}_R\rangle)$ is the set of strings such that no 3 bs occur in the string, no matter how many as intervene (note the above string $abbaaabab$ is not in this language; $abaaab$, for example, is). Because they restrict how members on T may appear in a language, we will sometimes refer to members of R as *restrictions* on symbols on the tier. For the closure properties of the TSL class and its relation to other formal language classes, see [6].

We say a grammar $G = \langle T, R\rangle$ is *canonical* if and only if T is as small as it can be without changing the language. The notion of canonical grammar leads to important properties a learning algorithm can use to learn the tier.

Definition 5 (Canonical TSL_k grammar). *A TSL_k grammar $G = \langle T, R\rangle$ is* canonical *iff for any TSL_k grammar $G' = \langle T', R'\rangle$, $L(G) = L(G')$ and $G \neq G'$ implies $T \subset T'$.*

Example 6. Let $\Sigma = \{a, b, c\}$. Let $G = \langle \{b\}_T, \{bb\}_R\rangle$; $L(G)$ is the strings of any number of as and cs but at most one b. G is canonical as no TSL_2 grammar for $L(G)$ has a smaller tier. For example, $L(\langle \{a, b\}_{T'}, \{bb\}_{R'}\rangle) = L(G')$ but $T \subset T'$.

Note that, under this definition, the canonical grammar for Σ^* is $\langle \emptyset, \emptyset\rangle$, which does not specify restrictions on any $\sigma \in \Sigma$, as the empty set is the smallest tier needed to describe Σ^* (note that this is the unique case in which R can be empty in a canonical grammar). Likewise, the canonical grammar for the empty language is $\langle \emptyset, \{\lambda\}\rangle$ for $k = 0$, $\langle \emptyset, \{\rtimes, \ltimes\}\rangle$ for $k = 1$, and $\langle \emptyset, \{\rtimes\ltimes\}\rangle$ for $k > 1$.

Several existing learning results pertain to the TSL languages. First, given T, learning R is identical to SL learning [6] procedure outlined in Sect. 3.1 [6]. An interesting question, however, is whether or not T can also be learned. As Σ is finite, the set of possible Ts is finite, and so the class of possible TSL languages for a given Σ and k is finite, and thus can be learned via an enumerative method [2]. Thus, in principle, there is a method for learning T. However, as TSL grammars appear to be relevant to linguistic cognition and learning [5,11], it is of interest to pursue a non-enumerative method that meets the efficiency criteria in Sect. 2.1.

For TSL_2 languages, such a method does exist. The Tier-based Strictly 2-Local Inference Algorithm (2TSLIA) of [9] can learn TSL_2 languages in quartic time with a data sample bounded by a constant. Essentially, the 2TSLIA does this by recursively removing symbols in Σ from its hypothesis for T and checking the tier 2-factors present in the data based on this new guess for the tier.

The algorithm described in the following section improves on this result in two ways. One, it can learn a TSL_k language given any k. Two, it accomplishes this in quadratic time by removing the recursive step.

3.3 Some Useful Properties of Canonical TSL Grammars

Given a canonical grammar $\langle T, R\rangle$, Lemmas 7 and 9 give important properties of restricted members of T and nonmembers of T, respectively. We henceforth assume factors are of strings in $\rtimes\Sigma^*\ltimes$ (e.g., ignoring all $u_1 \rtimes u_2$ where $u_1 \neq \lambda$).

Lemma 7. *If $G = \langle T, R\rangle$ is a canonical TSL_k grammar, then for all $\sigma \in T$ which appear in R (i.e., for which there is at least one $u_1\sigma u_2 \in R$), there is at least one $v_1\sigma v_2 \in R$ such that $v_1v_2 \in \texttt{fac}_{k-1}(L(G))$.*

Proof. Consider any grammar G and $L = L(G)$ for which there exists a $\sigma \in T$ that appears in R such that *for all* $v_1\sigma v_2 \in R$, $v_1v_2 \notin \texttt{fac}_{k-1}(L)$. We show there is a $G' = \langle T', R' \rangle$ such that $\sigma \notin T'$ but $L(G') = L$. Thus any such G is not canonical (and so conversely for any canonical grammar, Lemma 1 must hold).

First, if $v_1v_2 \notin \texttt{fac}_{k-1}(L)$, then all tier k-factors containing it must be banned. This means that either $v_1v_2 = \rtimes v_3 \ltimes$ and $v_1v_2 \in R$, or for all $\tau \in (T \cup \{\rtimes, \ltimes\})$, both $\tau v_1 v_2 \in R$ and $v_1 v_2 \tau \in R$. Because for this σ *for all* $w_1 \sigma w_2 \in R$ it is the case that $w_1 w_2 \notin L$, the previous sentence applies recursively. That is, if $v_1 v_2 \tau = v_1' \sigma v_2'$, then for all $\tau' \in (T \cup \{\rtimes, \ltimes\}), v_1' v_2' \tau' \in R$ and $\tau' v_1' v_2' \in R$. Thus for any string $v = t_0 \sigma t_1 \sigma \ldots t_{n-1} \sigma t_n \in R$ consisting of n σs interpolated with $n+1$ strings $t_i \in ((T \cup \{\rtimes, \ltimes\}) - \{\sigma\})^*$, then $u t_0 t_1 \ldots t_n u' \in R$ for all strings $u, u' \in ((T \cup \{\rtimes, \ltimes\}) - \{\sigma\})^*$ such that $u t_0 t_1 \ldots t_n u' \in \texttt{fac}_k((T - \{\sigma\})^*)$. In other words, for all $u t_0 \ldots t_n u' \in \texttt{fac}_k(\rtimes (T - \{\sigma\})^* \ltimes)$, $u t_0 \ldots t_n u' \in R$.

Now consider $G' = \langle T', R' \rangle$ that is identical to G except that σ has been removed from R' and T'; i.e. $R' = R - \{w | w = v_1 \sigma v_2$ for some $v_1, v_2 \in \texttt{fac}_k(T^*)\}$ and $T' = T - \{\sigma\}$. Let $L' = L(G')$. We show that $L' = L$.

For $L' \subseteq L$, note that $R' \subset R$ and, because there is no $v_1 \sigma v_2 \in R'$, for all $v \in R'$, $\texttt{erase}_{T'}(v) = \texttt{erase}_T(v)$. So if there is some $w \in \Sigma^*$ s.t. there is a $v \in R'$ and $v \in \texttt{fac}_k(\texttt{erase}_{T'}(w))$, $v \in R$ and $u \in \texttt{fac}_k(\texttt{erase}_T(w))$. Thus $w \notin L'$ implies $w \notin L$. For $L \subseteq L'$, take any $v = t_0 \sigma t_1 \sigma \ldots t_{n-1} \sigma t_n \in R$ (where each t_i is a string in $((T \cup \{\rtimes, \ltimes\}) - \{\sigma\})^*$) and some $w \in \Sigma^*$ where $v \in \texttt{fac}_k(\texttt{erase}_T(w))$. As shown above, for all $u t_0 \ldots t_n u' \in \texttt{fac}_k((T - \{\sigma\})^*)$, $u t_0 \ldots t_n u' \in R$, and so also $u t_0 \ldots t_n u' \in R'$. Thus there is some $u t_0 t_1 \ldots t_n u' \in R'$ such that $u t_0 t_1 \ldots t_n u' \in \texttt{fac}_k(\texttt{erase}_{T'}(w))$, and so $w \notin L$ implies $w \notin L'$. Thus, $L(G) = L(G')$ but $T \not\subseteq T'$, so G is not canonical. □

Example 8. Consider $G = \langle \{b, a\}_T, \{bab\}_R \rangle$. This is canonical for $k = 3$, and satisfies Lemma 7. For example, for a, bab is a banned 3-factor but bb is an allowed 2-factor in $L(G)$ (witnessed by the string $abba \in L(G_2)$) and for b, ab is an allowed 2-factor (as $aab \in L(G_2)$). Consider then G' which is identical except bb is not a 2-factor in $L(G')$. This means that $L(G') = \langle \{a, b\}_{T'}, \{bab, \rtimes bb, bb\ltimes, bba, abb\}_{R'} \rangle$, where R' bans all tier 3-factors that contain bb. However, $L(G')$ is not canonical, as $L(G') = L(\langle \{b\}, \{\rtimes bb, bbb, bb\ltimes\} \rangle)$, and $\{b\} \subset T'$.

Lemma 9. *For a canonical TSL$_k$ grammar G, the following hold iff $\sigma \notin T$:*

1. $\forall v_1 v_2 \in \texttt{fac}_{k-1}(L(G)), v_1 \sigma v_2 \in \texttt{fac}_k(L(G))$.
2. $\forall v_1 \sigma v_2 \in \texttt{fac}_{k+1}(L(G)), v_1 v_2 \in \texttt{fac}_k(L(G))$.

Proof. Let $L = L(G)$. ($\rightarrow$) This follows from the definition of a TSL grammar. For (1), if $\sigma \notin T$, then for any $w = w_1 v_1 v_2 w_2 \in L$, there is also a $w' = w_1 v_1 \sigma v_2 w_2 \in L$. This is because when $\sigma \notin T$, $\texttt{erase}_T(w) = \texttt{erase}_T(w')$, and thus the two strings are equivalent with respect to G. The same applies to (2): if $\sigma \notin T$, then for any $w' = w_1 v_1 \sigma v_2 w_2 \in L$, there is also a $w = w_1 v_1 v_2 w_2 \in L$.

($\leftarrow$) We show that for any σ that is a member of T, either (1) or (2) is false. There are two important cases for $\sigma \in T$. Either there is some $v_1 \sigma v_2 \in R$, or there is no such member of R and σ is thus unrestricted. For the case in which there *does* exist a $v_1 \sigma v_2 \in R$, it follows directly from Lemma 7 that (1) is false, because we know that there is some $u_1 u_2 \in \texttt{fac}_{k-1}(L(G))$ for which $u_1 \sigma u_2 \in R$, which implies that $u_1 \sigma u_2 \notin \texttt{fac}_k(L(G))$.

For any $\sigma \in T$ for which there is *not* some $v_1\sigma v_2 \in R$, (2) will always be false as long as R is nonempty. Consider any $v_1'v_2' \in R$. It must be true that $v_1'\sigma v_2' \in \mathtt{fac}_{k+1}(L)$, because any $u \in \mathtt{fac}_k(v_1'\sigma v_2')$ necessarily contains σ, and thus $u \notin R$. However, because $v_1'v_2' \in R$, $v_1'v_2' \notin \mathtt{fac}_k(L)$ by the definition of a TSL grammar, and so (2) is false. □

Example 10. For $\Sigma = \{a, b, c\}$, consider $G = \langle \{a, b, c\}_T, \{bab\}_R \rangle$. For b, (1) is false because bb is a 2-factor in $L(G)$, but bab is not a 3-factor in $L(G)$. For c, (2) is false because $bcab$ is a 4-factor in $L(G)$ but bab is not a 3-factor.

4 The Tier-Based Strictly k-Local Inference Algorithm

We can now define an efficient learning algorithm for learning a TSL$_k$ language, for any k, by taking advantage of the properties of canonical TSL$_k$ grammars proven in Lemmas 7 and 9 in Sect. 3.3. The algorithm is given below in Algorithm 1. Proofs of its correctness and efficiency are given in Sect. 5.

Data: A finite input sample $I \subset \Sigma^*$, a positive integer k
Result: A k-TSL grammar $G = \langle T, R \rangle$
Initialize $T = \Sigma$;
foreach $\sigma \in T$ **do**
  if a) $\forall v_1v_2 \in \mathtt{fac}_{k-1}(I), v_1\sigma v_2 \in \mathtt{fac}_k(I)$ and
    b) $\forall v_1\sigma v_2 \in \mathtt{fac}_{k+1}(I), v_1v_2 \in \mathtt{fac}_k(I)$ **then**
    remove σ from T
  end
end
Initialize R to $\mathtt{fac}_k(T^*)$;
foreach $u \in R$, if $u \in \mathtt{fac}_k(I)$ **do** remove u from R;

Algorithm 1: The Tier-based Strictly k-Local Inference Algorithm

Recall from Lemma 9 that, for a language L whose canonical grammar is $G = \langle T, R \rangle$, for any $\sigma \in \Sigma$, $\sigma \notin T$ if and only if (1) $\forall v_1v_2 \in \mathtt{fac}_{k-1}(L), v_1\sigma v_2 \in \mathtt{fac}_k(L)$ and (2) $\forall v_1\sigma v_2 \in \mathtt{fac}_{k+1}(L), v_1v_2 \in \mathtt{fac}_k(L)$. Given a set of input data I, the algorithm searches for exactly these pairs for each $\sigma \in \Sigma$. If all such pairs are present in I, then σ is removed from the algorithm's hypothesis for the tier. In this way, the algorithm can identify members of Σ that have the properties established in Lemma 9 and correctly remove them from the tier.

To describe the algorithm in more detail, it first sets its hypothesis for the tier to Σ. Then, in the first **foreach** loop, it cycles through each $\sigma \in \Sigma$, searching for the above information. Specifically, for every v_1v_2 in the $k-1$-factors of I, it searches for $v_1\sigma v_2$ in the k-factors of I, in order to determine whether σ is permitted to co-occur with every $k-1$-factor that is otherwise unrestricted. Likewise, for every $v_1\sigma v_2$ in the $k+1$-factors of I, the algorithm searches for v_1v_2 in the k-factors of I, in order to determine that there is no k-factor whose occurrence in the language is *dependent* on the intervening σ. If it finds all such pairs, then it removes σ from its hypothesis for the tier. Having calculated a hypothesis for the tier, it then calculates a hypothesis for R by initializing its hypothesis to the full set of possible k-factors of T^* and then removing from this hypothesis any tier k-factor it finds in the k-factors of I. In other words, all tier k-factors not seen in I will appear in the algorithm's hypothesis for R.

Example 11. Consider a case in which $k = 3$, $\Sigma = \{a, b\}$, and the target language is $L(G_*)$ where $G_* = \langle \{b\}_{T_*}, \{bbb\}_{R_*} \rangle$ and the algorithm is given as an input a sample I from L where $I = \{\lambda, a, b, bb, aaa, bab, abba, aabaabaa\}$. Given I, the algorithm will return a grammar $G = \langle T, R \rangle$ where $T = T_*$ and $R = R_*$. To see how, Table 1 lists the $k-1$-factors, k-factors, and $k+1$-factors of I.

First, the algorithm initializes its hypothesis T to $\{a, b\}$, then in the first **foreach** loop checks if either a or b meets the conditions in the **if** statement for removal from T. Say the algorithm first considers a. In condition (a) of the **if** statement, the algorithm checks that for every $v_1 v_2 \in \texttt{fac}_{k-1}(I)$, $v_1 a v_2 \in \texttt{fac}_k(I)$. This is true in all cases: for example, $\rtimes a \in \texttt{fac}_{k-1}(I)$ (row (b) in Table 1), and $\rtimes aa \in \texttt{fac}_k(I)$ (row (e)); also, $bb \in \texttt{fac}_{k-1}(I)$ (row (d)), and $abb, bab, bba \in \texttt{fac}_k(I)$ (rows (g), (f), and (g), respectively). Thus, a satisfies condition (a) of the **if** statement. Next, condition (b) in the **if** statement checks that, for every $v_1 a v_2 \in \texttt{fac}_{k+1}(I)$, $v_1 v_2 \in \texttt{fac}_k(I)$. This is also true: for example, $\rtimes aaa \in \texttt{fac}_{k+1}(I)$ (row (e)) and $\rtimes aa \in \texttt{fac}_k(I)$ (also row (e); also, $abba \in \texttt{fac}_{k+1}(I)$ (row (g)) and $bba, abb \in \texttt{fac}_k(I)$ (also row (g)). So a also satisfies condition (b) of the **if** statement. It is thus removed from T.

This, however, does not occur with b. In condition (a) of the **if** statement, the algorithm will check to see if the $k-1$-factor bb (which appears in row (c)) has a corresponding k-factor bbb. This does not appear in I. In fact, no sample of $L(G_*)$ will contain bbb as a 3-factor, as $bbb \in R_*$. Thus b will remain on T.

Having checked through each symbol in Σ for removal from T, the algorithm then calculates its hypothesis for R in the second **foreach** loop. First, it initializes R to all possible tier k-factors; in this case, this is $\{\rtimes\ltimes, \rtimes b\ltimes, \rtimes bb, bb\ltimes, bbb\}$. Note that all but bbb are attested in Table 1, so the **foreach** loop will remove all but bbb from R. Thus, the algorithm returns a grammar $\langle T, R \rangle = \langle T_*, R_* \rangle$.

Of course, the algorithm can only accurately determine if a symbol σ is on the tier if the data in I is somehow representative of the target language L. Definition 12 below defines a set D of data that I must contain in order for it to be representative of L. The following section will then prove that any such *representative sample* is a *characteristic* sample, in the sense defined in Sect. 2.1.

Definition 12 (Representative sample). *For a TSL$_k$ language L whose canonical grammar is $G = \langle T, R \rangle$, $S = \textit{fac}_k(T^*) - R$, $P = \{\sigma \mid v_1 \sigma v_2 \in R\}$, a set D is a* representative sample *of L if it meets the following conditions:*

1. ***Non-tier element condition.*** *For all non-tier elements $\sigma \notin T$,*
   (a) $\forall v_1 v_2 \in \textit{fac}_{k-1}(L), \exists v_1 \sigma v_2 \in \textit{fac}_k(D)$.
   (b) $\forall v_1 \sigma v_2 \in \textit{fac}_{k+1}(L), \exists v_1 v_2 \in \textit{fac}_k(D)$.

Table 1. Breakdown of the factors of I from Example 11. Each row gives the new 2-, 3-, and 4-factors (i.e., the $k-1$-, k-, and $k+1$-factors) generated from each data point.

	Input string	k-1-factors	k-factors	k+1-factors
a.	λ	$\rtimes\ltimes$		
b.	a	$\rtimes a, a\ltimes$	$\rtimes a\ltimes$	
c.	b	$\rtimes b, b\ltimes$	$\rtimes b\ltimes$	
d.	bb	bb	$\rtimes bb, bb\ltimes$	$\rtimes bb\ltimes$
e.	aaa	aa	$\rtimes aa, aaa, aa\ltimes$	$\rtimes aaa, aaa\ltimes$
f.	bab	ba, ab	$\rtimes ba, bab, ab\ltimes$	$\rtimes bab, bab\ltimes$
g.	$abba$	ab, ba	$\rtimes ab, abb, bba, ba\ltimes$	$\rtimes abb, abba, bba\ltimes$
h.	$aabaabaa$	—	aab, aba, baa	$\rtimes aab, aaba, abaa, baa\ltimes$

2. ***The tier element condition.*** *For each $\sigma \in T$,*
   (a) if $\sigma \in P$, then $\exists v_1v_2 \in \mathtt{fac}_{k-1}(D)$ s.t. $v_1\sigma v_2 \in R$.
   (b) if $\sigma \notin P$, then $\exists v_1\sigma v_2 \in \mathtt{fac}_{k+1}(D)$, where $v_1v_2 \in R$.
3. ***Allowed tier k-factor condition.*** *For all $v \in S, \exists w \in D$ s.t. $v \in \mathtt{fac}_k(w)$.*

Essentially, Definition 12 states that a representative sample is a set that contains the relevant information for each $\sigma \in \Sigma$ to distinguish it as a non-member or member of the tier. The *non-tier element condition* ensures that for each $\sigma \notin T$, a representative sample includes in its k-factors at least one $v_1\sigma v_2$ for every v_1v_2 in the $k-1$-factors of L and at least one v_1v_2 for every $v_1\sigma v_1$ in the $k+1$-factors of L. Again, the presence of these k-factors was shown by Lemma 9 to be definitional for non-members of T.

For any $\sigma \in T$, the *tier element condition* ensures that the representative sample includes sufficient information to identify σ as a member of the tier. This is done by ensuring the inverse of Lemma 9 is true: that for σ for which such there is some $v_1\sigma v_2 \in R$ (and thus will never appear as a k-factor in a sample of L), there is some $v_1v_2 \in \mathtt{fac}_{k-1}(D)$. Note that Lemma 7 guarantees such a v_1v_2 to exist as a $k-1$-factor of L. For $\sigma \in T$ for which no such k-factor exists in R, part (b) of the tier element condition states that a representative sample must include some $v_1\sigma v_2$ as a $k+1$-factor, where $v_1v_2 \in R$. Thus, for any $\sigma \in T$, a representative sample includes information showing that σ does not obey the properties Lemma 9 establishes for non-tier elements.

Finally, the *allowed tier k-factor condition*, ensures that the representative sample includes all tier k-factors allowed by G.

5 Identification in Polynomial Time and Data

We now prove that the kTSLIA can correctly identify any TSL language in polynomial time and data. First, we establish its time complexity.

Lemma 13. *Given an input sample I of size n, kTSLIA runs in polynomial time complexity with respect to n.*

Proof. The algorithm needs to calculate the $k-1$-, k-, and $k+1$-factors of I, each of which (per Remark 4) takes time linear in n. Note also that the cardinality of each of these sets of factors is bound by n.

The first **foreach** loop is called exactly $|\Sigma|$ times. Checking condition (a) in this loop requires that for every $\sigma_1 \ldots \sigma_{k-1} \in \mathtt{fac}_{k-1}(I)$, the algorithm checks $\mathtt{fac}_k(I)$ for $v_1\sigma v_2 \in \mathtt{fac}_k(I)$ where $v_1 = \lambda, v_2 = \sigma_1 \ldots \sigma_{k-1}$, $v_1 = \sigma_1, v_2 = \sigma_2 \ldots \sigma_{k-1}$ $v_1 = \sigma_1\sigma_2, v_2 = \sigma_3 \ldots \sigma_{k-1}$, etc. Thus condition (a) requires, for each member of $\mathtt{fac}_{k-1}(I)$, $k+1$ passes through $\mathtt{fac}_k(I)$. This takes $n \cdot (k+1) \cdot n = (k+1) \cdot n^2$ steps. Checking condition (b) requires that, in the worst case, for each member of $\mathtt{fac}_{k+1}(I)$, the algorithm passes through $\mathtt{fac}_k(I)$ $k+1$ times, taking $(k+1) \cdot n^2$ steps. Since $\mathtt{fac}$ is calculated in linear time, the time complexity for this loop is therefore $\mathcal{O}(|\Sigma|2(k+1)n^2) = \mathcal{O}(n^2)$ since $|\Sigma|$ and k are constants.

The final step of the algorithm, identifying the permissible tier-based k-factors, requires one final run through the k-factors of I, which again takes n steps. In total, the algorithm runs in $\mathcal{O}(3n + n^2 + n) = \mathcal{O}(n^2)$ time. □

Lemma 14. *For a language L, the size of the representative sample D for L is polynomial with respect to the size of G for any grammar G of L.*

Proof. The non-tier condition requires that for each $\sigma \notin T$ and for each $v_1v_2 \in \mathtt{fac}_{k-1}(L)$, the sample minimally contains a $v_1\sigma v_2$ factor. The length of these strings equals $|\Sigma - T| \cdot |\Sigma|^{k-1} \cdot k$. Additionally, for every $\sigma \notin T$ and for each $v_1\sigma v_2 \in \mathtt{fac}_{k+1}(L)$, the sample includes minimally a v_1v_2 substring. The combined length of these strings is $|\Sigma - T| \cdot |\Sigma|^k \cdot (k+1)$. The tier condition requires that for each $\sigma \in T$ there is minimally either one string v_1v_2 such that $v_1\sigma v_2 \in R$ or one string $v_1\sigma v_2$ such that $v_1v_2 \in R$. The total length of these strings is at most $|T| \cdot (k+1)$. The allowed tier k-factor condition requires for each $u \in S$ that minimally u is contained in the sample. Hence the length of these words equals $|S|$. Altogether, there is therefore a sample D such that $||D|| = |\Sigma - T| \cdot |\Sigma|^{k-1} \cdot k + |\Sigma - T| \cdot |\Sigma|^k \cdot (k+1) + |T| \cdot (k+1) + |S|$. Since $|T|$ is bounded by $|\Sigma|$ and $|S|$ and $|R|$ bounded by $|\Sigma|^k$, $||D||$ is bounded by $\mathcal{O}(|\Sigma|^k)$. As $|\Sigma|$ and k are constant, $||D||$ is thus bounded by a constant. □

Lemma 15. *Given any superset I of a representative sample D for a TSL_k language L whose canonical grammar is $G = \langle T, R \rangle$, the kTSLIA will return a grammar $G' = \langle T', R' \rangle$ such that $T' = T$.*

Proof. This is essentially due to the fact that a representative sample is defined as one which contains the information established in Lemmas 7 and 9 as distinguishing symbols on the tier from non-tier symbols in a canonical TSL grammar. Let $L = L(G)$. We show that $\sigma \notin T$ implies $\sigma \notin T'$ and that $\sigma \in T$ implies $\sigma \in T'$, and thus that $T = T'$.

First, for any non-tier element $\sigma \notin T$, $\sigma \notin T'$ if and only if $\forall v_1v_2 \in \mathtt{fac}_{k-1}(I), v_1\sigma v_2 \in \mathtt{fac}_k(I)$ (condition (a) of the algorithm) and $\forall v_1\sigma v_2 \in \mathtt{fac}_{k+1}(I), v_1v_2 \in \mathtt{fac}_k(I)$ (condition (b) of the algorithm). Part (1a) of the non-tier element condition for the representative sample (Definition 12-1a) guarantees that for any possible $k-1$-factor v_1v_2 of L that $v_1\sigma v_2 \in \mathtt{fac}_k(D)$. (Such a

$k+1$ factor is guaranteed to exist in L by Lemma 9-2. Recall that if $\sigma \in T$, then $\texttt{erase}_T(v_1v_2) = \texttt{erase}_T(v_1\sigma v_2)$, and so G cannot distinguish between them; i.e. v_1v_2 appears in L iff $v_1\sigma v_2$ does as well). Thus for any superset I of D consistent with L, if $v_1v_2 \in \texttt{fac}_{k-1}(I)$ then $v_1\sigma v_2 \in \texttt{fac}_k(I)$. So σ satisfies condition (a).

Similarly, part (1b) of the non-tier element condition for the representative sample requires that for any $v_1v_2 \in \texttt{fac}_k(L)$, then $v_1\sigma v_2 \in \texttt{fac}_{k+1}(D)$. (Again, this is possible because G will not distinguish between v_1v_2 and $v_1\sigma v_2$, and so if $v_1v_2 \in \texttt{fac}_k(L)$, then $v_1\sigma v_2 \in \texttt{fac}_{k+1}(L)$). Thus, for any $v_1v_2 \in \texttt{fac}_k(I)$ that the algorithm encounters, it will also $v_1v_2 \in \texttt{fac}_k(I)$. Thus σ will also satisfy condition (b) and be taken off of the tier. Thus $\sigma \notin T$ implies $\sigma \notin T'$.

For $\sigma \in T$, if there is a $v_1\sigma v_2 \in R$, then part (2a) of the tier element condition for the representative sample (Definition 2-1a) requires that $v_1v_2 \in \texttt{fac}_{k-1}(D)$. Thus I is guaranteed to contain some $k-1$-factor v_1v_2 for which there will be no $v_1\sigma v_2 \in \texttt{fac}_k(I)$, as long as I is consistent with L. Thus σ will fail condition (a) of the algorithm for removal from the tier.

If there is no $v_1\sigma v_2 \in R$, then part (2b) of the tier element condition for the representative sample (Definition 2-2b) requires that there must be some $v_1v_2 \in R$ such that $v_1\sigma v_2 \in \texttt{fac}_{k+1}(D)$. (Such a $k+1$ factor is guaranteed to exist because, again, there are no restrictions on σ.) As any sample consistent with L will never contain v_1v_2, σ is guaranteed to fail condition (b) for removal from the tier.

Thus, in either situation σ fails one of the algorithm's conditions (a) and (b) for removal from the tier, and so $\sigma \in T$ implies $\sigma \in T'$. Thus $T = T'$. □

Lemma 16. *Given any superset I of a representative sample D for a TSL_k language L whose canonical grammar is $G = \langle T, R\rangle$, the kTSLIA will return a grammar $G' = \langle T', R'\rangle$ such that $R' = R$.*

Proof. By Lemma 15, $T = T'$. Thus, in the last two lines of the algorithm R' is initialized to $\texttt{fac}_k(T'^*) = \texttt{fac}_k(T^*)$, and the final **foreach** loop will correctly locate all $u \in \texttt{fac}_k(T^*)$ found in D. By Definition 2 of the representative sample, D will contain all allowable tier substrings in $S = \texttt{fac}_k(T^*) - R$. These will thus all be removed from R' by the algorithm, and so $R' = \texttt{fac}_k(T^*) - S = R$. □

Lemma 17. *A representative sample D for L is a characteristic sample for L.*

Proof. From Lemmas 15 and 16, given a superset of D the kTSLIA will return a grammar $G' = \langle T', R'\rangle$ such that $T' = T$ and $R' = R$, where $\langle T, R\rangle$ is the canonical grammar for L. Thus $L(G') = L$. □

Theorem 18. *For any TSL_k language L, the kTSLIA identifies L in polynomial time and data.*

Proof. From Lemmas 13, 14, and 17. □

6 Discussion and Conclusion

The main contributions of this paper have been twofold. One, it redefined the notion of a canonical TSL_k grammar, and proved several resulting important properties of members and non-members of the tier. Two, it established an algorithm which uses these properties that is guaranteed to induce a TSL_k grammar in polynomial time and data.

Future work can now examine how results can be applied directly to natural language learning, the context that TSL languages were initially designed to model. While this paper has established, based on the aforementioned properties of members and non-members of the tier, a characteristic sample for the kTSLIA, it remains to be seen whether or not this characteristic sample appears in natural language data. Future work can examine to what extent this information is present in phonological corpora, and discuss what modifications may be necessary for the algorithm to be successful in these situations (as done in [8] for the 2TSLIA). Furthermore, while the learner presented here is fundamentally categorical and thus brittle in the face of noisy data, future work can build on the results here to create a stochastic version of the kTSLIA.

References

1. García, P., Vidal, E., Oncina, J.: Learning locally testable languages in the strict sense. In: Proceedings of Workshop on Algorithmic Learning Theory, pp. 325–338 (1990)
2. Gold, M.E.: Language identification in the limit. Inf. Control **10**, 447–474 (1967)
3. Heinz, J.: The inductive learning of phonotactic patterns. Ph.D. thesis, University of California, Los Angeles (2007)
4. Heinz, J.: Learning long-distance phonotactics. Linguist. Inq. **41**, 623–661 (2010)
5. Heinz, J.: Computational phonology part I: foundations. Lang. Linguist. Compass **5**(4), 140–152 (2011)
6. Heinz, J., Rawal, C., Tanner, H.G.: Tier-based strictly local constraints for phonology. In: Proceedings of 49th Annual Meeting of the Association for Computational Linguistics, pp. 58–64. Association for Computational Linguistics, Portland, June 2011
7. de la Higuera, C.: Characteristic sets for polynomial grammatical inference. Mach. Learn. **27**(2), 125–138 (1997)
8. Jardine, A.: Learning tiers for long-distance phonotactics. In: Proceedings of 6th Conference on Generative Approaches to Language Acquisition North America (GALANA 2015), pp. 60–72 (2016)
9. Jardine, A., Heinz, J.: Learning tier-based strictly 2-local languages. Trans. Assoc. Comput. Linguist. **4**, 87–98 (2016)
10. Jurafsky, D., Martin, J.H.: Speech and Language Processing, 2nd edn. Pearson Prentice Hall, Upper Saddle River (2009)
11. McMullin, K.: Tier-based locality in long-distance phonotactics: learnability and typology. Ph.D. thesis, University of British Columbia (2016)
12. McMullin, K., Hansson, G.Ó: Long-distance phonotactics as tier-based strictly 2-local languages. In: Proceedings of 2014 Annual Meeting on Phonology. Linguistic Society of America, Washington, DC (2016)

13. McNaughton, R., Papert, S.: Counter-Free Automata. MIT Press, Cambridge (1971)
14. Nevins, A.: Locality in Vowel Harmony. No. 55 in Linguistic Inquiry Monographs. MIT Press, Cambridge (2010)
15. Odden, D.: Adjacency parameters in phonology. Language **70**(2), 289–330 (1994)
16. Rogers, J., Heinz, J., Fero, M., Hurst, J., Lambert, D., Wibel, S.: Cognitive and sub-regular complexity. In: Morrill, G., Nederhof, M.-J. (eds.) FG 2012-2013. LNCS, vol. 8036, pp. 90–108. Springer, Heidelberg (2013). doi:10.1007/978-3-642-39998-5_6
17. Rogers, J., Pullum, G.: Aural pattern recognition experiments and the subregular hierarchy. J. Log. Lang. Inf. **20**, 329–342 (2011)

The Strong, Weak, and Very Weak Finite Context and Kernel Properties

Makoto Kanazawa[1(✉)] and Ryo Yoshinaka[2]

[1] National Institute of Informatics and SOKENDAI, Tokyo 101–8430, Japan
kanazawa@nii.ac.jp
[2] Graduate School of Information Sciences, Tohoku University, Sendai, Miyagi 980–8579, Japan

Abstract. We identify the properties of context-free grammars that exactly correspond to the behavior of the dual and primal versions of Clark and Yoshinaka's distributional learning algorithm and call them the *very weak finite context/kernel property*. We show that the very weak finite context property does not imply Yoshinaka's *weak finite context property*, which has been assumed to hold of the target language for the dual algorithm to succeed. We also show that the weak finite context property is genuinely weaker than Clark's *strong finite context property*, settling a question raised by Yoshinaka.

Keywords: Grammatical inference and algorithmic learning · Distributional learning · Finite context property · Finite kernel property · Context-free languages

1 Introduction

Clark [2] and Yoshinaka [8] pioneered an approach to efficient learning of context-free languages under the paradigm of *polynomial-time identification in the limit from positive data and membership queries*, which they called *distributional learning*.[1] The idea of distributional learning was based on the assumption that the target language has a context-free grammar each of whose nonterminals is *characterized* either by a finite set of strings or by a finite set of *contexts* (i.e., pairs of strings). There are strong and weak variants to this notion of characterization: A nonterminal X is *strongly* characterized by a set C of contexts if the strings derived from X are exactly those that can appear in all contexts from C; X is strongly characterized by a set K of strings if X is strongly characterized by the set of contexts in which all elements of K can appear. The *weak* notion of characterization is obtained by replacing "the strings derived from X" in this definition by their *closure*, i.e., "the strings that can appear in every context in which all strings derived from X can appear". A context-free grammar G has the *strong* (resp. *weak*) *finite context property (FCP)* if each nonterminal of G is

[1] Clark and Yoshinaka have used the term "distributional learning" more loosely in connection with a number of different learning paradims (see [5] for a survey).

F. Drewes et al. (Eds.): LATA 2017, LNCS 10168, pp. 77–88, 2017.
DOI: 10.1007/978-3-319-53733-7_5

strongly (resp. weakly) characterized by a finite set of contexts; G has the *strong* (resp. *weak*) *finite kernel property (FKP)* if each nonterminal of G is strongly (resp. weakly) characterized by a finite set of strings. The *dual* variant of the distributional learner uses finite sets of contexts as nonterminals and succeeds under the assumption that the target grammar has the weak FCP, while the *primal* variant uses finite sets of strings as nonterminals and assumes that the target grammar has the weak FKP. Distributional learning, both in its dual and primal variants, has since been extended to string and tree grammar formalisms that are "context-free" in a broad sense of the term [4,5,9,11].

Despite the naturalness and wide applicability of the approach, there is a notable discrepancy between the assumption of the (weak) FCP/FKP and the behavior of the learning algorithm. For, in hypothesizing a rule, what the algorithm tries to check is the "local" requirement that the rule be *valid* under the presumption that each nonterminal in the rule is strongly characterized by itself. For example, when the dual algorithm constructs a binary rule $C_0 \to C_1C_2$, where each C_i is a finite set of contexts, it checks whether the available evidence is consistent with the assumption $C_0^{\triangleleft} \supseteq C_1^{\triangleleft}C_2^{\triangleleft}$, where $C_i^{\triangleleft}$ denotes the set of strings that can appear in each context from C_i in the target language. (Note that the definition of the set $C_i^{\triangleleft}$ refers to the target language, not to any grammar for it.) In contrast, the weak or strong FCP/FKP of a context-free grammar is a "global" property of the grammar, since it refers to the set of strings derived from each nonterminal, something that you cannot determine just by looking at each individual rule in isolation.

The original idea of Clark [2] was to identify each nonterminal with a *closed* set of strings (i.e., a set that is its own closure). Thus, he employed the strong variant of the finite context property. Yoshinaka [8] recognized the possibility that the set of strings derived from a nonterminal in the hypothesized grammar may not be a closed set, and introduced the weak variants of the FCP and FKP. In his later paper [10] on distributional learning of conjunctive grammars, Yoshinaka mentioned as an open problem the question of whether the context-free grammars with the strong FCP generate the same languages as the context-free grammars with the weak FCP. However, the question of whether the weak FCP and FKP are weak enough, i.e., whether the two variants of the distributional learner always converge to a grammar with the weak FCP/FKP, does not seem to have attracted much attention.

In fact, the properties of context-free grammars that exactly correspond to the behavior of the dual and primal variants of the distributional learner are easy to state; we call them the *very weak FCP/FKP*. The dual/primal algorithm converges to a correct grammar for the target language when the latter has a grammar satisfying the very weak FCP/FKP, and the grammar it converges to always satisfies the very weak FCP/FKP. As we show below, the very weak FKP turns out to be equivalent to the weak FKP, and the primal algorithm is guaranteed to converge to a grammar with the weak FKP. In contrast, the very weak FCP is genuinely weaker than the weak FCP. We exhibit a language that has a context-free grammar with the very weak FCP but has no context-free grammar with the weak FCP. The fact that the dual algorithm succeeds on such languages has not been recognized so far. We also show that a similar separation holds between the weak and strong variants of both the FCP and the FKP. This negatively settles the above-mentioned open problem of Yoshinaka [10].

2 Preliminaries

We adopt the standard definition of context-free grammars (as in [1]), except that we allow them to have multiple initial nonterminals. Thus, a context-free grammar (CFG) is a 4-tuple $G = (N, \Sigma, P, I)$, where $I \subseteq N$ is the set of initial nonterminals. If A is a nonterminal of G, we write $L(G, A)$ for $\{w \in \Sigma^* \mid A \Rightarrow_G^* w\}$, the set of terminal strings derived from A. Then the language of G is $L(G) = \bigcup_{A \in I} L(G, A)$. We write $C(G, A)$ for $\{(u, v) \in \Sigma^* \times \Sigma^* \mid S \Rightarrow_G^* uAv$ for some $S \in I\}$.

Let $G = (N, \Sigma, P, I)$ be a CFG. It is well known that G can be thought of as a system of equations where the nonterminals are viewed as variables ranging over $\mathscr{P}(\Sigma^*)$. This system contains the equation $A = \alpha_1 \cup \cdots \cup \alpha_k$ for each nonterminal A, where $\alpha_1, \ldots, \alpha_k$ list the right-hand sides of the productions with A on the left-hand side. A sequence of sets $(X_A)_{A \in N}$ is a *fixed point* of G if assigning the value X_A to each A satisfies all these equations. The sequence $(X_A)_{A \in N}$ is a *pre-fixed point* of G if it instead satisfies $A \supseteq \alpha_1 \cup \ldots \cdots \cup \alpha_k$. Equivalently, $(X_A)_{A \in N}$ is a pre-fixed point of G if for each production $A \to w_0 A_1 w_1 \ldots A_n w_n$ in P (with $w_i \in \Sigma^*$ and $A_i \in N$), it holds that $X_A \supseteq w_0 X_{A_1} w_1 \ldots X_{A_n} w_n$. It is known that the sequence $(L(G, A))_{A \in N}$ is the *least fixed point* as well as the *least pre-fixed point* of G under the partial order of componentwise inclusion.

3 Three Variants of the Finite Context and Kernel Properties

We begin by reviewing some important notions from Clark's *syntactic concept lattice* [3]. Let $L \subseteq \Sigma^*$ be given. For $C \subseteq \Sigma^* \times \Sigma^*$ and $K \subseteq \Sigma^*$, we put

$$C^{\langle L|} = \{x \in \Sigma^* \mid uxv \in L \text{ for all } (u, v) \in C\},$$
$$K^{|L\rangle} = \{(u, v) \in \Sigma^* \times \Sigma^* \mid uKv \subseteq L\}.$$

When the language L is understood from context, these are simply written $C^{\triangleleft}$ and $K^{\triangleright}$. For a set $K \subseteq \Sigma^*$, its *closure* is $K^{\triangleright\triangleleft}$. The function $(\cdot)^{\triangleright\triangleleft}$ is indeed a closure operator in the sense that (i) $K \subseteq K^{\triangleright\triangleleft}$, (ii) $K_1 \subseteq K_2$ implies $K_1^{\triangleright\triangleleft} \subseteq K_2^{\triangleright\triangleleft}$, and (iii) $K^{\triangleright\triangleleft\triangleright\triangleleft} = K^{\triangleright\triangleleft}$. A set $K \subseteq \Sigma^*$ is *closed* if $K = K^{\triangleright\triangleleft}$; equivalently, K is closed if and only if there exists a $C \subseteq \Sigma^* \times \Sigma^*$ such that $K = C^{\triangleleft}$. (These notions are all relative to the given language L.) Note that L is always closed relative to L, since $L^{\triangleright}$ always contains $(\varepsilon, \varepsilon)$. (We write ε for the empty string.)

An important property of the closure operator $(\cdot)^{\triangleright\triangleleft}$ is the following [3]: for $X, Y \subseteq \Sigma^*$,

$$(XY)^{\triangleright\triangleleft} = (X^{\triangleright\triangleleft} Y^{\triangleright\triangleleft})^{\triangleright\triangleleft}. \tag{1}$$

Let $G = (N, \Sigma, P, I)$ be a CFG, and let the operators $\triangleleft$ and $\triangleright$ be understood relative to $L(G)$. A pre-fixed point $(X_A)_{A \in N}$ of G is *sound* if $\bigcup_{A \in I} X_A = L(G)$.

We abbreviate "sound pre-fixed point" to "SPP". It is easy to see that if $(X_A)_{A \in N}$ is an SPP of G, then $uX_Av \subseteq L(G)$ for all $(u, v) \in C(G, A)$. Since $(L(G, A))_{A \in N}$ is the least pre-fixed point of G, it is the least SPP.

Proposition 1. *If $(X_A)_{A \in N}$ is an SPP, then so is $(X_A^{\triangleright\triangleleft})_{A \in N}$.*

Proof. This easily follows from the fact that $(w_0 X_{A_1}^{\triangleright\triangleleft} w_1 \ldots X_{A_n}^{\triangleright\triangleleft} w_n)^{\triangleright\triangleleft}$ equals $(w_0 X_{A_1} w_1 \ldots X_{A_n} w_n)^{\triangleright\triangleleft}$, which in turn is a consequence of (1). □

Since $(L(G, A)^{\triangleright\triangleleft})_{A \in N}$ is the least pre-fixed point consisting entirely of closed sets, it is the least such SPP. It need not be the greatest SPP of G. In fact, it is not hard to see that the greatest SPP may not exist.

Let k be a natural number, and let $L \subseteq \Sigma^*$. A set $X \subseteq \Sigma^*$ is *k-context-generated* relative to L if $X = C^{\langle L|}$ for some $C \subseteq \Sigma^* \times \Sigma^*$ such that $|C| \leq k$. We say that X is *k-kernel-generated* relative to L if $X = K^{|L\rangle\langle L|}$ for some $K \subseteq \Sigma^*$ such that $|K| \leq k$. A sequence of sets is k-context-generated (k-kernel-generated) if each of its component sets is k-context-generated (k-kernel-generated).

We say that G has

- the *strong k-finite context property* (resp. *strong k-finite kernel property*) if $(L(G, A))_{A \in N}$ is k-context-generated (resp. k-kernel-generated) relative to $L(G)$;
- the *weak k-finite context property* (resp. *weak k-finite kernel property*) if $(L(G, A)^{\triangleright\triangleleft})_{A \in N}$ is k-context-generated (resp. k-kernel-generated) relative to $L(G)$;
- the *very weak k-finite context property* (resp. *very weak k-finite kernel property* if G has an SPP that is k-context-generated (resp. k-kernel-generated) relative to $L(G)$.

We abbreviate "finite context property" to "FCP" and "finite kernel property" to "FKP". Clearly, a CFG G has the strong k-FCP (k-FKP) if and only if G has the weak k-FCP (k-FKP) and in addition $L(G, A)$ is a closed set relative to $L(G)$ for each nonterminal A of G. It is also obvious that the weak k-FCP (k-FKP) implies the very weak k-FCP (k-FKP). We say that G has the strong/weak/very weak FCP/FKP when G has the strong/weak/very weak k-FCP/k-FKP for some k.

What Clark [2] called the finite context property was what we here call the strong finite context property. The weak finite context property was introduced by Yoshinaka [8] and adopted by Leiß [6].

Proposition 2. (i) *There is a language that has a CFG with the strong 1-FKP but has no CFG with the very weak FCP.*
(ii) *There is a language that has a CFG with the strong 1-FCP but has no CFG with the very weak FKP.*

Proof. (i). Let

$$L = L_1 \cup L_2, \quad L_1 = \{a^m c b^{2m} \mid m \in \mathbb{N}\}, \quad L_2 = \{a^m d b^n \mid n \leq m \leq 2n\}.$$

Let G be the following CFG with initial nonterminals S_1 and S_2:

$$S_1 \to aS_1bb \mid c, \quad S_2 \to aS_2b \mid aaS_2b \mid d.$$

Then $L(G, S_1) = L_1 = \{c\}^{\rhd\lhd}$ and $L(G, S_2) = L_2 = \{d\}^{\rhd\lhd}$. So $L(G) = L$ and G has the strong 1-FKP.

Now let G' be any CFG for L. Applying the pumping lemma to $a^p cb^{2p}$ for a sufficiently large p, we get

$$S \Rightarrow_{G'}^* a^{i_1} E b^{j_1}, \quad E \Rightarrow_{G'}^+ a^i E b^j, \quad E \Rightarrow_{G'}^* a^{i_2} c b^{j_2}$$

with $i + j > 0$, $i_1 + i + i_2 = p$, and $j_1 + j + j_2 = 2p$, for some nonterminal E and initial nonterminal S. Since $a^{i_1+ni+i_2} cb^{j_1+nj+j_2} \in L$ for all $n \in \mathbb{N}$, we must have $j = 2i$, which implies $i > 0$. By way of contradiction, assume that G' has an SPP whose component for E is $C_E^{\lhd}$ for some finite $C_E \subseteq \Sigma^* \times \Sigma^*$. We must have

$$L \supseteq a^{i_1} C_E^{\lhd} b^{j_1}, \quad C_E^{\lhd} \supseteq a^i C_E^{\lhd} b^{2i}, \quad C_E^{\lhd} \supseteq \{a^{i_2} cb^{j_2}\}.$$

By the last inclusion, every element of C_E must be of the form (a^{n-i_2}, b^{2n-j_2}) for some n such that $n \geq i_2$ and $2n \geq j_2$. Take an m large enough that $m \geq 2n$ for all n such that $(a^{n-i_2}, b^{2n-j_2}) \in C_E$. Then for all such n,

$$2m + 2n - j_2 \leq 3m \leq 3m + n - i_2 \leq 4m \leq 2(2m + 2n - j_2),$$

which implies $a^{3m} db^{2m} \in C_E^{\lhd}$. But since $L \supseteq a^{i_1+ni} C_E^{\lhd} b^{j_1+2ni}$ for all $n \in \mathbb{N}$, we get $a^{i_1+ni+3m} db^{j_1+2ni+2m} \in L$ and hence $i_1 + ni + 3m \geq j_1 + 2ni + 2m$ for all n, which contradicts $i > 0$.

(ii). Let $L = \{a^m b^n \mid m \neq n\}$. Let G be the following CFG with a unique initial nonterminal S:

$$S \to A \mid B \mid aSb, \quad A \to a \mid aA, \quad B \to b \mid bB.$$

Then $L(G, S) = L = \{(\varepsilon, \varepsilon)\}^{\lhd}, L(G, A) = a^+ = \{(\varepsilon, ab)\}^{\lhd}, L(G, B) = b^+ = \{(ab, \varepsilon)\}^{\lhd}$, so G has the strong 1-FCP.

Now suppose that L has a CFG with the very weak FKP. Then $L = K_1^{\rhd\lhd} \cup \cdots \cup K_n^{\rhd\lhd}$ for some finite sets $K_1, \ldots, K_n \subseteq \Sigma^*$. Clearly, $K_i \subseteq L$ for $i = 1, \ldots, n$. Let $p = \max\{|m - n| \mid a^m b^n \in K_i \text{ for some } i\}$. Then for each i, $K_i^{\rhd} \supseteq \{(a^m, b^n) \mid |m - n| > p\}$, which implies $K_i^{\rhd\lhd} \subseteq \{a^m b^n \mid |m - n| \leq p\}$. This is a contradiction, since $L \not\subseteq \{a^m b^n \mid |m - n| \leq p\}$. □

4 Distributional Learning

The distributional learner has access to an infinite stream of positive examples and the membership oracle for the target language L_*. Let $\rhd$ and $\lhd$ be understood relative to L_*.

The dual algorithm forms productions of the form $C_0 \to w_0 C_1 w_1 \ldots C_n w_n$, where each nonterminal C_i is a finite set of contexts (u, v) contained in the input positive data D (i.e., $uwv \in D$ for some w). Such a production is *valid* if

$$C_0^{\lhd} \supseteq w_0 C_1^{\lhd} w_1 \ldots C_n^{\lhd} w_n.$$

The membership of a string in $C_i^{\lhd}$ can be determined by a membership query, but since $C_i^{\lhd}$ is in general infinite, the validity of a production cannot be determined in finite time. At each stage, the algorithm uses only those productions that are *valid on* the set E of all substrings of the positive examples, in the sense that

$$C_0^{\lhd} \supseteq w_0(E \cap C_1^{\lhd})w_1 \dots (E \cap C_n^{\lhd})w_n.$$

Testing this condition for all candidate productions can be done with a polynomial number of membership queries if there is a fixed bound on n and the cardinality of each C_i. Since E continues to grow, if the output of the algorithm stabilizes on a particular grammar, all its productions will be valid.

The primal algorithm in contrast constructs productions of the form $K_0 \to w_0 K_1 w_1 \dots K_n w_n$ where each K_i is a finite set of strings w drawn from the input positive data D (i.e., $uwv \in D$ for some u, v). Such a production is *valid* if $K_0^{\rhd\lhd} \supseteq w_0 K_1^{\rhd\lhd} w_1 \dots K_n^{\rhd\lhd} w_n$. It is not difficult to see that this condition is equivalent to

$$K_0^{\rhd} \subseteq (w_0 K_1 w_1 \dots K_n w_n)^{\rhd}.$$

In hypothesizing a production, the primal algorithm checks that it is *valid on* the set J of all contexts contained in the input positive data, in the following sense:

$$J \cap K_0^{\rhd} \subseteq (w_0 K_1 w_1 \dots K_n w_n)^{\rhd}.$$

Again, this ensures the validity of all productions in the limit.

Algorithm 1. Dual learner for CFGs.

Parameters: Positive integers r, k;
Data: A positive presentation $t_1, t_2, \dots$ of $L_* \subseteq \Sigma^*$; membership oracle for L_*;
Result: A sequence of grammars $G_1, G_2, \dots$;

let $D_0 := \varnothing$; $E_0 := \varnothing$; $J_0 := \varnothing$; $H_0 := \varnothing$; $G_0 := (\varnothing, \Sigma, \varnothing, \varnothing)$;
for $i = 1, 2, \dots$ **do**
  let $D_i := D_{i-1} \cup \{t_i\}$; $E_i := \mathrm{Sub}(D_i)$;
  if $D_i \nsubseteq L(G_{i-1})$ **then**
    let $J_i := \mathrm{Con}(D_i)$; $H_i := \mathrm{Sub}^{\leq r+1}(D_i)$;
  else
    let $J_i := J_{i-1}$; $H_i := H_{i-1}$;
  output $G_i := (N_i, \Sigma, P_i, I_i)$ where
    $N_i = \{C \subseteq J_i \mid 1 \leq |C| \leq k\}$,
    $P_i = \{C_0 \to w_0 C_1 w_1 \dots C_n w_n \mid (w_0, w_1, \dots, w_n) \in H_i,$
      $C_0, C_1, \dots, C_n \in N_i, C_0 \to w_0 C_1 w_1 \dots C_n w_n$ is valid on $E_i\}$,
    $I_i = \{C \in N_i \mid E_i \cap C^{\langle L_* |} \subseteq L_*\}$;

Exact formulations of the two algorithms are given in Algorithms 1 and 2.[2] In the algorithms, $\mathrm{Sub}(D) = \{w \in \Sigma^* \mid uwv \in D \text{ for some } u, v\}$, $\mathrm{Sub}^n(D) =$

[2] The present formulations follow [4].

$\{(w_1, \ldots, w_n) \in (\Sigma^*)^n \mid u_0 w_1 u_1 \ldots w_n u_n \in D$ for some $u_0, \ldots, u_n\}$, $\mathrm{Sub}^{\leq m}(D) = \bigcup_{1 \leq n \leq m} \mathrm{Sub}^n(D)$, and $\mathrm{Con}(D) = \{(u, v) \in \Sigma^* \times \Sigma^* \mid uwv \in D$ for some $w\}$.

Algorithm 2. Primal learner for CFGs.

Parameters: Positive integers r, k;
Data: A positive presentation $t_1, t_2, \ldots$ of $L_* \subseteq \Sigma^*$; membership oracle for L_*;
Result: A sequence of grammars $G_1, G_2, \ldots$;

let $D_0 := \varnothing; E_0 := \varnothing; J_0 := \varnothing; H_0 := \varnothing; G_0 := (\varnothing, \Sigma, \varnothing, \varnothing)$;
for $i = 1, 2, \ldots$ **do**
  let $D_i := D_{i-1} \cup \{t_i\}$; $J_i := \mathrm{Con}(D_i)$;
  if $D_i \nsubseteq L(G_{i-1})$ **then**
    let $E_i := \mathrm{Sub}(D_i)$; $H_i := \mathrm{Sub}^{\leq r+1}(D_i)$;
  else
    let $E_i := E_{i-1}$; $H_i := H_{i-1}$;
  output $G_i := (N_i, \Sigma, P_i, I_i)$ where
   $N_i = \{K \subseteq E_i \mid 1 \leq |K| \leq k\}$,
   $P_i = \{K_0 \to w_0 K_1 w_1 \ldots K_n w_n \mid (w_0, w_1, \ldots, w_n) \in H_i,$
     $K_0, K_1, \ldots, K_n \in N_i, K_0 \to w_0 K_1 w_1 \ldots K_n w_n$ is valid on $J_i\}$,
   $I_i = \{K \in N_i \mid K \subseteq L_*\}$;

We say that the dual or primal learner *converges to G on L_** if, given a positive presentation (i.e., enumeration) of L_* and the membership oracle for L_*, the output of the learner eventually stabilizes on G.

Theorem 3. *Suppose that the dual learner converges to a grammar G on L_*. Then $L(G) = L_*$ and G has the very weak k-FCP.*

Proof. Let $G = (N, \Sigma, P, I)$. It is easy to see that $D_i \subseteq L(G_i)$ holds at each stage, so $L_* \subseteq L(G)$. Since every element of $\mathrm{Sub}(L_*)$ eventually appears in E_i, each production of G must be valid. Hence the sequence $(C^{\langle L_* |})_{C \in N}$ is a pre-fixed point of G. By the same token, we must have $C^{\langle L_* |} \subseteq L_*$ for all $C \in I$. So $\bigcup_{C \in I} C^{\langle L_* |} \subseteq L_* \subseteq L(G)$. Since $(L(G, C))_{C \in N}$ is the least pre-fixed point of G, $L(G) = \bigcup_{C \in I} L(G, C) \subseteq \bigcup_{C \in I} C^{\langle L_* |}$. Hence $L(G) = L_*$ and $(C^{\langle L(G) |})_{C \in N}$ is an SPP of G, which means that G has the very weak k-FCP. □

Similarly, we have

Theorem 4. *Suppose that the primal learner converges to a grammar G on L_*. Then $L(G) = L_*$ and G has the very weak k-FKP.*

The following theorems are clear from the existing proof of correctness of the dual and primal learners (see, e.g., [4]).

Theorem 5. *Let G be a CFG each of whose productions has at most r nonterminals on the right-hand side. If G has the very weak k-FCP, then the dual learner converges to a grammar for $L(G)$ on $L(G)$.*

Theorem 6. *Let G be a CFG each of whose productions has at most r nonterminals on the right-hand side. If G has the very weak k-FKP, then the primal learner converges to a grammar for $L(G)$ on $L(G)$.*

5 The Strong vs. Weak Finite Context and Kernel Properties

We write x^R for the reversal of a string x, and $|x|_a$ for the number of occurrences of a symbol a in x. Let

$$\begin{aligned}
\Sigma &= \{a, b, c, d, e, \#, \$\},\\
L &= L_1 \cup L_2 \cup L_3,\\
L_1 &= \{w_1\#w_2\#\ldots\#w_n\$w_n^R\ldots w_2^R w_1^R \mid n \geq 1, w_1, \ldots, w_n \in \{a,b\}^*\},\\
L_2 &= \{wyc^i d^i e^j z \mid w, z \in \{a,b\}^*, y \in (\#\{a,b\}^*)^*, i, j \geq 0, |w|_a \geq |w|_b\},\\
L_3 &= \{wyc^i d^j e^j z \mid w, z \in \{a,b\}^*, y \in (\#\{a,b\}^*)^*, i, j \geq 0, |w|_a \leq |w|_b\}.
\end{aligned}$$

Lemma 7. *Every CFG G for L has a nonterminal E such that $L(G, E)$ is not a closed set relative to L.*

Proof. Let G be a CFG for L. By applying Ogden's [7] lemma[3] to a derivation tree of a sufficiently long string in L_1 of the form $a^p b^p \# a^p \$ a^p b^p a^p$, we obtain

$$\begin{aligned}
&S_1 \Rightarrow_G^+ a^{m_1} A a^{l_1}, &&A \Rightarrow_G^+ a^{n_1} A a^{n_1}, &&A \Rightarrow_G^+ a^{m_2} b^{m_3} B b^{l_3} a^{l_2},\\
&B \Rightarrow_G^+ b^{n_2} B b^{n_2}, &&B \Rightarrow_G^+ b^{m_4} \# a^{m_5} D a^{l_5} b^{l_4}, &&D \Rightarrow_G^+ a^{m_6} \$ a^{l_6},
\end{aligned}$$

for some $n_1, n_2, m_1, m_2, m_3, m_4, m_5, m_6 \geq 1, l_1, l_2, l_3, l_4, l_5, l_6 \geq 0$ such that $m_1 + n_1 + m_2 = m_3 + n_2 + m_4 = m_5 + m_6 = l_1 + n_1 + l_2 = l_3 + n_2 + l_4 = l_5 + l_6 = p$, where S_1 is an initial nonterminal. We show that $L(G, D)$ is not a closed set.

Let $(u, v) \in L(G, D)^{\triangleright}$. Then $ua^{m_6}\$a^{l_6}v \in L$. Since $y\$z \in L$ implies $yc^i d^i e^i z \in L$ for every $y, z \in \Sigma^*$ and $i \geq 0$, we have $ua^{m_6} c^i d^i e^i a^{l_6} v \in L$ for every $i \geq 0$. This shows

$$\{a^{m_6} c^i d^i e^i a^{l_6} \mid i \geq 0\} \subseteq L(G, D)^{\triangleright\triangleleft}. \tag{2}$$

On the other hand, since

$$S_1 \Rightarrow_G^* a^{m_1} (a^{n_1})^i a^{m_2} b^{m_3} (b^{n_2})^j b^{m_4} \# a^{m_5} D a^{l_5} b^{l_4} (b^{n_2})^j b^{l_3} a^{l_2} (a^{n_1})^i a^{l_1}$$

for all $i, j \geq 0$, there are $w, w', z, z' \in \{a,b\}^*$ such that $|w|_a > |w|_b, |w'|_a < |w'|_b$. and

$$S_1 \Rightarrow_G^* w\#a^{m_5} Dz, \quad S_1 \Rightarrow_G^* w'\#a^{m_5} Dz', \tag{3}$$

[3] It is clear from Ogden's proof that the lemma is really about one particular derivation tree of a context-free grammar. If p is the constant of Ogden's lemma for G, we obtain the required decomposition of the derivation tree by first marking the initial a^p, then the b^p preceding $\#$, and then the a^p immediately following $\#$.

Now suppose $a^{m_6}c^id^je^ka^{l_6} \in L(G,D)^{\rhd\lhd}$. Since (3) implies $(w\#a^{m_5}, z) \in L(G,D)^{\rhd}$ and $(w'\#a^{m_5}, z') \in L(G,D)^{\rhd}$, we must have $w\#a^{m_5}a^{m_6}c^id^je^ka^{l_6}z \in L_2$ and $w'\#a^{m_5}a^{m_6}c^id^je^ka^{l_6}z \in L_3$. It follows that

$$a^{m_6}c^id^je^ka^{l_6} \in L(G,D)^{\rhd\lhd} \text{ only if } i = j = k. \tag{4}$$

By (2) and (4), $L(G,D)^{\rhd\lhd} \cap a^{m_6}c^*d^*e^*a^{l_6} = \{a^{m_6}c^id^ie^ia^{l_6} \mid i \geq 0\}$, which implies that $L(G,D)^{\rhd\lhd}$ is not context-free. Therefore, $L(G,D) \neq L(G,D)^{\rhd\lhd}$ and $L(G,D)$ is not a closed set. □

The above lemma implies that L has no CFG that has either the strong FCP or the strong FKP.

Lemma 8. *There is a CFG for L that has both the weak 2-FCP and the weak 2-FKP.*

Proof. Let G be the following CFG, where S_1, S_2, S_3 are the initial nonterminals.

$$\begin{array}{ll}
S_1 \to \$ \mid aS_1a \mid bS_1b \mid \#S_1, & C \to \varepsilon \mid cC, \\
Q \to \varepsilon \mid aQbQ \mid bQaQ, & J \to \varepsilon \mid dJe, \\
F \to Q\# \mid Fa \mid Fb \mid F\#, & S_2 \to HE \mid FS_2 \mid QS_2 \mid aS_2 \mid S_2a \mid S_2b, \\
H \to \varepsilon \mid cHd, & S_3 \to CJ \mid FS_3 \mid QS_3 \mid bS_3 \mid S_3a \mid S_3b. \\
E \to \varepsilon \mid Ee, &
\end{array}$$

We have

$$\begin{aligned}
L(G,S_1) &= L_1, \\
L(G,S_1)^{\rhd} &= \{(w_1\#w_2\#\ldots\#w_n, w_n^R\ldots w_2^Rw_1^R) \mid n \geq 1, w_1,\ldots,w_n \in \{a,b\}^*\}, \\
L(G,S_1)^{\rhd\lhd} &= L_1 \cup \{yc^id^ie^iz \mid y \in \{a,b,\#\}^*, z \in \{a,b\}^*, i \geq 0\} \\
&= \{(a\#,a),(b\#,b)\}^{\lhd} = \{\$\}^{\rhd\lhd}, \\
L(G,Q) &= \{w \in \{a,b\}^* \mid |w|_a = |w|_b\} = \{(\varepsilon,\#cd),(a,b\#de)\}^{\lhd} = \{\varepsilon, ab\}^{\rhd\lhd}, \\
L(G,F) &= \{w\#y \mid w \in \{a,b\}^*, |w|_a = |w|_b, y \in \{a,b,\#\}^*\} \\
&= \{(\varepsilon,cd),(\varepsilon,ade)\}^{\lhd} = \{\#, ab\#\}^{\rhd\lhd}, \\
L(G,H) &= \{c^id^i \mid i \geq 0\} = \{(a\#c,d)\}^{\lhd} = \{\varepsilon, cd\}^{\rhd\lhd}, \\
L(G,E) &= e^* = \{(a\#cd,e)\}^{\lhd} = \{\varepsilon, e\}^{\rhd\lhd}, \\
L(G,C) &= c^* = \{(b\#c,de)\}^{\lhd} = \{\varepsilon, c\}^{\rhd\lhd}, \\
L(G,J) &= \{d^ie^i \mid i \geq 0\} = \{(b\#d,e)\}^{\lhd} = \{\varepsilon, de\}^{\rhd\lhd}, \\
L(G,S_2) &= L_2, \\
L(G,S_2)^{\rhd} &= \{(wy,z) \mid w,z \in \{a,b\}^*, y \in (\#\{a,b\}^*)^*, |w|_a \geq |w|_b\}, \\
L(G,S_2)^{\rhd\lhd} &= L_2 \cup \{vc^id^ie^iz \mid v \in \{a,b,\#\}^*, z \in \{a,b\}^*, i \geq 0\} \\
&= \{(\varepsilon,\varepsilon),(a\#,b)\}^{\lhd} = \{cda\}^{\rhd\lhd}, \\
L(G,S_3) &= L_3,
\end{aligned}$$

$$\begin{aligned}L(G,S_3)^{\triangleright} &= \{(wy,z) \mid w,z \in \{a,b\}^*, y \in (\#\{a,b\}^*)^*, |w|_a \le |w|_b\},\\ L(G,S_3)^{\triangleright\triangleleft} &= L_3 \cup \{vc^id^ie^iz \mid v \in \{a,b,\#\}^*, z \in \{a,b\}^*, i \ge 0\}\\ &= \{(\varepsilon,\varepsilon),(b\#,a)\}^{\triangleleft} = \{\#de\}^{\triangleright\triangleleft}.\end{aligned}$$

This shows that G has both the weak 2-FCP and the weak 2-FKP. □

Theorem 9. *There is a language that has a CFG with both the weak 2-FCP and the weak 2-FKP but has no CFG with either the strong FCP or the strong FKP.*

6 The Weak vs. Very Weak Finite Context and Kernel Properties

Proposition 10. *If a language L has a CFG with the very weak k-FKP, then L has a CFG with the weak k-FKP.*

Proof. Let $G = (N, \Sigma, P, I)$ be a CFG and let $L = L(G)$. Suppose that $K_A \subseteq \Sigma^*$ is a finite set for each $A \in N$ such that $|K_A| \le k$ and $(K_A^{|L\rangle\langle L|})_{A\in N}$ is an SPP for G. Let $G' = (N, \Sigma, P', I)$, where $P' = P \cup \{A \to w \mid A \in N, w \in K_A\}$. Then $(L(G', A))_{A\in N}$ is the least pre-fixed point $(X_A)_{A\in N}$ of G such that $K_A \subseteq X_A$. Since $K_A \subseteq K_A^{|L\rangle\langle L|}$, this implies $L(G', A) \subseteq K_A^{|L\rangle\langle L|}$ for each $A \in N$. As a consequence, $L(G') \subseteq \bigcup_{A\in I} K_A^{|L\rangle\langle L|} = L$. Clearly, $L = L(G) \subseteq L(G')$, so $L(G') = L$. Since $K_A \subseteq L(G', A)$, we get $K_A^{|L\rangle\langle L|} \subseteq L(G', A)^{|L\rangle\langle L|}$ and hence $K_A^{|L\rangle\langle L|} = L(G', A)^{|L\rangle\langle L|}$. This shows that G' has the weak k-FKP. □

The proof of Proposition 10 shows that Theorem 4 can be strengthened to

Corollary 11. *If the primal learner converges to a grammar G on L_*, then $L(G) = L_*$ and G has the weak FKP.*

Let

$$\begin{aligned}\Sigma' &= \{a,b,c,d,e,f,\#,\$,\%\},\\ L' &= L_1 \cup L_2 \cup L_3 \cup L_4 \cup L_5,\\ L_4 &= \{v\$zc^k\%f^l \mid v \in \{a,b,\#\}^*, z \in \{a,b\}^*, k,l \ge 0\},\\ L_5 &= \{vc^id^ie^jzc^k\%f^l \mid v \in \{a,b,\#\}^*, z \in \{a,b\}^*, i,j,k,l \ge 0, j \ne k\},\end{aligned}$$

where L_1, L_2, L_3 are as defined in Sect. 5.

Lemma 12. *There is a CFG for L' that has the very weak 2-FCP.*

Proof. Let G' be the extension of the grammar G in the proof of Lemma 8 with the following additional productions:

$$\begin{aligned}&T \to \varepsilon \mid Ta \mid Tb, && S_{4,5} \to \$TC\% \mid HU\% \mid aS_{4,5} \mid bS_{4,5} \mid \#S_{4,5} \mid S_{4,5}f.\\ &U \to EeT \mid TcC \mid eUc,\end{aligned}$$

The nonterminals $T, U, S_{4,5}$ are new and $S_{4,5}$ is an initial nonterminal. All the old nonterminals except S_1 continue to be (weakly) characterized by the same sets of contexts as before, but we now have

$$\begin{aligned} L(G', S_1)^{\triangleright} &= \{(w_1\#w_2\#\dots\#w_n, w_n^R \dots w_2^R w_1^R) \mid n \geq 1, w_1, \dots, w_n \in \{a,b\}^*\} \\ &\quad \cup \{(v, zc^k\%f^l) \mid v \in \{a,b,\#\}^*, z \in \{a,b\}^*, k, l \geq 0\}, \\ L(G', S_1)^{\triangleright\triangleleft} &= L(G', S_1) = L_1, \end{aligned}$$

where of course $\triangleright, \triangleleft$ are now relative to L'. For the new nonterminals, we have

$$\begin{aligned} L(G', T) &= \{a,b\}^* = \{(\$, a\%)\}^{\triangleleft}, \\ L(G', U) &= \{e^j z c^k \mid z \in \{a,b\}^*, j, k \geq 0, j \neq k\} = \{(e, c\%)\}^{\triangleleft}, \\ L(G', S_{4,5}) &= L_4 \cup L_5 = \{(\varepsilon, f)\}^{\triangleleft}. \end{aligned}$$

Now if we let

$$\begin{aligned} X_{S_1} &= C(G', S_1)^{\triangleleft} \\ &= \{(w_1\#w_2\#\dots\#w_n, w_n^R \dots w_2^R w_1^R) \mid n \geq 1, w_1, w_2, \dots, w_n \in \{a,b\}^*\}^{\triangleleft} \\ &= L_1 \cup \{vc^i d^i e^i z \mid v \in \{a,b,\#\}^*, z \in \{a,b\}^*, i \geq 0\}, \end{aligned}$$

then we have $X_{S_1} \supseteq \{\$\} \cup aX_{S_1}a \cup bX_{S_1}b \cup \#X_{S_1}$, so X_{S_1} together with (the closures of) the languages of the other nonterminals constitute an SPP for G'. Since $X_{S_1} = \{(a\#, a), (b\#, b)\}^{\triangleleft}$, this shows that G' has the very weak 2-FCP. □

Lemma 13. *There is no CFG for L' that has the weak FCP.*

Proof. Let G be any CFG for L'. As in the proof of Lemma 7, we obtain

$$\begin{aligned} S &\Rightarrow_G^* a^{m_1}(a^{n_1})^i a^{m_2} b^{m_3} (b^{n_2})^j b^{m_4} \# a^{m_5} D a^{l_5} b^{l_4} (b^{n_2})^j b^{l_3} a^{l_2} (a^{n_1})^i a^{l_1}, \\ D &\Rightarrow_G^+ a^{m_6} \$ a^{l_6}, \end{aligned}$$

for every i and j, where S is an initial nonterminal, D is a nonterminal, and $n_1, n_2 \geq 1$. It is easy to see that

$$\begin{aligned} L(G, D) &\subseteq \{a,b,\#\}^*(\{\$\} \cup \{c^i d^i e^i \mid i \geq 0\})\{a,b\}^*, \\ L(G, D)^{\triangleright} &\subseteq \{a^{m_6}\$a^{l_6}\}^{\triangleright} \\ &\subseteq \{a,b,\#\}^* \times \{a,b\}^*(\{\varepsilon\} \cup c^*\%f^*). \end{aligned}$$

Since $L(G, D)$ is context-free, there must be a k_1 such that

$$L(G, D) \cap \{a,b,\#\}^* c^i d^i e^i \{a,b\}^* = \varnothing \text{ for all } i > k_1.$$

It follows that $\{(\varepsilon, c^i\%) \mid i > k_1\} \subseteq L(G, D)^{\triangleright}$ and so

$$L(G, D)^{\triangleright\triangleleft} \cap \{a,b,\#\}^* c^i d^i e^i \{a,b\}^* = \varnothing \text{ for all } i > k_1.$$

However, for any finite set $W \subseteq L(G, D)^{\triangleright}$, there is a k_2 such that $W \cap (\{a,b,\#\}^* \times \{a,b\}^* c^i \% f^*) = \varnothing$ for all $i > k_2$, which implies $\{c^i d^i e^i \mid i > k_2\} \subseteq W^{\triangleleft}$. It follows that $L(G, D)^{\triangleright\triangleleft} \neq W^{\triangleleft}$ for any finite W. □

Theorem 14. *There is a language that has a CFG with the very weak 2-FCP but has no CFG with the weak FCP.*

7 Conclusion

The basic idea of distributional learning has been to let a finite set of contexts/strings determine (the distributions of) the strings derived from each nonterminal. We have shown that while this is indeed a necessary condition for the primal learner, the dual learner may succeed in the absence of such a characterizing finite set of contexts.

References

1. Aho, A.V., Ullman, J.D.: The Theory of Parsing, Translation, and Compiling, vol. I. Prentice-Hall, Englewood Cliffs (1972)
2. Clark, A.: Learning context free grammars with the syntactic concept lattice. In: Sempere, J.M., García, P. (eds.) ICGI 2010. LNCS (LNAI), vol. 6339, pp. 38–51. Springer, Heidelberg (2010). doi:10.1007/978-3-642-15488-1_5
3. Clark, A.: The syntactic concept lattice: another algebraic theory of the context-free languages? J. Log. Comput. **25**(5), 1203–1229 (2015). First published online: July 30, 2013
4. Clark, A., Kanazawa, M., Kobele, G.M., Yoshinaka, R.: Distributional learning of some nonlinear tree grammars. Fundamenta Informaticae **146**(4), 339–377 (2016)
5. Clark, A., Yoshinaka, R.: Distributional learning of context-free and multiple context-free grammars. In: Heinz, J., Sempere, J.M. (eds.) Topics in Grammatical Inference, pp. 143–172. Springer, Berlin (2016)
6. Leiß, H.: Learning context free grammars with the finite context property: a correction of A. Clark's algorithm. In: Morrill, G., Muskens, R., Osswald, R., Richter, F. (eds.) Formal Grammar 2014. LNCS, vol. 8612, pp. 121–137. Springer, Heidelberg (2014). doi:10.1007/978-3-662-44121-3_8
7. Ogden, W.: A helpful result for proving inherent ambiguity. Math. Syst. Theory **2**(3), 191–194 (1968)
8. Yoshinaka, R.: Towards dual approaches for learning context-free grammars based on syntactic concept lattices. In: Mauri, G., Leporati, A. (eds.) DLT 2011. LNCS, vol. 6795, pp. 429–440. Springer, Heidelberg (2011). doi:10.1007/978-3-642-22321-1_37
9. Yoshinaka, R.: General perspectives on distributionally learnable classes. In: Kuhlmann, M., Kanazawa, M., Kobele, G.M. (eds.) Proceedings of the 14th Meeting on the Mathematics of Language, pp. 87–98. Association for Computational Linguistics, Stroudsburg (2015)
10. Yoshinaka, R.: Learning conjunctive grammars and contextual binary feature grammars. In: Dediu, A.-H., Formenti, E., Martín-Vide, C., Truthe, B. (eds.) LATA 2015. LNCS, vol. 8977, pp. 623–635. Springer, Heidelberg (2015). doi:10.1007/978-3-319-15579-1_49
11. Yoshinaka, R., Kanazawa, M.: Distributional learning of abstract categorial grammars. In: Pogodalla, S., Prost, J.-P. (eds.) LACL 2011. LNCS (LNAI), vol. 6736, pp. 251–266. Springer, Heidelberg (2011). doi:10.1007/978-3-642-22221-4_17

Automata and Logics

$\mathbb{N}$-Memory Automata over the Alphabet $\mathbb{N}$

Benedikt Brütsch, Patrick Landwehr(✉), and Wolfgang Thomas

Chair of Computer Science 7, RWTH Aachen University,
Ahornstr. 55, 52074 Aachen, Germany
{bruetsch,landwehr,thomas}@cs.rwth-aachen.de

Abstract. The concept of $\mathbb{N}$-memory automaton over the alphabet $\mathbb{N}$ is studied. We show a result on robustness of this model (by a connection to MSO-logic), give a discussion on its expressive power and closure properties, and show among other decidability results the solvability of the non-emptiness problem. We conclude with perspectives for applications and some open questions.

Keywords: Automata and logic · Infinite alphabet

1 Introduction

Much of the theory of automata and formal languages is based on the assumption that words and languages are formed over a given finite alphabet – indeed, the notion "alphabet" is usually considered as pointing to a finite set of symbols.

Automata over infinite alphabets were first proposed in the 1990s, notably the finite memory automata of Kaminski and Francez [9]. A more recent interest is triggered by two areas of applications, namely database theory where it is reasonable to work over infinite data spaces, and the verification of hybrid systems where infinite value domains enter. In this context several automata models were proposed, such as the data automata of Bojańczyk et al. [2], the G-automata of Bojańczyk et al. [3] and the ordered data automata of Tan [12,13]; see also the survey [10]. An important criterion for an automaton model over infinite alphabets to be useful is, besides a finite presentation, the solvability of the non-emptiness problem.

A weakness of the automata mentioned above is the fact that they can compare letters in a given word only in restricted ways, either just by equality or inequality, or (as in [12]) also by special conditions regarding their order. For example, over the alphabet $\mathbb{N}$ the "increasing words" of the form $12\dots k$ are not recognizable in the frameworks of [2,9,12]. In order to be able to test such conditions on increase and decrease of values in a word, the model of "progressive grid automaton" (PGA) was introduced in [7], still keeping decidability of the non-emptiness problem.

Let us recall the PGA model, which is later extended in the present paper to what we call "$\mathbb{N}$-memory automata". Here we always use $\mathbb{N}$ as the typical infinite alphabet. A word $n_1 \dots n_k \in \mathbb{N}^*$ is coded by a grid structure where each of the k

F. Drewes et al. (Eds.): LATA 2017, LNCS 10168, pp. 91–102, 2017.
DOI: 10.1007/978-3-319-53733-7_6

columns represents a number. The number n is coded by a column carrying base symbol #, n symbols 1, and then an infinite sequence of symbols $\perp$. Figure 1 shows the grid coding the word 4 2 0 4 3.

A PGA scans such a word by traversing the corresponding grid in three-way mode: Starting at the bottom, it analyzes the first column by moving up and down, then at some position on this column moves to the right, starting there the analysis of the second column, again in two-way mode, before jumping to the next column, etc. The input is accepted if a final state is reached when the last column has been left by a jump to the right. It is easy to see that an automaton of this kind can check, for example, whether the letters of the input word form a weakly increasing sequence, or whether the first and the last letter coincide. The test whether there are two positions with the same letter (= number) requires a nondeterministic PGA (to guess the first of the two positions).

If a PGA leaves a column at a certain height and enters there the next column, it implicitly uses the set $\mathbb{N}$ as a memory structure (or $Q \times \mathbb{N}$, when we also incorporate the finite state space Q of the automaton): entering a column coding number n in state p at height i and leaving it in state q at height j means to update the memory $Q \times \mathbb{N}$ from (p, i) to (q, j) upon reading the input n. This connection between (p, i), n, and (q, j) is more easily and without involvement of technicalities expressible in the structure $\mathcal{N}$ of the natural numbers with successor, using monadic second-order logic (MSO-logic). We just can write down a formula $\varphi_{p,q}(x, y, z)$ that is true in the structure $\mathcal{N} = (\mathbb{N}, \mathrm{Succ})$ for numbers i, n, j iff the above change of state from (p, i) via n to (q, j) is possible. One can associate with any PGA a finite set of MSO-formulas (namely for all combinations (p, q) of control states) that describe the transition relation of the PGA over columns. However, the converse fails, as explained in Sect. 3; hence, in the model of PGAs, the steps from one column to the next are not "expressively complete" with respect to MSO-logic.

⋮	⋮	⋮	⋮	⋮
$\perp$	$\perp$	$\perp$	$\perp$	$\perp$
1	$\perp$	$\perp$	1	$\perp$
1	$\perp$	$\perp$	1	1
1	1	$\perp$	1	1
1	1	$\perp$	1	1
#	#	#	#	#

Fig. 1. Grid representation of the word 4 2 0 4 3

In the present paper we extend PGAs in order to capture precisely MSO-logic for the transition between columns, while keeping all the desired properties offered by PGAs. We call this model $\mathbb{N}$-memory automaton. Rather than using the height at which a column is entered as memory, $\mathbb{N}$-memory automata involve tokens that are placed on a given column. A column coding the number n is scanned from the bottom, and the initial memory content i is captured by a "memory marker" on position i. The automaton also has a "memory update token" at its disposal, and the position j where this token resides at the end of the processing of this column (possibly after having been repositioned multiple times) gives the new memory content. $\mathbb{N}$-memory automata are a proper extension of PGAs; for example the set of words $i0i$ (shown not to be PGA-recognizable in [7]) is easily recognizable by an $\mathbb{N}$-memory automaton.

After presenting the formal definitions in the subsequent section, we discuss the expressive power of ℕ-memory automata. Then we show (as a first main result) the expressive equivalence with MSO-logic (regarding the transition relation). This establishes a bridge to logic that facilitates later arguments, and it documents some robustness of the concept of ℕ-memory automaton. We then establish the (rather weak) closure properties both in the deterministic and nondeterministic version, and show results on decidability and undecidability. Finally we briefly treat ω-languages over the alphabet ℕ and related applications.

Some results of the present paper have been stated without proof in [4] where an application to infinite games is treated.

2 Definitions

2.1 ℕ-Memory Automata

We introduce ℕ-memory automata in a top-down fashion, using two steps. The global structure is described first, the local one (dealing with individual transitions) in a second step.

Definition 1. *An* ℕ-memory automaton $\mathcal{A}$ *is a tuple* (Q, Δ, q_0, F) *where* Q *is a finite set of states,* $\Delta \subseteq ((Q \times \mathbb{N}) \times \mathbb{N} \times (Q \times \mathbb{N}))$ *is a transition relation defined by a transition automaton (as explained below),* $q_0 \in Q$ *is the initial state, and* $F \subseteq Q$ *is the set of final states.*

The automaton $\mathcal{A}$ is called deterministic if for all $(q_1, h_1) \in Q \times \mathbb{N}$ and all $n \in \mathbb{N}$ there exists at most one $(q_2, h_2) \in Q \times \mathbb{N}$ with $((q_1, h_1), n, (q_2, h_2)) \in \Delta$.

An *accepting run* of an ℕ-memory automaton $\mathcal{A}$ on a word $w_1 \dots w_k \in \mathbb{N}^*$ is a sequence $\rho = (p_0, h_0), \dots, (p_k, h_k) \in (Q \times \mathbb{N})^*$ with $p_0 = q_0$, $h_0 = 0$, $p_k \in F$, and $((p_i, h_i), w_{i+1}, (p_{i+1}, h_{i+1})) \in \Delta$ for all $0 \leq i < k$.

The automaton $\mathcal{A}$ accepts a word w if there exists an accepting run of $\mathcal{A}$ on w. The language recognized by $\mathcal{A}$ is $L(\mathcal{A}) := \{w \in \mathbb{N}^* \mid \mathcal{A} \text{ accepts } w\}$. A language $L \subseteq \mathbb{N}^*$ is (deterministically) ℕ-memory recognizable, if there exists a (deterministic) ℕ-memory automaton $\mathcal{A}$ with $L = L(\mathcal{A})$.

Definition 2. *A* transition automaton $\mathcal{A}_\Delta$ *is a tuple* (S, Q, R, s_0, s_H) *where* S *is a finite set of states,* Q *is a finite set of labels,* $s_0 \in S$ *is the initial state,* s_H *is the halting state, and* $R \subseteq S \times (Q^? \times \{\#, 1, \bot\} \times Q^?) \times S \times (\{\uparrow, \downarrow\} \cup Q)$ *is the transition relation. (Here* $Q^?$ *is the set* $Q \cup \{\diamond\}$ *with* $\diamond$ *indicating the absence of a label from* Q*.)*

A transition automaton $\mathcal{A}_\Delta$ is called deterministic if for all $s \in S$ and all $x \in (Q^? \times \{\#, 1, \bot\} \times Q^?)$ there exists at most one $(s, x, s', d) \in R$.

The automaton $\mathcal{A}_\Delta$ works on a single column of a grid (see Fig. 1). A triple $x \in (Q^? \times \{\#, 1, \bot\} \times Q^?)$ refers to the (absence of the) memory marker, the current column letter, and the (absence of the) memory update token. In each step, $\mathcal{A}_\Delta$ can move upwards or downwards or reposition the memory update token to the current height (and possibly change its label). Formally, the memory update token is a pair $m_u = (q_u, h_u) \in Q \times \mathbb{N}$, where q_u is the label and h_u is the height of the token. A *configuration* of $\mathcal{A}_\Delta$ is a tuple $(s, h, m_u) \in S \times \mathbb{N} \times (Q \times \mathbb{N})$, indicating the current state s, the current height h, and the current memory update token m_u. Altogether, $\mathcal{A}_\Delta$ is said to produce the memory update token $(q_u, h_u) \in Q \times \mathbb{N}$ on a column labeled $n \in \mathbb{N}$ from the memory marker $(q_{in}, h_{in}) \in Q \times \mathbb{N}$ if there exists a sequence $\rho = c_0, \ldots, c_k$ of configurations such that

- $c_0 = \big(s_0, 0, (q_{in}, 0)\big)$,
- for all $0 \leq i < k$ if $c_i = (s_i, h_i, m_u^i)$ and $c_{i+1} = (s_{i+1}, h_{i+1}, m_u^{i+1})$ then $\big(s_i, (q_{in}[h_i = h_{in}], \gamma(n, h_i), q_u^i[h_i = h_u^i]), s_{i+1}, d\big) \in R$, where:[1]
  - $d = \uparrow$, $h_{i+1} = h_i + 1$ and $m_u^{i+1} = m_u^i = (q_u^i, h_u^i)$,
  - or $d = \downarrow$, $h_{i+1} = h_i - 1$ and $m_u^{i+1} = m_u^i = (q_u^i, h_u^i)$,
  - or $d = q$, $h_{i+1} = h_i$, $m_u^i = (q_u^i, h_u^i)$ and $m_u^{i+1} = (q, h_i)$.
- $c_k = \big(s_H, h, (q_u, h_u)\big)$ for an arbitrary $h \in \mathbb{N}$.

This sequence ρ is called a run of $\mathcal{A}_\Delta$.

The transition automaton $\mathcal{A}_\Delta$ defines the set of triples $((q_1, h_1), n, (q_2, h_2))$ such that $\mathcal{A}_\Delta$ produces (q_2, h_2) on a column labeled n from (q_1, h_1), so it can be used to represent the transition relation of an $\mathbb{N}$-memory automaton. Note that if an $\mathbb{N}$-memory automaton is deterministic then the associated $\mathcal{A}_\Delta$ is *functional* (i.e., giving a unique result) but need not be deterministic. If we want to emphasize that $\mathcal{A}_\Delta$ is deterministic we call $\mathcal{A}$ *strongly deterministic*.

2.2 MSO-$\mathbb{N}$-Memory Automata

In order to reduce the technicalities of the previous definition, we introduce MSO-$\mathbb{N}$-memory automata, where the description of the transitions is done in a logical framework. We use here MSO-logic over the structure $\mathcal{N} = (\mathbb{N}, \mathrm{Succ})$ of the natural numbers with the successor relation. (For MSO-logic see e.g. [14].)

Definition 3. *An MSO-$\mathbb{N}$-memory automaton $\mathcal{A}$ is a tuple $\mathcal{A} = (Q, \Phi, q_0, F)$ where Q is a finite set of states, Φ is a family of MSO-formulas $\varphi_{p_1,p_2}(x, y, z)$, $q_0 \in Q$ is the initial state and $F \subseteq Q$ is a set of final states.*

The family of MSO-formulas Φ is called functional if for all $(q_1, h_1) \in Q \times \mathbb{N}$ and all $n \in \mathbb{N}$ there exists at most one $(q_2, h_2) \in Q \times \mathbb{N}$ with $\mathcal{N} \models \varphi_{q_1,q_2}[h_1, n, h_2]$. In this case we call $\mathcal{A}$ deterministic.

An *accepting run* of an MSO-$\mathbb{N}$-memory automaton $\mathcal{A}$ on the word $w_1 \ldots w_k \in \mathbb{N}^*$ is a sequence $\rho = (p_0, h_0), \ldots, (p_k, h_k) \in (Q \times \mathbb{N})^*$ with $p_0 = q_0$, $h_0 = 0$ and such that $\mathcal{N} \models \varphi_{p_i,p_{i+1}}[h_i, w_{i+1}, h_{i+1}]$ for all $0 \leq i < k$, and $p_k \in F$.

The automaton $\mathcal{A}$ accepts w if there exists an accepting run of $\mathcal{A}$ on w. The language recognized by $\mathcal{A}$ is $L(\mathcal{A}) := \{w \in \mathbb{N}^* \mid \mathcal{A} \text{ accepts } w\}$.

---

[1] We use the notation $q[condition]$ to indicate q if the condition is satisfied and $\diamond$ otherwise. We set $\gamma(n, h)$ to be $\#$ if $h = 0$, 1 if $0 < h \leq n$, and $\perp$ if $h > n$.

3 Remarks on Expressive Power

In this section we discuss the expressive power of ℕ-memory automata, giving examples and a comparison to related models.

As a first remark, we note that the restriction to finite alphabets (formally, the restriction of the input letters to a finite initial segment $[0, n]$ of the natural numbers) yields the well-known model of counter automata.

A simple language recognized by a deterministic ℕ-memory automaton is the set of words $\{1\ 2\ 3\ \ldots\ k \mid k \geq 1\}$. Similarly we can recognize the set of words having a subsequence of successive numbers leading from the first letter 1 to the last letter, i.e., of the form $1\mathbb{N}^*2\mathbb{N}^*3\mathbb{N}^* \ldots k$. Further examples are the set of words where successive numbers differ by 1 and the set of words where odd and even numbers alternate. Nondeterminism can be invoked (and is needed, as we shall see in Sect. 5) in order to check the existence of several occurrences of the same letter (= number).

It is instructive to compare ℕ-memory automata with closely related models considered in recent literature; we mention here the $\mathcal{N}$-MSO-automata (see [1,7]), the strong automata of [11], the progressive grid automata (PGA) of [7] and the ordered data automata of [12]. In the $\mathcal{N}$-MSO-automata we just have a finite state space and transitions from a state p to a state q as specified by an MSO-formula $\varphi_{p,q}(y)$; a transition from p via n to q is executable if the number n satisfies this formula in $\mathcal{N}$. This model allows information flow from letter to letter only via its states and thus cannot recognize a simple language such as $\{ii \mid i \geq 0\}$. In a strong automaton the transitions are specified in a more general way, by formulas $\varphi_{p,q}(x, y)$ that impose a condition on the input number n (as interpretation of y) in relation to the previous input number m (as interpretation of x). This amounts to using MSO-ℕ-memory automata in a special way, namely where the memory update token is always placed on the position of the current input letter m (to allow a comparison with the next input letter n). The first example language as mentioned above is clearly recognizable in this way, but the set of words of the form $k\mathbb{N}^+k$ is not. Comparing ℕ-memory automata with PGAs, it is obvious that each PGA can be simulated by an ℕ-memory automaton (use the position where a column is left as the position where the memory update token is placed). On the other hand, in PGAs the initial position from where a column is analyzed is available only at the start of a computation. Thus the ℕ-memory recognizable language of words $i0i$ is not PGA-recognizable (as shown formally in [7]): When the PGA starts on position i of the second column and moves to the bottom to check whether number 0 is the input, the initial position i is lost when moving to the third letter. The use of a memory marker repairs this defect. Finally, we note that ℕ-memory automata are incomparable in expressive power to the ordered data automata of [12]: The language of words $kmkm$ is recognized by the latter but not by the former, and the set of words $12 \ldots k$ provides the converse. Let us note that in the context of temporal logic, a formalism close to ℕ-memory automata appears in [6]; however there the comparison of values from ℕ is restricted to occurrences within a bounded time-interval – so a language as given by the expression $1\mathbb{N}^*2\mathbb{N}^*3\mathbb{N}^* \ldots k$ is not covered.

The use of tokens can be applied also in the definition of $\mathbb{N}$-memory transducers. Here an extra token is employed which is placed at the position that gives the respective output number (in the sense of a Mealy automaton). For definitions and an application we refer to [4].

4 An Equivalence Result and a Normal Form

We show that $\mathbb{N}$-memory automata and MSO-$\mathbb{N}$-memory automata have the same expressive power:

Theorem 4. *A language $L \subseteq \mathbb{N}^*$ is (strongly deterministically) $\mathbb{N}$-memory recognizable if and only if it is recognizable by a (deterministic) MSO-$\mathbb{N}$-memory automaton.*

First, using a standard approach as found, e.g., in [14], we show how to construct an MSO-formula from a given transition automaton.

Lemma 5. *Let $\mathcal{A}_\Delta$ be a (functional) transition automaton. There exists a (functional) family of MSO-formulas $(\varphi_{p_1,p_2}(x,y,z))_{p_1,p_2 \in Q}$ such that for all $q_{in}, q_u \in Q$ and all $h_{in}, h_u, n \in \mathbb{N}$ it holds that $\mathcal{N} \models \varphi_{q_{in},q_u}[h_{in}, n, h_u]$ if and only if $\mathcal{A}_\Delta$ produces (q_u, h_u) from (q_{in}, h_{in}) on a column labeled n.*

Proof. In a first step one can construct an MSO-formula describing partial runs of the transition automaton, disregarding the placement of the memory update token. That is an MSO-formula $\psi_{s_1,s_2,q_{in},q_u}$ with five free variables such that $\mathcal{N} \models \psi_{s_1,s_2,q_{in},q_u}[h_1, h_2, h_{in}, h_u, n]$ iff the transition automaton $\mathcal{A}_\Delta$ can reach from state s_1 on height h_1 the state s_2 on height h_2 by using only $\uparrow$ and $\downarrow$ transitions, while working on a column labeled n with the memory marker (q_{in}, h_{in}) and the token (q_u, h_u) present. The idea behind this formula is to quantify over a set of heights for each state $s \in S$ and define that if these sets are closed under the transition relation R and include height h_1 for state s_1 they will also include height h_2 for state s_2.

Using this formula, we then are able to describe partial runs with a single placement of the memory update token at the end. And finally we can define an MSO-formula expressing the existence of a complete run. We obtain a functional family of MSO-formulas if $\mathcal{A}_\Delta$ is functional. □

Now we turn to the more interesting direction of the theorem.

Lemma 6. *Let $(\varphi_{p_1,p_2}(x,y,z))_{p_1,p_2 \in Q}$ be a family of MSO-formulas. There exists a transition automaton $\mathcal{A}_\Delta$, such that for all $q_{in}, q_u \in Q$ and all $h_{in}, h_u, n \in \mathbb{N}$ it holds that $\mathcal{N} \models \varphi_{q_{in},q_u}[h_{in}, n, h_u]$ if and only if $\mathcal{A}_\Delta$ produces (q_u, h_u) from (q_{in}, h_{in}) on a column labeled n.*

Proof. For each MSO-formula φ_{p_1,p_2}, there exists a nondeterministic Büchi automaton $\mathcal{B}_{p_1,p_2}$ accepting precisely those ω-words for which φ_{p_1,p_2} evaluates to true [14]. Note that $\mathcal{B}_{p_1,p_2}$ will enter a loop (either accepting or rejecting) after it has read the memory marker, the memory update token and the height of the column. Thus, we can transform each $\mathcal{B}_{p_1,p_2}$ into an NFA $\mathcal{C}_{p_1,p_2}$ that accepts or rejects after reading only a finite prefix of the ω-word.

Finally, we can use these NFAs to construct the transition automaton $\mathcal{A}_\Delta$ as follows: First, $\mathcal{A}_\Delta$ places an arbitrary memory update token on an arbitrary height and moves back down again to height 0. From there it guesses p_1 and p_2, simulates the corresponding NFA $\mathcal{C}_{p_1,p_2}$ and enters the halting state if $\mathcal{C}_{p_1,p_2}$ accepts. □

This concludes the proof of Theorem 4 as far as nondeterministic automata are concerned. To cover the deterministic case, we shall prove the subsequent two lemmas. Let us first note, however, a normal form for nondeterministic ℕ-memory automata, obtained as a consequence of the constructions in Lemmas 5 and 6, where we can restrict the use of nondeterminism:

Corollary 7. *For each ℕ-memory recognizable language L there exists a nondeterministic ℕ-memory automaton recognizing L such that its underlying transition automaton $\mathcal{A}_\Delta$ behaves as follows:*

1. *It places the memory update token nondeterministically at an arbitrary height.*
2. *Then it moves back to height 0 and continues from a fixed state $s_0' \in S$.*
3. *Finally $\mathcal{A}_\Delta$ deterministically moves only upwards (i.e., it only uses transitions in $\Delta_\uparrow := S \times (Q^? \times \{\#, 1, \perp\} \times Q^?) \times S \times \{\uparrow\}$).*

Now we show that every deterministically ℕ-memory recognizable language can be recognized by an ℕ-memory automaton whose transition automaton is not only functional but deterministic (and thus conclude the proof of Theorem 4). We start with an interesting property of deterministic ℕ-memory automata.

Lemma 8. *If $\mathcal{A} = (Q, \Delta, q_0, F)$ is a deterministic ℕ-memory automaton, then there exists a $B \in \mathbb{N}$ such that for all $q_{in} \in Q$ and $h_{in}, n \in \mathbb{N}$ the uniquely defined $q_u \in Q$ and $h_u \in \mathbb{N}$ with $((q_{in}, h_{in}), n, (q_u, h_u)) \in \Delta$ fulfill that $h_u \in [0, \ldots, B] \cup [h_{in} - B, \ldots, h_{in} + B] \cup [n - B, \ldots, n + B]$.*

Proof. W.l.o.g. we can assume that $\mathcal{A}$ fulfills the property of Corollary 7. Define $B := m^2$ where m is the number of states of the underlying transition automaton $\mathcal{A}_\Delta$. Let us assume that there is $((q_{in}, h_{in}), n, (q_u, h_u)) \in \Delta$ with $h_u \notin [0, \ldots, B] \cup [h_{in} - B, \ldots, h_{in} + B] \cup [n - B, \ldots, n + B]$. If $h_u > max(h_{in}, n) + B$ then there exists a state repetition in the final one-way part of the run between h_{in} or n and h_u. Thus there also is an accepting run that produces a different memory update token. This is a contradiction to $\mathcal{A}$ being deterministic. On the other hand, if $h_u < max(h_{in}, n)$ we still know that $|h_u - 0|$, $|h_u - n|$ and $|h_u - h_{in}|$ are all larger than B. We assume that $h_{in} < h_u < n$ (all other cases are quite similar). Because $h_u - h_{in} > B > m$ there is a state repetition in the one-way part of the run of $\mathcal{A}_\Delta$ between h_{in} and h_u. Let $k \leq m$ be the size of this state repetition. Since $n - h_u > B = m^2$, there also exists a state repetition between h_u and n of a size $k \cdot r$ that is a multiple of k. Then by a pumping argument (by duplicating the first state repetition r times while deleting the second one), there is also an accepting run that produces the memory update token $(q_u, h_u + kr)$ from the memory marker (q_{in}, h_{in}) on the column of height n. This is again a contradiction to the fact that $\mathcal{A}$ is deterministic. □

Using this property we can now prove the following lemma.

Lemma 9. *An* $\mathbb{N}$*-memory automaton* $\mathcal{A} = (Q, \Delta, q_0, F)$ *is deterministic iff there exists a deterministic transition automaton* $\mathcal{A}_\Delta$ *defining* Δ*.*

Proof. We only address the direction from left to right. By Lemma 5 and the construction in the proof of Lemma 6 it is possible to define for a given transition relation the NFAs $\mathcal{C}_{p_1,p_2}$ that accept precisely those words that correspond to valid transitions. If $\mathcal{A}$ is deterministic, then by Lemma 8, the memory update token can only be at finitely many possible heights (in bounded intervals). Thus, we can define an NFA that first guesses this relative height (one of the three possible intervals and the position within that interval) then guesses p_1 and p_2 and finally simulates the correspondig automaton $\mathcal{C}_{p_1,p_2}$. In each step of this simulation, the automaton has to check whether its current position is the guessed height of the memory update token. To obtain the desired automaton, we transform this NFA into a DFA. It remains to place the memory update token at the correct height, which can be extracted from the final state reached by the DFA. □

5 Closure Properties

Our results are summarized in Fig. 2. We first consider Boolean operations and then concatenation and iteration.

Theorem 10. *The class of* $\mathbb{N}$*-memory recognizable languages is closed under union but neither under intersection nor complement. The class of deterministically* $\mathbb{N}$*-memory recognizable languages is closed under complement but neither under union nor intersection.*

The closure under union in the case of nondeterministic $\mathbb{N}$-memory automata is trivial. For the closure under complement in the deterministic case, the idea is to exchange the final and non-final states. The problem that the given automaton may reject a word just by lack of a run is overcome by introducing a sink state.

Applying de Morgan's laws it remains to show that neither deterministic nor nondeterministic $\mathbb{N}$-memory automata are closed under intersection. Consider the languages $L_1 := \{w \in \mathbb{N}^* \mid w_1 = w_3\}$ and $L_2 := \{w \in \mathbb{N}^* \mid w_2 = w_4\}$, both recognizable by deterministic $\mathbb{N}$-memory automata. Let us consider the language $L := L_1 \cap L_2$. Assume that there exists an $\mathbb{N}$-memory automaton $\mathcal{A}$ recognizing L and assume that it is in a normalized form according to Corollary 7. Let $m \in \mathbb{N}$ be bigger than the number of states in the associated transition automaton. Consider a run of $\mathcal{A}$ on the word $i\ell i\ell$ where $i = m$ and $\ell = 4m^2$. The memory marker on the fourth column is on a height $h_{in4} \geq \ell - m$. Otherwise there would be a state repetition of size $k \leq m$ during the one-way computation of the transition automaton between h_{in4} and ℓ. By a pumping argument, this would imply that $\mathcal{A}$ accepts the word $i\ell ij$ with $j = \ell - k$. Using a similar argument we know that the memory marker on the third column is on a height $h_{in3} \geq \ell - 2m$. But then it holds that $|h_{in3} - i| \geq m^2$ and $|i - 0| \geq m$. Thus there is a state repetition of size $k < m$ during the one-way computation of the transition automaton on the third column between heights 0 and i as well as a state repetition with a size that is a multiple of k (say $r \cdot k$), between heights i and h_{in3}. Therefore by another pumping argument similar to the one in the proof of Lemma 8, it follows that $\mathcal{A}$ accepts the word $i\ell j\ell$ with $j = i + kr$, which gives a contradiction. □

Theorem 11. *The class of* ℕ*-memory recognizable languages is closed under concatenation and iteration, whereas the class of deterministically* ℕ*-memory recognizable languages is neither closed under concatenation nor under iteration.*

The first statement holds because of the nondeterminism of ℕ-memory automata. For the second statement consider the deterministic ℕ-memory recognizable language $L = \{k\mathbb{N}^*k \mid k \in \mathbb{N}\}$. Assume that there exists a deterministic ℕ-memory automaton $\mathcal{A}$ recognizing $L \cdot L$. Consider the run of $\mathcal{A}$ on the word $w := iiij$ for letters i and j. Note that $\mathcal{A}$ has to accept $wi, wj \in L \cdot L$, but must reject wm for all other letters m $(i \neq m \neq j)$. Since $\mathcal{A}$ is deterministic it cannot remember both i and j. This can be shown with a pumping argument analogous to the one in the proof of Theorem 10. By the same argument, L^* is not deterministically ℕ-memory recognizable. □

	det.	n.det.
Union (∪)	NO	YES
Intersection (∩)	NO	NO
Complement (¬)	YES	NO
Concatenation (·)	NO	YES
Iteration (*)	NO	YES

Fig. 2. Closure properties of ℕ-memory recognizable languages

	det.	n.det.
non-emptiness	YES	YES
membership	YES	YES
universality	YES	NO
inclusion	NO	NO
empty intersection	NO	NO
equivalence	?	NO
deterministic	—	NO

Fig. 3. Decidability results for ℕ-memory automata

6 Decision Problems

In this section we discuss the decidability of some decision problems for ℕ-memory automata. The results are displayed in Fig. 3.

Theorem 12. *The non-emptiness problem for* ℕ*-memory automata is decidable.*

For the proof we apply a reduction to the decision problem of the MSO-theory of $\mathcal{N} = (\mathbb{N}, \mathrm{Succ})$. This theory was shown to be decidable by Büchi in 1962 [5]. Starting with an MSO-ℕ-memory automaton $\mathcal{A}$, we present an MSO-formula

$\varphi_{\mathcal{A}}$ which is true in $\mathcal{N}$ iff $\mathcal{A}$ accepts at least one word. To describe the existence of a run of $\mathcal{A}$ we first define a formula $\Psi_{q,q'}(h,h')$ that is true in the structure $\mathcal{N}$ iff there exists a word on which $\mathcal{A}$ starting in state q on height h will finally reach state q' on height h'. Assume that the set of states of $\mathcal{A}$ is $\{1,\ldots,n\}$.

$$\Psi_{q,q'}(h,h') := \forall X_1 \ldots \forall X_n((X_q(h) \wedge \Theta(X_1,\ldots,X_n)) \rightarrow X_{q'}(h'))$$

where $\Theta(X_1,\ldots,X_n)$ describes the transitive closure of the transition relation defined by the family of MSO-formulas $(\varphi_{p,q})_{p,q}$.

$$\Theta(X_1,\ldots,X_n) := \forall h_1 \forall h_2 (\bigwedge_{q_1,q_2 \in Q} (X_{q_1}(h_1) \wedge \exists y \varphi_{q_1,q_2}(h_1,y,h_2)) \rightarrow X_{q_2}(h_2))$$

We can set $\varphi_{\mathcal{A}} := \exists h_f \bigvee_{q_f \in F} \Psi_{q_0,q_f}(0,h_f)$ to obtain the desired formula. □

Note that the membership problem (whether a given $\mathbb{N}$-memory automaton $\mathcal{A}$ accepts a given word w) is solvable by enhancing $\mathcal{A}$ with a test whether the sequence of scanned letters matches w and then checking for non-emptiness.

For deterministic $\mathbb{N}$-memory automata, Theorem 12 implies the decidability of the universality problem, due to the fact that deterministic $\mathbb{N}$-memory automata can effectively be complemented (cf. Theorem 10). This, however, does not extend to nondeterministic $\mathbb{N}$-memory automata. We just invoke the undecidability of the universality problem for the weaker model of progressive grid automata, shown in [7]. It follows that also the equivalence problem and the inclusion problem for nondeterministic $\mathbb{N}$-memory automata are undecidable.

Theorem 13. *The empty intersection problem for deterministic* $\mathbb{N}$*-memory automata is undecidable.*

Proof. We apply an easy reduction from the halting problem for 2-register machines. Given a register machine $\mathcal{R}$, we construct two deterministic $\mathbb{N}$-memory automata $\mathcal{A}_1$ and $\mathcal{A}_2$. For an input sequence $r_0 s_0 r_1 s_1 \ldots r_n s_n$, $\mathcal{A}_1$ verifies that $r_0 r_1 \ldots r_n$ is the sequence of values of the first register along a halting computation of $\mathcal{R}$. Analogously, $\mathcal{A}_2$ checks the sequence $s_0 s_1 \ldots s_n$. The automata keep track of the current instruction in their control states and remember the last register value (of the respective register) using the memory marker. □

It follows that the inclusion problem for deterministic $\mathbb{N}$-memory automata is undecidable, since deterministic $\mathbb{N}$-memory automata are effectively closed under complement. We leave as an open question whether the equivalence problem is decidable.

Theorem 14. *The problem to determine for a given nondeterministic* $\mathbb{N}$*-memory automaton whether there exists an equivalent deterministic* $\mathbb{N}$*-memory automaton is undecidable.*

For the proof we apply a reduction from the universality problem, adapting a proof given by Ginsburg et al. [8] for one-way stack automata.

We mention that it is even undecidable whether a given deterministic $\mathbb{N}$-memory automaton $\mathcal{A}$ is equivalent to a nondeterministic one $\mathcal{B}$ for which one knows that $L(\mathcal{B})$ is deterministically $\mathbb{N}$-memory recognizable. This is analogous to the case of pushdown automata.

7 Extension to Infinite Words and Related Applications

In applications regarding the algorithmic verification or synthesis of state-based systems, it is often appropriate to consider non-terminating computations. In the present context, it is thus useful to consider infinite words over $\mathbb{N}$; so we add a third dimension of infinity beyond using infinite alphabets and infinite memory spaces. We briefly touch this topic without entering details.

The extension of $\mathbb{N}$-memory automata to infinite words, using the standard acceptance conditions (Büchi condition, Muller condition, parity condition), is obvious by referring to the finite space Q of control states of an $\mathbb{N}$-memory automaton. In contrast to the theory of regular ω-languages, each deterministic model mentioned here has strictly weaker expressive power than the corresponding nondeterministic model; this is clear from the example language $\{ukvk\alpha \mid k \geq 0, u, v \in \mathbb{N}^*, \alpha \in \mathbb{N}^\omega\}$. On the other hand, the solvability of the non-emptiness problem holds in all these cases. This is seen by adapting the last formula in the proof of Theorem 12 to the desired acceptance condition.

The latter fact opens the possibility to (moderate) applications in program verification. In the standard setting, the verification problem is the intersection problem "$L(\text{Sys}) \cap L(\neg\text{Spec}) = \emptyset$?" where $L(\text{Sys})$ and $L(\neg\text{Spec})$ are the ω-languages that capture the set of possible system runs and the undesired system runs (described by the negation of the specification), respectively. While the intersection problem is undecidable for $\mathbb{N}$-memory automata in general, we can solve this problem in the special case where the specification is definable by deterministic Muller- or parity $\mathcal{N}$-MSO-automata (as mentioned in Sect. 3). So we can conclude: *The verification problem is decidable for systems defined in terms of nondeterministic Muller or parity* $\mathbb{N}$*-memory automata and specifications defined by deterministic Muller or parity* $\mathcal{N}$*-MSO-automata.*

A second type of application is concerned with program synthesis. Here the specification is a condition on pairs of ω-words, the input stream and the output stream of a program, and the fundamental question is whether a program (an automaton) exists that can transform arbitrary input streams into output streams letter-by-letter such that the specification is satisfied (Church's Synthesis Problem). In a nice analogy to the case of finite-state systems where the Büchi-Landweber Theorem provides a positive solution, we can show the corresponding result for specifications given by deterministic parity $\mathbb{N}$-memory automata, using $\mathbb{N}$-memory transducers as indicated in Sect. 3. The details can be found in [4].

8 Conclusion

We have studied the concept of $\mathbb{N}$-memory automata, a natural model for processing words over the alphabet $\mathbb{N}$, extending the progressive grid automata of [7]. $\mathbb{N}$-memory automata were shown to be a "robust" concept by its close relation to MSO-logic. It may have algorithmic applications due to the solvability of the non-emptiness problem, but also has rather weak closure properties.

The present approach calls for a number of extensions, some of which have been carried out in (so far unpublished) bachelor and master theses at RWTH Aachen University. For example, the alphabet $\mathbb{N}$ may be replaced by the set Σ^* of words over a finite alphabet, by the set of finite trees over a finite label alphabet, or in general by some "alphabet structure" together with some logic for the definition of transitions. Another type of generalization concerns $\mathbb{N}$-memory automata over (finite or infinite) trees instead of words.

References

1. Bès, A.: An application of the Feferman-Vaught theorem to automata and logics for words over an infinite alphabet. Logical Methods Comput. Sci. **4**(1) (2008)
2. Bojańczyk, M., David, C., Muscholl, A., Schwentick, T., Segoufin, L.: Two-variable logic on data words. ACM Trans. Comput. Logic **12**(4), 27 (2011)
3. Bojańczyk, M., Klin, B., Lasota, S.: Automata theory in nominal sets. Logical Methods Comput. Sci. **10**(3) (2014)
4. Brütsch, B., Thomas, W.: Playing games in the Baire space. In: Brihaye, T., Delahaye, B., Jezequel, L., Markey, N., Srba, J. (eds.) Proceedings of Cassting Workshop on Games for the Synthesis of Complex Systems, EPTCS, vol. 220, pp. 13–25 (2016)
5. Büchi, J.R.: On a decision method in restricted second order arithmetic. In: Nagel, E., Suppes, P., Tarski, A. (eds.) Proceedings of the 1960 International Congress on Logic, Methodology and Philosophy of Science, Studies in Logic and the Foundations of Mathematics, vol. 44, pp. 1–11. Elsevier, Amsterdam (1966)
6. Carapelle, C., Feng, S., Kartzow, A., Lohrey, M.: Satisfiability of ECTL* with tree constraints. In: Beklemishev, L.D., Musatov, D.V. (eds.) CSR 2015. LNCS, vol. 9139, pp. 94–108. Springer, Heidelberg (2015). doi:10.1007/978-3-319-20297-6_7
7. Czyba, C., Spinrath, C., Thomas, W.: Finite automata over infinite alphabets: two models with transitions for local change. In: Potapov, I. (ed.) DLT 2015. LNCS, vol. 9168, pp. 203–214. Springer, Heidelberg (2015). doi:10.1007/978-3-319-21500-6_16
8. Ginsburg, S., Greibach, S.A., Harrison, M.A.: One-way stack automata. J. ACM **14**(2), 389–418 (1967)
9. Kaminski, M., Francez, N.: Finite-memory automata. Theoret. Comput. Sci. **134**(2), 329–363 (1994)
10. Segoufin, L.: Automata and logics for words and trees over an infinite alphabet. In: Ésik, Z. (ed.) CSL 2006. LNCS, vol. 4207, pp. 41–57. Springer, Heidelberg (2006). doi:10.1007/11874683_3
11. Spelten, A., Thomas, W., Winter, S.: Trees over infinite structures and path logics with synchronization. In: Yu, F., Wang, C. (eds.) Proceedings of INFINITY 2011, EPTCS, vol. 73, pp. 20–34 (2011)
12. Tan, T.: An automata model for trees with ordered data values. In: Proceedings of LICS 2012, pp. 586–595. IEEE Computer Society (2012)
13. Tan, T.: Extending two-variable logic on data trees with order on data values and its automata. ACM Trans. Comput. Log. **15**(1), 8 (2014)
14. Thomas, W.: Languages, automata, and logic. In: Rozenberg, G., Salomaa, A. (eds.) Handbook of Formal Languages, pp. 389–455. Springer, Berlin (1997)

An Automata View to Goal-Directed Methods

Lisa Hutschenreiter[1(✉)] and Rafael Peñaloza[2]

[1] Technische Universität Dresden, Dresden, Germany
lisa.hutschenreiter@tu-dresden.de
[2] Free University of Bozen-Bolzano, Bolzano, Italy
rafael.penaloza@unibz.it

Abstract. Consequence-based and automata-based algorithms encompass two families of approaches that have been thoroughly studied as reasoning methods for many logical formalisms. While automata are useful for finding tight complexity bounds, consequence-based algorithms are typically simpler to describe, implement, and optimize. In this paper, we show that consequence-based reasoning can be reduced to the emptiness test of an appropriately built automaton. Thanks to this reduction, one can focus on developing efficient consequence-based algorithms, obtaining complexity bounds and other benefits of automata methods for free.

1 Introduction

In logic-based knowledge representation, the knowledge from a domain is encoded using a finite set of axioms, expressed and interpreted in a suitable logic, that restrict the ways in which the domain symbols can be used. To keep the representation task feasible, only the most relevant portions of the knowledge are explicitly represented, while other consequences of these axioms are only implicitly available. The task of making this implicit knowledge explicit is usually known as *reasoning*.

For practical applications, it is fundamental to have effective reasoning methods. Ideally, these should be optimal w.r.t. the computational complexity of the reasoning problem, easy to implement, and behave well in practice. Keeping these desiderata in mind, many reasoning algorithms have been developed over the years. These can be broadly classified into two approaches: the automata-based, and the tableaux-based approaches. In a nutshell, the automata-based approach constructs an automaton that accepts all relevant models of a knowledge base. An emptiness test can then be used to decide whether a given (implicit) consequence can be derived from it. On the other hand, tableaux methods apply rules to extend the explicit knowledge until the consequence is derived. They can thus be thought of as "goal-directed" approaches. Consequence-based algorithms fall into this latter category, where rule applications have a limited effect.

Automata-based methods provide formal tools for understanding the theoretical properties and limitations of reasoning in the underlying logical formalism. They have been successfully used to prove tight (worst-case) complexity

L. Hutschenreiter—Supported by the DFG Graduiertenkolleg 1763 (QuantLA).

F. Drewes et al. (Eds.): LATA 2017, LNCS 10168, pp. 103–114, 2017.
DOI: 10.1007/978-3-319-53733-7_7

bounds [2]. They also provide an elegant solution for dealing with supplemental reasoning problems that can be seen as weighted model counting problems [4,20]. However, with a few notable exceptions [11], automata-based methods are not suitable for efficient implementations due to the match between their best-case and their worst-case behaviour.

Due to their goal-directed behaviour, tableaux-based methods are the basis of some of the most efficient implementations of reasoning algorithms available. However, extending these methods to handle supplemental reasoning problems is far from obvious, and might even lead to non-terminating procedures [5]. In fact, the known method for transforming a consequence-based algorithm into a supplemental reasoning procedure requires the application of an NP-hard propositional entailment test on *every* step of the execution, potentially damaging the overall complexity of the methods [6]. This is especially negative if one takes into account that the supplemental extensions of automata-based methods typically preserve the original complexity.

In this paper, we combine the benefits of consequence-based and automata-based methods to overcome their respective drawbacks. More precisely, we show that every consequence-based algorithm can be effectively transformed into an automaton deciding the same reasoning problem. Thus, one can focus on designing and implementing an efficient consequence-based algorithm and take advantage of this transformation to obtain tight complexity bounds and extensions to supplemental reasoning provided by the automata-based view.

Throughout this paper, we consider a general notion of consequence-based algorithm, which makes our results applicable to a wide range of settings. To improve readability, we use as a running example a known method for deciding subsumption in the description logic $\mathcal{EL}$.

2 Consequence-Based Algorithms

We consider a general notion of consequence-based algorithms as automated reasoning methods. The family of these methods, also called *ground tableaux* in the literature [5], encompasses many well-known algorithms, such as DPLL [8], congruence closure [19], and the prominent methods for reasoning in $\mathcal{EL}$ [1] and other description logics [13]. As a running example for all our notions, we will adapt the consequence-based algorithm for deciding subsumption first presented in $\mathcal{EL}$ from [14]. Thus we briefly recall this logic and its reasoning problem.

$\mathcal{EL}$ is a lightweight description logic whose main building blocks are *concepts* and *roles*. Given two disjoint infinite sets N_C and N_R of *concept names* and *role names*, respectively, $\mathcal{EL}$ *concepts* are constructed using the grammar rule $C ::= A \mid \top \mid C \sqcap C \mid \exists r.C$, where $A \in N_C$ and $r \in N_R$. An $\mathcal{EL}$ *TBox* is a finite set of *general concept inclusions (GCIs)* of the form $C \sqsubseteq D$, where C, D are $\mathcal{EL}$ concepts. The semantics of this logic is based on interpretations, which are pairs of the form $\mathcal{J} = (\Lambda^{\mathcal{J}}, \cdot^{\mathcal{J}})$, with $\Lambda^{\mathcal{J}}$ a non-empty set called the *domain* and $\cdot^{\mathcal{J}}$ the *interpretation function* that maps every concept name A to a subset $A^{\mathcal{J}} \subseteq \Lambda^{\mathcal{J}}$ and every role name r to a binary relation $r^{\mathcal{J}} \subseteq \Lambda^{\mathcal{J}} \times \Lambda^{\mathcal{J}}$. This function is extended to $\mathcal{EL}$ concepts by defining $\top^{\mathcal{J}} := \Lambda^{\mathcal{J}}$, $(C \sqcap D)^{\mathcal{J}} := C^{\mathcal{J}} \cap D^{\mathcal{J}}$, and $(\exists r.C)^{\mathcal{J}} := \{\lambda \in \Lambda^{\mathcal{J}} \mid \exists \mu \in C^{\mathcal{J}}.(\lambda, \mu) \in r^{\mathcal{J}}\}$. The interpretation $\mathcal{J}$ *satisfies* the GCI $C \sqsubseteq D$ iff $C^{\mathcal{J}} \subseteq D^{\mathcal{J}}$. It is a *model* of the TBox $\mathcal{T}$ if it satisfies all GCIs in $\mathcal{T}$. The concept C is *subsumed* by the concept D w.r.t. the TBox $\mathcal{T}$ if every model of $\mathcal{T}$ also satisfies the GCI $C \sqsubseteq D$.

We now define the notion of consequence-based algorithm. To remain as general as possible, for the rest of this paper we consider that we have two arbitrary (but fixed) sets $\mathfrak{I}$ of *inputs* and $\mathfrak{T}$ of *axioms*. We denote by $\mathscr{P}_{\mathsf{fin}}(\mathfrak{T})$ the set of all finite subsets of $\mathfrak{T}$. The different inputs in $\mathfrak{I}$ will be usually denoted by calligraphic letters like $\mathcal{I}$, and the axioms with lower-case letters; e.g., s.[1] We start by defining the consequences that will be decided by our algorithms.

Definition 1 (property). *A* consequence property *(or* property *for short) is a binary relation* $\mathcal{P} \subseteq \mathfrak{I} \times \mathscr{P}_{\mathsf{fin}}(\mathfrak{T})$ *such that if* $(\mathcal{I}, \mathcal{T}) \in \mathcal{P}$*, then* $(\mathcal{I}, \mathcal{T}') \in \mathcal{P}$ *for all* $\mathcal{T} \subseteq \mathcal{T}' \in \mathscr{P}_{\mathsf{fin}}(\mathfrak{T})$.

In other words, we are interested in deciding whether a given input $\mathcal{I}$ is entailed by a finite set of axioms $\mathcal{T}$ through a monotone relation. We use monotonicity in the standard logical sense in which new information can only generate more consequences, but never negate previously entailed ones. Throughout this paper we call pairs of the form $(\mathcal{I}, \mathcal{T})$ *axiomatized inputs.*

Consider for example the subsumption problem in $\mathcal{EL}$. In this case, the set $\mathfrak{T}$ of axioms consists of all possible GCIs $C \sqsubseteq D$. $\mathfrak{I}$ is the class of all possible subsumption relations, which will be denoted by $C \sqsubseteq^? D$ to distinguish them from the axioms in the TBox. The property $\mathcal{P}$ refers to the entailment of subsumption relations; that is, $(C \sqsubseteq^? D, \mathcal{T}) \in \mathcal{P}$ iff C is subsumed by D w.r.t. $\mathcal{T}$.

Depending on the specific shape of the property $\mathcal{P}$, there exist many different approaches for deciding whether a given axiomatized input $(\mathcal{I}, \mathcal{T})$ belongs to $\mathcal{P}$ or not. We focus on a class of decision methods which we call consequence-based algorithms.

Definition 2 (consequence-based algorithm). *Let* $\mathfrak{I}$ *be a set of inputs, and* $\mathfrak{T}$ *a set of axioms. A* consequence-based algorithm *for* $\mathfrak{I}$ *and* $\mathfrak{T}$ *is a tuple of the form* $S = (\Sigma, \cdot^S, \mathcal{R}, \mathcal{C})$ *where*

- Σ *is a set called the* signature*;*
- $\cdot^S$ *is the* initialization function *that maps every* $\mathcal{I} \in \mathfrak{I}$ *and every* $t \in \mathfrak{T}$ *to a finite subset of* Σ*;*
- $\mathcal{R}$ *is a set of* rules *of the form* $(B_0, \mathcal{S}) \to B$*, where* B_0 *and* B *are finite subsets of* Σ *and* $\mathcal{S} \in \mathscr{P}_{\mathsf{fin}}(\mathfrak{T})$*; and*
- $\mathcal{C}$ *is a set of finite subsets of* Σ*, which are called* clashes.

The idea of a consequence-based algorithm is to decide a property by making explicit all the consequences of the given axiomatized input. The explicit knowledge derived during the execution of the algorithm S is preserved in S-states.

[1] In the literature (e.g. [5]) the sets of axioms allowed are sometimes restricted to satisfy an *admissibility* criterion. As this criterion is irrelevant for our methods, we leave it out for the sake of simplicity.

Formally, given a consequence-based algorithm $S = (\Sigma, \cdot^S, \mathcal{R}, \mathcal{C})$, an *S-state* is a pair $\mathfrak{S} = (A, \mathcal{T})$ where A is a finite subset of Σ and $\mathcal{T} \in \mathscr{P}_{\mathsf{fin}}(\mathfrak{T})$. We call the elements of A in such an S-state *assertions*.

Given the axiomatized input $(\mathcal{I}, \mathcal{T})$, the decision procedure begins with the *initial S-state* $(\mathcal{I}, \mathcal{T})^S$ defined by $(\mathcal{I}, \mathcal{T})^S := (\mathcal{I}^S \cup \bigcup_{t \in \mathcal{T}} t^S, \mathcal{T})$. That is, the initial S-state contains all the assertions obtained by applying the initialization function to the input $\mathcal{I}$ and the axioms in $\mathcal{T}$. Notice that the second component of this S-state is the same set of axioms $\mathcal{T}$. As we will see, the algorithm never modifies this set. However, preserving the information of the set of axioms used will be helpful in the following sections. The first component of the S-state $\mathfrak{S}$ is iteratively extended through rule applications, which depend exclusively on the assertions and axioms appearing in $\mathfrak{S}$.

Definition 3 (rule application). *Let $\mathfrak{S} = (A, \mathcal{T})$ be an S-state. The rule $\mathsf{R} : (B_0, \mathcal{S}) \to B$ is* applicable *to $\mathfrak{S}$ iff (i) $\mathcal{S} \subseteq \mathcal{T}$, (ii) $B_0 \subseteq A$; and (iii) $B \not\subseteq A$. The* application *of* R *to $\mathfrak{S}$ yields the new S-state $\mathfrak{S}' := (A \cup B, \mathcal{T})$. In this case, we write $\mathfrak{S} \to_{\mathsf{R}} \mathfrak{S}'$, or $\mathfrak{S} \to_S \mathfrak{S}'$ if the specific rule applied is irrelevant.*

As usual, the reflexive and transitive closure of $\to_S$ is denoted by $\xrightarrow{*}_S$.

Starting from the initial state, consequence-based algorithms apply rules in a *not-care non-deterministic* manner until a *saturated* state is reached; that is, a state for which no rule is applicable. In this case, the not-care non-determinism means that whenever more than one rule can be applied to a given state, any one of them can be chosen. Finally, the set of clashes $\mathcal{C}$ is used to decide the property once a saturated S-state is reached: the axiomatized input is *accepted* (i.e., it belongs to the property $\mathcal{P}$) if and only if it contains a clash.

A consequence-based algorithm decides a property $\mathcal{P}$ if it always terminates and the resulting saturated S-state contains a clash whenever the axiomatized input belongs to $\mathcal{P}$. This notion is formalized next.

Definition 4 (correct). *The consequence-based algorithm $S = (\Sigma, \cdot^S, \mathcal{R}, \mathcal{C})$ is* correct *for the property $\mathcal{P}$ iff for every axiomatized input $\Gamma = (\mathcal{I}, \mathcal{T})$, the following two conditions hold:*

1. *S terminates on Γ; that is, there exists no infinite chain of rule applications $\mathfrak{S}_0 \to_S \mathfrak{S}_1 \to_S \cdots$ starting with $\mathfrak{S}_0 = \Gamma$; and*
2. *for every chain of rule applications $\mathfrak{S}_0 \xrightarrow{*}_S \mathfrak{S}_n$ with $\mathfrak{S}_0 = \Gamma$ and $\mathfrak{S}_n$ a saturated S-state, $\Gamma \in \mathcal{P}$ iff $\mathfrak{S}_n$ contains a clash.*

Example 5. A consequence-based algorithm for deciding subsumption in $\mathcal{EL}$ is given by $S_{\mathcal{EL}} = (\Sigma, \cdot^{S_{\mathcal{EL}}}, \mathcal{R}, \mathcal{C})$, where

- $\Sigma := \{C \sqsubseteq D, C \sqsubseteq^? D \mid C, D$ are $\mathcal{EL}$ concepts$\}$;
- for every GCI in $\mathfrak{T}$, $(C \sqsubseteq D)^{S_{\mathcal{EL}}} := \{C \sqsubseteq C, C \sqsubseteq \top\}$;
- for every $C \sqsubseteq^? D \in \mathfrak{I}$, $(C \sqsubseteq^? D)^{S_{\mathcal{EL}}} := \{C \sqsubseteq^? D\}$;
- the set of rules $\mathcal{R}$ is depicted in Fig. 1; and
- $\mathcal{C} := \{\{C \sqsubseteq D, C \sqsubseteq^? D\}\}$

	B_0	$\mathcal{S}$	$\rightarrow$	B
$\mathsf{R}_\sqcap^-$:	$\{C \sqsubseteq D_1 \sqcap D_2\}$	$\emptyset$	$\rightarrow$	$\{C \sqsubseteq D_1, C \sqsubseteq D_2\}$
$\mathsf{R}_\sqcap^+$:	$\{C \sqsubseteq D_1, C \sqsubseteq D_2\}$	$\emptyset$	$\rightarrow$	$\{C \sqsubseteq D_1 \sqcap D_2\}$
$\mathsf{R}_\exists$:	$\{E \sqsubseteq \exists r.C, C \sqsubseteq D\}$	$\emptyset$	$\rightarrow$	$\{E \sqsubseteq \exists r.D\}$
$\mathsf{R}_\sqsubseteq$:	$\{C \sqsubseteq D\}$	$\{D \sqsubseteq E\}$	$\rightarrow$	$\{C \sqsubseteq E\}$

Fig. 1. Rules for the consequence-based algorithm $S_{\mathcal{EL}}$

Intuitively, the algorithm makes all the relevant subsumption relations that follow from the TBox $\mathcal{T}$ explicit by applying the rules. The input subsumption relation, whose entailment is being decided, is kept in the set of assertions to be able to produce a clash when it is derived through the application of rules. The correctness of this algorithm has been shown in [14].

Notice that the second condition from Definition 4 requires that the algorithm yields the same answer regardless of the order in which the rules were applied. This corresponds to the not-care non-determinism mentioned above. As a consequence, any order chosen suffices for deciding whether a property holds or not; i.e., there is no need to backtrack if a saturated S-state without a clash is found. In fact, for consequence-based algorithms, the second condition is equivalent to requiring that there exists one sequence of rule applications that leads to a saturated state with a clash. More precisely, for every axiomatized input Γ and saturated S-states $\mathfrak{S}, \mathfrak{S}'$, if $\Gamma^S \xrightarrow{*}_S \mathfrak{S}$ and $\Gamma^S \xrightarrow{*}_S \mathfrak{S}'$, then $\mathfrak{S}$ and $\mathfrak{S}'$ must be equivalent. This can be easily seen from the fact that whenever a rule $(B_0, \mathcal{S}) \rightarrow B$ is applicable in an S-state, it remains applicable to any successive S-state until all the assertions in B have been introduced, which has the same effect as having applied the rule before-hand. Once again, this in particular means that the order in which the rules are applied is irrelevant for deriving a clash or not.

For supplemental reasoning, it is often important to know all the possible ways in which clashes can be generated by rule applications (see Sect. 5). In order to keep track of the different orders that have already been followed, extensions of consequence-based algorithms developed for dealing with these problems require the use of an NP oracle [5].

3 Tree Automata

We briefly recall the basic notions of tree automata. These automata receive finite trees of a fixed arity k with identified successors as inputs. For the rest of this paper, given a positive integer k, we will denote by K the set $\{1, \ldots, k\}$. As is usual, we identify the nodes in a k-ary tree by words in K^*: the root node is identified by the empty word ε, and the i-th successor of the node $u \in \mathsf{K}^*$ is identified by the word ui for all $i \in \mathsf{K}$.

Definition 6 (finite tree). *A* finite k-ary tree *is a finite subset $t \subseteq \mathsf{K}^*$ such that for every node $ui \in t$ it holds that (i) $u \in t$, and (ii) $uj \in t$ for all $j, 1 \leq j \leq i$.*

Intuitively, Condition (i) states that the parent of every node belongs to the tree; this in particular means that a non-empty tree will always contain the root node ε. The second condition ensures that all the successors of a node are adequately identified by the smallest possible natural numbers without gaps. We say that a tree is *full* if every node is either a *leaf* (i.e., has no successors), or has exactly k successors.

A *labelled tree* is a tree $t \subseteq \mathsf{K}^*$ extended with a labelling function lab. If the labels belong to a given set Q, we will often denote labelled trees as a function $\mathsf{lab} : t \to Q$. For this paper, we focus on tree automata that receive full finite unlabelled trees of a fixed arity k as inputs.

Definition 7 (finite tree automaton). *A* finite tree automaton *of arity k is a tuple $\mathcal{A} = (Q, \Delta, I, F)$ where*

- *Q is a finite set, whose elements are called* states;
- *$\Delta \subseteq Q^{k+1}$ is the* transition relation;
- *$I \subseteq Q$ is the set of* initial states; *and*
- *$F \subseteq Q$ is the set of* final states.

A run *of this automaton on the full unlabelled finite tree t is a labelled tree of the form $\mathsf{lab} : t \to Q$ such that for every non-leaf node $u \in t$, it holds that $(\mathsf{lab}(u), \mathsf{lab}(u1), \ldots, \mathsf{lab}(uk)) \in \Delta$. This run is* successful *iff for every leaf node $u \in t$, $\mathsf{lab}(u) \in F$.*

The *emptiness problem* for finite tree automata refers to the problem of deciding whether there exists a finite unlabelled tree t and a successful run on t with $\mathsf{lab}(\varepsilon) \in I$. In this case, we say that the automaton is *non-empty*. We often refer to successful runs with $\mathsf{lab}(\varepsilon) \in I$ as *accepting*. It is well known that the emptiness problem can be solved in polynomial time on the number of states. This general bound can be in fact improved to *linear* time in the number of states through a bottom-up approach that identifies the states that may appear in a successful run—we call these *good* states. All final states are clearly good. Further good states can be iteratively found by adding all states $q \in Q$ such that there is a transition of the form $(q, q_1, \ldots, q_k) \in \Delta$ where every $q_i, 1 \leq i \leq k$ is a good state. This iteration detects an initial state that is good if and only if the automaton is non-empty.

4 From Consequence-Based to Automata

We now show how to translate any given consequence-based algorithm S into a finite tree automaton of an appropriate arity in such a manner that the emptiness test of the latter can be used to verify whether an axiomatized input Γ belongs to the property decided by the former or not.

For this section we consider an arbitrary but fixed consequence-based algorithm $S = (\Sigma, \cdot^S, \mathcal{R}, \mathcal{C})$. We fix the constant $k := \max\{|B_0| \mid (B_0, \mathcal{S}) \to B \in \mathcal{R}\}$. In the following, whenever we refer to a tree, we implicitly assume that it is a finite k-ary tree, where k is defined as before.

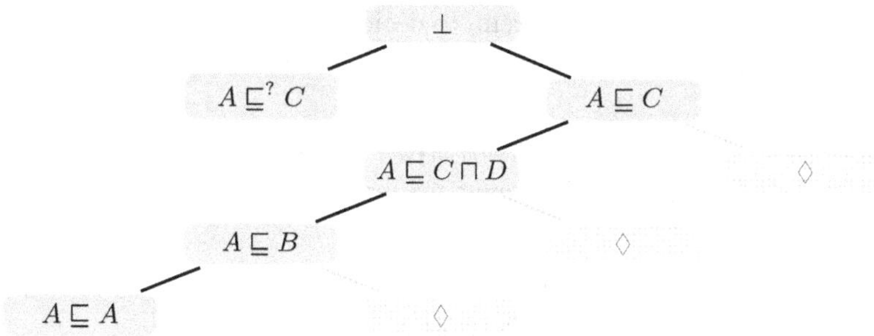

Fig. 2. A derivation tree for $(A \sqsubseteq^? C, \{A \sqsubseteq B, B \sqsubseteq C \sqcap D\})$ and its binary padding.

We can assume w.l.o.g. that all the rules in $\mathcal{R}$ are of the form $(B_0, \mathcal{S}) \to \{\sigma\}$ with $\sigma \in \Sigma$; that is, a rule application adds only one alphabet symbol as a consequence. To see this, notice that the rule $(B_0, \mathcal{S}) \to B$ can be equivalently replaced in $\mathcal{R}$ by the set of rules $\{(B_0, \mathcal{S}) \to \{\sigma\} \mid \sigma \in B\}$. Similarly, we assume that the set of clashes $\mathcal{C}$ contains only the singleton $\{\bot\}$. Otherwise, we can extend the set of rules $\mathcal{R}$ to include $(C, \emptyset) \to \{\bot\}$ for every $C \in \mathcal{C}$. This extension does not change the behaviour of the algorithm S, as it will still detect the presence of a clash by verifying whether the new symbol $\bot$ was derived. For example, we can change the rule $\mathsf{R}_\sqcap^-$ of the consequence-based algorithm $S_{\mathcal{EL}}$ (see Example 5) into two rules that derive $C \sqsubseteq D_1$ and $C \sqsubseteq D_2$, respectively, and add a new rule $\mathsf{R}_c : (\{C \sqsubseteq D, C \sqsubseteq^? D\}, \emptyset) \to \{\bot\}$ to satisfy the aforementioned assumptions without compromising its correctness for deciding subsumption relations.

Under these assumptions, we can view the possible derivations of the clash $\bot$ as labelled trees, where each node is labelled with an assertion from Σ, the root node is labelled by $\bot$, and the children of each node represent the set of assertions needed to apply a rule that generates them.

Definition 8 (derivation tree). *A* derivation tree *for the axiomatized input $\Gamma = (\mathcal{I}, \mathcal{T})$ w.r.t. the consequence-based algorithm S is a labelled finite k-ary tree $\mathsf{lab} : t \to \Sigma$ such that the following conditions hold:*

1. $\mathsf{lab}(\varepsilon) = \bot$;
2. *for every leaf node $u \in t$, $\mathsf{lab}(u) \in \Gamma^S$; and*
3. *for every non-leaf node $u \in t$ with i successors, there exists a rule of the form $(\{\mathsf{lab}(u1), \ldots, \mathsf{lab}(ui)\}, \mathcal{S}) \to \{\mathsf{lab}(u)\}$ in $\mathcal{R}$ such that $\mathcal{S} \subseteq \mathcal{T}$.*

Example 9. Consider again the algorithm $S_{\mathcal{EL}}$ for deciding subsumption in $\mathcal{EL}$ from Example 5. Since the rules in $S_{\mathcal{EL}}$ have at most two assertions as prerequisite for application, derivation trees for this algorithm will be binary. If we want to decide whether A is subsumed by C w.r.t. the TBox $\mathcal{T} = \{A \sqsubseteq B, B \sqsubseteq C \sqcap D\}$, we will call $S_{\mathcal{EL}}$ with the axiomatized input $\Gamma = (A \sqsubseteq^? C, \mathcal{T})$. A derivation tree for this input w.r.t. $S_{\mathcal{EL}}$ is depicted in Fig. 2 (ignore the nodes labelled with $\Diamond$ for the moment). Notice that there are only two leaf nodes, labelled with $A \sqsubseteq^? C$ and $A \sqsubseteq A$. Both of them belong to $\Gamma^{S_{\mathcal{EL}}}$.

As shown by the following theorem, to decide whether the axiomatized input Γ belongs to the property $\mathcal{P}$, it suffices to check for the existence of a derivation tree.

Theorem 10. *Let S be a consequence-based algorithm that is correct for the property $\mathcal{P}$, and $\Gamma = (\mathcal{I}, \mathcal{T})$ an axiomatized input. Then $\Gamma \in \mathcal{P}$ iff there exists a derivation tree for Γ w.r.t. S.*

Proof. Let $\mathfrak{S} = (A, \mathcal{T})$ be a saturated S-state such that $\Gamma^S \xrightarrow{*}_S \mathfrak{S}$. It suffices to show that $\bot \in A$ iff there exists a derivation tree for Γ w.r.t. S.
(if) Assume first that $\mathsf{lab} : t \to \Sigma$ is a derivation tree. We show by induction on the tree structure that $\mathsf{lab}(u) \in A$ holds for all $u \in t$. First, for all leaf nodes u, we have by definition that $\mathsf{lab}(u) \in \Gamma^S \subseteq A$. For the induction step consider a node u such that all its successors satisfy the property. By Condition 3 of Definition 8, there exists a rule $(\{\mathsf{lab}(u1), \ldots, \mathsf{lab}(ui)\}, \mathcal{S}) \to \{\mathsf{lab}(u)\}$ in $\mathcal{R}$ with $\mathcal{S} \subseteq \mathcal{T}$. Since this rule is not applicable to $\mathfrak{S}$, it must be the case that $\mathsf{lab}(u) \in A$, which finishes the induction proof. In particular, this means that $\mathsf{lab}(\varepsilon) = \bot \in A$.
(only if) Assume now that $\bot \in A$. We construct a derivation tree $\mathsf{lab} : t \to \Sigma$ recursively as follows. First set $\mathsf{lab}(\varepsilon) := \bot$. For each node $u \in t$ do the following. If $\mathsf{lab}(u) \in \Gamma^S$, then u is a leaf node. Otherwise, since $\mathsf{lab}(u) \in A$, there exists a rule $(B_0, \mathfrak{S}) \to \{\mathsf{lab}(u)\} \in \mathcal{R}$ with $B_0 \subseteq A$ and $\mathcal{S} \subseteq \mathcal{T}$ such that for all predecessors v of u it holds that $\mathsf{lab}(v) \notin B_0$. Let $B_0 = \{b_1, \ldots, b_n\}$. Then we add n new nodes $u_1, \ldots, u_n$ to t with $\mathsf{lab}(ui) := b_i$ for all $i, 1 \leq i \leq n$. It is easy to see that this construction yields a derivation tree for Γ. □

Based on this result, we will construct an automaton that produces derivation trees as its accepting runs. If such a run exists—i.e., if the automaton is not empty—then the axiomatized input belongs to the property.

Recall that we are interested only in consequence-based algorithms that can correctly decide a given property $\mathcal{P}$. In particular, this means that the algorithm S must terminate on all axiomatized inputs Γ. It is thus reasonable to assume that for every such axiomatized input $\Gamma = (\mathcal{I}, \mathcal{T})$, there exists a finite subset $\Sigma_\Gamma \subseteq \Sigma$ of signature symbols that contains Γ^S and $\bot$, and is closed under rule applications w.r.t. the axioms in $\mathcal{T}$. In other words, Σ_Γ is a known over-approximation of all the symbols that will be used during the execution of the consequence-based algorithm. Such a set may e.g., be known from the proof of termination. For example, many reasoning algorithms—including $S_{\mathcal{EL}}$ from our running example—satisfy the *subformula property* that states that all assertions derived during the rule applications are subformulas of the input provided; i.e., of the concepts appearing in the TBox and in the subsumption relation to be verified.

We will use the transitions from the automaton to search for the preconditions of a rule application, which correspond to the successor nodes in a derivation tree. Notice, however, that while tree automata accept only *full* k-ary trees, nodes in a derivation tree can have less than k successors. To solve this issue, we will complete the trees through a distinguished new symbol $\lozenge \notin \Sigma$, that will be used as padding for labelling all the irrelevant nodes from the input tree.

Let $\mathsf{R} : (B_0, \mathcal{S}) \rightarrow \{\sigma\} \in \mathcal{R}$ with $B_0 = \{b_1, \ldots, b_n\}, 1 \leq n \leq k$. We define the tuple $\delta_{\mathsf{R}} := (\sigma, b_1, \ldots, b_n) \times \{\Diamond\}^{k-n}$; that is, the trailing $n - k$ symbols in the tuple δ_{R} are filled with the special symbol $\Diamond$. Using these notions, we can now construct the family of automata $\mathcal{A}_S$.

Definition 11. **($\mathcal{A}_S$).** *Let $S = (\Sigma, \cdot^S, \mathcal{R}, \{\{\bot\}\})$ be a consequence-based algorithm for $\mathfrak{I}$ and $\mathfrak{T}$, and $\Gamma = (\mathcal{I}, \mathcal{T})$ be an axiomatized input. The finite tree automaton $\mathcal{A}_S(\Gamma) = (Q, \Delta, I, F)$ is defined by*

- $Q := \Sigma_\Gamma \cup \{\Diamond\}$
- $\Delta = \{\delta_{\mathsf{R}} \mid \mathsf{R} : (B_0, \mathcal{S}) \rightarrow \{\sigma\} \in \mathcal{R}, \mathcal{S} \subseteq \mathcal{T}\}$
- $I := \{\bot\}$
- $F := \Gamma^S \cup \{\Diamond\}$.

Our goal is to prove that if S is correct for the property $\mathcal{P}$, then for every axiomatized input Γ, it holds that $\Gamma \in \mathcal{P}$ iff $\mathcal{A}_S(\Gamma)$ has a successful run lab on some finite unlabelled tree with $\mathsf{lab}(\varepsilon) = \bot$. To achieve this, it would suffice to prove that the automaton is non-empty iff there exists at least one derivation tree. We will in fact provide a stronger result and show that the accepting runs of $\mathcal{A}_S(\Gamma)$ correspond exactly to the (padded) derivation trees of Γ w.r.t. S.

We start by showing that all successful runs that label the root node with $\bot$ correspond to derivation trees. Given a run $\mathsf{lab} : t \rightarrow Q$ of $\mathcal{A}_S(\Gamma)$ we define the sub-tree $t_\Sigma \subseteq t$ as the set of all nodes not labelled with $\Diamond$; in other words, $t_\Sigma := \{u \in t \mid \mathsf{lab}(u) \in \Sigma\}$. Since Δ does not have any transition with $\Diamond$ in the head, the tree t_Σ is well-defined. The labelled tree $\mathsf{lab}_\Sigma : t_\Sigma \rightarrow \Sigma$ is defined by restricting the labelling function lab to the nodes of t_Σ only. Formally, $\mathsf{lab}_\Sigma(u) = \mathsf{lab}(u)$ for all $u \in t_\Sigma$. Notice that by construction, no node in t_Σ can be labelled with the distinguished symbol $\Diamond$.

Lemma 12. *If $\mathsf{lab} : t \rightarrow Q$ is an accepting run of $\mathcal{A}_S(\Gamma)$, then $\mathsf{lab}_\Sigma : t_\Sigma \rightarrow \Sigma$ is a derivation tree for Γ w.r.t. S.*

Proof. Since $\mathsf{lab} : t \rightarrow Q$ is an accepting run, it follows that $\mathsf{lab}(\varepsilon) = \bot \in \Sigma$, and hence also $\mathsf{lab}_\Sigma(\varepsilon) = \bot$. Moreover, lab is successful. Thus, for every node $u \in t_\Sigma$, if u is a leaf, then u was also a leaf in t and thus $\mathsf{lab}_\Sigma(u) \in \Gamma^S$. If u is not a leaf, then there is a transition $(\mathsf{lab}(u), \mathsf{lab}(u1), \ldots, \mathsf{lab}(uk)) \in \Delta$. By construction, this transition is of the form $(\sigma, b_1, \ldots, b_n) \times \{\Diamond\}^{k-n}$ for some rule $(\{b_1, \ldots, b_n\}, \mathcal{S}) \rightarrow \{\sigma\} \in \mathcal{R}$ with $\mathcal{S} \subseteq \mathcal{T}$, $n \leq k$. Thus lab_Σ satisfies also the third condition from Definition 8. □

Conversely, every derivation tree can be padded to form a full tree by adding the necessary nodes labelled with $\Diamond$. If $\mathsf{lab} : t \rightarrow \Sigma$ is a derivation tree, we construct the tree $t_\Diamond$ by adding all missing nodes needed to have a full tree from t; that is, $t_\Diamond := t \cup \{uj \mid u1 \in t, 1 \leq j \leq k\}$. The labelling function $\mathsf{lab}_\Diamond : t_\Diamond \rightarrow Q$ extends lab by mapping all new nodes to $\Diamond$:

$$\mathsf{lab}_\Diamond(u) := \begin{cases} \mathsf{lab}(u) & \text{if } u \in t \\ \Diamond & \text{otherwise} \end{cases}$$

For instance, the gray nodes and edges in Fig. 2 show the padding for the derivation tree described in Example 9.

Lemma 13. *If* $\mathsf{lab} : t \to \Sigma$ *is a derivation tree for* Γ *w.r.t.* S*, then* $\mathsf{lab}_\Diamond : t_\Diamond \to Q$ *is a successful run of* $\mathcal{A}_S(\Gamma)$ *on* $t_\Diamond$ *and* $\mathsf{lab}_\Diamond(\varepsilon) = \bot \in I$.

Proof. First, since $\varepsilon \in t$, we immediately have that $\mathsf{lab}_\Diamond(\varepsilon) = \mathsf{lab}(\varepsilon) = \bot$, where the last equality follows from the first condition in Definition 8. Similarly, for every leaf node $u \in t_\Diamond$, if $u \in t$, then $\mathsf{lab}_\Diamond(u) = \mathsf{lab}(u) \in \Gamma^S$ and if $u \notin t$, then $\mathsf{lab}_\Diamond(u) = \Diamond$. In both cases, $\mathsf{lab}_\Diamond(u) \in F = \Gamma^S \cup \{\Diamond\}$. We now only need to show that for every non-leaf node u it holds that $(\mathsf{lab}_\Diamond(u), \mathsf{lab}_\Diamond(u1), \ldots, \mathsf{lab}_\Diamond(uk)) \in \Delta$. Notice first that the nodes in $t_\Diamond$ that are labelled with $\Diamond$ are all leafs. Hence, all non-leaf nodes of this extended tree existed already in the derivation tree t. Given such a non-leaf node $u \in t$, by the conditions of derivation trees, we know that there exists a rule $\mathsf{R} : (\{\mathsf{lab}(u1), \ldots, \mathsf{lab}(un)\}, \mathcal{S}) \to \{\mathsf{lab}(u)\} \in \mathcal{R}$ with $\mathcal{S} \subseteq \mathcal{T}$, and $1 \leq n \leq k$. Hence, $\delta_\mathsf{R} \in \Delta$. But

$$\begin{aligned}\delta_\mathsf{R} &:= (\mathsf{lab}(u), \mathsf{lab}(u1), \ldots, \mathsf{lab}(un)) \times \{\Diamond\}^{k-n} \\ &= (\mathsf{lab}_\Diamond(u), \mathsf{lab}_\Diamond(u1), \ldots, \mathsf{lab}_\Diamond(uk)),\end{aligned}$$

which concludes the proof. □

From these two lemmas it follows that the family of automata $\mathcal{A}_S(\Gamma)$ decides the same property as the consequence-based algorithm S.

Theorem 14. *Let* S *be a consequence-based algorithm that is correct for the property* $\mathcal{P}$*. For every axiomatized input* Γ *it holds that* $\Gamma \in \mathcal{P}$ *iff* $\mathcal{A}_S(\Gamma)$ *is non-empty.*

Recall from the last paragraph of Sect. 3 that the emptiness test iteratively constructs the set of all good states, starting from the final states, making the transition relation explicit, and at the end verifies whether an initial state is good. In the case of the automaton $\mathcal{A}_S(\Gamma)$, the final states are exactly those from Γ^S; the transition relation emulates the rules from S, and the only initial state is $\bot$ expressing that there is a clash found. Thus, the execution of the consequence-based algorithm S over the axiomatized input Γ is in fact an application of the emptiness test of the automaton $\mathcal{A}_S(\Gamma)$.

As mentioned already, the relationship between a consequence-based algorithm S and its associated family of automata $\mathcal{A}_S$ is much stronger. Rather than merely checking whether the execution of S over Γ yields the clash $\bot$, the automaton $\mathcal{A}_S(\Gamma)$ accepts all possible derivation trees. These trees can be seen as different proofs for the existence of a clash, and hence for the derivation of the properties. Notice that each of these proofs may require the presence of different axioms to trigger the rule applications. By tracing these axioms through the rule applications, it is possible to understand the axiomatic causes for this derivation, which is a fundamental task for many non-standard reasoning tasks that have been studied for many different formalisms.

5 Supplemental Reasoning

The automata $\mathcal{A}_S(\Gamma)$ can be seen as dual constructions to the axiomatic automata from [4]. Similar to that approach, associating a weight to every transition of the automaton—i.e., to every rule application of the original algorithm S—one can define the weight of every derivation tree. By extension, every axiomatized input is associated to the weight obtained from aggregating the weights of all its derivation trees. Supplemental reasoning refers to the task of computing the weight of each axiomatized input according to different interpretations.

Some of the typical examples of supplemental reasoning are axiom pinpointing [6,12,22] and MUS enumeration [7,15,18], in which the goal is to compute all the sets of axioms that entail the consequence, and its weaker version of lean kernel computation [16,17]; probabilistic logics with distribution semantics [21]; access control [3] and reasoning with meta-knowledge [9], to name a few.

An automaton that decides a property through an emptiness test can be modified into a weighted automaton [10] as described in [4] to solve these supplemental reasoning tasks through a so-called *behaviour computation* execution. Interestingly, if the weights of the automaton (which arise from the supplemental reasoning task under consideration) form a distributive lattice, then the behaviour of this automaton can be computed in polynomial time. That is, supplemental reasoning is as expensive as standard reasoning, when the underlying reasoning method is automata-based.

6 Conclusions

We have shown that reasoning with consequence-based methods can be reduced to the emptiness test of an automaton that accepts all the derivation trees of the former. In fact, the execution of a consequence-based method and the emptiness test of its associated automaton can be seen as two faces of the same process. This duality seamlessly combines the benefits of both approaches. On the one hand, we have a method that is easy to describe, implement, and optimize; and on the other, we have the complexity bounds and supplemental reasoning extensions that automata provide. As a simple application of our techniques, we obtain the first pinpointing extension of the consequence-based approach for $\mathcal{EL}$. Further similar results can be attained by instantiating our framework.

One important consideration for future work is to consider the application of non-deterministic rules in consequence-based methods. We notice, however, that tree automata can only provide deterministic complexity classes, due to their polynomial-time emptiness test. Thus, the benefits of translating non-deterministic procedures into automata are less obvious.

References

1. Baader, F., Brandt, S., Lutz, C.: Pushing the $\mathcal{EL}$ envelope. In: Proceedings of IJCAI 2005. Morgan Kaufmann, Edinburgh (2005)

2. Baader, F., Hladik, J., Peñaloza, R.: Automata can show PSPACE results for description logics. Inf. Comput. **206**(9–10), 1045–1056 (2008)
3. Baader, F., Knechtel, M., Peñaloza, R.: Context-dependent views to axioms and consequences of semantic web ontologies. J. Web Semant. **12–13**, 22–40 (2012)
4. Baader, F., Peñaloza, R.: Automata-based axiom pinpointing. J. Autom. Reason. **45**(2), 91–129 (2010)
5. Baader, F., Peñaloza, R.: Axiom pinpointing in general tableaux. J. Log. Comput. **20**(1), 5–34 (2010)
6. Baader, F., Peñaloza, R., Suntisrivaraporn, B.: Pinpointing in the description logic $\mathcal{EL}^+$. In: Hertzberg, J., Beetz, M., Englert, R. (eds.) KI 2007. LNCS (LNAI), vol. 4667, pp. 52–67. Springer, Heidelberg (2007). doi:10.1007/978-3-540-74565-5_7
7. Belov, A., Lynce, I., Marques-Silva, J.: Towards efficient MUS extraction. AI Commun. **25**(2), 97–116 (2012)
8. Davis, M., Putnam, H.: A computing procedure for quantification theory. J. ACM **7**(3), 201–215 (1960)
9. Dividino, R.Q., Schenk, S., Sizov, S., Staab, S.: Provenance, trust, explanations - and all that other meta knowledge. KI **23**(2), 24–30 (2009)
10. Droste, M., Gastin, P.: Weighted automata and weighted logics. Theoret. Comput. Sci. **380**(1–2), 69–86 (2007)
11. Gastin, P., Oddoux, D.: Fast LTL to Büchi automata translation. In: Berry, G., Comon, H., Finkel, A. (eds.) CAV 2001. LNCS, vol. 2102, pp. 53–65. Springer, Heidelberg (2001). doi:10.1007/3-540-44585-4_6
12. Kalyanpur, A., Parsia, B., Horridge, M., Sirin, E.: Finding all justifications of OWL DL entailments. In: Aberer, K., et al. (eds.) ASWC/ISWC -2007. LNCS, vol. 4825, pp. 267–280. Springer, Heidelberg (2007). doi:10.1007/978-3-540-76298-0_20
13. Kazakov, Y.: Consequence-driven reasoning for Horn SHIQ ontologies. In: Boutilier, C. (ed.) Proceedings of IJCAI 2009, pp. 2040–2045 (2009)
14. Kazakov, Y., Krötzsch, M., Simančík, F.: The incredible ELK: from polynomial procedures to efficient reasoning with $\mathcal{EL}$ ontologies. J. Autom. Reason. **53**, 1–61 (2014)
15. Kleine Büning, H., Kullmann, O.: Minimal unsatisfiability and autarkies. In: Handbook of Satisfiability, pp. 339–401 (2009)
16. Kullmann, O.: Investigations on autark assignments. Discret. Appl. Math. **107**(1–3), 99–137 (2000)
17. Kullmann, O., Lynce, I., Marques-Silva, J.: Categorisation of clauses in conjunctive normal forms: minimally unsatisfiable sub-clause-sets and the lean kernel. In: Biere, A., Gomes, C.P. (eds.) SAT 2006. LNCS, vol. 4121, pp. 22–35. Springer, Heidelberg (2006). doi:10.1007/11814948_4
18. Liffiton, M.H., Previti, A., Malik, A., Marques-Silva, J.: Fast, flexible MUS enumeration. Constraints **21**(2), 223–250 (2016)
19. Nieuwenhuis, R., Oliveras, A.: Fast congruence closure and extensions. Inf. Comput. **205**(4), 557–580 (2007)
20. Peñaloza, R.: Using sums-of-products for non-standard reasoning. In: Dediu, A.-H., Fernau, H., Martín-Vide, C. (eds.) LATA 2010. LNCS, vol. 6031, pp. 488–499. Springer, Heidelberg (2010). doi:10.1007/978-3-642-13089-2_41
21. Riguzzi, F., Bellodi, E., Lamma, E., Zese, R.: Probabilistic description logics under the distribution semantics. Semant. Web **6**(5), 477–501 (2015)
22. Schlobach, S., Cornet, R.: Non-standard reasoning services for the debugging of description logic terminologies. In: Proceedings of IJCAI 2003, pp. 355–362. Morgan Kaufmann (2003)

A Calculus of Cyber-Physical Systems

Ruggero Lanotte[1(✉)] and Massimo Merro[2]

[1] Dipartimento di Scienza e Alta Tecnologia, Università dell'Insubria, Como, Italy
ruggero.lanotte@uninsubria.it
[2] Dipartimento di Informatica, Università degli Studi di Verona, Verona, Italy
massimo.merro@univr.it

Abstract. We propose a hybrid process calculus for modelling and reasoning on *cyber-physical systems* (CPSs). The dynamics of the calculus is expressed in terms of a *labelled transition system* in the SOS style of Plotkin. This is used to define a *bisimulation-based* behavioural semantics which support compositional reasonings. Finally, we prove run-time properties and system equalities for a non-trivial case study.

Keywords: Process calculus · Cyber-physical system · Semantics

1 Introduction

Cyber-Physical Systems (CPSs) are integrations of networking and distributed computing systems with physical processes, where feedback loops allow physical processes to affect computations and vice versa. For example, in real-time control systems, a hierarchy of *sensors*, *actuators* and *control processing components* are connected to control stations. Different kinds of CPSs include supervisory control and data acquisition (SCADA), programmable logic controllers (PLC) and distributed control systems.

The *physical plant* of a CPS is often represented in the literature by means of a *discrete-time state-space model*[1] consisting of two equations of the form

$$\begin{aligned} x_{k+1} &= Ax_k + Bu_k + w_k \\ y_k &= Cx_k + e_k \end{aligned}$$

where $x_k \in \mathbb{R}^n$ is the current *(physical) state*, $u_k \in \mathbb{R}^m$ is the *input* (i.e., the control actions implemented through actuators) and $y_k \in \mathbb{R}^p$ is the *output* (i.e., the measurements from the sensors). The *uncertainty* $w_k \in \mathbb{R}^n$ and the *measurement error* $e_k \in \mathbb{R}^p$ represent perturbation and sensor noise, respectively, and A, B, and C are matrices modelling the dynamics of the physical system. The *next state* x_{k+1} depends on the current state x_k and the corresponding control actions u_k, at the sampling instant $k \in \mathbb{N}$. Note that, the state x_k cannot be directly observed: only its measurements y_k can be observed.

The physical plant is supported by a communication network through which the sensor measurements and actuator data are exchanged with the *controller(s)*, i.e., the *cyber* component, also called logics, of a CPS.

[1] See [17] for a tassonomy of the time-scale models used to represent CPSs.

F. Drewes et al. (Eds.): LATA 2017, LNCS 10168, pp. 115–127, 2017.
DOI: 10.1007/978-3-319-53733-7_8

The range of CPSs applications is rapidly increasing and already covers several domains: automotive, avionics, energy conservation, environmental monitoring, critical infrastructure control, etc. However, there is still a lack of research on the modelling and validation of CPSs through formal methodologies that might allow to model the interactions among the system components, and to verify the correctness of a CPS, as a whole, before its practical implementation. A straightforward utilisation of these techniques is for *model-checking*, i.e. to statically assess whether the current system deployment behaves as expected. However, they can also be an important aid for system planning, for instance to decide whether different deployments are behavioural equivalent.

In this paper, we propose a contribution in the area of *formal methods* for CPSs, by defining a *hybrid process calculus*, called CCPS, with a clearly-defined *behavioural semantics* for specifying and reasoning on CPSs. In CCPS, systems are represented as terms of the form $E \bowtie P$, where E denotes the *physical plant* (also called environment) of the system, containing information on state variables, actuators, sensors, evolution law, etc., while P represents the *cyber component of the system*, i.e., the *controller* that governs sensor reading and actuator writing, as well as channel-based communication with other cyber components. Thus, channels are used for logical interactions between cyber components, whereas sensors and actuators make possible the interaction between cyber and physical components. Despite this conceptual similarity, messages transmitted via channels are "consumed" upon reception, whereas actuators' states (think of a valve) remains unchanged until its controller modifies it.

CCPS is equipped with a *labelled transition semantics* (LTS) that satisfies some standard time properties such as: *time determinism*, *patience*, *maximal progress*, and *well-timedness*. Based on our LTS, we define a natural notion of *weak bisimilarity*. As a main result, we prove that our bisimilarity is a congruence and it is hence suitable for *compositional reasoning*. We are not aware of similar results in the context of CPSs. Finally, we provide a non-trivial *case study*, taken from an engineering application, and use it to illustrate our definitions and our semantic theory for CPSs. Here, we wish to remark that while we have kept the example simple, it is actually far from trivial and designed to show that various CPSs can be modelled in this style.

In this extended abstract, proofs are omitted; full details can be found in [10].

Outline. In Sect. 2, we give syntax and operational semantics of CCPS. In Sect. 3, we provide a bisimulation equivalence for CCPS, and prove its compositionality. In Sect. 4, we propose a case study, and prove for it run-time properties as well as system equalities. In Sect. 5, we discuss related and future work.

2 The Calculus

In this section, we introduce our *Calculus of Cyber-Physical Systems* CCPS. Let us start with some preliminary notations. We use $x, x_k \in \mathcal{X}$ for *state variables*; $c, d \in \mathcal{C}$ for *communication channels*, $a, a_k \in \mathcal{A}$ for *actuator devices*, and

$s, s_k \in \mathcal{S}$ for *sensors devices*. *Actuator names* are metavariables for actuator devices like *valve*, *light*, etc. Similarly, *sensor names* are metavariables for sensor devices, e.g., a sensor *thermometer* that measures, with a given precision, a state variable called *temperature*. *Values*, ranged over by $v, v' \in \mathcal{V}$, are built from basic values, such as Booleans, integers and real numbers; they also include names.

Given a generic set of names $\mathcal{N}$, we write $\mathbb{R}^{\mathcal{N}}$ to denote the set of functions assigning a real value to each name in $\mathcal{N}$. For $\xi \in \mathbb{R}^{\mathcal{N}}$, $n \in \mathcal{N}$ and $v \in \mathbb{R}$, we write $\xi[n \mapsto v]$ to denote the function $\psi \in \mathbb{R}^{\mathcal{N}}$ such that $\psi(m) = \xi(m)$, for any $m \neq n$, and $\psi(n) = v$. Given $\xi_1 \in \mathbb{R}^{\mathcal{N}_1}$ and $\xi_2 \in \mathbb{R}^{\mathcal{N}_2}$ such that $\mathcal{N}_1 \cap \mathcal{N}_2 = \emptyset$, we denote with $\xi_1 \uplus \xi_2$ the function in $\mathbb{R}^{\mathcal{N}_1 \cup \mathcal{N}_2}$ such that $(\xi_1 \uplus \xi_2)(x) = \xi_1(x)$, if $x \in \mathcal{N}_1$, and $(\xi_1 \uplus \xi_2)(x) = \xi_2(x)$, if $x \in \mathcal{N}_2$. Finally, given $\xi \in \mathbb{R}^{\mathcal{N}}$ and a set of names $\mathcal{M} \subseteq \mathcal{N}$, we write $\xi|_{\mathcal{M}}$ for the restriction of function ξ to the set $\mathcal{M}$.

In CCPS, a *cyber-physical system* consists of two components: a *physical environment* E that encloses all physical aspects of a system (state variables, physical devices, evolution law, etc.) and a *cyber component*, represented as a concurrent process P that interacts with the physical devices (sensors and actuators) of the system, and can communicate, via channels, with other processes of the same CPS or with processes of other CPSs.

We write $E \bowtie P$ to denote the resulting CPS, and use M and N to range over CPSs. Let us formally define physical environments.

Definition 1 (Physical Environment). *Let $\hat{\mathcal{X}} \subseteq \mathcal{X}$ be a set of state variables, $\hat{\mathcal{A}} \subseteq \mathcal{A}$ be a set of actuators, and $\hat{\mathcal{S}} \subseteq \mathcal{S}$ be a set of sensors. A* physical environment *E is 7-tuple $\langle \xi_x, \xi_u, \xi_w, evol, \xi_e, meas, inv \rangle$, where:*

- $\xi_x \in \mathbb{R}^{\hat{\mathcal{X}}}$ *is the* state function,
- $\xi_u \in \mathbb{R}^{\hat{\mathcal{A}}}$ *is the* actuator function,
- $\xi_w \in \mathbb{R}^{\hat{\mathcal{X}}}$ *is the* uncertainty function,
- $evol : \mathbb{R}^{\hat{\mathcal{X}}} \times \mathbb{R}^{\hat{\mathcal{A}}} \times \mathbb{R}^{\hat{\mathcal{X}}} \to 2^{\mathbb{R}^{\hat{\mathcal{X}}}}$ *is the* evolution map,
- $\xi_e \in \mathbb{R}^{\hat{\mathcal{S}}}$ *is the* sensor-error function,
- $meas : \mathbb{R}^{\hat{\mathcal{X}}} \times \mathbb{R}^{\hat{\mathcal{S}}} \to 2^{\mathbb{R}^{\hat{\mathcal{S}}}}$ *is the* measurement map,
- $inv : \mathbb{R}^{\hat{\mathcal{X}}} \to \{\mathsf{true}, \mathsf{false}\}$ *is the* invariant function.

All the functions defining an environment are total functions.

The *state function* ξ_x returns the current value (in $\mathbb{R}$) associated to each state variable of the system. The *actuator function* ξ_u returns the current value associated to each actuator. The *uncertainty function* ξ_w returns the uncertainty associated to each state variable. Thus, given a state variable $x \in \hat{\mathcal{X}}$, $\xi_w(x)$ returns the maximum distance between the real value of x and its representation in the model. Both the state function and the actuator function are supposed to change during the evolution of the system, whereas the uncertainty function is supposed to be constant.

Given a state function, an actuator function, and an uncertainty function, the *evolution map evol* returns the set of next *admissible state functions*. This function models the *evolution law* of the physical system, where changes made on actuators may reflect on state variables. Since we assume an uncertainty in our models, the evolution map does not return a single state function but a set of possible state functions. Note that we admit evolution maps that are not necessarily linear. Note also that, although the uncertainty function is constant, it can be used in the evolution map in an arbitrary way, with different weights.

The *sensor-error function* ξ_{e} returns the maximum error associated to each sensor. Again due to the presence of the sensor-error function, the *measurement map meas* returns a set of admissible measurement functions rather than a single one.

Finally, the *invariant function inv* represents the conditions that the state variables must satisfy to allow for the evolution of the system. A CPS whose state variables don't satisfy the invariant is in *deadlock*.

Let us now formalise in CCPS the cyber components of CPSs. We extend the *timed process algebra TPL* [8] with two constructs: one to read values detected at sensors, and one to write values on actuators.

Definition 2 (Processes). *Processes are defined by the grammar:*
$P, Q \ ::= \ \mathsf{nil} \ \big| \ \mathsf{idle}.P \ \big| \ P \parallel Q \ \big| \ \lfloor \pi.P \rfloor Q \ \big| \ [b]\{P\},\{Q\} \ \big| \ P\backslash c \ \big| \ X \ \big| \ \mathsf{rec}\, X.P.$

We write nil for the *terminated process*. The process $\mathsf{idle}.P$ sleeps for one time unit and then continues as P. We write $P \parallel Q$ to denote the *parallel composition* of concurrent processes P and Q. The process $\lfloor \pi.P \rfloor Q$, with $\pi \in \{\mathsf{snd}\, c\langle v\rangle, \mathsf{rcv}\, c(x), \mathsf{read}\, s(x), \mathsf{write}\, a\langle v\rangle\}$, denotes *prefixing with timeout*. Thus, $\lfloor \mathsf{snd}\, c\langle v\rangle.P \rfloor Q$ sends the value v on channel c and, after that, it continues as P; otherwise, if no communication partner is available within one time unit, it evolves into Q. The process $\lfloor \mathsf{rcv}\, c(x).P \rfloor Q$ is the obvious counterpart for channel reception. The process $\lfloor \mathsf{read}\, s(x).P \rfloor Q$ reads the value v detected by the sensor s, whereas $\lfloor \mathsf{write}\, a\langle v\rangle.P \rfloor Q$ writes the value v on the actuator a. The process $P\backslash c$ is the channel restriction operator of CCS. The process $[b]\{P\},\{Q\}$ is the standard conditional, where b is a decidable guard. For simplicity, as in CCS, we identify $[b]\{P\},\{Q\}$ with P, if b evaluates to true, and $[b]\{P\},\{Q\}$ with Q, if b evaluates to false. In processes of the form $\mathsf{idle}.Q$ and $\lfloor \pi.P \rfloor Q$, the occurrence of Q is said to be *time-guarded*. The process $\mathsf{rec}\, X.P$ denotes *time-guarded recursion* as all occurrences of the process variable X may only occur time-guarded in P.

In the two constructs $\lfloor \mathsf{rcv}\, c(x).P \rfloor Q$ and $\lfloor \mathsf{read}\, s(x).P \rfloor Q$, the variable x is said to be *bound*. Similarly, the process variable X is bound in $\mathsf{rec}\, X.P$. This gives rise to the standard notions of *free/bound (process) variables* and *α-conversion*. We identify processes up to α-conversion (similarly, we identify CPSs up to renaming of state variables, sensor names, and actuator names). A term is *closed* if it does not contain free (process) variables, and we assume to always work with closed processes: the absence of free variables is preserved at run-time. As further notation, we write $T\{^v/_x\}$ for the substitution of the variable x with the value v in any expression T of our language. Similarly, $T\{^P/_X\}$ is the substitution of the process variable X with the process P in T.

The syntax of our CPSs is slightly too permissive as a process might use sensors and/or actuators which are not defined in the physical environment.

Definition 3 (Well-formedness). *Given a process P and an environment $E = \langle \xi_{\rm x}, \xi_{\rm u}, \xi_{\rm w}, evol, \xi_{\rm e}, meas, inv \rangle$, the CPS $E \bowtie P$ is* well-formed *if: (i) for any sensor s mentioned in P, the function $\xi_{\rm e}$ is defined in s; (ii) for any actuator a mentioned in P, the function $\xi_{\rm u}$ is defined in a.*

Hereafter, we will always work with well-formed networks.

Finally, we assume a number of *notational conventions*. We write $\pi.P$ instead of $\mathsf{rec}\, X.\lfloor \pi.P \rfloor X$, when X does not occur in P. We write $\mathsf{snd}\, c$ (resp. $\mathsf{rcv}\, c$) when channel c is used for pure synchronisation. For $k \geq 0$, we write $\mathsf{idle}^k.P$ as a shorthand for $\mathsf{idle}.\mathsf{idle}.\ldots\mathsf{idle}.P$, where the prefix idle appears k consecutive times. Given $M = E \bowtie P$, we write $M \parallel Q$ for $E \bowtie (P \parallel Q)$, and $M\backslash c$ for $E \bowtie P\backslash c$.

2.1 Labelled Transition Semantics

In this section, we provide the dynamics of CCPS in terms of a *labelled transition system (LTS)* in the SOS style of Plotkin. In Definition 4, for convenience, we define some auxiliary operators on environments.

Definition 4. *Let $E = \langle \xi_{\rm x}, \xi_{\rm u}, \xi_{\rm w}, evol, \xi_{\rm e}, meas, inv \rangle$ be a physical environment.*

- $read\_sensor(E, s) = \{\xi(s) : \xi \in meas(\xi_{\rm x}, \xi_{\rm e})\}$
- $update\_act(E, a, v) = \langle \xi_{\rm x}, \xi_{\rm u}[a \mapsto v], \xi_{\rm w}, evol, \xi_{\rm e}, meas, inv \rangle$
- $next(E) = \bigcup_{\xi \in evol(\xi_{\rm x}, \xi_{\rm u}, \xi_{\rm w})} \{\langle \xi, \xi_{\rm u}, \xi_{\rm w}, evol, \xi_{\rm e}, meas, inv \rangle\}$
- $inv(E) = inv(\xi_{\rm x})$.

The operator $read\_sensor(E, s)$ returns the set of possible measurements detected by sensor s in the environment E; it returns a set of possible values rather than a single value due to the error $\xi_{\rm e}(s)$ of sensor s. $update\_act(E, a, v)$ returns the new environment in which the actuator function is updated in such a manner to associate the actuator a with the value v. $next(E)$ returns the set of the next admissible environments reachable from E, by an application of the evolution map. $inv(E)$ checks whether the state variables satisfy the invariant (here, with an abuse of notation, we overload the meaning of the function inv).

In Table 1, we provide standard transition rules for processes. Here, the meta-variable λ ranges over labels in the set $\{\mathsf{idle}, \tau, \overline{c}v, cv, a!v, s?v\}$. The symmetric counterparts of rules (Com) and (Par) are omitted.

In Table 2, we lift the transition rules from processes to systems. All rules have a common premise $inv(E)$: a CPS can evolve only if the invariant is satisfied, otherwise it is deadlocked. Here, actions, ranged over by α, are in the set $\{\tau, \overline{c}v, cv, \mathsf{idle}\}$. These actions denote: non-observable activities (τ); observable logical activities, *i.e.*, channel transmission ($\overline{c}v$ and cv); the passage of time (idle). Rules (Out) and (Inp) model transmission and reception, with an external system, on a channel c. Rule (SensRead) models the reading of the current data detected at sensor s. Rule (ActWrite) models the writing of a value v on an actuator a. Rule (Tau) lifts non-observable actions from processes to systems. A similar lifting occurs in rule (Time) for timed actions, where $next(E)$ returns

Table 1. LTS for processes

$$\text{(Outp)}\ \frac{-}{\lfloor \mathsf{snd}\, c\langle v\rangle.P\rfloor Q \xrightarrow{\overline{c}v} P} \qquad \text{(Inpp)}\ \frac{-}{\lfloor \mathsf{rcv}\, c(x).P\rfloor Q \xrightarrow{cv} P\{^v/_x\}}$$

$$\text{(Write)}\ \frac{-}{\lfloor \mathsf{write}\, a\langle v\rangle.P\rfloor Q \xrightarrow{a!v} P} \qquad \text{(Read)}\ \frac{-}{\lfloor \mathsf{read}\, s(x).P\rfloor Q \xrightarrow{s?v} P\{^v/_x\}}$$

$$\text{(Com)}\ \frac{P \xrightarrow{\overline{c}v} P' \quad Q \xrightarrow{cv} Q'}{P \parallel Q \xrightarrow{\tau} P' \parallel Q'} \qquad \text{(Par)}\ \frac{P \xrightarrow{\lambda} P' \quad \lambda \neq \mathsf{idle}}{P \parallel Q \xrightarrow{\lambda} P' \parallel Q}$$

$$\text{(ChnRes)}\ \frac{P \xrightarrow{\lambda} P' \quad \lambda \notin \{cv, \overline{c}v\}}{P\backslash c \xrightarrow{\lambda} P'\backslash c} \qquad \text{(Rec)}\ \frac{P\{^{\mathsf{rec}\, X.P}/_X\} \xrightarrow{\lambda} Q}{\mathsf{rec}\, X.P \xrightarrow{\lambda} Q}$$

$$\text{(TimeNil)}\ \frac{-}{\mathsf{nil} \xrightarrow{\mathsf{idle}} \mathsf{nil}} \qquad \text{(Delay)}\ \frac{-}{\mathsf{idle}.P \xrightarrow{\mathsf{idle}} P}$$

$$\text{(Timeout)}\ \frac{-}{\lfloor \pi.P\rfloor Q \xrightarrow{\mathsf{idle}} Q} \qquad \text{(TimePar)}\ \frac{P \xrightarrow{\mathsf{idle}} P' \quad Q \xrightarrow{\mathsf{idle}} Q' \quad P \parallel Q \not\xrightarrow{\tau}}{P \parallel Q \xrightarrow{\mathsf{idle}} P' \parallel Q'}$$

Table 2. LTS for CPSs

$$\text{(Out)}\ \frac{P \xrightarrow{\overline{c}v} P' \quad inv(E)}{E \bowtie P \xrightarrow{\overline{c}v} E \bowtie P'} \qquad \text{(Inp)}\ \frac{P \xrightarrow{cv} P' \quad inv(E)}{E \bowtie P \xrightarrow{cv} E \bowtie P'}$$

$$\text{(SensRead)}\ \frac{P \xrightarrow{s?v} P' \quad inv(E) \quad v \in read\_sensor(E, s)}{E \bowtie P \xrightarrow{\tau} E \bowtie P'}$$

$$\text{(ActWrite)}\ \frac{P \xrightarrow{a!v} P' \quad inv(E) \quad E' = update\_act(E, a, v)}{E \bowtie P \xrightarrow{\tau} E' \bowtie P'}$$

$$\text{(Tau)}\ \frac{P \xrightarrow{\tau} P' \quad inv(E)}{E \bowtie P \xrightarrow{\tau} E \bowtie P'} \qquad \text{(Time)}\ \frac{P \xrightarrow{\mathsf{idle}} P' \quad E \bowtie P \not\xrightarrow{\tau} \quad inv(E) \quad E' \in next(E)}{E \bowtie P \xrightarrow{\mathsf{idle}} E' \bowtie P'}$$

the set of possible environments for the next time slot. Thus, by an application of rule (Time) a CPS moves to the next physical state, in the next time slot.

Below, we report a few desirable time properties which hold in our calculus: (a) *time determinism*, (b) *maximal progress*, (c) *patience*, and (d) *well-timedness* (symbol $\equiv$ denotes standard *structural congruence* for timed processes [8,13]).

Theorem 5 (Time Properties). *Let $M = E \bowtie P$ an arbitrary CPS.*

(a) If $M \xrightarrow{\mathsf{idle}} \hat{E} \bowtie Q$ and $M \xrightarrow{\mathsf{idle}} \tilde{E} \bowtie R$, then $\{\hat{E}, \tilde{E}\} \subseteq next(E)$ and $Q \equiv R$.
(b) If $M \xrightarrow{\tau} M'$ then there is no M'' such that $M \xrightarrow{\mathsf{idle}} M''$.
(c) If $M \xrightarrow{\mathsf{idle}} M'$ for no M' then either $next(E) = \emptyset$ or $inv(M) = \mathsf{false}$ or there is N such that $M \xrightarrow{\tau} N$.
(d) There is k such that whenever $M \xrightarrow{\alpha_1} .. \xrightarrow{\alpha_n} N$, with $\alpha_i \neq \mathsf{idle}$, then $n \leq k$.

Well-timedness [4,13] ensures the absence of infinite instantaneous traces which would prevent the passage of time, and hence the physical evolution of a CPS. The proof of this property relies on time-guardedness of recursive processes.

3 Bisimulation

Once defined the labelled transition semantics, we are ready to define our bisimulation-based behavioural equality for CPSs. We recall that the only *observable activities* in CCPS are: time passing and channel communication. As a consequence, the capability to observe physical events depends on the capability of the cyber components to recognise those events by acting on sensors and actuators, and then signalling them using (unrestricted) channels.

We adopt a standard notation for weak transitions: we write $\Rightarrow$ for the reflexive and transitive closure of τ-actions, namely $(\xrightarrow{\tau})^*$, whereas $\xRightarrow{\alpha}$ means $\Longrightarrow\xrightarrow{\alpha}\Longrightarrow$, and finally $\xRightarrow{\hat{\alpha}}$ denotes $\Rightarrow$ if $\alpha = \tau$ and $\xRightarrow{\alpha}$ otherwise.

Definition 6 (Bisimulation). *A binary symmetric relation $\mathcal{R}$ over CPSs is a bisimulation if $M \mathrel{\mathcal{R}} N$ and $M \xrightarrow{\alpha} M'$ implies that there exists N' such that $N \xRightarrow{\hat{\alpha}} N'$ and $M' \mathrel{\mathcal{R}} N'$. We say that M and N are bisimilar, written $M \approx N$, if $M \mathrel{\mathcal{R}} N$ for some bisimulation $\mathcal{R}$.*

A main result of the paper is that our bisimilarity can be used to compare CPSs in a compositional manner. In particular, our bisimilarity is preserved by parallel composition of (non-interfering) CPSs, by parallel composition of (non-interfering) processes, and by channel restriction.

Two CPSs do not interfere with each other if they have a disjoint physical plant. Thus, let $E^i = \langle \xi_{\mathrm{x}}^i, \xi_{\mathrm{u}}^i, \xi_{\mathrm{w}}^i, evol^i, \xi_{\mathrm{e}}^i, meas^i, inv^i \rangle$ with sensors in $\hat{\mathcal{S}}_i$, actuators in $\hat{\mathcal{A}}_i$, and state variables in $\hat{\mathcal{X}}_i$, for $i \in \{1, 2\}$. If $\hat{\mathcal{S}}_1 \cap \hat{\mathcal{S}}_2 = \emptyset$ and $\hat{\mathcal{A}}_1 \cap \hat{\mathcal{A}}_2 = \emptyset$ and $\hat{\mathcal{X}}_1 \cap \hat{\mathcal{X}}_2 = \emptyset$, then we define the *disjoint union* of the environments E_1 and E_2, written $E_1 \uplus E_2$, to be the environment $\langle \xi_{\mathrm{x}}, \xi_{\mathrm{u}}, \xi_{\mathrm{w}}, evol, \xi_{\mathrm{e}}, meas, inv \rangle$ such that: $\xi_{\mathrm{x}} = \xi_{\mathrm{x}}^1 \uplus \xi_{\mathrm{x}}^2$, $\xi_{\mathrm{u}} = \xi_{\mathrm{u}}^1 \uplus \xi_{\mathrm{u}}^2$, $\xi_{\mathrm{w}} = \xi_{\mathrm{w}}^1 \uplus \xi_{\mathrm{w}}^2$, $\xi_{\mathrm{e}} = \xi_{\mathrm{e}}^1 \uplus \xi_{\mathrm{e}}^2$, and

$$\begin{aligned} evol(\xi, \psi, \phi) &= \{\xi' = \xi_1 \uplus \xi_2 \,:\, \xi_i \in evol^i(\xi|_{\hat{\mathcal{X}}_i}, \psi|_{\hat{\mathcal{A}}_i}, \phi|_{\hat{\mathcal{X}}_i}), \text{ for } i \in \{1, 2\}\} \\ meas(\xi, \psi) &= \{\xi' = \xi_1 \uplus \xi_2 \,:\, \xi_i \in meas^i(\xi|_{\hat{\mathcal{X}}_i}, \psi|_{\hat{\mathcal{S}}_i}), \text{ for } i \in \{1, 2\}\} \\ inv(\xi) &= inv^1(\xi|_{\hat{\mathcal{X}}_1}) \wedge inv^2(\xi|_{\hat{\mathcal{X}}_2}). \end{aligned}$$

Definition 7. *Let $M_i = E_i \bowtie P_i$, for $i \in \{1, 2\}$. We say that M_1 and M_2 do not interfere with each other if E_1 and E_2 have disjoint sets of state variables, sensors and actuators. In this case, we write $M_1 \uplus M_2$ to denote the CPS defined as $(E_1 \uplus E_2) \bowtie (P_1 \parallel P_2)$.*

A similar but simpler definition can be given for processes. Let $M = E \bowtie P$, a non-interfering process Q is a process which does not interfere with the plant E as it never accesses its sensors and/or actuators. Thus, in the system $M \parallel Q$ the process Q cannot interfere with the physical evolution of M. However, process Q can definitely affect the observable behaviour of the whole system by communicating on channels. Notice that, as we only consider well-formed CPSs (Definition 3), a non-interfering processes is basically a (pure) TPL process [8].

Definition 8. *A* non-interfering *process never acts on sensors and/or actuators.*

Now, everything is in place to prove the compositionality of our bisimilarity.

Theorem 9 (Congruence). *Let M and N be two CPSs.*

1. *$M \approx N$ implies $M \uplus O \approx N \uplus O$, for any non-interfering CPS O;*
2. *$M \approx N$ implies $M \parallel P \approx N \parallel P$, for any non-interfering process P;*
3. *$M \approx N$ implies $M \backslash c \approx M \backslash c$, for any channel c.*

As we will see in the next section, these compositional properties will be very useful when reasoning about complex systems.

4 Case Study

In this section, we model in CCPS an engine, called *Eng*, whose temperature is maintained within a specific range by means of a cooling system. The physical environment *Env* of the engine is constituted by: (i) a state variable *temp* containing the current temperature of the engine; (ii) an actuator *cool* to turn on/off the cooling system; (iii) a sensor s_{t} (such as a thermometer or a thermocouple) measuring the temperature of the engine; (iv) an uncertainty $\delta = 0.4$ associated to the only variable *temp*; (v) a simple evolution law that increases (resp., decreases) the value of *temp* of one degree per time unit if the cooling system is inactive (resp., active)—the evolution law is obviously affected by the uncertainty δ; (vi) an error $\epsilon = 0.1$ associated to the only sensor s_{t}; (vii) a measurement map to get the values detected by sensor s_{t}, up to its error ϵ; (viii) an invariant function saying that the system gets faulty when the temperature gets out of the range $[0, 30]$.

Formally, $Env = \langle \xi_{\mathrm{x}}, \xi_{\mathrm{u}}, \xi_{\mathrm{w}}, evol, \xi_{\mathrm{e}}, meas, inv \rangle$ with:

- $\xi_{\mathrm{x}} \in \mathbb{R}^{\{temp\}}$ and $\xi_{\mathrm{x}}(temp) = 0$;
- $\xi_{\mathrm{u}} \in \mathbb{R}^{\{cool\}}$ and $\xi_{\mathrm{u}}(cool) = \mathsf{off}$; for the sake of simplicity, we can assume ξ_{u} to be a mapping $\{cool\} \to \{\mathsf{on}, \mathsf{off}\}$ such that $\xi_{\mathrm{u}}(cool) = \mathsf{off}$ if $\xi_{\mathrm{u}}(cool) \geq 0$, and $\xi_{\mathrm{u}}(cool) = \mathsf{on}$ if $\xi_{\mathrm{u}}(cool) < 0$;
- $\xi_{\mathrm{w}} \in \mathbb{R}^{\{temp\}}$ and $\xi_{\mathrm{w}}(temp) = 0.4 = \delta$;
- $evol(\xi_{\mathrm{x}}^i, \xi_{\mathrm{u}}^i, \xi_{\mathrm{w}}) = \big\{ \xi : \xi(temp) = \xi_{\mathrm{x}}^i(temp) + heat(\xi_{\mathrm{u}}^i, cool) + \gamma \ \wedge \ \gamma \in [-\delta, +\delta] \big\}$, where $heat(\xi_{\mathrm{u}}^i, cool) = -1$ if $\xi_{\mathrm{u}}^i(cool) = \mathsf{on}$ (active cooling), and $heat(\xi_{\mathrm{u}}^i, cool) = +1$ if $\xi_{\mathrm{u}}^i(cool) = \mathsf{off}$ (inactive cooling);
- $\xi_{\mathrm{e}} \in \mathbb{R}^{\{s_{\mathrm{t}}\}}$ and $\xi_{\mathrm{e}}(s_{\mathrm{t}}) = 0.1 = \epsilon$;
- $meas(\xi_{\mathrm{x}}^i, \xi_{\mathrm{e}}) = \big\{ \xi : \xi(s_{\mathrm{t}}) \in [\xi_{\mathrm{x}}^i(temp) - \epsilon \,,\, \xi_{\mathrm{x}}^i(temp) + \epsilon] \big\}$;
- $inv(\xi_{\mathrm{x}}) = \mathsf{true}$ if $0 \leq \xi_{\mathrm{x}}(temp) \leq 30$; $inv(\xi_{\mathrm{x}}) = \mathsf{false}$, otherwise.

The cyber component of *Eng* consists of a process *Ctrl* which models the controller activity. Intuitively, process *Ctrl* senses the temperature of the engine at each time interval. When the sensed temperature is above 10, the controller activates the coolant. The cooling activity is maintained for 5 consecutive time units. After that time, if the temperature does not drop below 10 then the controller transmits its *ID* on a specific channel for signalling a *warning*, it keeps cooling for another 5 time units, and then checks again the sensed temperature; otherwise, if the sensed temperature is not above the threshold 10, the controller turns off the cooling and moves to the next time interval. Formally,[2]

$$\begin{aligned} \mathit{Ctrl} &= \mathsf{rec}\, X.\mathsf{read}\, s_t(x).[x > 10]\{\mathit{Cooling}\}, \{\mathsf{idle}.X\} \\ \mathit{Cooling} &= \mathsf{write}\; \mathit{cool}\langle \mathsf{on}\rangle.\mathsf{rec}\, Y.\mathsf{idle}^5.\mathsf{read}\, s_t(x). \\ &\quad [x > 10]\{\mathsf{snd}\; \mathit{warning}\langle \mathrm{ID}\rangle.Y\}, \{\mathsf{write}\; \mathit{cool}\langle \mathsf{off}\rangle.\mathsf{idle}.X\}. \end{aligned}$$

The whole engine is defined as: $\mathit{Eng} = \mathit{Env} \bowtie \mathit{Ctrl}$, where *Env* is the physical environment defined before.

Our operational semantics allows us to formally prove a number of *run-time properties* of our engine. For instance, the following proposition says that our engine never reaches a warning state and never deadlocks.

Proposition 10. *Let Eng be the CPS defined before. If* $\mathit{Eng} \xrightarrow{\alpha_1} \dots \xrightarrow{\alpha_n} \mathit{Eng}'$, *for some* Eng', *then* $\alpha_i \in \{\tau, \mathsf{idle}\}$, *for* $1 \le i \le n$, *and there is* Eng'' *such that* $\mathit{Eng}' \xrightarrow{\alpha} \mathit{Eng}''$, *for some* $\alpha_i \in \{\tau, \mathsf{idle}\}$.

Actually, we can be quite precise on the temperature reached by the engine before and after the cooling activity: in each of the 5 time slots of cooling, the temperature will drop of a value laying in the interval $[1-\delta, 1+\delta]$, where δ is the uncertainty of the model. Formally,

Proposition 11. *For any execution of Eng, we have:*

- *when Eng* turns on *the cooling, the value of the state variable temp ranges over* $(10-\epsilon\,,\, 11+\epsilon+\delta]$*;*
- *when Eng* turns off *the cooling, the value of the variable temp ranges over* $(10-\epsilon-5*(1+\delta)\,,\, 11+\epsilon+\delta-5*(1-\delta)]$.

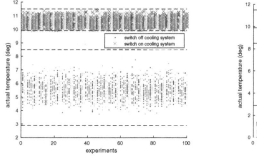

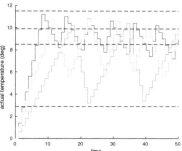

Fig. 1. Simulations in MATLAB of the engine *Eng*

In Fig. 1, the left graphic collects a campaign of 100 simulations, lasting 250 time units each, showing that the value of the state variable *temp* when the

[2] We recall that $\pi.P$ is a shorthand for $\mathsf{rec}\, X.\lfloor \pi.P \rfloor X$, when X does not occur in P.

cooling system is turned on (resp., off) lays in the interval $(9.9, 11.5]$ (resp., $(2.9, 8.5]$); these bounds are represented by the dashed horizontal lines. Since $\delta = 0.4$, these results are in line with those of Proposition 11. The right graphic shows three examples of possible evolutions of the state variable *temp*.

Now, the reader may wonder whether it is possible to design a variant of our engine which meets the same specifications with better performances. For instance, an engine consuming less coolant. Let us consider the variant: of the engine described before:

$$\overline{Eng} \;=\; \overline{Env} \bowtie Ctrl$$

where $\overline{Env}$ is the same as Env except for the evolution map, as we set $heat(\xi^i_{\mathrm{u}}, cool) = -0.8$ if $\xi^i_{\mathrm{u}}(cool) = \mathsf{on}$. This means that in $\overline{Eng}$ we reduce the power of the cooling system by 20%. In Fig. 2, we report the results of our simulations over 10000 runs lasting 10000 time units each. From this graph, $\overline{Eng}$ saves in average more than 10% of coolant with respect to *Eng*. So, the new question is: are these two engines behavioural equivalent? Do they meet the same specifications?

Our bisimilarity provides us with a precise answer to these questions.

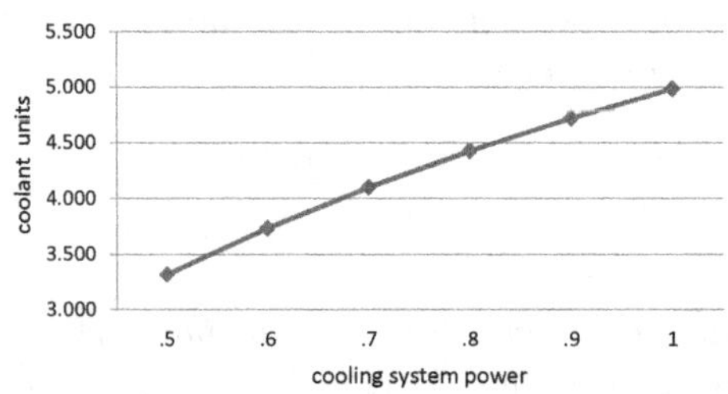

Fig. 2. Simulations in MATLAB of coolant consumption

Proposition 12. *The two variants of the engine are bisimilar:* $Eng \approx \overline{Eng}$.

At this point, one may wonder whether it is possible to improve the performances of our engine even further. For instance, by reducing the power of the cooling system by a further 10%, by setting $heat(\xi^i_{\mathrm{u}}, cool) = -0.7$ if $\xi^i_{\mathrm{u}}(cool) = \mathsf{on}$. We can formally prove that this is not the case.

Proposition 13. *Let* $\widehat{Eng}$ *be the same as Eng, except for the evolution map, in which* $heat(\xi^i_{\mathrm{u}}, cool) = -0.7$ *if* $\xi^i_{\mathrm{u}}(cool) = \mathsf{on}$. *Then,* $Eng \not\approx \widehat{Eng}$.

This is because the CPS $\widehat{Eng}$ may experience a warning, while *Eng* may not.

Finally, we show how we can use the compositionality of our behavioural semantics (Theorem 9) to deal with bigger CPSs. Suppose that *Eng* denotes the modelisation of an airplane engine. We could define in CCPS a very simple *airplane control system* that checks whether the left engine (Eng_{L}) and the right engine (Eng_{R}) are signalling warnings. The whole CPS is defined as follows:

$$Airplane \;=\; ((Eng_{\mathrm{L}} \uplus Eng_{\mathrm{R}}) \parallel Check)\backslash warning$$

where $Eng_{\mathrm{L}} = Eng\{^{\mathrm{L}}/_{\mathrm{ID}}\}\{^{temp\_l}/_{temp}\}\{^{cool\_l}/_{cool}\}\{^{s_{t\_l}}/_{s_t}\}$, and, similarly, $Eng_{\mathrm{R}} = Eng\{^{\mathrm{R}}/_{\mathrm{ID}}\}\{^{temp\_r}/_{temp}\}\{^{cool\_r}/_{cool}\}\{^{s_{t\_r}}/_{s_t}\}$, and process *Check* is defined as:

$$\begin{aligned}
Check &= \mathsf{rec}\, X.\lfloor \mathsf{rcv}\ warning(x).[x = \mathrm{L}]\{Check_1^{\mathrm{L}}\}, \{Check_1^{\mathrm{R}}\}\rfloor X \\
Check_i^{id} &= \lfloor \mathsf{rcv}\ warning(y).[y \neq id]\{\mathsf{snd}\ alarm.\mathsf{idle}.X\}, \{\mathsf{idle}.Check_{i+1}^{id}\}\rfloor\, Check_{i+1}^{id} \\
Check_5^{id} &= \lfloor \mathsf{rcv}\ warning(z).[z \neq id]\{\mathsf{snd}\ alarm.\mathsf{idle}.X\}, \{\mathsf{snd}\ failure\langle id\rangle.\mathsf{idle}.X\}\rfloor \\
&\quad\ \mathsf{snd}\ failure\langle id\rangle.X
\end{aligned}$$

for $1 \leq i \leq 5$. Intuitively, if one of the two engines is in a warning state then the process $Check_i^{id}$, for $id \in \{\mathrm{L}, \mathrm{R}\}$, checks whether also the second engine moves into a warning state, in the following 5 time intervals (i.e. during the cooling cycle). If both engines gets in a warning state then an *alarm* is sent, otherwise, if only one engine is facing a warning then the airplane control system yields a *failure* signalling which engine is not working properly.

So, since we know that $Eng \approx \overline{Eng}$, the final question becomes the following: can we safely equip our airplane with the more performant engines, $\overline{Eng_{\mathrm{L}}}$ and $\overline{Eng_{\mathrm{R}}}$, in which $heat(\xi_{\mathrm{u}}^i, cool) = -0.8$ if $\xi_{\mathrm{u}}^i(cool) = \mathsf{on}$, without affecting the whole observable behaviour of the airplane? The answer is "yes", and this result can be formally proved by applying Proposition 12 and Theorem 9.

Proposition 14. *Let* $\overline{Airplane} = ((\overline{Eng_{\mathrm{L}}} \uplus \overline{Eng_{\mathrm{R}}}) \parallel Check)\backslash warning$. *Then,* $Airplane \approx \overline{Airplane}$.

5 Related and Future Work

A number of approaches have been proposed for modelling CPSs using formal methods. For instance, *hybrid automata* [1] combine finite state transition systems with discrete variables (whose values capture the state of the modelled discrete or cyber components) and continuous variables (whose values capture the state of the modelled continuous or physical components).

Hybrid process algebras [2,5,7,15] are a powerful tool for reasoning about physical systems, and provide techniques for analysing and verifying protocols for hybrid automata. CCPS shares some similarities with the ϕ-calculus [15], a hybrid extension of the π-calculus. In the ϕ-calculus, a hybrid system is represented as a pair (E, P), where E is the environment and P is the process interacting with the environment. Unlike CCPS, in ϕ-calculus, given a system (E, P) the process P can dynamically change both the evolution law and the invariant of the system. However, the ϕ-calculus does not have a representation of physical devices and measurement law. Concerning behavioural semantics, the ϕ-calculus is equipped with a weak bisimilarity between systems that is not compositional.

In the HYPE process algebra [7], the continuous part of the system is represented by appropriate variables whose changes are determined by active influences (i.e., commands on actuators). The authors defines a *strong* bisimulation that extends the *ic-bisimulation* of [2]. Unlike ic-bisimulation, the bisimulation in HYPE is preserved by a notion of parallel composition that is slightly more permissive than ours. However, bisimilar systems in HYPE must always have the same influence. Thus, in HYPE we cannot compare CPSs sending different commands on actuators, as we do in Proposition 12.

Vigo et al. [16] proposed a calculus for wireless-based cyber-physical systems endowed with a theory to study cryptographic primitives, together with explicit notions of communication failure and unwanted communication. The calculus does not provide any notion of behavioural equivalence.

Lanese et al. [9] proposed an untimed calculus of IoT devices. The calculus does not contain any representation of the physical environment, and the bisimilarity is not preserved by parallel composition (compositionality is recovered by significantly strengthening the discriminating power of the bisimilarity).

Lanotte and Merro [11] extended and generalised the work of [9] in a timed setting by providing a bisimulation-based semantic theory that is suitable for compositional reasoning. As in [9], the physical environment is not represented.

Bodei et al. [3] proposed an untimed process calculus for IoT systems supporting a control flow analysis to track how data spread from sensors to the logics of the network, and how physical data are manipulated. Sensors and actuators are modelled as value-passing CCS channels. No behavioural equivalence is defined.

As regards future works, we believe that our paper can lay and streamline *theoretical foundations* for the development of formal and automated tools to verify CPSs before their practical implementation. To that end, we will consider applying, possibly after proper enhancements, existing tools and frameworks for automated verification, such as Maude [14] and SMC UPPAAL [6]. Finally, in [12], we developed an extended version of CCPS to provide a formal study of a variety of *cyber-physical attacks* targeting physical devices. Again, the final goal is to develop formal and automated tools to analyse security properties of CPSs.

Acknowledgements. We thank Riccardo Muradore for providing us with simulations in MATLAB of our case study. We thank the anonymous reviewers for valuable comments.

References

1. Alur, R., Courcoubetis, C., Henzinger, T.A., Ho, P.-H.: Hybrid automata: an algorithmic approach to the specification and verification of hybrid systems. In: Grossman, R.L., Nerode, A., Ravn, A.P., Rischel, H. (eds.) HS 1991-1992. LNCS, vol. 736, pp. 209–229. Springer, Heidelberg (1993). doi:10.1007/3-540-57318-6_30
2. Bergstra, J.A., Middleburg, C.A.: Process algebra for hybrid systems. TCS **335**(2–3), 215–280 (2005)
3. Bodei, C., Degano, P., Ferrari, G.-L., Galletta, L.: Where do your iot ingredients come from? In: Lluch Lafuente, A., Proença, J. (eds.) COORDINATION 2016. LNCS, vol. 9686, pp. 35–50. Springer, Heidelberg (2016). doi:10.1007/978-3-319-39519-7_3
4. Cerone, A., Hennessy, M., Merro, M.: Modelling MAC-layer communications in wireless systems. Logical Meth. Comput. Sci. **11**(1:18), 1–59 (2015)
5. Cuijpers, P., Reniers, M.: Hybrid process algebra. JLAP **62**(2), 191–245 (2005)

6. David, A., Larsen, K.G., Legay, A., Mikučionis, M., Wang, Z.: Time for statistical model checking of real-time systems. In: Gopalakrishnan, G., Qadeer, S. (eds.) CAV 2011. LNCS, vol. 6806, pp. 349–355. Springer, Heidelberg (2011). doi:10.1007/978-3-642-22110-1_27
7. Galpin, V., Bortolussi, L., Hillston, J.: HYPE: hybrid modelling by composition of flows. Formal Aspects Comput. **25**(4), 503–541 (2013)
8. Hennessy, M., Regan, T.: A process algebra for timed systems. I&C **117**(2), 221–239 (1995)
9. Lanese, I., Bedogni, L., Di Felice, M.: Internet of things: a process calculus approach. In: Shin, S., Maldonado, J. (eds.) ACM SAC 2013, pp. 1339–1346. ACM (2013)
10. Lanotte, R., Merro, M.: A calculus of cyber-physical systems. CoRR abs/1612.00484 (2016)
11. Lanotte, R., Merro, M.: A semantic theory of the internet of things. In: Lluch Lafuente, A., Proença, J. (eds.) COORDINATION 2016. LNCS, vol. 9686, pp. 157–174. Springer, Heidelberg (2016). doi:10.1007/978-3-319-39519-7_10
12. Lanotte, R., Merro, M., Muradore, R., Viganò, L.: A formal approach to cyber-physical attacks. CoRR abs/1611.01377 (2016)
13. Merro, M., Ballardin, F., Sibilio, E.: A timed calculus for wireless systems. TCS **412**(47), 6585–6611 (2011)
14. Ölveczky, P.C., Meseguer, J.: Semantics and pragmatics of real-time maude. High.-Order Symb. Comput. **20**(1–2), 161–196 (2007)
15. Rounds, W.C., Song, H.: The ϕ-calculus: a language for distributed control of reconfigurable embedded systems. In: Maler, O., Pnueli, A. (eds.) HSCC 2003. LNCS, vol. 2623, pp. 435–449. Springer, Heidelberg (2003). doi:10.1007/3-540-36580-X_32
16. Vigo, R., Nielson, F., Nielson, H.R.: Broadcast, denial-of-service, and secure communication. In: Johnsen, E.B., Petre, L. (eds.) IFM 2013. LNCS, vol. 7940, pp. 412–427. Springer, Heidelberg (2013). doi:10.1007/978-3-642-38613-8_28
17. Zacchia Lun, Y., D'Innocenzo, A., Malavolta, I., Di Benedetto, M.D.: Cyber-physical systems security: a systematic mapping study. CoRR abs/1605.09641 (2016)

Combinatorics on Words, Compression, and Pattern Matching

Efficient Pattern Matching in Elastic-Degenerate Texts

Costas S. Iliopoulos, Ritu Kundu(✉), and Solon P. Pissis

Department of Informatics, King's College London, London WC2R 2LS, UK
{costas.iliopoulos,ritu.kundu,solon.pissis}@kcl.ac.uk

Abstract. Motivated by applications in bioinformatics, in what follows, we extend the notion of gapped strings to *elastic-degenerate strings*. An elastic-degenerate string can been seen as an ordered collection of solid (standard) strings interleaved by *elastic-degenerate symbols*; each such symbol corresponds to a set of two or more variable-length solid strings. In this article, we present an algorithm for solving the pattern matching problem with a solid pattern and an elastic-degenerate text running in $\mathcal{O}(N + \alpha\gamma mn)$ time; where m is the length of the pattern; n and N are the length and total size of the elastic-degenerate text, respectively; α and γ are parameters, respectively representing the maximum number of strings in any elastic-degenerate symbol of the text and the maximum number of elastic-degenerate symbols spanned by any occurrence of the pattern in the text. The space used by the proposed algorithm is $\mathcal{O}(N)$.

Keywords: String processing algorithms · Degenerate strings · Indeterminate strings · Elastic-degenerate strings · Gapped strings

1 Introduction

Uncertainty in sequential data (strings) can be characterised using various representations. One such representation is a *degenerate string*, which is defined by the existence of one or more positions that are represented by sets of symbols from an alphabet Σ, unlike a solid (or deterministic, standard) string characterised by a single symbol at each position. For instance, $\begin{bmatrix}\texttt{a}\\\texttt{b}\end{bmatrix}\texttt{ac}\begin{bmatrix}\texttt{b}\\\texttt{c}\end{bmatrix}\texttt{a}\begin{bmatrix}\texttt{a}\\\texttt{b}\\\texttt{c}\end{bmatrix}$ is a degenerate string of length 6 over $\Sigma = \{\texttt{a,b,c}\}$; and abaababa is a solid string of length 8 over $\Sigma = \{\texttt{a,b}\}$. When a string is solid, we simply refer to it as string.

A *gapped string* is another way to capture uncertainty: it is an ordered collection of standard strings separated by variable-length gaps defined by an ordered collection of intervals [4]. Simply, a gapped string P can be represented as follows [15]: $P = P_1 *^{a_1,b_1} P_2 *^{a_2,b_2} P_3 \cdots *^{a_{\ell-1},b_{\ell-1}} P_\ell$, where $*$ is a *wildcard* symbol (also called *don't care* symbol or *hole*) that matches any symbol in alphabet Σ; $\forall i \in [1,\ell]$ each P_i is a string over Σ; and $\forall i \in [1,\ell-1]$ each pair (a_i, b_i) represents the gap (minimum and maximum number of wildcard symbols, respectively) between two consecutive strings P_i and P_{i+1}.

This work was partially supported by the British Council funded INSPIRE Project.

F. Drewes et al. (Eds.): LATA 2017, LNCS 10168, pp. 131–142, 2017.
DOI: 10.1007/978-3-319-53733-7_9

Here we introduce another representation to encapsulate uncertainty in sequential data—which we call *elastic-degenerate strings*—by extending and combining the ideas of gapped strings and degenerate strings. An *elastic-degenerate string* is a string such that an *elastic-degenerate symbol* can occur at one or more positions; each such symbol corresponds to a set of two or more variable-length strings. Another way to visualise an elastic-degenerate string is to see it as an ordered collection of $k > 1$ strings interleaved by $k - 1$ elastic-degenerate symbols. For instance, $\texttt{bc} \begin{bmatrix} \texttt{ab} \\ \texttt{aab} \\ \texttt{aca} \end{bmatrix} \texttt{ca} \begin{bmatrix} \texttt{abcab} \\ \texttt{cba} \end{bmatrix} \texttt{bb}$ is an example of an elastic-degenerate string over $\Sigma = \{\texttt{a},\texttt{b},\texttt{c}\}$.

This generalisation of the concept of *degeneracy* is motivated by several data mining problems [10] which can be reduced to the core task of discovering occurrences of one or more patterns in a text that can best be described as an ordered collection of strings interleaved by sets of variable-length strings.

More specifically, in genomics an important class of problems is to study within-species genetic variation; state-of-the-art solutions for this class comprises of matching (*mapping*) short strings (called *reads*) to a longer genomic sequence (canonical *reference genome* obtained through assembly). Owing to the high diversity among biologically relevant genomic regions in many organisms, the population level complexities cannot be captured by the linear structure of a reference genome (see [11]). Consequently, the recent research trend has shifted towards using alternative representations of genomic sequence for population-based genome assembly [2,5,8,12]. One such representation that encodes a set of related genomes with variations in the reference genome itself (called Population Reference Genome in [12]), can be seen as an elastic-degenerate string.

The problem of pattern matching and discovery in the context of gapped strings has been studied extensively using combinatorial approaches (see [14] and references therein). However, a gapped string, which specifies the constraint on only the length of the gap between two consecutive strings P_i and P_{i+1}, differs from an elastic-degenerate string because the later precisely defines the possible strings (of varying lengths) that can exist between P_i and P_{i+1}. This precise identification of allowed strings in a gap makes the matching problem, in the context of elastic-degenerate strings, algorithmically more challenging.

In this article, we not only formalise the concept of elastic-degenerate strings but also present an efficient—in terms of both time and space—algorithm to solve the pattern matching problem in a given elastic-degenerate text. To the best of our knowledge, no other work, heretofore, explores the problem accounting for *elastic-degeneracy* in the text. In the next section, we introduce the basic definitions and establish the notions of elastic-degeneracy that will be used throughout. The algorithmic tools required to build the solution are described in Sect. 3. In Sect. 4, we formally define the problem along with presenting the algorithm. The algorithm is analysed in Sect. 5. Finally, the article is concluded in Sect. 6 with some remarks and future proposals.

2 Terminology and Technical Background

We begin with basic definitions and notation. We think of a *string* X of *length* $n = |X|$ as an array $X[1\,..\,n]$, where every $X[i]$, $1 \le i \le n$, is a *symbol* drawn from some fixed *alphabet* Σ of size $|\Sigma| = \mathcal{O}(1)$. The *empty string* of length 0 is denoted by ε. Σ^* denotes the set of all strings over alphabet Σ including the empty string ε. A string Y is a *factor* of a string X if there exist two strings U and V, such that $X = UYV$. We say that there is an *occurrence* of Y in X, or simply, that Y *occurs* in X, when Y is a factor of X. The starting position of an occurrence, say i, is called *head* of the occurrence and its ending position $i + |Y| - 1$ is called *tail* of the occurrence. Note that an empty string occurs at each position in a given string. Consider the strings X, Y, U, and V, such that $X = UYV$. If $U = \varepsilon$, then Y is a *prefix* of X. If $V = \varepsilon$, then Y is a *suffix* of X.

A *degenerate symbol* $\tilde{\sigma}$ over an alphabet Σ is a non-empty subset of Σ, i.e., $\tilde{\sigma} \subseteq \Sigma$ and $\tilde{\sigma} \neq \emptyset$. $|\tilde{\sigma}|$ denotes the size of the set and we have $1 \le |\tilde{\sigma}| \le |\Sigma|$. A *degenerate string* is built over the potential $2^{|\Sigma|} - 1$ non-empty subsets of symbols of Σ. In other words, a degenerate string $\tilde{X} = \tilde{X}[1\,..\,n]$ is a string such that every $\tilde{X}[i]$ is a degenerate symbol, $1 \le i \le n$. If $|\tilde{x}[i]| = 1$, that is, $\tilde{X}[i]$ represents a single symbol of Σ, we say that $\tilde{X}[i]$ is a *solid* symbol and i is a *solid position*. Otherwise $\tilde{X}[i]$ and i are said to be a *non-solid symbol* and a *non-solid position*, respectively. For example, $\begin{bmatrix}\mathtt{a}\\\mathtt{b}\end{bmatrix}\mathtt{ac}\begin{bmatrix}\mathtt{b}\\\mathtt{c}\end{bmatrix}\mathtt{a}\begin{bmatrix}\mathtt{a}\\\mathtt{b}\\\mathtt{c}\end{bmatrix}$ is a degenerate string of length 6 over $\Sigma = \{\mathtt{a},\ \mathtt{b},\ \mathtt{c}\}$. A string consisting of only solid symbols is called a *solid string* or, simply, a string.

Now we give the terminology to build the concept of elastic-degeneracy by presenting the following definitions and examples.

Definition 1 (Seed: S). *A seed S is a (possibly empty) string over Σ.*

Definition 2 (Elastic-Degenerate Symbol: ξ). *An elastic-degenerate symbol ξ, over a given alphabet Σ, is a set of two or more strings over Σ (i.e. $\xi \subseteq \Sigma^*$ and $|\xi| > 1$). An elastic-degenerate symbol ξ is denoted by $\begin{bmatrix}E_1\\E_2\\\vdots\\E_{|\xi|}\end{bmatrix}$, where each E_i, $1 \le i \le |\xi|$, is a solid string. The minimum (resp. maximum) length in ξ, denoted by $|\xi|_{min}$ (resp. $|\xi|_{max}$), is the length of the shortest (resp. longest) string in the set.*

Definition 3 (Elastic-Degenerate String: $\hat{X}$). *An elastic-degenerate string $\hat{X}$, over a given alphabet Σ, is a sequence $S_1\xi_1S_2\xi_2S_3\dots S_{k-1}\xi_{k-1}S_k$, where S_i, $1 \le i \le k$, is a seed and ξ_i, $1 \le i \le k-1$ is an elastic-degenerate symbol.*

An elastic degenerate string $\hat{X}$ can be visualised as follows:

$$\hat{X} = S_1 \begin{bmatrix}E_{1,1}\\E_{1,2}\\\vdots\\E_{1,|\xi_1|}\end{bmatrix} S_2 \begin{bmatrix}E_{2,1}\\E_{2,2}\\\vdots\\E_{2,|\xi_2|}\end{bmatrix} S_3\dots S_{k-1} \begin{bmatrix}E_{k-1,1}\\E_{k-1,2}\\\vdots\\E_{k-1,|\xi_{k-1}|}\end{bmatrix} S_k.$$

Example 1. $\hat{X} = \texttt{abbc} \begin{bmatrix} ab \\ aab \\ acca \end{bmatrix} \texttt{cca} \begin{bmatrix} aabcab \\ cba \end{bmatrix} \texttt{bb}$ *is an elastic-degenerate string, where we have the following:*

- *Three seeds:* $S_1 = \texttt{abbc}$, $S_2 = \texttt{cca}$, *and* $S_3 = \texttt{bb}$.
- *Two elastic-degenerate symbols:*
  $\xi_1 = \begin{bmatrix} ab \\ aab \\ acca \end{bmatrix}$ *and* $\xi_2 = \begin{bmatrix} aabcab \\ cba \end{bmatrix}$.
- *For* ξ_1*:* $E_{1,1} = \texttt{ab}$, $E_{1,2} = \texttt{aab}$, $E_{1,3} = \texttt{acca}$*; minimum length is* 2 *(length of* $E_{1,1}$*); and maximum length is* 4 *(length of* $E_{1,3}$*).*
- *For* ξ_2*:* $E_{2,1} = \texttt{aabcab}$, $E_{2,2} = \texttt{cba}$*; minimum length is* 3 *(length of* $E_{2,2}$*); and maximum length is* 6 *(length of* $E_{2,1}$*).*

Observe the use of $\hat{X}$ to distinguish an elastic-degenerate string from a solid string X or a degenerate string $\tilde{X}$. In the following, we define three characteristics of a given elastic-degenerate string $\hat{X}$ with k seeds.

Definition 4 (Total Size: $\|\hat{X}\|$). *The total size of* $\hat{X}$*, denoted by* $\|\hat{X}\|$*, is defined as the sum of the total length of its seeds and the total length of all the strings in each of its elastic-degenerate symbols:* $\|\hat{X}\| = \sum_{i=1}^{k} |S_i| + \sum_{i=1}^{k-1} \sum_{j=1}^{|\xi_i|} |E_{i,j}|$.

Definition 5 (Length: $|\hat{X}|$). *The length of* $\hat{X}$*, denoted by* $|\hat{X}|$*, is defined as the sum of the total length of its seeds and the total number of its elastic-degenerate symbols:* $|\hat{X}| = \sum_{i=1}^{k} |S_i| + k - 1$.

Informally, the total number of positions in $\hat{X}$ is its length considering an elastic-degenerate symbol to occupy only one position. Intuitively, a position belonging to some seed will be called *solid position* and that of an elastic-degenerate symbol will be called *elastic-degenerate position.* In the running example, the total length of the seeds is 9; hence, $\|\hat{X}\| = 9+(2+3+4)+(6+3) = 27$, while $|\hat{X}| = 9 + 2 = 11$. The first a occurs at (solid) position 1, followed by b at (solid) position 2 and so on; $\xi_1$and ξ_2 are at (elastic-degenerate positions) 5 and 9, respectively; the last b is at (solid) position 11.

Definition 6 (Possibility-Set: $\Re$). *For the elastic-degenerate string* $\hat{X} = S_1\xi_1S_2\xi_2S_3 \ldots S_{k-1}\xi_{k-1}S_k$*, its possibility-set* $\Re$ *is defined as*

$$\Re = \{S_1E_{1,r_1}S_2E_{2,r_2} \ldots E_{k-1,r_{k-1}}S_k\} \ \forall r_i, 1 \le i \le k-1 \text{ such that } 1 \le r_i \le |\xi_i|.$$

Informally, the *possibility-set* $\Re$ of $\hat{X}$ is the set of all possible solid strings obtained from $\hat{X}$. A solid string can be obtained by replacing each of the elastic-degenerate symbols with one of its constituent strings. In the running example, $\Re =$ {abbc<u>ab</u>cca<u>aabcab</u>bb, abbc<u>ab</u>cca<u>cba</u>bb, abbc<u>aab</u>cca<u>aabcab</u>bb, abb<u>aab</u>cca<u>cba</u>bb, abbc<u>acca</u>cca<u>aabcab</u>bb, abbc<u>acca</u>cca<u>cba</u>bb}. Note that constituent strings replacing the elastic-degenerate symbols have been underlined for clarity.

We are now in a position to define *matching* and *occurrence* in the context of elastic-degenerate strings.

Definition 7 (Matching). *An elastic-degenerate string $\hat{X}$ with k seeds and a solid string Y are said to match, denoted by $\hat{X} \simeq Y$, if, and only if, there exists a solid string $S = S_1 E_{1,r_1} S_2 E_{2,r_2} \ldots E_{k-1,r_{k-1}} S_k, 1 \le r_i \le |\xi_i|$, obtained from $\hat{X}$ (i.e. $S \in \Re$ of $\hat{X}$), such that $S = UYV$, where $U, V \in \Sigma^*$, satisfying:*

$$\begin{cases} U = \varepsilon,\ V = \varepsilon & \text{if } S_1 \neq \varepsilon,\ S_k \neq \varepsilon \\ E_{1,r_1} \neq \varepsilon,\ V = \varepsilon,\ U \text{ is either empty or a prefix of } E_{1,r_1} & \text{if } S_1 = \varepsilon,\ S_k \neq \varepsilon \\ E_{k-1,r_{k-1}} \neq \varepsilon,\ U = \varepsilon,\ V \text{ is either empty or a suffix of } E_{k-1,r_{k-1}} & \text{if } S_1 \neq \varepsilon,\ S_k = \varepsilon \\ E_{1,r_1} \neq \varepsilon,\ U \text{ is either empty or a prefix of } E_{1,r_1}, & \\ \quad E_{k-1,r_{k-1}} \neq \varepsilon,\ V \text{ is either empty or a suffix of } E_{k-1,r_{k-1}} & \text{if } S_1 = \varepsilon,\ S_k = \varepsilon. \end{cases}$$

Informally, we say that $\hat{X}$ and Y match such that Y starts at the first position of $\hat{X}$ if the position is solid or as a suffix of one of its non-empty strings if it is elastic-degenerate; and Y ends at the last position of $\hat{X}$ if the position is solid or as a prefix of one of its non-empty strings if it is elastic-degenerate.

Example 2. *Consider $\hat{X}$ as given in Example 1. For string $Y =$ abbcabccacbabb we have that $\hat{X} \simeq Y$.*

Definition 8 (Occurrence). *In an elastic-degenerate string (text) $\hat{T}$, a solid string (pattern) P is said to have an occurrence starting and ending at positions i and j respectively, if $P \simeq \hat{T}[i\,..\,j]$. An occurrence is represented as the pair of starting position i (head) and ending position j (tail).*

For consistency with the intuitive meaning of an occurrence, we say that P occurs at the position of some elastic-degenerate symbol (say ξ_i) of $\hat{T}$, if it is a factor of any of the constituent strings of ξ_i.

Example 3. *Consider a pattern $P =$ cabbcb and a text $\hat{T}$ as follows:*

$$aacabbcbbc \begin{bmatrix} a \\ aab \\ acca \end{bmatrix} bb \begin{bmatrix} c \\ acabbcbb \\ cba \end{bmatrix} bacabbc \begin{bmatrix} b \\ cabb \\ bbc \\ aacabb \end{bmatrix} cbc.$$

All the occurrences of P in $\hat{T}$ are given below.

Occurrence:	(3, 8)	(10,15)	(11,14)	(11,15)	(14,14)	(17,22)	(22,24)
Strings chosen:	-	ξ_1: a ξ_2: c	ξ_1: acca ξ_2: cba	ξ_1: acca ξ_2: c	ξ_2: acabbcbb	ξ_3: b or ξ_3: bbc	ξ_3: cabb or ξ_3: aacabb

Note that more than one occurrence of P can start at the same starting position but their ending positions are different: for instance, $(11, 14)$ and $(11, 15)$ in Example 3. Also, note that different strings in the same elastic-degenerate symbols can lead to the same occurrence: for instance, the same pair of head and tail as happened for occurrences $(17, 22)$ and $(22, 24)$ in Example 3.

Example 4. *Here, we illustrate the case, where an elastic-degenerate string has the empty string as a seed. Consider a pattern $P =$ babbcb and a text $\hat{T}$ as follows:*

$$\hat{T} = ab \begin{bmatrix} bcab \\ abb \end{bmatrix} \begin{bmatrix} ab \\ cbb \\ abc \end{bmatrix} cca \begin{bmatrix} bb \\ cb \end{bmatrix} ca.$$

There is an occurrence of P at $(2, 4)$ of $\hat{T}$.

3 Algorithmic Tools

In this section, we briefly introduce a fundamental data structure, which supports a wide variety of string matching operations, and a well-known pattern matching algorithm. Both the data structure and the pattern matching algorithm will be used extensively by the proposed algorithm.

Suffix Tree

The *suffix tree* $\mathbb{S}(X)$ of a non-empty string X of length n is a compact trie representing all the suffixes of X such that $\mathbb{S}(X)$ has n leaves labelled from 1 to n. Additionally, each edge is labelled with a symbol of Σ. For any $i, 1 \leq i \leq n$, the concatenation of the edge labels on the path from the root of $\mathbb{S}(X)$ to leaf i is precisely the suffix $X[i \mathinner{..} n]$. For any two suffixes $U = X[i \mathinner{..} n]$ and $V = X[j \mathinner{..} n]$ of X, if W is the *longest common prefix* (LCP) of U and V, then the path in $\mathbb{S}(X)$ corresponding to W is the same for U and V. In other words, the depth of the *least common ancestor* (LCA) of the two leaves is the same as the length of the LCP of the suffixes represented by those leaves. For a general introduction to suffix trees, see [3].

The construction of the suffix tree $\mathbb{S}(X)$ for string X of length n over a fixed-sized alphabet takes $\mathcal{O}(n)$ time and space using one of the algorithms in [13,17,18]. Once the suffix tree of X has been constructed, it can be used to support queries that return all *Occ* occurrences of a given string (called pattern) of length m in time $\mathcal{O}(m + Occ)$. In addition, the LCA of any two leaves of $\mathbb{S}(X)$, thus the length of the LCP of any two suffixes of X, can be computed in constant time after a linear-time pre-processing [7,16]. A *generalised suffix tree* is a suffix tree for a set of strings [1,6].

KMP Algorithm and Failure Function

Knuth, Morris, and Pratt (KMP) introduced a linear-time algorithm for pattern matching in [9]; that is, an algorithm for finding all occurrences of a pattern P in a text T. The KMP algorithm follows the Naïve approach for this problem, that is, it slides P across T. Additionally, it pre-processes P by computing a *failure function* f that indicates the maximum possible shift using previously performed symbol comparisons. Specifically, the *failure function* $f(i)$ is defined as the length of the longest prefix of P that is a suffix of $P[1 \mathinner{..} i]$. By using the failure function, it achieves an optimal search time of $\mathcal{O}(n)$ after $\mathcal{O}(m)$-time pre-processing, where n is the length of T and $m < n$ is the length of P.

4 Algorithm for Pattern Matching in Elastic-Degenerate Texts

4.1 Problem Definition

Problem. PATTERN MATCHING IN ELASTIC-DEGENERATE TEXTS
Input: *An elastic-degenerate text* $\hat{T} = S_1\xi_1S_2\ldots\xi_{k-1}S_k$ *of length* n *and total size* N*, a pattern* P *of length* $m < N$.
Output: *All the occurrences of* P *in* $\hat{T}$.

By definition, all the occurrences of the pattern P in the text $\hat{T}$ fall under the following cases:

1. P entirely lies in some seed.
2. P entirely lies in some string of an elastic-degenerate symbol.
3. P spans across one or more elastic-degenerate symbols. This can further be seen as:
   (a) P starts in some seed.
   (b) P starts in some string of an elastic-degenerate symbol.

For instance, consider Example 3: the occurrences $(3, 8)$ and $(14, 14)$ fall into Case 1 and Case 2, respectively; $(10, 15)$ and $(17, 22)$ fall into Case $3(a)$; $(11, 14)$, $(11, 15)$, and $(22, 24)$ fall into Case $3(b)$.

4.2 Algorithm

Note that a naïve solution to this problem would be to find the pattern occurrences in the possibility-set $\Re$ of $\hat{T}$ using the KMP algorithm; this time is exponential in the number of elastic-degenerate symbols. In this section, we present an efficient algorithm that makes use of the KMP algorithm and the suffix tree data structure. Clearly, the KMP algorithm can easily report the occurrences corresponding to the Cases 1 and 2. Case 3 requires some additional processing and data structures. The algorithm works in two stages, outlined below.

Stage 1: Pre-processing. Pre-process the pattern P to compute its failure-function as required by the KMP algorithm. In addition, create the generalised suffix tree $\mathbb{S}_S$ for the set $\{P, S_1, S_2, \ldots, S_k\}$ of strings corresponding to all the seeds of $\hat{T}$, as well as the generalised suffix tree $\mathbb{S}_\xi$ for the set $\{P\} \cup \xi_1 \cup \xi_2 \cup \ldots \cup \xi_{k-1}$ of strings corresponding to all the strings in each of the elastic-degenerate symbols of $\hat{T}$. Furthermore, pre-process these two suffix trees so as to answer LCA queries in constant time.

Stage 2: Search. Start searching the pattern P in the text $\hat{T}$ using the KMP algorithm, comparing the symbols and using the failure function to shift the pattern on a mismatch. The starting position of an occurrence being tested may be either solid or elastic-degenerate; we call the two types of occurrences as *Type* 1 and *Type* 2, respectively. We consider the two types separately as follows.

Type 1: Solid Starting Position. Consider a situation when an occurrence starting from a position (say *pos*) that lies in some seed S_i is being tested. Proceed normally comparing the corresponding symbols of P and S_i; and shifting the pattern using failure function on a mismatch. As soon as the elastic-degenerate symbol ξ_i is encountered (suppose corresponding position in the pattern is p), abort the KMP algorithm (for this test). Check each of the strings of ξ_i (i.e. $E_{i,j}$) whether or not it occurs in the pattern at position p, using LCA queries on $\mathbb{S}_\xi$, and *tick* (mark) the tails of the found occurrences. This can be realised by maintaining a Boolean array of size m, which we denote by $\mathbb{T}_i$.

Next, Procedure 1 (given formally below) is executed. Each ticked position of $\mathbb{T}_i$ is tried to extend by testing whether S_{i+1} occurs adjacent to it (using LCA queries on $\mathbb{S}_S$). For each such found occurrence of S_{i+1}, occurrences of strings of ξ_{i+1} are checked using the suffix tree $\mathbb{S}_\xi$ and their tails are ticked in $\mathbb{T}_{i+1}$. The procedure will then be repeated for $\mathbb{T}_{i+1}$; this continues recursively until there is no tail marked in some call.

Once the process ends (reporting all the occurrences of P starting from *pos*, if any), the failure function corresponding to the position where the KMP algorithm was aborted (i.e. p) is used to shift the pattern and the KMP algorithm resumes. It is to be noted that an occurrence of P is implied if the length returned by the LCA query between the pattern starting from some ticked-tail t and either of the following hits the boundary of the pattern:

- some seed S_i;
- any string $E_{i,j}$ of some elastic-degenerate symbol ξ_i.

Figure 1 elucidates the description given above.

Procedure 1. Procedure to extend ticked tails in a given $\mathbb{T}_i$ and reporting the occurrences found, if any.

```
Extend(T_i)
input  : A boolean array T_i of size m indicating ticked tails to be extended.
output: Reporting the found occurrences and preparing T_{i+1} for the next recursive call.
  isNonEmpty ← false;
  forall indices t of T_i which are ticked do
      l_s ← | LCA(P[t+1..m], S_{i+1}[1..|S_{i+1}|]) |;
      if (l_s + t) == m then                                        // Pattern ends
          Report the occurrence;
      else if l_s = |S_{i+1}| then                                  // S_{i+1} occurs here
          e ← t + |S_{i+1}|;
          forall E_{i+1,j} in ξ_{i+1} do
              l_e ← | LCA(P[e+1..m], E_{i+1,j}[1..|E_{i+1,j}|]) |;
              if (l_e + e) == m then                                // Pattern ends
                  Report the occurrence (if not reported already);
              else if l_e = |E_{i+1,j}| then                        // E_{i+1,j} occurs here
                  Mark e + |E_{i+1,j}| − 1 in T_{i+1};
                  isNonEmpty ← true;
  if isNonEmpty then
      Extend(T_{i+1});
```

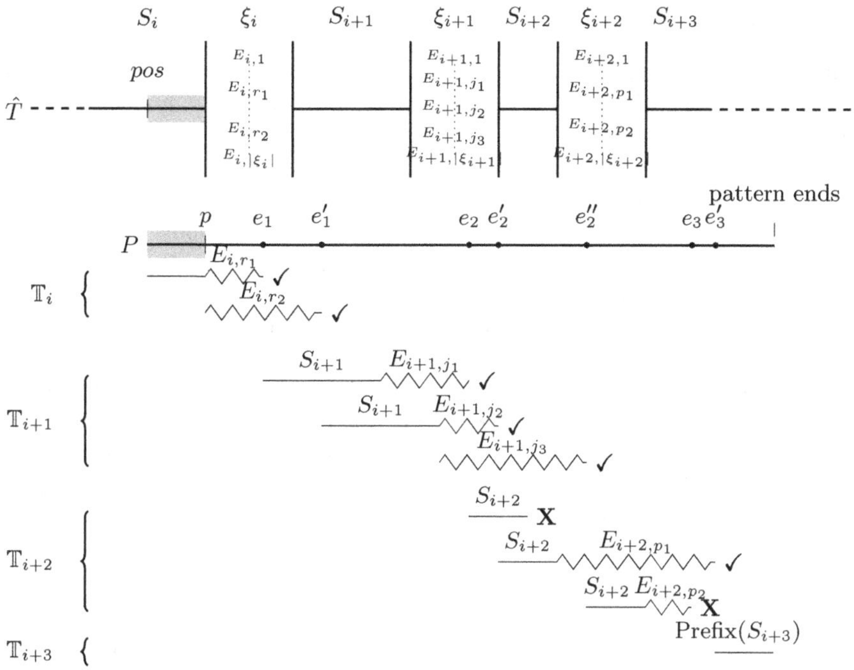

Fig. 1. An illustration of how the algorithm works for Type 1 occurrences. Strings in elastic-degenerate symbols are shown as zigzag, while solid lines depict the seeds. Symbol **X** denotes that this path could not be extended further while the symbol ✓ represents a ticked tail.

Type 2: Elastic-Degenerate Starting Position. Consider a situation when the starting position of an occurrence to be tested is an elastic-degenerate symbol ξ_i. This case can be processed in a similar fashion as the one described for Type 1, with the only difference being the manner in which tails are ticked initially.

Begin by applying the KMP algorithm for each $E_{i,j}$ to achieve two purposes: finding the occurrences of P in $E_{i,j}$ and ticking the last position of $E_{i,j}$ for which a prefix of P appears as a suffix of $E_{i,j}$. The ticked tails obtained in that way are then extended by Procedure 1 recursively and occurrences are reported. After the Procedure 1 ends, the KMP algorithm resumes and the testing starts at the beginning of the seed S_{i+1}.

5 Analysis

In this section, we discuss the correctness of the algorithm and analyse its space and time complexity.

5.1 Correctness

Consider an occurrence (i, j). If the occurrence falls under the Case 1 (resp. Case 2) then $j = i + m - 1$ (resp. $j = i$) for some fixed i. Thus, the number of occurrences falling under either Case 1 or Case 2 is bounded by $\mathcal{O}(n)$. On the other hand, for occurrences under Case 3, let parameter γ represent the maximum number of elastic-degenerate symbols spanned by any occurrence (i, j). Note that γ captures the possibility that the elastic-degenerate symbols contain empty strings. As there can be maximum m prefixes going past an elastic-degenerate position, the number of occurrences per starting position i are bounded by $\mathcal{O}(\gamma m)$. Thus the total number of distinct occurrences (i, j) is bounded by $\mathcal{O}(\gamma mn)$.

The correctness of the presented algorithm is straightforward as every starting position of the text is being tested for potential occurrences exhaustively. While the occurrences corresponding to the Cases 1 and $3(a)$ are covered by Type 1, Type 2 investigates all occurrences associated with Case 2 and Case $3(b)$. Thus all the occurrences of P in $\hat{T}$ are reported.

5.2 Space Complexity

The space required by both, the failure-function and ticked tails array, is $\mathcal{O}(m)$. The suffix tree $\mathbb{S}_S$ uses $\mathcal{O}(m + \sum_{i=1}^{k} |S_i|)$ space and the suffix tree $\mathbb{S}_\xi$ uses $\mathcal{O}(m + \sum_{i=1}^{k-1} \sum_{j=1}^{|\xi_i|} |E_{i,j}|)$ space. This leads to the total space required to be $\mathcal{O}(N)$, as $\sum_{i=1}^{k} |S_i| + \sum_{i=1}^{k-1} \sum_{j=1}^{|\xi_i|} |E_{i,j}| = N$ and $m < N$.

5.3 Time Complexity

The time taken by the pre-processing stage is $\mathcal{O}(N)$ as the failure function can be computed in $\mathcal{O}(m)$ time and construction of both the suffix trees (along with their pre-processing required to answer LCA queries in constant time) can be done in $\mathcal{O}(N)$ time.

The search stage uses the KMP algorithm over each seed and each string of every elastic-degenerate symbol in the text to report the occurrences for Case 1 and Case 2; and to search the beginning of the occurrence for Case 3. Thus the time consumed by the KMP algorithm is $\mathcal{O}(\sum_{i=1}^{k} |S_i| + \sum_{i=1}^{k-1} \sum_{j=1}^{|\xi_i|} |E_{i,j}|) = \mathcal{O}(N)$.

Procedure 1 can be analysed as follows. Intuitively, for every ticked position in the pattern (which can at most be m), an LCA query is used to find whether the corresponding seed occurs at the ticked position or not; a found such occurrence is then tried to extend by another LCA query with each of the strings in the following elastic-degenerate symbol. Let parameter α represent the maximum number of strings in any elastic-degenerate symbol of the text. This extension step for each ticked position will be carried out at most α times. More specifically, the outer loop of the procedure runs m times and the inner one takes $\mathcal{O}(\alpha)$ time, as each LCA query takes constant time. Thus, each recursive call requires $\mathcal{O}(m\alpha)$ time. The number of recursive calls depends on the number of the elastic-degenerate symbols spanned by the occurrence of P being tested. In other words, if an occurrence spans across i elastic-degenerate symbols, there will be i recursive calls to the procedure. If γ is the maximum such i, Procedure 1 executes in $\mathcal{O}(\alpha\gamma m)$ time in total for each starting position.

Initial ticking of the tails in Type 1 needs $\mathcal{O}(\alpha)$ time. For Type 2, initial ticking is done by KMP algorithm (already accounted above). In the worst case, Procedure 1 will be called from each of the n starting positions of the text, leading to an overall time-complexity of the algorithm to be $\mathcal{O}(N + \alpha\gamma mn)$. In other words, the algorithm takes $\mathcal{O}(N + \alpha\gamma mn)$ time to find and report $\mathcal{O}(\gamma mn)$ number of possible occurrences of the pattern.

6 Final Remarks

Motivated by applications in bioinformatics, we extended the notion of gapped strings to elastic-degenerate strings. In particular, we presented an efficient algorithm for pattern matching in elastic-degenerate texts. Given a solid pattern and an elastic-degenerate text the presented algorithm runs in $\mathcal{O}(N + \alpha\gamma mn)$ time; where m is the length of the given pattern; n and N are the length and total size of the given elastic-degenerate text, respectively; α and γ are parameters, respectively representing the maximum number of strings in any elastic-degenerate symbol of the text and the maximum number of elastic-degenerate symbols spanned by any occurrence of the pattern in the text.

Note that in applications involving gene sequence variation data, α represents the number of sequences in the multiple sequence alignment of the similar sequences and γ represents the number of genetic variation-sites falling in a full occurrence. The values of these parameters can be small and so the presented algorithm is expected to work very fast in practice. The space used by the algorithm is linear in the size of the input.

A proof-of-concept implementation of this algorithm (that has been tested for efficiency using synthetic data similar to the datasets used in genomics) can be accessed at https://github.com/Ritu-Kundu/ElDeS. Due to lack of space, experimental results are not included in the current version; they will be added in the full version of this article.

References

1. Amir, A., Farach, M., Galil, Z., Giancarlo, R., Park, K.: Dynamic dictionary matching. J. Comput. Syst. Sci. **49**(2), 208–222 (1994). http://www.sciencedirect.com/science/article/pii/S0022000005800479
2. Church, D.M., Schneider, V.A., Steinberg, K.M., Schatz, M.C., Quinlan, A.R., Chin, C.S., Kitts, P.A., Aken, B., Marth, G.T., Hoffman, M.M., Herrero, J., Mendoza, M.L.Z., Durbin, R., Flicek, P.: Extending reference assembly models. Genome Biol. **16**(1), 13 (2015). http://dx.doi.org/10.1186/s13059-015-0587-3

3. Crochemore, M., Hancart, C., Lecroq, T.: Algorithms on Strings, 392 p. Cambridge University Press, Cambridge (2007)
4. Crochemore, M., Sagot, M.F.: Motifs in Sequences: Localization and Extraction, pp. 47–97. Marcel Dekker, New York (2004)
5. Dilthey, A., Cox, C., Iqbal, Z., Nelson, M.R., McVean, G.: Improved genome inference in the MHC using a population reference graph. Nat. Genet. **47**(6), 682–688 (2015). Technical report, http://dx.doi.org/10.1038/ng.3257
6. Gusfield, D.: Algorithms on Strings, Trees, and Sequences: Computer Science and Computational Biology. Cambridge University Press, New York (1997)
7. Harel, H.T., Tarjan, R.E.: Fast algorithms for finding nearest common ancestors. SIAM J. Comput. **13**(2), 338–355 (1984)
8. Huang, L., Popic, V., Batzoglou, S.: Short read alignment with populations of genomes. Bioinformatics **29**(13), i361–i370 (2013). http://bioinformatics.oxfordjournals.org/content/29/13/i361.abstract
9. Knuth, D.E., Morris Jr., J.H., Pratt, V.R.: Fast pattern matching in strings. SIAM J. Comput. **6**(2), 323–350 (1977). http://dx.doi.org/10.1137/0206024
10. Li, Y., Bailey, J., Kulik, L., Pei, J.: Efficient matching of substrings in uncertain sequences. In: Zaki, M.J., Obradovic, Z., Tan, P., Banerjee, A., Kamath, C., Parthasarathy, S. (eds.) Proceedings of 2014 SIAM International Conference on Data Mining, 24–26 April 2014, pp. 767–775. SIAM, Philadelphia (2014). http://dx.doi.org/10.1137/1.9781611973440.88
11. Liu, Y., Koyutürk, M., Maxwell, S., Xiang, M., Veigl, M., Cooper, R.S., Tayo, B.O., Li, L., LaFramboise, T., Wang, Z., Zhu, X., Chance, M.R.: Discovery of common sequences absent in the human reference genome using pooled samples from next generation sequencing. BMC Genomics **15**(1), 685 (2014). http://dx.doi.org/10.1186/1471-2164-15-685
12. Maciuca, S., del Ojo Elias, C., McVean, G., Iqbal, Z.: A natural encoding of genetic variation in a burrows-wheeler transform to enable mapping and genome inference. In: Frith, M., Storm Pedersen, C.N. (eds.) WABI 2016. LNCS, vol. 9838, pp. 222–233. Springer, Heidelberg (2016). doi:10.1007/978-3-319-43681-4_18
13. McCreight, E.M.: A space-economical suffix tree construction algorithm. J. ACM (JACM) **23**(2), 262–272 (1976)
14. Pissis, S.P.: MoTeX-II: structured MoTif eXtraction from large-scale datasets. BMC Bioinform. **15**(1), 235 (2014). http://dx.doi.org/10.1186/1471-2105-15-235
15. Rahman, M.S., Iliopoulos, C.S., Lee, I., Mohamed, M., Smyth, W.F.: Finding patterns with variable length gaps or don't cares. In: Chen, D.Z., Lee, D.T. (eds.) COCOON 2006. LNCS, vol. 4112, pp. 146–155. Springer, Heidelberg (2006). doi:10.1007/11809678_17
16. Schieber, B., Vishkin, U.: On finding lowest common ancestors: simplification and parallelization. SIAM J. Comput. **17**(6), 1253–1262 (1988). http://dx.doi.org/10.1137/0217079
17. Ukkonen, E.: On-line construction of suffix trees. Algorithmica **14**(3), 249–260 (1995)
18. Weiner, P.: Linear pattern matching algorithms. In: Proceedings of 14th IEEE Annual Symposium on Switching and Automata Theory, pp. 1–11. Institute of Electrical Electronics Engineer (1973)

Integrated Encryption in Dynamic Arithmetic Compression

Shmuel T. Klein[1] and Dana Shapira[2(✉)]

[1] Computer Science Department, Bar Ilan University, Ramat Gan, Israel
tomi@cs.biu.ac.il
[2] Department of Computer Science and Mathematics, Ariel University, Ariel, Israel
shapird@gmail.com

Abstract. A compression cryptosystem based on adaptive arithmetic coding is proposed, in which the updates of the frequency tables for the underlying alphabet are done selectively, according to some secret key K. We give empirical evidence that the compression performance is not hurt, and discuss also aspects of the system being used as an encryption method.

1 Introduction

Some of the main concerns of communication over a network are security, space savings of the transformed information, and processing speed. These challenges can be overcome by means of encryption and compression of the involved data. Data *compression* focuses on representing the given data in fewer bits, while *encryption* concentrates on protecting information from third parties by transforming the data into a secure ciphertext. Although compression and encryption are two different disciplines, their goals are achieved for both by removing redundancies. We refer to a system combining the two disciplines as a *Compression Cryptosystem*. We suggest, in this research, a Compression Cryptosystem based on *arithmetic coding* that provides security as well as a data transfer rate increase, by generating a data file of reduced size.

Coding schemes like Huffman coding, that use a fixed set of codewords to represent the sequence of symbols in some given input file, are easily breakable by a simple chosen plaintext attack [1]. This type of attack is easiest for the attacker and most difficult for the cipher to withstand. Huffman coding schemes are able to cope with communication errors such as bit losses and changes: even if following such an error, the actually decoded text differs from the original encoded one, synchronization is generally regained after a small number of erroneous codewords [2]. Arithmetic coding schemes, however, are rendered inoperable at the loss of a single bit. The dependence of the encoded message upon all the previously transmitted characters ensures that even a minor discrepancy between the model actually used for encoding and that assumed for the decoding will, in the long run, produce nonsensical output.

Simultaneous compression and encryption can be achieved by either embedding compression into encryption algorithms as in [3], or by adding cryptographic

F. Drewes et al. (Eds.): LATA 2017, LNCS 10168, pp. 143–154, 2017.
DOI: 10.1007/978-3-319-53733-7_10

features into compression schemes, as we suggest here. The combination of arithmetic coding with data security was already suggested long ago by Jones [4] and Witten and Cleary [5]. Jones's implementation uses fixed source symbol probabilities but is flexible in the choice of source and code alphabets. Bergen and Hogan [1] investigate the security provided by static arithmetic coding, and show how the attacker can determine both the ordering of the symbols in the cumulative frequency table, and the actual value of the symbol frequencies, by feeding repeated binary substrings as the input to the algorithm.

Witten and Cleary [5] refer to the model as a very large key, without which decryption is impossible, and claim that an adaptive scheme provides protection of messages from a casual observer and against chosen plaintext attacks. This claim is justified in the work of Bergen and Hogan [6], where the authors consider adaptive arithmetic coding, in which all symbols are initialized to have unit frequencies, maintaining frequency counts adaptively, and halving the frequencies once the total cumulative frequency exceeds some fixed maximum value. Instead of attempting to discover the present state of the model, the attacker rather takes control of the model and is able to match his model to the one under attack by allowing decryption until the model is re-initialized.

In [7], a key controls the interval splitting of arithmetic coding, but the scheme suffers from an attack based on known plaintext [8] by using the fact that the same key is used to encode many messages. In [9], the authors show that even an improved version that uses different keys for encrypting different messages is still insecure under ciphertext-only attacks. Randomized arithmetic coding was proposed in [10], which is inefficient in terms of compression when compared to the traditional "compress-then-encrypt" approach. Utilizing chaotic systems for arithmetic coding was suggested in [11], where the secret key controls both the position and the direction of the line segments in the piecewise linear chaotic map. Klein et al. [12] suggest several heuristics for using compression as a data encryption method in order to prevent illegal use of copyright material.

Fraenkel and Klein [13] suggest methods for increasing the cryptographic security of ciphertexts containing variable length prefix free codes. Their methods are based on the NP-completeness of various decoding problems involving these ciphertexts, such that there is probably no polynomial algorithm for breaking the code.

In [14] a cryptosystem is used to provide security for mobile SMS communication. This system first compresses the SMS and then uses RSA for encryption. A compression cryptosystem especially suited for secure transmission of medical information such as images, audio, video etc. is proposed in [15], which is only suitable for short enough messages, as efficiency drops when the length of the message increases. In addition, the system requires a very large public key which makes it very difficult to use in several practical application. Singh and Gilhotra [16] use private key encryption based on static arithmetic coding. The data is first compressed and only then encrypted to provide security.

Cleary et al. [17] consider static arithmetic coding with a binary alphabet and show that for a chosen plaintext attack, $w + 2$ symbols are sufficient to uniquely determine a w-bit probability. Obviously, they deal with a very simplified version of arithmetic coding, while in our method, many more parts of the system remain unknown, besides the single probability. Duan et al. [18] propose a dynamic arithmetic coding method based on a Markov model for joint encryption and compression. The ith symbol is encoded based on a Markov chain of order 0 or 1, possibly permuting the relevant conditional probabilities in the model depending on a given secret key. Similarly to their scheme, we also update the model based on a secret key, but we ignore the dependency between consecutive characters.

In this paper we suggest a cryptosystem based on arithmetic coding. Although simultaneous arithmetic coding and encryption was already studied, most of these schemes are found insecure and especially inefficient in terms of compression. Unlike previous research, preliminary empirical results give evidence that our proposed algorithm provides security without hurting the compression efficiency. Section 2 describes our proposed method and Sect. 3 reports the experiments we have performed.

2 Proposed Method

We consider a cryptosystem, to be described below, which we imagine as being superimposed upon an adaptive arithmetic coder. Given is a plaintext $T = t_1 t_2 \cdots t_n$ of length n characters, drawn from an alphabet Σ of fixed size s. The text will be encoded using adaptive arithmetic coding, producing a compressed text $B = b_1 b_2 \cdots b_m$ of length m bits.

Arithmetic coding represents a message to be encoded by a sub-interval $[low, high)$ of $[0, 1)$. For an initially empty string T, the algorithm starts with the basic interval $[0, 1)$, which is increasingly narrowed as more characters from T are processed. The narrowing procedure is based on partitioning the current interval into sub-segments according to the probabilities of the characters in Σ.

For example, if $\Sigma = \{\mathsf{a}, \mathsf{b}, \mathsf{c}\}$ and the probabilities are 0.2, 0.7 and 0.1, respectively, a possible partition could be into the segments $[0, 0.2)$, $[0.2, 0.9)$ and $[0.9, 1)$. If the first character of T is b, the current interval after processing b is $[0.2, 0.9)$. In subsequent steps, the same procedure is applied after appropriate scaling. So if the second character of T is c, to which the last 10% of the initial interval have been assigned, the current interval after processing bc will be $[0.83, 0.9)$, the last 10% of the current interval $[0.2, 0.9)$. After processing 3 characters bcb, the interval would be $[0.844, 0.893)$.

The longer the text T, the narrower will the corresponding interval be, thus the more bits will usually be needed to represent any real number in it. To save space and since there will often be some overlap between the representations of the real numbers low and $high$ (in the last example, they both start with 0.8), the final encoding will not be the resulting interval itself, but rather a single real number within it. This suffices to allow decoding by reversing the above procedure, if some external stopping condition is added, like transmitting an end-of-text character or the length of the text. For the above example, one could choose, say, 0.86, or, even better, 0.875, which is the number with the shortest binary representation, 0.111, in the interval $[0.844, 0.893) = [0.1101100, 0.1110010)$.

In the static variant of arithmetic coding just described, the partition of $[0, 1)$ into sub-segments is fixed throughout the process. A dynamic variant calls for updating these segments adaptively, according to the probability distribution of the alphabet within the prefix of the text that has already been processed. In fact, the general step of the dynamic variant consists of two independent actions:

1. compute the new interval as a function of the current one, the current character and the currently assumed distribution of probabilities;
2. update the model by incrementing the frequency of the current character and adjusting the relative sizes of all the intervals in the partition accordingly.

The encryption we suggest is based on the fact that the model updates of the second action above are done selectively, not necessarily at every step. The exact subset of the processing steps at which the model is altered is controlled by a secret key K. Specifically, if $K = k_0 k_1 \cdots k_{t-1}$ is the standard binary representation of key K, where its length t is chosen large enough, say, $t = 512$ or more, then the model will be updated at step i, that is, after encoding the ith character, for $i \geq 1$, if and only if $k_{(i-1) \bmod t} = 1$. The algorithm for encrypting a given message M according to a secret key K is presented in Fig. 1.

```
encode(M, K)
1      n ←— |M|
2      t ←— |K|
3      initialize the interval to be [0, 1) with uniform distribution of the alphabet symbols
4      for i ←— 1 to n
4.1          compute the new interval as a function of:
                  the current interval
                  m_i (the current character)
                  the currently assumed distribution of probabilities
4.2          if k_((i-1) mod t) = 1 then
4.2.1             update the model
4.3          else
4.3.1             the new partition into intervals is the current one
5      return some value in the current interval
```

Fig. 1. Cryptosystem based on dynamic arithmetic encoding

The beginning of the encoding may introduce some weakness of the process, as the initial model of uniform distribution is not a secret. This might facilitate attempts of an attacker to incrementally decrypt at least the beginning of the encoded message. To avoid this flaw, the plaintext could be preceded by some known text of a predefined size, say, the thousand first characters of *Moby Dick*. This prefix is then used just to tune the encryption and decryption processes to a safe initialization of the boundaries of the intervals. The real encoding only starts when the original plaintext is processed. The rationale behind prepending a long enough known text, is that we expect that after updating the model selectively several times according to a secret key, the chances for the decryption model assumed by the attacker to be perfectly synchronized with the actual encryption model, without the knowledge of the secret key, are negligible, despite the fact that the characters are also known to the adversary. Thus, decoding errors will eventually appear, which in turn will initiate a snowball effect, as sporadic mistakes at the beginning will trigger even more errors subsequently, and the cumulative impact in the long run may destroy any similarity to the original text. The alternative of guessing a random key with 2^{512} potential variants is obviously ruled out.

We thus expect not to hurt the compression efficiency on the one hand, yet to provide strong enough encryption on the other hand in the long run. Indeed, dynamic arithmetic coding in particular, and all adaptive compression methods in general, are based on the assumption that the distribution of the characters in the text starting from the current position onwards will be similar to the distribution in the part of the text preceding this current position. This leads to the intuition that a longer history window will always be preferable to a shorter one. This will, however, not always be the case. It might well happen, in particular for non-homogeneous texts, that basing the prediction of the character probabilities on a random subset of n of the $2n$ most recently read characters may yield a compression performance that is not inferior, and sometimes even better, than using just the last n characters as basis.

It is easy to construct a worst case example in which any deviation from the standard model of considering the full history (or in case of limited memory, a bounded size window with a suffix of the history), will give deteriorated compression performance. Consider, for instance, a text of the form ababababa$\cdots$, consisting of strictly alternating characters of a binary alphabet. An adaptive arithmetic encoder will produce a uniform probability distribution $(\frac{1}{2}, \frac{1}{2})$ for any standard (even) sized history window. However, if the model is based on choosing n of the $2n$ last seen characters, according to some secret key K, then the uniform distribution will be obtained only if exactly half of the chosen characters are a and half are b. Assuming the values of K are randomly chosen, the probability of this event is

$$\frac{\binom{n}{n/2}\binom{n}{n/2}}{\binom{2n}{n}} \simeq \frac{2}{\sqrt{\pi\, n}},$$

where we have used Stirling's approximation. Thus for $k = 512$, only in 5% of the cases will the exactly uniform model be obtained. Nevertheless, this worst case behavior is restricted to such artificial texts, and our empirical tests of several real language texts suggest that the loss incurred by turning to a selective updating procedure as suggested is hardly noticeable.

3 Empirical Results

We considered four texts of different languages and sizes, each encoded as a sequence of characters. *ebib* is the Bible (King James version) in English, in which the text was stripped of all punctuation signs; *ftxt* is the French version of the European Union's JOC corpus, a collection of pairs of questions and answers on various topics used in the ARCADE evaluation project [19]; *sources* is formed by C/Java source codes obtained by concatenating .c, .h and .java files of the linux-2.6.11.6 distributions; and *English* is the concatenation of English text files selected from the etext02 to etext05 collections of the Gutenberg Project, from which the headers related to the project were deleted so as to leave just the real text.

3.1 Compression Performance

We have assumed that basing the prediction of the character probabilities on a random subset of bits will not hurt the compression performance. We therefore compared our method to traditional dynamic arithmetic coding, which uses the entire portion of the file that has already been processed to predict the current character, and measured their compression performance.

Table 1 presents information on the compression performance of the data files involved. The second column presents the original file size in MB. The third column gives the size of the file, in MB, compressed by adaptive arithmetic coding without any key, that is, using the full history window. The fourth column shows the difference in size, in bytes, of the compressed file, when the updates of the model are done according to a randomly chosen key as suggested. Interestingly, there was a loss, albeit a negligibly small one, in all our tests. The last column gives the ratio of the loss to the size of the file.

Table 1. Information about the used datasets

File	Full size MB	Compressed size MB	Absolute loss bytes	Relative loss
ebib	3.5	1.8	56	3×10^{-5}
ftxt	7.6	4.2	316	7×10^{-5}
sources	200.0	136.6	436	3×10^{-6}
English	1024.0	579.3	437	7×10^{-7}

As can be seen, there is hardly any noticeable difference in size between the files obtained by using the standard adaptive arithmetic code, and that with the selective updating. Timing results for both encoding and decoding were also almost identical for both variants.

3.2 Uniformity

As to security, any reasonably compressed or encrypted file should consist of a sequence of bits that is not distinguishable from a randomly generated binary sequence. A criterion for such randomness could be that the probability of occurrence, within the compressed file, of any substring of length m bits should be

2^{-m}, for all $m \geq 1$, that is, the probability for 1 or 0 are both 0.5, the probabilities for 00, 01, 10 and 11 are 0.25, etc. We checked this fact on all our compressed test files, for all values of m up to 8, and found distributions that are very close to uniform, with small fluctuations, for both methods of the original arithmetic coding and that with our selective updates. We bring here only the data for the file *ebib*; the results for the other files were practically identical.

The left part of Fig. 2 plots the probability of occurrence of 8-bit strings as a function of their possible values 0 to 255. As expected, the probabilities fluctuate within a narrow interval centered at $\frac{1}{256} = 0.0039$. All the possible bit-positions have been taken into account, so the strings were not necessarily byte aligned. The solid line corresponds to the method with a secret key suggested herein, whereas the broken line is the distribution for the original arithmetic coding. As can be seen, these distributions can be equally considered as uniform, and there seems to be no obvious deterioration of the uniformity due to the selective choice of the update steps.

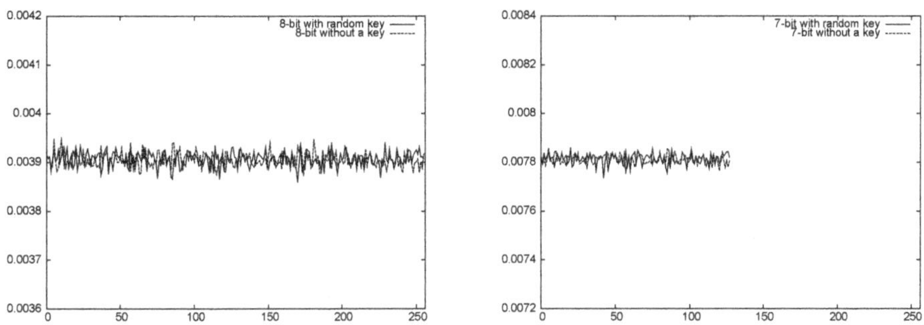

Distribution for 8-bit Distribution for 7-bit

Fig. 2. Probability of occurrence of 8- and 7-bit substrings as function of their value.

The right part of Fig. 2 repeats the test with 7-bit strings. Here the values are in the range $[0, 127]$, and the probabilities fluctuate around $\frac{1}{128} = 0.0078$. Similar graphs would be produced for the other values of m. For $m \leq 3$, the probabilities are shown in Table 2.

To get a more quantitative judgement of the intuitive impression that these values are evenly spread, we calculated the standard deviation of the distribution of the 2^m values for each value of m. Usually, the standard deviation σ is of the order of magnitude of the average μ, so their ratio $\frac{\sigma}{\mu}$ may serve as a measure of the skewness of the distribution. Table 3 gives this ratio for $1 \leq m \leq 8$, for both the standard adaptive arithmetic coding with model updates after every encoded character, and for the selective model we proposed. As can be seen, the ratio is very small in all cases, of the order of $\frac{1}{1000}$, suggesting that the distributions are indeed very close to uniform.

Table 2. Probability of occurrence of 3-, 2- and 1-bit substrings as function of their value.

value	Standard arithmetic			Selective updates		
	$m = 3$	$m = 2$	$m = 1$	$m = 3$	$m = 2$	$m = 1$
0	0.12503	0.25002	0.50011	0.12507	0.25010	0.500005004
1	0.12498	0.25009	0.49989	0.12503	0.24991	0.499994996
2	0.12510	0.25009		0.12491	0.24991	
3	0.12499	0.24981		0.12499	0.25009	
4	0.12498			0.12503		
5	0.12511			0.12488		
6	0.12499			0.12499		
7	0.12482			0.12499		

Table 3. Ratio $\frac{\sigma}{\mu}$ of standard deviation to average within the set of 2^m values for $m = 1, \ldots, 8$.

m	8	7	6	5	4	3	2	1
Standard	0.00383	0.00251	0.00164	0.00125	0.00094	0.00072	0.00053	0.00030
Selective	0.00135	0.00042	0.00207	0.00182	0.00059	0.00013	0.00003	0.00001

3.3 Cryptographic Attacks

Uniformity is a necessary, but not sufficient condition for a secure system. There might be other possible attacks that could render the method vulnerable. For our following experiment we wanted to check the ability of the adversary to predict the partition of [0,1) into intervals according to the probabilities of the characters, without knowledge of the key. This is important, because in a chosen cleartext attack, an adversary would know at each stage the true distribution of the characters in the already processed prefix of the text, which could possibly help to infer from it the stages at which the model has been updated, and thereby guess the secret key on which the encryption is based. We are therefore interested in measuring, at each stage, the size of the overlapping parts of the subintervals of all characters, between two possible partitions: the one induced by the entire history processed so far, and the one corresponding to the subset of updating steps according to the secret key.

Figure 3 illustrates what we mean by overlap. The interval $[0, 1)$ is shown, partitioned into 5 segments, corresponding to an alphabet $\{\mathsf{a}, \mathsf{b}, \mathsf{c}, \mathsf{d}, \mathsf{e}\}$ of 5 characters, but with slightly differing boundaries in the upper and lower parts of the figure. Overlapping parts of segments assigned to the same character are emphasized. Our measure for the overall overlap is the cumulative size of the boldfaced sub-intervals, 0.714 in this example.

Figure 4 plots this overlap for the partitions of $[0, 1)$ into sub-intervals according to:

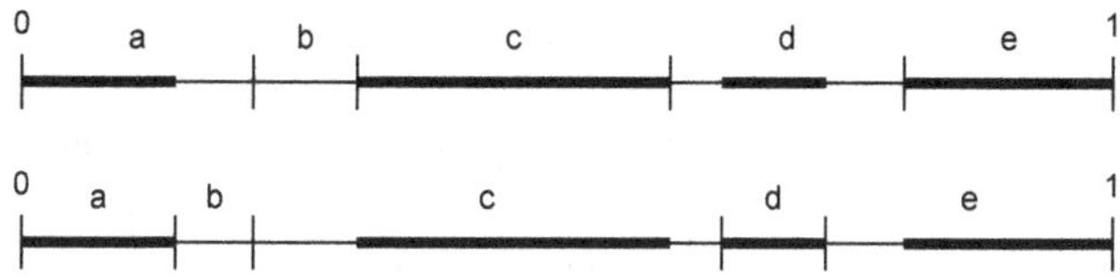

Fig. 3. Overlapping intervals.

1. a model updating the partition after each character read;
2. a model updating the partition selectively, according to some secret key.

The test text for this figure is the beginning of *Moby Dick*, which we have used to initiate the frequency table prior to the processing of the cleartext itself. As can be seen, the overlap is large at the beginning, but quickly drops to a level of about 10%, which is reached after roughly 100 characters. Then the overlap slowly rises until reaching a value of about 0.76 for 10000 processed characters. Indeed, the initial prefixes of the text are too short to be representative samples of the general text; but as more characters are accumulated, even the distribution within a subsample will be increasingly similar to that of the entire set. A similar phenomenon can be observed when considering several independent sources describing the distribution of the characters in "standard" English. Almost all will agree that the order of the characters will be E, T, A, O, I, N,, and will give quite similar values for their probabilities.

Returning to the suggested compression cryptosystem, the overlap after 1000 characters is roughly around 0.3, which means that an adversary guessing the partition, or basing it on the full distribution of all the characters in the prefixed *Moby Dick* sample, will have, for each processed characters, a chance of about 0.7 for being wrong. The probability for correct guesses in all of the 10 first attempts is thus less than 0.000006, and a single wrong guess will imply many more subsequently.

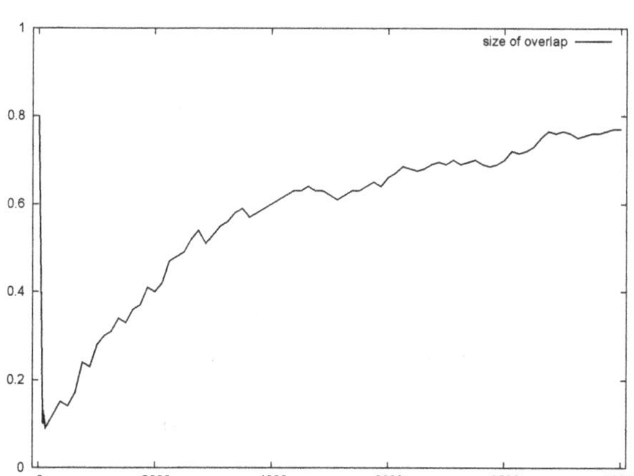

Fig. 4. Size of overlap as a function of the number of processed characters.

In the last test, we checked the sensitivity of the system to variations in the secret key. The measure of similarity between two image files proposed in [18] is the normalized number of differing pixels. Since we consider encrypted files which are not images, we shall use the normalized Hamming distance: let $A = a_1 \cdots a_n$ and $B = b_1 \cdots b_m$ be two bitstrings and assume $n \geq m$. First extend B by zeros so that both strings are of the same length n. The normalized Hamming distance is then defined by $\frac{1}{n}\sum_{i=1}^{n}(a_i \text{ XOR } b_i)$. Figure 5 plots these values for prefixes of size n, for $1 \leq n \leq 1000$ of the file *ebib*: the first plot considers two independently generated random keys, for the second and third plots the same key is used, with just the first or last bit flipped. In any case, one sees that the produced cipherfiles are completely different, with the number of differences in corresponding bits rapidly tending to the expected value $\frac{1}{2}$. The values of the ratio for the three tests at the end of the file (after processing 1.8 MB) were 0.499894, 0.500004 and 0.499995, respectively. We conclude that the suggested selective update procedure of the model is extremely sensitive to even small alterations: all produced files pass the above randomness tests, are practically of the same size, and are completely different from each other.

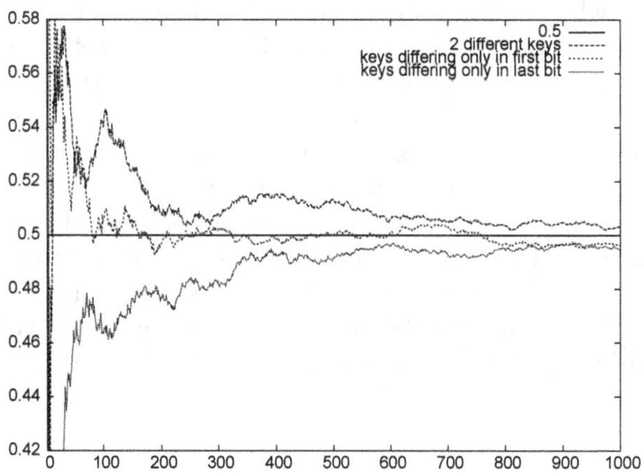

Fig. 5. Normalized Hamming distance.

4 Conclusion

A standard way to devise a compression cryptosystem is to compress the text and only then encrypt the compressed form. The alternative of encrypting first and then compressing would not be effective, as a reasonably encrypted file lacks any easily detectable redundancy and thus would not be compressible at all. We have suggested a way to combine the compression and encryption transformations in a single step, by using selective update steps in the maintained adaptive model. Experiments show that neither the compression performance, nor the running time are hurt. Moreover, the randomness of our ciphertext suggests that decryption is hard without the knowledge of the key.

Several aspects are left for future research and we shall mention only two:

1. Using repeatedly the same key K might give an attacker the opportunity to try to guess K by some chosen plaintext or other attack. This can be overcome by considering K as the seed of some random number generator. For example, use a large constant randomly chosen prime P and a large constant a and choose a new K at each iteration by $K \leftarrow a^K \bmod P$. Going backwards then means calculating the discrete log. So there is hardly any addition in encoding or decoding time, but an enemy cannot do any analysis since every block of 512 chars uses a different key.
2. We assumed that the order of the characters is constant and known (say alphabetic). If this is risky (maybe there is, or will be, some chosen plaintext or other attack based on this knowledge), it has been suggested to permute the alphabet at every step. But this is costly. We suggest using the key K also to permute the alphabet at every step.

References

1. Bergen, H.A., Hogan, J.M.: Data security in a fixed-model arithmetic coding compression algorithm. Comput. Secur. **11**(5), 445–461 (1992)
2. Klein, S.T., Shapira, D.: Pattern matching in Huffman encoded texts. Inf. Process. Manage. **41**(4), 829–841 (2005)
3. Wong, K., Yuen, C.H.: Embedding compression in chaos based cryptography. IEEE Trans. Circuits Syst.-II Expr. Briefs **55**(11), 1193–1197 (2008)
4. Jones, C.B.: An efficient coding system for long source sequences. IEEE Trans. Inf. Theory **27**, 280–291 (1981)
5. Witten, I.H., Cleary, J.G.: On the privacy afforded by adaptive text compression. Comput. Secur. **7**(4), 397–408 (1988)
6. Bergen, H.A., Hogan, J.M.: A chosen plaintext attack on an adaptive arithmetic coding compression algorithm. Comput. Secur. **12**(2), 157–167 (1993)
7. Wen, J., Kim, H., Villasenor, J.: Binary arithmetic coding with key based interval splitting. IEEE Trans. Signal Process. Lett. **13**(2), 69–72 (2006)
8. Jakimoski, G., Subbalakshmi, K.: Cryptanalysis of some multimedia encryption schemes. IEEE Trans. Multimed. **10**(3), 330–338 (2008)
9. Katti, R.S., Vosoughi, A.: On the security of key based interval splitting arithmetic coding with respect to message indistinguishability. IEEE Trans. Inf. Forensics Secur. **7**(3), 895–903 (2012)
10. Grangetto, M., Magli, E., Olmo, G.: Multimedia selective encryption by means of randomized arithmetic coding. IEEE Trans. Multimed. **8**(5), 905–917 (2006)
11. Wong, K., Lin, Q., Chen, J.: Simultaneous arithmetic coding and encryption using chaotic maps. IEEE Trans. Circuits Syst.-II Expr. Briefs **57**(2), 146–150 (2010)
12. Klein, S.T., Bookstein, A., Deerwester, S.: Storing text retrieval systems on cd-rom: compression and encryption considerations. ACM Trans. Inf. Syst. **7**(3), 230–245 (1989)

13. Fraenkel, A.S., Klein, S.T.: Complexity aspects of guessing prefix codes. Algorithmica **12**(4), 409–419 (1994)
14. Mahmoud, T.M., Abdel-Latef, B.A., Ahmed, A.A., Mahfouz, A.M.: Hybrid compression encryption technique for securing sms. Int. J. Comput. Sci. Secur. (IJCSS) **3**(6), 473–481 (2009)
15. Ojha, D.B., Sharma, A., Dwivedi, A., Pande, N., Kumar, A.: Space age approach to transmit medical image with code base cryptosystem over noisy channel. Int. J. Eng. Sci. Technol. **2**(12), 7112–7117 (2010)
16. Singh, A., Gilhotra, R.: Data security using private key encryption system based on arithmetic coding. Int. J. Netw. Secur. Appl. (IJNSA) **3**(3), 58–67 (2011)
17. Cleary, J.G., Irvine, S.A., Rinsma-Melchert, I.: On the insecurity of arithmetic coding. Comput. Secur. **14**(2), 167–180 (1995)
18. Duan, L., Liao, X., Xiang, T.: A secure arithmetic coding based on Markov model. Commun. Nonlinear Sci. Numer. Simul. **16**(6), 2554–2562 (2011)
19. Véronis, J., Langlais, P.: Evaluation of parallel text alignment systems: the ARCADE project. In: Véronis, J. (ed.) Parallel Text Processing, pp. 369–388. Kluwer Academic Publishers, Dordrecht (2000)

Two-Dimensional Palindromes and Their Properties

Manasi S. Kulkarni(✉) and Kalpana Mahalingam

Department of Mathematics Indian Institute of Technology Madras, Chennai 600036, India
ma16ipf01@smail.iitm.ac.in, kmahalingam@iitm.ac.in

Abstract. A two-dimensional word (2D) is a rectangular finite array of letters from the alphabet Σ. A 2D word is said to be a 2D palindrome if it is equal to its reverse image. In this paper, we study some combinatorial properties of 2D palindromes. In particular, we provide a sufficient condition under which a 2D word is said to be a 2D palindrome, discuss the necessary and sufficient condition under which a 2D word can be decomposed into 2D palindromes, and find the relation between the set of all 2D palindromes and the set of all 2D primitive words. We also show that the set of all 2D palindromes is not a recognizable language, and study a special class of 2D palindromes, namely 2D palindrome square words.

Keywords: Combinatorics on words · Two-Dimensional words · Two-Dimensional palindromes · Recognizable languages · Primitivity · Symmetry

1 Introduction

Identification of symmetric patterns in digital images and non-rigid shapes is one of the most interesting problems in image processing, [6,11,16]. It has numerous applications ranging from face recognition technologies to biology. In [14], authors provide an algorithm that detects and measures the bilateral symmetry of an image of arbitrary dimension and discuss its application in medical image processing. The relation of the field of image processing to genetic algorithms has been established in [8] by discussing a global optimization algorithm to detect the local reflectional symmetry in grey level images. To extract a set of significant features of a human face, face recognition technologies exploits the symmetry characteristics of human face, [3]. One of the symmetrical characteristic that can be of interest is the palindromic property in images.

Thus, it is of natural interest to extend the concept of palindromes to two-dimension that in some sense possesses a symmetrical property. Palindromes are one of the most important category of words that have been extensively studied in formal language theory and combinatorics on words. (A non-empty word w is a palindrome if it is equal to its mirror image, i.e., $w = mi(w)$.) The

F. Drewes et al. (Eds.): LATA 2017, LNCS 10168, pp. 155–167, 2017.
DOI: 10.1007/978-3-319-53733-7_11

formal notion of 2D palindromes was first introduced by Berthé and Vuillon [2] in order to characterize 2D Sturmian sequences in terms of 2D palindromes. 2D palindromes are also studied in [4] where authors provide an algorithm for searching 2D words for maximal 2D palindromes.

In this paper, we attempt to study 2D palindrome words and 2D palindrome languages from combinatorics on words point of view rather than algorithmic or formal language perspective. We study the relation between 2D palindromes and 2D primitive words, discuss the decomposition of a 2D primitive word into 2D palindromes and prove the non-recognizability of the set of all 2D palindromes.

The paper is organized as follows: In Sect. 2, we provide the basic definitions and notations for words in single as well as two dimension along with providing formal definitions of prefix, suffix and subword of a 2D word, and a 2D primitive word. In Sect. 3, we recall the definition of a 2D palindrome, and prove various properties of these words including the relation between 2D palindromes and 2D primitive words (Proposition 11), the non-recognizability of the set of all 2D palindromes (Sect. 3.2). We discuss a special class of 2D palindromes in Sect. 3.1 with concluding remarks in Sect. 4.

2 Basic Definitions and Notations

An alphabet Σ is a finite non-empty set of symbols. Σ^* denotes the set of all words over Σ including the empty word λ. Σ^+ is the set of all non-empty words over Σ. The length of a word $u \in \Sigma^*$ (i.e., the number of symbols in a word) is denoted by $|u|$. The reversal of $u = a_1 a_2 \cdots a_n$ is defined to be a string $u^R = a_n \cdots a_2 a_1$ where $a_i \in \Sigma$ for $1 \leq i \leq n$. A word u is said to be a palindrome or 1D palindrome if $u = u^R$. A word w is said to be primitive if $w = u^n$ implies $n = 1$ and $w = u$. For all other concepts in the formal language theory and combinatorics on words, the reader is referred to [7,10,17].

2.1 Two-Dimensional Words

Definition 1. *A two-dimensional word or block (also called a picture) $w = [w_{i,j}]_{1 \leq i \leq m, 1 \leq j \leq n}$ over an alphabet Σ of size (m,n) is defined to be a two-dimensional rectangular finite array of letters:*

$$w = \begin{matrix} w_{1,1} & w_{1,2} & \cdots & w_{1,n-1} & w_{1,n} \\ w_{2,1} & w_{2,2} & \cdots & w_{2,n-1} & w_{2,n} \\ \vdots & \vdots & \ddots & \vdots & \vdots \\ w_{m-1,1} & w_{m-1,2} & \cdots & w_{m-1,n-1} & w_{m-1,n} \\ w_{m,1} & w_{m,2} & \cdots & w_{m,n-1} & w_{m,n} \end{matrix}$$

In case of 2D words, an empty word is a word of the size $(0,0)$, and we use the same notation, λ to denote such a word. The set of all 2D (rectangular) words including the empty word λ over Σ is denoted by Σ^{**}, whereas Σ^{++} is the set of all non-empty 2D words over Σ. A 2D language over Σ is a subset of Σ^{**}.

Note that, the words of size $(m, 0)$ and $(0, m)$ for $m > 0$ are not defined. We recall the following definition of the concatenation operation between 2D words, and 2D languages.

Definition 2 [5]. *Let u and v be two words over an alphabet Σ of size (m_1, n_1) and (m_2, n_2), respectively with $m_1, n_1, m_2, n_2 > 0$:*

$$u = \begin{matrix} u_{1,1} & \cdots & u_{1,n_1} \\ \vdots & & \vdots \\ u_{m_1,1} & \cdots & u_{m_1,n_1} \end{matrix}, \quad v = \begin{matrix} v_{1,1} & \cdots & v_{1,n_2} \\ \vdots & & \vdots \\ v_{m_2,1} & \cdots & v_{m_2,n_2} \end{matrix}$$

1. *The column catenation of u and v (denoted by $\oplus$) is a partial operation, defined if $m_1 = m_2 = m$, and it is given by*

$$u \oplus v = \begin{matrix} u_{1,1} & \cdots & u_{1,n_1} & v_{1,1} & \cdots & v_{1,n_2} \\ \vdots & & \vdots & \vdots & & \vdots \\ u_{m,1} & \cdots & u_{m,n_1} & v_{m,1} & \cdots & v_{m,n_2} \end{matrix}$$

   The column closure of u (denoted by $u^{*\oplus}$) is defined as $u^{*\oplus} = \bigcup_{i\geq 0} u^{i\oplus}$ where $u^{0\oplus} = \lambda, u^{1\oplus} = u, u^{n\oplus} = u \oplus u^{(n-1)\oplus}$.

2. *The row catenation of u and v (denoted by $\ominus$) is a partial operation defined if $n_1 = n_2 = n$, and it is given by*

$$u \ominus v = \begin{matrix} u_{1,1} & \cdots & u_{1,n} \\ \vdots & & \vdots \\ u_{m_1,1} & \cdots & u_{m_1,n} \\ v_{1,1} & \cdots & v_{1,n} \\ \vdots & & \vdots \\ v_{m_2,1} & \cdots & v_{m_2,n} \end{matrix}$$

   The row closure of u (denoted by $u^{*\ominus}$) is defined as $u^{*\ominus} = \bigcup_{i\geq 0} u^{i\ominus}$ where $u^{0\ominus} = \lambda, u^{1\ominus} = u, u^{n\ominus} = u \ominus u^{(n-1)\ominus}$.

It is clear that the operations of row and column catenation are associative but not commutative. Moreover, the column and row catenation of u and the empty word λ is always defined and λ is a neutral element for both the operations.

The definitions of column catenation (row catenation, respectively) and column closure (row closure, respectively) of words can be extended to languages in a similar fashion.

Definition 3

1. *Let $u, v \in \Sigma^{++}$ be two words of size (m_1, n_1) and (m_2, n_2) respectively. Then the operation of a dual-catenation, $\oplus$ is defined as*

$$u \oplus v = \begin{cases} u \ominus v & \text{if } n_1 = n_2 \\ u \oplus v & \text{if } m_1 = m_2 \\ \{u \ominus v, u \oplus v\} & \text{if } (m_1, n_1) = (m_2, n_2). \end{cases}$$

2. Let $x \in \Sigma^{++}$, then

$$x^{k\oplus} = \{(x^{k_1\ominus})^{k_2\oplus} : \textit{for all } 1 \leq k_1, k_2 \leq k \textit{ such that } k_1k_2 = k\}.$$

In lieu of above definition, we use the convention $u \oplus v \in X$ for some set X to represent $u \oplus v$ to be an element of X if $m_1 = m_2$ or $n_1 = n_2$, or to represent $u \oplus v$ to be a subset of X if $(m_1, n_1) = (m_2, n_2)$.

In [1], prefix of a 2D word w is defined to be a rectangular sub-block (sub-block of a block w of size (m, n) is any block of size (h, k) in w where $h \leq m, k \leq n$) that contains one corner of w, whereas suffix of w is defined to be a rectangular sub-block that contains the diagonally opposite corner of w. However, in this paper we consider prefix of a 2D word w to be a rectangular sub-block that contains only the top left corner of w, and suffix of w to be a rectangular sub-block that contains only the bottom right corner of w. Formally,

Definition 4. *Given $u \in \Sigma^{**}$, $v \in \Sigma^{**}$ is said to be a prefix of u (respectively, suffix of u), denoted by $v \leq_p u$ (respectively $v \leq_s u$) if $u = (v \ominus x) \oplus y$ or $u = (v \oplus x) \ominus y$ (respectively, $u = y \oplus (x \ominus v)$ or $u = y \ominus (x \oplus v)$) for $x, y \in \Sigma^{**}$. Furthermore, v is said to be a proper prefix of u (respectively proper suffix of u) denoted by $v <_p u$ (respectively $v <_s u$) if either $x \neq \lambda$ or $y \neq \lambda$, or both $x, y \in \Sigma^{++}$.*

Similarly, given $u \in \Sigma^{**}$, $v \in \Sigma^{**}$ is said to be a subword (respectively, proper subword) of u, denoted by $v \leq_{sw} u$ (respectively, $v <_{sw} u$) if $u = x \oplus (x' \ominus v \ominus y') \oplus y$ or $u = x \ominus (x' \oplus v \oplus y') \ominus y$ for $x, x', y, y' \in \Sigma^{**}$ (respectively, if any of x, x', y, y' are non-empty).

A 2D word $w \in \Sigma^{++}$ is said to be 2D-*primitive* if $w = x^{k\oplus}$ implies that $k = 1$ and $w = x$, [9]. By Q_{2d}, let us denote the set of all 2D primitive words. Also, if $w = x^{k\oplus}$ and x is 2D primitive, then x is said to be a 2D-*primitive root* of w denoted by $\rho_{2d}(w)$.

Definition 5. *Let $w = [w_{i,j}]$ be a 2D word of size (m, n).*

- *The clockwise rotation of w denoted by w^{CR} is defined as $w^{CR} = A_1 \ominus A_2 \ominus \cdots \ominus A_n$ where $A_k = w_{m,k} \oplus w_{m-1,k} \oplus \cdots \oplus w_{2,k} \oplus w_{1,k}$ for $1 \leq k \leq n$*
- *The counter-clockwise rotation of w denoted by w^{ACR} is defined as $w^{ACR} = B_n \ominus B_{n-1} \ominus \cdots \ominus B_1$ where $B_{k'} = w_{1,k'} \oplus w_{2,k'} \oplus \cdots \oplus w_{m-1,k'} \oplus w_{m,k'}$ for $1 \leq k' \leq n$.*

3 Two-Dimensional Palindromes

In this section, we recall the definition of a 2D palindromes and, study some basic properties of 2D palindromes. We give a sufficient condition for a 2D word to be a 2D palindrome. The relation between 2D palindromes and 1D palindromes, as well as the relation between the set of all 2D palindromes and the set of all 2D primitive words is given. In order to define 2D palindromes, we recall the definition of the reverse of a 2D word.

Definition 6 [2]. *Let $w = [w_{i,j}]$ be a 2D word of size (m, n). The reverse image of w, i.e., w^R is defined as:*

$$w^R = \begin{matrix} w_{m,n} & w_{m,n-1} & \cdots & w_{m,2} & w_{m,1} \\ w_{m-1,n} & w_{m-1,n-1} & \cdots & w_{m-1,2} & w_{m-1,1} \\ \vdots & \vdots & \ddots & \vdots & \vdots \\ w_{2,n} & w_{2,n-1} & \cdots & w_{2,2} & w_{2,1} \\ w_{1,n} & w_{1,n-1} & \cdots & w_{1,2} & w_{1,1} \end{matrix}$$

If w is equal to its reverse image w^R, then w is said to be a *two-dimensional palindrome*, [2,4]. By P_{2d} we denote the set of all 2D palindromes over an alphabet Σ. In [2], 2D palindromes are referred to as *centrosymmetric factors*, while in [4] they are referred to as *rect2DP*.

Example 7. Let $\Sigma = \{a, b, c\}$. Then $w = \begin{matrix} a\,b\,b\,c \\ b\,c\,b\,a \\ a\,b\,c\,b \\ c\,b\,b\,a \end{matrix}$ is a 2D palindrome.

Observation: Consider a 2D palindrome $w = [w_{i,j}]$ of size (m, n) over an alphabet Σ. Then concatenation of rows i and $m-i+1$ of w for $1 \leq i \leq m$ written as a string is a 1D palindrome. Similar property holds for concatenation of columns j and $n-j+1$ for $1 \leq j \leq n$.

The notions of conjugacy and commutativity are one of the most basic notions studied and used in combinatorics on words, [12]. The fundamental results associated with these notions are extended to their 2D counterpart in [9]. These results play a major role in proving some of the properties of 2D palindromes.

A 2D word u is said to be a *conjugate* of another 2D word w if $u \oplus v = v \oplus w$ for some $v \in \Sigma^{++}$. Two words $u, v \in \Sigma^{++}$ are said to be commutative if $u \oplus v = v \oplus u$. The following results provides a characterization of 2D words that are conjugates of each other, and 2D words that commute.

Lemma 8 [9]. *Let $u, v, w \in \Sigma^{++}$ be words of size $(m_1, n_1), (m_2, n_2)$ and (m_3, n_3) respectively where $m_1, m_2, m_3, n_1, n_2, n_3 \geq 1$. Then $u \oplus v = v \oplus w$ implies that for $k \geq 0$, $x \in \Sigma^{++}$ and $y \in \Sigma^{**}$,*

1. *If $m_1 = m_2 = m_3$, then $u = x \oplus y$, $v = (x \oplus y)^{k\oplus} \oplus x$, $w = y \oplus x$.*
2. *If $n_1 = n_2 = n_3$, then $u = x \ominus y$, $v = (x \ominus y)^{k\ominus} \ominus x$, $w = y \ominus x$.*

Lemma 9 [9]. *Let $u, v \in \Sigma^{++}$. Then $u \oplus v = v \oplus u$ implies that u and v share a common 2D primitive root.*

It is known that for $u \in \Sigma^*$, u is a palindrome if and only if $u = (xy)^i x$ for some palindromes $x, y \in \Sigma^*$ and $i \geq 1$, [18]. Proposition 10 provides only a sufficient condition for a 2D word to be a palindrome.

Proposition 10. *If $u = (x \oplus y)^{i\oplus} \oplus x$ where $x, y \in P_{2d}$ and $i \geq 1$ then $u \in P_{2d}$.*

However, converse of the above proposition is not true in general. For example,

$$u = \begin{matrix} a & b & c \\ c & a & c \\ c & b & a \end{matrix}$$

is a 2D palindrome, but there does not exist any $x, y \in P_{2d}$ such that $u = (x \oplus y)^{i\oplus} \oplus x$.

Note that, for any $u \in \Sigma^{++}$, $u \in P_{2d}$ if and only if $\rho_{2d}(u) \in P_{2d}$. Consider the set of all non-empty 2D palindromes, denoted by P^1_{2d}, i.e., $P^1_{2d} = P_{2d} \backslash \lambda$. It is clear that $\rho_{2d}(P^1_{2d}) \subseteq P_{2d}$. Also, $P_{2d} \cap Q_{2d} \subseteq \rho_{2d}(P^1_{2d})$. Hence we have the following result.

Proposition 11. $\rho_{2d}(P^1_{2d}) = P_{2d} \cap Q_{2d}$.

The following theorem provides a necessary and sufficient condition such that the dual catenation of two non-empty 2D palindromes is a 2D palindrome.

Theorem 12. *Let $u \in P^1_{2d}$ and $v \in \Sigma^{++}$. The following statements are equivalent:*

1. $\{v, u \oplus v\} \subseteq P_{2d}$;
2. $\rho_{2d}(u) = \rho_{2d}(v)$;
3. $\{v, u^{i\oplus} \oplus v^{i\oplus}\} \subseteq P_{2d}$ *for some* $i, j \geq 1$;
4. $u^{*\oplus} \oplus v^{*\oplus} \subseteq P_{2d}$.

Proof. (1) ⇒ (2): Let $u, v, u \oplus v \in P_{2d}$. Then $u \oplus v = (u \oplus v)^R = v^R \oplus u^R = v \oplus u$ and hence by Lemma 9, $\rho_{2d}(u) = \rho_{2d}(v)$.

(2) ⇒ (4): Let $\rho_{2d}(u) = \rho_{2d}(v)$. Since $u \in P_{2d}$, $\rho_{2d}(u) \in P_{2d}$. Consider $u^{i\oplus} \oplus v^{j\oplus}$ such that $i, j \geq 0$ and $i + j \geq 0$. Since $\rho_{2d}(u) = \rho_{2d}(v)$, $\rho_{2d}(u^{i\oplus} \oplus v^{j\oplus}) = \rho_{2d}(u) \in P_{2d}$. Hence $u^{i\oplus} \oplus v^{j\oplus} \in P_{2d}$ and thus $u^{*\oplus} \oplus v^{*\oplus} \subseteq P_{2d}$.

(4) ⇒ (1) and (4) ⇒ (3): Follows immediately.

(3) ⇒ (2): Let $v, u^{i\oplus} \oplus v^{j\oplus} \in P_{2d}$ for $i, j \geq 1$. This implies $u^{i\oplus} \oplus v^{j\oplus} = [u^{i\oplus} \oplus v^{j\oplus}]^R = [v^{j\oplus}]^R \oplus [u^{i\oplus}]^R = v^{j\oplus} \oplus u^{i\oplus}$ which by Lemma 9 further implies that $\rho_{2d}(u^{i\oplus}) = \rho_{2d}(u) = \rho_{2d}(v) = \rho_{2d}(v^{j\oplus})$. □

In the following result we state the relationship between the set of all 2D palindromes and the set of all 2D primitive words.

Proposition 13. *Let $u, v \in \Sigma^{++}$. Then $u \oplus v \in P_{2d} \cap Q_{2d}$ implies that either $u \notin P_{2d}$ or $v \notin P_{2d}$.*

Proposition 14. *Let $u \in P_{2d}$ and $p \in \Sigma^{++}$ such that $p \leq_p u$. Then $u^{i\oplus} \oplus p^{j\oplus} \in P_{2d}$ for some $i, j \geq 1$ iff $\rho_{2d}(u) = \rho_{2d}(p)$.*

We state the relationship between 2D palindromes and 1D palindromes in the following proposition.

Proposition 15. *Every 2D palindrome can be written as a palindrome and vice versa.*

Lemma 8 gives a characterization of 2D words that are conjugates of each other under the operation of dual catenation. The following result illustrates that a 2D word v can be decomposed in terms of 2D palindromes if it is a conjugate of its reverse, v^R.

Lemma 16. *If* $u \oplus v = v^R \oplus u$, *then* $v = y \oplus x$, $u = (x \oplus y)^{k\oplus} \oplus x$ *for* $x, y \in P_{2d}$ *and* $k \geq 0$.

In the following we calculate the total number of 2D palindromes of a given size over an alphabet of fixed size.

Observation: Consider all 2D palindromes of size (m, n) and $|\Sigma| = t$. Then

1. If $m = 2k$, then the total number of 2D palindrome words over Σ is t^{kn}.
2. If $m = 2k+1$, then the total number of 2D palindrome words over Σ is $t^{nk+k'}$ where if n' is even, then $n = 2k'$ and if n is odd then $n = 2k' - 1$.

Propositions 17 and 18 provides a necessary and sufficient condition under which a 2D word can be decomposed as a dual catenation of two non-empty 2D palindromes.

Proposition 17. *Let* $x, v, y \in \Sigma^{++}$ *be such that* $x \oplus y \in P_{2d}$. *If* $x \oplus v \oplus y \in P_{2d}$ *then* $v = v_1 \oplus v_2$ *such that* $v_1, v_2 \in P_{2d}$.

Proof. Let $x \oplus y \in P_{2d}$ and $x \oplus v \oplus y \in P_{2d}$. Let the sizes of x, v, y be $(m_1, n_1), (m_2, n_2), (m_3, n_3)$ respectively. Then we have following cases:

Case 1: $(m_1, n_1) = (m_3, n_3)$. Since $x \oplus y, x \oplus v \oplus y \in P_{2d}$, $x \oplus y = (x \oplus y)^R = y^R \oplus x^R$ and $x \oplus v \oplus y = (x \oplus v \oplus y)^R = y^R \oplus v^R \oplus x^R$ which implies that $x = y^R$ and $v = v^R$.

Case 2: Without loss of generality, let us assume that $m_1 = m_2 = m_3$. The case when $n_1 = n_2 = n_3$ can be proved similarly. Let $n_1 < n_3$.

Case 2(a): $n_3 \leq n_1 + n_2$. Since $x \oplus y = x \obar y \in P_{2d}$, i.e., $x \obar y = y^R \obar x^R$, we get $y^R = x \obar y_1$ and $y_2 = x^R$ for $y = y_1 \obar y_2$ where $y_1, y_2 \in \Sigma^{++}$ which implies $y_2^R \obar y_1^R = x \obar y_1$ which further implies $y_1 = y_1^R$ and $x = y_2^R$. Also, since $x \oplus v \oplus y = x \obar v \obar y \in P_{2d}$, i.e., $x \obar v \obar y = y^R \obar v^R \obar x^R$, we get $y^R = x \obar v_1$ and $v^R \obar x^R = v_2 \obar y$ for $v = v_1 \obar v_2$ where $v_1, v_2 \in \Sigma^{++}$. This implies $v_2 \obar y = v^R \obar x^R = (v_1 \obar v_2)^R \obar x^R = v_2^R \obar v_1^R \obar x^R$ which further implies $v_2 \in P_{2d}$. Also, $y^R = x \obar v_1$, i.e., $y_2^R \obar y_1^R = x \obar v_1$ which together with $y_2 = x^R$ implies $v_1 = y_1^R \in P_{2d}$. Thus $v = v_1 \obar v_2$ where $v_1, v_2 \in P_{2d}$.

Case 2(b): $n_3 > n_1 + n_2$. We know from Case 2(a) that $x \obar y \in P_{2d}$ implies $y_1 \in P_{2d}$ and $y_2 = x^R$ for $y = y_1 \obar y_2$ where $y_1, y_2 \in \Sigma^{++}$. Also, we have $x \obar v \obar y = y^R \obar v^R \obar x^R$. This implies $y^R = x \obar v \obar y' = y''^R \obar y'^R$ and $y'' = v^R \obar x^R$ for $y = y' \obar y''$ which further implies $y' \in P_{2d}$ where $y', y'' \in \Sigma^{++}$. Also, $x \obar y = x \obar y' \obar y'' = x \obar y' \obar v^R \obar x^R = x \obar v \obar y' \obar x^R = y^R \obar x^R$ which by size argument implies $y' \obar v^R = v \obar y'$ and by Lemma 16 there exists $\alpha, \beta \in P_{2d}$ such that $y' = \alpha \obar (\beta \obar \alpha)^{i\obar}$ and $v = \alpha \obar \beta$ for $i \geq 0$.

Case 3: $n_1 \geq n_3$. The proof is similar to that of Case 2. □

Proposition 18. *Let $u, v \in \Sigma^{++}$ such that $u \in P_{2d}$, and either $u \oplus v \in P_{2d}$ or $v \oplus u \in P_{2d}$, then $v = x \oplus y$ where $x, y \in P_{2d}$.*

The following lemma shows the uniqueness of decomposition of a 2D primitive word into 2D palindromes.

Lemma 19. *For $x, y \in \Sigma^{++} \cap P_{2d}$, let $u = x \oplus y \in Q_{2d}$. Then $u \notin P_{2d}$, and x and y are unique such words.*

Proof. Assume that $u \in P_{2d}$. Then $u = x \oplus y = y^R \oplus x^R = y \oplus x$ which by Lemma 9 implies that $\rho_{2d}(x) = \rho_{2d}(y)$ which further implies that $u \notin Q_{2d}$, a contradiction. Thus $u \notin P_{2d}$.

Assume that there exists $\alpha, \beta \in \Sigma^{++} \cap P_{2d}$ such that $u = x \oplus y = \alpha \oplus \beta$, and $x \neq \alpha$, $y \neq \beta$. Let the sizes of x, y, α, β be $(m_1, n_1), (m_2, n_2), (m_1', n_1'), (m_2', n_2')$, respectively, for $m_1, n_1, m_2, n_2, m_1', n_1', m_2', n_2' \geq 1$. Let us assume that $m_1 = m_2 = m_1' = m_2'$. The case when $n_1 = n_2 = n_1' = n_2'$ can be proved similarly. Let $n_1 < n_1'$. Then $\alpha = x \oplus x' = x'^R \oplus x = \alpha^R$ and $y = x' \oplus \beta = \beta \oplus x'^R = y^R$ for $x' \in \Sigma^{++}$. Thus $u = x \oplus y = (x \oplus \beta) \oplus x'^R = x'^R \oplus (x \oplus \beta) = \alpha \oplus \beta$ which by Lemma 9 implies $\rho_{2d}(x \oplus \beta) = \rho_{2d}(x'^R)$ which further implies that $u \notin Q_{2d}$, a contradiction. Hence $x = \alpha$ and $y = \beta$. The case when $n_1 \geq n_1'$ will lead to the same contradiction. □

3.1 2D Palindrome Square Words

In this subsection, we study a special class of 2D palindromes namely *2D palindrome square words* which are 2D palindrome words of size (n, n) with some extra conditions as follows:

Definition 20. *Consider a 2D palindrome word $w = [w_{i,j}]$ of size (n, n), then w is said to be a 2D palindrome square word if $w_{i,j} = w_{j,i} = w_{k,l} = w_{l,k}$ where $k = n + 1 - j$ and $l = n + 1 - i$.*

In [4], 2D palindrome square words are referred to as *sq2DP* and defined as those 2D words that admit four symmetries, which are, identity, two diagonal reflections, and 180° rotation. (The first occurrence of 2D palindrome square word can be dated back to at least 79 AD with the discovery of famous "Sator Square", [15].)

Example 21. Let $\Sigma = \{a, b, c\}$, then $w = \begin{matrix} c & b & a \\ b & a & b \\ a & b & c \end{matrix}$ is a 2D palindrome square word of size $(3, 3)$.

In the last section, we have seen that any 2D palindrome can be written as a palindrome and vice versa. Similarly, every 2D palindrome square word can be written as a palindrome. However, every palindrome need not necessarily be written as 2D palindrome square word as demonstrated by the following example.

Example 22. Let $\Sigma = \{a, b, c\}$. Then $w = abcba$ is a palindrome, but w cannot be written as a 2D palindrome square word.

The following lemma follows immediately from the definition and hence the proof is omitted.

Lemma 23. *Let $w \in \Sigma^{++}$ be a 2D palindrome square word of size (n, n) given by $w = [w_{i,j}]$ Then, $p = w_{i,1}w_{i,2}\cdots w_{i,n-1}w_{i,n} = w_{n-(i-1),n}w_{n-(i-1),n-1} \cdots w_{n-(i-1),2}w_{n-(i-1),1} = w_{n,n-(i-1)}w_{n-1,n-(i-1)}\cdots w_{2,n-(i-1)}w_{1,n-(i-1)} = w_{1,i}w_{2,i}\cdots w_{n-1,i}w_{n,i}$.*

The following proposition demonstrates the construction of a 2D palindrome square word of size (n, n) from a 2D palindrome square word of size $(n+1, n+1)$.

Proposition 24. *Let $w \in \Sigma^{++}$ be a 2D palindrome square word of size $(n + 1, n + 1)$. Then a 2D palindrome square word u of size (n, n) can be constructed from w as follows:*

1. *If $n + 1 = 2k + 1$ and $w = A_1 \ominus \cdots \ominus A_k \ominus A_{k+1} \ominus A_{k+2} \ominus \cdots \ominus A_{2k+1}$ where $A_i = w_{i,1} \obar \cdots \obar w_{i,k} \obar w_{i,k+1} \obar w_{i,k+2} \obar \cdots \obar w_{i,2k+1}$ for $1 \le i \le 2k + 1$, then $u = A'_1 \ominus \cdots \ominus A'_k \ominus A'_{k+2} \ominus \cdots \ominus A'_{2k+1}$ where $A'_j = w_{j,1} \obar \cdots \obar w_{j,k} \obar w_{j,k+2} \obar \cdots \obar w_{j,2k+1}$ for $1 \le j \le k$ and $k + 2 \le j \le 2k + 1$.*
2. *If $n + 1 = 2k$ and $w = B_1 \ominus \cdots \ominus B_k \ominus B_{k+1} \ominus B_{k+2} \ominus \cdots \ominus B_{2k}$ where $B_i = w_{i,1} \obar \cdots \obar w_{i,k} \obar w_{i,k+1} \obar w_{i,k+2} \obar \cdots \obar w_{i,2k}$ for $1 \le i \le 2k$ then, $u = B'_1 \ominus \cdots \ominus B'_k \ominus B'_{k+2} \ominus \cdots B'_{2k}$ where $B'_j = w_{j,1} \obar \cdots w_{j,k} \obar w_{j,k+2} \obar w_{j,2k}$ for $1 \le j \le k - 1$, $B'_k = w_{k,1} \obar \cdots \obar w_{k,k} \obar w_{k+1,k+2} \obar \cdots w_{k+1,2k}$, $B'_j = w_{j,1} \obar \cdots \obar w_{j,k-1} \obar w_{j,k+1} \obar \cdots \obar w_{j,2k}$ for $k + 2 \le j \le 2k$.*

We demonstrate Proposition 24 using the following example.

Example 25. From $w \in \Sigma^{++}$ which is a 2D palindrome square word, we construct u, and then from u, v is constructed such that u and v are 2D palindromes. Note that, the letters in bold denote the letters to be deleted.

$$w = \begin{array}{cccccc} e & s & c & \mathbf{a} & p & e \\ s & c & o & \mathbf{q} & n & p \\ c & o & r & \mathbf{t} & \mathbf{q} & \mathbf{a} \\ \mathbf{a} & \mathbf{q} & \mathbf{t} & \mathbf{r} & o & c \\ p & n & \mathbf{q} & o & c & s \\ e & p & \mathbf{a} & c & s & e \end{array}, \quad u = \begin{array}{ccccc} e & s & \mathbf{c} & p & e \\ s & c & \mathbf{o} & n & p \\ \mathbf{c} & \mathbf{o} & \mathbf{r} & \mathbf{o} & \mathbf{c} \\ p & n & \mathbf{o} & c & s \\ e & p & \mathbf{c} & s & e \end{array}, \quad v = \begin{array}{cccc} e & s & p & e \\ s & c & n & p \\ p & n & c & s \\ e & p & s & e \end{array}$$

Lemma 26. *Let $w \in \Sigma^{++}$ be a 2D palindrome square word of size (n, n) then every row of $w \obar w^{CR}$ and every column of $w \ominus w^{CR}$ is a 2D palindrome. Similar property holds for $w^{CR} \oplus w$, $w \oplus w^{ACR}$, $w^{ACR} \oplus w$.*

However, the above lemma does not hold in case of general 2D palindromes that are not 2D palindrome square words as demonstrated by the following example.

Example 27. Let $\Sigma = \{a, b, c\}$ and for a given $w \in \Sigma^{++}$ one can observe that none of the rows of $w \oplus w^{CR}$ are 2D palindromes.

$$w = \begin{matrix} a & b & c \\ c & a & c \\ c & b & a \end{matrix}, \quad w \oplus w^{CR} = \begin{matrix} a & b & c & c & c & a \\ c & a & c & b & a & b \\ c & b & a & a & c & c \end{matrix}$$

Observation: Let $|\Sigma| = t$ and consider all 2D palindrome square words of size (m, m). Then,

1. The total number of 2D palindrome square words of size $(2k, 2k)$ is $t^{k(k+1)}$.
2. The total number of 2D palindrome square words of size $(2k+1, 2k+1)$ is $t^{(k+1)^2}$.

3.2 Non-Recognizability of the Set of 2D Palindromes

The class of regular 2D languages is the smallest class of 2D languages over an alphabet Σ containing all singleton languages, and thus it is believed that the class of recognizable 2D (picture) languages is a two-dimensional equivalent of regular word languages, [13]. It is known that the set of all palindromes is not regular but a context-free language. In this subsection we prove the non-recognizability of the set of all 2D palindromes.

Let $w = [w_{i,j}]$ be a 2D word of size (m, n). Let us call the square 2D word of size $(2, 2)$ a tile. By $B_{2,2}(w)$, let us denote the set of all tiles/subwords of w of size $(2, 2)$. Let w' be a word of size $(m+2, n+2)$ obtained from w by surrounding w with a special boundary symbol # such that $\# \notin \Sigma$.

For a 2D word w of size (m, n), the projection by mapping π of w is a 2D word $w' \in \Sigma^{**}$ such that $w'_{i,j} = \pi(w_{i,j})$, for all $1 \leq i \leq m, 1 \leq j \leq n$. Similarly, the projection by mapping π of a 2D language L is the language $L' = \{w' : w' = \pi(w)\ \forall w \in L\}$.

Definition 28 [5]**.** *Let Γ be a finite alphabet. A 2D language $L \subseteq \Gamma^{**}$ is local if there exists a finite set Θ of tiles over the alphabet $\Gamma \cup \{\#\}$ such that $L = \{w \in \Gamma^{**} : B_{2,2}(w') \subseteq \Theta\}$, whereas Γ is called a local alphabet.*

Definition 29. *A tiling system (TS) is a 4-tuple $\tau = (\Sigma, \Gamma, \Theta, \pi)$, where Σ and Γ are two finite alphabets, Θ is a finite set of tiles over the alphabet $\Gamma \cup \{\#\}$ and $\pi : \Gamma \to \Sigma$ is a projection.*

A tiling system τ is said to recognize a language L, denoted by $L = L(\tau)$, if $L = \pi(L')$ where L' is the underlying local language. A language $L \subseteq \Sigma^{**}$ is said to be *recognizable* if there exists a tiling system $\tau = (\Sigma, \Gamma, \Theta, \pi)$ such that $L = L(\tau)$.

The following lemma is analogous to the Pumping lemma for regular languages.

Lemma 30 [5] *(Horizontal Iteration Lemma). Let L be a recognizable two-dimensional language. Then there is a function $\varphi : \mathbb{N} \to \mathbb{N}$ such that if p is a word in L such that the number of rows of p, $|p|_{row} = n$ and the number of columns of p, $|p|_{col} > \varphi(n)$, we may write $p = x \oplus q \oplus y$ with $|x \oplus q|_{col} \leq \varphi(n)$ and $|y|_{col} \geq 1$; and for all $i \geq 0$, word $x \oplus q^{i\oplus} \oplus y$ is in L. Furthermore, $\varphi(n) \leq \gamma^n$, $n \in \mathbb{N}$, where γ is the size of any local alphabet used to represent L.*

Theorem 31. *The set of all 2D palindromes, P_{2d} is not a recognizable 2D language.*

Proof. We prove the result by contradiction. By $|p|_{row}$ and by $|p|_{col}$, let us denote the number of rows and columns of a 2D word p, respectively.

Let us assume that P_{2d} is recognizable. Then, let $\tau = (\Sigma, \Gamma, \Theta, \pi)$ be a tiling system that recognizes P_{2d} such that $\Sigma = \{a, c\}$, $\Gamma = \{0, 1, 2\}$ and $\pi : \tau \to \Sigma$ be such that $\pi(0) = \pi(1) = a$ and $\pi(2) = c$. Thus, the size of local alphabet, $\gamma = 3$.

For $p \in P_{2d}$, let $|p|_{row} = 2k$. Then by Horizontal Iteration Lemma, there exists a function $\varphi : \mathbb{N} \to \mathbb{N}$ such that $\varphi(2k) \leq 3^{2k}$, $|p|_{col} = 3^{2k+2} + 1 > \varphi(2k)$, and we can write $p = x \oplus q \oplus y$ with $|x \oplus q|_{col} \leq \varphi(2k)$ and $|y|_{col} \geq 1$; and for all $i \geq 0$, $x \oplus q^{i\oplus} \oplus y$ is in L.

Now, we have $l_2(p) = 3^{2k+2} + 1 = (2k' + 1) + 1$, and it is easy to observe that k' will always be even. Also, it can be verified that $\varphi(2k) < k'$. Let,

$$p = [(a \oplus c) \ominus (c \oplus a)]^{k\ominus}\}^{\frac{k'}{2}\oplus} \oplus (a \oplus a)^{2k\ominus} \oplus \{[(a \oplus c) \ominus (c \oplus a)]^{k\ominus}\}^{\frac{k'}{2}\oplus}.$$

We can write $p = p_1^{\frac{k'}{2}\oplus} \oplus p_2 \oplus p_1^{\frac{k'}{2}\oplus}$ where $p_1 = [(a \oplus c) \ominus (c \oplus a)]^{k\ominus}$ and $p_2 = (a \oplus a)^{2k\ominus}$. Clearly $p_2 \in P_{2d}$, and since p_1 has a 2D primitive root $((a \oplus c) \ominus (c \oplus a))$ which is a 2D palindrome, $p_1 \in P_{2d}$, and hence $p \in P_{2d}$. Since $\varphi(2k) < k'$ and $|x \oplus q|_{col} \leq \varphi(2k)$, q must be a subword of $\{[(a \oplus c) \ominus (c \oplus a)]^{k\ominus}\}^{\frac{k'}{2}\oplus}$ with $|q|_{col} \leq k'$. Thus we have following four cases:

Case 1: $q = (a \ominus c)^{k\ominus} \oplus q_1 \oplus (a \ominus c)^{k\ominus}$ where $q_1 \in \Sigma^{**}$. Then for $i = 2$, $x \oplus q^{2\oplus} \oplus y = x \oplus [(a \ominus c)^{k\ominus} \oplus q_1 \oplus (a \ominus c)^{k\ominus}]^{2\oplus} \oplus y = p_1^{m\oplus} \oplus p_2 \oplus p_3^{\frac{k'}{2}\oplus}$ where $m > \frac{k'}{2}$. This implies $x \oplus q^{2\oplus} \oplus y \notin P_{2d}$, a contradiction. The other cases can be proved similarly.

Case 2: $q = (a \ominus c)^{k\ominus} \oplus q_2 \oplus (c \ominus a)^{k\ominus}$ where $q_2 \in \Sigma^{**}$.

Case 3: $q = (c \ominus a)^{k\ominus} \oplus q_3 \oplus (c \ominus a)^{k\ominus}$ where $q_3 \in \Sigma^{**}$.

Case 4: $q = (c \ominus a)^{k\ominus} \oplus q_4 \oplus (a \ominus c)^{k\ominus}$ where $q_4 \in \Sigma^{**}$.

Since all the four cases lead to a contradiction, our assumption was incorrect, and hence P_{2d} is not recognizable. □

4 Conclusions

In this paper, we studied a special class of 2D words, namely 2D palindromes and 2D palindrome square words. In particular, we showed its relation with other types of 2D words, such as 2D primitive words, counted the number of 2D words give the size of an alphabet and proved the non-recognizability of the set of all 2D palindromes. We also studied the properties of special class of 2D palindromes, namely 2D palindrome square words.

Further directions of research include detailed investigation of important notions in combinatorics on words including, square free and cube freeness, exploration of the concept of 2D words and languages under the more generalized involution mappings, and extension of two fundamental results in combinatorics, namely, Fine-Wilf theorem and Lyndon-Schützenberger equation.

References

1. Amir, A., Benson, G.: Two-dimensional periodicity in rectangular arrays. SIAM J. Comput. **27**(1), 90–106 (1998)
2. Berthé, V., Vuillon, L.: Palindromes and two-dimensional Sturmian sequences. J. Automata Lang. Comb. **6**(2), 121–138 (2001)
3. De Natale, F.G.B., Giusto, D.D., Maccioni, F.: A symmetry-based approach to facial features extraction. In: Proceedings of 13th International Conference on Digital Signal Processing, vol. 2, pp. 521–525 (1997)
4. Geizhals, S., Sokol, D.: Finding maximal 2-dimensional palindromes. In: Grossi, R., Lewenstein, M. (eds.) 27th Annual Symposium on Combinatorial Pattern Matching (CPM 2016), vol. 54, pp. 19:1–19:12 (2016)
5. Giammarresi, D., Restivo, A.: Two-dimensional languages. In: Rozenberg, G., Salomaa, A. (eds.) Handbook of Formal Languages, pp. 215–267. Springer, Heidelberg (1997)
6. Hooda, A., Bronstein, M.M., Bronstein, A.M., Horaud, R.P.: Shape palindromes: analysis of intrinsic symmetries in 2D articulated shapes. In: Bruckstein, A.M., Haar Romeny, B.M., Bronstein, A.M., Bronstein, M.M. (eds.) SSVM 2011. LNCS, vol. 6667, pp. 665–676. Springer, Heidelberg (2012). doi:10.1007/978-3-642-24785-9_56
7. Hopcroft, J.E., Ullman, J.D.: Formal Languages and Their Relation to Automata. Addison-Wesley Longman Inc., Boston (1969)
8. Kiryati, N., Gofman, Y.: Detecting symmetry in grey level images: the global optimization approach. Int. J. Comput. Vision **29**(1), 29–45 (1998)
9. Kulkarni, M.S., Mahalingam, K.: Two-dimensional primitive words. Manuscript (in preparation)
10. Lothaire, M.: Combinatorics on Words. Cambridge University Press, Cambridge (1997)
11. Loy, G., Eklundh, J.-O.: Detecting symmetry and symmetric constellations of features. In: Leonardis, A., Bischof, H., Pinz, A. (eds.) ECCV 2006. LNCS, vol. 3952, pp. 508–521. Springer, Heidelberg (2006). doi:10.1007/11744047_39
12. Lyndon, R.C., Schützenberger, M.P.: The equation $a^m = b^n c^p$ in a free group. Mich. Math. J. **9**(4), 289–298 (1962)
13. Matz, O.: Recognizable vs. regular picture languages. In: Bozapalidis, S., Rahonis, G. (eds.) CAI 2007. LNCS, vol. 4728, pp. 112–121. Springer, Heidelberg (2007). doi:10.1007/978-3-540-75414-5_7
14. O'Mara, D., Owens, R.: Measuring bilateral symmetry in digital images. In: Proceedings of 1996 IEEE TENCON Digital Signal Processing Applications, vol. 1, pp. 151–156 (1996)

15. Pickover, C.A.: The Zen of Magic Squares, Circles, and Stars: An Exhibition of Surprising Structures Across Dimensions. Princeton University Press, Princeton (2002)
16. Raviv, D., Bronstein, A.M., Bronstein, M.M., Kimmel, R.: Symmetries of non-rigid shapes. In: 2007 IEEE 11th International Conference on Computer Vision. pp. 1–7 (2007)
17. Yu, S.S.: Languages and Codes. Tsang Hai Book Publishing Co., Taichung (2005)
18. Yu, S.S.: Palindrome words and reverse closed languages. Int. J. Comput. Math. **75**(4), 389–402 (2000)

Complexity

Complexity of Left-Ideal, Suffix-Closed and Suffix-Free Regular Languages

Janusz A. Brzozowski and Corwin Sinnamon(✉)

David R. Cheriton School of Computer Science, University of Waterloo, Waterloo, ON N2L 3G1, Canada
brzozo@uwaterloo.ca, sinncore@gmail.com

Abstract. A language L over an alphabet Σ is suffix-convex if, for any words $x, y, z \in \Sigma^*$, whenever z and xyz are in L, then so is yz. Suffix-convex languages include three special cases: left-ideal, suffix-closed, and suffix-free languages. We examine complexity properties of these three special classes of suffix-convex regular languages. In particular, we study the quotient/state complexity of boolean operations, product (concatenation), star, and reversal on these languages, as well as the size of their syntactic semigroups, and the quotient complexity of their atoms.

Keywords: Different alphabets · Left ideal · Most complex · Quotient/state complexity · Regular language · Suffix-closed · Suffix-convex · Suffix-free · Syntactic semigroup · Transition semigroup · Unrestricted complexity

1 Introduction

Suffix-Convex Languages. Convex languages were introduced in 1973 [27], and revisited in 2009 [1]. For $w, x, y \in \Sigma^*$, if $w = xy$, then y is a *suffix* of w. A language L is *suffix-convex* if, whenever z and xyz are in L, then yz is also in L, for all $x, y, z \in \Sigma^*$. Suffix-convex languages include three well-known subclasses: left-ideal, suffix-closed, and suffix-free languages. A language L is a *left ideal* if it is non-empty and satisfies the equation $L = \Sigma^* L$. Left ideals play a role in pattern matching: If one is searching for all words ending with words in some language L in a given text (a word over Σ^*), then one is looking for words in $\Sigma^* L$. Left ideals also constitute a basic concept in semigroup theory. A language L is *suffix-closed* if, whenever w is in L and x is a suffix of w, then x is also in L, for all $w, x \in \Sigma^*$. The complement of every suffix-closed language not equal to Σ^* is a left ideal. A language is *suffix-free* if no word in the language is a suffix of another word in the language. Suffix-free languages (with the exception of $\{\varepsilon\}$, where ε is the empty word) are suffix codes. They have many applications, and have been studied extensively; see [2] for example.

This work was supported by the Natural Sciences and Engineering Research Council of Canada grant No. OGP0000871.

F. Drewes et al. (Eds.): LATA 2017, LNCS 10168, pp. 171–182, 2017.
DOI: 10.1007/978-3-319-53733-7_12

Quotient/State Complexity. If Σ is an alphabet and $L \subseteq \Sigma^*$ is a language such that every letter of Σ appears in some word of L, then the *(left) quotient* of L by a word $w \in \Sigma^*$ is $w^{-1}L = \{x \mid wx \in L\}$. A language is regular if and only if it has a finite number of distinct quotients. So the number of quotients of L, the *quotient complexity* $\kappa(L)$ [3] of L, is a natural measure of complexity for L. A concept equivalent to quotient complexity is the *state complexity* [28] of L, which is the number of states in a complete minimal deterministic finite automaton (DFA) with alphabet Σ recognizing L. We refer to quotient/state complexity simply as *complexity.*

If L_n is a regular language of complexity n, and $\circ$ is a unary operation, then the *complexity of* $\circ$ is the maximal value of $\kappa(L_n^\circ)$, expressed as a function of n, as L_n ranges over all regular languages of complexity n. Similarly, if L'_m and L_n are regular languages of complexities m and n respectively, $\circ$ is a binary operation, then the *complexity of* $\circ$ is the maximal value of $\kappa(L'_m \circ L_n)$, expressed as a function of m and n, as L'_m and L_n range over all regular languages of complexities m and n. The complexity of an operation is a lower bound on its time and space complexities, and has been studied extensively; see [3,4,28].

In the past the complexity of a binary operation was studied under the assumption that the arguments of the operation are *restricted* to be over the same alphabet, but this restriction was removed in [5]. We study both the restricted and unrestricted cases.

Witnesses. To find the complexity of a unary operation we find an upper bound on this complexity, and languages that meet this bound. We require a language L_n for each $n \geqslant k$, that is, a sequence $(L_k, L_{k+1}, \dots)$, where k is a small integer, because the bound may not hold for small values of n. Such a sequence is a *stream* of languages. For a binary operation we require two streams. Sometimes the same stream can be used for both operands; in general, however, this is not the case. For example, the bound for union is mn, and it cannot be met by languages from one stream if $m = n$ because $L_n \cup L_n = L_n$ and the complexity is n instead of n^2.

Dialects. For all common binary operations on regular languages the second stream can be a "dialect" of the first, that is it can "differ only slightly" from the first, and all the bounds can still be met [4]. Let $\Sigma = \{a_1, \dots, a_k\}$ be an alphabet ordered as shown; if $L \subseteq \Sigma^*$, we denote it by $L(a_1, \dots, a_k)$ to stress its dependence on Σ. A *dialect* of L is obtained by deleting letters of Σ in the words of L, or replacing them by letters of another alphabet Σ'. More precisely, for a partial injective map $\pi \colon \Sigma \mapsto \Sigma'$, we obtain a dialect of L by replacing each letter $a \in \Sigma$ by $\pi(a)$ in every word of L, or deleting the word entirely if $\pi(a)$ is undefined. We write $L(\pi(a_1), \dots, \pi(a_k))$ to denote the dialect of $L(a_1, \dots, a_k)$ given by π, and we denote undefined values of π by "$-$". For example, if $L(a, b, c) = \{a, ab, ac\}$, then $L(b, -, d)$ is the language $\{b, bd\}$. Undefined values at the end of the alphabet are omitted. A similar definition applies to DFAs. Our definition of dialect is more general than that of [7,12], where only the case $\Sigma' = \Sigma$ was allowed.

Most Complex Streams. It was proved that there exists a stream $(L_3, L_4, \dots)$ of regular languages which together with some dialects meets all the complexity bounds for reversal, (Kleene) star, product (concatenation), and all binary boolean operations [4,5]. Moreover, this stream meets two additional complexity bounds: the size of the syntactic semigroup, and the complexities of atoms (discussed later). A stream of deterministic finite automata (DFAs) corresponding to a most complex language stream is a *most complex DFA stream.* In defining a most complex stream we try to minimize the size of the union of the alphabets of the dialects required to meet all the bounds.

Most complex streams are useful in the designs of systems dealing with regular languages and finite automata. To know the maximal sizes of automata that can be handled by the system it suffices to use the most complex stream to test all the operations.

It is known that there is a most complex stream of left ideals that meets all the bounds in both the restricted [7,12] and unrestricted [12] cases, but a most complex suffix-free stream does not exist [14].

Our Contributions

1. We derive a new left-ideal stream from the most complex left-ideal stream and show that it meets all the complexity bounds except that for product.
2. We prove that the complement of the new left-ideal stream is a most complex suffix-closed stream.
3. We find a new suffix-free stream that meets the bounds for star, product and boolean operations; it has simpler transformations than the known stream.
4. Our witnesses for left-ideal, suffix-closed, and suffix-free streams are all derived from one most complex regular stream.

2 Background

Finite Automata. A *deterministic finite automaton (DFA)* is a quintuple $\mathcal{D} = (Q, \Sigma, \delta, q_0, F)$, where Q is a finite non-empty set of *states*, Σ is a finite non-empty *alphabet*, $\delta\colon Q \times \Sigma \to Q$ is the *transition function*, $q_0 \in Q$ is the *initial* state, and $F \subseteq Q$ is the set of *final* states. We extend δ to a function $\delta\colon Q \times \Sigma^* \to Q$ as usual. A DFA $\mathcal{D}$ *accepts* a word $w \in \Sigma^*$ if $\delta(q_0, w) \in F$. The language accepted by $\mathcal{D}$ is denoted by $L(\mathcal{D})$. If q is a state of $\mathcal{D}$, then the language L^q of q is the language accepted by the DFA $(Q, \Sigma, \delta, q, F)$. A state is *empty* if its language is empty. Two states p and q of $\mathcal{D}$ are *equivalent* if $L^p = L^q$. A state q is *reachable* if there exists $w \in \Sigma^*$ such that $\delta(q_0, w) = q$. A DFA is *minimal* if all of its states are reachable and no two states are equivalent. Usually DFAs are used to establish upper bounds on the complexity of operations and also as witnesses that meet these bounds.

A *nondeterministic finite automaton (NFA)* is a quintuple $\mathcal{D} = (Q, \Sigma, \delta, I, F)$ where Q, Σ and F are defined as in a DFA, $\delta\colon Q \times \Sigma \to 2^Q$ is the *transition function*, and $I \subseteq Q$ is the *set of initial states.* An *ε-NFA* is an NFA in which transitions under the empty word ε are also permitted.

Transformations. We use $Q_n = \{0, \ldots, n-1\}$ as our basic set with n elements. A *transformation* of Q_n is a mapping $t\colon Q_n \to Q_n$. The *image* of $q \in Q_n$ under t is denoted by qt. If s and t are transformations of Q_n, their composition is denoted $(qs)t$ when applied to $q \in Q_n$. Let $\mathcal{T}_{Q_n}$ be the set of all n^n transformations of Q_n; then $\mathcal{T}_{Q_n}$ is a monoid under composition.

For $k \geqslant 2$, a transformation (permutation) t of a set $P = \{q_0, q_1, \ldots, q_{k-1}\} \subseteq Q$ is a *k-cycle* if $q_0 t = q_1, q_1 t = q_2, \ldots, q_{k-2} t = q_{k-1}, q_{k-1} t = q_0$. This k-cycle is denoted by $(q_0, q_1, \ldots, q_{k-1})$. A 2-cycle (q_0, q_1) is called a *transposition.* A transformation that sends all the states of P to q and acts as the identity on the remaining states is denoted by $(P \to q)$ the transformation $(Q_n \to p)$ is called *constant.* If $P = \{p\}$ we write $(p \to q)$ for $(\{p\} \to q)$. The identity transformation is denoted by $\mathbb{1}$. The notation $(_i^j\ q \to q+1)$ denotes a transformation that sends q to $q+1$ for $i \leqslant q \leqslant j$ and is the identity for the remaining states. the notation $(_i^j\ q \to q-1)$ is defined similarly.

Semigroups. The *Myhill congruence* $\approx_L$ [25] (also known as the *syntactic congruence*) of a language $L \subseteq \Sigma^*$ is defined on Σ^+ as follows: For $x, y \in \Sigma^+, x \approx_L y$ if and only if $wxz \in L \Leftrightarrow wyz \in L$ for all $w, z \in \Sigma^*$. The quotient set $\Sigma^+/{\approx_L}$ of equivalence classes of $\approx_L$ is a semigroup, the *syntactic semigroup* T_L of L.

Let $\mathcal{D} = (Q_n, \Sigma, \delta, 0, F)$ be a DFA. For each word $w \in \Sigma^*$, the transition function induces a transformation δ_w of Q_n by w: for all $q \in Q_n$, $q\delta_w = \delta(q, w)$. The set $T_{\mathcal{D}}$ of all such transformations by non-empty words is the *transition semigroup* of $\mathcal{D}$ under composition [26]. Sometimes we use the word w to denote the transformation it induces; thus we write qw instead of $q\delta_w$. We extend the notation to sets: if $P \subseteq Q_n$, then $Pw = \{pw \mid p \in P\}$. We also find write $P \xrightarrow{w} Pw$ to indicate that the image of P under w is Pw.

If $\mathcal{D}$ is a minimal DFA of L, then $T_{\mathcal{D}}$ is isomorphic to the syntactic semigroup T_L of L [26], and we represent elements of T_L by transformations in $T_{\mathcal{D}}$. The size of this semigroup has been used as a measure of complexity [4,18,21,24].

Atoms. Atoms are defined by a left congruence, where two words x and y are equivalent if $ux \in L$ if and only if $uy \in L$ for all $u \in \Sigma^*$. Thus x and y are equivalent if $x \in u^{-1}L$ if and only if $y \in u^{-1}L$. An equivalence class of this relation is an *atom* of L [17]. Thus an atom is a non-empty intersection of complemented and uncomplemented quotients of L. The number of atoms and their complexities were suggested as possible measures of complexity of regular languages [4], because all the quotients of a language, and also the quotients of atoms, are always unions of atoms [16,17,22].

Our Key Witness. The stream $(\mathcal{D}_n(a, b, c) \mid n \geqslant 3)$ of Definition 1 and Fig. 1 was introduced in [4]. It will be used as a component in all the classes of languages examined in this paper. It was shown in [4] that this stream together with some dialects is most complex for restricted operations, and also for unrestricted operations if an input d that induces the identity transformation is added [5,12].

Definition 1. *For* $n \geqslant 3$, *let* $\mathcal{D}_n = \mathcal{D}_n(a, b, c) = (Q_n, \Sigma, \delta_n, 0, \{n-1\})$, *where* $\Sigma = \{a, b, c\}$, *and* δ_n *is defined by* $a\colon (0, \ldots, n-1)$, $b\colon (0, 1)$, $c\colon (n-1 \to 0)$.

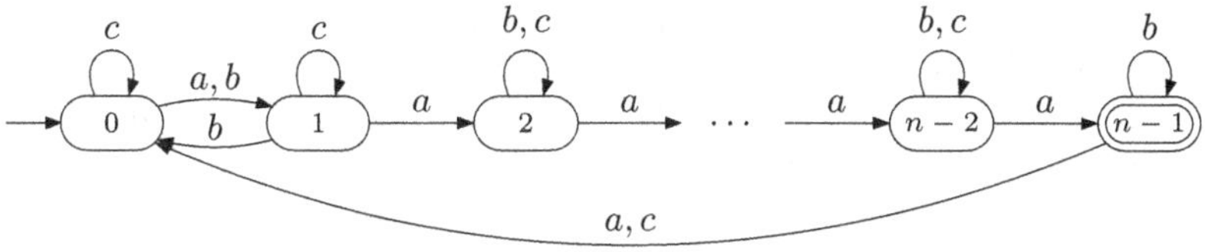

Fig. 1. Minimal DFA of a most complex regular language.

3 Left Ideals

The following stream was studied in [18] and also in [6,7,13]. This stream is most complex when the two alphabets are the same in binary operations [7]. It is also most complex for unrestricted operations [12].

Definition 2. *For $n \geqslant 4$, let $\mathcal{D}_n = \mathcal{D}_n(a,b,c,d,e) = (Q_n, \Sigma, \delta_n, 0, \{n-1\})$, where $\Sigma = \{a,b,c,d,e\}$, and δ_n is defined by transformations $a\colon (1,\dots,n-1)$, $b\colon (1,2)$, $c\colon (n-1 \to 1)$, $d\colon (n-1 \to 0)$, and $e\colon (Q_n \to 1)$. See Fig. 2. Let $L_n = L_n(a,b,c,d,e)$ be the language accepted by $\mathcal{D}_n$.*

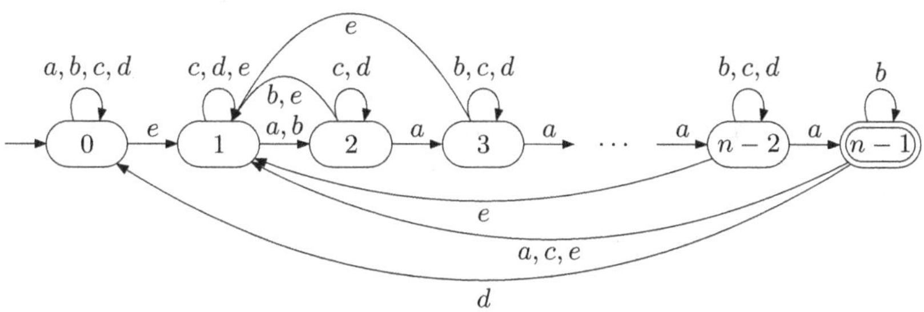

Fig. 2. Minimal DFA of a most complex left ideal $L_n(a,b,c,d,e)$.

Theorem 3 (Most Complex Left Ideals [7,12]). *For each $n \geqslant 4$, the DFA of Definition 2 is minimal. The stream $(L_n(a,b,c,d,e) \mid n \geqslant 4)$ with some dialect streams is most complex in the class of regular left ideals.*

1. *The syntactic semigroup of $L_n(a,b,c,d,e)$ has cardinality $n^{n-1}+n-1$.*
2. *Each quotient of $L_n(a,-,-,d,e)$ has complexity n.*
3. *The reverse of $L_n(a,-,c,d,e)$ has complexity $2^{n-1}+1$, and $L_n(a,-,c,d,e)$ has $2^{n-1}+1$ atoms.*
4. *For each atom A_S of $L_n(a,b,c,d,e)$, the complexity $\kappa(A_S)$ satisfies:*

$$\kappa(A_S) = \begin{cases} n, & \text{if } S = Q_n; \\ 2^{n-1}, & \text{if } S = \emptyset; \\ 1 + \sum_{x=1}^{|S|} \sum_{y=1}^{n-|S|} \binom{n-1}{x}\binom{n-x-1}{y-1}, & \text{otherwise.} \end{cases}$$

5. *The star of* $L_n(a,-,-,-,e)$ *has complexity* $n+1$.
6. (a) *Restricted product:* $\kappa(L'_m(a,-,-,-,e)L_n(a,-,-,-,e)) = m+n-1$.
   (b) *Unrestricted product:* $\kappa(L'_m(a,b,-,d,e)L_n(a,d,-,c,e)) = mn+m+n$.
7. (a) *Restricted complexity:* $\kappa(L'_m(a,-,c,-,e) \circ L_n(a,-,e,-,c)) = mn$.
   (b) *Unrestricted complexity:* $\kappa(L'_m(a,b,-,d,e) \circ L_n(a,d,-,c,e)) = (m+1)(n+1)$ *if* $\circ \in \{\cup, \oplus\}$), $mn+m$ *if* $\circ = \setminus$, *and* mn *if* $\circ = \cap$.

   In both cases the bounds for boolean operations are the same as those for regular languages.

We now define a new left-ideal witness similar to the witness in Definition 2.

Definition 4. *For* $n \geqslant 4$, *let* $\mathcal{E}_n = \mathcal{E}_n(a,b,c,d,e) = (Q_n, \Sigma, \delta_n, 0, \{1,\dots,n-1\})$, *where* Σ *and the transformations induced by its letters are as in* $\mathcal{D}_n$ *of Definition 2. Let* $M_n = M_n(a,b,c,d,e)$ *be the language accepted by* $\mathcal{E}_n$.

Theorem 5 (Nearly Most Complex Left Ideals). *For each* $n \geqslant 4$, *the DFA of Definition 4 is minimal and its language* $M_n(a,b,c,d,e)$ *is a left ideal of complexity* n. *The stream* $(M_n(a,b,c,d,e) \mid n \geqslant 4)$ *with some dialect streams meets all the complexity bounds for left ideals, except those for product.*

Proof. It is easily verified that $\mathcal{E}_n(a,-,-,d,e)$ is minimal; hence $M_n(a,b,c,d,e)$ has complexity n. M_n is a left ideal because, for each letter ℓ of Σ, and each word $w \in \Sigma^*$, $w \in M_n$ implies $\ell w \in M_n$. We prove all the claims of Theorem 3 except the claims in Item 6.

1. **Semigroup.** The transition semigroup is independent of the set of final states; hence it has the size of the DFA of the most complex left ideal.
2. **Quotients.** Obvious.
3. **Reversal.** The upper bound of $2^{n-1}+1$ was proved in [8], and it was shown in [17] that the number of atoms is the same as the complexity of the reverse. Applying the standard NFA construction for reversal, we reverse every transition in DFA $\mathcal{E}_n$ and interchange the final and initial states, yielding the NFA in Fig. 3, where the initial states (unmarked) are $Q_n \setminus \{0\}$.
   We perform the subset construction. Set $Q_n \setminus \{0\}$ is initial. From $\{q_1,\dots,q_k\}$, $1 \leqslant q_1 \leqslant q_k$, we delete q_i, $q_1 \leqslant q_i \leqslant q_k \leqslant n-1$, by applying $a^{q_i}da^{n-1-q_i}$. Thus all 2^{n-1} subsets of $Q_n \setminus \{0\}$ can be reached, and Q_n is reached from the initial state $\{1\}$ by e. For any distinct $S,T \subseteq Q_n$ with $q \in S \setminus T$, either $q=0$, in which case S is final and T is non-final, or $Sa^{q-1}e = Q_n$ and $Ta^{q-1}e = \emptyset$. Hence all $2^{n-1}+1$ states are pairwise distinguishable.
4. **Atoms.** The upper bounds in Theorem 3 for left ideals were derived in [6]. The proof of [6] that these bounds are met applies also to our witness M_n.
5. **Star.** The upper bound $n+1$ was proved in [8]. To construct an NFA recognizing $(M_n(a,-,-,d,e))^*$ we add a new initial state $0'$ which is also final and has the same transitions as the former initial state 0. We then add an ε-transition from each final state of $\mathcal{E}(a,-,-,d,e)$ to the initial state $0'$. The language recognized by the new NFA $\mathcal{N}$ is $(M_n(a,-,-,d,e))^*$. The final state $\{0'\}$ in the subset construction for $\mathcal{N}$ is distinguishable from every other final state, since it rejects a, whereas other final states accept it.

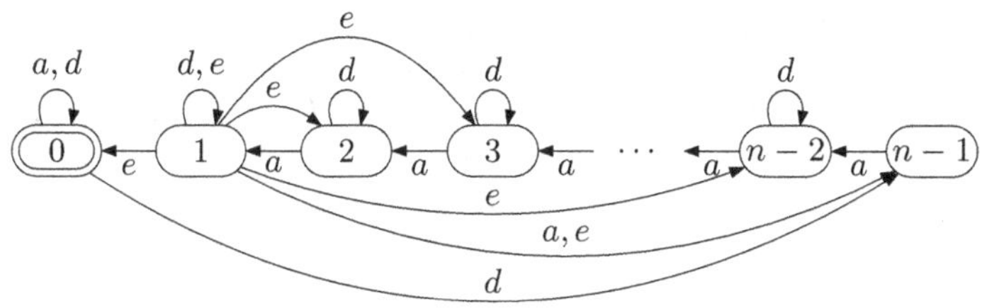

Fig. 3. NFA for reversal of $M_n(a, -, -, d, e)$.

6. **Product.** Not applicable.
7. **Boolean Operations.** *Proof sketch; omitted proofs can be found in* [11].
   (a) Restricted complexity: The upper bound of mn is the same as for regular languages. We show that $M'_m(a, b, -, d, e) \circ M_n(a, e, -, d, b)$ has complexity mn. Using the standard construction for boolean operations, we consider the direct product of $\mathcal{E}'_m(a, b, -, d, e)$ and $\mathcal{E}_n(a, e, -, d, b)$. The set of final states of the direct product varies depending on $\circ \in \{\cup, \oplus, \setminus, \cap\}$.
   It is easy to see that all mn states are reachable. We then verify for each operation that every two states in the direct product are distinguishable.
   (b) Unrestricted complexity: To produce a DFA recognizing $M'_m(a, b, c, d, e) \circ M_n(a, e, f, d, b)$, we add an empty state $\emptyset'$ to $\mathcal{E}'_m(a, b, c, d, e)$, and send all the transitions from any state of Q'_m under f to $\emptyset'$. Similarly add an empty state $\emptyset$ to $\mathcal{E}_n(a, e, f, d, b)$ and send all the transitions from any state of Q_n under c to $\emptyset$. Now the DFAs are over $\{a, b, c, d, e, f\}$ and we take their direct product. By the restricted case all the states of $Q'_m \times Q_n$ are reachable and distinguishable using words in $\{a, b, d, e\}^*$. Let $R_{\emptyset'} = \{(\emptyset', q) \mid q \in Q_n\}$ and $C_\emptyset = \{(p', \emptyset) \mid p' \in Q'_m\}$. States of $R_{\emptyset'} \cup C_\emptyset \cup \{(\emptyset', \emptyset)\}$ are easily seen to be reachable.
   Union. Here all $(m+1)(n+1)$ states turn out to pairwise distinguishable.
   Symmetric Difference. Same as union.
   Difference. States of $R_{\emptyset'} \cup \{(\emptyset', \emptyset)\}$ are empty and therefore equivalent. However, since the alphabet of $M'_m(a, b, c, d, e) \setminus M_n(a, e, f, d, b)$ is $\{a, b, c, d, e\}$ we omit f, delete the states of $R_{\emptyset'} \cup \{(\emptyset', \emptyset)\}$, and have a DFA over $\{a, b, c, d, e\}$ accepting $M'_m(a, b, c, d, e) \setminus M_n(a, e, f, d, b)$. The $mn+m$ remaining states are pairwise distinguishable.
   Intersection. States of $R_{\emptyset'} \cup C_\emptyset \cup \{(\emptyset', \emptyset)\}$ are empty and therefore equivalent. Since the alphabet of $M'_m(a, b, c, d, e) \cap M_n(a, e, f, d, b)$ is $\{a, b, d, e\}$, we omit c and f, delete the states of $R_{\emptyset'} \cup C_\emptyset \cup \{(\emptyset', \emptyset)\}$, and have a DFA over $\{a, b, d, e\}$ accepting $M'_m(a, b, c, d, e) \cap M_n(a, e, f, d, b)$. By the restricted case, all mn states are pairwise distinguishable. □

4 Suffix-Closed Languages

The complexity of suffix-closed languages was studied in [9] in the restricted case, and the syntactic semigroup of these languages, in [13,15,18]; however, most complex suffix-closed streams have not been examined.

Definition 6. *For $n \geqslant 4$, let $\mathcal{D}_n = \mathcal{D}_n(a,b,c,d,e) = (Q_n, \Sigma, \delta_n, 0, \{0\})$, where $\Sigma = \{a,b,c,d,e\}$, and δ_n is defined by transformations $a\colon (1,\dots,n-1)$, $b\colon (1,2)$, $c\colon (n-1 \to 1)$, $d\colon (n-1 \to 0)$, $e\colon (Q_n \to 1)$. Let $L_n = L_n(a,b,c,d,e)$ be the language accepted by $\mathcal{D}_n$; this language is the complement of the left ideal of Definition 4. The structure of $\mathcal{D}_n(a,b,c,d,e)$ is shown in Fig. 4.*

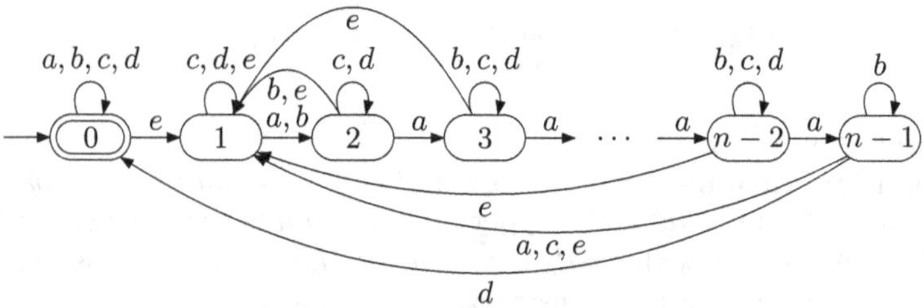

Fig. 4. Minimal DFA $\mathcal{D}_n(a,b,c,d,e)$ of Definition 6.

Theorem 7 (Most Complex Suffix-Closed Languages). *For each $n \geqslant 4$, the DFA of Definition 6 is minimal and its language $L_n(a,b,c,d,e)$ is suffix-closed and has complexity n. The stream $(L_n(a,b,c,d,e) \mid n \geqslant 4)$ with some dialect streams is most complex in the class of suffix-closed languages.*

1. *The syntactic semigroup of $L_n(a,b,c,d,e)$ has cardinality $n^{n-1}+n-1$. Moreover, fewer than five inputs do not suffice to meet this bound.*
2. *All quotients of $L_n(a,-,-,d,e)$ have complexity n.*
3. *The reverse of $L_n(a,-,-,d,e)$ has complexity $2^{n-1}+1$, and $L_n(a,-,-,d,e)$ has $2^{n-1}+1$ atoms.*
4. *For each atom A_S of $L_n(a,b,c,d,e)$, the complexity $\kappa(A_S)$ satisfies:*

$$\kappa(A_S) = \begin{cases} n, & \text{if } S = \emptyset; \\ 2^{n-1}, & \text{if } S = Q_n; \\ 1 + \sum_{x=1}^{|S|} \sum_{y=1}^{n-|S|} \binom{n-1}{y}\binom{n-y-1}{x-1}, & \text{if } \{0\} \subseteq S \subsetneq Q_n. \end{cases}$$

5. *The star of $L_n(a,-,-,d,e)$ has complexity n.*
6. *(a) Restricted complexity: $\kappa(L'_m(a,b,-,d,e)L_n(a,e,-,d,b)) = mn - n + 1$.*
   (b) Unrestricted complexity: $\kappa(L'_m(a,b,c,d,e)L_n(a,e,f,d,b)) = mn + m + 1$.
7. *(a) Restricted complexity: $\kappa(L'_m(a,b,-,d,e) \circ L_n(a,e,-,d,b)) = mn$ for $\circ \in \{\cup, \oplus, \cap, \setminus\}$.*
   (b) Unrestricted complexity: $\kappa(L'_m(a,b,c,d,e) \circ L_n(a,e,f,d,b)) = (m+1)(n+1)$ if $\circ \in \{\cup, \oplus\}$, it is $mn+m$ if $\circ = \setminus$, and mn if $\circ = \cap$.

The above results for syntactic complexity, reversal, complexity of atoms, and restricted boolean operations follow easily from Theorem 5.

5 Suffix-Free Languages

The complexity of suffix-free languages was studied in detail in [10,14,19,20,23]. For completeness we present a short summary of some of those results. The main result of [14] is a proof that *a most complex suffix-free language does not exist.* Since every suffix-free language has an empty quotient, the restricted and unrestricted cases for binary operations coincide.

For $n \geqslant 6$, the transition semigroup of the DFA defined below is the largest transition semigroup of a minimal DFA accepting a suffix-free language.

Definition 8. *For $n \geqslant 4$, we define the DFA $\mathcal{D}_n(a,b,c,d,e) = (Q_n, \Sigma, \delta, 0, F)$, where $Q_n = \{0,\dots,n-1\}$, $\Sigma = \{a,b,c,d,e\}$, δ is defined by the transformations $a\colon (0 \to n-1)(1,\dots,n-2)$, $b\colon (0 \to n-1)(1,2)$, $c\colon (0 \to n-1)(n-2 \to 1)$, $d\colon (\{0,1\} \to n-1)$, $e\colon (Q \setminus \{0\} \to n-1)(0 \to 1)$, and $F = \{q \in Q_n \setminus \{0,n-1\} \mid q \text{ is odd}\}$. For $n = 4$, a and b coincide, and we can use $\Sigma = \{b,c,d,e\}$. Let the transition semigroup of $\mathcal{D}_n$ be $\mathbf{T}^{\geqslant 6}(n)$.*

The main result for this witness is the following theorem:

Theorem 9 (Semigroup, Quotients, Reversal, Atoms, Boolean Ops.). *Consider DFA $\mathcal{D}_n(a,b,c,d,e)$ of Definition 8; its language $L_n(a,b,c,d,e)$ is a suffix-free language of complexity n. Moreover, it meets the following bounds:*

1. *For $n \geqslant 6$, $L_n(a,b,c,d,e)$ meets the bound $(n-1)^{n-2} + n - 2$ for syntactic complexity, and at least five letters are required to reach this bound.*
2. *The quotients of $L_n(a,-,-,-,e)$ have complexity $n-1$, except for L which has complexity n, and the empty quotient which has complexity 1.*
3. *For $n \geqslant 4$, the reverse of $L_n(a,-,c,-,e)$ has complexity $2^{n-2}+1$, and $L_n(a,-,c,-,e)$ has $2^{n-2}+1$ atoms.*
4. *Each atom A_S of $L_n(a,b,c,d,e)$ has maximal complexity:*

$$\kappa(A_S) = \begin{cases} 2^{n-2}+1, & \text{if } S = \emptyset; \\ n, & \text{if } S = \{0\}; \\ 1 + \sum_{x=1}^{|S|} \sum_{y=0}^{n-2-|S|} \binom{n-2}{x}\binom{n-2-x}{y}, & \emptyset \neq S \subseteq \{1,\dots,n-2\}. \end{cases}$$

5. *For $n,m \geqslant 4$, the complexity of $L_m(a,b,-,d,e) \circ L_n(b,a,-,d,e)$ is $mn-(m+n-2)$ if $\circ \in \{\cup,\oplus\}$, $mn-(m+2n-4)$ if $\circ = \setminus$, and $mn-2(m+n-3)$ if $\circ = \cap$.*
6. *A language which has a subsemigroup of $\mathbf{T}^{\geqslant 6}(n)$ as its syntactic semigroup cannot meet the bounds for star and product.*

The DFA defined below has the largest transition semigroup when $n \in \{4,5\}$. The transition semigroup of this DFA is $\mathbf{T}^{\leqslant 5}(n)$, and at least n letters are required to generate it.

Definition 10. *For $n \geqslant 4$, $\mathcal{D}_n(a,b,c_1,\dots,c_{n-2}) = (Q_n, \Sigma_n, \delta, 0, \{n-2\})$, where $Q_n = \{0,\dots,n-1\}$, $\Sigma_n = \{a,b,c_1,\dots,c_{n-2}\}$, δ is given by $a\colon (0 \to n-1)(1,\dots,n-2)$, $b\colon (0 \to n-1)(1,2)$, and $c_p\colon (p \to n-1)(0 \to p)$ for $1 \leqslant p \leqslant n-2$.*

We now define a DFA based on Definition 10, but with only three inputs.

Definition 11. *For $n \geqslant 4$, define the DFA $\mathcal{D}_n = (Q_n, \Sigma, \delta, 0, \{n-2\})$, where $Q_n = \{0, \ldots, n-1\}$, $\Sigma = \{a, b, c\}$, and δ is defined by a: $(0 \to n-1)(1, \ldots, n-2)$, b: $(0 \to n-1)(1, 2)$, c: $(1, n-1)(0 \to 1)$. See Fig. 5.*

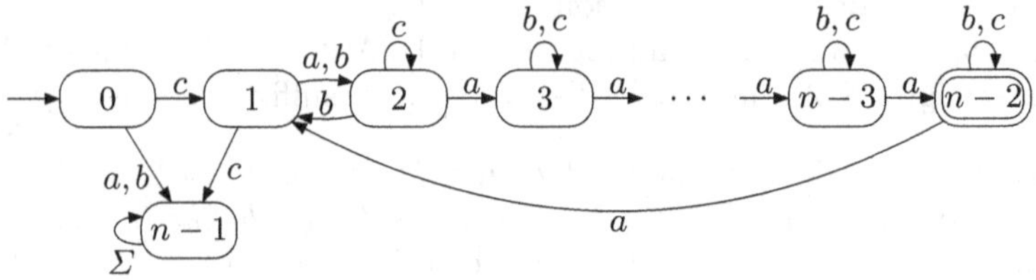

Fig. 5. Witness for star, product, and boolean operations.

Theorem 12 (Star, Product, Boolean Operations). *Let $\mathcal{D}_n(a, b, c)$ be the DFA of Definition 11, and let the language it accepts be $L_n(a, b, c)$. Then L_n and its permutational dialects meet the bounds for star, product, and boolean operations as follows:*

1. *For $n \geqslant 4$, $(L_n(a, b, c))^*$ meets the bound $2^{n-2} + 1$.*
2. *For $m, n \geqslant 4$, $L'_m(a, b, c)L_n(c, a, b)$ meets the bound $(m-1)2^{n-2} + 1$.*
3. *For $m, n \geqslant 4$, but $(m, n) \neq (4, 4)$, the complexity of $L'_m(a, b, c) \circ L_n(b, a, c)$ is $mn-(m+n-2)$ if $\circ \in \{\cup, \oplus\}$, $mn-(m+2n-4)$ if $\circ = \setminus$, and $mn-2(m+n-3)$ if $\circ = \cap$.*

The transition semigroup of the DFA of Definition 13 below is a also a subsemigroup of $\mathbf{T}^{\leqslant 5}(n)$, and its language also meets the bounds for product, star and boolean operations. The advantage of this DFA is that its witnesses use only two letters for star and only two letters (but three transformations) for boolean operations. Its disadvantages are the rather complex transformations. For more details see [14]. The DFA of Definition 11 seems to us more natural.

Definition 13. *For $n \geqslant 6$, we define the DFA $\mathcal{D}_n = (Q_n, \Sigma, \delta, 0, \{1\})$, where $Q_n = \{0, \ldots, n-1\}$, $\Sigma = \{a, b, c\}$, and δ is defined by the transformations a: $(0 \to n-1)(1, 2, 3)(4, \ldots, n-2)$, b: $(2 \to n-1)(1 \to 2)(0 \to 1)(3, 4)$, c: $(0 \to n-1)(1, \ldots, n-2)$.*

6 Conclusions

We have examined the complexity properties of left-ideal, suffix-closed, and suffix-free languages together because they are all special cases of suffix-convex languages. We have used the same most complex regular language as a basic component in all three cases.

Our results are summarized in Table 1. The largest bounds are shown in boldface type. Recall that for regular languages we have the following results:

Table 1. Complexities of special suffix-convex languages

	Left-ideal	Suffix-closed	Suffix-free
Semigroup	$\mathbf{n^{n-1}+n-1}$	$\mathbf{n^{n-1}+n-1}$	$(n-1)^{n-2}+n-2$
Reverse	$\mathbf{2^{n-1}+1}$	$\mathbf{2^{n-1}+1}$	$2^{n-2}+1$
Star	$n+1$	n	$\mathbf{2^{n-2}+1}$
Product restricted	$m+n-1$	$mn-n+1$	$\mathbf{(m-1)2^{n-2}+1}$
Product unrestricted	$mn+m+n$	$mn+m+1$	$\mathbf{(m-1)2^{n-2}+1}$
∪ *restricted*	$\mathbf{mn}$	$\mathbf{mn}$	$mn-(m+n-2)$
∪ *unrestricted*	$\mathbf{(m+1)(n+1)}$	$\mathbf{(m+1)(n+1)}$	$mn-(m+n-2)$
⊕ *restricted*	$\mathbf{mn}$	$\mathbf{mn}$	$mn-(m+n-2)$
⊕ *unrestricted*	$\mathbf{(m+1)(n+1)}$	$\mathbf{(m+1)(n+1)}$	$mn-(m+n-2)$
\ *restricted*	$\mathbf{mn}$	$\mathbf{mn}$	$mn-(m+2n-4)$
\ *unrestricted*	$\mathbf{mn+m}$	$\mathbf{mn+m}$	$mn-(m+2n-4)$
∩ *restr.* and *unrestr.*	$\mathbf{mn}$	$\mathbf{mn}$	$mn-2(m+n-3)$

semigroup: n^n; reverse: 2^n; star: $2^{n-1}+2^{n-2}$; product, restricted: $(m-1)2^n+2^{n-1}$; unrestricted: $m2^n+2^{n-1}$; ∪ and ⊕, restricted: mn; unrestricted: $(m+1)(n+1)$; \, restricted: mn; unrestricted: $mn+m$; ∩, restricted: mn; unrestricted: mn.

The complexities for left ideals are the same as those for suffix-closed languages, except for star and product, and the complexities of boolean operations for these two classes are the same as those for arbitrary regular languages. The complexities of suffix-free languages are smaller than those of left ideals and suffix-closed languages, except for star and product.

References

1. Ang, T., Brzozowski, J.A.: Languages convex with respect to binary relations, and their closure properties. Acta Cybern. **19**(2), 445–464 (2009)
2. Berstel, J., Perrin, D., Reutenauer, C.: Codes and Automata (Encyclopedia of Mathematics and its Applications). Cambridge University Press, Cambridge (2010)
3. Brzozowski, J.A.: Quotient complexity of regular languages. J. Autom. Lang. Comb. **15**(1/2), 71–89 (2010)
4. Brzozowski, J.A.: In search of the most complex regular languages. Int. J. Found. Comput. Sci. **24**(6), 691–708 (2013)
5. Brzozowski, J.: Unrestricted state complexity of binary operations on regular languages. In: Câmpeanu, C., Manea, F., Shallit, J. (eds.) DCFS 2016. LNCS, vol. 9777, pp. 60–72. Springer, Heidelberg (2016). doi:10.1007/978-3-319-41114-9_5
6. Brzozowski, J.A., Davies, S.: Quotient complexities of atoms in regular ideal languages. Acta Cybern. **22**(2), 293–311 (2015)
7. Brzozowski, J.A., Davies, S., Liu, B.Y.V.: Most complex regular ideal languages. Discrete Math. Theoret. Comput. Sci. **18**(3) (2016). Paper #5
8. Brzozowski, J.A., Jirásková, G., Li, B.: Quotient complexity of ideal languages. Theoret. Comput. Sci. **470**, 36–52 (2013)

9. Brzozowski, J.A., Jirásková, G., Zou, C.: Quotient complexity of closed languages. Theory Comput. Syst. **54**, 277–292 (2014)
10. Brzozowski, J.A., Li, B., Ye, Y.: Syntactic complexity of prefix-, suffix-, bifix-, and factor-free regular languages. Theoret. Comput. Sci. **449**, 37–53 (2012)
11. Brzozowski, J.A., Sinnamon, C.: Complexity of left-ideal, suffix-closed, and suffix-free regular languages (2016). http://arxiv.org/abs/1610.00728
12. Brzozowski, J.A., Sinnamon, C.: Unrestricted state complexity of binary operations on regular and ideal languages (2016). http://arxiv.org/abs/1609.04439
13. Brzozowski, J., Szykuła, M.: Upper bounds on syntactic complexity of left and two-sided ideals. In: Shur, A.M., Volkov, M.V. (eds.) DLT 2014. LNCS, vol. 8633, pp. 13–24. Springer, Heidelberg (2014). doi:10.1007/978-3-319-09698-8_2
14. Brzozowski, J., Szykuła, M.: Complexity of suffix-free regular languages. In: Kosowski, A., Walukiewicz, I. (eds.) FCT 2015. LNCS, vol. 9210, pp. 146–159. Springer, Heidelberg (2015). doi:10.1007/978-3-319-22177-9_12. Full paper at http://arxiv.org/abs/1504.05159
15. Brzozowski, J.A., Szykuła, M., Ye, Y.: Syntactic complexity of regular ideals, (September 2015). http://arxiv.org/abs/1509.06032
16. Brzozowski, J.A., Tamm, H.: Quotient complexities of atoms of regular languages. Int. J. Found. Comput. Sci. **24**(7), 1009–1027 (2013)
17. Brzozowski, J.A., Tamm, H.: Theory of átomata. Theoret. Comput. Sci. **539**, 13–27 (2014)
18. Brzozowski, J., Ye, Y.: Syntactic complexity of ideal and closed languages. In: Mauri, G., Leporati, A. (eds.) DLT 2011. LNCS, vol. 6795, pp. 117–128. Springer, Heidelberg (2011). doi:10.1007/978-3-642-22321-1_11
19. Cmorik, R., Jirásková, G.: Basic operations on binary suffix-free languages. In: Kotásek, Z., Bouda, J., Černá, I., Sekanina, L., Vojnar, T., Antoš, D. (eds.) MEMICS 2011. LNCS, vol. 7119, pp. 94–102. Springer, Heidelberg (2012). doi:10.1007/978-3-642-25929-6_9
20. Han, Y.S., Salomaa, K.: State complexity of basic operations on suffix-free regular languages. Theoret. Comput. Sci. **410**(27–29), 2537–2548 (2009)
21. Holzer, M., König, B.: On deterministic finite automata and syntactic monoid size. Theoret. Comput. Sci. **327**(3), 319–347 (2004)
22. Iván, S.: Complexity of atoms, combinatorially. Inform. Process. Lett. **116**(5), 356–360 (2016)
23. Jirásková, G., Olejár, P.: State complexity of union and intersection of binary suffix-free languages. In: Bordihn, H., et al. (eds.) NMCA, pp. 151–166. Austrian Computer Society (2009)
24. Krawetz, B., Lawrence, J., Shallit, J.: State complexity and the monoid of transformations of a finite set. In: Domaratzki, M., Okhotin, A., Salomaa, K., Yu, S. (eds.) CIAA 2004. LNCS, vol. 3317, pp. 213–224. Springer, Heidelberg (2005). doi:10.1007/978-3-540-30500-2_20
25. Myhill, J.: Finite automata and representation of events. Wright Air Development Center. Technical report, pp. 57–624 (1957)
26. Pin, J.E.: Syntactic semigroups. In: Rozenberg, G., Salomaa, A. (eds.) Handbook of Formal Languages. vol. 1: Word, Language, Grammar, pp. 679–746. Springer, New York (1997)
27. Thierrin, G.: Convex languages. In: Nivat, M. (ed.) Automata, Languages and Programming, pp. 481–492. North-Holland (1973)
28. Yu, S.: State complexity of regular languages. J. Autom. Lang. Comb. **6**, 221–234 (2001)

On the Complexity of Hard Enumeration Problems

Nadia Creignou[1], Markus Kröll[2(✉)], Reinhard Pichler[2], Sebastian Skritek[2], and Heribert Vollmer[3]

[1] Aix-Marseille University, CNRS, Marseille, France
creignou@lif.univ-mrs.fr
[2] TU Wien, Vienna, Austria
{kroell,pichler,skritek}@dbai.tuwien.ac.at
[3] Leibniz Universität Hannover, Hannover, Germany
vollmer@thi.uni-hannover.de

Abstract. Complexity theory provides a wealth of complexity classes for analyzing the complexity of decision and counting problems. Despite the practical relevance of enumeration problems, the tools provided by complexity theory for this important class of problems are very limited. In particular, complexity classes analogous to the polynomial hierarchy and an appropriate notion of problem reduction are missing. In this work, we lay the foundations for a complexity theory of hard enumeration problems by proposing a hierarchy of complexity classes and by investigating notions of reductions for enumeration problems.

1 Introduction

While decision problems often ask for the *existence of a solution* to some problem instance, enumeration problems aim at outputting *all solutions*. In many domains, enumeration problems are thus the most natural kind of problems. Just take the database area (usually the user is interested in all answer tuples and not just in a yes/no answer) or diagnosis (where the user wants to retrieve possible explanations, and not only whether one exists) as two examples. Nevertheless, the complexity of enumeration problems is far less studied than the complexity of decision problems.

It should be noted that even simple enumeration problems may produce big output. To capture the intuition of easy to enumerate problems – despite a possibly exponential number of output values – various notions of tractable enumeration classes have been proposed in [13]. The class DelayP ("polynomial delay") contains all enumeration problems where, for given instance x, (1) the time to compute the first solution, (2) the time between outputting any two solutions, and (3) the time to detect that no further solution exists, are all polynomially bounded in the size of x. The class IncP ("incremental polynomial time") contains those enumeration problems where, for given instance x, the time to compute the next solution and for detecting that no further solution exists is polynomially bounded in the size of both x and of the already computed

F. Drewes et al. (Eds.): LATA 2017, LNCS 10168, pp. 183–195, 2017.
DOI: 10.1007/978-3-319-53733-7_13

solutions. Obviously, the relationship $\mathsf{DelayP} \subseteq \mathsf{IncP}$ holds. In [17], the proper inclusion $\mathsf{DelayP} \subsetneq \mathsf{IncP}$ is mentioned. For these tractable enumeration classes, a variety of membership results exist, a few examples are [2,6,9,14,15].

There has also been work on intractable enumeration problems. Intractability of enumeration is typically proved by showing intractability of a related decision problem rather than directly proving lower bounds by relating one enumeration problem to the other. Tools for a more fine-grained analysis of intractable enumeration problems are missing to date. For instance, up to now we are not able to make a differentiated analysis of the complexity of the following typical enumeration problems:

$\Pi_k\mathrm{SAT}^e$ / $\Sigma_k\mathrm{SAT}^e$
INSTANCE: $\psi = \forall x_1 \exists x_2 \ldots Q_k x_k \phi(\boldsymbol{x}, \boldsymbol{y})$ / $\psi = \exists x_1 \forall x_2 \ldots Q_k x_k \phi(\boldsymbol{x}, \boldsymbol{y})$
OUTPUT: All assignments for $\boldsymbol{y}$ such that ψ is true

This is in sharp contrast to decision problems, where the polynomial hierarchy is crucial for a detailed complexity analysis. As a matter of fact, it makes a big difference, if an NP-hard problem is in NP or not. Indeed, NP-complete problems have an efficient transformation into SAT and can therefore be solved by making use of powerful SAT-solvers. Similarly, problems in Σ_2^P can be solved by using ASP-solvers. Finally, also for problems on higher levels of the polynomial hierarchy, the number of quantifier alternations in the QBF-encoding matters when using QBF-solvers. For counting problems, an analogue of the polynomial hierarchy has been defined in form of the $\# \cdot \mathcal{C}$–classes with $\mathcal{C} \in \{\mathsf{P}, \mathsf{coNP}, \Pi_2^P, \ldots\}$ [12,19]. For enumeration problems, no such analogue has been studied.

Goal and Results. The goal of this work is to lay the foundations for a complexity theory of hard enumeration problems by defining appropriate complexity classes for intractable enumeration and a suitable notion of problem reductions. We propose to extend tractable enumeration classes by oracles. We will thus get a hierarchy of classes $\mathsf{DelayP}^{\mathcal{C}}$, $\mathsf{IncP}^{\mathcal{C}}$, where various complexity classes $\mathcal{C}$ are used as oracles. As far as the definition of an appropriate notion of reductions is concerned, we follow the usual philosophy of reductions: if some enumeration problem can be reduced to another one, then we can use this reduction together with an enumeration algorithm for the latter problem to solve the first one. We observe that two principal kinds of reductions are used for decision problems, namely many-one reductions and Turing reductions. Similarly, we shall define a more declarative-style and a more procedural-style notion of reduction for enumeration problems. Our results are summarized below. All missing proof details can be found in the full version of this article [5].

- *Enumeration complexity classes.* In Sect. 3, we introduce a hierarchy of complexity classes of intractable enumeration via oracles and prove that it is strict unless the polynomial hierarchy collapses.
- *Declarative-style reductions.* In Sect. 4, we introduce a declarative-style notion of reductions. While they enjoy some desirable properties, we do not succeed in exhibiting complete problems under this reduction.

- *Procedural-style reductions and completeness results.* In Sect. 5, we introduce a procedural-style notion of reductions and show that they remedy some shortcomings of the declarative-style notion. In particular we prove completeness results. We obtain a Schaefer-like dichotomy complexity classification for the enumeration of models of generalized CNF-formulas.

2 Preliminaries

In the following, Σ denotes a finite alphabet and R denotes a polynomially bounded, binary relation $R \subseteq \Sigma^* \times \Sigma^*$, i.e., there is a polynomial p such that for all $(x, y) \in R$, $|y| \leq p(|x|)$. For every string x, $R(x) = \{y \in \Sigma^* \mid (x, y) \in R\}$. A string $y \in R(x)$ is called a *solution* for x. With a polynomially bounded, binary relation R, we can associate several natural problems:

EXIST_R INSTANCE: $x \in \Sigma^*$ QUESTION: Exists $y \in \Sigma^*$ s.t. $(x, y) \in R$?	EXIST-ANOTHERSOL_R / ANOTHERSOL_R INSTANCE: $x \in \Sigma^*, Y \subseteq R(x)$ OUTPUT: Is $(R(x) \setminus Y) \neq \emptyset$? / $y \in R(x) \setminus Y$ or declare that no such y exists.
CHECK_R INSTANCE: $(x, y) \in \Sigma^* \times \Sigma^*$ QUESTION: Is $(x, y) \in R$?	EXTSOL_R INSTANCE: $(x, y) \in \Sigma^* \times \Sigma^*$ QUESTION: Is there some (possibly empty) $y' \in \Sigma^*$ such that $(x, yy') \in R$?

A binary relation R also gives rise to an enumeration problem, which aims at outputting the function $\mathsf{Sol}_R : \Sigma^* \to 2^{\Sigma^*}, x \mapsto \{y \in \Sigma^* \mid (x, y) \in R\}$.

ENUM_R INSTANCE: $x \in \Sigma^*$ OUTPUT: $R(x) = \{y \in \Sigma^* \mid (x, y) \in R\}$.

We assume the reader to be familiar with the polynomial hierarchy – the complexity classes P, NP, coNP and, more generally, Δ_k^P, Σ_k^P, and Π_k^P for $k \in \{0, 1, \dots\}$. For a definition of the counting hierarchy $\# \cdot \mathcal{C}$ via the complexity of the CHECK_R problem, we refer to [12].

In Sect. 1, we have already recalled two important tractable enumeration complexity classes, DelayP and IncP from [13]. Note that in [17,18], these classes are defined slightly differently by allowing only those ENUM_R problems in DelayP and IncP where the corresponding CHECK_R problem is in P. We adhere to the definition of tractable enumeration classes from [13].

A complexity class $\mathcal{C}$ is *closed under a reduction* $\leq_r$ if, for any two binary relations R_1 and R_2 we have that $R_2 \in \mathcal{C}$ and $R_1 \leq_r R_2$ implies $R_1 \in \mathcal{C}$. Furthermore, a reduction $\leq_r$ is *transitive* if for any three binary relations R_1, R_2, R_3, it is the case that $R_1 \leq_r R_2$ and $R_2 \leq_r R_3$ implies $R_1 \leq_r R_3$.

3 Complexity Classes

In contrast to counting complexity, defining a hierarchy of enumeration problems via the CHECK_R problem of binary relations R is not appropriate. This can be seen by considering artificial problems obtained by padding the set of solutions of any problem with an exponential number of fake (and trivial to produce) solutions. While these fake solutions do not change the complexity of the check problem, enumerating these exponentially many fake solutions first gives an enumeration algorithm enough time to search for the non trivial ones.

Thus, we need an alternative approach for defining meaningful enumeration complexity classes. To this end, we first fix our computation model. We have already observed in the previous section that an enumeration problem may produce exponentially big output. Hence, the runtime and also the space requirements of an enumeration algorithm may be exponential in the input. Therefore, it is common (cf. [17]) to use the RAM model as a computational model, because a RAM can access parts of exponential-size data in polynomial time. We restrict ourselves here to polynomially bounded RAM machines, i.e., throughout the computation of such a machine, the size of the content of each register is polynomially bounded in the size of the input.

For enumeration, we will also make use of RAM machines with an output-instruction, as defined in [17]. This model can be extended further by introducing decision oracles. The input to the oracle is stored in special registers and the oracle takes consecutive non-empty registers as input. Moreover, following [1], we use a computational model that does not delete the input of an oracle call once such a call is made. For a detailed definition, refer to [17] or [5]. It is important to note that due to the exponential runtime of an enumeration algorithm and the fact that the input to an oracle is not deleted when the oracle is executed, the input to an oracle call may eventually become exponential as well. Clearly, this can only happen if exponentially many consecutive special registers are non-empty, since we assume also each special register to be polynomially bounded.

Using this we define a collection of enumeration complexity classes via oracles:

Definition 1 (enumeration complexity classes). *Let* ENUM_R *be an enumeration problem, and* $\mathcal{C}$ *a decision complexity class. Then we say that:*

- ENUM_$R \in \mathsf{DelayP}^{\mathcal{C}}$ *if there is a RAM machine* M *with an oracle* L *in* $\mathcal{C}$ *such that* M *enumerates* ENUM_R *with polynomial delay. The class* $\mathsf{IncP}^{\mathcal{C}}$ *is defined analogously.*
- ENUM_$R \in \mathsf{DelayP}_p^{\mathcal{C}}$ *if there is a RAM machine* M *with an oracle* L *in* $\mathcal{C}$ *such that for any instance* x*,* M *enumerates* $R(x)$ *with polynomial delay and the size of the input to every oracle call is polynomially bounded in* $|x|$*.*

Note that the restriction of the oracle inputs to polynomial size only makes sense for $\mathsf{DelayP}^{\mathcal{C}}$, where we have a discrepancy between the polynomial restriction (w.r.t. the input x) on the time between two consecutive solutions are output and the possibly exponential size (w.r.t. the input x) of oracle calls. No such discrepancy exists for $\mathsf{IncP}^{\mathcal{C}}$, where the same polynomial upper bound w.r.t. the already computed solutions (resp. all solutions) applies both to the allowed time and to the size of the oracle calls.

We now prove several properties of these complexity classes. First, we draw a connection between the complexity of enumeration and decision problems.

It turns out that in order to study the class $\mathsf{DelayP}_p^{\mathcal{C}}$ the ExtSol_R problem is most relevant. Indeed, the standard enumeration algorithm [6,17], which outputs the solutions in lexicographical order, gives the following relationship.

Proposition 2. *Let R be a binary relation, $k \geq 0$, and $\mathcal{C} \in \{\Delta_k^P, \Sigma_k^P\}$. If* ExtSol_$R \in \mathcal{C}$ *then* Enum_$R \in \mathsf{DelayP}_p^{\mathcal{C}}$.

An important class of search problems are those for which search reduces to decision, the so-called self-reducible problems. This notion can be captured by the following definition.

Definition 3 (self-reducibility). *Let $\leq_T$ denote Turing reductions. We say that a binary relation R is* self-reducible, *if* ExtSol_$R \leq_T$ Exist_R,

For self-reducible problems the above proposition can be refined as follows.

Proposition 4. *Let R be a binary relation, which is self-reducible, and $k \geq 0$. Then the following holds:* Exist_$R \in \Delta_k^P$ *if and only if* Enum_$R \in \mathsf{DelayP}_p^{\Delta_k^P}$.

The above proposition gives a characterization of the class $\mathsf{DelayP}_p^{\Delta_k^P}$ in terms of the complexity of decision problems in the case of self-reducible relations. Analogously, the notion of "enumeration self-reducibility" introduced by Kimelfeld and Kolaitis [14] allows a characterization of the class $\mathsf{IncP}^{\Delta_k^P}$.

Definition 5 ([14], enumeration self-reducibility). *A binary relation R is* enumeration self-reducible *if* AnotherSol_$R \leq_T$ Exist-AnotherSol_R.

Proposition 6. *Let R be a binary relation, which is enumeration self-reducible, and $k \geq 0$. Then the following holds:* Exist-AnotherSol_$R \in \Delta_k^P$ *if and only if* Enum_$R \in \mathsf{IncP}^{\Delta_k^P}$.

We now prove that our classes provide strict hierarchies under the assumption that the polynomial hierarchy is strict.

Theorem 7. *Let $k \geq 0$. Then, unless the polynomial hierarchy collapses to the $(k+1)$-st level,*

$$\mathsf{DelayP}_p^{\Sigma_k^P} \subsetneq \mathsf{DelayP}_p^{\Sigma_{k+1}^P}, \mathsf{DelayP}^{\Sigma_k^P} \subsetneq \mathsf{DelayP}^{\Sigma_{k+1}^P} \text{ and } \mathsf{IncP}^{\Sigma_k^P} \subsetneq \mathsf{IncP}^{\Sigma_{k+1}^P}$$

Proof. Let $k \geq 0$, let L be a Σ_{k+1}^P-complete problem. Define a relation $R_L = \{(x,1) \mid x \in L\}$. It is clear that Check_R_L is Σ_{k+1}^P-complete. Moreover, the enumeration problem Enum_R_L is in $\mathsf{DelayP}_p^{\Sigma_{k+1}^P}$ (thus also in $\mathsf{DelayP}^{\Sigma_{k+1}^P}$ and $\mathsf{IncP}^{\Sigma_{k+1}^P}$). Assume that Enum_$R_L \in \mathsf{DelayP}_p^{\Sigma_k^P}$ (or Enum_$R_L \in \mathsf{DelayP}^{\Sigma_k^P}$ or Enum_$R_L \in \mathsf{IncP}^{\Sigma_k^P}$). Then Check_$R_L$ can be decided in polynomial time using a Σ_k^P-oracle, meaning that Check_$R_L \in \Delta_{k+1}^P$ and thus the polynomial hierarchy collapses to the $(k+1)$-st level.

The following proposition states that the complexity classes based on DelayP_p and DelayP, respectively, are very likely to be distinct. We refer to the definition of the exponential hierarchy in [11]. We only recall here that $\Delta_{k+1}^{\mathsf{EXP}}$ denotes the class of decision problems decidable in exponential time with a Σ_k^P-oracle.

Proposition 8. *Let $k \geq 0$. If $\mathsf{EXP} \subsetneq \Delta_{k+1}^{\mathsf{EXP}}$, then $\mathsf{DelayP}_p^{\Sigma_k^P} \subsetneq \mathsf{DelayP}^{\Sigma_k^P} \not\subseteq \mathsf{DelayP}_p^{\Sigma_{k+1}^P}$.*

I.e., the lower computational power of DelayP_p compared with DelayP or IncP cannot be compensated by equipping the lower class with a slightly more powerful oracle. While complementing this result, we now also show that in contrast, the lower computational power of DelayP compared with IncP can be compensated by equipping the lower class with a slightly more powerful oracle.

Theorem 9. *Let $k \geq 0$. Then the following holds.*

1. $\mathsf{DelayP}_p^{\Sigma_{k+1}^P} \not\subseteq \mathsf{DelayP}^{\Sigma_k^P}$ *and* $\mathsf{DelayP}_p^{\Sigma_{k+1}^P} \not\subseteq \mathsf{IncP}^{\Sigma_k^P}$*, unless the polynomial hierarchy collapses to the $(k+1)$-st level.*
2. $\mathsf{DelayP}^{\Delta_{k+1}^P} = \mathsf{IncP}^{\Sigma_k^P}$.

Proof (Idea). The first claim follows from the proof of Theorem 7. For the second claim, the inclusion $\mathsf{DelayP}^{\Delta_{k+1}^P} \subseteq \mathsf{IncP}^{\Sigma_k^P}$ holds since the incremental delay with access to a Σ_k^P-oracle gives enough time to compute the answers of a Δ_{k+1}^P-oracle. To show that $\mathsf{DelayP}^{\Delta_{k+1}^P} \supseteq \mathsf{IncP}^{\Sigma_k^P}$, let $\text{ENUM\_}R \in \mathsf{IncP}^{\Sigma_k^P}$ and $\mathcal{A}$ be a corresponding enumeration algorithm. We define a decision problem $\text{ANOTHERSOLEXT}_R^{<^*}$ that, on an input $y_1, \ldots, y_n, y', x \in \Sigma^*$, decides whether y' is the prefix of the $(n+1)$-st output of $\mathcal{A}(x)$. Since $\mathcal{A}$ witnesses the membership $\text{ENUM\_}R \in \mathsf{IncP}^{\Sigma_k^P}$, it follows that $\text{ANOTHERSOLEXT}_R^{<^*} \in \Delta_{k+1}^P$, and using this language as an oracle, we have that $\text{ENUM\_}R \in \mathsf{DelayP}^{\Delta_{k+1}^P}$.

Concerning the effect of the allowed input size to the oracles, observe that it follows immediately that $\mathsf{DelayP}^{\Delta_{k+1}^P} \neq \mathsf{DelayP}^{\Sigma_k^P}$, but $\mathsf{DelayP}_p^{\Delta_{k+1}^P} = \mathsf{DelayP}_p^{\Sigma_k^P}$.

4 Declarative-Style Reductions

As far as we know, only a few kinds of reductions between enumeration problems have been investigated so far. One such reduction is implicitly described in [7]. It establishes a bijection between sets of solutions. A different approach introduced in [3] relaxes this condition and allows non-bijective reduction functions. We go further in that direction in proposing a declarative style reduction relaxing the isomorphism requirement while closing the relevant enumeration classes.

Definition 10 (reduction $\leq_e$). *Let $R_1, R_2 \subseteq \Sigma^*$ be binary relations. Then we define $\text{ENUM\_}R_1 \leq_e \text{ENUM\_}R_2$ if there exist a function $\sigma : \Sigma^* \to \Sigma^*$ computable in polynomial time and a relation $\tau \subseteq \Sigma^* \times \Sigma^* \times \Sigma^*$, s.t. for all $x \in \Sigma^*$ the following holds. For $y \in \Sigma^*$, let $\tau(x, y, -) := \{z \in \Sigma^* \mid (x, y, z) \in \tau\}$ and for $z \in \Sigma^*$, let $\tau(x, -, z) := \{y \in \Sigma^* \mid (x, y, z) \in \tau\}$. Then:*

1. $\mathsf{Sol}_{R_1}(x) = \bigcup_{y \in \mathsf{Sol}_{R_2}(\sigma(x))} \tau(x, y, -)$;
2. $\forall y \in \mathsf{Sol}_{R_2}(\sigma(x))$, *we have* $\emptyset \subsetneq \tau(x, y, -) \subseteq \mathsf{Sol}_{R_1}(x)$ *and* $\tau(x, y, -)$ *can be enumerated with polynomial delay in* $|x|$;
3. $\forall z \in \mathsf{Sol}_{R_1}(x)$, *we have* $\tau(x, -, z) \subseteq \mathsf{Sol}_{R_2}(\sigma(x))$ *and the size of* $\tau(x, -, z)$ *is polynomially bounded in* $|x|$.

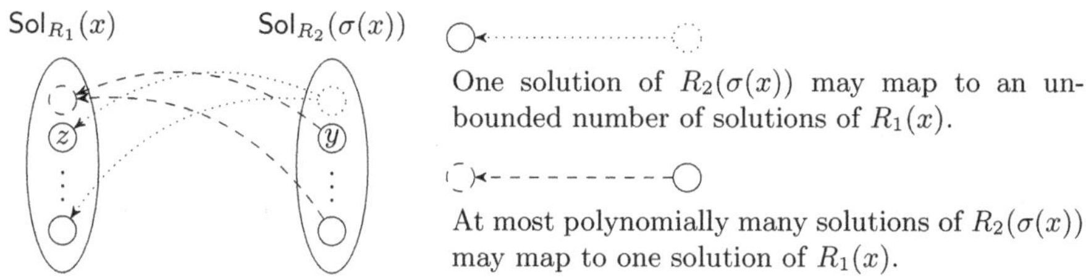

Sol$_{R_1}(x)$
Sol$_{R_2}(\sigma(x))$
z
y
One solution of $R_2(\sigma(x))$ may map to an unbounded number of solutions of $R_1(x)$.
At most polynomially many solutions of $R_2(\sigma(x))$ may map to one solution of $R_1(x)$.

Fig. 1. Illustration of relation τ from Definition 10.

Intuitively, τ establishes a relationship between instances x, solutions $y \in \mathsf{Sol}_{R_2}(\sigma(x))$ and solutions $z \in \mathsf{Sol}_{R_1}(x)$. We can thus use τ to design an enumeration algorithm for $\mathsf{Sol}_{R_1}(x)$ via an enumeration algorithm for $\mathsf{Sol}_{R_2}(\sigma(x))$. The conditions imposed on τ have the following meaning: By condition 1, the solutions $\mathsf{Sol}_{R_1}(x)$ can be computed by iterating through the solutions $y \in \mathsf{Sol}_{R_2}(\sigma(x))$ and computing $\tau(x, y, -) \subseteq \mathsf{Sol}_{R_1}(x)$. Conditions 2 and 3 make sure that the delay of enumerating $\mathsf{Sol}_{R_1}(x)$ only differs by a polynomial from the delay of enumerating $\mathsf{Sol}_{R_2}(\sigma(x))$: condition 2 ensures that, for every y, the set $\tau(x, y, -)$ can be enumerated with polynomial delay and that we never encounter a "useless" y (i.e., a solution $y \in \mathsf{Sol}_{R_2}(\sigma(x))$ which is associated with no solution $z \in \mathsf{Sol}_{R_1}(x)$). In principle, we may thus get duplicates z associated with different values of y. However, condition 3 ensures that each z can be associated with at most polynomially many values y. Using a priority queue storing all z that are output, we can avoid duplicates, c.f. the proof of Proposition 12 or [17]. Figure 1 illustrates τ.

Example 11. The idea of the relation τ can also be nicely demonstrated on an $\leq_e$ reduction from 3-COLOURABILITY^e to 4-COLOURABILITY^e (enumerating all valid 3- respectively 4-colourings of a graph). We intentionally choose this reduction since there is no bijection between the solutions of the two problems.

Recall the classical many-one reduction between these problems, which takes a graph G and defines a new graph G' by adding an auxiliary vertex v and connecting it to all the other ones. This reduction can be extended to a $\leq_e$ reduction with the following relation τ: With every graph G in the first component of τ, we associate all valid 4-colourings (using 0, 1, 2, and 3) of G' in the third component of τ. With each of those we associate the corresponding 3-colouring of G in the second component. They are obtained from the 4-colourings by first making sure that v is coloured with 3 (by "switching" the colour of v with 3) and then by simply reading off the colouring of the remaining vertices.

The reductions $\leq_e$ have two desirable important properties, as stated next.

Proposition 12. *Let $\mathcal{C} \in \{\Sigma_k^P, \Delta_k^P \mid k \geq 0\}$. The classes* $\mathsf{DelayP}_p^{\mathcal{C}}$, $\mathsf{DelayP}^{\mathcal{C}}$, *and* $\mathsf{IncP}^{\mathcal{C}}$ *are closed under $\leq_e$. In addition, the reductions $\leq_e$ are transitive.*

Nevertheless their main drawback is that it is very unlikely that completeness results under $\leq_e$ reductions can be obtained, since even the most natural problems are not complete under such a reduction.

Proposition 13. *Let $k \geq 1$. The problem $\Sigma_k\mathrm{SAT}^e$ is not complete for* $\mathsf{DelayP}_p^{\Sigma_k^P}$ *under $\leq_e$ reductions unless the polynomial hierarchy collapses to the kth level.*

5 Procedural-Style Reductions and Completeness Results

Although Turing reductions are too strong to show completeness results for classes in the polynomial hierarchy, Turing style reductions turn out to be meaningful in our case. In this section we introduce two types of reductions that are motivated by Turing reductions. Both of them are able to reduce between enumeration problems for which the reduction $\leq_e$ seems to be too weak.

Towards this goal, we first have to define the concept of RAMs with an *oracle for enumeration problems*. The intuition behind the definition of such enumeration oracle machines is the following: For algorithms (i.e., Turing machines or RAMs in the case of enumeration) using a decision oracle for the language L, we usually have a special instruction that given an input x decides in one step whether $x \in L$, and then executes the next step of the algorithm accordingly. For an algorithm $\mathcal{A}$ using an enumeration oracle, an input x to some ENUM_R-oracle returns in a single step (using the instruction NOO, see the definition below) a single element of $\mathsf{Sol}_R(x)$, and then $\mathcal{A}$ can proceed according to this output.

Definition 14 (Enumeration Oracle Machines). *Let* ENUM_R *be an enumeration problem. An* Enumeration Oracle Machine with an enumeration oracle ENUM_R (EOM_R) *is a RAM with a sequence of new registers $O^e(0), O^e(1), \ldots$ and a new instruction* NOO *(next Oracle output). An EOM_R is* oracle-bounded *if the size of all inputs to the oracle is at most polynomial in the size of the input to the EOM_R.*

When executing NOO, the machine writes – in one step – some $y_i \in \mathsf{Sol}_R(x)$ to the accumulator A, where x is the word stored in $O^e(0), O^e(1), \ldots$ and y_i is defined as follows:

Definition 15 (Next Oracle Output). *Let R be a binary relation, $\pi_1, \pi_2, \ldots$ be the run of an EOM_R and assume that the kth instruction is* NOO, *i.e., $\pi_k =$* NOO. *Denote with x_i the word stored in $O^e(0), O^e(1), \ldots$ at step i. Let $K = \{\pi_i \in \{\pi_1, \ldots, \pi_{k-1}\} \mid \pi_i = \mathsf{NOO}$ and $x_i = x_k\}$. Then the* oracle output *y_k in π_k is defined as an arbitrary $y_k \in \mathsf{Sol}_R(x_k)$ s.t. y_k has not been the oracle output in any $\pi_i \in K$. If no such y_k exists, then the oracle output in π_k is undefined.*

When executing NOO *in step π_k, if the oracle output y_k is undefined, then the accumulator A contains some special symbol in step π_{k+1}. Otherwise in step π_{k+1} the accumulator A contains y_k.*

Observe that since an EOM M^e is a polynomially bounded RAM and the complete oracle output is stored in the accumulator A, only such oracle calls are allowed where the size of each oracle output is guaranteed to be polynomially in the size of the input of M^e.

Using EOMs, we can now define another type of reductions among enumerations problems, reminiscent of classical Turing reductions. I.e., we say that one problem Enum_R_1 reduces to another problem Enum_R_2 if Enum_R_1 can be solved by an EOM using Enum_R_2 as an enumeration oracle.

Definition 16 (Reductions $\leq_D$, $\leq_I$). *Let R_1 and R_2 be binary relations.*

- *We say that* Enum_$R_1 \leq_D$ Enum_R_2 *if there is an oracle-bounded EOM_R_2 that enumerates R_1 in* DelayP *and is independent of the order in which the* Enum_R_2 *oracle enumerates its answers.*
- *We say that* Enum_$R_1 \leq_I$ Enum_R_2 *if there is an EOM_R_2 that enumerates R_1 in* IncP *and is independent of the order in which the* Enum_R_2 *oracle enumerates its answers.*

For $\leq_D$, we required the EOM_R_2 to be oracle-bounded. We would like to point out that this restriction is essential: if we drop it, then the classes $\mathsf{DelayP}^{\mathcal{C}}$ are not closed under the resulting reduction. They are, however, closed under the reductions as defined above.

Proposition 17. *Let $\mathcal{C} \in \{\Sigma_k^P, \Delta_k^P \mid k \geq 0\}$. The classes $\mathsf{DelayP}^{\mathcal{C}}$ and $\mathsf{DelayP}_p^{\mathcal{C}}$ are closed under $\leq_D$. The classes $\mathsf{IncP}^{\mathcal{C}}$ are closed under $\leq_I$.*

We note that all of these properties still hold when there is no oracle at all, i.e., for the classes DelayP and IncP.

Proposition 18. *The reductions $\leq_D$ and $\leq_I$ are transitive.*

Now, unlike for $\leq_e$, the next theorem shows that the reductions $\leq_D$ and $\leq_I$ induce complete problems for the enumeration complexity classes introduced in Sect. 3.

Theorem 19. *Let R be a binary relation and $k \geq 1$ such that* Exist_R *is Σ_k^P-complete.*

- Enum_R *is $\mathsf{DelayP}_p^{\Sigma_k^P}$-hard under $\leq_D$ reductions.*
- Enum_R *is $\mathsf{IncP}^{\Sigma_k^P}$-hard under $\leq_I$ reductions.*
- *If R is self-reducible, then* Enum_R *is $\mathsf{DelayP}_p^{\Sigma_k^P}$-complete under $\leq_D$ reductions and $\mathsf{IncP}^{\Sigma_k^P}$-complete under $\leq_I$ reductions.*

Proof (Idea). Let $\textsc{Enum\_}R' \in \mathsf{DelayP}_p^L$ for some $L \in \Sigma_k^P$, and assume that z is the input to an L-oracle when enumerating $\mathsf{Sol}_{R'}(x)$ for some $x \in \Sigma^*$. As $\textsc{Exist\_}R$ is Σ_k^P-complete and the enumeration is oracle-bounded, z can be transformed to an equivalent instance z' of $\textsc{Exist\_}R$ in time polynomial only in $|x|$. Therefore by calling the $\textsc{Enum\_}R$-oracle once and by checking whether $\mathsf{Sol}_R(z') = \emptyset$, one can decide whether $z \in L$. The membership $\textsc{Enum\_}R \in \mathsf{DelayP}_p^{\Sigma_k^P}$ in the case of self-reducibility follows by Proposition 2.

As a consequence, the enumeration problems $\Sigma_k\mathrm{SAT}^{\mathrm{e}}$ and also $\Pi_k\mathrm{SAT}^{\mathrm{e}}$ are natural complete problems for our enumeration complextiy classes:

Corollary 20. *Let $k \geq 0$. Then*

1. *$\Sigma_{k+1}\mathrm{SAT}^{\mathrm{e}}$ is complete for $\mathsf{DelayP}_p^{\Sigma_{k+1}^P}$ under $\leq_D$ reductions.*
2. *$\Pi_k\mathrm{SAT}^{\mathrm{e}}$ and $\Sigma_{k+1}\mathrm{SAT}^{\mathrm{e}}$ are complete for $\mathsf{IncP}^{\Sigma_{k+1}^P}$ under $\leq_I$ reductions.*

Observe that, under different reductions, $\Sigma_k\mathrm{SAT}^{\mathrm{e}}$ is complete for both, $\mathsf{IncP}^{\Sigma_k^P}$ and for the presumably smaller class $\mathsf{DelayP}_p^{\Sigma_k^P}$. This provides additional evidence that the two reductions nicely capture $\mathsf{IncP}^{\Sigma_k^P}$ and $\mathsf{DelayP}_p^{\Sigma_k^P}$, respectively. Also from Corollary 20 it follows as a special case that $\mathsf{IncP}^{\Sigma_0^P}$ and $\mathsf{IncP}^{\Sigma_1^P}$ are equivalent under $\leq_I$ reductions: Clearly, $\Sigma_0\mathrm{SAT}^{\mathrm{e}} = \Pi_0\mathrm{SAT}^{\mathrm{e}}$, since in both cases the formulas are quantifier free and one asks for all satisfying truth assignments. Now by the theorem we know that both, $\Sigma_1\mathrm{SAT}^{\mathrm{e}}$ and $\Pi_0\mathrm{SAT}^{\mathrm{e}}$, and thus also $\Sigma_0\mathrm{SAT}^{\mathrm{e}}$, are complete for $\mathsf{IncP}^{\Sigma_1^P}$. As a result we have that the enumeration variant of the traditional SAT problem is $\mathsf{IncP}^{\mathsf{NP}}$-complete.

Roughly speaking Theorem 19 says that any self-reducible enumeration problem whose corresponding decision problem is hard, is hard as well. An interesting question is whether there exist easy decision problems for which the corresponding enumeration problem is hard. We answer positively to this question in revisiting, in our framework, a classification theorem obtained for the enumeration of generalized satisfiability [4]. It is convenient to first introduce some notation.

A *logical relation* of arity k is a relation $R \subseteq \{0,1\}^k$. A *constraint*, C, is a formula $C = R(x_1, \ldots, x_k)$, where R is a logical relation of arity k and the x_i's are variables. An assignment m of truth values to the variables *satisfies* the constraint C if $\big(m(x_1), \ldots, m(x_k)\big) \in R$. A *constraint language* Γ is a finite set of nontrivial logical relations. A *Γ-formula* ϕ is a conjunction of constraints using only logical relations from Γ. A Γ-formula ϕ is satisfied by an assignment $m : \mathrm{var}(\phi) \rightarrow \{0,1\}$ if m satisfies all constraints in ϕ.

Throughout the text we refer to different types of Boolean relations following Schaefer's terminology, see [4,16]. We say that a constraint language is *Schaefer* if every relation in Γ is either Horn, dualHorn, bijunctive, or affine.

$\mathrm{SAT}(\Gamma)^{\mathrm{e}}$	
INSTANCE:	ϕ a Γ-formula
OUTPUT:	all satisfying assignments of ϕ

The following theorem gives the complexity of this problem according to Γ.

Theorem 21. *Let Γ be a finite constraint language. If Γ is Schaefer, then* $\mathrm{SAT}(\Gamma)^e$ *is in* DelayP*, otherwise it is* $\mathsf{DelayP}_p^{\mathsf{NP}}$*-complete under* $\leq_D$ *reductions.*

Proof. The polynomial cases were studied in [4]. Let us now consider the case where Γ is not Schaefer. Membership of $\mathrm{SAT}(\Gamma)^e$ in $\mathsf{DelayP}_p^{\mathsf{NP}}$ is clear. For the hardness, let us introduce T and F as the two unary constant relations $\mathrm{T} = \{1\}$ and $\mathrm{F} = \{0\}$. According to Schaefer's dichotomy theorem [16], deciding whether a $\Gamma \cup \{\mathrm{F}, \mathrm{T}\}$-formula is satisfiable is NP-complete. Since this problem is self-reducible, according to Theorem 19, $\mathrm{SAT}(\cup\{\mathrm{F}, \mathrm{T}\})^e$ is $\mathsf{DelayP}_p^{\mathsf{NP}}$-complete under $\leq_D$ reductions. From the proof given in [4] it is easy to see that if Γ is not Schaefer, then $\mathrm{SAT}(\cup\{\mathrm{F}, \mathrm{T}\})^e \leq_D \mathrm{SAT}(\Gamma)^e$, thus concluding the proof.

To come back to the above discussion, we point out that there exist constraint languages Γ such that the decision problem $\mathrm{SAT}(\Gamma)$ is in P, while the enumeration problem $\mathrm{SAT}(\Gamma)^e$ is $\mathsf{DelayP}_p^{\mathsf{NP}}$-complete, namely 0-valid or 1-valid constraint languages that are not Schaefer.

A rather surprising completeness result is the following.

Proposition 22. *Let* $\mathrm{CIRCUMSCRIPTION}^e$ *denote the problem of enumerating all subset minimal models of a boolean formula. Then* $\mathrm{CIRCUMSCRIPTION}^e$ *is* $\mathsf{IncP}^{\mathsf{NP}}$*-complete under* $\leq_I$ *reductions.*

What makes this result surprising is the discrepancy from the behaviour of the counting variant of the problem: The counting variant of $\mathrm{CIRCUMSCRIPTION}^e$ is a prototypical $\# \cdot \mathsf{coNP}$-complete problem [8], and thus of the same hardness as the counting variant of $\Pi_1\mathrm{SAT}^e$. However, for enumeration we have that $\mathrm{CIRCUMSCRIPTION}^e$ shows the same complexity as $\Sigma_1\mathrm{SAT}^e$, which is considered to be lower than that of $\Pi_1\mathrm{SAT}^e$.

Observe that $\mathrm{CIRCUMSCRIPTION}^e$ is very unlikely to be self-reducible: In fact, the problem of deciding if a partial truth assignment can be extended to a subset minimal model is Σ_2^P-complete [10], while deciding the existence of a minimal model is clearly NP-complete. Thus $\mathrm{CIRCUMSCRIPTION}^e$ is not self-reducible unless the polynomial hierarchy collapses to the first level.

6 Conclusion

We introduced a hierarchy of enumeration complexity classes, extending the well-known tractable enumeration classes DelayP and IncP, just as the Δ_k^P-classes of the polynomial-time hierarchy extend the class P. We show that under reasonable complexity assumptions these hierarchies are strict. We introduced a type of reduction among enumeration problems under which the classes in our hierarchies are closed and which allow to exhibit complete problems. For well-studied problems like Boolean CSPs in the Schaefer framework or circumscription, we obtain completeness results for the associated enumeration problems. Up to now, lower bounds for enumeration problems were only of the form "ENUM_R is not in DelayP (or IncP) unless P $\neq$ NP". Our work provides a framework which allows us to pinpoint the complexity of such problems in a better way in terms of completeness.

Acknowledgments. This work was supported by the Vienna Science and Technology Fund (WWTF) through project ICT12-015, the Austrian Science Fund (FWF): P25207-N23, P25518-N23, I836-N23, W1255-N23 and the French Agence Nationale de la Recherche, AGGREG project reference ANR-14-CE25-0017-01.

References

1. Arora, S., Barak, B.: Computational Complexity: A Modern Approach. Cambridge University Press, Cambridge (2009)
2. Bagan, G., Durand, A., Grandjean, E.: On acyclic conjunctive queries and constant delay enumeration. In: Duparc, J., Henzinger, T.A. (eds.) CSL 2007. LNCS, vol. 4646, pp. 208–222. Springer, Heidelberg (2007). doi:10.1007/978-3-540-74915-8_18
3. Brault-Baron, J.: De la pertinence de l'énumération : complexité en logiques propositionnelle et du premier ordre. (The relevance of the list: propositional logic and complexity of the first order). Ph.D. thesis, University of Caen Normandy, France (2013). https://tel.archives-ouvertes.fr/tel-01081392
4. Creignou, N., Hébrard, J.J.: On generating all solutions of generalized satisfiability problems. Informatique Théorique et Applications **31**(6), 499–511 (1997)
5. Creignou, N., Kröll, M., Pichler, R., Skritek, S., Vollmer, H.: On the complexity of hard enumeration problems. CoRR abs/1610.05493 (2016), http://arxiv.org/abs/1610.05493
6. Creignou, N., Vollmer, H.: Parameterized complexity of weighted satisfiability problems: decision, enumeration, counting. Fundam. Inform. **136**(4), 297–316 (2015). http://dx.doi.org/10.3233/FI-2015-1159
7. Durand, A., Grandjean, E.: First-order queries on structures of bounded degree are computable with constant delay. ACM Trans. Comput. Log. **8**(4), 21/1–21/19 (2007). http://doi.acm.org/10.1145/1276920.1276923
8. Durand, A., Hermann, M., Kolaitis, P.G.: Subtractive reductions and complete problems for counting complexity classes. Theor. Comput. Sci. **340**(3), 496–513 (2005)
9. Durand, A., Schweikardt, N., Segoufin, L.: Enumerating answers to first-order queries over databases of low degree. In: Proceedings of PODS 2014, pp. 121–131. ACM (2014)
10. Eiter, T., Gottlob, G.: The complexity of logic-based abduction. J. ACM **42**(1), 3–42 (1995)
11. Hemachandra, L.A.: The strong exponential hierarchy collapses. In: Proceedings of STOC 1987, pp. 110–122. ACM (1987)
12. Hemaspaandra, L.A., Vollmer, H.: The satanic notations: counting classes beyond #P and other definitional adventures. SIGACT News **26**(1), 2–13 (1995)
13. Johnson, D.S., Papadimitriou, C.H., Yannakakis, M.: On generating all maximal independent sets. Inf. Process. Lett. **27**(3), 119–123 (1988)
14. Kimelfeld, B., Kolaitis, P.G.: The complexity of mining maximal frequent subgraphs. ACM Trans. Database Syst. **39**(4), 32:1–32:33 (2014). http://doi.acm.org/10.1145/2629550

15. Lucchesi, C.L., Osborn, S.L.: Candidate keys for relations. J. Comput. Syst. Sci. **17**(2), 270–279 (1978)
16. Schaefer, T.J.: The complexity of satisfiability problems. In: Proceedings of STOC 1978, pp. 216–226. ACM Press (1978)
17. Strozecki, Y.: Enumeration complexity and matroid decomposition. Ph.D. thesis, Universite Paris Diderot - Paris 7, December 2010. http://www.prism.uvsq.fr/~ystr/these_strozecki
18. Strozecki, Y.: On enumerating monomials and other combinatorial structures by polynomial interpolation. Theory Comput. Syst. **53**(4), 532–568 (2013)
19. Toda, S.: PP is as hard as the polynomial-time hierarchy. SIAM J. Comput. **20**(5), 865–877 (1991)

Consensus String Problem for Multiple Regular Languages

Yo-Sub Han[1], Sang-Ki Ko[2(✉)], Timothy Ng[3], and Kai Salomaa[3]

[1] Department of Computer Science, Yonsei University, 50, Yonsei-Ro, Seodaemun-Gu, Seoul 120-749, Republic of Korea
emmous@yonsei.ac.kr

[2] Department of Computer Science, University of Liverpool, Liverpool L69 3BX, UK
sangkiko@liverpool.ac.uk

[3] School of Computing, Queen's University, Kingston, ON K7L 3N6, Canada
{ng,ksalomaa}@queensu.ca

Abstract. The consensus string (or center string, closest string) of a set S of strings is defined as a string which is within a radius r from all strings in S. It is well-known that the consensus string problem for a finite set of equal-length strings is NP-complete. We study the consensus string problem for multiple regular languages. We define the consensus string of languages $L_1, \ldots, L_k$ to be within distance at most r to some string in each of the languages $L_1, \ldots, L_k$. We also study the complexity of some parameterized variants of the consensus string problem. For a constant k, we give a polynomial time algorithm for the consensus string problem for k regular languages using additive weighted finite automata. We show that the consensus string problem for multiple regular languages becomes intractable when k is not fixed. We also examine the case when the length of the consensus string is given as part of input.

Keywords: Consensus string problem · Computational complexity · Regular languages · Edit-distance

1 Introduction

In bioinformatics, the multiple sequence alignment is a process of finding an optimal alignment from its multiple reads to find a correct biological sequence [10,21]. See Fig. 1 for example. Moreover, it is a very important task to find the *consensus sequence* for detecting data commonalities from a set of strings in many practical applications such as coding theory [5,7], data compression [8], and so forth.

There have been several definitions of a consensus string for a set of strings. Frances and Litman defined the consensus string based on the concept of the *radius* [7]. The radius of a string w with respect to a set S of strings is the smallest number r such that the distance between w and any string in S is

F. Drewes et al. (Eds.): LATA 2017, LNCS 10168, pp. 196–207, 2017.
DOI: 10.1007/978-3-319-53733-7_14

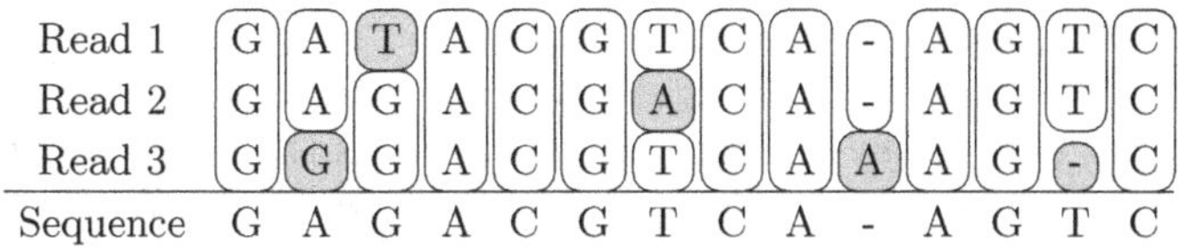

Read 1 G A T A C G T C A - A G T C
Read 2 G A G A C G A C A - A G T C
Read 3 G G G A C G T C A A A G - C
Sequence G A G A C G T C A - A G T C

Fig. 1. The correct biological sequence can be estimated as the consensus sequence derived from the multiple sequence alignment from its reads

bounded by r. It is known that the consensus string problem based on radius is NP-complete even when the strings are given over the binary alphabet [7]. Sim and Park considered a different consensus string problem where they try to minimize the sum of distances between w and all strings in S, which is the *consensus error*. They showed that the consensus string problem based on the consensus error is NP-complete when the penalty matrix is a metric [25].

Amir et al. [1] examined the consensus string problem by considering both distance sum and radius, where the distance sum is the sum of distances from the strings in the given set to the consensus string and the radius is the largest distance from the set to the consensus string. They presented efficient polynomial time algorithms for the set of three strings. Amir et al. [2] studied the consensus string problem for other string metrics such as the swap metric and the reversal metric and showed that the problem is NP-hard for the swap metric and APX-hard for the reversal metric.

Since there is no polynomial-time solution for the consensus string problem unless $P = NP$, many researchers studied approximation algorithms and fixed-parameter tractability [10,16]. Stojanovic et al. [26] proposed a linear-time algorithm when the radius is one. Gramm et al. [9,10] designed the first fixed-parameter algorithm whose time complexity is $O(kl + kr^{r+1})$ where k is the number of strings, l is the length of strings, and r is the radius, which yields a linear-time algorithm for a constant r. For more details on fixed-parameter tractability of the consensus string problem, we refer the reader to [10,16,21].

We consider the consensus string problem for multiple regular languages, that is, to compute the consensus string which is within a given radius to the given regular languages. We use the Levenshtein distance (edit-distance) as a distance function for strings instead of the Hamming distance since the regular languages may be infinite and thus containing strings of unequal length.[1]

Given k regular languages given by NFAs or DFAs (nondeterministic or deterministic finite-state automata) and a radius r, we define the consensus string problem which decides the existence of a consensus string of radius r. We show that the problem is PSPACE-complete in general, and also when the radius r is fixed. We also establish that the problem becomes polynomial-time decidable when k is fixed using additive weighted finite automata. Lastly, we study a special case when the length l of the consensus string is given as input.

[1] The Hamming distance is only for strings of equal length.

2 Preliminaries

In the following Σ is always a finite alphabet, Σ^* is the set of strings over Σ, and ε is the empty string. The length of a string w is $|w|$. When there is no danger of confusion, a singleton set $\{w\}$ is denoted simply as w. The set of nonnegative integers is $\mathbb{N}_0$. For $n \in \mathbb{N}_0$, $\text{bin}(n) \in \{0,1\}^*$ is the string giving the binary representation of n.

A *nondeterministic finite automaton* (NFA) is a tuple $A = (Q, \Sigma, \delta, q_0, F)$ where Q is a finite set of states, Σ is an alphabet, δ is a multi-valued transition function $\delta : Q \times \Sigma \to 2^Q$, $q_0 \in Q$ is the initial state, and $F \subseteq Q$ is a set of final states. We extend the transition function δ to a function $Q \times \Sigma^* \to 2^Q$ in the usual way. A string $w \in \Sigma^*$ is *accepted* by A if $\delta(q_0, w) \cap F \neq \emptyset$ and the language recognized by A consists of all strings accepted by A. The automaton A is a *deterministic finite automaton* (DFA) if, for all $q \in Q$ and $a \in \Sigma^*$, $\delta(q, a)$ either consists of one state or is undefined.

The reader can find more details on finite automata and regular languages in the text by Shallit [24] or the survey by Yu [27].

2.1 Distance Measures and Neighbourhoods

Intuitively, a distance measure on strings is a numerical description of how far apart two strings are. We view a distance on strings as a function from $\Sigma^* \times \Sigma^*$ to the nonnegative rationals that has value zero only for two identical strings, is symmetric, and satisfies the triangle inequality [6]. For our purposes it is sufficient to consider *integral distances* [20] where the values are integers. We define that a function $d : \Sigma^* \times \Sigma^* \to \mathbb{N}_0$ is a *distance* if it satisfies, for all $x, y, z \in \Sigma^*$,

(i) $d(x, y) = 0$ if and only if $x = y$,
(ii) $d(x, y) = d(y, x)$,
(iii) $d(x, z) \leq d(x, y) + d(y, z)$.

The *neighbourhood* of radius r of a language L is the set

$$E(L, d, r) = \{x \in \Sigma^* : (\exists y \in L)\ d(x, y) \leq r\}.$$

A distance d is said to be *finite* if the neighbourhood of any given radius of an individual string with respect to d is finite. A distance d is *additive* [3] if for every factorization $w = w_1 w_2$ and radius $r \geq 0$,

$$E(w, d, r) = \bigcup_{r_1 + r_2 = r} E(w_1, d, r_1) \cdot E(w_2, d, r_2).$$

Additive distances preserve regularity in the sense that the neighbourhood of a regular language is always regular [3].

The Levenshtein distance [15], a.k.a. the *edit-distance* d_e [4,11,13,22] is an example of an additive distance. By the elementary edit operations on strings we mean an operation that replaces an alphabet symbol by another alphabet symbol (substitution), a deletion of an alphabet symbol or an insertion of an alphabet symbol into a string. The edit-distance between strings s_1 and s_2 is the smallest number of elementary edit operations that transform s_1 into s_2. More generally, we can associate a non-negative cost to each elementary edit operation and then define the edit-distance between s_1 and s_2 as the smallest cost of all sequences of elementary edit operations that transform string s_1 into string s_2.

Unless otherwise mentioned, in the following we assume that elementary edit operations are all associated a unit cost. Our results would not change significantly if we use more general costs for the elementary edit operations.

We recall a result on the nondeterministic state complexity of edit-distance neighbourhoods. The result is originally due to Povarov [23] who states it for the Hamming distance neighbourhoods. However, exactly the same construction works for a general edit-distance where the costs of elementary edit operations are non-negative integers [20]. We add to the statement of the result a time bound needed for the construction.

Proposition 1 [20,23]. *Let A be an NFA with n states and $r \in \mathbb{N}$. The neighbourhood of $L(A)$ of radius r with respect to the edit-distance d_e can be recognized by an NFA B with $n \cdot (r+1)$ states. The NFA B can be constructed in time that depends polynomially on n and r.*

2.2 Additive Weighted Finite Automata

An additive weighted finite automaton model has been used by Ng et al. [19] to recognize the neighbourhood of an NFA language. Since we need to recognize an intersection of neighbourhoods we extend the model to a multi-component weighted finite automaton where the states are k-tuples and transition weights are k-tuples of integers. The original definition allows real weights but integer weights will be sufficient for our purposes.

Definition 2. *An* additive k-component weighted finite automaton *(additive k-WFA) is a 6-tuple $A = (Q, \Sigma, \gamma, \omega, q_0, F)$ where $Q = P_1 \times \cdots \times P_k$, $k \in \mathbb{N}$, and each P_i is a finite set of states, Σ is an alphabet, $\gamma : Q \times (\Sigma \cup \{\varepsilon\}) \to 2^Q$ is the transition function, $\omega : Q \times (\Sigma \cup \{\varepsilon\}) \times Q \to \mathbb{N}_0^k$ is a partial weight function where $\omega(q_1, a, q_2)$ is defined if and only if $q_2 \in \gamma(q_1, a)$, ($a \in \Sigma \cup \{\varepsilon\}$), $q_0 \in Q$ is the initial state, and $F \subseteq Q$ is the set of accepting states.*

Strictly speaking, the transitions of γ are also determined by the domain of the partial function ω. By a transition of an additive k-WFA A on symbol $a \in \Sigma$ we mean a triple (q_1, a, q_2) such that $q_2 \in \gamma(q_1, a)$, $q_1, q_2 \in Q$. A computation path α of the additive k-WFA A along a string $w = a_1 a_2 \cdots a_m$, $a_i \in \Sigma$, $i = 1, \ldots, m$, from state s_1 to s_2 is a sequence of transitions that spells out the string w,

$$\alpha = (q_0, a_1, q_1)(q_1, a_2, q_2) \cdots (q_{m-1}, a_m, q_m), \tag{1}$$

where $s_1 = q_0$, $s_2 = q_m$, and $q_i \in \gamma(q_{i-1}, a_i)$, $1 \leq i \leq m$.

In the following, we use componentwise notation for addition and inequality for k-tuples in $\mathbb{N}_0^k$. Let $(x_1, \ldots, x_k), (y_1, \ldots, y_k) \in \mathbb{N}_0^k$. Then, $(x_1, \ldots, x_k) + (y_1, \ldots, y_k) = (x_1 + y_1, \ldots, x_k + y_k)$, and $(x_1, \ldots, x_k) \leq (y_1, \ldots, y_k)$ if and only if $x_i \leq y_i$, $i = 1, \ldots, k$.

The weight of the computation path α as in Eq. (1) is

$$\omega(\alpha) = \sum_{i=1}^{m} \omega(q_{i-1}, a_i, q_i) \in \mathbb{N}_0^k.$$

We let $\Theta(s_1, w, s_2)$ denote the set of all computation paths along a string w from state s_1 to state s_2. The *language recognized by the additive k-WFA A within the weight bound $r \geq 0$* is the set of strings for which there exists a computation path that is accepted by A and each component of the weight is at most r. Formally, we define

$$L(A, r) = \{w \in \Sigma^* : (\exists f \in F)(\exists \alpha \in \Theta(q_0, w, f))\ \omega(\alpha) \leq (r, \ldots, r)\}.$$

3 Consensus String for Multiple Regular Languages

We define that the consensus string of languages $L_1, \ldots, L_k$ is a string that is within a given edit-distance r from a string in each of the languages.

Definition 3 (consensus string of multiple languages). *Let $L_i \subseteq \Sigma^*, 1 \leq i \leq k$ be k languages over an alphabet Σ. Then, a string w is a radius r consensus of the languages $L_1, L_2, \ldots, L_k$, if $\min\{d_e(w, w_i) \mid w_i \in L_i\} \leq r$ for all $1 \leq i \leq k$.*

The following lemma is an immediate consequence of the definition.

Lemma 4. *Let $r, k \in \mathbb{N}$. Languages $L_1, \ldots, L_k$ have a radius r consensus string if and only if $\bigcap_{i=1}^{k} E(L_i, d_e, r) \neq \emptyset$.*

We will consider the algorithmic problem of determining the existence of a consensus string of radius r for given k regular languages. We consider also uniform variants of the problem where the values k and/or r will be given as part of the input. The terminology for talking about different variants of the problem is defined next.

Definition 5. *Let $k, r \in \mathbb{N}_0$ be fixed. The (k, r)-consensus string problem for NFAs (respectively, for given DFAs) is the problem of determining, for given NFAs (respectively, for DFAs) $A_1, \ldots, A_k$*

$$\textit{whether or not } L(A_1), \ldots, L(A_k) \textit{ have a radius } r \textit{ consensus string.} \quad (2)$$

For a fixed $r \in \mathbb{N}_0$, the $(*, r)$-consensus string problem for NFAs is the problem of determining whether (2) holds for given $k \in \mathbb{N}$ and NFAs $A_1, \ldots, A_k$. For a fixed $k \in \mathbb{N}$, the $(k, *)$-consensus string problem for NFAs asks whether (2) holds for given $r \in \mathbb{N}$ and NFAs $A_1, \ldots, A_k$, and the $(*, *)$-consensus problem for NFAs is the same problem where both k and r are part of the input.

The $(*, r)$- (respectively, $(k, *)$-, $(*, *)$-) consensus string problem for DFAs is defined analogously by restricting the input automata to be DFAs.

3.1 The $(*, r)$-Consensus String Problem for NFAs

Using Proposition 1 it is easy to see that the (k, r)-consensus string problem for NFAs can be solved in polynomial time. In Sect. 3.2, more generally, we show that the $(k, *)$-consensus string problem for NFAs has a polynomial time algorithm. On the other hand, the $(*, 0)$-consensus string problem for DFAs is the standard DFA intersection emptiness problem and is known to be PSPACE-complete [12,14]. Below we show that, for any $r \in \mathbb{N}$, the $(*, r)$-consensus string problem is PSPACE-complete.

Lemma 6. *For $r \in \mathbb{N}$, the $(*, r)$-consensus string problem for DFAs is PSPACE-complete.*

Proof. For given k and DFAs $A_1, \ldots, A_k$, by Proposition 1, we can construct in polynomial space NFAs B_i recognizing the neighbourhood $E(L(A_i), d_e, r)$, $i = 1, \ldots, k$, since r is a constant. Then, the intersection emptiness of the NFAs B_i can be decided in polynomial space.

For the hardness result, we reduce the DFA intersection emptiness problem to the $(*, r)$-consensus string problem for DFAs. Let $C_1, \ldots, C_k$ be DFAs over an alphabet Σ. We construct DFAs $D_1, \ldots, D_k$ such that $D_1, \ldots, D_k$ have a radius r consensus string if and only if $\bigcap_{i=1}^{k} L(C_i) \neq \emptyset$.

Let $h : \Sigma^* \rightarrow \Sigma^*$ be a morphism defined by the condition $h(\sigma) = \sigma^{2r+1}$ for all $\sigma \in \Sigma$. Let D_i, $1 \leq i \leq k$, be a DFA for the language $h(L(C_i))$. If $\bigcap_{i=1}^{k} L(C_i) = \emptyset$, $L(D_1), \ldots, L(D_k)$ cannot have a radius r consensus because a block of $2r + 1$ symbols cannot be converted to a different block in r edit steps. Conversely, if $w \in \bigcap_{i=1}^{k} L(C_i)$, then $h(w)$ is a radius 0 consensus string for $L(D_1), \ldots, L(D_k)$. □

The first part of the proof works equally well for NFAs and we have

Corollary 7. *For a constant $r \in \mathbb{N}$, the $(*, r)$-consensus string problem for NFAs is PSPACE-complete.*

The proof of Lemma 6 explicitly constructs NFAs for the neighbourhoods $E(L(A_i), d_e, r)$. In the case where the radius r is part of the input this construction cannot be completed in polynomial space and the proof does not imply that the $(*, *)$-consensus string problem is in PSPACE. In Sect. 3.2, we give a different PSPACE algorithm for the $(*, *)$-consensus string problem.

It is known that the intersection emptiness for unary NFAs or DFAs is NP-complete [12] and this implies, as in the proof of Lemma 6, that for all $r \in \mathbb{N}$, the $(*, r)$-consensus string problem for unary DFAs is NP-hard.

Theorem 8. *For a constant $r \in \mathbb{N}$, the $(*, r)$-consensus string problem for unary NFAs is NP-complete.*

Proof. We first show that the $(*, r)$-consensus string problem for unary NFAs over $\Sigma = \{0\}$ is in NP. Suppose that we have k unary NFAs from A_1 to A_k and $A_i, 1 \leq i \leq k$ has m_i states. If there is a radius r consensus string for unary

NFAs $A_1, \ldots A_k$, then the intersection of the neighbourhood $\cap_{i=1}^{k} E(L(A_i), d_e, r)$ is not empty. Since we can construct the neighbourhood $E(L(A_i), d_e, r)$ of unary NFA A_i with $m_i + r$ states, we have an upper bound m on the number of states of $\cap_{i=1}^{k} E(L(A_i), d_e, r)$ as follows: $m = \prod_{i=1}^{k}(m_i + r)$.

This implies that if there is a radius r consensus string for unary NFAs $A_1, \ldots A_k$, then there exists a consensus string whose length is bounded by m. Hence, we can nondeterministically guess a string $w = 0^n, n \leq m$ which is a radius r consensus string of unary NFAs. We can test whether or not $w \in E(L(A_i), d_e, r), 1 \leq i \leq k$ in time bounded by a polynomial in $|\text{bin}(n)|$ by successively squaring and multiplying matrices for the transition function. Since $|\text{bin}(n)| \leq |\text{bin}(m)| = O(\log m)$, we can verify that the unary string w is a radius r consensus string of unary NFAs in time bounded by a polynomial in the size of NFAs.

For the hardness, we reduce the intersection emptiness of unary NFAs to the $(*, r)$-consensus string problem for unary NFAs as in the proof of Lemma 6. □

Finally, we note that since the emptiness problem for two context-free languages is undecidable, similarly as in Lemma 6, it follows that for all $k \geq 2$ and $r \geq 0$ the (k, r)-consensus problem for context-free languages is undecidable.

Corollary 9. *For all $k \geq 2$ and $r \geq 0$ the (k, r)-consensus problem for context-free languages is undecidable.*

3.2 The $(k, *)$-Consensus String Problem for NFAs

In this section we consider the consensus string problem where the number of NFAs is fixed. Proposition 1 yields "small" NFAs for radius r neighbourhoods of regular languages. However, the NFAs are still too big to yield a polynomial time algorithm if the size of the input is counted to be the length of the binary representation of r. On the other hand, if the distance r is given in unary, then the above approach yields polynomial time algorithm and we consider this case first.

By the $(k, *\text{unary})$-consensus string problem, we mean a variant of the $(k, *)$-consensus string problem for NFAs where the radius r is given in unary notation,

Lemma 10. *For a constant $k \in \mathbb{N}$, the $(k, *\text{unary})$-consensus string problem for NFAs can be decided in polynomial time.*

Proof. Consider NFAs A_i with m_i states, $i = 1, \ldots, k$. By Proposition 1, the neighbourhood $E(L(A_i), d_e, r)$ has an NFA B_i with $m_i \cdot (r+1)$ states, $1 \leq i \leq k$, and B_i can be constructed in time that depends polynomially on m_i and r. An NFA C for $\bigcap_{i=1}^{k} L(B_i)$ can be obtained from the NFAs B_i, $1 \leq i \leq k$, using the standard cross-product construction and emptiness of $L(C)$ can be tested in polynomial time. The claim follows by Lemma 4. □

Note that if the radius r is given in binary the proof of Lemma 10 does not yield a polynomial time algorithm because the NFAs B_i are too large to write down. Next we extend the polynomial time algorithm of the standard $(k,*)$-consensus string problem for NFAs. Given NFAs $A_1, \ldots, A_k$ and r, we again, roughly speaking, need to decide non-emptiness of $\bigcap_{i=1}^{k} E(L(A_i), d_e, r)$. However, instead of NFAs (with a number of states that depends exponentially on the size of the representation of r) we use a weighted finite automaton where the number of states is independent of r.

We obtain a construction for the weighted finite automaton by modifying the proof of the following lemma from [19].

Lemma 11 [19]. *Let $N = (Q, \Sigma, \delta, q_0, F)$ be an NFA with n states, d an additive quasi-distance, and $R \geq 0$ is a constant. There exists an additive WFA A with n states such that for any $0 \leq r \leq R$,*

$$L(A, r) = E(L(N), d, r)$$

Furthermore, the WFA A can be constructed in time $O(n^3)$.

Note that Lemma 11 assumes that the radius is a constant and for this reason we have to be a little careful to check that the construction can be done in time that depends polynomially on the length of the binary representation of r. Furthermore, Lemma 11 deals only with one component WFAs (the case $k = 1$) but changing the construction for k components is straightforward. On the other hand, the construction for Lemma 11 allows the use of a general additive quasi-distance, and we are dealing with the simpler case of edit-distance where a neighbourhood of a string is always finite.

Lemma 12. *Let $k \in \mathbb{N}$ be fixed. Let $B_i = (S_i, \Sigma, \delta_i, s_{i,0}, F_i), i = 1, \ldots, k$ be an NFA with m_i states and $r \in \mathbb{N}$. There exists an additive k-WFA A with $\prod_{i=1}^{k} m_i$ states such that*

$$L(A, r) = \bigcap_{i=1}^{k} E(L(B_i), d_e, r) \tag{3}$$

Furthermore, the additive k-WFA A can be constructed in time that depends polynomially on the sizes of the NFAs B_i, $1 \leq i \leq k$, and $|\text{bin}(r)|$.

Proof. We define an additive k-WFA $A = (Q, \Sigma, \gamma, \omega, q_0, F)$, where $Q = S_1 \times \cdots \times S_k$, $q_0 = (s_{1,0}, \ldots, s_{k,0})$, $F = F_1 \times \cdots \times F_k$ and the transitions of γ and the weight function are defined as follows.

The transition function γ is defined by setting, for $(s_1, \ldots, s_k) \in Q$, $b \in \Sigma \cup \{\varepsilon\}$,

$$\begin{aligned} &\gamma((s_1, \ldots, s_k), b) = \\ &\quad \{(s'_1, \ldots, s'_k) : (\exists x \in \Sigma^*)\ s'_i \in \delta_i(s_i, x), 1 \leq i \leq k, \text{ and } d_e(b, x) \leq r\}. \end{aligned} \tag{4}$$

That is, for each two states of A we add a transition on $b \in \Sigma \cup \{\varepsilon\}$ if there is a string $x \in \Sigma^*$ within edit-distance at most r from the symbol b that in the NFAs B_i transform the components of the first state to the components of the second state. The transition $(\mathbf{s}, b, \mathbf{s}')$, $\mathbf{s} = (s_1, \ldots, s_k)$, $\mathbf{s}' = (s'_1, \ldots, s'_k)$, in A has weight

$$\omega((\mathbf{s}, b, \mathbf{s}')) = \min_{x \in \Sigma^*} \{d_e(b, x) : s'_i \in \delta(s_i, x), i = 1, \ldots, k\}. \quad (5)$$

The correctness of the construction (i.e., that Eq. (3) holds) is verified as in [19] and we only need to check that the construction, for non-constant r, can be done in time that is polynomial in the m_i's and $|\text{bin}(r)|$ (whereas in [19] the radius was treated as a constant).

For $s_i, s'_i \in S_i$ and $b \in \Sigma \cup \{\varepsilon\}$, to check whether there exists a string x such that $s'_i \in \delta_i(s_i, x)$ and $d_e(x, b) \leq r$ we determine whether the shortest path in B_i from s_i to s'_i has length at most r, or length at most $r + 1$ if $b \in \Sigma$ and the path contains an occurrence of b. This can be done in time that depends polynomially on m_i and $|\text{bin}(r)|$. Then, the transitions of γ (4) can be computed by repeating this procedure $(\Pi_{i=1}^k m_i)^2$ times.

For each two tuples $\mathbf{s} = (s_1, \ldots, s_k)$ and $\mathbf{s}' = (s'_1, \ldots, s'_k)$ that will have a γ-transition on $b \in \Sigma \cup \{\varepsilon\}$, the process finds the string x which transforms components of $\mathbf{s}$ into components of $\mathbf{s}'$ in the NFAs B_i and minimizes the distance $d_e(b, x)$, and this allows us to compute also the weights in (5). Note that although the length of x may be superpolynomial in $|\text{bin}(r)|$, the length is upper bounded by the values m_i which are the sizes of the input NFAs. □

We need one more technical lemma.

Lemma 13. *Let $k \in \mathbb{N}$ be fixed. Given an additive k-WFA A with n states and $r \in \mathbb{N}$, we can decide in time that is polynomial in n and in $|\text{bin}(r)|$ whether or not $L(A, r) = \emptyset$.*

Proof. We use a polynomial time graph reachability algorithm to check whether a final state of A is reachable from the initial state, and the computation keeps track of the smallest cumulative weight of the path traversed up to that point. Recall that each state of A is a k-tuple of states.

Let $A = (Q, \Sigma, \gamma, \omega, q_0, F)$ be the given additive k-WFA. In stage one, the algorithm marks the states of A reachable from $q_0 = (q_{0,1}, \ldots, q_{0,k})$ in a single transition. Each of these states $q = (q_1, \ldots, q_k)$ is marked by a k-tuple $(w_1, \ldots, w_k)$, where w_i is the smallest weight of a transition that reaches q_i from $q_{0,i}$. The marking process is then repeated $n - 1$ times as follows.

Suppose states $p_1, \ldots, p_r$ are marked at the ith stage ($i \leq n - 2$) where the cumulative weight of p_i is w_i. In stage $i + 1$ the algorithm marks states $p'_1, \ldots, p'_s$ reachable from a state among $p_1, \ldots, p_r$ with a single transition. Each state $p'_i = (p'_{i,1}, \ldots, p'_{i,k})$ will have a weight tuple $w'_i = (w'_{i,1}, \ldots, w'_{i,k})$ where for $1 \leq \ell \leq k$, we have

$$w_{i,\ell} = \min(\{w_{j,\ell} + \omega(p_{j,\ell}, b, p'_{i,\ell}) \mid 1 \leq j \leq r, b \in \Sigma \cup \{\varepsilon\}\} \cup \{r + 1\}).$$

Note that weight $r + 1$ is used as an error value indicating that the computation path has failed.

If at some point a final state is marked with a weight where each component is at most r, the algorithm answers "yes". The algorithm is correct because

$L(A, r) \neq \emptyset$ if and only if A has a computation of weight at most r leading to a final state on a string of length at most $n-1$. The number of steps of the marking algorithm is upper bounded by $O(kn^2)$ (when the size of the alphabet Σ is viewed as a constant). The individual weight additions can be done in time linear in $|\text{bin}(r)|$. □

Now we present a polynomial time algorithm for the $(k, *)$-consensus string problem.

Theorem 14. *For a constant $k \in \mathbb{N}_0$, the $(k, *)$-consensus string problem for NFAs can be solved in polynomial time.*

As a corollary we extend the result of Lemma 6 for the $(*, *)$-consensus string problem.

Corollary 15. *The consensus string problem for NFAs (or DFAs) is PSPACE-complete.*

3.3 Finding a Consensus String of Given Length

Interestingly, if we are given the length $l \in \mathbb{N}_0$ of a consensus string in unary, then the computational complexity of the problem becomes NP-complete. We use a reduction from the classical consensus string problem which is already proven to be NP-complete. First, we give the definition of the classical consensus string problem. Note that the distance function d_H denotes the Hamming distance.

Definition 16. *Let $S \subseteq \Sigma^l$ be a finite set of strings of length l. Then, a string w is a radius r consensus of S, if $d_H(w, s) \leq r$ for all $s \in S$.*

Then, given $\ell, r \in \mathbb{N}$ and a set $S \subseteq \Sigma^l$, it is NP-complete to decide whether or not there exists a radius r consensus of S [7]. The problem remains NP-complete even when $|\Sigma| = 2$.

However, because we are considering the edit-distance for our variant of the consensus string problem, first we need to reduce the Hamming distance to the edit-distance. Manthey and Reischuk [17] have shown that it is possible to reduce the Hamming distance to the edit-distance when only binary strings are considered. Here we first show that we can reduce the Hamming distance to the edit-distance in a much simpler way by introducing one more character.

Lemma 17. *Let w, w' be a strings of length l over Σ and $h : \Sigma^* \to (\Sigma \cup \{\$\})^*, \$ \notin \Sigma$ be a morphism defined by $h(\sigma) = \$^l\sigma$ for all $\sigma \in \Sigma$. Then, $d_H(w, w') = d_e(h(w), h(w'))$.*

The next lemma shows that the consensus string problem for multiple NFAs is NP-complete when the length ℓ of the consensus string is given in unary. The lemma is proved by a reduction from the classical consensus string problem and by relying on Lemma 17.

Lemma 18. *The consensus string problem for NFAs (or DFAs) is NP-complete if the length l of consensus string is given in unary.*

We also mention that the problem is still NP-complete if context-free languages are considered instead of regular languages since the edit-distance between a string and a context-free language described by a context-free grammar (CFG) can be computed in polynomial time [18].

Corollary 19. *The consensus string problem for context-free languages is NP-complete if the length l of consensus string is given in unary.*

However, the problem becomes PSPACE-complete if the length ℓ is given in binary.

Theorem 20. *The consensus string problem for NFAs (or DFAs) is PSPACE-complete if the length l of consensus string is given in binary.*

We also establish that the *fixed-length consensus problem*, where the length l of the consensus string is fixed, can be decided in polynomial time.

Corollary 21. *The fixed-length consensus string problem for NFAs (or DFAs) can be decided in $O(n \log n)$ time, where n is the size of NFAs (or DFAs).*

As a final note, we state that the fixed-length consensus string problem for context-free languages given by CFGs can be also decided in polynomial time.

Corollary 22. *The fixed-length consensus string problem for CFGs can be decided in $O(n \log n)$ time, where n is the size of CFGs.*

References

1. Amir, A., Landau, G.M., Na, J.C., Park, H., Park, K., Sim, J.S.: Efficient algorithms for consensus string problems minimizing both distance sum and radius. Theoret. Comput. Sci. **412**(39), 5239–5246 (2011)
2. Amir, A., Paryenty, H., Roditty, L.: On the hardness of the consensus string problem. Inf. Process. Lett. **113**(10–11), 371–374 (2013)
3. Calude, C.S., Salomaa, K., Yu, S.: Additive distances and quasi-distances between words. J. Univ. Comput. Sci. **8**(2), 141–152 (2002)
4. Choffrut, C., Pighizzini, G.: Distances between languages and reflexivity of relations. Theoret. Comput. Sci. **286**(1), 117–138 (2002)
5. Cohen, G.D., Honkala, I.S., Litsyn, S.N., Solé, P.: Long packing and covering codes. IEEE Trans. Inf. Theor. **43**(5), 1617–1619 (2006)
6. Deza, M.M., Deza, E.: Encyclopedia of Distances. Springer, Heidelberg (2009)
7. Frances, M., Litman, A.: On covering problems of codes. Theor. Comput. Syst. **30**(2), 113–119 (1997)
8. Graham, R.L., Sloane, N.J.A.: On the covering radius of codes. IEEE Trans. Inf. Theor. **31**(3), 385–401 (2006)
9. Gramm, J., Niedermeier, R., Rossmanith, P.: Exact solutions for closest string and related problems. In: Eades, P., Takaoka, T. (eds.) ISAAC 2001. LNCS, vol. 2223, pp. 441–453. Springer, Heidelberg (2001). doi:10.1007/3-540-45678-3_38

10. Gramm, J., Niedermeier, R., Rossmanith, P.: Fixed-parameter algorithms for closest string and related problems. Algorithmica **37**, 25–42 (2003)
11. Han, Y.-S., Ko, S.-K., Salomaa, K.: The edit-distance between a regular language and a context-free language. Int. J. Found. Comput. Sci. **24**(7), 1067–1082 (2013)
12. Holzer, M., Kutrib, M.: Descriptional and computational complexity of finite automata—a survey. Inf. Comput. **209**(3), 456–470 (2011)
13. Konstantinidis, S.: Computing the edit distance of a regular language. Inf. Comput. **205**(9), 1307–1316 (2007)
14. Kozen, D.: Lower bounds for natural proof systems. In: Proceedings of the 18th Annual Symposium on Foundations of Computer Science, pp. 254–266 (1977)
15. Levenshtein, V.I.: Binary codes capable of correcting deletions, insertions, and reversals. Sov. Phys. Dokl. **10**(8), 707–710 (1966)
16. Ma, B., Sun, X.: More efficient algorithms for closest string and substring problems. SIAM J. Comput. **39**(4), 1432–1443 (2010)
17. Manthey, B., Reischuk, R.: The intractability of computing the Hamming distance. Theoret. Comput. Sci. **337**(1–3), 331–346 (2005)
18. Myers, G.: Approximately matching context-free languages. Inf. Process. Lett. **54**, 85–92 (1995)
19. Ng, T., Rappaport, D., Salomaa, K.: Quasi-distances and weighted finite automata. In: Shallit, J., Okhotin, A. (eds.) DCFS 2015. LNCS, vol. 9118, pp. 209–219. Springer, Heidelberg (2015). doi:10.1007/978-3-319-19225-3_18
20. Ng, T., Rappaport, D., Salomaa, K.: State complexity of neighbourhoods and approximate pattern matching. In: Potapov, I. (ed.) DLT 2015. LNCS, vol. 9168, pp. 389–400. Springer, Heidelberg (2015). doi:10.1007/978-3-319-21500-6_31
21. Palopoli, L., Chen, Z.-Z., Ma, B., Wang, L.: A three-string approach to the closest string problem. J. Comput. Syst. Sci. **78**(1), 164–178 (2012)
22. Pighizzini, G.: How hard is computing the edit distance? Inf. Comput. **165**(1), 1–13 (2001)
23. Povarov, G.: Descriptive complexity of the hamming neighborhood of a regular language. In: Proceedings of the 1st International Conference on Language and Automata Theory and Applications, pp. 509–520 (2007)
24. Shallit, J.: A Second Course in Formal Languages and Automata Theory, 1st edn. Cambridge University Press, New York (2008)
25. Sim, J.S., Park, K.: The consensus string problem for a metric is NP-complete. J. Discret. Algorithms **1**(1), 111–117 (2003)
26. Stojanovic, N., Berman, P., Gumucio, D., Hardison, R., Miller, W.: A linear-time algorithm for the 1-mismatch problem. In: Dehne, F., Rau-Chaplin, A., Sack, J.-R., Tamassia, R. (eds.) WADS 1997. LNCS, vol. 1272, pp. 126–135. Springer, Heidelberg (1997). doi:10.1007/3-540-63307-3_53
27. Yu, S.: Regular languages. In: Rozenberg, G., Salomaa, A. (eds.) Handbook of Formal Languages, vol. 1, pp. 41–110. Springer, Berlin (1997)

The Weight in Enumeration

Johannes Schmidt[(✉)]

Jönköping International Business School,
Jönköping University, Jönköping, Sweden
johannes.schmidt@ju.se

Abstract. In our setting enumeration amounts to generate all solutions of a problem instance without duplicates. We address the problem of enumerating the models of B-formulæ. A B-formula is a propositional formula whose connectives are taken from a fixed set B of Boolean connectives. Without imposing any specific order to output the solutions, this task is solved. We completely classify the complexity of this enumeration task for all possible sets of connectives B imposing the orders of (1) non-decreasing weight, (2) non-increasing weight; the weight of a model being the number of variables assigned to 1. We consider also the weighted variants where a non-negative integer weight is assigned to each variable and show that this add-on leads to more sophisticated enumeration algorithms and even renders previously tractable cases intractable, contrarily to the constraint setting. As a by-product we obtain also complexity classifications for the optimization problems known as MIN-ONES and MAX-ONES which are in the B-formula setting two different tasks.

Keywords: Computational complexity · Enumeration · Non-decreasing weight · Polynomial delay · Post's lattice · MaxOnes

1 Introduction

We deal in this paper with algorithmic and complexity of *enumeration*, the task of generating all solutions of a problem instance. Over the last 15 years, in both practice and theory, one can observe a growing interest in studying enumeration problems which have previously been poorly studied compared to decision, optimization and counting problems. The main reason for this may lie in the huge increase of the size of the data computers are nowadays demanded and able to process in everyday applications.

It is in the meanwhile commonly agreed to consider an enumeration algorithm *efficient* if it has *polynomial delay* ([9,16]), *i.e.*, the time passing between outputs of two successive solutions is polynomial in the input size (while the total time of the output process is usually exponential, due to large solution sets). Variants and different degrees of efficiency in this context exist, see e.g. [9,19]. Known reductions for enumeration are essentially one-to-one parsimonious reductions, as opposed to counting complexity where a greater variety of useful reductions exist, see e.g. [3,7]. An interesting issue of enumeration is the order in which the

F. Drewes et al. (Eds.): LATA 2017, LNCS 10168, pp. 208–219, 2017.
DOI: 10.1007/978-3-319-53733-7_15

solutions are output. Imposing different orders for an enumeration process may drastically change the complexity, see e.g. [2,5,9].

We focus in this paper on the task of enumerating the models of a propositional formula. This task has already been addressed in the context of Boolean constraint satisfaction problems (CSPs). One considers here formulæ in generalized conjunctive normal form [15], also called Γ-*formulæ* where Γ is the *constraint language*. In [4] this task, EnumSAT for short, has been studied without imposing any special order. There is a polynomial delay algorithm if and only if the underlying constraint language Γ is either Horn, or dual Horn, or affine, or 2CNF, unless P = NP. It is worth mentioning that the algorithms underlying this result are all straight forward extensions of the corresponding decision procedures via the notion of *self-reducibility* [18] which naturally leads to lexicographic order. In the non-Boolean domain the self-reducible fragment does not deliver all tractable cases anymore [17] and things get much more involved.

Back to the Boolean domain, EnumSAT has also been considered imposing the order of non-decreasing weight (EnumSAT$_\uparrow$ for short), the weight of a model being the number of variables assigned to 1. The weight is a natural parameter in Boolean CSPs that can be assimilated to the cost of an assignment. Hence, the task EnumSAT$_\uparrow$ can be seen as the task of enumerating the cheapest solutions first, then the more expensive ones in order of increasing cost. In [5] the task EnumSAT$_\uparrow$ has been studied for Γ-formulæ. There is a polynomial delay algorithm to enumerate the models of a propositional Γ-formula by order of non-decreasing weight if and only if Γ is width-2-affine or Horn, unless P = NP. By duality in that context, the task of enumerating by order of non-increasing weight (EnumSAT$_\downarrow$) is tractable if and only if Γ is width-2-affine or dual Horn.

In this paper we reveal new tractable fragments of propositional logic for EnumSAT$_\uparrow$ and EnumSAT$_\downarrow$ by considering fragments of propositional logic by a different approach. A *B-formula* is a propositional formula whose connectives are taken from B, a fixed set of Boolean functions. This approach covers different fragments than the classical constraint approach, e.g. monotonic, self-dual, 0-separating of degree n. It has first been taken by Lewis [12] who showed that the satisfiability problem for B-formulæ, Sat(B) for short, is NP-complete if and only if the set B is able to express negation of implication ($x \wedge \neg y$), unless P = NP. Since then, a number of problems dealing with propositional formulæ have been parameterized by B-formulæ in order to get a finer classification of their complexity, e.g. equivalence [14], implication [1], circumscription [20], abduction [6].

In [2] the model enumeration problem has been studied in the context of B-circuits without imposing an order and imposing lexicographic order. Roughly speaking, a B-formula can be represented by a B-circuit without size-increase, but, in general, not vice versa. Therefore, tractability translates from B-circuits to B-formulæ, whereas this does not automatically hold for hardness results. We observe however that only slight modifications in the hardness proof from [2] suffice and one obtains the same classification for B-formulæ.

Our main contribution lies in complete classifications for EnumSAT$_\uparrow$ and EnumSAT$_\downarrow$. We show that the models of a B-formula can efficiently be enumerated by order of non-decreasing weight if and only if the connectives are either 0-separating, or affine, or conjunctive, or disjunctive, unless P = NP. We further show that we can efficiently enumerate by order of non-increasing weight if and only if the connectives are either 0-separating of degree 2, or monotone, or affine, unless P = NP. We also consider the weighted variants of $\text{ENUMSAT}_{\uparrow}$ and $\text{ENUMSAT}_{\downarrow}$ (denoted $\text{W-ENUMSAT}_{\uparrow}$ and $\text{W-ENUMSAT}_{\downarrow}$, respectively) where a weight function $w : \{x_1, \ldots, x_n\} \to \mathbb{N}$ assigns a non-negative integer weight to each variable and the weight of an assignment is the sum of the weights of the variables assigned to 1. We show that for $\text{W-ENUMSAT}_{\uparrow}$ the previously tractable fragment of 0-separating connectives now compounds intractable cases.

We also shed new light on the optimization problems known as MIN-ONES and MAX-ONES where the task is to find a model of minimal/maximal weight. We use these tasks, together with their weighted and non-trivial variants, to obtain hardness of the enumeration problems. These two tasks are in our setting not "the same": contrary to the classical constraint setting [10], no duality notion allows to easily derive the classification for MAX-ONES from the one for MIN-ONES, or vice versa. This is because the duality notion in our setting transforms MIN-ONES (find a satisfying assignment with minimal number of 1's) into the task of finding a non-satisfying assignment with maximal number of 1's. We show further that allowing weights on the variables renders previously tractable fragments intractable, contrarily to the classical constraint approach.

Among the algorithmic enumeration strategies we use, we apply a method we shall call *priority queue method*. It has first been used in [9] in order to enumerate all maximal independent sets of a graph in lexicographical order. This method turned out to be applicable in much more generality [5,11,16]. We use it to obtain various polynomial delay algorithms for $\text{ENUMSAT}_{\uparrow}$ and $\text{ENUMSAT}_{\downarrow}$ and their weighted variants.

We give another non-trivial enumeration algorithm for $\text{ENUMSAT}_{\downarrow}$ for the fragment of connectives that are 0-separating of degree 2 (Proposition 16) that may be intuitively best described by *nested* or *incremental bruteforce*: we use the Erdős-Ko-Rado Theorem [8] to obtain a combinatorial bound that allows us to *buy time* [17] from a relatively large number of models whose output process delivers then enough time to compute further, computationally more involving models that are stored and output afterwards.

The paper is organized as follows. In Sect. 2 we give the necessary preliminaries on complexity theory, propositional formulæ and clones of Boolean functions. In Sect. 3 we briefly look at model enumeration without order prescription. We treat the order of non-decreasing and non-increasing weight in Sects. 4 and 5 respectively. We conclude in Sect. 6. A version of this paper with full proofs can be found at https://arxiv.org/pdf/1612.00675.pdf.

2 Preliminaries

2.1 Complexity Theory

For the decision problems the arising complexity degrees encompass the classes P and NP. For our hardness results we employ logspace many-one reductions.

An *enumeration problem* E can be formalized by a triple $(I, Sol, \leq)$, where I are the instances, Sol is a function mapping each instance $x \in I$ to its set of solutions $Sol(x)$ and $\leq$ is a partial order (possibly empty) on the solution space. We say that an algorithm A solves an enumeration problem $E = (I, Sol, \leq)$ if for a given input $x \in I$, A generates one by one the elements of $Sol(x)$ without repetition such that for all $y, z \in Sol(x)$ such that $y < z$, A outputs y before z.

An enumeration algorithm runs in *polynomial delay* if the delay until the first solution is output and thereafter the delay between any two consecutive solutions is bounded by a polynomial $p(n)$ in the input size n. We denote *DelayP* the class of enumeration problems that admit a polynomial delay algorithm and *SpaceDelayP* those problems in DelayP that are solvable within polynomial space.

2.2 Propositional Formulæ

We assume familiarity with propositional logic. For a propositional formula φ we denote by $\mathrm{Vars}(\varphi)$ the set of variables occurring in φ. We represent an assignment $\sigma : \mathrm{Vars}(\varphi) \to \{0,1\}^n$ usually as a tuple over $\{0,1\}$ or when convenient by the set of variables assigned to 1, *i.e.*, the empty set corresponds to $\mathbf{0}$ and $\mathrm{Vars}(\varphi)$ to $\mathbf{1}$. A *model* for a formula φ is an assignment that satisfies φ. A *non-trivial* assignment is an assignment different from $\mathbf{0}$ and $\mathbf{1}$. The *complement* of an assignment σ is defined as $\overline{\sigma}(x) = 0 \Leftrightarrow \sigma(x) = 1$. We call a variable $x \in \mathrm{Vars}(\varphi)$ *fictive*, if the assignment $x = 0$ can be extended to a model of φ if and only if so can the assignment $x = 1$. We denote by $\varphi[\alpha/\beta]$ the formula obtained from φ by replacing all occurrences of α with β.

2.3 Clones of Boolean Functions

A *Boolean function* is an n-ary function $f : \{0,1\}^n \to \{0,1\}$. For technical reasons we consider only Boolean functions of arity > 0. It is not difficult but just technical to include also functions of arity 0 into our considerations. We denote the n-ary Boolean constants by C_0^n and C_1^n, respectively. When the arity is not relevant, we indicate them also by C_0 and C_1, keeping in mind that they have at least one fictive coordinate. An n-ary assignment m such that $f(m) = 1$ will be called *model* of f. A *clone* is a set of Boolean functions that is closed under superposition, *i.e.*, it contains all projections (that is, the functions $f(a_1, \ldots, a_n) = a_k$ for all $1 \leq k \leq n$ and $n \in \mathbb{N}$) and is closed under arbitrary composition. Let B be a finite set of Boolean functions. We denote by $[B]$ the smallest clone containing B and call B a *base* for $[B]$. In 1941 Post identified the set of all clones of Boolean functions [13]. He gave a finite base for each of the clones and showed that they form a lattice under the usual $\subseteq$-relation, hence the name *Post's lattice* (see, *e.g.*, Fig. 1). To define the clones we introduce the following notions, where f is an n-ary Boolean function:

- f is *c-reproducing* if $f(c, \ldots, c) = c$, $c \in \{0,1\}$.
- f is *monotonic* if $a_1 \leq b_1, \ldots, a_n \leq b_n$ implies $f(a_1, \ldots, a_n) \leq f(b_1, \ldots, b_n)$.

- f is *c-separating of degree k* if for all $A \subseteq f^{-1}(c)$ of size $|A| = k$ there exists an $i \in \{1, \ldots, n\}$ such that $(a_1, \ldots, a_n) \in A$ implies $a_i = c$, $c \in \{0, 1\}$.
- f is *c-separating* if f is c-separating of degree $|f^{-1}(c)|$.
- f is *self-dual* if $f \equiv \text{dual}(f)$, where $\text{dual}(f)(x_1, \ldots, x_n) := \neg f(\neg x_1, \ldots, \neg x_n)$.
- f is *affine* if $f \equiv x_1 \oplus \cdots \oplus x_n \oplus c$ with $c \in \{0, 1\}$.

A list of some clones with definitions and finite bases is given in Table 1.

We will often add some function $f \notin C$ to a clone C and consider the clone $C' = [C \cup \{f\}]$ generated out of C and f. With Post's lattice one can determine this C' quite easily: It is the lowest clone above C that contains f. We will use in particular the identities $[\mathsf{S}_{12} \cup \{\mathsf{C}_1\}] = \mathsf{S}_1$, $[\mathsf{D} \cup \{\mathsf{C}_1\}] = \mathsf{BF}$, $[\mathsf{R}_1 \cup \{\mathsf{C}_0\}] = \mathsf{BF}$, $[\mathsf{D}_1 \cup \{\mathsf{C}_1\}] = \mathsf{R}_1$, and $[\mathsf{S}_{10} \cup \{\mathsf{C}_1\}] = \mathsf{M}_1$.

A propositional formula using only connectives from B is called a *B-formula.*

Definition 1. *Let f be an n-ary Boolean function and let B be a set of Boolean functions. A B-formula φ with* $\text{Vars}(\varphi) = \{x_1, \ldots, x_k\}$ *is called* B-representation *of f if there is an index function $\pi : \{1, \ldots, n\} \to \{1, \ldots, k\}$ such that $\forall x_1, \ldots, x_k \in \{0, 1\}$ it holds $f(x_{\pi(1)}, \ldots, x_{\pi(n)}) = 1$ if and only if φ evaluates to* 1.

We note that such a B-representation exists for every $f \in [B]$. We note further that, if f does not contain fictive coordinates, then there is also a B-representation for f without fictive variables. We shall keep this in mind, since some problems we consider are not stable under introduction/elimination of fictive variables.

There is a canonical transformation of a B_1-formula φ_1 into a B-formula, if $B_1 \subseteq [B]$: replace every connective in φ_1 by its B-representation. Though, this may lead to an explosion of the formula size. This can happen when a B-representation for some $f \in [B]$ uses some input variable more than once and φ_1 is of linear nesting depth, see e.g. [6]. We will nevertheless use this transformation idea in order to obtain reductions. This is possible since in the cases we encounter, we are always able to (re-)write φ_1 as a formula of logarithmic nesting depth. We note that this is not possible in general. We call formulæ of logarithmic nesting depth *compact.*

3 Enumeration Without Order Prescription

We begin by looking at the model enumeration problem without order prescription.

Problem: ENUMSAT(B)
Instance: a B-formula φ
Question: generate all models of φ (without duplicates)

This problem has been studied in [2] considering B-circuits instead of B-formulæ. It is not difficult to observe that the algorithms from [2] also prove SpaceDelayP-membership for B-formulæ for the clones M, L, D and S_0^2. But we

Table 1. List of relevant Boolean clones with definitions and bases, where t_p^q denotes the q-ary p-threshold function and $d_1(x,y,z) = (x \wedge y) \vee (x \wedge \neg z) \vee (y \wedge \neg z)$.

Name	Definition	Base
BF	All Boolean functions	$\{x \wedge y, \neg x\}$
R_1	$\{f \mid f$ is 1-reproducing$\}$	$\{x \vee y, x = y\}$
R_2	$\mathsf{R}_0 \cap \mathsf{R}_1$	$\{\vee, x \wedge (y = z)\}$
M	$\{f \mid f$ is monotonic$\}$	$\{x \vee y, x \wedge y, \mathrm{C}_0, \mathrm{C}_1\}$
S_0^n	$\{f \mid f$ is 0-separating of degree $n\}$	$\{x \rightarrow y, t_2^{n+1}\}$
S_0	$\{f \mid f$ is 0-separating$\}$	$\{x \rightarrow y\}$
S_1	$\{f \mid f$ is 1-separating$\}$	$\{x \wedge \neg y\}$
S_{00}^n	$\mathsf{S}_0^n \cap \mathsf{R}_2 \cap \mathsf{M}$	$\{x \vee (y \wedge z), t_2^{n+1}\}$
S_{00}	$\mathsf{S}_0 \cap \mathsf{R}_2 \cap \mathsf{M}$	$\{x \vee (y \wedge z)\}$
S_{12}	$\mathsf{S}_1 \cap \mathsf{R}_2$	$\{x \wedge (y \rightarrow z)\}$
S_{10}	$\mathsf{S}_1 \cap \mathsf{R}_2 \cap \mathsf{M}$	$\{x \wedge (y \vee z)\}$
D	$\{f \mid f$ is self-dual$\}$	$\{(x \wedge \neg y) \vee (x \wedge \neg z) \vee (\neg y \wedge \neg z)\}$
D_1	$\mathsf{D} \cap \mathsf{R}_2$	$\{d_1\}$
D_2	$\mathsf{D} \cap \mathsf{M}$	$\{t_2^3\}$
L	$\{f \mid f$ is affine$\}$	$\{x \oplus y, \mathrm{C}_1\}$
V	$\{f \mid f$ is a disjunction of variables or constants$\}$	$\{x \vee y, \mathrm{C}_0, \mathrm{C}_1\}$
E	$\{f \mid f$ is a conjunction of variables or constants$\}$	$\{x \wedge y, \mathrm{C}_0, \mathrm{C}_1\}$

have to slightly modify the hardness proof from [2] in order to deal with the issue of possible exponential blowup. Hardness of EnumSAT(B) is inherited from SAT*(B), the non-trivial satisfiability problem for B-formulæ (given a B-formula, does it admit a non-trivial model m, *i.e.*, $m \notin \{\mathbf{0}, \mathbf{1}\}$?). A look at Post's lattice shows us that $\mathsf{S}_{12} \nsubseteq [B]$ if and only if either $[B] \subseteq \mathsf{M}$, or $[B] \subseteq \mathsf{L}$, or $[B] \subseteq \mathsf{D}$, or $[B] \subseteq \mathsf{S}_0^2$. The following proposition will therefore complete the classification.

Proposition 2. *Let* $\mathsf{S}_{12} \subseteq [B]$. *Then* SAT*($B$) *is* NP-*complete.*

Theorem 3. *Let B be a finite set of Boolean functions. Then* EnumSAT(B) *is*

1. NP-*hard if* $\mathsf{S}_{12} \subseteq [B]$,
2. *in* SpaceDelayP *otherwise (i.e.,* $[B] \subseteq \mathsf{M}$ *or* $[B] \subseteq \mathsf{L}$ *or* $[B] \subseteq \mathsf{D}$ *or* $[B] \subseteq \mathsf{S}_0^2$*).*

4 Enumeration by Order of Non-decreasing Weight

In this section we consider model enumeration by order of non-decreasing weight.

Problem: EnumSAT$_\uparrow$(B)
Instance: a B-formula φ
Question: generate all models of φ by order of non-decreasing weight

Proposition 4. *Let* $[B] \subseteq \mathsf{V}$ *or* $[B] \subseteq \mathsf{E}$ *or* $[B] \subseteq \mathsf{L}$ *or* $[B] \subseteq \mathsf{S}_0$. *Then* EnumSAT$_\uparrow$($B$) $\in$ SpaceDelayP.

Proof. The first three cases are easy. More interesting is the fourth case. Let φ be a B-formula with n variables. Since we are 0-separating, we know that there is a special variable, call it x_j, such that any assignment with $x_j = 1$ is a model.

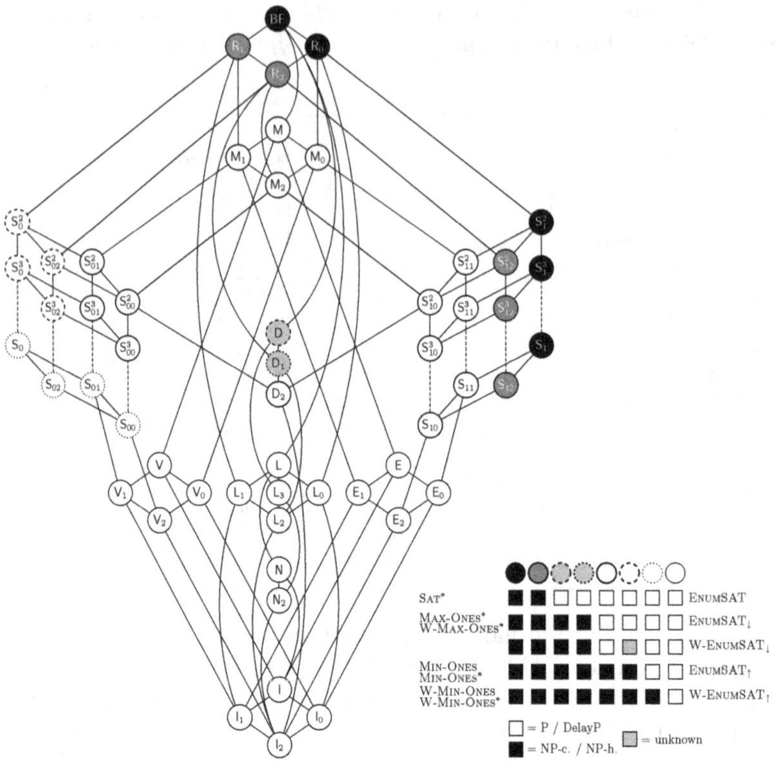

Fig. 1. The complexity of all problems from this paper illustrated on Post's Lattice.

The number of assignments of weight k with $x_j = 1$ (which all are satisfying assignments, we call them therefore *steady* models) is $\binom{n-1}{k-1}$, while the number of assignments of weight k with $x_j = 0$ is $\binom{n-1}{k}$. Since the factor between $\binom{n-1}{k-1}$ and $\binom{n-1}{k}$ is polynomial, the output process of the *steady* models delivers enough time to determine in the meanwhile the set of *unsteady* models, that is, models of weight k with $x_j = 0$. These can be stored and output afterwards. Note that this method uses exponential space. One can however obtain polynomial space (still maintaining polynomial delay) by not storing for each k the whole set of *unsteady* models, but by starting outputting them while still outputting the *steady* ones.

Solving EnumSAT$_\uparrow$ requires to efficiently solve Min-Ones, the task of computing a model of minimal weight. We will therefore inherit hardness from Min-Ones.

Proposition 5. *Let* $\mathsf{S}_{10} \subseteq [B]$ *or* $\mathsf{S}_{00}^n \subseteq [B]$ *for an* $n \geq 2$ *or* $\mathsf{D}_2 \subseteq [B]$. *Then* Min-Ones$(B)$ *is* NP*-hard.*

Proof. In the all three cases we reduce from MIN-ONES(positive-2CNF) (NP-hard according to [10]). The second and third case are technically involving, where we deal with the q-ary p-threshold function.

Theorem 6. *Let B be a finite set of Boolean functions. Then* ENUMSAT$_{\uparrow}(B)$

1. *is* NP*-hard if* $\mathsf{S}_{00}^n \subseteq [B]$ *for some* $n \geq 2$ *or* $\mathsf{D}_2 \subseteq [B]$ *or* $\mathsf{S}_{10} \subseteq [B]$,
2. *is in* SpaceDelayP *otherwise (i.e.,* $[B] \subseteq \mathsf{S}_0$ *or* $[B] \subseteq \mathsf{V}$ *or* $[B] \subseteq \mathsf{L}$ *or* $[B] \subseteq \mathsf{E}$*).*

We turn to the weighted variant.
The following method will deliver us several tractability results.

Theorem 7 (Priority queue method [9,16]**).** *Let $E = (I, Sol, \leq)$ be an enumeration problem. If it holds*

1. *for each $x \in I$, $\leq$ restricted to $Sol(x)$ is total and computable in polynomial time in $|x|$,*
2. *it can be determined in polynomial time in $|x|$ whether $Sol(x)$ is non-empty and if so, then $\min(Sol(x))$ is computable in polynomial time in $|x|$,*
3. *there is a binary function f such that for all $x \in I$ and for all $y \in Sol(x)$ holds:*
   (a) *$f(x, y)$ is computable in polynomial time in $|x|$*
   (b) *$f(x, y) \subseteq Sol(x)$*
   (c) *if $y \neq \min(Sol(x))$ then there is a $z \in Sol(x)$ such that $z < y$ and $y \in f(x, z)$,*

then $E \in$ DelayP.

Proof. Correctness of the following algorithm is not difficult to observe.

```
if Sol(x) = ∅ then return 'no'
Q = newPriorityQueue(≤)
compute ℓ := min(Sol(x))
Q.enqueue(ℓ)
while Q is not empty do
   ℓ := Q.dequeue
   output ℓ
   compute L := f(x, ℓ)
   for all z ∈ L do
      if z > ℓ then Q.enqueue(z)
   end for
end while
```

The priority queue is supposed to eliminate duplicates. Note that this method may run in exponential space.

In order to apply the method to the partial order induced by the weight of assignments, it suffices to extend it to a total order, for instance by the lexicographical order on assignments.

Proposition 8. *Let* $[B] \subseteq \mathsf{V}$ *or* $[B] \subseteq \mathsf{E}$. *Then* W-ENUMSAT$_{\uparrow}(B) \in$ DelayP.

Proof. In the first case a B-formula can be seen as disjunction of variables and constants. All assignments are models, with the possible exception of $\mathbf{0}$. Thus, we reduce our problem to

Problem: SUBSETSUM
Instance: A sequence of non-negative integers $C = (w_1, \ldots, w_n) \in \mathbb{N}^n$
Question: generate all subsets $S \subseteq \{1, \ldots, n\}$ by non-decreasing weight $\delta(S)$, where $\delta(S) = \sum_{i \in S} w_i$

This task can be solved in polynomial delay and polynomial space by a dynamic programming method if the weights on the variables are polynomially bounded [5]. Otherwise, the priority queue method from Theorem 7 is applicable with $f(C, S) = \{S \cup \{i\} \mid i \in \{1, \ldots, n\}\}$.

In the second case a B-formula can be seen as conjunction of variables and constants. If this disjunction contains a constant C_0, then there are no models. Otherwise $\mathbf{1}$ is the only model, up to fictive variables occurring in constants C_1. Again, we reduce our problem to SUBSETSUM as in the previous case.

Proposition 9. *Let* $[B] \subseteq \mathsf{L}$. *Then* W-ENUMSAT$_{\uparrow}(B) \in$ DelayP.

Proof. Apply Theorem 7 with $f(\varphi, m) = \{m \cup \{x\} \mid x \text{ fictive}\} \cup \{m \cup \{x, y\} \mid x, y \text{ not fictive and } m \cap \{x, y\} = \emptyset\}$.

The following previously tractable fragment becomes intractable.

Proposition 10. *Let* $\mathsf{S}_{00} \subseteq [B]$. *Then* W-MIN-ONES$(B)$ *is* NP*-hard.*

Proof. Via a reduction from MIN-ONES$(B \cup \{\mathrm{C}_0\})$, replacing C_0 by a fresh variable of big weight.

Theorem 11. *Let B be a finite set of Boolean functions.* W-ENUMSAT$_{\uparrow}(B)$

1. *is* NP*-hard if* $\mathsf{S}_{00} \subseteq [B]$ *or* $\mathsf{D}_2 \subseteq [B]$ *or* $\mathsf{S}_{10} \subseteq [B]$,
2. *is in* DelayP *otherwise (i.e.,* $[B] \subseteq \mathsf{V}$ *or* $[B] \subseteq \mathsf{L}$ *or* $[B] \subseteq \mathsf{E}$*).*

5 Enumeration by Order of Non-increasing Weight

In this section we consider model enumeration by order of non-increasing weight.

Problem: ENUMSAT$_{\downarrow}(B)$
Instance: a B-formula φ
Question: generate all models of φ by order of non-increasing weight

Analogously to Proposition 4 we obtain SpaceDelayP-membership for disjunctive, conjunctive, affine, or 0-separating formulæ.

Proposition 12. *Let* $[B] \subseteq \mathsf{V}$ *or* $[B] \subseteq \mathsf{E}$ *or* $[B] \subseteq \mathsf{L}$ *or* $[B] \subseteq \mathsf{S}_0$. *Then* ENUMSAT$_{\downarrow}(B) \in$ SpaceDelayP.

For monotone formulæ in general we apply once more the priority queue method.

Proposition 13. *Let* $[B] \subseteq \mathsf{M}$. *Then* $\textsc{EnumSAT}_{\downarrow}(B) \in \text{DelayP}$.

Proof. Apply Theorem 7 with $f(\varphi, m) = \{m\backslash\{x\} \mid m\backslash\{x\} \models \varphi\}$.

We now address one of the rare cases where the priority queue method is not applicable and still we obtain tractability. We use for this the following classical result from combinatorics.

Theorem 14 (Erdős-Ko-Rado Theorem [8]**).** *Let* $n \geq 2r$ *and* A *be a family of distinct subsets of* $\{1, \ldots, n\}$ *such that each subset is of size* r *and each pair of subsets intersects. Then it holds*

$$|A| \leq \binom{n-1}{r-1}.$$

Lemma 15. *Let* $f \in \mathsf{S}_0^2$ *be an* n*-ary Boolean function and let* k *be an integer such that* $n/2 \leq k \leq n$. *Then the number of models of weight* k *is at least* $\binom{n-1}{k-1}$.

Proposition 16. *Let* $[B] \subseteq \mathsf{S}_0^2$. *Then* $\textsc{EnumSAT}_{\downarrow}(B) \in \text{DelayP}$.

Proof. In a first step we give a description of the enumeration scheme for the weight range n down to $n/2$.

We start with weight n: there is one such assignment which is also a model (all functions in S_0^2 are 1-reproducing). We continue with an inductive argument (for $n/2 \leq k < n$): assume that we know for weight k exactly the set of models S_k. By Lemma 15, we have $\binom{n-1}{k-1} \leq |S_k| \leq \binom{n}{k}$. The total time needed to output these models is something polynomial in $|S_k|$. This delivers enough time to bruteforce all assignments of the next weight level $k-1$: There are $\binom{n}{k-1}$ such assignments to be tested, and the factor between $\binom{n}{k-1}$ and $|S_k|$ is obviously polynomially bounded in n. Summed up, while outputting (with polynomial delay) the models of weight k, we can compute the set of models of weight $k-1$. Repeated application of this allows to enumerate with polynomial delay all models in the weight range n down to $n/2$ by order of non-increasing weight.

The models in the weight range $n/2$ down to 0 can be computed and stored during the first step: When during the first step an assignment a is tested, also test its complement, $\overline{a}$, which lies then in the weight range $n/2$ down to 0. If $\overline{a}$ is a model, put it on a stack. After step 1 has finished, output all the assignments from the stack.

We turn to the intractable cases. Solving $\textsc{EnumSAT}_{\downarrow}$ requires to efficiently solve $\textsc{Max-Ones}^*$, the task of computing a model of maximal weight different from **1**. The hardness of this task will therefore deliver us hardness of $\textsc{EnumSAT}_{\downarrow}$. The hardness of $\textsc{Max-Ones}^*$ is obtained from $\textsc{Sat}^*$ and the following problem.

Problem: Inverse-Root-Weight-Sat
Instance: a 3CNF-formula φ of n variables
Question: does φ admit a model of weight $\geq n - \sqrt{n}$?

Lemma 17. Inverse-Root-Weight-Sat *is* NP*-complete. If the number of variables is assumed to be a power of* 3 *it remains* NP*-complete.*

Proposition 18. *Let* $\mathsf{S}_{12} \subseteq [B]$ *or* $\mathsf{D}_1 \subseteq [B]$. *Then* $\text{Max-Ones}^*(B)$ *is* NP*-hard.*

Proof. In the first case we reduce from $\text{Sat}^*(B)$ via $\varphi \mapsto (\varphi, 1)$ and conclude with Proposition 2. In the second case we have a technically involving reduction from Inverse-Root-Weight-Sat.

Theorem 19. *Let B be a finite set of Boolean functions. Then* $\text{EnumSAT}_\downarrow(B)$

1. *is* NP*-hard if* $\mathsf{S}_{12} \subseteq [B]$ *or* $\mathsf{D}_1 \subseteq [B]$,
2. *is in* DelayP *otherwise (i.e.,* $[B] \subseteq \mathsf{S}_0^2$ *or* $[B] \subseteq \mathsf{M}$ *or* $[B] \subseteq \mathsf{L}$*), where* $\text{EnumSAT}_\downarrow(X) \in$ SpaceDelayP *for* $X \in \{\mathsf{V}, \mathsf{E}, \mathsf{L}, \mathsf{S}_0\}$

Lastly, a look at the weighted variant, where we obtain only partial results.

Proposition 20. *Let* $[B] \subseteq \mathsf{S}_0$ *or* $[B] \subseteq \mathsf{M}$. *Then* $\text{W-EnumSAT}_\downarrow(B) \in$ DelayP.

Proof. Apply Theorem 7 with $f(\varphi, m) = \{m \backslash \{x\} \mid m \backslash \{x\} \models \varphi\}$.

Proposition 21. *Let* $[B] \subseteq \mathsf{L}$. *Then* $\text{W-EnumSAT}_\downarrow(B) \in$ DelayP.

Proof. Analogously to Proposition 9.

The following tractability indicates that also $\text{W-EnumSAT}_\downarrow(\mathsf{S}_0^2)$ might be tractable. However, none of the above algorithmic strategies seems to work out.

Proposition 22. *Let* $[B] \subseteq \mathsf{S}_0^2$. *Then* $\text{W-Max-Ones}^*(B) \in$ P.

6 Conclusion

In this paper we provided complete complexity classifications of the problem of enumerating all satisfying assignments of a propositional B-formula for every set B of allowed connectives, imposing the orders of non-decreasing weight and non-increasing weight. We also considered the weighted variant, where the variables are assigned a non-negative integer weight. We obtained a complete classification for the weighted variant when imposing the order of non-decreasing weight and remained with one open case for the order of non-increasing weight when the connectives are 0-separating of degree 2. Interesting are the polynomial delay algorithms we obtained. They either rely on combinatorial bounds allowing a brute force approach, or on the use of a priority queue which necessarily leads to an exponential space usage. Future research could affront the open case, but should also investigate the question of exponential space: can it be avoided, or is it inherent to these problems, in particular to SubSetSum without polynomial bounds on the weights?

Acknowledgements. The author would like to thank Johan Thapper for combinatorial support.

References

1. Beyersdorff, O., Meier, A., Thomas, M., Vollmer, H.: The complexity of propositional implication. Inf. Process. Lett. **109**(18), 1071–1077 (2009)
2. Böhler, E., Creignou, N., Galota, M., Reith, S., Schnoor, H., Vollmer, H.: Complexity classifications for different equivalence and audit problems for Boolean circuits. Logical Methods Comput. Sci. **8**(3) (2012). https://lmcs.episciences.org/1172
3. Bulatov, A.A., Dyer, M.E., Goldberg, L.A., Jalsenius, M., Jerrum, M., Richerby, D.: The complexity of weighted and unweighted #csp. J. Comput. Syst. Sci. **78**(2), 681–688 (2012)
4. Creignou, N., Hébrard, J.-J.: On generating all solutions of generalized satisfiability problems. ITA **31**(6), 499–511 (1997)
5. Creignou, N., Olive, F., Schmidt, J.: Enumerating all solutions of a Boolean CSP by non-decreasing weight. In: Sakallah, K.A., Simon, L. (eds.) SAT 2011. LNCS, vol. 6695, pp. 120–133. Springer, Heidelberg (2011). doi:10.1007/978-3-642-21581-0_11
6. Creignou, N., Schmidt, J., Thomas, M.: Complexity classifications for propositional abduction in post's framework. J. Log. Comput. **22**(5), 1145–1170 (2012)
7. Durand, A., Hermann, M., Kolaitis, P.G.: Subtractive reductions and complete problems for counting complexity classes. Theor. Comput. Sci. **340**(3), 496–513 (2005)
8. Erdős, P., Ko, C., Rado, R.: Intersection theorem for system of finite sets. Quart. J. Math. Oxford Ser. **12**, 313–318 (1961)
9. Johnson, D.S., Papadimitriou, C.H., Yannakakis, M.: On generating all maximal independent sets. Inf. Process. Lett. **27**(3), 119–123 (1988)
10. Khanna, S., Sudan, M., Williamson, D.P.: A complete classification of the approximability of maximization problems derived from Boolean constraint satisfaction. In: STOC, pp. 11–20 (1997)
11. Kimelfeld, B., Sagiv, Y.: Incrementally computing ordered answers of acyclic conjunctive queries. In: Etzion, O., Kuflik, T., Motro, A. (eds.) NGITS 2006. LNCS, vol. 4032, pp. 141–152. Springer, Heidelberg (2006). doi:10.1007/11780991_13
12. Lewis, H.: Satisfiability problems for propositional calculi. Math. Syst. Theory **13**, 45–53 (1979)
13. Post, E.: The two-valued iterative systems of mathematical logic. Ann. Math. Stud. **5**, 1–122 (1941)
14. Reith, S.: On the complexity of some equivalence problems for propositional calculi. In: Rovan, B., Vojtáš, P. (eds.) MFCS 2003. LNCS, vol. 2747, pp. 632–641. Springer, Heidelberg (2003). doi:10.1007/978-3-540-45138-9_57
15. Schaefer, T.J.: The complexity of satisfiability problems. In: Proceedings 10th Symposium on Theory of Computing, pp. 216–226. ACM Press (1978)
16. Schmidt, J.: Enumeration: Algorithms and complexity. Preprint (2009). http://www.thi.uni-hannover.de/fileadmin/forschung/arbeiten/schmidt-da.pdf
17. Schnoor, H., Schnoor, I.: Enumerating all solutions for constraint satisfaction problems. In: Thomas, W., Weil, P. (eds.) STACS 2007. LNCS, vol. 4393, pp. 694–705. Springer, Heidelberg (2007). doi:10.1007/978-3-540-70918-3_59
18. Schnorr, C.: Optimal algorithms for self-reducible problems. In: ICALP, pp. 322–337 (1976)
19. Strozecki, Y.: Enumeration complexity and matroid decomposition. Ph.D. thesis (2010)
20. Thomas, M.: The complexity of circumscriptive inference in post's lattice. In: Erdem, E., Lin, F., Schaub, T. (eds.) LPNMR 2009. LNCS (LNAI), vol. 5753, pp. 290–302. Springer, Heidelberg (2009). doi:10.1007/978-3-642-04238-6_25

Finite Automata

Minimization of Finite State Automata Through Partition Aggregation

Johanna Björklund[1(✉)] and Loek Cleophas[1,2]

[1] Department of Computing Science, Umeå University, Umeå, Sweden
johanna@cs.umu.se, loek@fastar.org
[2] Department of Information Science, Stellenbosch University, Stellenbosch, South Africa

Abstract. We present a minimization algorithm for finite state automata that finds and merges bisimulation-equivalent states, identified through partition aggregation. We show the algorithm to be correct and run in time $O(n^2d^2|\Sigma|)$, where n is the number of states of the input automaton M, d is the maximal outdegree in the transition graph for any combination of state and input symbol, and $|\Sigma|$ is the size of the input alphabet. The algorithm is slower than those based on partition refinement, but has the advantage that intermediate solutions are also language equivalent to M. As a result, the algorithm can be interrupted or put on hold as needed, and the derived automaton is still useful. Furthermore, the algorithm essentially searches for the maximal model of a characteristic formula for M, so many of the optimisation techniques used to gain efficiency in SAT solvers are likely to apply.

1 Introduction

Finite-state automata form one of the key concepts of theoretical computer science, and their computational and representational complexity is the subject of a great body of work. In the case of *deterministic* finite state automata (DFA), there is for every DFA M a minimal language-equivalent DFA M', and this M' is canonical with respect to the recognized language. In the general, non-deterministic case, no analogous result exists. In fact, NFA minimization is PSPACE complete [14] and the solution is not guaranteed to be unique. Moreover, given an NFA with n states, the minimization problem cannot be efficiently approximated within a factor $o(n)$, unless P = PSPACE [9].

Since NFA minimization is inherently difficult, attention has turned to efficient heuristic language minimization algorithms, that often, if not always, perform well. In this category we find bisimulation minimization. Intuitively, two states are bisimulation equivalent if every transition that can be made from one of them, can be mirrored starting from the other. More formally, an equivalence relation $\mathcal{E}$ on the states Q of a NFA M is a bisimulation relation if the following holds: (i) the relations respects the separation in M of final and non-final states, and (ii) for every $p, q \in Q$ such that $(p, q) \in \mathcal{E}$, if $p' \in Q$ can be reached from p on the symbol a, then there exists a $q' \in Q$ that can be reached from q on a, and $(p', q') \in \mathcal{E}$.

F. Drewes et al. (Eds.): LATA 2017, LNCS 10168, pp. 223–235, 2017.
DOI: 10.1007/978-3-319-53733-7_16

The transitive closure of the union of two bisimulation relations is again a bisimulation relation, so there is a unique coarsest bisimulation relation $\mathcal{E}$ of every NFA M. When each equivalence class of $\mathcal{E}$ is merged into a single state, the result is a smaller but language-equivalent NFA. If M is deterministic, then this approach coincides with regular DFA minimization. The predominant method of finding $\mathcal{E}$ is through partition refinement. The states are initially divided into final and non-final states, and the algorithm resolves contradictions to the bisimulation condition by refining the partition until a fixed point is reached. This method is fast, and requires $O(m \log n)$ computation steps [17], where m is the size of M's transition function. The drawback is that up until termination, merging equivalence classes into states will not preserve the recognized language.

In Sect. 4, we present an NFA minimization algorithm in which also the intermediate solutions are language-equivalent with M. Similarly to previous approaches, the algorithm computes the coarsest bisimulation relation $\mathcal{E}$ on M. However, the initial partition is entirely made up of singleton classes, and these are repeatedly merged until a fixed point is reached. The algorithm runs in time $O(n^2 d^2 |\Sigma|)$, where d is the maximal outdegree in the transition graph for any combination of state and input symbol, and Σ is the input alphabet.

The use of aggregation was inspired by a family of minimization algorithms for DFA (see Sect. 1.1), and we lift the technique non-deterministic devices. In the deterministic case, our algorithm runs in $O(n^2 |\Sigma|)$, which is the same as for the fastest aggregation-based DFA minimisation algorithms.

Another contribution is the computational approach: we derive a characteristic propositional-logic formula w_M for the input automaton M, in which the variables are pairs of states. The algorithm entails finding the maximal model $\hat{v}$ of w_M, in the sense that $\hat{v}$ assigns 'true' to as many variables as possible. We show that if w_M is satisfiable, then $\hat{v}$ is unique and efficiently computable by a greedy algorithm, and $\hat{v}$ encodes the coarsest bisimulation relation on M.

1.1 Related Work

DFA minimization has been studied extensively since the 1950s [10,12,15]. Ten Eikelder observed that the equivalence problem for recursive types can be formulated as a DFA reachability problem, and gave a recursive procedure for deciding equivalence for a pair of DFA states [19]. This procedure was later used by Watson to formulate a DFA minimization algorithm that works through partition aggregation [20]. The algorithm runs in exponential time, and two mutually exclusive optimization methods were discussed in [21]. One uses memoziation to limit the number of recursive invocations; the other bases the implementation on the union-find data structure [2,11,18]. The latter method reduces the complexity from $O(|\Sigma|^{n-2} n^2)$ to $O(\alpha(n^2) n^2)$, where $\alpha(n)$, rougly speaking, is the inverse of Ackermann's function. The value of this function is less than 5 for $n \leq 2^{2^{16}}$, so it can be treated as a constant. The original version of the algorithm has been lifted to deterministic tree automata (a generalisation of finite state automata) both as an imperative sequential algorithm and in terms of communicating sequential processes [7]. In [8, Chapter 7], Daciuk continues the discussion of aggregation-based DFA minimization, starting from the work reported in [21]. He simplifies the presentation and generally improves the algorithm, including the removal of an incorrect combination of memoization and restricted recursion depth. The fact that this combination was problematic had been pointed out by Marco Almeida, and is also reported in [3]; Almeida had found apparently rare DFA cases in which the Watson-Daciuk algorithm returned non-minimal DFAs. In [3], Almeida et al. also present a simpler version, doing away with presumably costly dependency list management. Assuming a constant alphabet size, they state that their algorithm has a worst-case running time of $O\big(\alpha(n^2)n^2\big)$ for all practical cases, yet also claim it to be faster than the Watson-Daciuk one. Based on Almeida's reporting, Daciuk in [8, Section 7.4] provides a new version, presented as a compromise between the corrected Watson-Daciuk and the Almeida-Moreira-Reis algorithm, but does not discuss its efficiency. NFA minimisation has also received much attention, but we restrict ourselves to heuristics that compute weaker relations than the actual Nerode congruence (recalled in Sect. 2). In [17], three partition refinement algorithms were presented, one of which is essentially bisimulation minimization for NFA. The technique was revived in [1], then in the domain of finite-state tree automata. The paper was soon followed by bisimulation-minimization algorithms for weighted and unranked tree automata [4,5], and also algorithms based on more general simulation relations [1,13]. This work is to the best of our knowledge the first in which the bisimulation relation is computed through aggregation.

2 Preliminaries

Sets and Numbers. We write $\mathbb{N}$ for the set of natural numbers including 0. For $n \in \mathbb{N}$, $[n] = \{i \in \mathbb{N} \mid 1 \leq i \leq n\}$. Thus, in particular, $[0] = \emptyset$. The cardinality of a set S is written $|S|$ and the powerset of S by $pow(S)$.

Relations. A binary relation is an equivalence relation if it is reflexive, symmetric and transitive. Let $\mathcal{E}$ and $\mathcal{F}$ be equivalence relations on S. We say that $\mathcal{F}$ is *coarser* than $\mathcal{E}$ (or equivalently: that $\mathcal{E}$ is a *refinement* of $\mathcal{F}$), if $\mathcal{E} \subseteq \mathcal{F}$. The *equivalence class* of an element s in S with respect to $\mathcal{E}$ is the set $[s]_\mathcal{E} = \{s' \mid (s, s') \in \mathcal{E}\}$. Whenever $\mathcal{E}$ is obvious from the context, we simply write $[s]$ instead of $[s]_\mathcal{E}$. It should be clear that $[s]$ and $[s']$ are equal if s and s' are in relation $\mathcal{E}$, and disjoint otherwise, so $\mathcal{E}$ induces a partition $(S/\mathcal{E}) = \{[s] \mid s \in S\}$ of S. We denote the identity relation $\{(s, s) \mid s \in S\}$ on S by $\mathcal{I}_S$.

Strings. An alphabet is a finite nonempty set. The empty string is denoted by ε. For an alphabet Σ, a string is a sequence of symbols from Σ, in other words, an element of Σ^*. A string language is a subset of Σ^*.

Finite Automata. A *non-deterministic finite state automaton* (or NFA, for short) is a tuple $M = (Q, \Sigma, \delta, Q_I, Q_F)$, where Q is a finite set of *states*; Σ is an alphabet of *input symbols*; $\delta = (\delta_f)_{f\in\Sigma}$ is a family of transition functions $\delta_f : Q \to pow(Q)$; $Q_I \subseteq Q$ is a set of *initial states*; and $Q_F \subseteq Q$ is a set of *final states*. The size of M is $|M| = |\delta|$.

We immediately extend δ to $(\hat{\delta}_w)_{w\in\Sigma^*}$ where $\hat{\delta}_w : pow(Q) \to pow(Q)$ as follows: For every $w \in \Sigma^*$ and $P \subseteq Q$,

$$\hat{\delta}_w(P) = \begin{cases} P & \text{if } w = \varepsilon, \text{ and} \\ \bigcup_{p\in P} \hat{\delta}_{w'}(\delta_f(p)) & \text{if } w = fw' \text{ for some } f \in \Sigma, \text{and } w' \in \Sigma^*. \end{cases}$$

The language recognised by M is $\mathcal{L}(M) = \{w \in \Sigma^* \mid \hat{\delta}_w(Q_I) \cap Q_F \neq \emptyset\}$. From here on, we identify δ with $\hat{\delta}$. If $|Q_I| \leq 1$, and if $|\delta_f(\{q\})| \leq 1$ for every $f \in \Sigma$ and $q \in Q$, then M is said to be *deterministic*.

Let $\mathcal{E}$ be an equivalence relation on Q. The *aggregated* NFA with respect to $\mathcal{E}$ is the NFA $(M/\mathcal{E}) = ((Q/\mathcal{E}), \Sigma, \delta', Q'_I, Q'_F)$ given by $\delta'_f([q]) = \{[p] | p \in \delta_f(q)\}$ for every $q \in Q$ and $f \in \Sigma$; $Q'_I = \{[q] \mid q \in Q_I\}$; and $Q'_F = \{[q] | q \in Q_F\}$.

The *right language* of $q \in Q$ is $\overrightarrow{\mathcal{L}}(q) = \{w \in \Sigma^* \mid \delta_w(\{q\}) \cap Q_F \neq \emptyset\}$. The Nerode congruence [16] is the coarsest *congruence relation* $\mathcal{E}$ on Q w.r.t the right-languages $\overrightarrow{\mathcal{L}}(q)$; i.e. $\mathcal{E}(p, q)$ if and only if $\overrightarrow{\mathcal{L}}(p) = \overrightarrow{\mathcal{L}}(q)$ for all $p, q \in Q$.

Propositional Logic. We assume that the reader is familiar with propositional logic, but recall a few basics to fix the terminology. The Boolean values *true* and *false* are written as $\top$ and $\bot$, respectively, and we use $\mathbb{B}$ for $\{\top, \bot\}$. Let L be a propositional logic over the logical variables V, and let $\mathrm{WF}(L)$ be the set of well-formed formulas over L. An *interpretation* of L is a partial function $V \to \mathbb{B}$. Given interpretations v and v', we say that v' is an *extension* of v if $v'(\pi) = v(\pi)$ for all $\pi \in dom(v)$. The set of all such extensions is written $\mathrm{Ext}(v)$.

A *substitution* of formulas for variables is a set $\{x_1 \leftarrow w_1, \ldots, x_n \leftarrow w_n\}$, where each $x_i \in X$ is a distinct variable and each $w_i \in \mathrm{WF}(L)$ is a formula. The *empty* substition is defined by the empty set.

Let $\theta = \{x_1 \leftarrow w_1, \ldots, x_n \leftarrow w_n\}$ and $\sigma = \{y_1 \leftarrow w'_1, \ldots, y_k \leftarrow w'_k\}$ be two substitutions. Let X and Y be the sets of variables substituted for in θ and σ, respectively. The *composition* $\theta\sigma$ of θ and σ is the substitution $\{x_i \leftarrow w_i\sigma \mid x_i \in X\} \cup \{y_j \leftarrow w_j \mid y_j \in Y \setminus X\}$. The *application* of θ to a formula w is denoted $w\theta$ and defined by (simultaneously) replacing every occurrence of each x_i in w by the corresponding w_i. Finally, given a set of formulas $W \subseteq \mathrm{WF}(L)$, we let $W\theta = \{w\theta \mid w \in W\}$.

Every interpretation v of L can be seen as a substitution, in which $\pi \in dom(v)$ is replaced by $v(\pi)$. This allows us to extend v to a function $\mathrm{WF}(L) \to \mathbb{B}$ where $v(w) = \top$ if wv is a tautology, $v(w) = \bot$ if wv is a contradiction, and $v(w)$ is undefined otherwise. The formula w is *resolved* by v if $v(w) \in \{\top, \bot\}$, and v is a *model* for w if $v(w) = \top$. The set of models of w is denoted by $\mathrm{Mod}(w)$.

3 Logical Framework

In this section, we express the problem of finding the coarsest simulation relation on a finite automaton, as a problem of computing the maximal model of a propositional-logic formula. Due to space restrictions, the argumentation is kept at an intuitive level[1].

From here on, let $M = (Q, \Sigma, \delta, Q_I, Q_F)$ be a fixed but arbitrary NFA.

Definition 1 (Bisimulation, cf. [6] [Definition 3.1]). *Let $\mathcal{E}$ be a relation on Q. It is a* bisimulation relation *on M if for every $(p, q) \in \mathcal{E}$, (1) $p \in Q_F$ if and only if $q \in Q_F$; and (2) for every symbol $f \in \Sigma$,*

$$\begin{array}{rl} \textit{for every } p' \in \delta_f(p) \textit{ there is a } q' \in \delta_f(q) & \textit{such that } (p', q') \in \mathcal{E} \\ \textit{and for every } q' \in \delta_f(q) \textit{ there is a } p' \in \delta_f(p) & \textit{such that } (p', q') \in \mathcal{E}. \end{array}$$

Condition 2 of Definition 1 can be expressed in a propositional logic, in which the variables are pairs of automata states. The variable corresponding to the pair $\langle p, q \rangle$ is true if and only if p and q satisfy Condition 2.

Definition 2 (Characteristic formula). *Let $V_M = \{\langle p, q \rangle \mid p, q \in Q\}$ be a set of propositional variables. For $\pi = \langle p, q \rangle \in V_M$ and $f \in \Sigma$, we denote by w_π^f the negation-free CNF formula*

$$\bigwedge_{p' \in \delta_f(p)} \bigvee_{q' \in \delta_f(q)} \langle p', q' \rangle \quad \wedge \quad \bigwedge_{q' \in \delta_f(q)} \bigvee_{p' \in \delta_f(p)} \langle p', q' \rangle$$

and by w_π the formula $\bigwedge_{f \in \Sigma} w_\pi^a$. Observe that w_π is negation-free. Finally, we denote by w_M the conjunction $\bigwedge_{\pi \in V_M} \pi \to w_\pi$.

We could also model Condition 1 in the formula w_M, but that would introduce negations and require a more complex algorithm than that which we are to present. To find the coarsest bisimulation relation for M, we instead start out from a partial interpretation of V_M satisfying Condition 1 of Definition 1 and search for a 'maximal' extension that also satisfies Condition 2. By 'maximal' we mean that it assigns as many variables as possible the value $\top$.

Definition 3 (Maximal model). *Let v and v' be interpretations of V_M. Then $v \vee v'$ denotes the interpretation of V_M given by $(v \vee v')(\pi) = v(\pi) \vee v'(\pi)$, for every $\pi \in V_M$. We say that $v \in Mod(w)$ is* maximal *if $v \vee v' = v$ for every $v' \in Ext(v) \cap Mod(w)$.*

Due to the structure of w_M, its models are closed under variable-wise 'or'. In other words, if $v, v' \in \text{Mod}(w_M)$, then $v \vee v' \in \text{Mod}(w_M)$. From this we conclude that when a solution exists, it is unique.

Lemma 1. *Let v be a partial interpretation of V_M. If $Ext(v) \cap Mod(w_M) \neq \emptyset$, then there is a $\hat{v} \in Ext(v)$ that is a maximal model for w_M, and $\hat{v}$ is unique.*

[1] Detailed proofs are provided in the technical report available for download at https://www8.cs.umu.se/research/uminf/index.cgi?year=2016&number=18.

To translate our logical models back into the domain of bisimulation relations, we introduce the notion of their *associated relations.*

Definition 4 (Associated relation). *We associate with every (partial) interpretation v of V_M a relation $\sim_v$ on V_M, given by $p \sim_v q \iff v(\langle p, q\rangle) = \top$. We say that the interpretation v is reflexive, symmetric, and transitive, respectively, whenever $\sim_v$ is.*

Note that Definition 4 makes no difference between a state pair π for which $v(\pi) = \bot$, and a state pair for which v is undefined.

If v is an arbitrary model for w_M, then its associated relation need not be an equivalence relation, but for the maximal model, it is.

Lemma 2. *Let v be a partial interpretation of V_M such that $\sim_v$ is an equivalence relation, and let $\hat{v}$ be an extension of v that is a maximal model of V_M, then also $\sim_{\hat{v}}$ is an equivalence relation.*

We introduce a partial interpretation v_0 to reflect Condition 1 of Definition 1 and use this as the starting point for our search.

Definition 5. *Let v_0 be the partial interpretation of V_M such that*

$$v_0(\langle p, p\rangle) = \top \text{ for every } p \in Q$$
$$v_0(\langle p, q\rangle) = \bot \text{ for every } p, q \in Q \text{ with } p \in Q_F \not\equiv q \in Q_F$$

and v_0 undefined on all other state pairs.

Lemma 3. *$v_0 \in Mod(w_M)$ and $\sim_{v_0}$ is an equivalence relation.*

Theorem 1. *There is a unique maximal extension $\hat{v}$ of v_0 in $Mod(w_M)$, and the relation $\sim_{\hat{v}}$ is the coarsest bisimulation relation on M.*

4 Algorithm

Aggregation-based algorithms for automata minimization start with a singleton partition, in which each state is viewed as a separate equivalence class, and iteratively merge partitions found to be equivalent. When all states are mutually distinguishable, the algorithm terminates. We use the same approach for the more general problem of minimizing NFAs with respect to bisimulation equivalence. The procedure is outlined in Algorithm 1 and the auxiliary Algorithm 2.

The input to Algorithm 1 is an NFA $M = (Q, \Sigma, \delta, Q_I, Q_F)$. The algorithm computes an interpretation $\hat{v}$ of the set of variables $V_M = \{(p, q) \mid p, q \in Q\}$, where $\hat{v}(\pi) = \top$ means that π is a pair of equivalent states, and $\hat{v}(\pi) = \bot$ that π is a pair of distinguishable states. The interpretation $\hat{v}$ is an extension of v_0 as in Definition 5, and a maximal model for the characteristic formula w_M. Due to the structure of w_M such a model can, as we shall see, be computed greedily.

The construction of $\hat{v}$ is done by incrementally building up a substitution σ_i that replaces state pairs by logical formulas. This is done in such a way that

Algorithm 1. Aggregation-based bisimulation minimization algorithm

1: **function** $minimize(M)$
2: $\sigma_0 ::= \{\langle q, q\rangle \leftarrow \top \mid q \in Q\} \cup \{\langle p, q\rangle \leftarrow \bot \mid (p \in Q_F) \not\equiv (q \in Q_F)\}$
3: **for** $\pi \in V_M \setminus dom(\sigma_i)$ **do**
4: $equiv(\pi, \{\pi\})$
5: **end for**
6: **return** $(M/\sim_{\sigma_i})$
7: **end function**

Algorithm 2. Point-wise computation of $\pi \in V_M$

function $equiv(\pi, S)$
while $\exists \pi' \in var(w_\pi) \setminus dom(\sigma_i) \setminus S$ and $w_\pi\sigma_i$ is not resolved **do**
$equiv(\pi', S \cup \{\pi'\})$
end while
if $w_\pi\sigma_i$ is resolved **then**
$\sigma_{i+1} ::= \sigma_i\{\pi \leftarrow w_\pi\sigma_i\}$
else
$\sigma_{i+1} ::= \sigma_i\{\pi \leftarrow w_\pi\sigma_i\{\pi \leftarrow \top\}\}$
end if
end function

(i) the substitution is eventually a total function, and (ii) no right-hand side of the substitution contains a variable that is also in the domain of the substitution. In combination, this means that when the algorithm terminates, the logical value of every variable is resolved to $\top$ or $\bot$. The substitution thus comes to represent a total interpretation of V_M. In the computations, σ_i is a global variable. It is initialised such that it substitutes $\top$ for each pair of identical states, and $\bot$ for each pair of states that differ in their finality (see Line 2 of Algorithm 1). Following this initialisation, the function *equiv* (see Algorithm 2) is called for each pair of states not yet resolved by the substitution.

Function *equiv* has two parameters: the pair of states π for which equivalence or distinguishability should be determined, and a set S of such pairs. This set consists of pairs of states that are under investigation in earlier, though not yet completed invocations of the function. In other words, S contains pairs that are higher up in the call hierarchy. The function recursively invokes itself with those pairs of states that occur as a variable in formula w_π, but which have note yet been resolved, nor form part of the call stack S. After these calls have been completed and we have exited the while loop, $w_\pi\sigma_i$ may or may not have been resolved. If it has, then we extend the substitution with the appropriate substitution rule, that is, one which replaces occurrences of π by the value of $w_\pi\sigma_i$. If $w_\pi\sigma_i$ has *not* been resolved, then we first rewrite $w_\pi\sigma_i$ by replacing every occurrence of π by $\top$ and then extend the substitution with a rule substituting π by $w_\pi\sigma_i\{\pi \leftarrow \top\}$. These operations clear cyclic dependencies, and the maximal model for the updated formula is the maximal model for the original one.

4.1 Correctness

It can be shown that throughout the computation, $var(w_\pi\sigma_i) \cap dom(\sigma_i) = \emptyset$, for every $\pi \in V_M$; i.e. during every point of the computation, the set of variables that occur in the domain of σ_i is disjoint from the set of variables that occur in $w_\pi\sigma_i$, $\pi \in V_M$. This avoids circular dependencies, and helps us prove that eventually, every variable will be resolved. Intuitively, it holds because every time we update σ_i by adding a particular π to its domain, the assignment on Line 8 clears π from w_π in such a way that $\text{Mod}(w_M\sigma_i)$ is kept unchanged. Furthermore, it is always the case that $\hat{v}(v_0(w_M)) = \hat{v}(w_M\sigma_i)$.

We now make the following observation: Let σ_t be σ_i at the point of termination. Let $\overline{\sigma_t}$ be the interpretation of V_M given by $\overline{\sigma_t}(\pi) \equiv w_\pi\sigma_t$. Since $var(w_\pi\sigma_t) = \emptyset$, for every $\pi \in V_M$, the interpretation $\overline{\sigma_t}$ is total.

Theorem 2. *Algorithm 1 terminates, and when it does, the relation $\sim_{\overline{\sigma_t}}$ is the unique coarsest bisimulation equivalence on M.*

4.2 Complexity

Let us now discuss the efficient implementation of Algorithm 1. The key idea is to keep the representation of the characteristic formula and the computed substitutions small by linking shared structures, rather than copying them. We use the parameter r to capture the amount of nondeterminism in M. It is defined as $r = max_{q \in Q, f \in \Sigma} |\delta_f(q)|$. In particular, $r \leq 1$ whenever M is deterministic.

Let us denote the *union* of all w_π, $\pi \in V_M$, i.e. that appear as right-hand sides in w_M, by rhs_M. In the update of σ_i on Line 8, some of these formulas may be copied into others, so the growth of $rhs_M\sigma_i$ is potentially exponential. For the sake of compactness we therefor represent $rhs_M\sigma_i$ as a directed acyclic graph (DAG) and allow node sharing between formulas. In the initial DAG, only nodes representing variables and the logical constants $\top$ and $\bot$ are shared, but as the algorithm proceeds, greater parts of the graph come to overlap. The construction is straight-forward but has many steps, so readers that are satisfied with a high-level view may want to continue to Theorem 3.

Definition 6 (DAG representation of formulas). *Let L be the proposition logic $(V_M, \{\vee, \wedge, \top, \bot\})$ and let $w \in WF(L)$. The (rooted, labelled)* DAG representation *$D(w)$ of w is recursively defined. For every $x \in V_M \cup \{\top, \bot\}$,*

$$D(x) = (\{v\}, \emptyset, \{(v, x)\}) \text{ with } root(D(x)) = v.$$

The DAG $D(x)$ thus consists of a single node v labelled x, and v is the root of $D(x)$. For $\otimes \in \{\vee, \wedge\}$ and $w, w' \in WF(L)$, we derive $D(w \otimes w')$ from $D(w) = (V, E, l)$ and $D(w') = (V', E', l')$ by letting

$$\begin{aligned} D(w \otimes w') = (&V \cup V' \cup \{v\}, \\ &E \cup E' \cup \{(v, root(D(w))),\ (v, root(D(w')))\}, \\ &l \cup l' \cup \{(v, \otimes)\}), \end{aligned}$$

where $root(D(w \otimes w')) = v$, and then merging leaf nodes with identical labels.

Given the above definition, we obtain the many-rooted DAG representation $D(rhs_M)$ of rhs_M by taking the disjoint union of $D(w_\pi)$, $w_\pi \in rhs_M$, and merging all leaf nodes that have identical labels. Thus, for each state pair π and for each of $\top$ and $\bot$, there is a single leaf node in $D(rhs_M)$.

Throughout the computation, we maintain a DAG representing $D(rhs_M\sigma_i)$. This is initialised to $D(rhs_M\emptyset)$ and then immediately updated to $D(rhs_M\sigma_0)$. On top of this DAG, we assume that for each pair π, we have a reference $ref_{rhs}(\pi)$ to w_π, i.e. to the corresponding right hand side representation in the DAG. Part of the initial DAG is depicted in Fig. 1.

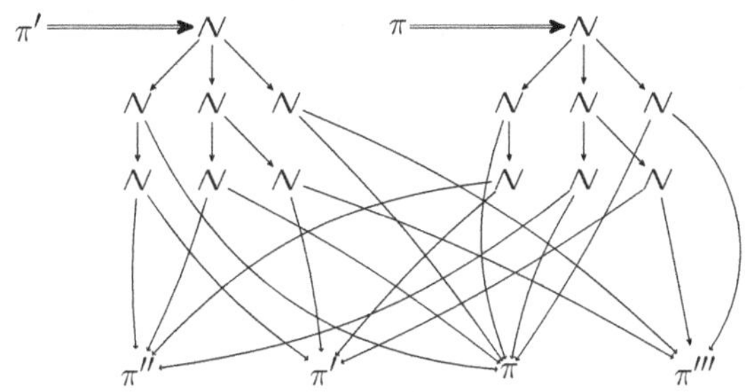

Fig. 1. A tiny example DAG $D(rhs_M\sigma_i)$ with state-pair variables π' and π. References ref_{rhs} are depicted by double-lined arrows. $\wedge\!\!\vee$ denotes a node labeled by either $\wedge$ or $\vee$.

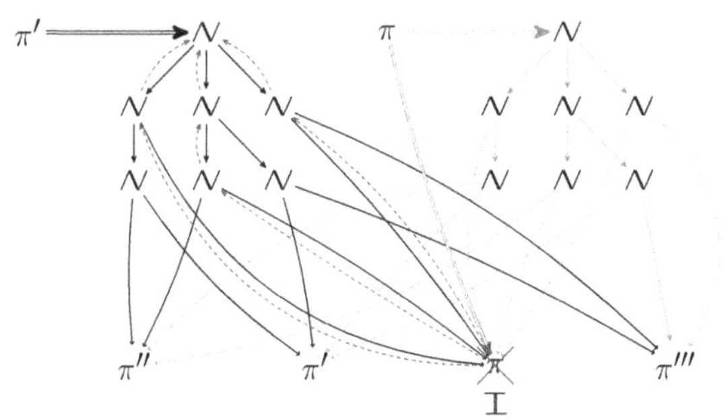

Fig. 2. The update of the DAG $D(rhs_M\sigma_i)$ in the case where π gets resolved to either $\top$ or $\bot$. The symbol $\wedge\!\!\vee$ denotes a node labeled by either $\wedge$ or $\vee$, and the symbol $\top\!\!\!\bot$ one labelled by $\top$ or $\bot$. The update to w_π for the aforementioned case is depicted in cyan (new edges, node relabelling, and propagation) and gray (removed edges and nodes).

During the computation, the graph $D(rhs_M\sigma_i)$ is reorganised by changing the targets of certain edges, but $D(rhs_M\sigma_i)$ does not grow. The exceptions are a potential once-off addition of $\top$ and $\bot$ labelled nodes during initialisation in

Algorithm 1, and the addition of a single outgoing edge to each of the initial leave nodes. Moreover, every time a variable is resolved, $D(rhs_M\sigma_i)$ is updated to reflect this; while the $ref_{rhs}(\pi)$'s will continue to point at $w_\pi\sigma_i$, expression $w_\pi\sigma_i$ changes to reflect the latest σ_i, and will be simplified as much as possible.

There are two kinds of updates to a variable that can occur in our algorithm. The first is the resolution of $w_\pi\sigma$ to either $\top$ or $\bot$, which happens during initialisation of σ on Line 2 of Algorithm 1, on Line 6 of Algorithm 2, and possibly on Line 8 of that algorithm as well. In this case, as sketched in Fig. 2, three things must happen to the graph $D(rhs_M\sigma_i)$ to ensure that it reflects the updated $w_\pi\sigma_{i+1}$: Firstly, formula $w_\pi\sigma_i$ in $D(rhs_M\sigma_i)$ must be replaced by $\top$ or $\bot$ as the case may be. Thus, the graph $D(rhs_M\sigma_i)$ is modified to remove the nodes and edges of such $w_\pi\sigma_i$. Secondly, the unique shared leaf node representing π in the DAG must be re-labeled to $\top$ or $\bot$. Thirdly, this re-labeling must be propagated upwards along each DAG branch leading to this node, now labeled $\top$ respectively $\bot$, as this resolution of π may lead subtrees rooted further up this branch to resolve to either $\bot$ or $\top$ as well. In the case of $\bot$, if the immediate parent is labeled by $\wedge$, then it can be resolved to (i.e. replaced by a reference to) $\bot$. If the parent is instead labelled $\vee$, then we can simplify the graph by deleting the edge and if it was the last edge, also resolving the parent to $\bot$. In the case of $\top$ and parent $\vee$, the parent can be resolved to $\top$. In the case of $\top$ with parent $\wedge$, a simplification is possible by deleting the edge between them, and if it was the last edge, resolving the parent to $\top$. This processes continues upwards through the DAG until no more simplifications and resolutions are possible.

The second kind of update, sketched in Fig. 3, is that corresponding to Line 8 of Algorithm 2 extending σ_i by a substitution for π by $w_\pi\sigma_i\{\pi \leftarrow \top\}$ in case the latter does *not* correspond to $\bot$ or $\top$. Again, a number of things must

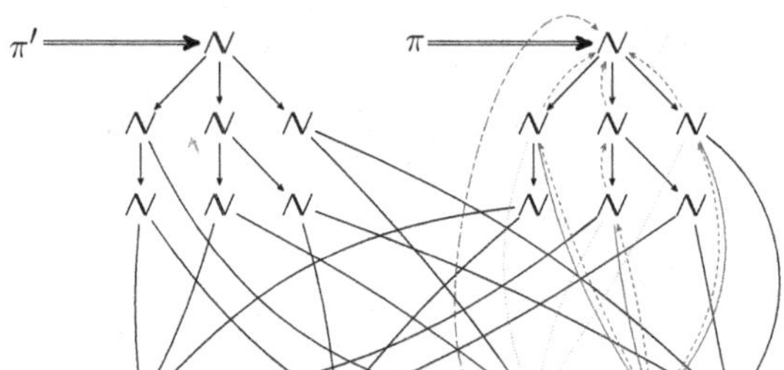

Fig. 3. The update of the DAG $D(rhs_M\sigma_i)$ in the case where π gets resolved to either $\top$ or $\bot$. The symbol $\wedge\!\!\!\vee$ denotes a node labeled by either $\wedge$ or $\vee$, and the symbol $\top\!\!\!\bot$ one labelled by $\top$ or $\bot$. Cyan indicates new edges in w_π, as well as the following upward propagation to simplify $w_\pi\sigma_{i+1}$. The leftmost oddly dashed arrow depicts the replacement of leaf node π's label by a reference to the simplified $w_\pi\sigma_{i+1}$. Removed edges in $w_\pi\sigma_{i+1}$ are depicted dotted in gray. Note that if upward propagation reaches the root of the DAG part representing $w_\pi\sigma_{i+1}$, then the propagation continues upwards through the DAG part for $w'_\pi\sigma_{i+1}$. This is similar to the case shown in Fig. 2.

happen to $D(rhs_M \sigma_i)$. Firstly, references in $w_\pi \sigma_i$ to the unique shared leaf node for π itself must be replaced by references to $\top$. Secondly, this change must be propagated upwards along each DAG branch leading to this reference to $\top$, as this local resolution of π may either simplify (in case of $\wedge$) or resolve (in case of $\vee$) subtrees rooted further up in $rhs_M \sigma_i$. The resulting modified right hand side $w_\pi \sigma_{i+1}$ may either resolve to $\top$, or still be a proper tree. In the first case, the unique shared leaf node representing π in the DAG is re-labeled to $\top$. This change is then propagated upwards, as described in the previous paragraph. In the second case, the node π may still be used in right-hand sides other than $w_\pi \sigma_{i+1}$, and is there replaced by a reference to the modified $w_\pi \sigma_{i+1}$.

In combination, these graph manipulations permit an efficient implementation of Algorithm 1.

Theorem 3 (Complexity). *Algorithm 1 is in* $O(n^2 r^2 |\Sigma|)$.

Recall that bisimulation minimization coincides with classical minimization in the case of DFA. Since $r \leq 1$ for such devices, the run time of our algorithm is comparable to that of the algorithm in [21].

4.3 Lazy Evaluation

We argued from the outset that one advantage of the aggregation approach is that also intermediate solutions are language-equivalent with the original automaton. Let us now show that every time that the call hierarchy returns to the level of Algorithm 1 (i.e., the function *minimize*), the status of all pairs on which *equiv* has been called is known.

We use $var(\sigma_i)$ as shorthand for $\cup_{\pi \in dom(\sigma_i)} var(\sigma_i(\pi))$.

Lemma 4. *Throughout the computation, the following invariants hold: Firstly,* $var(\sigma_i) \subseteq S$*. Secondly, from the point the function* equiv *has reached Line 5 on the pair* π*, we have* $var(w_\pi \sigma_i) \subseteq S$ *for every subsequent* σ_i.

Theorem 4. *Every time the process control returns to* minimize*, every pair* π *on which equiv has been called is resolved.*

5 Conclusion

We have presented a minimization algorithm for NFA that identifies and merges bisimulation-equivalent states. In terms of running time, it is as efficient as any existing aggregation-based minimisation algorithm for DFA, but less efficient than current refinement-based minimisation algorithms for NFA. However, compared to the latter group, it has the advantage that intermediate solutions are usable for language-preserving reduction of the input automaton M. Thus, implementations can be interrupted in time-constrained settings, to save memory by transforming the input to a reduced, not necessarily minimal, equivalent automaton.

The algorithm is the first to compute the coarsest bisimulation relation on M through partition aggregation. Also the logical framework used for representation and computation appears to be new for this application. For this reason, the investigation of optimization techniques similar to those used in SAT solvers is an interesting future endeavour. Furthermore the generalization of the algorithm to, e.g., nondeterministic graph automata could be considered.

Certain highly connected automata might lead the algorithm to only converge in the final iteration. As future work, an empirical investigation of its behaviour on various automata would also be interesting.

References

1. Abdulla, P.A., Holík, L., Kaati, L., Vojnar, T.: A uniform (bi-)simulation-based framework for reducing tree automata. Electron. Notes Theor. Comput. Sci. **251**, 27–48 (2009)
2. Aho, A.V., Hopcroft, J.E., Ullman, J.D.: The design and analysis of computer algorithms. Addison-Wesley, Reading (1974)
3. Almeida, M., Moreira, N., Reis, R.: Incremental DFA minimisation. RAIRO - Theor. Inform. Appl. **48**(2), 173–186 (2014)
4. Björklund, J., Maletti, A., May, J.: Backward and forward bisimulation minimization of tree automata. Theor. Comput. Sci. **410**(37), 3539–3552 (2009)
5. Björklund, J., Maletti, A., Vogler, H.: Bisimulation minimisation of weighted automata on unranked trees. Fundamenta Informatica **92**(1–2), 103–130 (2009)
6. Buchholz, P.: Bisimulation relations for weighted automata. Theor. Comput. Sci. **393**(13), 109–123 (2008)
7. Cleophas, L., Kourie, D.G., Strauss, T., Watson, B.W.: On minimizing deterministic tree automata. In: Holub, J., Žďárek, J. (eds.) Prague Stringology Conference, Prague, Czech Republic, pp. 173–182 (2009)
8. Daciuk, J.: Optimization of Automata. Gdańsk University of Technology Publishing House, Gdańsk (2014)
9. Gramlich, G., Schnitger, G.: Minimizing NFA's and regular expressions. J. Comput. Syst. Sci. **73**(6), 908–923 (2007)
10. Hopcroft, J.E.: An $n \log n$ algorithm for minimizing the states in a finite automaton. In: Kohavi, Z. (ed.) The Theory of Machines and Computations, pp. 189–196. Academic Press (1971)
11. Hopcroft, J.E., Ullman, J.D.: Set merging algorithms. SIAM J. Comput. **2**(4), 294–303 (1973)
12. Huffman, D.A.: The synthesis of sequential switching circuits. J. Franklin Inst. **257**, 161–190, 275–303 (1954)
13. Maletti, A.: Minimizing weighted tree grammars using simulation. In: Yli-Jyrä, A., Kornai, A., Sakarovitch, J., Watson, B. (eds.) FSMNLP 2009. LNCS (LNAI), vol. 6062, pp. 56–68. Springer, Heidelberg (2010). doi:10.1007/978-3-642-14684-8_7
14. Meyer, A.R., Stockmeyer, L.J.: The equivalence problem for regular expressions with squaring requires exponential space. In: 13th Annual IEEE Symposium on Switching and Automata Theory, pp. 125–129 (1972)
15. Moore, E.F.: Gedanken-experiments on sequential machines. Automata Stud. **34**, 129–153 (1956). Princeton University Press, Princeton, New Jersey
16. Nerode, A.: Linear automaton transformations. Proc. Am. Math. Soc. **9**(4), 541–544 (1958)
17. Paige, R., Tarjan, R.: Three partition refinement algorithms. SIAM J. Comput. **16**(6), 973–989 (1987)

18. Tarjan, R.E.: Efficiency of a good but not linear set union algorithm. J. ACM **22**(2), 215–225 (1975)
19. ten Eikelder, H.: Some algorithms to decide the equivalence of recursive types. Technical report 93/32, Department of Mathematics and Computer Science, Technische Universiteit Eindhoven (1991)
20. Watson, B.W.: Taxonomies and toolkits of regular language algorithms. Ph.D. thesis, Department of Mathematics and Computer Science, TU Eindhoven (1995)
21. Watson, B.W., Daciuk, J.: An efficient incremental DFA minimization algorithm. Nat. Lang. Eng. **9**(1), 49–64 (2003)

Derivatives and Finite Automata of Expressions in Star Normal Form

Haiming Chen[1(✉)] and Ping Lu[2]

[1] State Key Laboratory of Computer Science,
Institute of Software Chinese Academy of Sciences, Beijing 100190, China
chm@ios.ac.cn

[2] BDBC, Beihang University, Beijing 100191, China
luping@buaa.edu.cn

Abstract. This paper studies derivatives and automata for expressions in star normal form as defined by Brüggemann-Klein. For an expression in star normal form, the paper shows that the derivatives are either $\emptyset$ or unique, while in general Berry and Sethi's result shows the derivatives are either $\emptyset$ or similar. It is known that the partial derivative automaton and the follow automaton are two small automata, each of which is a quotient of the position automaton. For the relation between the partial derivative and follow automata, however, Ilie and Yu stated that a rigorous analysis is necessary but difficult. The paper tackles the issue, and presents several results. Our work shows that there are different conditions under which the relation of the two automata can be different.

Keywords: Regular expressions · Finite automata · Derivatives · Partial derivatives · Star normal form

1 Introduction

Finite automata are basic for efficient implementation and application of regular expressions. Derivatives are a fundamental concept for regular expressions and a useful tool to study automata construction from regular expressions. This paper studies derivatives and automata of regular expressions in star normal form, defined by Brüggemann-Klein [3]. It is known that every regular expression can be transformed into star normal form in linear time [3], and several algorithms depend on star normal form (e. g., [3,8]).

Derivatives of regular expressions were introduced by Brzozowski [5]. The notion was generalized to partial derivatives by Antimirov [1]. There has been no result about derivatives particular for expressions in star normal form. Among the many constructions of ϵ-free non-deterministic finite automata (NFA) from regular expressions, we consider *position automata* proposed separately by Glushkov [10] and McNaughton and Yamada [12], *partial derivative* or *equation*

Work supported by the National Natural Science Foundation of China under Grant No. 61472405.

F. Drewes et al. (Eds.): LATA 2017, LNCS 10168, pp. 236–248, 2017.
DOI: 10.1007/978-3-319-53733-7_17

automata using partial derivatives [1], and *follow automata* proposed by Ilie and Yu [11]. The position automaton has size at most quadratic and can be computed in quadratic time [3,9,14]. Berry and Sethi [2] showed a natural connection between the position automaton and the derivatives. The partial derivative automaton has also been proved to be equivalent to the automaton constructed from the prebase [13]. Champarnaud and Ziadi [7] proposed a quadratic algorithm for computing the partial derivative automata which improved very much the original algorithm [1], and proved that the partial derivative automaton is a quotient of the position automaton. Ilie and Yu [11] proposed a simplified proof of the result. Lombardy and Sakarovitch [15] gave another proof in the more general setting of expressions with multiplicity which applies to present Boolean case. Recently Ilie and Yu [11] introduced the follow automaton which can be computed in quadratic time, and proved that the follow automaton is a quotient of the position automaton. Champarnaud, Nicart and Ziadi presented another quadratic algorithm [8] for computing the follow automaton.

The paper first shows that, for an expression in star normal form, the derivatives of the marked expression (see Sect. 2 for the explanation of marked expression) with respect to word of the form wa for any word w and a fixed symbol a are either $\emptyset$ or unique, while Berry and Sethi's result [2] establishes that in general the above derivatives are either $\emptyset$ or similar. This uniqueness of derivatives is of course an attractive property.

The paper then discusses the relation between the partial derivative and follow automata. It has been known that both the partial derivative and follow automata are quotients of the position automaton. The question is what is the relation between the first two automata. In [11] Ilie and Yu compared some examples and stated that "a more rigorous comparison" between the automata "should be done" but "seems difficult". Champarnaud et al. [6] gave a condition ("normalized" regular expressions) under which the partial derivative automaton is a quotient of the follow automaton[1]. The paper gives several conditions for the following relations between the two automata: (1) the partial derivative automaton is a quotient of the follow automaton, (2) the converse, and (3) the two automata are isomorphic. Our work thus shows, for the first time, there are different conditions under which the relation of the two automata is different.

In concrete, it first presents several simple characterizations, in terms of derivatives, of the above relations between the two automata. Then based on the structure of expressions, we find conditions that are connected to the relations, and give several properties of the conditions. We show that for an expression in star normal form satisfying *CONC* condition (see Sect. 4), the partial derivative automaton is a quotient of the follow automaton. Compared with the work in [6], the *CONC* condition is more general (meaning that it allows more expressions than normalized regular expressions), and captures more adequately the nature of expressions for which the resulting partial derivative and follow automata

[1] This quotient result, however, is not given in [6]. In [6] the main theorem (Theorem 4, p.11) states for a "normalized" regular expression, the size of the partial derivative automaton is smaller than the size of the follow automaton.

retain the above quotient relation. For example, none of the expressions given in Example 37 are normalized regular expressions, while they all satisfy *CONC* condition, and for each of the expressions the partial derivative automaton is a quotient of the follow automaton. See Sect. 4 for a discussion. We further present conditions for some special situations, in which the two automata are isomorphic or the follow automaton is a quotient of the partial derivative automaton. Since regular expressions can be transformed to star normal form in linear time, we can easily get the smaller automaton when one of the above conditions is satisfied.

Section 2 introduces basic notations and notions. Derivatives for expressions in star normal form are considered in Sect. 3. Section 4 focuses on the relation of partial derivative and follow automata. Section 5 gives concluding remarks.

2 Preliminaries

We assume the reader to be familiar with basic regular language and automata theory, e.g., from [16]. We introduce here only some notations and notions used later in the paper.

Let Σ be an alphabet of symbols. The empty word is denoted by ε. The set of all finite words over Σ is denoted by Σ^*. A regular expression over Σ is $\emptyset, \varepsilon$ or $a \in \Sigma$, or is the union E_1+E_2, the concatenation E_1E_2, or the star E_1^* for regular expressions E_1 and E_2. For a regular expression E, the language specified by E is denoted by $L(E)$. Define $\lambda(E) = \varepsilon$ if $\varepsilon \in L(E)$ and $\emptyset$ otherwise. The size of E is denoted by $|E|$ and is the length of E when written in postfix (parentheses are not counted). The number of symbol occurrences in E, or the alphabetic width of E, is denoted by $\|E\|$. The symbols that occur in E, which is the smallest alphabet of E, is denoted by Σ_E. We assume that rules $E+\emptyset = \emptyset+E = E, E\emptyset = \emptyset E = \emptyset$, and $E\varepsilon = \varepsilon E = E$ (rules-$\emptyset\varepsilon$) hold in the paper.

For a regular expression we can mark symbols with subscripts so that in the marked expression each marked symbol occurs only once. For example $(a_1 + b_2)^* a_3 b_4 (a_5 + b_6)$ is a marking of the expression $(a+b)^* ab(a+b)$. The marking of an expression E is denoted by $\overline{E}$. The same notation will also be used for dropping of subscripts from the marked symbols: $\overline{\overline{E}} = E$. We extend the notation for words and automata in the obvious way. It will be clear from the context whether $\bar{\cdot}$ adds or drops subscripts.

For an expression E over Σ, we define the following sets: $first(E) = \{a \mid aw \in L(E), a \in \Sigma, w \in \Sigma^*\}, last(E) = \{a \mid wa \in L(E), w \in \Sigma^*, a \in \Sigma\}, follow(E, a) = \{b \mid uabv \in L(E), u, v \in \Sigma^*, b \in \Sigma\}$ for $a \in \Sigma$.

Define $followlast(E) = \{b \mid vbw \in L(E), v \in L(E), v \neq \varepsilon, b \in \Sigma, w \in \Sigma^*\}$. An expression E is in *star normal form* (SNF) [4] if, for each starred subexpression H^* of E, $followlast(\overline{H}) \cap first(\overline{H}) = \emptyset$ and $\varepsilon \notin L(H)$. It is known that regular expressions can be transformed to SNF in linear time [3].

A finite automaton is a quintuple $M = (Q, \Sigma, \delta, q_0, F)$, where Q is a finite set of states, Σ is the alphabet, $\delta \subseteq Q \times \Sigma \times Q$ is the transition mapping, q_0 is the start state, and $F \subseteq Q$ is the set of accepting states. Denote the language accepted by the automaton M by $L(M)$.

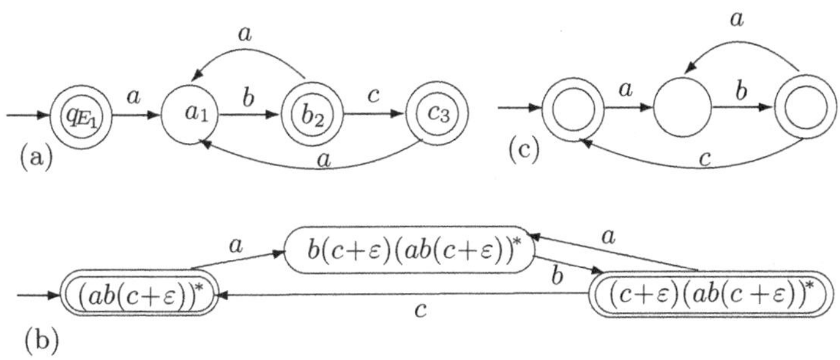

Fig. 1. (a) $M_{\text{pos}}(E_1)$, (b) $M_{\text{pd}}(E_1)$, and (c) $M_{\text{f}}(E_1)$, corresponding to $E_1 = (ab(c+\varepsilon))^*$.

Let $\equiv \subseteq Q \times Q$ be an equivalence relation. We say that $\equiv$ is right invariant w.r.t. M iff (1) $\equiv \subseteq (Q-F)^2 \cup F^2$ and (2) for any $p, q \in Q, a \in \Sigma$, if $p \equiv q$, then $p_1 \equiv q_1$ for $p_1 \in \delta(p,a), q_1 \in \delta(q,a)$. If $\equiv$ is right invariant, then we can define a quotient automaton $M/_{\equiv}$ in the usual way.

The position automaton was introduced independently by Glushkov [10] and McNaughton and Yamada [12]. The *position automaton* of E is $M_{\text{pos}}(E) = (Q_{\text{pos}}, \Sigma, \delta_{\text{pos}}, q_E, F_{\text{pos}})$, where $Q_{\text{pos}} = \Sigma_{\overline{E}} \cup \{q_E\}$, $\delta_{\text{pos}}(q_E, a) = \{x \mid x \in first(\overline{E}), \overline{x} = a\}$ for $a \in \Sigma$, $\delta_{\text{pos}}(x, a) = \{y \mid y \in follow(\overline{E}, x), \overline{y} = a\}$ for $x \in \Sigma_{\overline{E}}$ and $a \in \Sigma$, $F_{\text{pos}} = last(\overline{E}) \cup \{q_E\}$ if $\lambda(E) = \varepsilon$, or $last(\overline{E})$ otherwise.

For further purpose we set $last_0(\overline{E})$ equal to $last(\overline{E})$ if $\varepsilon \notin L(E)$ and $last(\overline{E}) \cup \{q_E\}$ otherwise, and extend $follow(\overline{E}, q_E) = first(\overline{E})$.

Example 1. The position automaton $M_{\text{pos}}(E_1)$ for the regular expression $E_1 = (ab(c+\varepsilon))^*$ is shown in Fig. 1(a).

As shown by Glushkov [10] and McNaughton and Yamada [12], $L(M_{\text{pos}}(E)) = L(E)$. $M_{\text{pos}}(E)$ can be computed in quadratic time [3,9,14].

Below we introduce deravatives.

Definition 2 (Brzozowski [5]). *Given a regular expression E and a symbol a, the derivative $a^{-1}(E)$ of E w.r.t. a is defined inductively as follows:*

$$a^{-1}(\emptyset) = a^{-1}(\varepsilon) = \emptyset$$
$$a^{-1}(b) = \varepsilon \text{ if } b = a, \ \emptyset \text{ otherwise}$$
$$a^{-1}(F+G) = a^{-1}(F) + a^{-1}(G)$$
$$a^{-1}(FG) = a^{-1}(F)G + a^{-1}(G) \text{ if } \lambda(F) = \varepsilon, \ a^{-1}(F)G \text{ otherwise}$$
$$a^{-1}(F^*) = a^{-1}(F)F^*$$

Derivative w.r.t. a word is computed by $\varepsilon^{-1}(E) = E$, $(wa)^{-1}(E) = a^{-1}(w^{-1}(E))$.

Definition 3 (Antimirov [1]). *Given a regular expression E and a symbol a, the set of partial derivatives $\partial_a(E)$ of E w.r.t. a is defined as follows:*[2]

$$\begin{aligned}
&\partial_a(\emptyset) = \partial_a(\varepsilon) = \emptyset\\
&\partial_a(b) = \{\varepsilon\} \text{ if } b = a,\ \emptyset \text{ otherwise}\\
&\partial_a(F+G) = \partial_a(F) \cup \partial_a(G)\\
&\partial_a(FG) = \partial_a(F)G \cup \partial_a(G) \text{ if } \lambda(F) = \varepsilon,\ \partial_a(F)G \text{ otherwise}\\
&\partial_a(F^*) = \partial_a(F)F^*
\end{aligned}$$

Partial derivative w.r.t. a word is computed by $\partial_\varepsilon(E) = \{E\}$, $\partial_{wa}(E) = \bigcup_{p\in\partial_w(E)} \partial_a(p)$. The language denoted by $\partial_w(E)$ is $L(\partial_w(E)) = \bigcup_{p\in\partial_w(E)} L(p)$.

It is proved in [1] that the cardinality of the set $PD(E) = \cup_{w\in\Sigma^*}\partial_w(E)$ of all partial derivatives of a regular expression E is less than or equal to $\|E\|+1$.

The *partial derivative* or *equation automaton* [1] constructed by partial derivatives is $M_{\text{pd}}(E) = (PD(E), \Sigma, \delta_{\text{pd}}, E, \{q \in PD(E) \mid \varepsilon \in L(q)\})$, where $\delta_{\text{pd}}(q, a) = \partial_a(q)$, for any $q \in PD(E), a \in \Sigma$. An example is shown in Fig. 1(b).

It is proved that for a regular expression, the partial derivative automaton is a quotient of the position automaton [7,11]. Another proof is given by Lombardy and Sakarovitch [15], which is in the more general setting of expressions with multiplicity but still applies to present case (multiplicities over the Boolean semiring).

Expressions with distinct symbols are called linear. For any expression E, $\overline{E}$ is the linearized version of E. For linear expressions from Brzozowski [5] and Berry and Sethi [2] the following fact is easily derived.

Proposition 4. *Let E be linear. Given $a \in \Sigma_E$, for all words w,*

1. If $E = E_1 + E_2$, then

$$(wa)^{-1}(E_1+E_2) = \begin{cases} (wa)^{-1}(E_1) \text{ if } a \in \Sigma_{E_1}\\ (wa)^{-1}(E_2) \text{ if } a \in \Sigma_{E_2}\end{cases} \quad (1)$$

2. If $E = E_1E_2$, then

$$(wa)^{-1}(E_1E_2) = \begin{cases} (wa)^{-1}(E_1)E_2 & \text{if } a \in \Sigma_{E_1}\\ (va)^{-1}(E_2) & \text{if } w = uv, \lambda(u^{-1}(E_1)) = \varepsilon, a \in \Sigma_{E_2},\\ & u \in \Sigma_{E_1}^*, v \in \Sigma_{E_2}^*\\ \emptyset & \text{otherwise}\end{cases} \quad (2)$$

3 Derivatives of Expressions in SNF

Two regular expressions E_1 and E_2 which reduce to the same expression using associativity, commutativity, and idempotence of + are called *ACI-similar* [5],

[2] $RF = \{EF | E \in R\}$ for a set R of regular expressions and a regular expression F.

which is denoted by $E_1 \sim_{aci} E_2$. Berry and Sethi [2] have shown that, for a marked expression $\overline{E}$, given a fixed $x \in \Sigma_{\overline{E}}$, $(wx)^{-1}(\overline{E})$ is either $\emptyset$ or unique modulo $\sim_{aci}$ for all words w. In [2], based on this a natural connection between the position automaton and derivatives is set up.

Here, we further show that, if E is in SNF then the ACI-similarity in the above is unnecessary.

Proposition 5. *For a marked expression $\overline{E}$, if E is in SNF then given a fixed $x \in \Sigma_{\overline{E}}$, $(wx)^{-1}(\overline{E})$ is either $\emptyset$ or unique for all words w.*

Proof. We prove it by induction on the structure of $\overline{E}$. The cases for $\overline{E} = \varepsilon, \emptyset, x$, $x \in \Sigma_{\overline{E}}$, are obvious.

1. $\overline{E} = \overline{E_1} + \overline{E_2}$. By Eq. (1), if x is in $\overline{E_1}$, then $(wx)^{-1}(\overline{E_1})$, and the inductive hypothesis applies to it. The case for x in $\overline{E_2}$ follows in the same way.
2. $\overline{E} = \overline{E_1}\,\overline{E_2}$. If x is in $\overline{E_1}$, then by Eq. (2) $(wx)^{-1}(\overline{E}) = (wx)^{-1}(\overline{E_1})\overline{E_2}$, and the inductive hypothesis applies to it. Otherwise, x is in $\overline{E_2}$ and $(wx)^{-1}(\overline{E}) = (vx)^{-1}(E_2)$ for some $w = uv$ or $(wx)^{-1}(\overline{E}) = \emptyset$. Therefore the inductive hypothesis applies to it.
3. $\overline{E} = \overline{E_1}^*$. From [5] and [2] $(wx)^{-1}(\overline{E})$ is a sum of subterms of the form $(vx)^{-1}(\overline{E_1})\overline{E_1}^*$ where $wx = uvx$. We show that there is at most one non-null subterm.

Suppose there are non-null subterms $(v_1x)^{-1}(\overline{E_1})\overline{E_1}^*$ and $(v_2x)^{-1}(\overline{E_1})\overline{E_1}^*$. If $v_1 \neq v_2$, suppose $|v_1| < |v_2|$. Let $wx = a_1a_2\ldots a_t$. We can suppose $v_1x = a_{r_1}\ldots a_t, v_2x = a_{r_2}\ldots a_{r_1}\ldots a_t, 1 \leq r_2 < r_1 \leq t$. Since $(v_1x)^{-1}(\overline{E_1}) \neq \emptyset$, we have $a_{r_1} \in first(\overline{E_1})$. Since $(v_2x)^{-1}\overline{E_1}) \neq \emptyset$, there exists a word w_1, such that $a_{r_2}\ldots a_{r_1}\ldots a_tw_1 \in L(\overline{E_1})$. Then $a_{r_1} \in follow(\overline{E_1}, a_{r_1-1})$.

A careful analysis on the derivation of $(wx)^{-1}(\overline{E})$ shows that if $(v_1x)^{-1}(\overline{E_1}) \neq \emptyset$, then either $\varepsilon \in L((a_{r_1-1})^{-1}(\overline{E_1}))$ or $\varepsilon \in L((a_n\ldots a_{r_1-1})^{-1}(\overline{E_1}))$ for some $n < a_{r_1-1}$. In either case, we have $a_{r_1-1} \in last(\overline{E_1})$. Note the symbols and positions are in one-one correspondence for $\overline{E}$. Therefore E is not in SNF, which is a contradiction.

If $v_1 = v_2$, then $v_1x = v_2x = a_{r_1}\ldots a_t, 2 < r_1 \leq t$. Similarly, a careful analysis on $(wx)^{-1}(\overline{E})$ shows that there must be $\varepsilon \in L((a_{n_1}\ldots a_i)^{-1}(\overline{E_1})), \varepsilon \in L((a_{n_2}\ldots a_i)^{-1}(\overline{E_1}))$ and $\varepsilon \in L((a_{n_3}\ldots a_{n_1-1})^{-1}(\overline{E_1})), n_2 < n_1 \leq i \leq r_1 - 1, n_3 < n_1$. So we have $a_{n_1} \in first(\overline{E_1}), a_{n_1} \in follow(\overline{E_1}, a_{n_1-1}), a_{n_1-1} \in last(\overline{E_1})$. Therefore E is not in SNF, which is a contradiction.

So there is at most one non-null subterm, and the inductive hypothesis applies to it. □

This uniqueness of derivatives is of course an attractive property. There have been several work relying on finding a unique representative for the set of non-null $(wx)^{-1}(\overline{E})$ [7,11]. If E is in SNF, then $(wx)^{-1}(\overline{E})$ is already unique.

Corollary 6. *If E is in SNF and there are non-null $(w_1)^{-1}(\overline{E})$ and $(w_2)^{-1}(\overline{E})$, such that $(w_1)^{-1}(\overline{E}) \sim_{aci} (w_2)^{-1}(\overline{E})$, then $(w_1)^{-1}(\overline{E}) = (w_2)^{-1}(\overline{E})$.*

From the proof of Proposition 5 above, it follows

Corollary 7. *If* $E = E_1^*$ *is in SNF, then for a non-null* $(wx)^{-1}(\overline{E})$, $(wx)^{-1}(\overline{E}) = (vx)^{-1}(\overline{E_1})\overline{E}$ *for some* $wx = uvx$.

4 Partial Derivative and Follow Automata

The *follow automaton* $M_f(E)$ was introduced by Ilie and Yu [11]. It is constructed by eliminating ε-transitions from an ε-automaton defined in [11]. We do not present the construction in detail here. An example is shown in Fig. 1(c). What is important here is the following.

Define the equivalence $\equiv_f \subseteq Q_{\text{pos}}^2$ by $x_1 \equiv_f x_2$ iff $x_1 \in last_0(\overline{E}) \Leftrightarrow x_2 \in last_0(\overline{E})$ and $follow(\overline{E}, x_1) = follow(\overline{E}, x_2)$. The equivalence relation is right invariant w.r.t. $M_{\text{pos}}(E)$. Define $M_1 \simeq M_2$ if M_1 and M_2 are isomorphic. It is known that

Proposition 8 [11]. $M_f(E) \simeq M_{\text{pos}}(E)/_{\equiv_f}$.

As we have mentioned, it is well-known that the partial derivative automaton is a quotient of the position automaton [7,11,15]. Here it is presented following [11]. For a letter $x \in \Sigma_{\overline{E}}$, denote $C_x(\overline{E})$ any expression $(wx)^{-1}(\overline{E}) \neq \emptyset$. Denote also $C_{q_E}(\overline{E}) = \overline{E}$ (q_E is the start state of the position automaton of E). For an SNF expression E, $C_x(\overline{E})$ is already unique. For general expressions assume that we find a proper representative for each $C_x(\overline{E})$ [7,11]. Define the equivalence $=_c \subseteq Q_{\text{pos}}^2$ by $x_1 =_c x_2$ iff $C_{x_1}(\overline{E}) = C_{x_2}(\overline{E})$. Define the equivalence $\equiv_c \subseteq Q_{\text{pos}}^2$ by $x_1 \equiv_c x_2$ iff $\overline{C_{x_1}(\overline{E})} = \overline{C_{x_2}(\overline{E})}$. Each of the equivalence relations is right invariant w.r.t. $M_{\text{pos}}(E)$. It is known that

Proposition 9. *(1)* $M_{\text{pd}}(E) \simeq M_{\text{pos}}(E)/_{\equiv_c}$; *(2)* $\overline{M_{\text{pd}}(\overline{E})} \simeq M_{\text{pos}}(E)/_{=_c}$.

From Propositions 8 and 9 both $M_{\text{pd}}(E)$ and $M_f(E)$ are always smaller than or equal to $M_{\text{pos}}(E)$. However, for the relation between $M_{\text{pd}}(E)$ and $M_f(E)$, Ilie and Yu [11] compared some examples and showed that it is difficult to give a theoretical analysis. Here we try to do so.

First we give characterizations of the different relations between the two automata. It is easy to see the following:

Lemma 10. *For any* $a \in \Sigma_{\overline{E}}$, *(1)* $first(C_a(\overline{E})) = follow(\overline{E}, a)$ [2], *and (2)* $a \in last_0(\overline{E}) \Leftrightarrow \lambda(C_a(\overline{E})) = \varepsilon$.

From Lemma 10 and the above definitions of the equivalence relations, the following are implied

Lemma 11. *(1)* $=_c \subseteq \equiv_f$; *(2)* $=_c \subseteq \equiv_c$.

Then we give a characterization of $=_c = \equiv_f$ as follows.

Proposition 12. *For an expression* E, *we have* $=_c = \equiv_f$ *iff* $\forall a, b \in Q_{\text{pos}}$, $first(C_a(\overline{E})) = first(C_b(\overline{E})) \wedge \lambda(C_a(\overline{E})) = \lambda(C_b(\overline{E})) \Rightarrow C_a(\overline{E}) = C_b(\overline{E})$.

Similarly the following are other characterizations.

Proposition 13. *For an expression* E*, we have* $=_c\ =\ \equiv_c$ *iff* $\forall a, b \in Q_{\mathrm{pos}}$, $\overline{C_a(\overline{E})} = \overline{C_b(\overline{E})} \Rightarrow C_a(\overline{E}) = C_b(\overline{E})$.

Proposition 14. *For an expression* E*, we have* $\equiv_c\ =\ \equiv_f$ *iff* $\forall a, b \in Q_{\mathrm{pos}}$, $\overline{C_a(\overline{E})} = \overline{C_b(\overline{E})} \Leftrightarrow first(C_a(\overline{E})) = first(C_b(\overline{E})) \wedge \lambda(C_a(\overline{E})) = \lambda(C_b(\overline{E}))$.

On the other hand, from Propositions 8, 9 and Lemma 11 it follows

Theorem 15. *For an expression* E*,*

(1) if $=_c = \equiv_f$*, then* $M_{\mathrm{pd}}(E)$ *is a quotient of* $M_{\mathrm{f}}(E)$*,* $\overline{M_{\mathrm{pd}}(\overline{E})} \simeq M_{\mathrm{f}}(E)$*; and*
(2) if $=_c = \equiv_c$*, then* $M_{\mathrm{f}}(E)$ *is a quotient of* $M_{\mathrm{pd}}(E)$*,* $\overline{M_{\mathrm{pd}}(\overline{E})} \simeq M_{\mathrm{pd}}(E)$*; and*
(3) if $\equiv_c = \equiv_f$*, then* $M_{\mathrm{pd}}(E) \simeq M_{\mathrm{f}}(E)$*.*

Example 16. Let $E_1 = aa^* + ba^*, E_2 = (a^* + \varepsilon)a^*a^*, E_3 = a^*$, one can verify that $M_{\mathrm{pd}}(E_1)$ is a quotient of $M_{\mathrm{f}}(E_1)$, $M_{\mathrm{f}}(E_2)$ is a quotient of $M_{\mathrm{pd}}(E_2)$, and $M_{\mathrm{pd}}(E_3) \simeq M_{\mathrm{f}}(E_3)$.

The above characterizations are given in terms of $C_x(\overline{E})$. Below we consider conditions in terms of the structure of expressions. We first prove the following Lemmas. Recall that we assume that the rules (rules-$\emptyset\varepsilon$) hold. It is known that the following property holds:

$$first(\overline{F+G}) = first(\overline{F}) \cup first(\overline{G}), first(\overline{F^*}) = first(\overline{F}),$$
$$first(\overline{FG}) = first(\overline{F}) \cup first(\overline{G}) \text{ if } \varepsilon \in L(F), first(\overline{F}) \text{ otherwise.}$$
$$last(\overline{F+G}) = last(\overline{F}) \cup last(\overline{G}), last(\overline{F^*}) = last(\overline{F}),$$
$$last(\overline{FG}) = last(\overline{F}) \cup last(\overline{G}) \text{ if } \varepsilon \in L(G), last(\overline{G}) \text{ otherwise.}$$
$$follow(\overline{F+G}, a) = \begin{cases} follow(\overline{F}, a), \text{ if } a \in \Sigma_{\overline{F}} \\ follow(\overline{G}, a), \text{ if } a \in \Sigma_{\overline{G}} \end{cases}$$
$$follow(\overline{FG}, a) = \begin{cases} follow(\overline{F}, a), & \text{if } a \in \Sigma_{\overline{F}} - last(\overline{F}) \\ follow(\overline{F}, a) \cup first(\overline{G}), & \text{if } a \in last(\overline{F}) \\ follow(\overline{G}, a), & \text{if } a \in \Sigma_{\overline{G}} \end{cases}$$
$$follow(\overline{F^*}, a) = \begin{cases} follow(\overline{F}, a), & \text{if } a \in \Sigma_{\overline{F}} - last(\overline{F}) \\ follow(\overline{F}, a) \cup first(\overline{F}), & \text{if } a \in last(\overline{F}) \end{cases}$$

Lemma 17. *For* $b \in \Sigma_{\overline{E}}$*, if* $follow(\overline{E}, b) = \emptyset$ *then* $b \in last(\overline{E})$*.*

Lemma 18. *For* $b \in \Sigma_{\overline{E}}$*,* $follow(\overline{E}, b) = \emptyset$ *iff* $\forall w \in \Sigma_{\overline{E}}^*$*,* $(wb)^{-1}(\overline{E}) = \emptyset$ *or* $(wb)^{-1}(\overline{E}) = \varepsilon$*.*

Lemma 19. *For* $\overline{E} = \overline{F} + \overline{G}$*,* $a \in \Sigma_{\overline{F}}$ *and* $b \in \Sigma_{\overline{G}}$*,* $a \equiv_f b \Leftrightarrow a =_c b$*.*

Definition 20. *For an expression E, the leftmost expression of E w.r.t. concatenation is $le(E) = le(F)$ if $E = FG$; E otherwise. We say an expression E is leftmost ε-reduced if $le(E)$ does not contain any subexpression $F+\varepsilon$ or $\varepsilon+F$ where $\lambda(F) = \varepsilon$. Obviously if $E = FG$ then E is leftmost ε-reduced iff F is leftmost ε-reduced.*

The expressions $a+\varepsilon$, $(a^*+\varepsilon)^*$, $a+(a^*+\varepsilon)b$, $b^*(a^*+\varepsilon)$, $(a+\varepsilon)+b^*$ are leftmost ε-reduced, while $a^*+\varepsilon$, $(a+\varepsilon)+\varepsilon$, $(a^*+\varepsilon)b^*$, $(\varepsilon+a^*)b$, $(a+b^*)+\varepsilon$ are not leftmost ε-reduced.

Definition 21. *For an expression E, and $b \in \Sigma_{\overline{E}}$, we denote $\psi_1(E,b)$ the following condition: $b \in last(\overline{E}) \Leftrightarrow \varepsilon \in L(\overline{E})$; and denote $\psi_2(E,b)$ the following condition: $first(\overline{E}) = follow(\overline{E}, b)$.*

Lemma 22. *The following are equivalent statements.*

(1) $q_E \equiv_f b$;
(2) $\psi_1(E,b)$ and $\psi_2(E,b)$;
(3) $\forall w \in \Sigma^*_{\overline{E}}$, if $(wb)^{-1}(\overline{E}) \neq \emptyset$ then $L((wb)^{-1}(\overline{E})) = L(\overline{E})$.

Definition 23. *For an expression E, we call the following the emptiness condition of E: If $le(\overline{E}) = \overline{F}^*, b \in last(\overline{F})$, and $first(\overline{F}^*) = follow(\overline{F}^*, b)$, then $followlast(\overline{F}) \cap first(\overline{F}) = \emptyset$.*

Lemma 24. *For an expression E and $b \in \Sigma_{\overline{E}}$, if $\psi_1(E,b)$, $\psi_2(E,b)$, E is leftmost ε-reduced, and satisfies the emptiness condition, then $\forall w \in \Sigma^*_{\overline{E}}$, if $(wb)^{-1}(\overline{E}) \neq \emptyset$ then $(wb)^{-1}(\overline{E}) = \overline{E}$.*

From the proof of the above lemma, it follows

Corollary 25. *For an expression E and $b \in \Sigma_{\overline{E}}$, if $\psi_1(E,b)$, $\psi_2(E,b)$, E is leftmost ε-reduced, and satisfies the emptiness condition, then E can be only of the form F^* or $T_n^* G_n \dots G_0, n \geq 0$, where $b \in \Sigma_{\overline{T}_n}$, and T_n^* satisfies the same conditions as for E.*

It is easy to see that $q_E =_c b$ equals the statement: $\forall w \in \Sigma^*_{\overline{E}}$, if $(wb)^{-1}(\overline{E}) \neq \emptyset$ then $(wb)^{-1}(\overline{E}) = \overline{E}$. Then from Lemmas 11 and 22 we have the following:

Lemma 26. *Given $b \in \Sigma_{\overline{E}}$, if $\forall w \in \Sigma^*_{\overline{E}}$, and whenever $(wb)^{-1}(\overline{E}) \neq \emptyset$ we have $(wb)^{-1}(\overline{E}) = \overline{E}$, then $\psi_1(\overline{E}, b)$ and $\psi_2(\overline{E}, b)$.*

Definition 27. *For any starred subexpression F^* of an expression E, we call the following the equivalence condition of E: If $a, b \in last(\overline{F})$ and $follow(\overline{F}^*, a) = follow(\overline{F}^*, b)$, then $follow(\overline{F}, a) = follow(\overline{F}, b)$.*

For an SNF expression, we have

Lemma 28. *Suppose F^* is in SNF. If $a, b \in last(\overline{F})$ and $follow(\overline{F}^*, a) = follow(\overline{F}^*, b)$, then $follow(\overline{F}, a) = follow(\overline{F}, b)$.*

Definition 29. *For an expression E, we call the following the CONC (Concatenation) condition of E: If $\psi_1(E,b)$ and $\psi_2(E,b)$ for some $b \in \Sigma_{\overline{E}}$ then E is leftmost ε-reduced and satisfies the emptiness condition; For any subexpression $\overline{FG}$ of $\overline{E}$, if $follow(\overline{F},a) = \emptyset$, $\psi_1(G,b)$ and $\psi_2(G,b)$ for some $a \in \Sigma_{\overline{F}}$ and $b \in \Sigma_{\overline{G}}$ then G is leftmost ε-reduced and satisfies the emptiness condition.*

The significance of the *CONC* condition can be seen from the following two lemmas.

Lemma 30. *For $\overline{E} = \overline{FG}$, $a \in \Sigma_{\overline{F}}$ and $b \in \Sigma_{\overline{G}}$, $a \equiv_f b$ iff $follow(\overline{F},a) = \emptyset$, $\psi_1(G,b)$ and $\psi_2(G,b)$.*

Lemma 31. *For $\overline{E} = \overline{FG}$, $a \in \Sigma_{\overline{F}}$ and $b \in \Sigma_{\overline{G}}$, if $follow(\overline{F},a) = \emptyset$, $\psi_1(G,b)$, $\psi_2(G,b)$, G is leftmost ε-reduced and satisfies the emptiness condition, then $a =_c b$.*

From Lemmas 11 and 30 it follows

Corollary 32. *For $\overline{E} = \overline{FG}$, $a \in \Sigma_{\overline{F}}$ and $b \in \Sigma_{\overline{G}}$, if $a =_c b$ then $follow(\overline{F},a) = \emptyset$, $\psi_1(G,b)$ and $\psi_2(G,b)$.*

The following is a sufficient condition for $=_c = \equiv_f$.

Theorem 33. *For an expression E satisfying CONC and equivalence conditions, we have $=_c = \equiv_f$.*

Note the restriction that final and non-final states cannot be $\equiv_f$-equivalent is essential, as shown by the expression $E = b^*a(b^*a)^*$. Let $\overline{E} = b_1^*a_2(b_3^*a_4)^*$. Then $C_{a_2}(\overline{E}) = C_{a_4}(\overline{E}) \neq C_{b_3}(\overline{E})$, $follow(\overline{E},a_2) = follow(\overline{E},b_3) = follow(\overline{E},a_4)$. However, $a_2, a_4 \in last(\overline{E})$ and $b_3 \notin last(\overline{E})$.

According to Lemma 28, we have

Corollary 34. *For an SNF expression E satisfying CONC condition, we have $=_c = \equiv_f$.*

Corollary 35. *For an expression E satisfying CONC and equivalence conditions, $\overline{M_{\text{pd}}(\overline{E})} \simeq M_{\text{f}}(E)$, and $M_{\text{pd}}(E)$ is a quotient of $M_{\text{f}}(E)$.*

Corollary 36. *For an SNF regular expression E satisfying CONC condition, $\overline{M_{\text{pd}}(\overline{E})} \simeq M_{\text{f}}(E)$, and $M_{\text{pd}}(E)$ is a quotient of $M_{\text{f}}(E)$.*

Example 37. Let $E_1 = a^*(a^* + \varepsilon)c^*, E_2 = a(a^* + \varepsilon + b), E_3 = (a^* + \varepsilon)b^*c^* + d$, they all are in SNF and satisfy *CONC* condition. One can verify that for each E_i, $=_c=\equiv_f$, and $M_{\text{pd}}(E_i)$ is a quotient of $M_{\text{f}}(E_i), i = 1, 2, 3$.

Also, the expressions E_1 in Example 1, E_1 and E_3 in Example 16 are in SNF and satisfy *CONC* condition, and their partial derivative automata are quotients of the follow automata.

Remark. Champarnaud et al. [6] has proposed a condition called "normalized" regular expressions, which requires that in an SNF expression no subexpression

$F + \varepsilon$ with $\lambda(F) = \varepsilon$ should exist. For a "normalized" regular expression the partial derivative automaton is a quotient of the follow automaton. A "normalized" expression is of course leftmost ε-reduced, and trivially satisfies *CONC* condition. Conversely, if an SNF expression satisfies *CONC* condition, it may not necessarily be a "normalized" expression. For example, none of expressions given in Example 37 are "normalized", while they all satisfy *CONC* condition, and for each of the expressions the partial derivative automaton is a quotient of the follow automaton. As the above example hints, for many expressions that are not "normalized", the quotient relation between the partial derivative automaton and the follow automaton still exists. Actually "normalized" expressions simply forbid the occurrence of any subexpression $F + \varepsilon$ where $\lambda(F) = \varepsilon$, but *CONC* condition only forbid the occurrence of the above subexpression in some sensitive positions in an expression. Therefore "normalized" expressions impose too strong restrictions on expressions to ensure the quotient. On the other hand, *CONC* condition captures more adequately the nature of expressions for which the partial derivative automaton is a quotient of the follow automaton.

We further present the following conditions for some special situations, concerning also $=_c$ and $\equiv_c$.

Condition 1. Let $E = F_1F_2 \dots F_n, F_r$ is of the form: a, a^*, $a^* + \varepsilon$ or $\varepsilon + a^*, a \in \Sigma, r = 1, \dots, n, n \geq 1$.

(a) F_1 is of the form a or a^*, and
(b) if $F_r = a$, then F_{r+1} is of the form b or b^*.

Theorem 38. *For a regular expression E satisfying Condition 1, we have $=_c = \equiv_f$, $=_c = \equiv_c$, and $\equiv_c = \equiv_f$.*

Condition 2. Let $E = F_1F_2 \dots F_n, n \geq 1$ the same as in Condition 1. The following is satisfied at least once:

(a) F_1 is of the form $a^* + \varepsilon$ or $\varepsilon + a^*$, or
(b) if $F_r = a$, then F_{r+1} is of the form $b^* + \varepsilon$ or $\varepsilon + b^*$.

Note Condition 2 is the negated one of Condition 1 w.r.t E.

Theorem 39. *For a regular expression E satisfying Condition 2, we have $=_c \neq \equiv_f$ and $=_c = \equiv_c$.*

Corollary 40. *For a regular expression E satisfying Condition 1, $M_{\mathrm{pd}}(E) \simeq M_{\mathrm{f}}(E) \simeq \overline{M_{\mathrm{pd}}(\overline{E})}$. For a regular expression E satisfying Condition 2, $M_{\mathrm{pd}}(E) \not\simeq M_{\mathrm{f}}(E), \overline{M_{\mathrm{pd}}(\overline{E})} \simeq M_{\mathrm{pd}}(E)$ and $M_{\mathrm{f}}(E)$ is a quotient of $M_{\mathrm{pd}}(E)$.*

For example, the expressions E_3 in Example 16 and E_1 in Example 37 satisfy Condition 1, and their partial derivative and follow automata are isomorphic. The expression E_2 in Example 16 satisfies Condition 2, and its follow automaton is a quotient of the partial derivative automaton.

If an expression E is linear, there is a one-one correspondence between the symbols in E and $\overline{E}$. Then for $C_a(\overline{E}) \neq C_b(\overline{E})$ it cannot be $\overline{C_a(\overline{E})} = \overline{C_b(\overline{E})}$. So

Theorem 41. *For a linear expression E, we have* $=_c = \equiv_c$.

Corollary 42. *For a linear expression E,* $\overline{M_{\mathrm{pd}}(\overline{E})} \simeq M_{\mathrm{pd}}(E)$*, and* $M_{\mathrm{f}}(E)$ *is a quotient of* $M_{\mathrm{pd}}(E)$.

For example, the expression E_1 in Example 1 is linear, so $=_c = \equiv_c$. We also know that for E_1 we have $=_c = \equiv_f$. Therefore $\equiv_c = \equiv_f$, that is, $M_{\mathrm{pd}}(E_1) \simeq M_{\mathrm{f}}(E_1)$. Similarly, for the expression E_3 in Example 37, we have $M_{\mathrm{pd}}(E_3) \simeq M_{\mathrm{f}}(E_3)$ since it is linear and from Example 37 for E_3 we have $=_c = \equiv_f$.

So far we have presented some conditions for the relations among $=_c, \equiv_c$ and $\equiv_f$, hence the relations between $M_{\mathrm{pd}}(E)$ and $M_{\mathrm{f}}(E)$. Since regular expressions can be transformed to SNF in linear time [3], we can easily get the smaller automaton when one of the above conditions is satisfied. Further, it would be interesting to find some more conditions, which remains as a further research.

5 Concluding Remarks

The paper discussed derivatives and automata for expressions in SNF. It showed that if an expression E is in SNF, then $(wx)^{-1}(\overline{E})$ is either $\emptyset$ or unique for all words w, which is a stronger property than Berry and Sethi's [2]. For a regular expression in SNF it presented several conditions for the quotient or isomorphism relation between the partial derivative and follow automata.

Several problems can be investigated as future work. For conditions based on the structure of expressions, although *CONC* condition allows more expressions, presently it is unclear whether it captures all expressions for which $M_{\mathrm{pd}}(E)$ is a quotient of $M_{\mathrm{f}}(E)$. As mentioned above, whether there are some more conditions for the relation between $M_{\mathrm{pd}}(E)$ and $M_{\mathrm{f}}(E)$ remains as a further research.

References

1. Antimirov, V.: Partial derivatives of regular expressions and finite automaton constructions. Theoret. Comput. Sci. **155**, 291–319 (1996)
2. Berry, G., Sethi, R.: From regular expressions to deterministic automata. Theoret. Comput. Sci. **48**, 117–126 (1986)
3. Brüggemann-Klein, A.: Regular expressions into finite automata. Theoret. Comput. Sci. **120**, 197–213 (1993)
4. Brüggemann-Klein, A., Wood, D.: One-unambiguous regular languages. Inf. Comput. **142**(2), 182–206 (1998)
5. Brzozowski, J.A.: Derivatives of regular expressions. J. ACM (JACM) **11**(4), 481–494 (1964)
6. Champarnaud, J.-M., Ouardi, F., Ziadi, D.: Normalized expressions and finite automata. Int. J. Algebra Comput. **17**(01), 141–154 (2007)
7. Champarnaud, J.-M., Ziadi, D.: Canonical derivatives, partial derivatives and finite automaton constructions. Theoret. Comput. Sci. **289**(1), 137–163 (2002)
8. Champarnaud, J.-M., Nicart, F., Ziadi, D.: Computing the follow automaton of an expression. In: Domaratzki, M., Okhotin, A., Salomaa, K., Yu, S. (eds.) CIAA 2004. LNCS, vol. 3317, pp. 90–101. Springer, Heidelberg (2005). doi:10.1007/978-3-540-30500-2_9

9. Chia-Hsiang, C., Paige, R.: From regular expressions to DFA's using compressed NFA's. Theoret. Comput. Sci. **178**(1), 1–36 (1997)
10. Glushkov, V.M.: The abstract theory of automata. Russ. Math. Surv. **16**(5), 1 (1961)
11. Ilie, L., Yu, S.: Follow automata. Inf. Comput. **186**, 146–162 (2003)
12. McNaughton, R., Yamada, H.: Regular expressions and state graphs for automata. IEEE Trans. Electron. Comput. **1**(EC–9), 39–47 (1960)
13. Mirkin, B.G.: An algorithm for constructing a base in a language of regular expressions. Eng. Cybern. **5**, 110–116 (1966)
14. Ponty, J.-L., Ziadi, D., Champarnaud, J.-M.: A new quadratic algorithm to convert a regular expression into an automaton. In: Raymond, D., Wood, D., Yu, S. (eds.) WIA 1996. LNCS, vol. 1260, pp. 109–119. Springer, Heidelberg (1997). doi:10.1007/3-540-63174-7_9
15. Lombardy, S., Sakarovitch, J.: Derivatives of rational expressions with multiplicity. Theoret. Comput. Sci. **332**(1–3), 141–177 (2005)
16. Yu, S.: Regular languages. In: Rozenberg, G., Salomaa, A. (eds.) Handbook of Formal Languages, vol. 1, pp. 41–110. Springer, Berlin (1997)

Finding DFAs with Maximal Shortest Synchronizing Word Length

Henk Don[2] and Hans Zantema[1,2(✉)]

[1] Department of Computer Science, TU Eindhoven,
P.O. Box 513, 5600 MB Eindhoven, The Netherlands
`h.zantema@tue.nl`
[2] Radboud University Nijmegen,
P.O. Box 9010, 6500 GL Nijmegen, The Netherlands
`h.don@math.ru.nl`

Abstract. It was conjectured by Černý in 1964 that a synchronizing DFA on n states always has a shortest synchronizing word of length at most $(n-1)^2$, and he gave a sequence of DFAs for which this bound is reached. In 2006 Trahtman conjectured that apart from Černý's sequence only 8 DFAs exist attaining the bound. He gave an investigation of all DFAs up to certain size for which the bound is reached, and which do not contain other synchronizing DFAs. Here we extend this analysis in two ways: we drop this latter condition, and we drop limits on alphabet size. For $n \leq 4$ we do the full analysis yielding 19 new DFAs with smallest synchronizing word length $(n-1)^2$, refuting Trahtman's conjecture. All these new DFAs are extensions of DFAs that were known before. For $n \geq 5$ we prove that none of the DFAs in Trahtman's analysis can be extended similarly. In particular, as a main result we prove that the Černý examples C_n do not admit non-trivial extensions keeping the same smallest synchronizing word length $(n-1)^2$.

1 Introduction

A *deterministic finite automaton (DFA)* over a finite alphabet Σ is called *synchronizing* if it admits a *synchronizing word.* Here a word $w \in \Sigma^*$ is called *synchronizing* (or directed, or reset) if starting in any state q, after processing w one always ends in one particular state q_s. So processing w acts as a reset button: no matter in which state the system is, it always moves to the particular state q_s. Now Černý's conjecture [4] states:

Every synchronizing DFA on n states admits a synchronizing word of length $\leq (n-1)^2$.

Surprisingly, despite extensive effort this conjecture is still open, and even the best known upper bound is still cubic in n. Černý himself [4] provided an upper bound of $2^n - n - 1$ for the length of the shortest synchronizing word. A substantial improvement was given by Starke [14], who was the first to give a cubic upper bound. The best known upper bound is $\frac{1}{6}(n^3 - n)$, established by Pin in

F. Drewes et al. (Eds.): LATA 2017, LNCS 10168, pp. 249–260, 2017.
DOI: 10.1007/978-3-319-53733-7_18

1983 [12], based on [10]. Since then for more than 30 years no progress for the general case has been made.

The conjecture has been proved for some particular classes of automata. For these results and some more partial answers, see [1,2,6,8,15]. For a survey on synchronizing automata and Černý's conjecture, we refer to [17].

In [4] Černý already gave DFAs for which the bound of the conjecture is attained: for $n \geq 2$ the DFA C_n is defined to consist of n states $1, 2, \ldots, n$, and two symbols a, b, acting by $\delta(i, a) = i + 1$ for $i = 1, \ldots, n-1$, $\delta(n, a) = 1$, and $\delta(i, b) = i$ for $i = 2, \ldots, n$, $\delta(1, b) = 2$. For $n = 4$ this is depicted on the right.

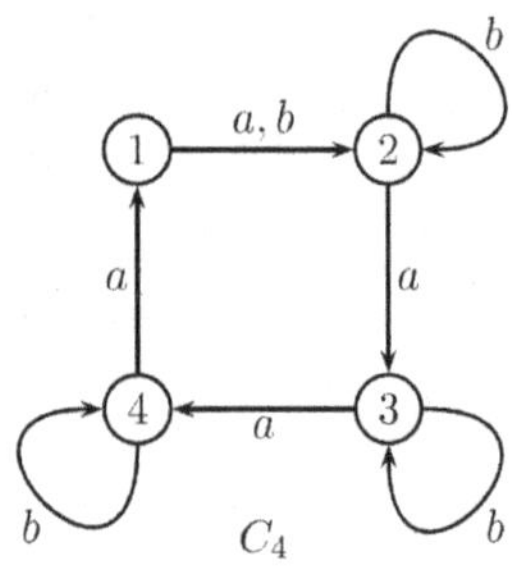

For C_n the string $w = b(a^{n-1}b)^{n-2}$ of length $|w| = (n-1)^2$ satisfies $qw = 2$ for all $q \in Q$, so is synchronizing. No shorter synchronizing word exists for C_n as is shown in [4], showing that the bound in Černý's conjecture is sharp.

The topic of this paper is to investigate all DFAs for which the bound is reached; these DFAs are called *critical*. A DFA for which the bound is exceeded is called *super-critical*, so Černý's conjecture states that no super-critical DFA exists. To exclude infinitely many trivial extensions, we only consider *basic* DFAs: no two distinct symbols act in the same way in the automaton, and no symbol acts as the identity. Obviously, adding the identity or copies of existing symbols has no influence on synchronization.

An extensive investigation was already done by Trahtman in [16]: by computer support and clever algorithms all critical DFAs on n states and q symbols were investigated for $3 \leq n \leq 7$ and $q \leq 4$, and for $n = 8, 9, 10$ and $q = 2$. Here a minimality requirement was added: examples were excluded if criticality may be kept after removing one symbol. Then up to isomorphism there are exactly 8 of them, apart from the basic Černý examples: 3 with 3 states, 3 with 4, one with 5 and one with 6. So apart from the basic Černý examples only 8 other critical DFAs were known. It was conjectured in [16] that no more exist, which is refuted in this paper by finding several more not satisfying the minimality condition, all being extensions of known examples. As one main result we prove that up to isomorphism for $n = 3$ there are exactly 15 basic critical DFAs and for $n = 4$ there are exactly 12 basic critical DFAs, 19 more than the four for $n = 3$ and the four for $n = 4$ that were known before.

Two typical examples are depicted on the right. The left one restricted to a, b is exactly C_3, while restricted to a, c it is exactly a DFA found in [16] that we call T3-1 in Sect. 3. So this example is a kind of

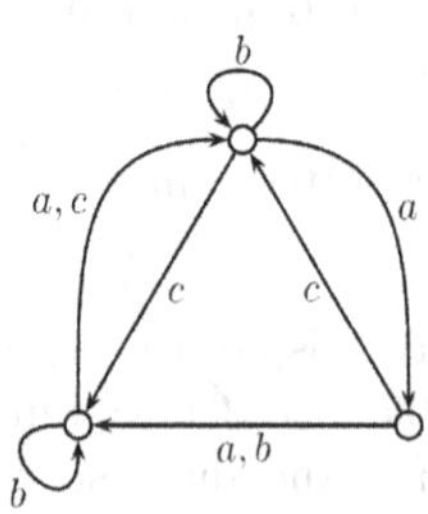

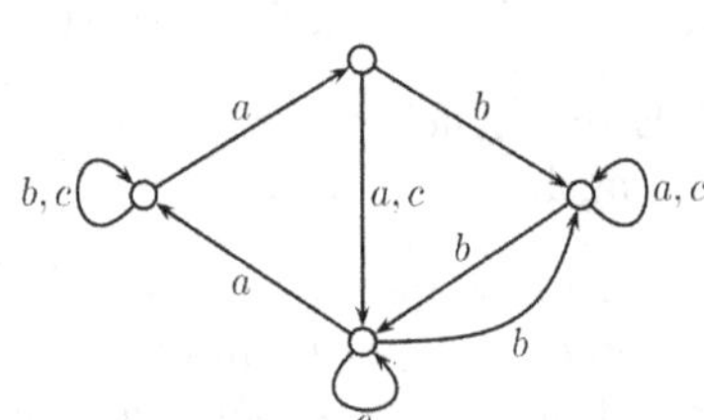

union of C_3 and T3-1. It has four distinct synchronizing words of the minimal length 4 described by $(b+c)aa(b+c)$, having two distinct synchronizing states.

The right one restricted to a, b is the example found in [5] that we call CPR in Sect. 3. However, the extra non-trivial symbol c does not occur in any known critical DFA on four states. It has eight distinct synchronizing words of the minimal length 9 described by $(b+c)aa(b+c)abaa(b+c)$, again having two distinct synchronizing states.

For $n \geq 5$, we wonder whether the minimal critical DFAs in Trahtman's analysis admit critical extensions just as for $n \leq 4$. The answer is negative. Apart from C_n these include only two minimal critical DFAs: one with 5 and one with 6 states, for which a simple computer search applies. For C_n this boils down to the main theorem stating that when adding an extra symbol to C_n not acting as the identity or as one of the existing symbols, always a strictly shorter synchronizing word can be obtained. The theorem is proved by a case analysis in how this extra symbol acts on the states.

This paper is organized as follows. In Sect. 2 we give some preliminaries. In Sect. 3 we consider DFAs of at most six states. First we give a self-contained analysis of all critical DFAs on ≤ 4 states. Next, for the known critical DFAs on five and six states we show that they do not admit critical extensions. The most substantial part is Sect. 4, where we prove our property for C_n for arbitrary n: C_n has no critical extension for $n \geq 5$. An extensive case analysis on how an extra non-trivial symbol c acts on the n states shows that this always yields a shorter synchronizing word. For some parts of the proofs we refer to the full version [7] of this paper. We conclude in Sect. 5.

2 Preliminaries

A *deterministic finite automaton (DFA)* over a finite alphabet Σ consists of a finite set Q of states and a map $\delta : Q \times \Sigma \to Q$.[1] A DFA is called *basic* if the mappings $q \mapsto \delta(a, q)$ are distinct for all $a \in \Sigma$, and are not the identity. For $w \in \Sigma^*$ and $q \in Q$ define qw inductively by $q\epsilon = q$ and $qwa = \delta(qw, a)$ for $a \in \Sigma$. So qw is the state where one ends when starting in q and applying δ-steps for the symbols in w consecutively, and qa is a short hand notation for $\delta(q, a)$. A word $w \in \Sigma^*$ is called *synchronizing* if a state $q_s \in Q$ exists such that $qw = q_s$ for all $q \in Q$. Stated in words: starting in any state q, after processing w one always ends in state q_s. A DFA on n states is *critical* if its shortest synchronizing word has length $(n-1)^2$; it is *super-critical* if its shortest synchronizing word has length $> (n-1)^2$. A critical DFA is *minimal* if it is not the extension of another critical DFA by one or more extra symbols; it is *maximal* if it does not admit a basic critical extension.

The basic tool to analyze synchronization is by exploiting the *power set automaton*. For any DFA (Q, Σ, δ) its power set automaton is the DFA $(2^Q, \Sigma, \delta')$ where $\delta' : 2^Q \times \Sigma \to 2^Q$ is defined by $\delta'(V, a) = \{q \in Q \mid \exists p \in V :$

[1] For synchronization the initial state and the set of final states in the standard definition may be ignored.

$\delta(p, a) = q\}$. For any $V \subseteq Q, w \in \Sigma^*$ we define Vw as above, using δ' instead of δ. From this definition one easily proves that $Vw = \{qw \mid q \in V\}$ for any $V \subseteq Q, w \in \Sigma^*$. A set of the shape $\{q\}$ for $q \in Q$ is called a *singleton*. So a word w is synchronizing if and only if Qw is a singleton. Hence a DFA is synchronizing if and only if its power set automaton admits a path from Q to a singleton, and the shortest length of such a path corresponds to the shortest length of a synchronizing word.

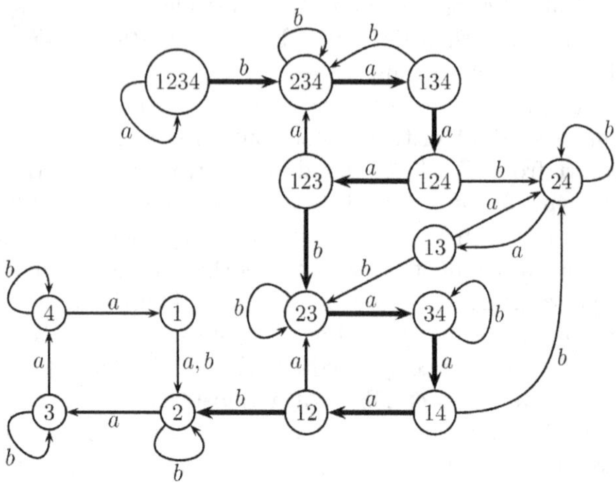

The power set automaton of C_4 is depicted on the right, in which indeed the unique shortest path from Q to a singleton (indicated by fat arrows from 1234 to 2) has length 9.

3 Small DFAs

3.1 Three States

First we give the minimal critical DFAs as presented in [16] on three states, apart from C_3:

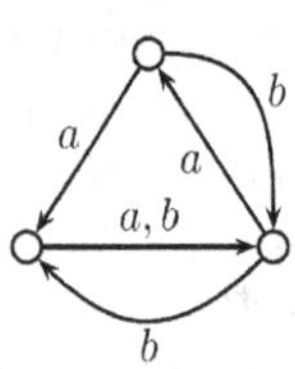

T3-1

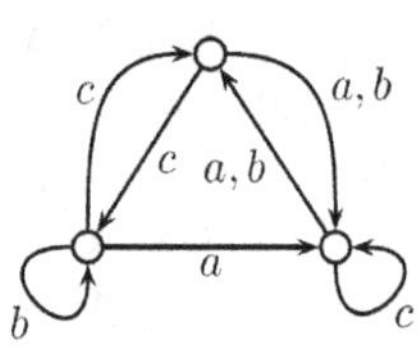

T3-2

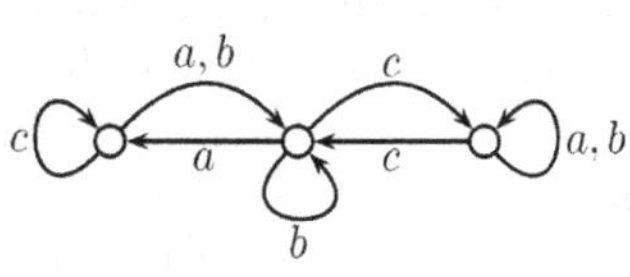

T3-3

We call them T3-1, T3-2 and T3-3, as they were found by Trahtman. They all have a unique synchronizing word of length 4, being *baab*, *acba*, *bacb*, respectively.

They can be combined to a single DFA A3 on five symbols a, b, c, d, e, depicted as follows.

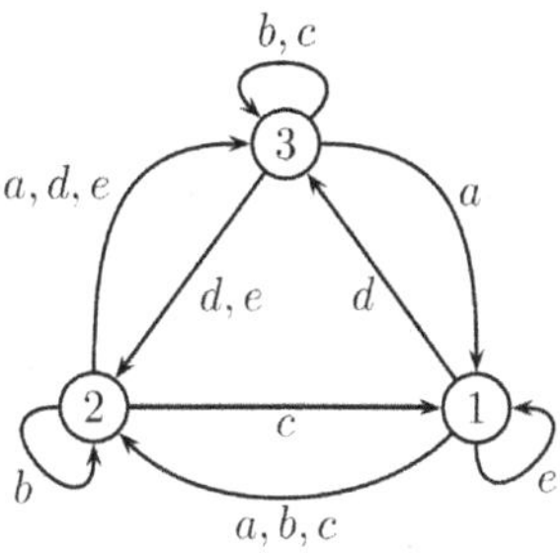

A3

Observe that A3 restricted to a, b coincides with C_3, A3 restricted to a, d coincides with T3-1, A3 restricted to c, d, e coincides with T3-2 and A3 restricted to b, c, e coincides with T3-3, so exactly the four minimal critical automata on three states from [16]. On the other hand, as all minimal basic critical DFAs on three states are contained in A3, A3 is the only maximal basic critical DFA on three states. It admits 16 synchronizing words of length 4, expressed by the regular expression $(b+d)(a+c)(a+e)(b+d)$, where state 2 is the synchronizing state if the word ends in b and state 3 if the word ends in d.

The relationship between A3 and critical DFAs is given in the following theorem.

Theorem 1. *No super-critical DFAs on three states exist, and a basic DFA on three states is critical if and only if up to isomorphism it is one of the 15 automata that can be obtained from A3 by removing zero or more symbols and keeping at least one of the sets* $\{a, b\}, \{a, d\}, \{b, c, e\}, \{c, d, e\}$ *of symbols.*

Proof. Let 1,2,3 be the three states. The automaton has a shortest synchronizing word of length ≥ 4 if and only if the shortest path from $\{1, 2, 3\}$ to a singleton in the power set automaton has length ≥ 4. There is a step from $\{1, 2, 3\}$ to a smaller set. Since the length of the shortest path is ≥ 4, this smaller set is not a singleton, so it is a pair; without loss of generality we may assume this is $\{2, 3\}$. Let b be the first symbol of a shortest synchronizing word, so $\{1, 2, 3\} \xrightarrow{b} \{2, 3\}$. Since the shortest path from $\{2, 3\}$ to a singleton consists of at least three steps, it meets the other two pairs and consists of exactly three steps, yielding shortest synchronizing word length 4. May be after swapping 2 and 3 we may assume this shortest path is $\{1, 2, 3\} \xrightarrow{b} \{2, 3\} \to \{1, 3\} \to \{1, 2\} \to$ singleton. As it is the shortest path, we conclude that for every symbol a we have

- either $\{1, 2, 3\} \xrightarrow{a} \{1, 2, 3\}$ or $\{1, 2, 3\} \xrightarrow{a} \{2, 3\}$,
- either $\{2, 3\} \xrightarrow{a} \{2, 3\}$ or $\{2, 3\} \xrightarrow{a} \{1, 3\}$, and
- not $\{1, 3\} \xrightarrow{a}$ singleton.

A small program investigates that among the $3^3 = 27$ possible symbol actions in a DFA on three states exactly 6 satisfy these properties: exactly the symbols a, b, c, d, e in A3 and the identity. So for all DFAs being a sub-automaton of A3 it holds that if it is synchronizing, then the shortest synchronizing word length is 4. Restricting A3 to either $\{a, b\}$, $\{a, d\}$, $\{b, c, e\}$ or $\{c, d, e\}$ yields one of the known synchronizing DFAs, so every extension is synchronizing too. Conversely, it is easily checked that all of these restrictions are minimal: all symbols are required for synchronization. This concludes the proof. □

As a consequence of Theorem 1 apart from the four minimal critical DFAs that were known on three states, we obtain 11 more that are not minimal.

3.2 Four States

First we give the minimal critical DFAs as presented in [16] on four states, apart from C_4. The first one is CPR, found by Černý, Piricka and Rosenauerova, [5], and has unique synchronizing word of length 9, being *baababaab*. The next two we call T4-1 and T4-2, as they were found by Trahtman. The DFA T4-1 has a unique synchronizing word of length 9, being *abcacabca*; for T4-2 there are 4 synchronizing words of length 9 represented by $acb(a+c)a(a+b)cba$.

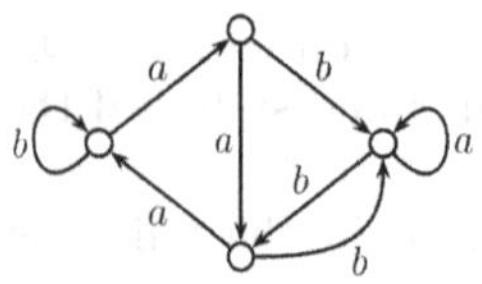

CPR

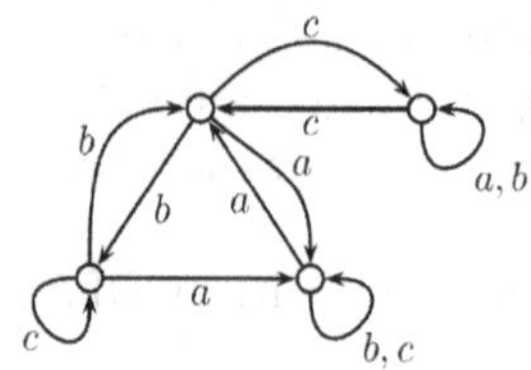

T4-1

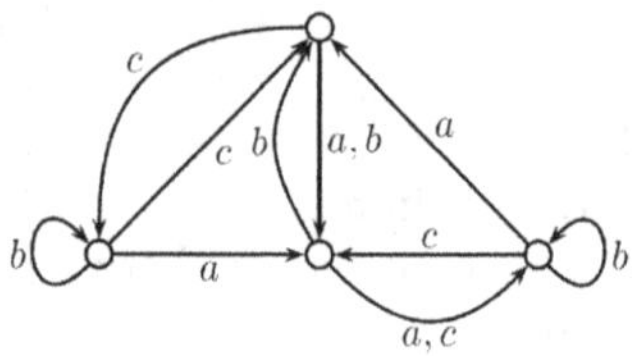

T4-2

In order to investigate all critical DFAs with four states, we introduce the DFA A4 on five symbols a, b, c, d, e, depicted as follows.

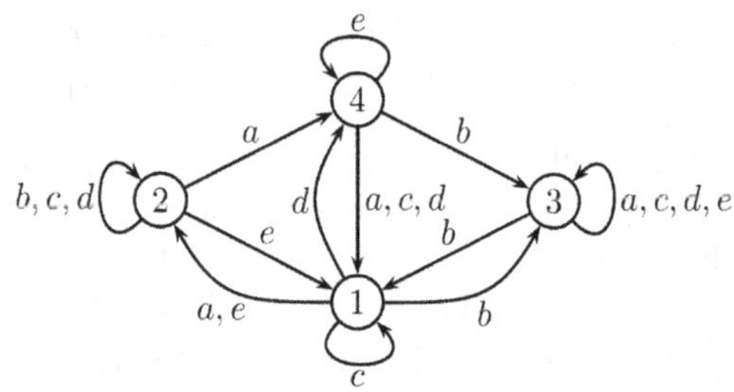

A4

Observe that A4 restricted to a, b coincides with CPR and A4 restricted to b, d, e coincides with T4-1, so together with C_4 and T4-2 exactly the four automata with four states from [16], being the minimal ones. On the other hand, C_4, T4-2 and A4 are the only maximal basic critical DFAs on four states. We will prove this in Theorem 2. The DFA A4 admits 256 synchronizing words of length 9, expressed by the regular expression $(b+c)(a+d)(a+e)(b+c)(a+e)b(a+d)(a+e)(b+c)$, where the synchronizing state is 1 or 3, depending on the last symbol. The relationship between A4 and critical DFAs is given in the following theorem.

Theorem 2. *No super-critical DFAs on four states exist, and a basic DFA on four states is critical if and only if up to isomorphism it is* C_4*, T4-2, or one of the 10 automata that can be obtained from A4 by removing zero or more symbols and keeping at least one of the sets* $\{a, b\}, \{b, d, e\}$ *of symbols.*

Proof. Let 1,2,3,4 be the four states. We have to prove that the shortest path in the power set automaton from $\{1, 2, 3, 4\}$ to a singleton never has length > 9 (this would be super-critical), and that length 9 only occurs in the cases indicated by the theorem. So assume this length is ≥ 9. Since there is a step from $\{1, 2, 3, 4\}$ to a smaller set, and since the length is ≥ 9, it is not to a pair since there are only 6 distinct pairs. So after one step only one element is removed from $\{1, 2, 3, 4\}$, say, 4. By the same argument also the next step in a shortest path to a singleton is not to a pair; by possibly renaming we may assume it is to $\{2,3,4\}$, so a shortest path is of the shape $\{1,2,3,4\} \xrightarrow{a_1} \{1,2,3\} \xrightarrow{a_2} \{2,3,4\} \to^{\geq 7}$ singleton.

The approach is to generate all solutions by a computer program. In order to reduce the search space, first we prove that for every symbol a we have

1. if $\{1,2,3,4\} \xrightarrow{a} V$ then $\{1,2,3\} \subseteq V$;
2. if $\{1,2,3\} \xrightarrow{a} V$ then either $V = \{1,2,3\}$ or $V = \{2,3,4\}$;
3. if $\{2,3,4\} \xrightarrow{a} V$ then $|V| = 3$.

We start by property 3. For the full version of the proof we refer to [7], including justification of correctness of the SMT approach. The idea is that if a symbol a exists such that $\{2,3,4\} \xrightarrow{a} \{p_1, q_1\}$, then the shortest path to a singleton meets all six possible unordered pairs. We collected a number of properties that follow from this assumption in a formula. Next we applied the SMT solver Yices [9] to this formula, that stated that this formula is unsatisfiable in a fraction of a second. So this yields a contradiction, proving property 3.

In order to prove properties 1 and 2, observe that from $a_1(\{1,2,3,4\}) = \{1,2,3\}$ we conclude that $x \neq y \in \{1,2,3,4\}$ exist such that $a_1(x) = a_1(y)$. Since $a_1(\{2,3,4\})$ consists of three elements by property 3, we have $\{x,y\} \not\subseteq \{2,3,4\}$, so $1 \in \{x,y\}$. If $a_1(\{1,2,3\})$ consists a two elements this gives rise to a shorter synchronizing sequence, so $\{x,y\} \not\subseteq \{1,2,3\}$, hence $4 \in \{x,y\}$. So $a_1(1) = a_1(4)$.

For property 1 assume that $\{1,2,3\} \not\subseteq V$ for $V = a(\{1,2,3,4\})$. Since $|V| = 3$, the set V is one of the three sets $\{2,3,4\}, \{1,2,4\}, \{1,3,4\}$. If it is $\{2,3,4\}$, we have a shorter synchronizing sequence; otherwise $\{1,4\} \subseteq V$, by which $|a_1(V)| = 2$, and this pair $a_1(V)$ can be reached in two steps a, a_1 from $\{1,2,3,4\}$. Both cases yield a contradiction, proving property 1.

The proof of property 2 is similar: if $V = a(\{1,2,3\})$ is not $\{1,2,3\}$ or $\{2,3,4\}$, then by $|V| = 3$ we have V is $\{1,2,4\}$ or $\{1,3,4\}$, so $|a_1(V)| = 2$ by $a_1(1) = a_1(4)$, and this pair $a_1(V)$ can be reached in three steps a_1, a, a_1 from $\{1,2,3,4\}$, contradicting property 3 stating that no shortest path from $\{1,2,3,4\}$ to a singleton reaches a pair in three steps.

It turns out that among the 256 functions from $\{1,2,3,4\}$ to itself exactly 18 satisfy properties 1, 2 and 3. This includes the identity that has to be excluded since that is not allowed in a basic DFA, leaving 17 functions. A straightforward computation in <10 s on the corresponding $2^{17} = 131072$ basic DFAs yields the shortest path lengths from $\{1,2,3,4\}$ to a singleton. As expected, no shortest path length longer than 9 is obtained, proving that no super-critical DFA on 4 states exists. Exactly 24 basic DFAs are obtained with shortest path length 9. These 24 automata exactly coincide with the 12 automata indicated in the theorem; each occurring twice up to swapping 2 and 3. □

As a consequence of Theorem 2 apart from the four minimal critical DFAs that were known on four states, we obtain 8 more that are not minimal. An alternative proof of Theorem 2 was given by de Bondt [3] by a direct computer search exploiting bounds on path lengths in the power set automaton; his approach also succeeded to prove that for $n = 5$ there are no more critical DFAs than the two that were known before.

3.3 Five and Six States

In Sect. 3 we saw that for $n = 3, 4$ a critical DFA may have a basic critical extension. We now claim that for $n \geq 5$ this does not occur any more for the known critical DFAs. In Section 4 we will prove that this holds for C_n for all $n \geq 5$. By Trahtman's investigation the only two more critical DFAs to consider are one on five states from Roman [13] and one on six states from Kari [11], depicted as follows.

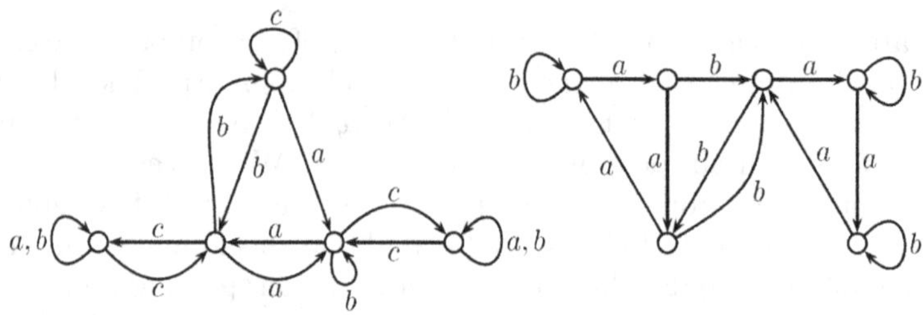

For Roman's DFA the shortest synchronizing word *abcacacbcaacabca* is unique; for Kari's DFA there are two shortest synchronizing words, described by *baababababbaba*$(baab + abaa)$*babaab*.

For $n = 5, 6$ we wrote a program that takes a DFA on n states and computes for all n^n ways to add a fresh symbol, the shortest path length in the power set automaton from the full set to a singleton. For both candidates it turns out that the only extensions keeping this shortest path length to be $(n-1)^2$ is by adding either a copy of one of the existing symbols, or a symbol that acts as the identity. This proves our claim.

To check our results, we also applied this approach to $n = 3, 4$: all 19 new critical DFAs from Theorems 1 and 2 were obtained as extensions of the earlier known DFAs.

4 Extending C_n

In this section we show that for all $n \geq 5$ the DFA C_n is maximal: it cannot be extended to a basic critical DFA. The main result of this section is the following:

Theorem 3. *Let $n \geq 5$ and let C_n^c be a basic extension of C_n by a symbol c. Then C_n^c admits a synchronizing word of length strictly less than $(n-1)^2$.*

This section is organized as follows: first we collect properties of C_n and its shortest synchronizing word. Then we assume that c is a permutation on Q. We will give a typical example that shows how to construct a shorter synchronizing word. Finally, in Lemma 6, we demonstrate how to generalize this.

4.1 Properties of C_n

Recall that C_n is defined by n states $1, 2, \ldots, n$, and two symbols a, b, acting by $qa = q + 1$ for $q = 1, \ldots, n-1$, $na = 1$, and $qb = q$ for $q = 2, \ldots, n$, $1b = 2$. It is well known that $w_n = b(a^{n-1}b)^{n-2}$ of length $|w_n| = (n-1)^2$ is its shortest synchronizing word. It is synchronizing since

$$Qb = \{2, 3, \ldots, n\} \tag{1}$$
$$\{2, 3, \ldots, k\}\, a^{n-1}b = \{2, 3, \ldots, k-1\}, \quad 3 \leq k \leq n. \tag{2}$$

The first part of this word defines the path

$$Q \xrightarrow{b} Q \setminus \{1\} \xrightarrow{a} Q \setminus \{2\} \xrightarrow{a} \ldots \xrightarrow{a} Q \setminus \{n\}. \tag{3}$$

We now extend the alphabet of the automaton by a non-trivial new symbol c. Here we will assume that c is a permutation, i.e. $|Qc| = n$, and show that in this case a shorter synchronizing word exists. The other cases use similar ideas and are covered in [7]. The general pattern in the arguments is as follows. The shortest synchronizing word w_n corresponds to a path from Q to a singleton in the power automaton of C_n. Take two sets $S, S' \subseteq Q$ on this path which are visited in this order. Let d be the distance from S to S', i.e.

$$d := \min\left\{|w| : Sw = S', w \in \{a, b\}^\star\right\}.$$

Now construct a word $w \in \{a, b, c\}^\star$ in the automaton C_n^c for which $Sw = S'$ and $|w| < d$. Then C_n^c admits a synchronizing word of length at most $|w_n| - d + |w| < (n-1)^2$.

4.2 Construction of a Shorter Synchronizing Word

If c defines a permutation on Q, we may assume that c satisfies:

$$qc \leq q + 1 \text{ for all } q \in Q. \tag{4}$$

Indeed, if $qc = q + k$ for some $q \in Q$ and $k \geq 2$, then $(Q \setminus \{q\})c = Q \setminus \{q + k\}$, which in view of (3) would imply existence of a synchronizing word shorter than $(n-1)^2$. The following lemma describes the structure of c.

Lemma 4. *If $|Q| = n \geq 1$ and c is a permutation on Q satisfying (4), then there exist numbers L (number of c-loops) and $1 \leq l_1, \ldots, l_L \leq n$ (lengths of c-loops) with $\sum_{i=1}^{L} l_i = n$ such that*

$$qc = \begin{cases} q - l_i + 1 & \text{if } q = l_1 + \ldots + l_i \text{ for some } 1 \leq i \leq L \\ q + 1 & \text{otherwise} \end{cases} \tag{5}$$

The proof of this lemma is straightforward and can be found in [7]. An illustration of the statement is given below.

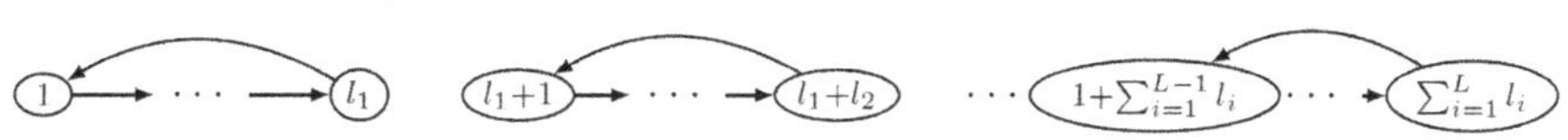

Note that $L = 1$ and $L = n$ are the trivial cases, because then $c = a$ or c is the identity. Before we give a general argument, we first give an example.

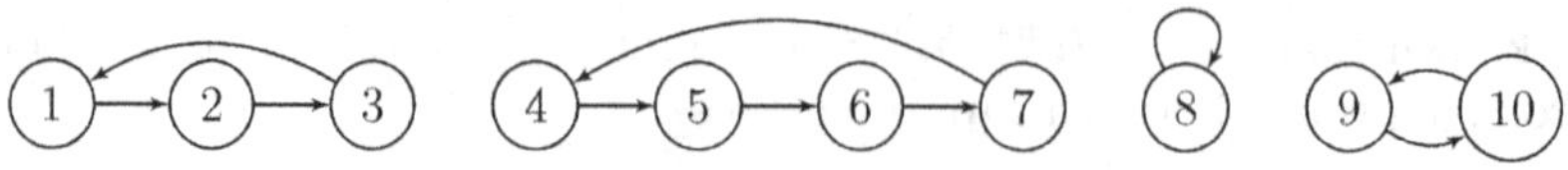

Example 5. Consider the automaton $C_{10}^c = \{Q, \Sigma, \delta\}$ with $Q = \{1, \ldots, 10\}$ and $\Sigma = \{a, b, c\}$. The actions of the symbols a and b are from the definition of C_n and c is the permutation shown above. Here we have four loops ($L = 4$) with lengths $l_1 = 3, l_2 = 4, l_3 = 1$ and $l_4 = 2$. We will show how to use the c-loop of length four to create a shorter synchronizing word. Consider the set $S = \{2, \ldots, 9\}$. We start by a greedy approach to reach a set of size 7:

$$Sa^3b = (\{1, 2\} \cup \{5, \ldots, 10\})\, b = \{2\} \cup \{5, \ldots, 10\}\,.$$

As a next step, we shift everything by using the symbol a until the isolated state $\{2\}$ ends up in the c-loop of length four:

$$(\{2\} \cup \{5, \ldots, 10\})\, a^3 = \{1, 2, 3\} \cup \{5\} \cup \{8, 9, 10\}$$

Since $\{1, 2, 3\}$ and $\{8, 9, 10\}$ are (unions of) full c-loops, they are invariant under c. Therefore, we can move the isolated state $\{5\}$ to the desired position:

$$(\{1, 2, 3\} \cup \{5\} \cup \{8, 9, 10\})\, c^3 = \{1, 2, 3, 4\} \cup \{8, 9, 10\}$$

Finally, we shift again by a power of a and apply b to get rid of one more state:

$$(\{1, 2, 3, 4\} \cup \{8, 9, 10\})\, a^3b = \{1, \ldots, 7\}\, b = \{2, \ldots, 7\} := S'.$$

We conclude that the word $w = a^3ba^3c^3a^3b$ has the property that $Sw = S'$. In C_{10} both S and S' are on the shortest path from Q to $\{2\}$ and by (1) the distance between them is equal to $2n = 20$. The word w has length $|w| = 14$, so in C_{10}^c there exists a synchronizing word of length at most $(10 - 1)^2 - 6 = 75$.

The idea of this example works in more generality if there is a c-loop of length at least 3, as is proved in the next lemma. If the longest loop has length 2, then basically we can do the same thing, but we need at least three c-loops to isolate a state.

Lemma 6. *Let $n \geq 5$ and let C_n^c be an extension of the automaton C_n by a symbol c as given in Lemma 4. If $2 \leq L \leq n-1$, then C_n^c admits a synchronizing word of length strictly less than $(n-1)^2$.*

Proof. Assume that $l_k \geq 3$ for some k and write $\Lambda^- = \sum_{i=1}^{k-1} l_i$, $\Lambda^+ = \sum_{i=k+1}^{L} l_i$, for the sum of the loop lengths before the kth loop and after the kth loop respectively. These sums can be zero if $k = 1$ or $k = L$. Define $\Lambda = \Lambda^- + \Lambda^+ = n - l_k \leq n - 3$. Since $L \geq 2$, we have $\Lambda \geq 1$. Take

$$S = \{2, 3, \ldots, n - l_k + 3\}\,, \quad S' = \{2, 3, \ldots, n - l_k + 1\}\,.$$

and define the word

$$w = a^{l_k - 1} b a^{\Lambda^-} c^{l_k - 1} a^{\Lambda^+} b. \tag{6}$$

We will show that $Sw = S'$. Write $S = S_1 \cup S_2$ with

$$S_1 = \{2, \ldots, n - l_k + 1\} = \{2, \ldots, 1 + \Lambda\},$$
$$S_2 = \{n - l_k + 2, n - l_k + 3\} = \{2 + \Lambda, 3 + \Lambda\}.$$

Then

$$\begin{aligned} S_1 w &= \{2, \ldots, 1 + \Lambda\}\, a^{l_k - 1} b a^{\Lambda^-} c^{l_k - 1} a^{\Lambda^+} b \\ &= \{l_k + 1, \ldots, n\}\, b a^{\Lambda^-} c^{l_k - 1} a^{\Lambda^+} b = \{l_k + 1, \ldots, n\}\, a^{\Lambda^-} c^{l_k - 1} a^{\Lambda^+} b \\ &= \left(\{1, \ldots, \Lambda^-\} \cup \{\Lambda^- + l_k + 1, \ldots, n\}\right) c^{l_k - 1} a^{\Lambda^+} b \\ &= \left(\{1, \ldots, \Lambda^-\} \cup \{\Lambda^- + l_k + 1, \ldots, n\}\right) a^{\Lambda^+} b \\ &= \{1, \ldots, \Lambda\}\, b = \begin{cases} \{2\} = \{1 + \Lambda\} & \text{if } \Lambda = 1 \\ \{2, \ldots, \Lambda\} & \text{if } \Lambda \geq 2, \end{cases} \end{aligned} \tag{7}$$

where sets of the form $\{x, \ldots, y\}$ with $x > y$ should be interpreted as being empty. This occurs if $\Lambda^- = 0$ or $\Lambda^+ = 0$. Furthermore

$$\begin{aligned} S_2 w &= \{2 + \Lambda, 3 + \Lambda\}\, a^{l_k - 1} b a^{\Lambda^-} c^{l_k - 1} a^{\Lambda^+} b = \{1, 2\}\, b a^{\Lambda^-} c^{l_k - 1} a^{\Lambda^+} b \\ &= \{2\}\, a^{\Lambda^-} c^{l_k - 1} a^{\Lambda^+} b = \{2 + \Lambda^-\}\, c^{l_k - 1} a^{\Lambda^+} b = \{1 + \Lambda^-\}\, a^{\Lambda^+} b \\ &= \{1 + \Lambda\}\, b = \{1 + \Lambda\}. \end{aligned} \tag{8}$$

It follows that the word w has the property

$$Sw = (S_1 \cup S_2) w = S_1 w \cup S_2 w = \{2, \ldots, \Lambda + 1\} = S'.$$

and its length is $|w| = l_k - 1 + 1 + \Lambda^- + l_k - 1 + \Lambda^+ + 1 = 2l_k + \Lambda = l_k + n < 2n$. In the automaton C_n the sets S and S' are both on the shortest path from Q to a singleton and the shortest path is defined by $S(a^{n-1}b)^2 = S'$. Since $|(a^{n-1}b)^2| = 2n > |w|$, the statement of the lemma follows.

The above proof fails if all loops have length at most 2. Using quite similar ideas, a proof for this case is given in the full version of this paper [7]. □

Proof of Theorem 3. The results of this section prove that C_n^c is sub-critical if c is a permutation. The case $|Qc| \leq n - 1$ is covered in [7]. □

5 Conclusions and Further Research

We investigated critical DFAs in two main ways: exploiting computer support we did a full investigation for $n = 3, 4$, and for $n \geq 5$ in classical mathematical style we proved that C_n does not admit non-trivial critical extensions. Further we showed that neither of two more known critical DFAs on 5 and 6 states admit non-trivial critical extensions. If Trahtman's investigation gives all minimal critical DFAs (which is a weaker form of his conjecture), our results give a full characterization of all critical DFAs. In contrast to what Trahtman expected, several minimal critical DFAs on 3 and 4 states can be combined and/or extended to critical DFAs. For all of these the minimal synchronizing word is not unique, and sometimes the synchronizing state is not unique.

Despite of extensive effort, Černý's conjecture is still open after more than half a century. Being a strengthening of this long standing open problem, a full characterization of all critical DFAs may not be tractable. More feasible challenges may include

- a full investigation for $n = 6$,
- proving or disproving that every non-minimal basic critical DFA admits multiple shortest synchronizing words,
- giving an upper bound on the number of symbols in a minimal critical DFA (all known examples have at most three).

References

1. Almeida, J., Margolis, S., Steinberg, B., Volkov, M.: Representation theory of finite semigroups, semigroup radicals and formal language theory. Trans. Am. Math. Soc. **361**, 1429–1461 (2009)
2. Béal, M.P., Berlinkov, M., Perrin, D.: A quadratic upper bound on the size of a synchronizing word in one-cluster automata. Int. J. Found. Comput. Sci. **22**, 277–288 (2011)
3. de Bondt, M.: Personal communication, December 2016
4. Černy, J.: Poznámka k homogénnym experimentom s konečnými automatmi. Matematicko-fyzikálny časopis, Slovensk. Akad. Vied **14**(3), 208–216 (1964)
5. Černy, J., Piricka, A., Rosenauerova, B.: On directable automata. Kybernetika **7**(4), 289–298 (1971)
6. Don, H.: The Černý conjecture and 1-contracting automata. Electron. J. Comb. **23**(3), P3.12 (2016)
7. Don, H., Zantema, H.: Finding DFAs with maximal shortest synchronizing word length (2016). http://arxiv.org/abs/1609.06853
8. Dubuc, L.: Sur les automates circulaires et la conjecture de Černý. RAIRO Inform. Theor. Appl. **32**, 21–34 (1998)
9. Dutertre, B., de Moura, L.: Yices: an SMT solver. http://yices.csl.sri.com/
10. Frankl, P.: An extremal problem for two families of sets. Eur. J. Comb. **3**, 125–127 (1982)
11. Kari, J.: A counterexample to a conjecture concerning synchronizing word in finite automata. EATCS Bull. **73**, 146–147 (2001)
12. Pin, J.E.: On two combinatorial problems arising from automata theory. Ann. Discret. Math. **17**, 535–548 (1983)
13. Roman, A.: A note on Černy conjecture for automata with 3-letter alphabet. J. Automata Lang. Comb. **13**(2), 141–143 (2008)
14. Starke, P.: Eine bemerkung über homogene experimente. Elektronische Informationverarbeitung und Kybernetik **2**, 257–259 (1966)
15. Steinberg, B.: The Černý conjecture for one-cluster automata with prime length cycle. Theoret. Comput. Sci. **412**(39), 5487–5491 (2011)
16. Trahtman, A.N.: An efficient algorithm finds noticeable trends and examples concerning the Černy conjecture. In: Královič, R., Urzyczyn, P. (eds.) MFCS 2006. LNCS, vol. 4162, pp. 789–800. Springer, Heidelberg (2006)
17. Volkov, M.V.: Synchronizing automata and the Černý conjecture. In: Martín-Vide, C., Otto, F., Fernau, H. (eds.) LATA 2008. LNCS, vol. 5196, pp. 11–27. Springer, Heidelberg (2008)

Lower Bound Methods for the Size of Nondeterministic Finite Automata Revisited

Hellis Tamm[1(✉)] and Brink van der Merwe[2]

[1] Institute of Cybernetics, Tallinn University of Technology, Akadeemia tee 21, 12618 Tallinn, Estonia
hellis@cs.ioc.ee

[2] Department of Computer Science, Stellenbosch University, Private Bag X1, Matieland 7602, South Africa
abvdm@cs.sun.ac.za

Abstract. We revisit the following lower bound methods for the size of a nondeterministic finite automaton: the fooling set technique, the extended fooling set technique, and the biclique edge cover technique, presenting these methods in terms of quotients and atoms of regular languages. Although the lower bounds obtained by these methods are not necessarily tight, some classes of languages for which tight bounds can be achieved, are known. We show that languages with maximal reversal complexity belong to the class of languages for which the fooling set technique provides a tight bound. We also show that the extended fooling set technique is tight for a subclass of unary cyclic languages.

1 Introduction

We revisit the following lower bound methods for the number of states of a nondeterministic finite automaton (NFA) of a regular language: the *fooling set technique* [5], the *extended fooling set technique* [1], and the *biclique edge cover technique* [7]. All these lower bound methods were considered by Gruber and Holzer [7], who defined the *dependency graph* of a language and showed that lower bounds obtained by these techniques can be achieved by inspecting this graph. They also pointed out that the dependency graph was implicitly defined already in the classical work on NFA minimization by Kameda and Weiner [10].

Atoms of regular languages are a recently introduced notion in language and automata theory [3]. We express the dependency graph of a language in terms of (left) quotients and atoms of the language, similarly to how the matrix used by the Kameda-Weiner method was recently reinterpreted [17]. We present the above-mentioned lower bound methods in terms of quotients and atoms. We then consider certain subsets of the sets of quotients and atoms, so-called *prime quotients* and *prime atoms*, and show that the lower bound methods can be presented in terms of prime quotients and prime atoms. We also state simple

This work was supported by the Estonian Ministry of Education and Research institutional research grant IUT33-13 and by the ERDF funded ICT National Programme project "Coinduction".

F. Drewes et al. (Eds.): LATA 2017, LNCS 10168, pp. 261–272, 2017.
DOI: 10.1007/978-3-319-53733-7_19

necessary conditions for a language to have a fooling set or an extended fooling set of some size, and derive upper bounds for the size of a fooling set and an extended fooling set for a language.

Lower bounds obtained by the above methods are not necessarily tight, that is, a minimal NFA of a language may have more states than the obtained bound. Some classes of regular languages for which tight bounds can be achieved, have been specified in [15]. Namely, it was shown in [15] that the lower bound provided by the fooling set technique can be tight for and only for *biseparable* languages, and the lower bound provided by the extended fooling set technique can be tight for any *biresidual* language. Both of these language classes were studied in [11]. However, the class of languages for which the extended fooling set technique can provide a tight bound, is larger than the class of biresidual languages.

We consider languages with *maximal reversal complexity*, studied in [13] and [14]. Equivalently, these are languages with maximal number of atoms [3]. We show that any such language is biseparable, and thus the fooling set technique provides a tight bound for minimal NFAs of these languages.

Finally, we consider unary cyclic languages [9] and show that the extended fooling set technique is tight for a subclass of this class of languages.

2 Automata, Quotients, and Atoms of Regular Languages

A *nondeterministic finite automaton (NFA)* is a quintuple $\mathcal{N} = (Q, \Sigma, \delta, I, F)$, where Q is a finite, non-empty set of *states*, Σ is a finite non-empty *alphabet*, $\delta : Q \times \Sigma \to 2^Q$ is the *transition function*, $I \subseteq Q$ is the set of *initial states*, and $F \subseteq Q$ is the set of *final states*. We extend the transition function to functions $\delta' : Q \times \Sigma^* \to 2^Q$ and $\delta'' : 2^Q \times \Sigma^* \to 2^Q$, using δ for all these functions. The *left language* of a state q of $\mathcal{N}$ is the set of words $w \in \Sigma^*$ such that $q \in \delta(I, w)$, and the *right language* of q is the set of words $w \in \Sigma^*$ such that $\delta(q, w) \cap F \neq \emptyset$. An NFA is *trim* if it does not have any state with the empty left or right language. The *language accepted* by an NFA $\mathcal{N}$ is $L(\mathcal{N}) = \{w \in \Sigma^* \mid \delta(I, w) \cap F \neq \emptyset\}$. Two NFAs are *equivalent* if they accept the same language. An NFA is *minimal* if it has a minimum number of states among all equivalent NFAs. The *reverse* of an NFA $\mathcal{N} = (Q, \Sigma, \delta, I, F)$ is the NFA $\mathcal{N}^R = (Q, \Sigma, \delta^R, F, I)$, where $q \in \delta^R(p, a)$ if and only if $p \in \delta(q, a)$ for $p, q \in Q$ and $a \in \Sigma$.

A *deterministic finite automaton (DFA)* is a quintuple $\mathcal{D} = (Q, \Sigma, \delta, q_0, F)$, where Q, Σ, and F are as in an NFA, $\delta : Q \times \Sigma \to Q$ is the transition function, and q_0 is the initial state. It is well known that for every regular language there is a unique minimal DFA.

The *left quotient*, or simply *quotient*, of a language L by a word $w \in \Sigma^*$ is the language $w^{-1}L = \{x \in \Sigma^* \mid wx \in L\}$. There is one *initial* quotient, $\varepsilon^{-1}L = L$. A quotient is *final* if it contains ε. We note here the fact that left quotients of L correspond to the states of the minimal DFA of L.

A *residual finite state automaton (RFSA)* is an NFA $\mathcal{N}$ such that for every state q of $\mathcal{N}$, the right language of q is a left quotient of $L(\mathcal{N})$.

An *atom* of a regular language L with quotients $K_0, \dots, K_{n-1}$ is any non-empty language of the form $\widetilde{K_0} \cap \cdots \cap \widetilde{K_{n-1}}$, where $\widetilde{K_i}$ is either K_i or $\overline{K_i}$, and $\overline{K_i}$ is the complement of K_i with respect to Σ^*. If $\overline{K_0} \cap \cdots \cap \overline{K_{n-1}}$ is an atom, then it is called the *negative* atom, all the other atoms are *positive*. Thus atoms of L are regular languages uniquely determined by L; they define a partition of Σ^*. It is easy to see that L has at most 2^n atoms. Every quotient K_i is a (possibly empty) union of atoms.

It is well known that quotients of L correspond to the equivalence classes of the *Nerode right congruence* $\equiv_L$ of L [12] defined as follows: for $x, y \in \Sigma^*$, $x \equiv_L y$ if for every $v \in \Sigma^*$, $xv \in L$ if and only if $yv \in L$. That is, the equivalence class $[x]_L$ of a word x with respect to $\equiv_L$ is the set of all words y such that $x^{-1}L = y^{-1}L$. Similarly, the *left congruence* ${}_L{\equiv}$ of L can be defined as follows: for $x, y \in \Sigma^*$, $x\,{}_L{\equiv}\,y$ if for every $u \in \Sigma^*$, $ux \in L$ if and only if $uy \in L$. It has been noticed that the left congruence classes are the atoms of L [8]. That is, the equivalence class ${}_L[x]$ of a word x with respect to ${}_L{\equiv}$ is an atom A_i of L, such that $x \in A_i$. This idea was also used in [2], where this equivalence is called the *atom congruence*. It was shown in [3] that atoms correspond to the states of an NFA called the *átomaton* of L, and that the reverse NFA of the átomaton of L is the minimal DFA of the reverse language L^R of L. Thus, there is a one-to-one correspondence between the atoms of L and the quotients of L^R.

3 Lower Bound Methods for the Size of NFA

There are two simple lower bound methods for the number of states of an NFA: the *fooling set technique* presented by Glaister and Shallit [5], and the *extended fooling set technique* introduced by Birget [1]. These methods can be presented, respectively, as the first and the second case of the following theorem:

Theorem 1. *Let $L \subseteq \Sigma^*$ be a regular language, and suppose there exists a set of pairs $P = \{(x_i, w_i) \mid 0 \leqslant i \leqslant p-1\}$ such that either*

1. (a) $x_i w_i \in L$ for $0 \leqslant i \leqslant p-1$,
(b) $x_j w_i \notin L$ for $0 \leqslant i, j \leqslant p-1$, $i \neq j$,
or
2. (a) $x_i w_i \in L$ for $0 \leqslant i \leqslant p-1$,
(b) $x_j w_i \notin L$ or $x_i w_j \notin L$ for $0 \leqslant i, j \leqslant p-1$, $i \neq j$,

holds. Then any NFA accepting L has at least p states.

The set P satisfying the conditions (a) and (b) in case 1 of Theorem 1 is called a *fooling set* of L, in case 2 it is called an *extended fooling set* of L. One can easily see that the fooling set technique is a special case of the extended fooling set technique. In fact, the latter one can provide better lower bounds for some languages. However, neither of these techniques nor the third technique that we describe next, provides necessarily a tight bound.

The third lower bound method that we consider is the *biclique edge cover technique* introduced by Gruber and Holzer [7]. Let $G = (X, Y, E)$ be a bipartite graph, with two sets of vertices X and Y, and the set of edges $E \subseteq X \times Y$. A set $C = \{H_0, H_1, \ldots\}$ of bipartite subgraphs of G is an *edge cover* of G if every edge $e \in E$ is an edge of some H_i. An edge cover C of G is a *biclique edge cover* if every H_i is a *biclique*, that is, if $H_i = (X_i, Y_i, E_i)$ with $E_i = X_i \times Y_i$. The *bipartite dimension* of G, denoted by $d(G)$, is the size of the smallest biclique edge cover of G if it exists and is infinite otherwise.

Gruber and Holzer [7] associated to any language $L \subseteq \Sigma^*$ and sets $X, Y \subseteq \Sigma^*$, a bipartite graph $G = (X, Y, E_L)$, where for $x \in X$ and $y \in Y$, $(x, y) \in E_L$ if and only if $xy \in L$. They introduced the biclique edge cover technique by the following theorem:

Theorem 2. *Let $L \subseteq \Sigma^*$ be a regular language, and suppose there exists a bipartite graph $G = (X, Y, E_L)$ with $X, Y \subseteq \Sigma^*$ for L. Then any NFA accepting L has at least $d(G)$ states.*

4 Quotient-Atom Graph and Matrix of a Language

Gruber and Holzer [7] defined a canonical graph, the *dependency graph* of a language L to be the bipartite graph $G_L = (X, Y, E_L)$, where X is the set of the Nerode right congruence classes of L, and Y is the set of the left congruence classes of L, and $([x]_L, {}_L[y]) \in E_L$ if and only if $xy \in L$.

Let L be a regular language. Let $K = \{K_0, \ldots, K_{n-1}\}$ be the set of quotients of L, and let $A = \{A_0, \ldots, A_{m-1}\}$ be the set of atoms of L. Since the classes of the Nerode equivalence of L correspond to the left quotients of L, and the classes of the left congruence of L are the atoms of L, we can define the dependency graph G_L of L in terms of quotients and atoms of L. To see this, we will show that the following proposition holds:

Proposition 1. *For any $x, y \in \Sigma^*$, $xy \in L$ if and only if $A_j \subseteq K_i$, where $K_i = x^{-1}L$ and $y \in A_j$.*

Proof. Let $x \in \Sigma^*$, and let $K_i = x^{-1}L$. By definition, $x^{-1}L = \{v \in \Sigma^* \mid xv \in L\}$. That is, for any $y \in \Sigma^*$, $xy \in L$ if and only if $y \in x^{-1}L$. Since the atoms of L partition Σ^*, we know that for every $y \in \Sigma^*$ there is exactly one atom A_j of L such that $y \in A_j$. Because every quotient of L is a union of atoms, we get that $y \in x^{-1}L$ if and only if $A_j \subseteq x^{-1}L$. Thus, $xy \in L$ if and only if $A_j \subseteq K_i$. □

By Proposition 1, we observe that the dependency graph of L can be expressed as the bipartite graph $G_L = (K, A, E_L)$, with $(K_i, A_j) \in E_L$ if and only if $A_j \subseteq K_i$. With this interpretation of the dependency graph, we can call it the *quotient-atom graph* of the language.

Based on [7], maximal fooling sets and extended fooling sets, as well as a smallest biclique edge cover for the language, can be found by inspecting the graph G_L. Especially, by [7] the bipartite dimension of the graph $G = (\Sigma^*, \Sigma^*, E_L)$ associated with L is equal to the bipartite dimension of G_L. This bipartite dimension is also called the bipartite dimension of L. Then the biclique edge cover technique can be presented by the following theorem:

Theorem 3. *Let $L \subseteq \Sigma^*$ be a regular language, and let the quotient-atom graph of L be $G_L = (K, A, E_L)$, with $(K_i, A_j) \in E_L$ if and only if $A_j \subseteq K_i$. Then any NFA accepting L has at least $d(G_L)$ states.*

Also, the fooling set technique and the extended fooling set technique can be expressed as the first and the second case, respectively, of the following theorem:

Theorem 4. *Let $L \subseteq \Sigma^*$ be a regular language, and suppose there exists a set of quotient-atom pairs $P = \{(K_i, A_i) \mid 0 \leqslant i \leqslant p-1\}$ such that either*

1. *(a) $A_i \subseteq K_i$ for $0 \leqslant i \leqslant p-1$,*
   (b) $A_i \not\subseteq K_j$ for $0 \leqslant i, j \leqslant p-1$, and $i \neq j$,
   or
2. *(a) $A_i \subseteq K_i$ for $0 \leqslant i \leqslant p-1$,*
   (b) $A_i \not\subseteq K_j$ or $A_j \not\subseteq K_i$ for $0 \leqslant i, j \leqslant p-1$, and $i \neq j$

holds. Then any NFA accepting L has at least p states.

Similarly to the classical definition of fooling sets, the set P satisfying the conditions (a) and (b) in case 1 of Theorem 4 can be called a fooling set in terms of quotients and atoms of L, in case 2 it is an extended fooling set of L.

It was pointed out in [7] and also discussed in [6] that the dependency graph of a language was implicitly defined already in the classical theory of NFA minimization by Kameda and Weiner [10]. They used the states of the minimal DFAs for a language L and its reverse L^R, to form a matrix, and based on the grids in this matrix, a minimal NFA was found.

The Kameda-Weiner method was reinterpreted recently in terms of quotients and atoms [17], and it was shown that Kameda-Weiner matrix can be viewed as the *quotient-atom matrix*, with the rows of the matrix corresponding to non-empty quotients of L and columns, to positive atoms of L. Then an (i, j) entry of the matrix is 1 if quotient K_i contains atom A_j as a subset, and 0 otherwise. Any grid $g = P \times R$ of this matrix is a direct product of a subset P of quotients with a subset R of atoms, such that every atom in R is a subset of every quotient in P. A grid $g = P \times R$ is *maximal* if for any grid $g' = P' \times R'$ such that $P \subseteq P'$ and $R \subseteq R'$, it holds that $P = P'$ and $R = R'$. A *cover* C of the matrix is a set $C = \{g_0, \dots, g_{k-1}\}$ of grids, such that every 1-entry (K_i, A_j) belongs to some grid g_i in C. A minimal cover has the minimal number of grids. Based on any grid cover C of the quotient-atom matrix, the Kameda-Weiner method constructs an NFA $\mathcal{N}_C$ which may or may not accept the language L. A cover C is called *legal* if $L(\mathcal{N}_C) = L$. To find a minimal NFA of a language L, the covers of the quotient-atom matrix of L are tested in the order of increasing size to see if they are legal. The first legal NFA is a minimal one.

It is easy to see that the quotient-atom matrix is another representation of the quotient-atom graph of the language, where the empty quotient and the negative atom (if they exist) have been removed, and with 1-entries of the matrix corresponding to the edges of the graph. For any grid $g = P \times R$ of the matrix, there is a corresponding bipartite graph $G = (P, R, E)$ with $E = P \times R$, that is, a biclique. Therefore, given any grid cover of the quotient-atom matrix, the set of corresponding bicliques forms a biclique edge cover of the quotient-atom graph.

5 Prime Quotients and Prime Atoms

Let L be a regular language, $K = \{K_0, \dots, K_{n-1}\}$ be the set of quotients, and $A = \{A_0, \dots, A_{m-1}\}$ be the set of atoms of L. A non-empty quotient K_i is *prime* if K_i is not a union of other quotients [4].

We know by the definition of an atom that any atom A_j can be presented as an intersection $A_j = \bigcap_{i \in S_j} K_i \cap \bigcap_{i \in \overline{S_j}} \overline{K_i}$, where $S_j \subseteq \{0, \dots, n-1\}$ and $\overline{S_j} = \{0, \dots, n-1\} \backslash S_j$. Thus, for an atom A_j, there is a corresponding set $\{K_i \mid i \in S_j\}$ of uncomplemented quotients in the intersection representing A_j, or equivalently, the set $\{K_i \mid A_j \subseteq K_i\}$. We say that any positive atom A_j is *prime* if the set of uncomplemented quotients in the intersection representing A_j is not a union of such sets of quotients corresponding to other atoms. Duality between the definitions of a prime quotient and a prime atom becomes more evident if we consider the quotient-atom matrix of L. Namely, prime quotients correspond to the rows of the quotient-atom matrix which are not unions of other rows, and prime atoms correspond to the columns of the matrix which are not unions of other columns.

We now consider a submatrix of the quotient-atom matrix, consisting of the rows and columns which correspond to the prime quotients and prime atoms, respectively. We call this matrix the *prime quotient-atom matrix*. Similarly, we can form a subgraph of the quotient-atom graph, with prime quotients and prime atoms as sets of vertices and corresponding edges between these vertices. We call this subgraph the *prime quotient-atom graph*.

Proposition 2. *Let $C = \{g_0, \dots, g_{k-1}\}$ be a minimal cover of the quotient-atom matrix, with $g_i = P_i \times R_i$ for $i = 0, \dots, k-1$. For every grid $g_i = P_i \times R_i$ in C, there is some prime quotient in P_i and some prime atom in R_i.*

Proof. Let $C = \{g_0, \dots, g_{k-1}\}$ be a minimal cover of the quotient-atom matrix, with $g_i = P_i \times R_i$ for $i = 0, \dots, k-1$. Suppose that there is some grid $g_i = P_i \times R_i$ in C, such that every quotient in P_i is not prime. Let $K_l \in P_i$ be any such quotient. Then it is easy to see that K_l can be covered by vertically extending those grids in C which involve prime quotients that are subsets of K_l. That is, for every prime quotient $K_p \subseteq K_l$, we replace any grid $g_h = P_h \times R_h$ such that $K_p \in P_h$, by the grid $g'_h = (P_h \cup \{K_l\}) \times R_h$. In this way, all entries of the grid g_i will finally also belong to some other (modified) grid in C, implying that we could remove g_i from C. Thus, C is not a minimal cover, a contradiction. A similar reasoning can be applied for the set R_i of atoms. □

Proposition 3. *There is a one-to-one correspondence between the sets of minimal covers of the quotient-atom matrix and the prime quotient-atom matrix, consisting of maximal grids.*

Proof. Let $C = \{g_0, \ldots, g_{k-1}\}$ be a minimal cover of the quotient-atom matrix consisting of maximal grids. By Proposition 2, every grid g_i in C involves some prime quotient and prime atom. Therefore, for every grid $g_i = P_i \times R_i$ in C, there is a corresponding grid $g'_i = P'_i \times R'_i$ of the prime quotient-atom matrix, where P'_i is the set of prime quotients in P_i and R'_i is the set of prime atoms in R_i, both P'_i and R'_i being non-empty. Clearly, the set $C' = \{g'_0, \ldots, g'_{k-1}\}$ is a grid cover of the prime quotient-atom matrix. We claim that C' is a minimal cover. Suppose that there is a cover C'' of the prime quotient-atom matrix consisting of fewer than k grids. Since any grid in C'' is also a grid of the quotient-atom matrix, it can be made maximal by possibly extending it horizontally and vertically. In this way, the quotient-atom matrix can be covered by the maximized versions of grids in C'', implying that C is not a minimal cover, a contradiction. Conversely, if we consider the set $C' = \{g'_0, \ldots, g'_{k-1}\}$ as the set of grids of the quotient-atom matrix, then by maximizing all grids g'_i, we obtain the original cover C.

Similarly, we can show that if $C' = \{g'_0, \ldots, g'_{k-1}\}$ is a minimal cover of the prime quotient-atom matrix, consisting of maximal grids, and if we consider these grids as grids of the full matrix, then by maximizing all grids g'_i, we get a minimal cover of the quotient-atom matrix. □

By Proposition 3, instead of looking for minimal covers of the quotient-atom matrix, one can search for minimal covers of the prime quotient-atom matrix. The same reasoning applies to searching for a minimal biclique edge cover of the quotient-atom graph and its prime version.

Let $K' \subseteq K$ be the set of prime quotients of L, and let $A' \subseteq A$ be the set of prime atoms of L. Then the biclique edge cover technique can be presented by the following theorem:

Theorem 5. *Let $L \subseteq \Sigma^*$ be a regular language, and let the prime quotient-atom graph of L be $G'_L = (K', A', E'_L)$, with $(K_i, A_j) \in E'_L$ if and only if $A_j \subseteq K_i$. Then any NFA accepting L has at least $d(G'_L)$ states, with $d(G'_L) = d(G_L)$.*

Next theorem shows that both of the fooling set techniques can also be expressed in terms of prime quotients and prime atoms:

Theorem 6. *If $P = \{(K_i, A_i) \mid 0 \leqslant i \leqslant p-1\}$ is a fooling set (an extended fooling set, respectively) for a regular language L, then there is a fooling set (an extended fooling set, respectively) $P' = \{(K'_i, A'_i) \mid 0 \leqslant i \leqslant p-1\}$ for L such that all K'_i's and A'_i's are prime.*

Proof. Let $L \subseteq \Sigma^*$ be a regular language, with a fooling set or an extended fooling set $P = \{(K_i, A_i) \mid 0 \leqslant i \leqslant p-1\}$. We show that every pair $(K_i, A_i) \in P$, where either K_i or A_i is not prime, can be replaced by a pair (K'_i, A'_i), such that both K'_i and A'_i are prime.

Consider any pair (K_i, A_i) in P. If K_i is not prime, then there is some prime quotient $K'_i \subseteq K_i$, such that $A_i \subseteq K'_i$. If P is a fooling set, then $A_j \not\subseteq K_i$ holds for every $j \neq i$, implying that $A_j \not\subseteq K'_i$ holds as well. If P is an extended fooling set, then either $A_j \not\subseteq K_i$ or $A_i \not\subseteq K_j$ holds for every $j \neq i$, implying that either

$A_j \not\subseteq K_i'$ or $A_i \not\subseteq K_j$ holds. We note that K_i' is not equal to any K_h, where $h \in \{0, \ldots, p-1\}$, because otherwise both $A_i \subseteq K_h$ and $A_h \subseteq K_i$ would hold for some $h \neq i$, implying that P could not be a (extended) fooling set. Thus we can replace (K_i, A_i) by (K_i', A_i) in P, and P will still be a fooling set, or an extended fooling set, respectively.

If A_i is not prime, then there is some prime atom A_i', such that $A_i' \subseteq K_i$. A similar reasoning as above will allow us to replace (K_i, A_i) by (K_i, A_i') in P, so that P remains to be a fooling set, or an extended fooling set, respectively. □

By Theorem 6, one can search for a fooling set or an extended fooling set for a language, looking at the prime quotient-atom matrix/graph, instead of the full version of the matrix/graph. Let a language L have n_p prime quotients and m_p prime atoms, and let $\min(n_p, m_p)$ denote a minimum of n_p and m_p. Clearly, the size of any fooling set or an extended fooling set for L is at most $\min(n_p, m_p)$. We note that the *canonical RFSA* [4] of L has n_p states, every state corresponding to some prime quotient of L, and symmetrically, the canonical RFSA of L^R has m_p states. Therefore, it is obvious that a minimal NFA of L (as well as of L^R) has at most $\min(n_p, m_p)$ states.

To conclude this section, we present simple necessary conditions for the prime quotient-atom matrix of L so that L has a fooling set or an extended fooling set of a certain size. As a corollary, upper bounds for the size of a fooling set and an extended fooling set for L are derived.

Proposition 4. *If L has a fooling set (an extended fooling set, respectively) of size p, then the prime quotient-atom matrix of L has at least $p(p-1)$ ($\frac{p(p-1)}{2}$, respectively) 0-entries.*

Proof. Let L have a fooling set of size p. Then by Theorem 6, there is a fooling set $P = \{(K_i, A_i) \mid 0 \leqslant i \leqslant p-1\}$, such that all K_i's and A_j's are prime. By Theorem 4, $A_i \not\subseteq K_j$ must hold for all $0 \leqslant i, j \leqslant p-1$, $i \neq j$. Therefore, for every pair of (K_i, A_i) and (K_j, A_j) such that $i \neq j$, both entries of the prime quotient-atom matrix corresponding to (K_i, A_j) and (K_j, A_i), must be 0. Since there are $\binom{p}{2} = \frac{p(p-1)}{2}$ such pairs, the total number of 0-entries in the matrix is at least $2\binom{p}{2} = p(p-1)$.

By a similar reasoning we get that if L has an extended fooling set of size p, then the prime quotient-atom matrix has at least $\frac{p(p-1)}{2}$ 0-entries. □

Corollary 1. *The size of a fooling set of L is at most $\frac{1+\sqrt{4r+1}}{2}$ and the size of an extended fooling set of L is at most $\frac{1+\sqrt{8r+1}}{2}$, where r is the number of 0-entries in the prime quotient-atom matrix of L.*

6 When Are the Lower Bounds Tight?

Lower bounds obtained by the fooling set techniques or the biclique edge cover technique are not necessarily tight. Denoting the maximal lower bounds obtained by the fooling set technique and the extended fooling set technique for L, by *fst*(L)

and $efst(L)$, respectively, the bipartite dimension of L by $d(L)$, and the *nondeterministic state complexity* of L, that is, the size of a minimal NFA of L, by $nsc(L)$, it is clear that the inequalities $fst(L) \leqslant efst(L) \leqslant d(L) \leqslant nsc(L)$ hold.

The subclass of regular languages for which the lower bound provided by the fooling set technique is tight, was characterized in [15]. Namely, it was shown that the fooling set technique can be tight for and only for languages accepted by a *biseparable* NFA defined in [11] as follows: a trim NFA $\mathcal{N} = (Q, \Sigma, \delta, I, F)$ is *separable* if for every state $q \in Q$ there is a word $u \in \Sigma^*$ such that $\delta(I, u) = \{q\}$, and $\mathcal{N}$ is *biseparable* if both $\mathcal{N}$ and $\mathcal{N}^R$ are separable.

We note that a partial result of the above characterization was presented in [6], where it was shown that tightness of the fooling set technique for a language implies that the language is biseparable.

It was also shown in [15] that the lower bound provided by the extended fooling set technique is tight for any language accepted by a *biresidual automaton (biRFSA)*, that is, an RFSA with its reverse automaton also being an RFSA. Such languages are called biRFSA languages. However, there are other languages for which the lower bound obtained by this technique is tight. We also note that a biseparable automaton is a special case of a biRFSA. Both of these automata and language classes were studied in [11], where it was shown that for a biRFSA language L, the canonical RFSA is a biRFSA and a minimal NFA, and the canonical RFSA of L^R is the reverse of the canonical RFSA of L.

A *factorization* of a language L is a pair (X, Y) of languages such that $XY \subseteq L$ and such that for any pair (X', Y') with $X \subseteq X'$ and $Y \subseteq Y'$, the equalities $X = X'$ and $Y = Y'$ hold.

We recall that there is a one-to-one correspondence between the atoms of L and the quotients of L^R (cf. the end of Sect. 2).

To show a relationship between biRFSAs and the prime quotients and prime atoms of a language L, we will make use of the notion of a *maximized atom* [16] which is defined for every atom A_i of L by $max(A_i) = \bigcap_{A_i \subseteq K_j} K_j$, where K_j's are the quotients of L, and the following result from [16]:

Proposition 5 ([16], Proposition 4, Part 2). *If A_i is an atom of a language L and Q_i is the corresponding quotient of L^R, then $(Q_i^R, max(A_i))$ is a factorization of L.*

Proposition 6. *A language L is a biRFSA language if and only if there is a one-to-one correspondence between the prime quotients K_i and the prime atoms A_i of L such that $K_i = max(A_i)$.*

Proof. Let L be a biRFSA language and let $\mathcal{C}$ be the canonical RFSA of L. Then $\mathcal{C}$ is a biRFSA such that for every state q_i of $\mathcal{C}$, the right language of q_i is some prime quotient K_i of L and the left language of q_i is the reverse of some prime quotient Q_i of L^R. Since by Proposition 5, $(Q_i^R, max(A_i))$ is a factorization of L, the equality $K_i = max(A_i)$ holds.

Conversely, if there is a one-to-one correspondence between the prime quotients K_i and the prime atoms A_i of L with $K_i = max(A_i)$, then by Proposition 5, (Q_i^R, K_i) is a factorization of L, implying that L is a biRFSA language. □

Since a biseparable automaton is a canonical biRFSA and because the fooling set technique is tight for and only for biseparable languages, we can state the following proposition as a consequence of Theorem 6:

Proposition 7. *The following statements are equivalent:*

1. *A language L is biseparable.*
2. *The fooling set technique is tight for L.*
3. *The prime quotient-atom matrix of L is the identity matrix (after ordering quotients and atoms appropriately).*

6.1 Languages with Maximal Reversal Complexity

In this subsection we consider an interesting subclass of biseparable languages. Let L be a regular language such that the minimal DFA of L has n states and the minimal DFA of L^R has 2^n states. Since it is well known that if the state complexity of a given language is n, then the state complexity of the reverse language is at most 2^n, L is a language of *maximal reversal complexity*. It is also known that L is a language with maximal number of atoms [3]. Such kind of languages have been studied in [13,14], however, a complete characterization of languages of maximal reversal complexity is still an interesting open problem.

Theorem 7. *If the state complexity of a language L is n, and the state complexity of L^R is 2^n, then L is biseparable.*

Proof. Indeed, if the minimal DFA of a language L has n states and the minimal DFA of L^R has 2^n states, then L has n quotients and 2^n atoms. All the quotients of L are prime, because for every quotient K_i there is an atom $\overline{K_0} \cap \cdots \cap \overline{K_{i-1}} \cap K_i \cap \overline{K_{i+1}} \cap \cdots \cap \overline{K_{n-1}}$ with only K_i uncomplemented and other quotients complemented. The corresponding set of atoms forms the set of prime atoms of L, and it is clear that every quotient of L contains exactly one prime atom as a subset. By Proposition 7, L is biseparable. □

By Proposition 7 and Theorem 7, the fooling set technique is tight for any language with maximal reversal complexity. We also note that since by [11], any biseparable NFA is a unique minimal NFA of a language, the minimal DFA of a language with maximal reversal complexity is a unique minimal NFA.

6.2 Unary Cyclic Languages

Let L be a regular language over a unary alphabet $\Sigma = \{a\}$, and let the minimal DFA of L be $\mathcal{D} = (Q, \Sigma, \delta, q_0, F)$ with a state set $Q = \{q_0, \ldots, q_{n-1}\}$ such that $\delta(q_i, a) = q_{i+1}$ for $i = 0, \ldots, n-2$, and $\delta(q_{n-1}, a) = q_0$. This kind of language is called a *unary cyclic* language. Minimal NFAs of unary cyclic languages were studied in [9], where also a lower bound for the size of an NFA of such a language was presented.

First, we note that any unary language L and its reverse L^R are the same languages. This fact implies that there is a one-to-one correspondence between the quotients and the atoms of a unary language, such that if we order the rows and columns of the quotient-atom matrix according to this correspondence, the matrix will be symmetric. More specifically, for example, we can use the order of rows corresponding to quotients, with the first row corresponding to $K_0 = L$, and the ith row corresponding to $K_{i-1} = a^{-1}K_{i-2}$, $i = 2, \ldots, n$, and the order of columns corresponding to a similar order of atoms, starting with the atom A_0 such that $\varepsilon \in A_0$, and using the ith column for the atom A_{i-1} such that $A_{i-2} \subseteq a^{-1}A_{i-1}$, $i = 2, \ldots, n$.

In the following we can assume that the quotient-atom matrix is symmetric, with the rows and columns ordered as described above. We state some easily verified properties of unary cyclic languages:

Proposition 8. *Let L be a unary cyclic language. The following statements hold:*

1. *The quotient-atom matrix of L and its prime version are the same matrices.*
2. *Every row and column of the quotient-atom matrix of L has k 1-entries and $n-k$ 0-entries, where n is the number of quotients and k is the number of final quotients of L.*

Let L be a unary cyclic language with the minimal DFA $\mathcal{D} = (Q, \Sigma, \delta, q_0, F)$ as described above. The following statement holds:

Proposition 9. *If there is a final state $q_i \in F$ of $\mathcal{D}$ such that for every $q_j \in F$ with $j \neq i$, the state $q_{(2i-j) \bmod n}$ is not final, then L has an extended fooling set of size n.*

Proof. Let there be a state $q_i \in F$ such that for every $q_j \in F$ with $j \neq i$, $q_{(2i-j) \bmod n} \in Q \setminus F$. We claim that the set $P = \{(K_k, A_l) \mid (k+l) \bmod n = i\} = \{(K_0, A_i), (K_1, A_{i-1}), \ldots, (K_i, A_0)\} \cup \{(K_{i+1}, A_{n-1}), \ldots, (K_{n-1}, A_{i+1})\}$ is an extended fooling set for L. Indeed, it is not difficult to see that because $q_i \in F$, the inclusions $A_i \subseteq K_0$, $A_{i-1} \subseteq K_1$, and other similar inclusions hold for all quotient-atom pairs in P. We can also notice that since for every final state q_j with $j \neq i$, the state $q_{(2i-j) \bmod n}$ is not final, for any two non-equal quotient-atom pairs $(K_{k_1}, A_{l_1}), (K_{k_2}, A_{l_2}) \in P$, either $A_{l_1} \not\subseteq K_{k_2}$ or $A_{l_2} \not\subseteq K_{k_1}$ must hold. Thus, P is an extended fooling set. □

Remark 1. We can use Proposition 9 to show that the bound for the size of an extended fooling set given by Corollary 1 is tight. Indeed, let $\mathcal{D} = (Q, \Sigma, \delta, q_0, F)$ be the minimal DFA of a unary cyclic language L with $Q = \{q_0, \ldots, q_{n-1}\}$, where n is odd, and with $F = \{q_0, \ldots, q_{(n-1)/2}\}$. Using $i = 0$ in Proposition 9, we get that L has an extended fooling set of size n. By Corollary 1, the size of an extended fooling set of L is at most $\frac{1+\sqrt{8n(n-1)/2+1}}{2} = n$.

We note that if the condition of Proposition 9 holds for a unary cyclic language L, then the extended fooling set technique is tight for L. Consequently, the minimal DFA $\mathcal{D}$ of L is a minimal NFA for L.

Proposition 10. *If a unary cyclic language L with n quotients has an extended fooling set of size n, then L has at most $\lceil \frac{n}{2} \rceil$ final quotients.*

Proof. Follows from Propositions 4 and 8. □

References

1. Birget, J.C.: Intersection and union of regular languages and state complexity. Inf. Process. Lett. **43**, 185–190 (1992)
2. Brzozowski, J., Davies, S.: Quotient complexities of atoms in regular ideal languages. Acta Cybernetica **22**(2), 293–311 (2015)
3. Brzozowski, J., Tamm, H.: Theory of átomata. Theoret. Comput. Sci. **539**, 13–27 (2014)
4. Denis, F., Lemay, A., Terlutte, A.: Residual finite state automata. Fundamenta Informaticae **51**, 339–368 (2002)
5. Glaister, I., Shallit, J.: A lower bound technique for the size of nondeterministic finite automata. Inf. Process. Lett. **59**, 75–77 (1996)
6. Gruber, H.: On the descriptional and algorithmic complexity of regular languages. Ph.D. thesis, Gießener dissertation, Fachbereich Mathematik und Informatik, Physik, Geographie, Justus-Liebig-Universität Gießen (D26) (2009)
7. Gruber, H., Holzer, M.: Finding lower bounds for nondeterministic state complexity is hard. In: Ibarra, O.H., Dang, Z. (eds.) DLT 2006. LNCS, vol. 4036, pp. 363–374. Springer, Heidelberg (2006). doi:10.1007/11779148_33
8. Iván, S.: Complexity of atoms, combinatorially. Inf. Process. Lett. **116**, 356–360 (2016)
9. Jiang, T., McDowell, E., Ravikumar, B.: The structure and complexity of minimal NFA's over a unary alphabet. Int. J. Found. Comput. Sci. **2**(2), 163–182 (1991)
10. Kameda, T., Weiner, P.: On the state minimization of nondeterministic finite automata. IEEE Trans. Comput. **C–19**(7), 617–627 (1970)
11. Latteux, M., Roos, Y., Terlutte, A.: Minimal NFA and biRFSA languages. RAIRO - Theoret. Inform. Appl. **43**(2), 221–237 (2009)
12. Nerode, A.: Linear automaton transformations. Proc. Am. Math. Soc. **9**, 541–544 (1958)
13. Salomaa, A., Wood, D., Yu, S.: On the state complexity of reversals of regular languages. Theoret. Comput. Sci. **320**, 315–329 (2004)
14. Salomaa, A.: Mirror images and schemes for the maximal complexity of nondeterminism. Fundamenta Informaticae **116**, 237–249 (2012)
15. Tamm, H.: Some minimality results on biresidual and biseparable automata. In: Dediu, A.-H., Fernau, H., Martín-Vide, C. (eds.) LATA 2010. LNCS, vol. 6031, pp. 573–584. Springer, Heidelberg (2010). doi:10.1007/978-3-642-13089-2_48
16. Tamm, H.: Generalization of the double-reversal method of finding a canonical residual finite state automaton. In: Shallit, J., Okhotin, A. (eds.) DCFS 2015. LNCS, vol. 9118, pp. 268–279. Springer, Heidelberg (2015). doi:10.1007/978-3-319-19225-3_23
17. Tamm, H.: New interpretation and generalization of the Kameda-Weiner method. In: 43rd International Colloquium on Automata, Languages, and Programming (ICALP 2016). Leibniz International Proceedings in Informatics (LIPIcs), vol. 55, pp. 116:1–116:12. Schloss Dagstuhl-Leibniz-Zentrum für Informatik, Dagstuhl (2016)

Grammars, Languages, and Parsing

Linear Parsing Expression Grammars

Nariyoshi Chida(✉) and Kimio Kuramitsu

Yokohama National University, Yokohama, Japan
nariyoshi-chida-pg@ynu.jp, kimio@ynu.ac.jp

Abstract. PEGs were formalized by Ford in 2004, and have several pragmatic operators (such as ordered choice and unlimited lookahead) for better expressing modern programming language syntax. Since these operators are not explicitly defined in the classic formal language theory, it is significant and still challenging to argue PEGs' expressiveness in the context of formal language theory. Since PEGs are relatively new, there are several unsolved problems. One of the problems is revealing a subclass of PEGs that is equivalent to DFAs. This allows application of some techniques from the theory of regular grammar to PEGs. In this paper, we define Linear PEGs (LPEGs), a subclass of PEGs that is equivalent to DFAs. Surprisingly, LPEGs are formalized by only excluding some patterns of recursive nonterminal in PEGs, and include the full set of ordered choice, unlimited lookahead, and greedy repetition, which are characteristic of PEGs. Although the conversion judgement of parsing expressions into DFAs is undecidable in general, the formalism of LPEGs allows for a syntactical judgement of parsing expressions.

Keywords: Parsing expression grammars · Boolean finite automata · Packrat parsing

1 Introduction

Deterministic finite automata (DFAs) are a simple and fundamental theory in the classic formal language, which allows pattern matching on the input without backtracking. This positive aspect is applied to the implementation of many regular expression engines such as Google RE2 [8] and grep leading to significantly improved performance.

Similarly, the DFA nature is used for faster parsing. For example, a partial conversion of *context-free grammars* (CFGs) into DFAs is studied with ANTLR3/4 by Parr *et al.* [15,16]. In this study, Parr *et al.* achieve better performance of a parser based on CFG by using the conversion. Concretely, the parser decides a nonterminal that should be expanded by using the DFA. That is, DFA conversions remove backtracking while parsing.

In this way, DFAs are used for faster parsing. To the best of our knowledge, however, DFAs are not used for parsing a *parsing expression grammar* (PEG) [7] yet. PEGs are a relatively new and popular foundation for describing syntax, formalized by Ford in 2004. PEGs look very similar to some of the EBNFs or

F. Drewes et al. (Eds.): LATA 2017, LNCS 10168, pp. 275–286, 2017.
DOI: 10.1007/978-3-319-53733-7_20

CFG-based grammar specifications, but differ significantly in that they have *unlimited lookahead* with syntactic predicates and deterministic behaviors with greedy repetition and prioritized choice. Due to these extended operators, PEGs can recognize highly nested languages such as $\{a^n\ b^n\ c^n \mid n > 0\}$, which is not possible in a CFG.

These extended operators raise an interesting and open question on the connection to the formal language theory. In particular, we have expected that a partial DFA conversion brings better performance benefits to the PEG-based parser generation as well as Parr *et al.* However, parsing expressions are obviously more expressive than DFAs, due to recursion which does not appear in regular expressions. Therefore, we require a subclass of PEGs that is equivalent to DFAs for applying DFA techniques to PEGs.

The main contribution of this paper is that we reveal a subclass of PEGs that is equivalent to DFAs. We formalize the subclass as *linear parsing expression grammars* (LPEGs). Surprisingly, LPEGs are formalized by excluding only some patterns of recursive nonterminal in PEGs, and include the full set of prioritized choice, unlimited lookahead, and greedy repetition, which are unique to PEGs. Furthermore, the formalism of LPEGs allows a partial conversion of a PEG into DFAs. Since converting into DFAs can eliminate backtracking, the partial conversion would lead to further optimization of the parser generator.

The rest of this paper proceeds as follows. Section 2 describes the formalism of LPEGs and shows the relationship between LPEGs and PEGs. Section 3 shows a regularity of LPEGs. Section 4 briefly reviews related work. Section 5 is the conclusion.

2 Linear PEG

In this section, we describe the formalism of *linear parsing expression grammars* (LPEGs). LPEGs are a subclass of PEGs equivalent to DFAs, and LPEGs are formalized by excluding patterns of recursive nonterminals that are followed by expressions. By the exclusion, the syntax of an LPEG is limited to right-linear. Thus, we can simply consider an LPEG as a PEG where the syntax is right-linear.

To begin with, we describe PEG operators in Sect. 2.1. Then, we show the formalism of LPEGs in Sect. 2.2. Finally, we describe language properties in Sect. 2.3.

2.1 PEG Operators

Table 1 shows the summary of PEG operators used throughout this paper.

The string 'abc' exactly matches the same input, while [abc] matches one of these terminals. The . operator matches any single terminal. The $e?$, $e*$, and $e+$ expressions behave as in common regular expressions, except that they are greedy and match until the longest position. The $e_1\ e_2$ attempts two expressions e_1 and e_2 sequentially, backtracking the starting position if either expression

Table 1. PEG operators

PEG	Type	Proc.	Description
' '	Primary	5	Matches text
[]	Primary	5	Matches character class
.	Primary	5	Any character
A	Primary	5	Non-terminal application
(e)	Primary	5	Grouping
$e?$	Unary suffix	4	Option
$e*$	Unary suffix	4	Zero-or-more repetitions
$e+$	Unary suffix	4	One-or-more repetitions
$\&e$	Unary prefix	3	And-predicate
$!e$	Unary prefix	3	Not-predicate
$e_1 e_2$	Binary	2	Sequence
e_1/e_2	Binary	1	Prioritized choice

fails. The choice e_1/e_2 first attempts e_1 and then attempts e_2 if e_1 fails. The expression $\&e$ attempts e without any terminal consuming. The expression $!e$ fails if e succeeds, but succeeds if e fails.

We consider the any character . expression to be a choice of all single terminals $(a/b/\dots/c)$ in Σ. As long as any special cases are not noted, we treat the any character as a syntax sugar of such a terminal choice.

Likewise, many convenient notations used in PEGs such as character class, option, and one or more repetition are treated as syntax sugars:

$$
\begin{array}{lll}
[abc] & = a/b/c & \text{character class} \\
e^+ & = ee^* & \text{one or more repetition} \\
e? & = e/\varepsilon & \text{option} \\
\&e & = !!e & \text{and-predicate}
\end{array}
$$

2.2 Definition of LPEGs

Definition 1. *A linear parsing expression grammar (LPEG) is defined by a 4-tuple $G = (N_G, \Sigma, P_G, e_s)$, where N_G is a finite set of nonterminals, Σ is a finite set of terminals, P_G is a finite set of production rules, and e_s is a linear parsing expression termed the start expression. A linear parsing expression e is a parsing expression with the syntax according to BNF shown in Fig. 1. p in Fig. 1 is a nonterminal-free parsing expression (n-free parsing expression). An n-free parsing expression p is a parsing expression such that the expression doesn't contain nonterminals. Each rule in P_G is a mapping from a nonterminal $A \in N_G$ to a linear parsing expression e. We write $P_G(A)$ to denote an associated expression e such that $A \leftarrow e \in P_G$.*

$$
\begin{array}{rcll}
e & ::= & p & \\
& | & p\ A & \\
& | & p\ e & \\
& | & e/e & \\
& | & !e\ e & \\
p & ::= & \varepsilon & \text{empty} \\
& | & a & \text{character} \\
& | & . & \text{any character} \\
& | & p\ p & \text{sequence} \\
& | & p/p & \text{prioritized choice} \\
& | & p* & \text{zero or more repetition} \\
& | & !p & \text{not-predicate}
\end{array}
$$

Fig. 1. Syntax of a linear parsing expression

We show two examples of an LPEG and an example of a PEG but not an LPEG.

Example 2. $G = (\{A, B\}, \{a, b, c\}, \{A \leftarrow aA/bB/c, B \leftarrow aB/bA/c\}, A)$ is an LPEG.

Example 3. $G = (\{A\}, \{a, b\}, \{A \leftarrow !(aA)aA/b\}, A)$ is an LPEG.

Example 4. $G = (\{A, B\}, \{a, b\}, \{A \leftarrow aAa/B*, B \leftarrow aB/b\}, A)$ is not an LPEG. Note that aAa and $B*$ are not derived from the above syntax.

All subsequent use of the unqualified term "grammar" refers specifically to linear parsing expression grammars as defined here, and the unqualified term "expression" refers to linear parsing expressions. We use the variables $a, b, c \in \Sigma$, $A, B, C \in N_G$, $x, y, z \in \Sigma^*$, and e for linear parsing expressions.

2.3 Language Properties

In this section, we define a language recognized by LPEGs. We use a function *consume* to define the language. $consume(e, x) = y$ denotes that the expression e succeeds on the input string x and consumes y. $consume(e, x) = f$ denotes that the expression e fails on the input string x.

Definition 5. *Let $G = (N_G, \Sigma, P_G, e_s)$ be an LPEG, let e be an expression. The language generated by e is a set of all strings over Σ:*

$$L_G(e) = \{x \mid x \in \Sigma^*,\ y \text{ is a prefix of } x,\ consume(e, x) = y\}.$$

Definition 6. *Let $G = (N_G, \Sigma, P_G, e_s)$ be an LPEG. The language generated by a grammar G is a set of all strings over Σ:*

$$L(G) = L_G(e_s).$$

3 Regularity

In this section, we prove that LPEGs are a class that is equivalent to DFAs. To prove this, we show that for any LPEG G there exists a DFA D such that $L(G) = L(D)$ and for any DFA D there exists an LPEG G such that $L(D) = L(G)$. We show the former in Sect. 3.1 and the latter in Sect. 3.2.

3.1 From LPEGs to DFAs

We show that for any LPEG G there exists a DFA D such that $L(G) = L(D)$. This can be proved by translating LPEGs into *boolean finite automata* (BFAs) [4].

A BFA is a generalized *nondeterministic finite automaton* (NFA). The difference between NFAs and BFAs is a representation of a state under transition. The state under transition on NFAs can be represented as a boolean function consisting of logical OR and boolean variables. On the other hand, the state under transition on BFAs can be represented as a boolean function consisting of logical AND, logical OR, logical NOT, constant values (i.e. $true$ and $false$), and boolean variables.

There are two reasons for using BFAs. One is to handle not-predicates. We can represent these predicates as a boolean function by using logical AND and logical NOT. Another reason is that BFAs can be converted into DFAs ([4], Theorem 2). Thus, LPEGs can be converted into DFAs if we can convert LPEGs into BFAs.

In the next section we describe basic definitions and notations of BFAs. In Sect. 3.1, we show that LPEGs can be converted into BFAs.

Boolean Finite Automata

Definition 7. *A* boolean finite automaton *(BFA) is a 5-tuple* $B = (Q, \Sigma, \delta, f^0, F)$. $Q = \{q_1, q_2, \ldots, q_n\}$ *is a finite non-empty set of states.* Σ *is a finite set of terminals.* $\delta : Q \times \Sigma \rightarrow V_Q$ *is a transition function that maps a state and a terminal into a boolean function of boolean variables that correspond to the states* $q_1, q_2, \ldots, q_n$ *in the set of boolean functions* V_Q. $f^0 \in V_Q$ *is an initial boolean function.* F *is a finite set of accepting states. We use* q_i *as a boolean variable that corresponds to a state* $q_i \in Q$.

Let f be a boolean function in V_Q. The transition function δ is extended to $V_Q \times \Sigma^*$ as follows:

$$\begin{aligned}
\delta(f, \epsilon) &= f \\
\delta(f, a) &= f(\delta(q_1, a), \ldots, \delta(q_n, a)) \\
\delta(f, aw) &= \delta(\delta(f, a), w)
\end{aligned}$$

A language accepted by a BFA is defined as follows:

Definition 8. *Let* B *be a BFA and* $x \in \Sigma^*$. $x \in L(B)$ *iff* $\delta(f^0, x)(c_1, \ldots, c_n) = true$, *where* $c_i = true$ *if* $q_i \in F$, *otherwise* $false$.

From LPEGs to BFAs. We show a conversion from an LPEG into a BFA. The conversion consists of three steps. In the first step, we modify an LPEG in order to simplify the conversion. In the second step, we convert a modified LPEG into a BFA. However, the BFA is incomplete in this step, since the conversion handles nonterminals as temporary boolean variables to avoid an infinite loop by recursions. In the final step, we replace the temporary boolean variables in a BFA with initial functions of the nonterminals.

First, we modify an LPEG by applying a modification function C_G shown in Definition 9. By applying the modification, new production rules for nonterminals in not-predicates are added to the LPEG. We apply this modification to LPEGs, because we consider a nonterminal A in a not-predicate and a nonterminal A that is not in a not-predicate as distinct.

Definition 9. *Let* $G = (N_G, \Sigma, P_G, e_s)$ *be an LPEG.* $C_G(G) = (N_G \cup N_{G'}, \Sigma, P_{G_1} \cup P_{G_2}, e_{s'})$, *where* $P_{G_1} = \{A \leftarrow C_n(e_A) \mid e_A \in P_G\}$, $P_{G_2} = \{A' \leftarrow e_{A'} \mid e_{A'} = copy(e_A), e_A \in P_G\}$, $N_{G'} = \{A' \mid e_{A'} \in P_{G_2}\}$, $e_{s'} = C_n(e_s)$.

In the modification function, we use an auxiliary function C_n. C_n is a function for modification of a production rule. We show the definition of C_n in Definition 10. In the following definition, we use a function *copy*. $copy(e) = e'$ denotes that a nonterminal A is renamed as A' if the nonterminal A is not already A' and the other expressions are same. We assume that there does not exist A' in an LPEG before the modification.

For example, $copy(aA/!(bB)b/c) = aA'/!(bB')b/c$ and $copy(copy(!(aA))) = copy(!(aA')) = !(aA')$.

Definition 10.

$$\begin{aligned} C_n(p) &= p \\ C_n(p\ A) &= p\ A \\ C_n(p\ e) &= p\ C_n(e) \\ C_n(e/e) &= C_n(e)/C_n(e) \\ C_n(!e\ e) &= !(copy(e))\ C_n(e) \end{aligned}$$

We show an example of the modification as follows:

Example 11. $G = (\{A, B\}, \{a, b, c, d\}, \{A \leftarrow !(aA/bB/c)d, B \leftarrow aB/b\}, A)$ is an LPEG. Then, $C_G(G) = (\{A, B, A', B'\}, \{a, b, c, d\}, P_{G_1} \cup P_{G_2}, A)$, where P_{G_1} consists of the following rules:

$$\begin{aligned} A &\leftarrow !(aA'/bB'/c)d \\ B &\leftarrow aB/b \end{aligned}$$

P_{G_2} consists of the following rules:

$$\begin{aligned} A' &\leftarrow !(aA'/bB'/c)d \\ B' &\leftarrow aB'/b \end{aligned}$$

Secondly, we describe the conversion from modified LPEGs to BFAs with temporary boolean variables. This is inspired by [13].

In this function, a set of accepting states is divided into two sets, F and P, in order to simplify the construction of BFAs. The set P is a set of accepting states for not-predicates. We assume that the names of boolean variables are distinct in the conversion. We write a temporary boolean variable of a nonterminal A as f_{tmp_A}. A function $\phi(f_1, f_2, F)$ converts the boolean function f_1 by replacing a boolean variable s in f_1 with $s \vee f_2$ if $s \in F$. For example, let $f_1 = (q_1 \wedge q_2) \vee q_3$, $f_2 = q_4$ and $F = \{q_2, q_3\}$, where q_1, q_2, q_3 and q_4 are boolean variables. Then, $\phi(f_1, f_2, F) = (q_1 \wedge (q_2 \vee q_4)) \vee (q_3 \vee q_4)$. A function *copy* used in $T_B(!e)$ is the same definition as in Definition 10. Note that the BFA converted by the following function accepts the full match of the expressions. A BFA that accepts the same language with the LPEG is written as $T_B(e_s\,.*)$.

$$
\begin{aligned}
T(G) &= (Q, \Sigma, \delta', f^0, F \cup P) \\
&\quad \textit{where} \quad (Q, \Sigma, \delta, f^0, F, P) = T_B(e_s) \\
&\quad \textit{and} \quad \delta' = \{((s, .), s) \mid s \in P\} \cup \delta \\
T_B(\epsilon) &= (\{s\}, \Sigma, \{\}, s, \{s\}, \{\}) \\
T_B(a) &= (\{s, t\}, \Sigma, \{((s, a), t)\}, s, \{t\}, \{\}) \\
T_B(!e) &= (Q \cup \{s\}, \Sigma, \delta, s \wedge \overline{f^0}, \{s\}, F \cup P) \\
&\quad \textit{where} \quad (Q, \Sigma, \delta, f^0, F, P) = T_B(\textit{copy}(e)) \\
T_B(e_1 e_2) &= (Q_1 \cup Q_2, \Sigma, \delta, \phi(f_1^0, f_2^0, F_1), F_2, P_1 \cup P_2) \\
&\quad \textit{where} \quad (Q_1, \Sigma, \delta_1, f_1^0, F_1, P_1) = T_B(e_1), \\
&\quad (Q_2, \Sigma, \delta_2, f_2^0, F_2, P_2) = T_B(e_2) \\
&\quad \textit{and} \quad \delta = \{((s, a), \phi(t, f_2^0, F_1)) \mid ((s, a), t) \in \delta_1\} \cup \delta_2 \\
T_B(e_1/e_2) &= T_B(e_1 \mid !e_1 e_2) \\
T_B(e_1 \mid e_2) &= (Q_1 \cup Q_2, \Sigma, \delta_1 \cup \delta_2, f_1^0 \vee f_2^0, F_1 \cup F_2, P_1 \cup P_2) \\
&\quad \textit{where} \quad (Q_1, \Sigma, \delta_1, f_1^0, F_1, P_1) = T_B(e_1) \\
&\quad \textit{and} \quad (Q_2, \Sigma, \delta_2, f_2^0, F_2, P_2) = T_B(e_2) \\
T_B(e*) &= T_B(e^{\star}\,!e) \\
T_B(e^{\star}) &= (Q \cup \{s\}, \Sigma, \delta', s \vee f^0, F \cup \{s\}, P) \\
&\quad \textit{where} \quad (Q, \Sigma, \delta, f^0, F, P) = T_B(e) \\
&\quad \textit{and} \quad \delta' = \{((s, a), \phi(t, f^0, F)) \mid ((s, a), t) \in \delta\} \\
T_B(A) &= \begin{cases} T_B(P_G(A)) \\ \texttt{(first time to apply the function to a nonterminal A)} \\ (\{\}, \Sigma, \{\}, f_{tmp_A}, \{\}, \{\}) \\ \texttt{(otherwise)} \end{cases}
\end{aligned}
$$

Basically, this conversion is based on Thompson's construction [17]. In this conversion, the construction of prioritized choices / and zero-or-more repetitions $*$ is reduced to the construction of alternations $\mid$ and zero-or-more repetitions $\star$ in a regular expression. We rewrite them precisely as follows:

$$e_1/e_2 \Rightarrow e_1 \mid\ !e_1e_2$$
$$e* \Rightarrow e^\star\,!e$$

$\alpha \Rightarrow \beta$ denotes rewriting α as β. For example, a/aa is rewritten as $a \mid (!a)aa$ and $a * a$ is rewritten as $a^\star\,(!a)a$.

In the rewriting of prioritized choices, the not-predicate $!e_1$ is added to the front of e_2. By the rewriting, e_2 does not match an input string when the input string matches e_1.

Furthermore, in the rewriting of zero-or-more repetitions, the not-predicate $!e$ is added to the back of $e^\star$. By this rewriting, we can eliminate the ambiguity of $e^\star$ and the repetition becomes a longest match.

The function T handles the nonterminals in the same way as a conversion from a right-linear grammar to an NFA [11]. In the conversion from a right-linear grammar to an NFA, a nonterminal is handled as an initial state of the NFA. In the same way, in the function T, a nonterminal is handled as an initial function of the BFA.

Finally, we replace temporary variables with the initial functions of the nonterminals. We show the replacement in the following example of conversion from an LPEG to a BFA.

Example 12. Let $G = (\{A\}, \{a, b\}, \{A \leftarrow aA/b\}, A)$ be an LPEG. The language of the LPEG $L(G) = \{a^ib \mid i \geq 0\}$.

First, we modify the LPEG G as follows: $G = C_G(G)$, where $C_G(G) = (\{A, A'\}, \{a, b\}, \{A \leftarrow aA/b, A' \leftarrow aA'/b\}, A)$.

Secondly, we convert the LPEG G to a BFA B with temporary boolean variables. As a result of the conversion, we get the BFA $B = (Q, \{a, b\}, \delta, q_0 \vee ((q_{11} \vee q_{12}) \wedge \overline{q_2}), \{q_{10}, q_{13}\})$, where δ is shown in Table 2. For simplicity, we consider transitions that are not in Table 2 return $false$.

Table 2. The transition function δ with temporary boolean variables

	$\delta(state, terminal)$	TERMINAL	
		a	b
STATE	q_0	$q_1 \vee f_{tmp_A}$	$false$
	q_2	$q_3 \vee (q_4 \vee ((q_8 \vee q_9) \wedge \overline{q_6}))$	$false$
	q_4	$q_5 \vee f_{tmp_{A'}}$	$false$
	q_6	$q_7 \vee f_{tmp_{A'}}$	$false$
	q_9	$false$	q_{10}
	q_{10}	q_{10}	q_{10}
	q_{12}	$false$	q_{13}

Finally, we replace temporary boolean variables with the initial functions. In this BFA, there are two temporary boolean variables, f_{tmp_A} and $f_{tmp_{A'}}$. f_{tmp_A} is replaced by $q_0 \vee ((q_{11} \vee q_{12}) \wedge \overline{q_2})$. $f_{tmp_{A'}}$ is replaced by $q_4 \vee ((q_8 \vee q_9) \wedge \overline{q_6})$. The transition function δ is shown in Table 3.

Table 3. The transition function δ

	$\delta(state, terminal)$	TERMINAL	
		a	b
STATE	q_0	$q_1 \vee q_0 \vee ((q_{11} \vee q_{12}) \wedge \overline{q_2})$	$false$
	q_2	$q_3 \vee (q_4 \vee ((q_8 \vee q_9) \wedge \overline{q_6}))$	$false$
	q_4	$q_5 \vee q_4 \vee ((q_8 \vee q_9) \wedge \overline{q_6})$	$false$
	q_6	$q_7 \vee q_4 \vee ((q_8 \vee q_9) \wedge \overline{q_6})$	$false$
	q_9	$false$	q_{10}
	q_{10}	q_{10}	q_{10}
	q_{12}	$false$	q_{13}

The BFA B accepts an input string b.

$$\begin{aligned}\delta(q_0 \vee ((q_{11} \vee q_{12}) \wedge \overline{q_2}), b) &= false \vee ((false \vee q_{13}) \wedge \overline{false}) \\ &= false \vee ((false \vee true) \wedge \overline{false}) \\ &= true\end{aligned}$$

In the same way, we can check that the BFA B rejects an input string a.

In order to define a function *consume* for BFAs, we define two evaluate function, $eval_F$ and $eval_P$. $eval_F$ takes a boolean function f and a set of accepting state F and returns a boolean function f' that replaced boolean variables $q_i \in F$ in f with $true$. For example, let $f = q_0 \wedge (q_1 \vee q_2)$ and $F = \{q_1\}$. Then $eval_F(f, F) = q_0 \wedge (true \vee q_2) = q_0 \wedge q_2$. $eval_P$ takes a boolean function f and a set of accepting state of not-predicates P and returns a boolean value that is a result of a replacement of a boolean variables $q_i \in P$ in f with $true$, otherwise $false$. For example, let $f = q_0 \wedge \overline{q_1}$ and $P = \{q_0\}$. Then, $eval_P(f, P) = true \wedge \overline{false} = true$.

We define a function *consume* for a BFA B. $consume(B, w) = x$ denotes that $eval_P(\delta(eval_F(\delta(f^0, x), F), y), P) = true$ for an input string $w = xyz$. $consume(B, w) = f$ if there is no such x.

Theorem 13. *Let* $G = (N_G, \Sigma, P_G, e_s)$ *be an LPEG modified by* C_G *in Definition 9. Let* $B = T((N_G, \Sigma, P_G, e_s\,.*))$ *and* B *has already replaced the temporary variables with initial functions. Then,* $L(G) = L(B)$.

Proof. The proof is by induction on the structure of linear parsing expression e. We assume that $T_B(e)$ is a BFA such that $consume(T_B(e), x) = consume(e, x)$, where $x \in \Sigma^*$.

Theorem 14. *For any LPEG* G *there exists a DFA* D *such that* $L(G) = L(D)$.

Proof. By Theorem 13, LPEGs can be converted into BFAs. BFAs can be converted into DFAs.

3.2 From a DFA to an LPEG

An arbitrary regular expression can be converted into a PEG [12,14]. In this section, we say that for any DFA D there exists an LPEG G such that $L(D) = L(G)$. To prove this, we show that a PEG converted from a regular expression by [12] is an LPEG, since DFAs can be converted into equivalent regular expressions [9].

Medeiros et al. studied the conversion and they showed the conversion function as a function Π [12]. The definition of the function Π is shown in Definition 15. The function $\Pi(r, G)$ takes a regular expression r and a continuation grammar $G = (N_G, \Sigma, P_G, e_s)$, and returns a PEG. The continuation grammar is defined by a PEG $G_0 = (\{\}, \Sigma, \{\}, \varepsilon)$ for the first application.

Definition 15 (in [12]).

$$
\begin{aligned}
\Pi(\epsilon, G) &= G\\
\Pi(a, G) &= (N_G, \Sigma, P_G, ae_s)\\
\Pi(r_1 r_2, G) &= \Pi(r_1, \Pi(r_2, G))\\
\Pi(r_1 \mid r_2, G) &= (N_G{}'', \Sigma, P_G{}'', e_s{}'/e_s{}'')\\
&\qquad \mathit{where} \quad (N_G{}'', \Sigma, P_G{}'', e_s{}'') = \Pi(r_2, (N_G{}', \Sigma, P_G{}', e_s))\\
&\qquad \mathit{and} \quad (N_G{}', \Sigma, P_G{}', e_s{}') = \Pi(r_1, G)\\
\Pi(r^\star, G) &= (N_G{}', \Sigma, P_G{}' \cup \{A \leftarrow e_s{}'/e_s\}, A) \ \mathit{with}\ A \notin N_G\\
&\qquad \mathit{and} \quad (N_G{}', \Sigma, P_G{}', e_s{}') = \Pi(r, (N_G \cup \{A\}, \Sigma, P_G, A))
\end{aligned}
$$

Theorem 16. *Let r be a regular expression and $\Pi(r, G_0) = G$. The PEG G is an LPEG.*

Proof. We assume that if G is an LPEG, then $\Pi(r, G)$ is also an LPEG. For any regular expression r, we check whether the assumption is correct. If so, $\Pi(r, G_0)$ is an LPEG since G_0 is obviously an LPEG.

1. Case $r = \epsilon$
   By induction hypothesis, G is an LPEG.
2. Case $r = a$
   By induction hypothesis, e_s is a linear parsing expression. Since $ae_s = pe$, (N_G, Σ, P_G, ae_s) is an LPEG.
3. Case $r = r_1 r_2$
   Since G is an LPEG, $\Pi(r_2, G)$ is an LPEG. Therefore, $\Pi(r_1, \Pi(r_2, G))$ is also an LPEG.
4. Case $r = r_1 \mid r_2$
   $\Pi(r_1, G)$ is an LPEG. Since e_s is a linear parsing expression, $\Pi(r_2, (N_G{}', \Sigma, P_G{}', e_s))$ is also an LPEG. Therefore, $e_s{}'$ and $e_s{}''$ are a linear parsing expression. Since $e_s{}'/e_s{}'' = e/e$, $(N_G{}'', \Sigma, P_G{}'', e_s{}'/e_s{}'')$ is an LPEG.
5. Case $r = r^\star$
   Since a nonterminal $A (A = pA)$ is a linear parsing expression, $(N_G \cup \{A\}, \Sigma, P_G, A)$ is an LPEG and $\Pi(r, (N_G \cup \{A\}, \Sigma, P_G, A))$ is also an LPEG. Since $e_s{}'/e_s = e/e$, $(N_G{}', \Sigma, P'_G \cup \{A \leftarrow e_s{}'/e_s\}, A)$ is an LPEG.

Hence, $\Pi(r, G_0)$ is an LPEG.

Theorem 17. *For any DFA D there exists an LPEG G such that $L(D) = L(G)$.*

Proof. A DFA D can be converted into a regular expression r. By Theorem 16, r can be converted into an LPEG.

Consequently, we derive the following theorem.

Theorem 18. *LPEGs are a class that is equivalent to DFAs.*

Proof. By Theorem 14, for any LPEG G there exists a DFA D such that $L(G) = L(D)$. In addition, by Theorem 17, for any DFA D there exists an LPEG G such that $L(D) = L(G)$. Hence, LPEGs are a class that is equivalent to DFAs.

4 Related Work

Birman and Ullman showed formalism of recognition schemes as TS and gTS [2,3]. TS and gTS were introduced in [1] as TDPL and GTDPL, respectively. A PEG is a development of GTDPL. In this paper, we showed a subclass of PEGs that is equivalent to DFAs, which would lead to more optimized PEG-based parser generator such as [10].

Morihata showed a translation of regular expression with positive and negative lookaheads into finite state automata [13]. He used a *boolean finite automata* (BFAs) [4], that is, *alternating finite automata* [5,6], to represent positive and negative lookaheads of regular expressions as finite automata. We showed that a PEG excluding nonterminals can be converted into an equivalent regular expression with positive and negative lookaheads. Therefore, these PEGs can be converted into a DFA by applying Morihata's translation. However, nonterminals were not covered. In this paper, we showed a translation to handle nonterminals on Morihata's translation.

5 Conclusion

In this study, we formalized a subclass of PEGs that is equivalent to DFAs. In the process of proving the equivalence of the class and DFAs, we showed the conversion from LPEGs into BFAs. Since BFAs can be converted into DFAs, we can convert these LPEGs into DFAs.

One of our motivations is to achieve speed up of runtime by processing a part of a PEG such that the part is regular by using DFAs. To achieve this, we have to check whether the part of a PEG is regular. However, this is undecidable. On the other hand, it is decidable whether a PEG is an LPEG. Thus, we can check whether the part of a PEG is an LPEG and convert the part into DFAs. Since DFAs eliminate backtracking, it would lead to further optimizations of the parser generator.

As a future study, we aim to propose an algorithm for detecting a part of a PEG such that backtracking becomes necessary.

References

1. Aho, A.V., Ullman, J.D.: The Theory of Parsing, Translation, and Compiling. Prentice-Hall Inc., Upper Saddle River (1972)
2. Birman, A.: The TMG recognition schema. Ph.D. thesis aAI7101582, Princeton, NJ, USA (1970)
3. Birman, A., Ullman, J.D.: Parsing algorithms with backtrack. Inf. Control **23**(1), 1–34 (1973). http://www.sciencedirect.com/science/article/pii/S0019995873908516
4. Brzozowski, J., Leiss, E.: On equations for regular languages, finite automata, and sequential networks. Theoret. Comput. Sci. **10**(1), 19–35 (1980). http://www.sciencedirect.com/science/article/pii/0304397580900699
5. Chandra, A.K., Kozen, D.C., Stockmeyer, L.J.: Alternation. J. ACM **28**(1), 114–133 (1981). http://doi.acm.org/10.1145/322234.322243
6. Fellah, A., Jürgensen, H., Yu, S.: Constructions for alternating finite automata. Int. J. Comput. Math. **35**(1–4), 117–132 (1990). http://dx.doi.org/10.1080/00207169008803893
7. Ford, B.: Parsing expression grammars: a recognition-based syntactic foundation. In: Proceedings of 31st ACM SIGPLAN-SIGACT Symposium on Principles of Programming Languages, pp. 111–122. ACM, New York (2004). http://doi.acm.org/10.1145/964001.964011
8. Google: Re2. https://github.com/google/re2
9. Hopcroft, J.E., Motwani, R., Ullman, J.D.: Introduction to Automata Theory, Languages, and Computation, 3rd edn. Addison-Wesley Longman Publishing Co., Inc., Boston (2006)
10. Kuramitsu, K.: Nez: practical open grammar language. In: Proceedings of 2016 ACM International Symposium on New Ideas, New Paradigms, and Reflections on Programming and Software, Onward! 2016, pp. 29–42. ACM, New York (2016). http://doi.acm.org/10.1145/2986012.2986019
11. Linz, P.: An Introduction to Formal Language and Automata. Jones and Bartlett Publishers Inc., USA (2006)
12. Medeiros, S., Mascarenhas, F., Ierusalimschy, R.: From regexes to parsing expression grammars. Sci. Comput. Program. Part A **93**, 3–18 (2014). http://www.sciencedirect.com/science/article/pii/S0167642312002171
13. Morihata, A.: Translation of regular expression with lookahead into finite state automaton. Comput. Softw. **29**(1), 1_147–1_158 (2012)
14. Oikawa, M., Ierusalimschy, R., Moura, A.L.D.: Converting regexes to parsing expression grammars
15. Parr, T., Fisher, K.: Ll(*): the foundation of the ANTLR parser generator. In: Proceedings of 32nd ACM SIGPLAN Conference on Programming Language Design and Implementation, PLDI 2011, pp. 425–436. ACM, New York (2011). http://doi.acm.org/10.1145/1993498.1993548
16. Parr, T., Harwell, S., Fisher, K.: Adaptive ll(*) parsing: the power of dynamic analysis. SIGPLAN Not. **49**(10), 579–598 (2014). http://doi.acm.org/10.1145/2714064.2660202
17. Thompson, K.: Programming techniques: regular expression search algorithm. Commun. ACM **11**(6), 419–422 (1968). http://doi.acm.org/10.1145/363347.363387

On Finite-Index Indexed Grammars and Their Restrictions

Flavio D'Alessandro[1,2(✉)], Oscar H. Ibarra[3], and Ian McQuillan[4]

[1] Department of Mathematics, Sapienza University of Rome, 00185 Rome, Italy
dalessan@mat.uniroma1.it
[2] Department of Mathematics, Boğaziçi University, 34342 Bebek, Istanbul, Turkey
[3] Department of Computer Science, University of California, Santa Barbara, CA 93106, USA
ibarra@cs.ucsb.edu
[4] Department of Computer Science, University of Saskatchewan, Saskatoon, SK S7N 5A9, Canada
mcquillan@cs.usask.ca

Abstract. The family, $\mathcal{L}(\mathsf{IND}_{\mathsf{LIN}})$, of languages generated by linear indexed grammars has been studied in the literature. It is known that the Parikh image of every language in $\mathcal{L}(\mathsf{IND}_{\mathsf{LIN}})$ is semi-linear. However, there are bounded semi-linear languages that are not in $\mathcal{L}(\mathsf{IND}_{\mathsf{LIN}})$. Here, we look at larger families of (restricted) indexed languages and study their properties, their relationships, and their decidability properties.

Keywords: Indexed languages · Finite-index · Full trios · Semi-linearity · Bounded languages · ET0L languages

1 Introduction

Indexed grammars [1,2] are a natural generalization of context-free grammars, where variables keep stacks of indices. Despite being all context-sensitive languages, the languages are still quite general as they can generate non-semi-linear languages [1]. Several restrictions have been studied that have desirable computational properties. Linear indexed grammars were first created, restricting the number of variables on the right hand side to be at most one [5]. Other restrictions include another system named exactly linear indexed grammars [6] (see also [17]), which are different than the first formalisms, although both are sufficiently restricted to only generate semi-linear languages. In this paper, we only examine the first formalism of linear indexed grammars.

The research of F. D'Alessandro was supported by a EC-FP7 Marie Curie-TÜBITAK Co-Funded Brain Circulation Scheme Project 2236 Fellowship. The research of O. H. Ibarra was supported, in part, by NSF Grant CCF-1117708. The research of I. McQuillan was supported, in part, by a grant from Natural Sciences and Engineering Research Council of Canada.

F. Drewes et al. (Eds.): LATA 2017, LNCS 10168, pp. 287–298, 2017.
DOI: 10.1007/978-3-319-53733-7_21

We study indexed grammars that are restricted to be finite-index, which is a generalization of linear indexed grammars [5]. Grammar systems that are k-*index* are restricted so that, for every word generated by the grammar, there is some successful derivation where at most k variables (or nonterminals) appear in every sentential form of the derivation [13,15]. A system is finite-index if it is k-index for some k. It has been found that that when restricting many different types of grammar systems to be finite-index, their languages coincide. This is the case for finite-index $\mathsf{ET0L}$, $\mathsf{EDT0L}$, context-free programmed grammars, ordered grammars, and matrix grammars.

We introduce the family, $\mathcal{L}(\mathsf{IND}_{\mathsf{FIN}})$, of languages generated by finite-index indexed grammars and study a sub-family, $\mathcal{L}(\mathsf{IND}_{\mathsf{UFIN}})$, of languages generated by uncontrolled finite-index indexed grammars, where every successful derivation has to be finite-index. These have been very recently studied under the name *breadth-bounded grammars*, where it was shown that this family is a semi-linear full trio. We also study a special case of the latter, called $\mathcal{L}(\mathsf{IND}_{\mathsf{UFIN}_1})$ that restricts branching productions. We then show the following:

1. All families are semi-linear full trios.
2. The following conditions are equivalent for a bounded language L:
   - $L \in \mathcal{L}(\mathsf{IND}_{\mathsf{UFIN}_1})$,
   - $L \in \mathcal{L}(\mathsf{IND}_{\mathsf{UFIN}})$,
   - L is bounded semi-linear,
   - L can be generated by a finite-index $\mathsf{ET0L}$ system,
   - L can be accepted by a DFA augmented with reversal-bounded counters,
3. Every finite-index $\mathsf{ET0L}$ language is in $\mathcal{L}(\mathsf{IND}_{\mathsf{FIN}})$.
4. $\mathcal{L}(\mathsf{CFL}) \subset \mathcal{L}(\mathsf{IND}_{\mathsf{LIN}}) \subset \mathcal{L}(\mathsf{IND}_{\mathsf{UFIN}_1}) \subseteq \mathcal{L}(\mathsf{IND}_{\mathsf{UFIN}}) \subset \mathcal{L}(\mathsf{IND}_{\mathsf{FIN}})$.
5. Containment and equality are decidable for bounded languages in $\mathcal{L}(\mathsf{IND}_{\mathsf{LIN}})$ and $\mathcal{L}(\mathsf{IND}_{\mathsf{UFIN}})$.

Due to space limitation, all proofs (except for the proofs of Lemma 16 and Proposition 23) are omitted. The full paper with all the proofs can be found at arXiv:1610.06366.

2 Preliminaries

We assume a basic background in formal languages and automata theory [9].

Let $\mathbb{N}^k$ be the additive free commutative monoid of non negative integers. If B is a subset of $\mathbb{N}^k$, $B^\oplus$ denotes the submonoid of $\mathbb{N}^k$ generated by B.

An *alphabet* is a finite set of symbols, and given an alphabet A, A^* is the free monoid generated by A. An element $w \in A^*$ is called a *word*, the empty word is denoted by λ, and any $L \subseteq A^*$ is a *language*. The *length* of a word $w \in A^*$ is denoted by $|w|$, and the number of a's, $a \in A$, in w is denoted by $|w|_a$, extended to subsets X of A by $|w|_X = \sum_{a\in X} |w|_a$.

Let $A = \{a_1, \ldots, a_t\}$ be an alphabet of t letters, and let $\psi : A^* \to \mathbb{N}^t$ be the corresponding *Parikh morphism* defined by $\psi(w) = (|w|_{a_1}, \ldots, |w|_{a_t})$ extended to languages $L \subseteq A^*$.

A set $B \subseteq \mathbb{N}^k$ is a *linear set* if there exists vectors $\mathbf{b}_0, \mathbf{b}_1, \ldots, \mathbf{b}_n$ of $\mathbb{N}^k$ such that $B = \mathbf{b}_0 + \{\mathbf{b}_1, \ldots, \mathbf{b}_n\}^{\oplus}$. Further, B is called a *semi-linear set* if $B = \bigcup_{i=1}^{m} B_i, m \geq 1$, for linear sets $B_1, \ldots, B_m$. A language $L \subseteq A^*$ is said to be *semi-linear* if the Parikh morphism applied to L gives a semi-linear set. A language family is said to be semi-linear if all languages in the family are semi-linear. Many known families are semi-linear, such as the regular languages, context-free (denoted by $\mathcal{L}(\mathsf{CFL})$, see [9]), and finite-index ET0L languages ($\mathcal{L}(\mathsf{ET0L}_{\mathsf{FIN}})$), see [13,14].

A language L is termed *bounded* if there exist non-empty words $u_1, \ldots, u_k$, with $k \geq 1$, such that $L \subseteq u_1^* \cdots u_k^*$. Let $\varphi : \mathbb{N}^k \to u_1^* \cdots u_k^*$ be the map defined as: for every tuple $(\ell_1, \ldots, \ell_k) \in \mathbb{N}^k$,

$$\varphi(\ell_1, \ldots, \ell_k) = u_1^{\ell_1} \cdots u_k^{\ell_k}.$$

The map φ is called the *Ginsburg map.*

Definition 1. *A bounded language $L \subseteq u_1^* \cdots u_k^*$ is said to be* bounded Ginsburg semi-linear *if there exists a semi-linear set B of $\mathbb{N}^k$ such that $\varphi(B) = L$.*

In the literature, bounded Ginsburg semi-linear has also been called just bounded semi-linear, but we will use the terminology bounded Ginsburg semi-linear henceforth in this paper.

A *full trio* is a language family closed under morphism, inverse morphism, and intersection with regular languages [3].

We will also relate our results to the languages accepted by one-way nondeterministic reversal-bounded multicounter machines (denoted by $\mathcal{L}(\mathsf{NCM})$), and to one-way deterministic reversal-bounded multicounter machines (denoted by $\mathcal{L}(\mathsf{DCM})$). These are NFAs (DFAs) augmented by a set of counters that can switch between increasing and decreasing a fixed number of times [10].

3 Restrictions on Indexed Grammars

We first recall the definition of indexed grammar introduced in [1] by following [9], Sect. 14.3 (see also [4] for a reference book on grammars).

Definition 2. *An indexed grammar is a 5-tuple $G = (V, T, I, P, S)$, where*

- *V, T, I are finite pairwise disjoint sets: the set of variables, terminals, and indices, respectively;*
- *P is a finite set of productions of the forms*

$$\textbf{(1)}\ A \to \nu, \quad \textbf{(2)}\ A \to Bf, \quad or \quad \textbf{(3)}\ Af \to \nu,$$

where $A, B \in V$, $f \in I$ and $\nu \in (V \cup T)^*$;
- *$S \in V$ is the start variable.*

Let us now define the derivation relation $\Rightarrow_G$ of G. Let ν be an arbitrary sentential form of G, $u_1 A_1 \alpha_1 u_2 A_2 \alpha_2 \cdots u_k A_k \alpha_k u_{k+1}$, with $A_i \in V, \alpha_i \in I^*, u_i \in T^*$. For a sentential form $\nu' \in (VI^* \cup T)^*$, we set $\nu \Rightarrow_G \nu'$ if one of the following three conditions holds:

(1) In P, there exists a production of the form (1) $A \to w_1 C_1 \cdots w_\ell C_\ell w_{\ell+1}$, $C_j \in V, w_j \in T^*$, such that in the sentential form ν, for some i with $1 \leq i \leq k$, one has $A_i = A$ and

$$\nu' = u_1 A_1 \alpha_1 \cdots u_i (w_1 C_1 \alpha_i \cdots w_\ell C_\ell \alpha_i w_{\ell+1}) u_{i+1} A_{i+1} \alpha_{i+1} \cdots u_k A_k \alpha_k u_{k+1}.$$

(2) In P, there exists a production of the form (2) $A \to Bf$ such that in the sentential form ν, for some i with $1 \leq i \leq k$, one has $A_i = A$ and $\nu' = u_1 A_1 \alpha_1 \cdots u_i (Bf\alpha_i) u_{i+1} A_{i+1} \alpha_{i+1} \cdots u_k A_k \alpha_k u_{k+1}$.

(3) In P, there exists a production of the form (3) $Af \to w_1 C_1 \cdots w_\ell C_\ell w_{\ell+1}$, $C_j \in V, w_j \in T^*$, such that in the sentential form ν, for some i with $1 \leq i \leq k$, one has $A_i = A$, $\alpha_i = f\alpha_i', \alpha_i' \in I^*$, and

$$\nu' = u_1 A_1 \alpha_1 \cdots u_i (w_1 C_1 \alpha_i' \cdots w_\ell C_\ell \alpha_i' w_{\ell+1}) u_{i+1} A_{i+1} \alpha_{i+1} \cdots u_k A_k \alpha_k u_{k+1}.$$

In this case, one says that the index f is consumed.

For every $n \in \mathbb{N}$, $\Rightarrow_G^n$ stands for the n-fold product of $\Rightarrow_G$ and $\Rightarrow_G^*$ stands for the reflexive and transitive closure of $\Rightarrow_G$. The language $L(G)$ generated by G is the set $L(G) = \{u \in T^* : S \Rightarrow_G^* u\}$.

Notation and Convention. *In the sequel we will adopt the following notation and conventions for an indexed grammar G.*

- *capital letters as $A, B, ...$etc will denote variables of G.*
- *the small letters e, f, as well as f_i, will be used to denote indices while α, β and γ, as well as its indexed version (as for instance α_i), will denote arbitrary words over I.*
- *Small letters as $a, b, c, ...$etc (as well as its indexed version) will denote letters of T and small letters as $u, v, w, r...$, etc (as well as its indexed version) will denote words over T.*
- *ν and μ, as well as ν_i and μ_i, will denote arbitrary sentential forms of G.*
- *in order to shorten the notation, according to Definition 2, if p is a production of G of the form (1) or (3), we will simply write $Af \to \nu, \quad f \in I \cup \{\lambda\}$, where it is understood that if $f = \lambda$, the production p has form (1) and if $f \in I$, the production p has form (3).*
- *a derivation of G of the form $\nu_0 \Rightarrow_{p_1} \nu_1 \Rightarrow_{p_2} \cdots \Rightarrow_{p_n} \nu_n$ will be also shortly denoted as $\Rightarrow_{p_1 \cdots p_n}$.*

The following set of definitions defines the main objects studied in this draft. Let G be an indexed grammar and let $L(G)$ be the language generated by G. The first definition is from [5].

Definition 3. *We say that G is* linear *if the right side component of every production of G has at most one variable. A language L is said to be* linear indexed *if there exists a linear indexed grammar G such that $L = L(G)$.*

Definition 4. *Given an integer $k \geq 1$, a derivation $\nu_0 \Rightarrow \nu_1 \Rightarrow \cdots \Rightarrow \nu_n$ of $G = (V, T, I, P, S)$, is said to be of* index-k *if $|\nu_i|_V \leq k$, for all i, $0 \leq i \leq n$.*

Definition 5. *Given an integer $k \geq 1$, G is said to be* of index-k *if, for every word $u \in L(G)$, there exists a derivation of u in G of index-k.*

A language L is said to be an indexed language of index-k *if there exists an indexed grammar G of index-k such that $L = L(G)$. An indexed language L is said to be* of finite-index *if L is of index-k, for some k.*

Definition 6. *An indexed grammar G is said to be* uncontrolled *index-k if, for every derivation $\nu_0 \Rightarrow \cdots \Rightarrow \nu_n$ generating $u \in L(G), |\nu_i|_V \leq k$, for all i, $0 \leq i \leq n$. G is uncontrolled finite-index if G is uncontrolled index-k, for some k. A language L is said to be an* uncontrolled finite-index indexed language *if there exists an uncontrolled finite-index grammar G such that $L = L(G)$.*

Remark 7. If G is a grammar of index-k_1, then G is a grammar of index-k_2, for every integer $k_1 \leq k_2$.

Remark 8. Definition 6 corresponds, in the case of context-free grammars, to the definition of nonterminal bounded grammar (cf [8], Sect. 5.7). We recall that nonterminal bounded grammars are equivalent to ultralinear grammars and thus provide a characterisation of the family of languages that are accepted by Finite-Turn pushdown automata.

Finally let us denote by

- $\mathcal{L}(\mathsf{IND_{LIN}})$ the family of linear indexed languages [5];
- $\mathcal{L}(\mathsf{IND_{UFIN}})$ the family of uncontrolled finite-index indexed languages;
- $\mathcal{L}(\mathsf{IND_{FIN}})$ the family of finite-index indexed languages.

A reminder that uncontrolled finite-index corresponds to breadth-bounded indexed grammars [18]. Therefore, the following is implied from this paper.

Theorem 9. *$\mathcal{L}(\mathsf{IND_{UFIN}})$ is a semi-linear full trio.*

The family $\mathcal{L}(\mathsf{IND_{LIN}})$ has been introduced in [5] where results of algebraic and combinatorial nature characterize the structure of its languages. Recall that a linear indexed grammar G is said to be *right linear indexed* if, according to Definition 2, in every production p of G of the form (1) or (3), the right hand component ν of p has the form $\nu = u$, or $\nu = uB$, where $u \in T^*, B \in V$. In [1] (see also [5]), the following theorem has been proved:

Theorem 10. *If L is an arbitrary language, L is context-free if and only if there exists a right linear indexed grammar G such that $L = L(G)$.*

From this, the following is evident.

Proposition 11. $\mathcal{L}(\mathsf{CFL}) \subset \mathcal{L}(\mathsf{IND_{LIN}}) \subset \mathcal{L}(\mathsf{IND_{UFIN}}) \subseteq \mathcal{L}(\mathsf{IND_{FIN}})$.

Indeed Theorem 10 provides the inclusion $\mathcal{L}(\mathsf{CFL}) \subseteq \mathcal{L}(\mathsf{IND_{LIN}})$. The inclusions $\mathcal{L}(\mathsf{IND_{LIN}}) \subseteq \mathcal{L}(\mathsf{IND_{UFIN}}) \subseteq \mathcal{L}(\mathsf{IND_{FIN}})$ come immediately from the definitions of the corresponding families. Now, for every $k \geq 1$, let $L_k = \{w^k : w \in A^*\}$. It is easy to construct a linear indexed grammar that generates L_2 so that

$L_2 \in \mathcal{L}(\mathsf{IND}_{\mathsf{LIN}}) \setminus \mathcal{L}(\mathsf{CFL})$ (cf, for instance, [5]). Moreover it is proved that $L_4 \notin \mathcal{L}(\mathsf{IND}_{\mathsf{LIN}})$ (see [5], Theorem 3.8). On the other hand, it is easily shown that $L_k \in \mathcal{L}(\mathsf{IND}_{\mathsf{UFIN}})$, $k \geq 0$.

Also, in [5], it is shown that for an alphabet T, $\$ \notin T$, and $A, B \subseteq T^*$, if $L = A\$B$ is a linear indexed language, then A or B is a context-free language. Then, let $T = \{a, b, c\}$, $A = \{a^n b^n c^n : n > 0\}$, and $B = \{a^n b^n c^n : n > 0\}$. Then $L = \{a^n b^n c^n \$ a^m b^m c^m : n, m > 0\}$. But since both A and B are not context-free, then L must not be linear indexed.

Next, closure under union is addressed with a straightforward adaptation of the first part of the proof of Theorem 6.1 of [9].

Lemma 12. *The families $\mathcal{L}(\mathsf{IND}_{\mathsf{FIN}})$ and $\mathcal{L}(\mathsf{IND}_{\mathsf{UFIN}})$ are closed under union.*

Next, we show that $\mathcal{L}(\mathsf{IND}_{\mathsf{FIN}})$ is a full trio, and the result also holds for $\mathcal{L}(\mathsf{IND}_{\mathsf{UFIN}})$ as well (shown in [18]). We will prove the more general fact that they are closed under rational transductions. The proof is structured using a chain of lemmas.

Lemma 13. *$\mathcal{L}(\mathsf{IND}_{\mathsf{UFIN}})$ and $\mathcal{L}(\mathsf{IND}_{\mathsf{FIN}})$ are closed under morphisms.*

Lemma 14. *$\mathcal{L}(\mathsf{IND}_{\mathsf{UFIN}})$ and $\mathcal{L}(\mathsf{IND}_{\mathsf{FIN}})$ are closed under intersection with regular languages.*

Next, we show closure under a inverse morphisms of a specific type.

Let T and T' be two alphabets with $T \subseteq T'$ and let $\widehat{\pi_T} : (T')^* \to T^*$ be the projection of $(T')^*$ onto T^*, that is the epi-morphism from $(T')^*$ onto T^* generated by the mapping $\pi_T : T' \to T \cup \{\lambda\}$

$$\forall\, \sigma \in T', \pi_T(\sigma) = \begin{cases} \lambda & \text{if } \sigma \notin T, \\ \sigma & \text{if } \sigma \in T \end{cases}.$$

In the sequel, for the sake of simplicity, we denote the projection $\widehat{\pi_T}$ by π_T. It is useful to remark that, for every $w \in T^*$ and $w' \in (T')^*$, with $w = a_1 \cdots a_n$, $n \geq 0$, $a_i \in T$,

$$w' \in \pi_T^{-1}(w) \Leftrightarrow w' = w_1 a_1 \cdots w_n a_n w_{n+1},\ w_i \in (T' \setminus T)^*. \tag{1}$$

Lemma 15. *If $L \in \mathcal{L}(\mathsf{IND}_{\mathsf{UFIN}})$ (resp. $\mathcal{L}(\mathsf{IND}_{\mathsf{FIN}})$) with $L \subseteq T^*$, then $\pi_T^{-1}(L) \in \mathcal{L}(\mathsf{IND}_{\mathsf{UFIN}})$ (resp. $\mathcal{L}(\mathsf{IND}_{\mathsf{FIN}})$).*

Next, it is possible to show closure under rational transductions.

Lemma 16. *Let T and T' be two alphabets. Let $\tau : T^* \to (T')^*$ be a rational transduction from T^* into $(T')^*$. If L is a language of T^* in the family $\mathcal{L}(\mathsf{IND}_{\mathsf{UFIN}})$ (resp. $\mathcal{L}(\mathsf{IND}_{\mathsf{FIN}})$), then $\tau(L) \in \mathcal{L}(\mathsf{IND}_{\mathsf{UFIN}})$ (resp. $\mathcal{L}(\mathsf{IND}_{\mathsf{FIN}})$).*

Proof. We will show it for $\mathcal{L}(\mathsf{IND}_{\mathsf{UFIN}})$. Let us first assume that $T \cap T' = \emptyset$. By a well known theorem for the representation of rational transductions (see [3], Chap. III, Theorem 4.1, see also [7]), there exists a regular set R over the alphabet $(T \cup T')$ such that

$$\tau = \{(\pi_T(u), \pi_{T'}(u)) : u \in R\},$$

where π_T and $\pi_{T'}$ are the projections of $(T \cup T')^*$ onto T^* and T'^* respectively.

From the latter, one has that, for every $u \in T^*$, $\tau(u) = \pi_{T'}(\pi_T^{-1}(u) \cap R)$, so that

$$\tau(L) = \bigcup_{u \in L} \tau(u) = \pi_{T'}(\pi_T^{-1}(L) \cap R). \tag{2}$$

Since, by hypothesis, $L \in \mathcal{L}(\mathsf{IND}_{\mathsf{UFIN}})$, the claim follows from (2), by applying Lemmas 13, 14, and 15.

Let us finally treat the case where T and T' are not disjoint. Let T'' be a copy of T with $T'' \cap T' = \emptyset$ and let $c_{T''} : (T')^* \to (T'')^*$ be the corresponding copying iso-morphism from $(T')^*$ onto $(T'')^*$. By applying the latter argument to the rational transduction $c_{T''}\tau : T^* \to (T'')^*$, one has $(c_{T''}\tau)(L) \in \mathcal{L}(\mathsf{IND}_{\mathsf{UFIN}})$. Since $c_{T''}^{-1}(c_{T''}\tau)(L) = \tau(L)$, then the claim follows from the latter by applying Lemma 13. □

Then the following is immediate:

Corollary 17. *$\mathcal{L}(\mathsf{IND}_{\mathsf{UFIN}})$ and $\mathcal{L}(\mathsf{IND}_{\mathsf{FIN}})$ are closed under inverse morphisms.*

By Lemmas 13, 14, and Corollary 17, we obtain:

Theorem 18. *The families $\mathcal{L}(\mathsf{IND}_{\mathsf{FIN}})$ and $\mathcal{L}(\mathsf{IND}_{\mathsf{UFIN}})$ are full trios.*

We now prove a result which extends the semi-linearity of a family of languages to a bigger family. If $\mathcal{C}$ is a full trio of semi-linear languages and $\mathcal{L}$ is the family of languages accepted by NCMs, let $\mathcal{C} \cap \mathcal{L} = \{L_1 \cap L_2 : L_1 \in \mathcal{C}, L_2 \in \mathcal{L}\}$.

Proposition 19. *Every language in $\mathcal{C} \cap \mathcal{L}$ has a semi-linear Parikh map.*

Note that the above proposition does not depend on how the languages in $\mathcal{C}$ are specified. It extends the semi-linearity of languages in $\mathcal{C}$ to a bigger family that can do some "counting". The proposition applies to all well-known full trios of semi-linear languages, in particular, to $\mathcal{C} = \mathcal{L}(\mathsf{IND}_{\mathsf{UFIN}})$.

Corollary 20. *Let $\mathcal{C}$ be a full trio whose closures under homomorphism, inverse homomorphism and intersection with regular sets are effective. Moreover, assume that for each L in $\mathcal{C}$, $\psi(L)$ can effectively be constructed. Then $\mathcal{C} \cap \mathcal{L}$ has a decidable emptiness problem.*

Note that $\mathcal{L}$ is also a full trio of semi-linear languages. It is easy to see that the proposition is not true if $\mathcal{L}$ is an arbitrary full trio of semi-linear languages. For example suppose $\mathcal{C} = \mathcal{L}$ is the family of languages accepted by 1-reversal NPDAs (= linear context-free languages). Let

$$L_1 = \{a^{n_1}\sharp \cdots \sharp a^{n_k}\$a^{n_k}\sharp \cdots \sharp a^{n_1} : k \geq 4, n_i \geq 1\},$$
$$L_2 = \{a^{n_1}\sharp \cdots \sharp a^{n_k}\$a^{m_k}\sharp \cdots \sharp a^{m_1} : k \geq 4,\ n_i,\ m_i \geq 1,\ m_j = n_{j+1},\ 1 \leq j < k\}.$$

Clearly, L_1 and L_2 can be accepted by 1-reversal NPDAs. But $\psi(L_1 \cap L_2)$ is $\{(a^n\sharp)^{k-1}a^n\$(a^n\sharp)^{k-1}a^n : n \geq 1,\ k \geq 4\}$ and it is not semi-linear.

Similarly, it is easy to show that the proposition does not hold when $\mathcal{C} = \mathcal{L}$ is the family of languages accepted by NFAs with one unrestricted counter (i.e., NPDAs with a unary stack alphabet in addition to a distinct bottom of the stack symbol which is never altered).

Finally, let $\mathcal{C}_1$ and $\mathcal{C}_2$ be any full trios of semi-linear languages. It is clear that $\mathcal{C}_1 \cup \mathcal{C}_2 = \{L_1 \cup L_2 \ :\ L_1 \in \mathcal{C}_1, L_2 \in \mathcal{C}_2\}$ is a semi-linear family. One can also show that $\mathcal{C}_1 \cdot \mathcal{C}_2 = \{L_1 L_2 \ :\ L_1 \in \mathcal{C}_1, L_2 \in \mathcal{C}_2\}$ is a semi-linear family.

4 Bounded Languages and Hierarchy Results

The purpose of this section is to demonstrate that all bounded Ginsburg semi-linear languages are in $\mathcal{L}(\mathsf{IND_{UFIN}})$ (thus implying they are in $\mathcal{L}(\mathsf{IND_{FIN}})$ as well), but not in $\mathcal{L}(\mathsf{IND_{LIN}})$.

Notice that the language L from Proposition 11 is a bounded Ginsburg semi-linear language. Thus, the following is true:

Proposition 21. *There are bounded Ginsburg semi-linear languages that are not in* $\mathcal{L}(\mathsf{IND_{LIN}})$.

Furthermore, it has been shown that in every semi-linear full trio, all bounded languages in the family are bounded Ginsburg semi-linear [12]. Further $\mathcal{L}(\mathsf{IND_{LIN}})$ is a semi-linear full trio [5]. Therefore, the bounded languages in $\mathcal{L}(\mathsf{IND_{LIN}})$ are strictly contained in the bounded languages contained in any family containing all bounded Ginsburg semi-linear languages. We only mention here three of the many such families mentioned in [12].

Corollary 22. *The bounded languages in* $\mathcal{L}(\mathsf{IND_{LIN}})$ *are strictly contained in the bounded languages from* $\mathcal{L}(\mathsf{NCM}), \mathcal{L}(\mathsf{DCM}), \mathcal{L}(\mathsf{ET0L_{FIN}})$.

Proposition 23. $\mathcal{L}(\mathsf{IND_{UFIN}})$ *contains all bounded Ginsburg semi-linear languages.*

Proof. We now prove that if L is a bounded Ginsburg semi-linear language, with $L \subseteq u_1^* \cdots u_k^*$, then $L \in \mathcal{L}(\mathsf{IND_{UFIN}})$. Since $\mathcal{L}(\mathsf{IND_{UFIN}})$ is closed under union by Lemma 12, it is enough to show it for a linear set B. Let B be a set of the form $B = \{\mathbf{b}_0 + x_1\mathbf{b}_1 + \cdots + x_\ell \mathbf{b}_\ell \ : x_1, \ldots, x_\ell \in \mathbb{N}\}$, where $\mathbf{b}_0, \mathbf{b}_1, \ldots, \mathbf{b}_\ell$, are vectors of $\mathbb{N}^k$. By denoting the arbitrary vector $\mathbf{b}_i$ as $(b_{i1}, \ldots, b_{ik})$, we write B as

$$\{(\mathbf{b}_{01} + x_1\mathbf{b}_{11} + \cdots + x_\ell \mathbf{b}_{\ell 1},\ \ldots,\ \mathbf{b}_{0k} + x_1\mathbf{b}_{1k} + \cdots + x_\ell \mathbf{b}_{\ell k}),\ : x_1, \ldots, x_\ell \in \mathbb{N}\},$$

so that the language $L = \varphi(B)$ becomes

$$u_1^{\mathbf{b}_{01}+x_1\mathbf{b}_{11}+\cdots+x_\ell\mathbf{b}_{\ell 1}} u_2^{\mathbf{b}_{02}+x_1\mathbf{b}_{12}+\cdots+x_\ell\mathbf{b}_{\ell 2}} \cdots u_k^{\mathbf{b}_{0k}+x_1\mathbf{b}_{1k}+\cdots+x_\ell\mathbf{b}_{\ell k}}, \tag{3}$$

where $x_1, \ldots, x_\ell \in \mathbb{N}$. Let us now define an indexed grammar G such that $L = L(G)$. Let $G = (V, T, I, P, S)$, where

$$V = \{S, Y, X_1, \ldots, X_k\}, \quad T = A, \quad I = \{e, f_1, f_2, \ldots, f_\ell\},$$

and the set P of productions is the following:

1. $P_{start} = (S \to Ye)$
2. For every $j = 1, \ldots, \ell$, $P_j = (Y \to Yf_j)$
3. $Q = (Y \to X_1 X_2 \cdots X_k)$
4. For every $i = 1, \ldots, k$ and for every $j = 1, \ldots, \ell$,

$$R_{i0} = (X_i e \to u_i^{b_{0i}}), \quad R_{ij} = (X_i f_j \to u_i^{b_{ji}} X_i).$$

Let us finally prove that $L = L(G)$ and G is an uncontrolled grammar. Let us first show that $L \subseteq L(G)$. Let $w \in L$. By (3), there exist $x_1, \ldots, x_\ell \in \mathbb{N}$ such that

$$w = u_1^{\mathbf{b}_{01}+x_1\mathbf{b}_{11}+\cdots+x_\ell\mathbf{b}_{\ell 1}} u_2^{\mathbf{b}_{02}+x_1\mathbf{b}_{12}+\cdots+x_\ell\mathbf{b}_{\ell 2}} \cdots u_k^{\mathbf{b}_{0k}+x_1\mathbf{b}_{1k}+\cdots+x_\ell\mathbf{b}_{\ell k}}.$$

Consider the derivation defined by the word over the alphabet P:

$$\mathcal{P} = P_{start} P_1^{x_1} P_2^{x_2} \cdots P_\ell^{x_\ell} Q Q_1 \cdots Q_k,$$

where, for every $i = 1, \ldots, k$, $Q_i = R_{i\ell}^{x_\ell} \cdots R_{i2}^{x_2} R_{i1}^{x_1} R_{i0}$. It is easily checked that $S \Rightarrow_{\mathcal{P}} w$. Indeed,
$S \Rightarrow_{P_{start}} Ye \Rightarrow_{P_1^{x_1} P_2^{x_2} \ldots P_\ell^{x_\ell}} Y f_\ell^{x_\ell} \cdots f_1^{x_1} e \Rightarrow_Q$
$X_1 f_\ell^{x_\ell} \cdots f_1^{x_1} e \cdots X_k f_\ell^{x_\ell} \cdots f_1^{x_1} e \Rightarrow_{Q_1} u_1^{\mathbf{b}_{01}+x_1\mathbf{b}_{11}+\cdots+x_\ell\mathbf{b}_{\ell 1}} X_2 \cdots X_k f_\ell^{x_\ell} \cdots f_1^{x_1} e$
$\Rightarrow_{Q_2} u_1^{\mathbf{b}_{01}+x_1\mathbf{b}_{11}+\cdots+x_\ell\mathbf{b}_{\ell 1}} u_2^{\mathbf{b}_{02}+x_1\mathbf{b}_{12}+\cdots+x_\ell\mathbf{b}_{\ell 2}} X_3 \cdots X_k f_\ell^{x_\ell} \cdots f_1^{x_1} e \Rightarrow_{Q_3 \cdots Q_k} w$,
so that $w \in L(G)$. Similarly, it can be shown that $L(G) \subseteq L$. □

Since it is known that in any semi-linear full trio, all bounded languages in the family are bounded Ginsburg semi-linear, the bounded languages in $\mathcal{L}(\mathsf{IND}_{\mathsf{UFIN}})$ coincide with several other families, including a deterministic machine model [12].

Corollary 24. *The bounded languages in $\mathcal{L}(\mathsf{IND}_{\mathsf{UFIN}})$ coincides with the bounded Ginsburg semi-linear languages, which coincides with the bounded languages in $\mathcal{L}(\mathsf{NCM}), \mathcal{L}(\mathsf{DCM}), \mathcal{L}(\mathsf{ET0L}_{\mathsf{FIN}})$ (and several other families listed in [12]).*

Also, since $\mathcal{L}(\mathsf{IND}_{\mathsf{LIN}})$ does not contain all bounded Ginsburg semi-linear languages by Proposition 21, but $\mathcal{L}(\mathsf{IND}_{\mathsf{UFIN}})$ does, the following is immediate:

Corollary 25. $\mathcal{L}(\mathsf{IND}_{\mathsf{LIN}}) \subset \mathcal{L}(\mathsf{IND}_{\mathsf{UFIN}})$.

Next, a restriction of $\mathcal{L}(\mathsf{IND}_{\mathsf{UFIN}})$ is studied and compared to the other families. And indeed, this family is quite general as it contains all bounded Ginsburg semi-linear languages in addition to some languages that are not in $\mathcal{L}(\mathsf{ET0L}_{\mathsf{FIN}})$.

Now let $p = (Af \to \nu) \in P$, with $f \in I \cup \{\lambda\}$, be a production. Then p is called *special* if the number of occurrences of variables of V in ν is at least 2, and *linear*, otherwise. Denote by $P_{\mathcal{S}}$ and $P_{\mathcal{L}}$ the sets of special and linear productions of P respectively. By Definition 6, a grammar G is uncontrolled finite-index if and only if the number of times special productions appear in every successful derivation of G is upper bounded by a given fixed integer.

Next, we will deal with uncontrolled grammars such that in every successful derivation of G, at most one special production occurs. The languages generated by such grammars form a family denoted $\mathcal{L}(\mathsf{IND}_{\mathsf{UFIN}_1})$. It is worth noticing that a careful rereading of the proof of Theorem 18 and Lemma 12 shows that they hold for $\mathcal{L}(\mathsf{IND}_{\mathsf{UFIN}_1})$ as well. Further, it is clear that only one special production is used in every derivation of a word in the proof of Proposition 23. Therefore, the following holds:

Proposition 26. *The family $\mathcal{L}(\mathsf{IND}_{\mathsf{UFIN}_1})$ is a union-closed full trio and it contains all bounded Ginsburg semi-linear languages.*

It is immediate from the definitions that $\mathcal{L}(\mathsf{IND}_{\mathsf{LIN}}) \subseteq \mathcal{L}(\mathsf{IND}_{\mathsf{UFIN}_1}) \subseteq \mathcal{L}(\mathsf{IND}_{\mathsf{UFIN}})$. Further, since $\mathcal{L}(\mathsf{IND}_{\mathsf{UFIN}_1})$ contains all bounded Ginsburg semi-linear languages by Proposition 26, but the linear indexed languages do not, by Proposition 21, the following holds:

Proposition 27. $\mathcal{L}(\mathsf{IND}_{\mathsf{LIN}}) \subset \mathcal{L}(\mathsf{IND}_{\mathsf{UFIN}_1}) \subseteq \mathcal{L}(\mathsf{IND}_{\mathsf{UFIN}})$.

Then the following is true from [12].

Corollary 28. *$\mathcal{L}(\mathsf{IND}_{\mathsf{UFIN}_1})$ is a semi-linear full trio containing all bounded Ginsburg semi-linear languages. Further, the bounded languages in $\mathcal{L}(\mathsf{IND}_{\mathsf{UFIN}_1})$ coincides with the bounded languages in $\mathcal{L}(\mathsf{IND}_{\mathsf{UFIN}})$, $\mathcal{L}(\mathsf{NCM})$, $\mathcal{L}(\mathsf{DCM})$, and $\mathcal{L}(\mathsf{ET0L}_{\mathsf{FIN}})$, and several others listed in [12].*

5 Some Examples, Separation, and Decidability Results

We start this section by giving an example that clarifies previous results.

Example 29. Let $L = \{a^n b^n c^n \$ a^n b^n c^n : n \in \mathbb{N}\}$. If $\varphi : \mathbb{N}^7 \to a^*b^*c^*\$^*a^*b^*c^*$, then $L = \varphi(B)$, where $B = \{\mathbf{b}_0 + n\mathbf{b}_1 : n \in \mathbb{N}\}$, with $\mathbf{b}_0 = (0,0,0,1,0,0,0)$ and $\mathbf{b}_1 = (1,1,1,0,1,1,1)$. It is worth noticing that, by the discussion preceding Proposition 21, L is not a linear indexed grammar. We define an uncontrolled finite-index grammar $G = (V,T,I,P,S)$ where $V = \{S, Y, X_1, X_2, X_3, X_4, X_5, X_6, X_7\}$, $T = \{a, b, c, \$\}$, $I = \{e, f\}$, and the set P of productions is:

$$P_{start} = S \to Ye,\ P = Y \to Yf,\ Q = Y \to X_1X_2 \cdots X_7$$

$$\begin{array}{llllll} X_1f \to aX_1 & X_2f \to bX_2 & X_3f \to cX_3 & X_4f \to X_4 & X_5f \to aX_5 & X_6f \to bX_6 \\ X_7f \to cX_7 & X_1e \to \varepsilon & X_2e \to \varepsilon & X_3e \to \varepsilon & X_4e \to \$ & X_5e \to \varepsilon \\ X_6e \to \varepsilon & X_7e \to \varepsilon. & & & & \end{array}$$

In general

$$\begin{aligned} &S \Rightarrow Ye \Rightarrow^n Yf^ne \Rightarrow X_1X_2X_3X_4X_5X_6X_7f^ne \\ &= X_1f^neX_2f^neX_3f^neX_4f^neX_5f^neX_6f^neX_7f^ne \Rightarrow^* a^nb^nc^n\$a^nb^nc^n. \end{aligned}$$

As the only freedom in derivations of G consists of how many times the rule P is applied and of trivial variations in order to perform the rules $X_if \to \sigma X_i, \sigma \in T \cup \{\varepsilon\}$, it should be clear that $L = L(G)$.

It is known that decidability of several properties holds for semi-linear trios where the properties are effective [11]. This is the case for $\mathcal{L}(\mathsf{IND}_{\mathsf{UFIN}})$, and also for $\mathcal{L}(\mathsf{IND}_{\mathsf{LIN}})$ [5].

Corollary 30. *Containment, equality, membership, and emptiness are decidable for bounded languages in* $\mathcal{L}(\mathsf{IND_{UFIN}})$ *and* $\mathcal{L}(\mathsf{IND_{LIN}})$.

Lastly, it is known that $\mathcal{L}(\mathsf{ET0L_{FIN}})$ cannot generate some context-free languages [16], but all context-free languages can be generated by indexed linear grammars by Theorem 10, which are all in $\mathcal{L}(\mathsf{IND_{UFIN_1}})$.

Corollary 31. *There are languages in* $\mathcal{L}(\mathsf{IND_{UFIN_1}})$ *and* $\mathcal{L}(\mathsf{IND_{LIN}})$ *that are not in* $\mathcal{L}(\mathsf{ET0L_{FIN}})$.

We provide an example of language in $\mathcal{L}(\mathsf{IND_{FIN}})$ whose Parikh image is not a semi-linear set.

Example 32. We construct a grammar of index 3, which is not uncontrolled, that generates the language $L = \{aba^2b \cdots a^nba^{n+1} \ : \ n \geq 1\}$. Let $G = (V, T, I, P, S)$ be the grammar where $V = \{S, A, B, X, X', X''\}$, $T = \{a, b\}$, $I = \{e, f, g\}$, and the set of productions of G are defined as:

- $p_0 = S \to Xe$, $\quad p_1 = X \to ABX'f$, $\quad p_2 = X' \to X$, $\quad p_3 = X' \to X''$,
- $p_4 = X''f \to aX''$, $\quad p_5 = X''e \to a$, $\quad p_6 = Af \to aA$, $\quad p_7 = Ae \to \varepsilon$,
- $p_8 = Bf \to B$, $\quad p_9 = Be \to \varepsilon$.

One can check that G is not uncontrolled and $L = L(G)$.

Corollary 33. *There are languages in* $\mathcal{L}(\mathsf{IND_{FIN}})$ *that are not semi-linear. Furthermore, there are bounded (and unary) languages in* $\mathcal{L}(\mathsf{IND_{FIN}})$ *that are not bounded Ginsburg semi-linear.*

This allows for the separation of $\mathcal{L}(\mathsf{IND_{UFIN}})$ (which only contains semi-linear languages) and $\mathcal{L}(\mathsf{IND_{FIN}})$.

Corollary 34. *The following holds:*

$$\mathcal{L}(\mathsf{CFL}) \subset \mathcal{L}(\mathsf{IND_{LIN}}) \subset \mathcal{L}(\mathsf{IND_{UFIN_1}}) \subseteq \mathcal{L}(\mathsf{IND_{UFIN}}) \subset \mathcal{L}(\mathsf{IND_{FIN}}).$$

Finally, we show that all finite-index ET0L languages are finite-index.

Proposition 35. $\mathcal{L}(\mathsf{ET0L_{FIN}}) \subset \mathcal{L}(\mathsf{IND_{FIN}})$.

It is an open question though as to how $\mathcal{L}(\mathsf{ET0L_{FIN}})$ compares to $\mathcal{L}(\mathsf{IND_{UFIN}})$. For finite-index ET0L, uncontrolled systems, defined similarly to our definition of uncontrolled, does not restrict languages accepted. Furthermore, it is known that $\mathcal{L}(\mathsf{ET0L_{FIN}})$ is closed under Kleene-$*$ [14] and therefore contains $\{a^nb^nc^n : n > 0\}^*$. But we conjecture that this language is not in $\mathcal{L}(\mathsf{IND_{UFIN}})$ despite being in $\mathcal{L}(\mathsf{IND_{FIN}})$ by the proposition above. This would imply that $\mathcal{L}(\mathsf{IND_{UFIN}})$ is incomparable with $\mathcal{L}(\mathsf{ET0L_{FIN}})$ by Corollary 31.

References

1. Aho, A.V.: Indexed grammars—an extension of context-free grammars. J. ACM **15**, 647–671 (1968)
2. Aho, A.V.: Nested stack automata. J. ACM **16**, 383–406 (1969)
3. Berstel, J.: Transductions and Context-Free Languages. B.B. Teubner, Stuttgart (1979)
4. Dassow, J., Păun, G.: Regulated Rewriting in Formal Language Theory. EATCS Monographs on Theoretical Computer Science, vol. 18. Springer, Berlin (1989)
5. Duske, J., Parchmann, R.: Linear indexed languages. Theoret. Comput. Sci. **32**(1–2), 47–60 (1984)
6. Gazdar, G.: Applicability of indexed grammars to natural languages. In: Reyle, U., Rohrer, C. (eds.) Natural Language Parsing and Linguistic Theories, vol. 35, pp. 69–94. Springer, Dordrecht (1988)
7. Ginsburg, S.: The Mathematical Theory of Context-Free Languages. McGraw-Hill, Inc., New York (1966)
8. Harrison, M.A.: Introduction to Formal Language Theory. Addison-Wesley Series in Computer Science. Addison-Wesley Pub. Co., Reading (1978)
9. Hopcroft, J.E., Ullman, J.D.: Introduction to Automata Theory, Languages, and Computation. Addison-Wesley, Reading (1979)
10. Ibarra, O.H.: Reversal-bounded multicounter machines and their decision problems. J. ACM **25**(1), 116–133 (1978)
11. Ibarra, O.H., McQuillan, I.: On bounded semilinear languages, counter machines, and finite-index ET0L. In: Han, Y.-S., Salomaa, K. (eds.) CIAA 2016. LNCS, vol. 9705, pp. 138–149. Springer, Heidelberg (2016). doi:10.1007/978-3-319-40946-7_12
12. Ibarra, O.H., McQuillan, I.: On families of full trios containing counter machine languages. In: Brlek, S., Reutenauer, C. (eds.) DLT 2016. LNCS, vol. 9840, pp. 216–228. Springer, Heidelberg (2016). doi:10.1007/978-3-662-53132-7_18
13. Rozenberg, G., Salomaa, A.: The Mathematical Theory of L Systems. Academic Press, Inc., New York (1980)
14. Rozenberg, G., Vermeir, D.: On ET0L systems of finite index. Inf. Control **38**, 103–133 (1978)
15. Rozenberg, G., Vermeir, D.: On the effect of the finite index restriction on several families of grammars. Inf. Control **39**, 284–302 (1978)
16. Rozoy, B.: The Dyck language $D_1'^*$ is not generated by any matrix grammar of finite index. Inf. Comput. **74**(1), 64–89 (1987)
17. Vijay-Shanker, K., Weir, D.J.: The equivalence of four extensions of context-free grammars. Math. Syst. Theor. **27**(6), 511–546 (1994)
18. Zetzsche, G.: An approach to computing downward closures. In: Halldórsson, M.M., Iwama, K., Kobayashi, N., Speckmann, B. (eds.) ICALP 2015. LNCS, vol. 9135, pp. 440–451. Springer, Heidelberg (2015). doi:10.1007/978-3-662-47666-6_35

A Derivational Model of Discontinuous Parsing

Mark-Jan Nederhof[1(✉)] and Anssi Yli-Jyrä[2]

[1] School of Computer Science, University of St Andrews, St Andrews, UK
markjan.nederhof@googlemail.com
[2] Department of Modern Languages, University of Helsinki, Helsinki, Finland
anssi.yli-jyra@helsinki.fi

Abstract. The notion of latent-variable probabilistic context-free derivation of syntactic structures is enhanced to allow heads and unrestricted discontinuities. The chosen formalization covers both constituent parsing and dependency parsing. The derivational model is accompanied by an equivalent probabilistic automaton model. By the new framework, one obtains a probability distribution over the space of all discontinuous parses. This lends itself to intrinsic evaluation in terms of perplexity, as shown in experiments.

Keywords: Parsing · Grammars · Weighted automata

1 Introduction

Much of traditional parsing theory considers a syntactic structure to be a tree in which siblings are linearly ordered, and a sentence is formed by the labels of the leaves from left to right. Whereas most English sentences can be given syntactic analyses that satisfy these constraints, other languages, especially those with more flexible word order such as German or Czech, do not let themselves be described easily, if at all, by using trees of this form. At the very least, these languages require types of syntactic trees with 'crossing edges', a phenomenon which is known formally as *discontinuity*.

In the theory of constituent parsing, leaf nodes in a parse tree are commonly words and punctuation tokens, and non-leaf nodes represent categories; one may also assign a special role to the nodes one level above the words, to represent parts of speech. In the theory of dependency parsing however, each node corresponds to a word or punctuation token, and can also be tagged with a part of speech; moreover, the parent-child edges are typically labeled by dependency relations. Discontinuity in dependency parsing is more specifically called *non-projectivity*.

One approach to obtaining discontinuous structures is to use formalisms that distinguish between derived trees and derivation trees, with discontinuity introduced through the interaction between the two kinds of trees. This approach has been explored in particular for tree adjoining grammars (TAGs) and linear context-free rewriting systems (LCFRSs). For TAG, see [10]. For LCFRS applied to dependency parsing see [12] and for LCFRS applied to constituent parsing

The second author has been funded by the Academy of Finland (Academy Research Fellowship; decision no 270354).

F. Drewes et al. (Eds.): LATA 2017, LNCS 10168, pp. 299–310, 2017.
DOI: 10.1007/978-3-319-53733-7_22

see [5]. In all of these cases, probability models may remain attached to grammar rules, as in the case of traditional probabilistic context-free parsing [8].

Another approach takes shift-reduce automata as starting point, with an additional mechanism for swapping elements in the stack [13,18]. Typically, there is a unique next parser action determined by a discriminative method, or there may be a probability distribution over a set of possible next actions. In the latter case, beam-search may be used to reduce the computational costs, by restricting attention to a bounded number of partial parses that locally seem most promising. In either case, parsing tends to be very fast.

However, it was shown for continuous parsing that models of syntax that rely on a probability distribution over actions of a shift-reduce parser are incomplete, in the sense that some probability distributions that can be expressed by probabilistic grammars cannot be expressed in terms of the corresponding automata [16]. Moreover, shift-reduce models tend to have many more parameters than grammatical models. Under certain conditions, this may lead to more accurate models [24] but when little training material is available, accurate estimation of the larger number of parameters may be infeasible. One way to deal with this is to derive the probabilities of parser actions directly from an underlying grammatical model [15].

The purpose of the current paper is to explore avenues towards similar theory for the discontinuous case. Concretely, we propose a grammatical, probabilistic model of discontinuous syntax, and show how this relates to an automaton model. This approach differs from an approach using TAG or LCFRS in that it retains a notion of immediate dominance that is context-free. Added to this is an independent model of discontinuity.

Our work has elements in common with, for example, [4,11,22], which also investigated discontinuity through a redefinition of context-free derivations. An important difference is that we aim to characterize 'typical' discontinuity in terms of a probabilistic model rather than in terms of a system of boolean constraints.

Other approaches, such as hybrid parsing [17], pseudo-projectivity [9,14,20], and the reversible splitting conversion of [2], are incomplete, in that allowed discontinuity is bounded by properties of the trained grammar, whereas our model provably allows for any discontinuity.

2 Trees

In the following, we define a type of trees that is able to represent both constituent structures and dependency structures with discontinuities. We assume that each substructure has a *head*. Heads are an inherent component of most definitions of dependency structures [6,7]. Most older definitions of constituent structures avoid the notion of heads altogether, whereas some more recent literature tends to at least involve heads in some way [3].

Let $\mathbb{N}^+ = \{1, 2, \dots\}$, and let $[n] = \{1, 2, \dots, n\}$ for $n \in \mathbb{N}^+$. Let Σ be a finite set of *terminals* and let N be a finite set of *labels*. Terminals correspond naively to tokens, although in reality they can represent open classes of distributionally similar tokens. Labels could represent categories, parts of speech, semantic roles, or even a combination of these.

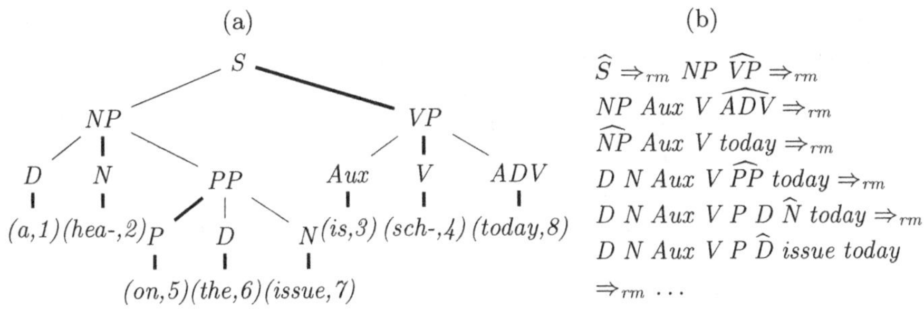

Fig. 1. Complete ph-tree for "*a hearing is scheduled on the issue today*" and corresponding rightmost derivation, assuming π is the identity function. Thick edges lead to heads and thin edges to dependents. Examples of headed rules used here are $NP \to D\langle N\rangle PP$ and $PP \to \varepsilon\langle P\rangle D\ N$ with ε here indicating absence of left dependents.

The set $H(\Sigma, N)$ of *headed trees* over Σ and N is defined inductively as follows. We have a *leaf* $(a, i) \in H(\Sigma, N)$ for each $a \in \Sigma$ and $i \in \mathbb{N}^+$. We also have $A(s_1 \cdots s_k, h, t_1 \cdots t_\ell) \in H(\Sigma, N)$ for each $A \in N$ and $s_1, \ldots, s_k, h, t_1, \ldots, t_\ell \in H(\Sigma, N)$. Nothing else is in $H(\Sigma, N)$.

In a leaf (a, i), the number i indicates an (input) position of the occurrence of a in a string of terminals. The set of all positions in a headed tree t is denoted by $pos(t)$. All of $s_1, \ldots, s_k$, h, $t_1, \ldots, t_\ell$ in a headed tree $t = A(s_1 \cdots s_k, h, t_1 \cdots t_\ell)$ will be referred to as *immediate subtrees* of t. We call subtree h the *head* of t, we call $s_1, \ldots, s_k$ its *left dependents* and $t_1, \ldots, t_\ell$ its *right dependents.*

The *head leaf* of $t = (a, i)$ is t itself and the head leaf of $t = A(s_1 \cdots s_k,\ h,\ t_1 \cdots t_\ell)$ is the head leaf of h. If (a, i) is the head leaf of t, then a is called the *head terminal* of t and i is called the *head position* of t.

A headed tree is a *positioned headed tree* (ph-tree) if no two leaves share the same position and if for every subtree $t = A(s_1 \cdots s_k, h, t_1 \cdots t_\ell)$, the sequence of the head positions of $s_1, \ldots, s_k$, h, $t_1, \ldots, t_\ell$ is strictly increasing. A ph-tree t is *complete* if $pos(t) = [n]$ for some $n \in \mathbb{N}^+$; see Fig. 1(a) for an example. The set of ph-trees is denoted by $P(\Sigma, N)$, and the set of complete ph-trees by $C(\Sigma, N)$. The *yield* of a ph-tree whose leaves are (a_1, k_1), ..., (a_m, k_m), arranged such that $k_1 < \ldots < k_m$, is the string $a_1 \cdots a_m$.

We call a ph-tree *unilexical* if each subtree is either a leaf or of the form $A(s_1 \cdots s_k, h, t_1 \cdots t_\ell)$, where h is a leaf and none of $s_1, \ldots, s_k$, $t_1, \ldots, t_\ell$ are leaves. A complete ph-tree that is unilexical would more commonly be called a dependency structure.

3 Headed Context-Free Grammars

In this section, we give a formalization of headed grammars that differs somewhat from related definitions in the literature, for example those of [1,3]. This is motivated by the need for a streamlined presentation that allows formulation of both discontinuous constituent parsing and non-projective dependency parsing. We also wish to incorporate the notion of latent variables, as this is an essential component of some state-of-the-art parsers [21].

A *headed context-free grammar* (HCFG) is a 6-tuple $(\Sigma, Q, q_{init}, R, N, \pi)$, where Σ is a finite set of terminals as before, Q is a finite set of *states*, $q_{init} \in Q$ is the *initial state*, and R is a set of *headed rules*. Also as before, N is a finite set of labels. The function π maps states to labels. Several states may be mapped to the same label, to accommodate for latent variables. However, in the examples and in the current experiments (Sect. 7), π is always the identity function.

A headed rule has the form $q \to \alpha\langle Z\rangle\beta$, where $q \in Q$, $Z \in \Sigma \cup Q$ and $\alpha, \beta \in (\Sigma \cup Q)^*$. Here q is called the *left-hand side*, and $\alpha\langle Z\rangle\beta$ the *right-hand side*, in which Z is the *head*, and the symbols in α and β are the left and right dependents, respectively. The set R of headed rules is potentially infinite, in which case we assume finite descriptions for the sets of strings α and β that may appear in rules of the form $q \to \alpha\langle Z\rangle\beta$, for given q and Z. Such descriptions would typically be finite automata.

Assuming a fixed HCFG, the binary relation $\Rightarrow$ has $\gamma_0\gamma_1 \cdots \gamma_k q \delta_0\delta_1 \cdots \delta_\ell \Rightarrow \gamma_0 X_1 \gamma_1 X_2 \cdots X_k \gamma_k Z \delta_0 Y_1 \delta_1 Y_2 \cdots Y_\ell \delta_\ell$ if $q \to X_1 \cdots X_k\langle Z\rangle Y_1 \cdots Y_\ell$ is a rule. Note that if we were to restrict $\gamma_1 \cdots \gamma_k$ and $\delta_0 \cdots \delta_{\ell-1}$ to be always ε, then we obtain the familiar notion of (continuous) context-free derivation. The reflexive, transitive closure of $\Rightarrow$ is denoted by $\Rightarrow^*$.

Where we speak of '*a derivation* $q_{init} \Rightarrow^* w$', we implicitly assume a certain sequence of rule applications that leads us from q_{init} to w, via intermediate *sentential forms*. This includes not only the identity of each applied rule, but also the occurrence of the state on which it is applied (a sentential form may contain several occurrences of the same state), and the locations where the left and right dependents are placed among the existing elements in the sentential form.

A derivation $q_{init} \Rightarrow^* w$ maps to a complete ph-tree as follows. First we enhance $w = a_1 \cdots a_n$ to $w' = (a_1, 1) \cdots (a_n, n)$, so that each terminal is coupled to its position in the derived string. In the same way, we construct a set of enhanced rules, on the basis of the rules that occur in the derivation. Concretely, for a rule ρ of the form $q \to X_1 \cdots X_k\langle Z\rangle Y_1 \cdots Y_\ell$, the set of enhanced rules contains all rules of the form $(q, i) \to (X_1, i_1) \cdots (X_k, i_k)\langle(Z, i)\rangle(Y_1, j_1) \cdots (Y_\ell, j_\ell)$, where $1 \leq i_1 < \ldots < i_k < i < j_1 < \ldots < j_\ell \leq n$. The set of such enhanced rules for given rule ρ will be denoted by $\rho^{(n)}$. Examples of enhanced rules relevant for Fig. 1 are $(S, 4) \to (NP, 2)\langle(VP, 4)\rangle\varepsilon$ and $(D, 6) \to \varepsilon\langle(the, 6)\rangle\varepsilon$. We can now extend the derivation $q_{init} \Rightarrow^* w$ in a unique way to a derivation $(q_{init}, i_0) \Rightarrow^* w'$, for some i_0, where we replace an application of a rule ρ by some rule $\rho' \in \rho^{(n)}$. In the enhanced derivation, we have made explicit in which position each terminal occurrence will end up, as well as made explicit the head position belonging to each state occurrence.

Next, we interpret the enhanced derivation as a tree structure, with the right-hand side elements of an enhanced rule being the children of the left-hand side. On this tree structure, we apply π, which amounts to replacing each (q, i) by

$\pi(q)$. In particular, if π is the identity function, as in the case of Fig. 1, then each (q, i) is simply replaced by q. Hereby, a derivation maps to a unique string w as well as to a unique complete ph-tree. For a given HCFG G, the string language $SL(G)$ generated by G is the set of all strings that can be derived and the tree language $TL(G)$ is the corresponding set of complete ph-trees.

The *permutation closure* of a string language $L \subseteq \Sigma^*$ is defined to be the language $perm(L)$ of strings that are permutations of a string in L. We extend permutation closure to rules as follows. If ρ is a rule $q \to \alpha\langle Z\rangle\beta$, then $perm(\rho)$ is the set of rules of the form $q \to \alpha'\langle Z\rangle\beta'$, where $\alpha' Z \beta'$ is a permutation of $\alpha Z \beta$; note that α' and β' need not be of the same length as α and β. The permutation closure of a HCFG G, denoted by $perm(G)$, is obtained by replacing its set of rules by the union of their permutation closures. It is easy to see that a language is a permutation closure of an epsilon-free context-free language (and thereby of an epsilon-free regular language) if and only if it is $SL(perm(G))$ for some HCFG G.

In practice, it is undesirable for a model of natural language syntax to allow indiscriminate permutation of left dependents or of right dependents, let alone indiscriminate swapping of left and right dependents. This motivates considering the following weaker alternative to permutation closure. It involves shuffling the descendents of a node with descendents of other nodes, while preserving the relative order of immediate subtrees. Formally, a complete ph-tree u_2 is a *shuffling* of a complete ph-tree u_1 if their yields, both of length n, are equal under some permutation f of positions in $[n]$ and if for every subtree of u_1 of the form $A(s_1 \cdots s_k, h, t_1 \cdots t_\ell)$, whose immediate subtrees have head positions $i_1, \ldots, i_k, i, j_1, \ldots, j_\ell$, there is a corresponding subtree of u_2 of the form $A(s'_1 \cdots s'_k, h', t'_1 \cdots t'_\ell)$, whose immediate subtrees have head positions $f(i_1), \ldots, f(i_k), f(i), f(j_1), \ldots, f(j_\ell)$. The *shuffle closure* of a set T of complete ph-trees, denoted by $shuffle(T)$, is obtained by replacing every tree $t \in T$ by the set of its shufflings. It is easy to see that $TL(G) = shuffle(TL_c(G))$ for every HCFG G, where $TL_c(G)$ is the tree language that results if $\Rightarrow$ is restricted to continuous derivation.

We have thus seen two ways of relating HCFG to continuous context-free grammar, one in terms of string languages, using the permutation closure, and one in terms of tree languages, using the shuffle closure.

4 Leftmost and Rightmost Derivations

Just as in established theory of context-free grammars, there can be several derivations for the same string and the same tree that differ only in the order in which states are rewritten. For the purpose of designing effective parsers and formulating consistent probability distributions, one traditionally restricts derivations to be either leftmost or rightmost. The behavior of top-down parsers most closely matches leftmost derivations, whereas bottom-up parsers typically match (reversed) rightmost derivations.

Restricting our discontinuous derivations to be either leftmost or rightmost is more involved than in established theory, because of the potentially non-local behavior of derivation steps. Although we could define leftmost and rightmost derivations for arbitrary HCFGs, the definitions become simpler if we restrict ourselves to HCFGs that are separated; a HCFG is called *separated* if terminals only occur in rules of the form $q \rightarrow \varepsilon\langle a\rangle\varepsilon$, where $a \in \Sigma$, and all other rules are of the form $q \rightarrow \alpha\langle r\rangle\beta$, where $r \in Q$ and $\alpha, \beta \in Q^*$. In a rightmost derivation, every sentential form is then split into a prefix and a suffix. The suffix consists entirely of terminals, whereas the prefix is in the set $\{\varepsilon\} \cup Q^*\hat{Q}Q^*$, where $\hat{Q} = \{\hat{q} \mid q \in Q\}$. In words, if the prefix is not the empty string, then it contains only states, of which exactly one has a hat.

The binary relation $\Rightarrow_{rm}$ ('*rm*' for 'rightmost') has $\gamma\hat{q}\delta w \Rightarrow_{rm} \gamma_0 q'_1 \gamma_1 q'_2 \cdots q'_k \gamma_k r' \delta_0 s'_1 \delta_1 s'_2 \cdots s'_\ell \delta_\ell w$ if $q \rightarrow q_1 \cdots q_k \langle r\rangle s_1 \cdots s_\ell$ is a rule, $\gamma = \gamma_0 \cdots \gamma_k \in Q^*$, $\delta = \delta_0 \cdots \delta_\ell \in Q^*$, $w \in \Sigma^*$, $q, q_1, \ldots, q_k, r, s_1, \ldots, s_\ell \in Q$, and $q'_1 \cdots q'_k r' s'_1 \cdots s'_\ell$ is obtained from $q_1 \cdots q_k r s_1 \cdots s_\ell$ by placing the hat on exactly one of these states.

The relation $\Rightarrow_{rm}$ further has $\gamma\hat{q}w \Rightarrow_{rm} \gamma' aw$ if $q \rightarrow \varepsilon\langle a\rangle\varepsilon$ is a rule, where $a \in \Sigma$, and $\gamma' = \gamma$ if $\gamma = \varepsilon$ and otherwise γ' is obtained from γ by placing the hat on exactly one of the states. A derivation starts from the sentential form $\widehat{q_{init}}$.

Perhaps counter-intuitively at first sight, our rightmost derivations do not necessarily rewrite the rightmost state. Instead, a rightmost derivation can be decomposed into several chains of rewrites, each of which ends in a step that is rightmost in the sense of adding one more terminal at the front of the suffix of terminals. After the first step in a single chain, each step rewrites a state introduced by the previous step. This constraint is enforced by placing a hat on a state to be rewritten next.

An example of a chain starts in the third line in Fig. 1(b), with $\widehat{NP}$. In the fourth line, *NP* has been rewritten to *D N PP*, of which the last obtains the hat. The chain ends when *issue* is added at the front of the terminal suffix, upon which another state from the sentential form obtains the hat, in this case the rightmost *D*, which starts a new chain.

Leftmost derivations are analogous. We can define SL_{lm}, TL_{lm}, SL_{rm} and TL_{rm} much as we defined *SL* and *TL*, now restricting the derivations to be leftmost or rightmost, respectively. Of central importance to later sections is:

Theorem 1. *For each HCFG G, we have* $SL(G) = SL_{lm}(G) = SL_{rm}(G)$, *and* $TL(G) = TL_{lm}(G) = TL_{rm}(G)$.

A proof can be given in terms of enhanced derivations, which can be rearranged to become rightmost (or leftmost for the symmetric case). For a string of length n, there are chains of rewrites, one for each $i = n, \ldots, 1$. In the chain for a certain i, only state occurrences are rewritten whose corresponding subtrees have yields that include the i-th terminal but not the j-th terminal in the string, for any $j > i$. Theorem 1 can be refined to formulate a surjective mapping from an arbitrary derivation to a rightmost derivation for the same tree. Moreover, if π is the identity function, then there is a bijective mapping from rightmost derivations to $TL(G)$.

5 The Automaton Model

This section defines a *discontinuous* shift-reduce parser, which computes (reversed) rightmost derivations of a separated HCFG. A *configuration* is a pair consisting of a *stack*, which is a string in $\{\varepsilon\} \cup Q^*\hat{Q}Q^*$, and a *remaining input*, which is a string in Σ^*.

The binary relation $\vdash$ is defined by two allowable steps. A *shift* is $(\gamma, aw) \vdash (\gamma'\hat{q}, w)$ if $q \to \varepsilon\langle a\rangle\varepsilon$ is a rule, and γ' results from γ by removing the occurrence of the hat if there is one (if not, then $\gamma = \varepsilon$). A *reduction* is $(\gamma_0 q'_1 \gamma_1 q'_2 \cdots q'_k \gamma_k r' \delta_0 s'_1 \delta_1 s'_2 \cdots s'_\ell \delta_\ell, w) \vdash (\gamma_0 \cdots \gamma_k \hat{q} \delta_0 \cdots \delta_\ell, w)$ if $q \to q_1 \cdots q_k \langle r\rangle s_1 \cdots s_\ell$ is a rule, and $q'_1 \cdots q'_k r' s'_1 \cdots s'_\ell$ contains exactly one hat, which is removed to give $q_1 \cdots q_k r\, s_1 \cdots s_\ell$. It differs from the usual definition of reduction in continuous parsing by the fact that the occurrences of symbols in the right-hand side of the used rule can be arbitrarily deep in the stack (but in the same relative order as in the rule). The location in the stack where the head is found determines the location of the left-hand side of the rule after the reduction.

A *computation* recognizing a string w is a sequence of steps $(\varepsilon, w) \vdash^* (\widehat{q_{init}}, \varepsilon)$. As $\vdash$ can be seen as the reversal of $\Rightarrow_{rm}$, it is not difficult to see that a string can be recognized if and only if it is in $SL(G)$, using Theorem 1. Further, computations can be enhanced to construct corresponding trees.

For the example from Fig. 1, the computation is:

$$
\begin{array}{lr}
(\varepsilon & , \textit{a hearing is scheduled on the issue today}) \vdash \\
(\widehat{D} & , \textit{hearing is scheduled on the issue today}) \vdash \\
(D\ \widehat{N} & , \textit{is scheduled on the issue today}) \vdash \ldots \vdash \\
(D\ N\ \mathit{Aux}\ V\ P\ \widehat{D} & , \textit{issue today}) \vdash \\
(D\ N\ \mathit{Aux}\ V\ P\ D\ \widehat{N} & , \textit{today}) \vdash \\
(D\ N\ \mathit{Aux}\ V\ \widehat{PP} & , \textit{today}) \vdash \\
(\widehat{NP}\ \mathit{Aux}\ V & , \textit{today}) \vdash \\
(NP\ \mathit{Aux}\ V\ \widehat{ADV} & , \varepsilon) \vdash \\
(NP\ \widehat{VP} & , \varepsilon) \vdash \\
(\widehat{S} & , \varepsilon)
\end{array}
$$

6 Probabilities

There may be many derivations for a given string, each of which determines one tree. In order to disambiguate, and choose one out of those derivations, and thereby one tree, one may impose a probability model, either on steps of the automaton, or on derivation steps. For reasons explained in Sect. 1, we here want to investigate the latter, as before for a fixed HCFG that is separated.

The task ahead is to define a probability distribution over the derivation steps that are possible for a sentential form $\gamma\hat{q}\delta w$. A derivation step is characterized first by a choice of a rule $q \to \alpha\langle r\rangle\beta$ or a rule $q \to \varepsilon\langle a\rangle\varepsilon$; the latter is only possible if $\delta = \varepsilon$. When a non-lexical rule $q \to \alpha\langle r\rangle\beta$ is applied, we also need to choose the way in which γ and δ are broken up, to accommodate for the placement of the elements of α and β, and we need to choose the state among those in $\alpha r \beta$ that will have the hat next. When a lexical rule $q \rightarrow \varepsilon\langle a\rangle\varepsilon$ is applied, we need to choose the state among those in the sentential form that will have the hat next.

In order to be able to estimate parameters effectively, we need to make a number of independence assumptions, which will become clear in the following. The probability of obtaining $\alpha_2 = \gamma_0 q'_1 \gamma_1 \cdots q'_k \gamma_k r' \delta_0 s'_1 \delta_1 \cdots s'_\ell \delta_\ell w$ in one step from $\alpha_1 = \gamma_0 \cdots \gamma_k \hat{q} \delta_0 \cdots \delta_\ell w$ through application of $q \rightarrow q_1 \cdots q_k \langle r \rangle s_1 \cdots s_\ell$, where the m-th state in $q'_1 \cdots q'_k r' s'_1 \cdots s'_\ell$ is the one with the hat, and B denoting the truth value of $\delta_0 \cdots \delta_\ell = \varepsilon$, can be approximated by:

$$\begin{aligned} p(\alpha_2 \mid \alpha_1) \approx\, & p_{rule}(q \rightarrow q_1 \cdots q_k \langle r \rangle s_1 \cdots s_\ell \mid q, B) \cdot \\ & p_{left}(|\gamma_0|, \ldots, |\gamma_k| \mid k, |\gamma_0 \cdots \gamma_k|) \cdot \\ & p_{right}(|\delta_0|, \ldots, |\delta_\ell| \mid \ell, |\delta_0 \cdots \delta_\ell|) \cdot \\ & p_{rule\_hat}(m \mid k, \ell) \end{aligned} \quad (1)$$

The use of p_{rule} embodies the independence assumption that the probability of applying a non-lexical rule for state q does not depend on the context, except for the question whether q is the rightmost state in the sentential form. This is because probability mass may be shared with application of a lexical rule in case $B = \mathbf{true}$, which is to be discussed later.

Further, $p_{left}(i_0, \ldots, i_k \mid k, i)$ is the probability that k left dependents are distributed over $i = i_0 + \ldots + i_k$ states, leaving i_0 states before the first left dependent, i_k after the last left dependent, and i_1, ..., i_{k-1} states between the corresponding pairs of consecutive left dependents. The meaning of $p_{right}(j_0, \ldots, j_\ell \mid \ell, j)$ is analogous. The assumption made here is that the probability of how the left and right dependents are interspersed with the existing states of the sentential form is independent of the identities of the involved states, and only their numbers matter. The motivation behind this assumption is to keep the model simple. Investigation of more refined models is a matter for future research.

Lastly, $p_{rule\_hat}(m \mid k, \ell)$ is the probability that with k left dependents, one head, and ℓ right dependents, the hat is placed on the m-th element, with $m \in [k + 1 + \ell]$. Once more, there is the independence assumption that the identities of the involved states do not matter.

The probability of obtaining $\alpha_2 = \gamma' a w$ from $\alpha_1 = \gamma \hat{q} w$ using a rule $q \rightarrow \varepsilon\langle a\rangle\varepsilon$, where the m-th state in γ' is the one with the hat, can be approximated by:

$$p(\alpha_2 \mid \alpha_1) \approx p_{rule}(q \rightarrow \varepsilon\langle a\rangle\varepsilon \mid q) \cdot p_{lex\_hat}(m \mid |\gamma|) \quad (2)$$

Here p_{rule} is implicitly conditional on $B = \mathbf{true}$, as lexical rules can only rewrite states that occur rightmost in the sentential form. Further, $p_{lex\_hat}(m \mid k)$ is the probability that the hat is placed on the m-th state of a string of k states. Once again, there is the independence assumption that the identities of the involved states do not matter.

We define p_{left} and p_{right} recursively, motivated by the assumption that the probability decreases exponentially with the number of existing states from the sentential form that are interspersed with the dependents. For $i \geq 0$ and $k \geq 0$:

$$p_{left}(i_0 \mid 0, i) = p_{left}(i_0, \ldots, i_k \mid k, 0) = 1 \tag{3}$$

$$p_{left}(i_0, \ldots, i_k, i_{k+1} + 1 \mid k+1, i+1) = P_{left} \cdot p_{left}(i_0, \ldots, i_k, i_{k+1} \mid k+1, i) \tag{4}$$

$$p_{left}(i_0, \ldots, i_k, 0 \mid k+1, i+1) = (1 - P_{left}) \cdot p_{left}(i_0, \ldots, i_k \mid k, i+1) \tag{5}$$

Here P_{left} is the probability that the next dependent is *not* placed rightmost among the available existing states in the sentential form, provided there are any. We have probability 1 if there are no more available states in the sentential form that can be skipped, or no more dependents. We define p_{right} in the same way, with constant P_{right}. By the same reasoning, we define $p_{rule\_hat}(m \mid k, \ell) = P_{rule\_hat}^{k+\ell+1-m} \cdot (1 - P_{rule\_hat})$ for $m > 1$ and $p_{rule\_hat}(m \mid k+\ell+1) = P_{rule\_hat}^{k+\ell+1-m}$ for $m = 1$. Here P_{rule_hat} can be seen as the probability that the hat is *not* placed on the next available state of a rule, from right to left, if there are at least two more available states. We have probability 1 if there is only one more state. We define p_{lex_hat} similarly, with constant P_{lex_hat}, which can be seen as the probability that the hat is *not* placed on the next available state in the sentential form, from right to left.

With the usual assumption of absence of useless rules, a sufficient condition for the above equations to specify a consistent probability model is that there is at least one rule $q \to \alpha\langle r\rangle\beta$ with non-empty β for each q. To illustrate the problem that is potentially caused if this requirement is not satisfied, assume the hat is placed on a state q in the sentential form that is not rightmost, and assume only lexical rules exist that have q as left-hand side. Then no rules at all are applicable, and probability mass is lost.

Such a problem in fact had to be solved for our experiments in Sect. 7 with dependency grammars, which are formalized in terms of rules $q_{init} \to \varepsilon\langle\overline{A}\rangle\varepsilon$, $\overline{A} \to \alpha\langle A\rangle\beta$, and $A \to \varepsilon\langle a\rangle\varepsilon$, where state A represents a part of speech and $\overline{A}$ is an auxiliary state for the same part of speech, α and β are strings of such auxiliary states for parts of speech, and a is a word. Dependency relations are ignored. For each A there is one smoothed bigram model p_{ld} for possible choices of left dependents α and one such model p_{rd} for right dependents β. To avoid problems caused by out-of-vocabulary words and inflection, probabilities of rules $A \to \varepsilon\langle a\rangle\varepsilon$ are ignored, so that conceptually the input consists of a string of parts of speech.

In order to then obtain a probability distribution over derivations, one needs to ensure that the hat cannot be given to a part of speech that is non-rightmost in the sentential form. This is achieved by adjusting the definitions of p_{rule_hat} and p_{lex_hat} to ignore parts of speech unless they are right-most in the sentential form. We further ensure that an auxiliary state $\overline{A}$ that occurs non-rightmost in the sentential form can only be rewritten using $\overline{A} \to \alpha\langle A\rangle\beta$ if $\alpha\beta \neq \varepsilon$, with probability $p_{ld}(\alpha \mid A) \cdot p_{rd}(\beta \mid A) \cdot C_{norm}(A)$, with the normalization factor $C_{norm}(A) = 1/(1 - p_{ld}(\varepsilon \mid A) \cdot p_{rd}(\varepsilon \mid A))$. For rightmost occurrences of $\overline{A}$ there is no such restriction on α and β and the normalization factor is not needed.

Table 1. Perplexity of the likelihood p, and some estimated parameters, for German, Norwegian, English and Hindi, for leftmost and for rightmost derivations.

	$\Rightarrow_{lm}$					$\Rightarrow_{rm}$				
	p	p_{lex_hat}	p_{rule_hat}	p_{left}	p_{right}	p	p_{lex_hat}	p_{rule_hat}	p_{left}	p_{right}
Ge	1.88	$4.0*10^{-3}$	$2.0*10^{-3}$	$1.3*10^{-1}$	$4.2*10^{-2}$	1.89	$6.0*10^{-4}$	$1.1*10^{-2}$	$1.0*10^{-2}$	$2.8*10^{-1}$
No	1.96	$5.8*10^{-4}$	$3.4*10^{-3}$	$5.0*10^{-1}$	$8.5*10^{-2}$	1.97	$2.1*10^{-3}$	$1.7*10^{-2}$	$5.1*10^{-3}$	$2.1*10^{-1}$
En	1.99	$4.8*10^{-4}$	$3.8*10^{-3}$	$5.2*10^{-1}$	$3.7*10^{-2}$	2.00	$1.1*10^{-3}$	$6.5*10^{-3}$	$4.5*10^{-3}$	$2.3*10^{-1}$
Hi	1.72	$2.3*10^{-3}$	$3.6*10^{-3}$	$5.7*10^{-1}$	$4.1*10^{-2}$	1.71	$3.9*10^{-4}$	$2.6*10^{-2}$	$9.6*10^{-3}$	$4.6*10^{-1}$

7 Evaluation

The number of derivations is exponential in the length of a sentence. This makes it infeasible to compute the most probable among all rightmost (or leftmost) derivations. One may use beam search or related pruning techniques to reduce running time. However, an extrinsic evaluation that determines the usual F1 score (combining precision and recall) would then say as much about the used techniques of pruning as it does about the underlying model.

Because our model defines a probability distribution, one may instead perform an intrinsic evaluation in terms of perplexity, which is the negative log likelihood of a test corpus, normalized by the size of that corpus, i.e. $\frac{-\sum_{t \in T} \log_2 p(t)}{\sum_{t \in T} |t|}$. Here T is the set of trees for the test corpus, p is the trained probability model of leftmost or rightmost derivations, and $|t|$ is the number of nodes in t. Perplexity was shown by [23] to be a good indicator of parsing accuracy.

An obvious question to investigate is whether there is a difference in perplexity between leftmost and rightmost derivations. For this, we considered four corpora from the Universal Dependencies treebank [19], taking the first 13000 trees from each training section and the first 950 trees from each testing section. All punctuation was removed and sentences consisting entirely of punctuation were ignored altogether. Table 1 presents perplexity and some of the parameters obtained by maximum likelihood estimation.

Note that the probabilities of p_{rule}, as determined by p_{ld} and p_{rd} and the probabilities of rules $q_{init} \rightarrow \varepsilon\langle\overline{A}\rangle\varepsilon$, are not affected by the direction of the derivations. They make the biggest contribution to the perplexity, so that total values for leftmost and right derivations become very similar. Table 2 therefore looks at the decomposition of the perplexity, into the contributions from p_{rule}, p_{lex_hat}, p_{rule_hat}, from p_{left} and p_{right} together, as well as the (negative) contribution from the normalization factor C_{norm}. Also this more detailed view does not reveal a clear preference for leftmost or rightmost derivations.

Table 2. Perplexity of the likelihood p decomposed.

		$\Rightarrow_{lm}$					$\Rightarrow_{rm}$				
	p_{rule}	p	p_{lex_hat}	p_{rule_hat}	$p_{left}*p_{right}$	C_{norm}	p	p_{lex_hat}	p_{rule_hat}	$p_{left}*p_{right}$	C_{norm}
Ge	1.86	1.88	$5.4*10^{-3}$	$2.9*10^{-3}$	$1.5*10^{-2}$	$-3.0*10^{-4}$	1.89	$8.3*10^{-3}$	$1.3*10^{-2}$	$1.2*10^{-2}$	$-1.6*10^{-3}$
No	1.92	1.96	$4.6*10^{-3}$	$7.0*10^{-3}$	$2.9*10^{-2}$	$-3.4*10^{-4}$	1.97	$1.8*10^{-2}$	$1.8*10^{-2}$	$2.1*10^{-2}$	$-5.5*10^{-3}$
En	1.98	1.99	$1.7*10^{-3}$	$1.1*10^{-3}$	$8.9*10^{-3}$	$-1.8*10^{-4}$	2.00	$4.6*10^{-3}$	$6.7*10^{-3}$	$5.5*10^{-3}$	$-1.4*10^{-3}$
Hi	1.67	1.72	$1.1*10^{-2}$	$6.4*10^{-3}$	$3.4*10^{-2}$	$-5.3*10^{-4}$	1.71	$1.7*10^{-3}$	$2.3*10^{-2}$	$2.0*10^{-2}$	$-1.7*10^{-3}$

8 Conclusion

Motivated by the ultimate aim of developing more accurate and robust parsers that can handle discontinuity, we have introduced a model of syntax that captures discontinuous derivation. Unlike previous models, it explicitly defines a probability distribution over the space of all discontinuous parses. We have shown that this allows evaluation in terms of perplexity.

References

1. Alshawi, H.: Head automata and bilingual tiling: translation with minimal representations. In: Proceedings of the Conference on 34th Annual Meeting of the Association for Computational Linguistics, Santa Cruz, California, USA, pp. 167–176, June 1996
2. Boyd, A.: Discontinuity revisited: an improved conversion to context-free representations. In: Proceedings of the Linguistic Annotation Workshop, at ACL 2007, Prague, Czech Republic, pp. 41–44, June 2007
3. Collins, M.: Head-driven statistical models for natural language parsing. Comput. Linguis. **29**(4), 589–637 (2003)
4. Daniels, M., Meurers, W.: Improving the efficiency of parsing with discontinuous constituents. In: Proceedings of NLULP 2002: The 7th International Workshop on Natural Language Understanding and Logic Programming, Datalogiske Skrifter, vol. 92, pp. 49–68, Roskilde Universitetscenter, Copenhagen (2002)
5. Evang, K., Kallmeyer, L.: PLCFRS parsing of English discontinuous constituents. In: Proceedings of the 12th International Conference on Parsing Technologies, Dublin, Ireland, pp. 104–116, October 2011
6. Gaifman, H.: Dependency systems and phrase-structure systems. Inf. Control **8**, 304–337 (1965)
7. Hays, D.: Dependency theory: a formalism and some observations. Language **40**(4), 511–525 (1964)
8. Jelinek, F., Lafferty, J., Mercer, R.: Basic methods of probabilistic context free grammars. In: Laface, P., De Mori, R. (eds.) Speech Recognition and Understanding – Recent Advances, Trends and Applications, pp. 345–360. Springer, Heidelberg (1992)
9. Kahane, S., Nasr, A., Rambow, O.: Pseudo-projectivity, a polynomially parsable non-projective dependency grammar. In: 36th Annual Meeting of the Association for Computational Linguistics and 17th International Conference on Computational Linguistics, vol. 1, Montreal, Quebec, Canada, pp. 646–652, August 1998
10. Kallmeyer, K., Kuhlmann, M.: A formal model for plausible dependencies in lexicalized tree adjoining grammar. In: Eleventh International Workshop on Tree Adjoining Grammar and Related Formalisms, pp. 108–116 (2012)
11. Kathol, A., Pollard, C.: Extraposition via complex domain formation. In: Proceedings of the Conference on 33rd Annual Meeting of the Association for Computational Linguistics, Cambridge, Massachusetts, USA , pp. 174–180, June 1995
12. Kuhlmann, M.: Mildly non-projective dependency grammar. Comput. Linguis. **39**(2), 355–387 (2013)
13. Maier, W.: Discontinuous incremental shift-reduce parsing. In: 53rd Annual Meeting of the Association for Computational Linguistics and 7th International Joint Conference on Natural Language Processing, vol. 1, Beijing, pp. 1202–1212, July 2015

14. McDonald, R., Pereira, F.: Online learning of approximate dependency parsing algorithms. In: Proceedings of the 11th Conference of the European Chapter of the Association for Computational Linguistics, Trento, Italy, pp. 81–88 (2006)
15. Nederhof, M.J., McCaffery, M.: Deterministic parsing using PCFGs. In: Proceedings of the 14th Conference of the European Chapter of the Association for Computational Linguistics, Gothenburg, Sweden, pp. 338–347 (2014)
16. Nederhof, M.J., Satta, G.: An alternative method of training probabilistic LR parsers. In: Proceedings of the Conference on 42nd Annual Meeting of the Association for Computational Linguistics, Barcelona, Spain, pp. 551–558, July 2004
17. Nederhof, M.J., Vogler, H.: Hybrid grammars for discontinuous parsing. In: The 25th International Conference on Computational Linguistics: Technical papers, Dublin, Ireland, pp. 1370–1381, August 2014
18. Nivre, J.: Non-projective dependency parsing in expected linear time. In: Proceedings of the Joint Conference of the 47th Annual Meeting of the ACL and the 4th International Joint Conference on Natural Language Processing of the AFNLP, Suntec, Singapore, pp. 351–359, August 2009
19. Nivre, J.: Towards a universal grammar for natural language processing. In: Gelbukh, A. (ed.) CICLing 2015. LNCS, vol. 9041, pp. 3–16. Springer, Heidelberg (2015). doi:10.1007/978-3-319-18111-0_1
20. Nivre, J., Nilsson, J.: Pseudo-projective dependency parsing. In: Proceedings of the Conference on 43rd Annual Meeting of the Association for Computational Linguistics, Ann Arbor, Michigan, pp. 99–106, June 2005
21. Petrov, S., Barrett, L., Thibaux, R., Klein, D.: Learning accurate, compact, and interpretable tree annotation. In: Proceedings of the 21st International Conference on Computational Linguistics and 44th Annual Meeting of the Association for Computational Linguistics, Sydney, Australia, pp. 433–440, July 2006
22. Reape, M.: A logical treatment of semi-free word order and bounded discontinuous constituency. In: Proceedings of the Conference on Fourth Conference of the European Chapter of the Association for Computational Linguistics, Manchester, England, pp. 103–110, April 1989
23. Søgaard, A., Haulrich, M.: On the derivation perplexity of treebanks. In: Proceedings of the Ninth International Workshop on Treebanks and Linguistic Theories, Tartu, Estonia, pp. 223–232, December 2010
24. Sornlertlamvanich, V., Inui, K., Tanaka, H., Tokunaga, T., Takezawa, T.: Empirical support for new probabilistic generalized LR parsing. J. Nat. Lang. Process. **6**(3), 3–22 (1999)

Cut Languages in Rational Bases

Jiří Šíma(✉) and Petr Savický

Institute of Computer Science, The Czech Academy of Sciences,
P.O.Box 5, 18207 Prague 8, Czech Republic
{sima,savicky}@cs.cas.cz

Abstract. We introduce a so-called cut language which contains the representations of numbers in a rational base that are less than a given threshold. The cut languages can be used to refine the analysis of neural net models between integer and rational weights. We prove a necessary and sufficient condition when a cut language is regular, which is based on the concept of a quasi-periodic power series. For a nonnegative base and digits, we achieve a dichotomy that a cut language is either regular or non-context-free while examples of regular and non-context-free cut languages are presented. We show that any cut language with a rational threshold is context-sensitive.

Keywords: Grammars · Quasi-periodic power series · Cut language

1 Cut Languages

We study so-called cut languages which contain the representations of numbers in a rational base [1,2,5–7,10,12–15] that are less than a given threshold. Hereafter, let a be a rational number such that $0 < |a| < 1$, which is the inverse of a base (radix) $1/a$ where $|1/a| > 1$, and let $B \subset \mathbb{Q}$ be a finite set of rational digits. We say that $L \subseteq \Sigma^*$ is a *cut language* over a finite alphabet $\Sigma \neq \emptyset$ if there is a bijection $b : \Sigma \longrightarrow B$ and a real threshold c such that

$$L = L_{<c} = \left\{ x_1 \ldots x_n \in \Sigma^* \;\middle|\; \sum_{i=0}^{n-1} b(x_{n-i}) a^i < c \right\} . \tag{1}$$

The cut languages can be used to refine the analysis of computational power of neural network models [17,23]. This analysis is satisfactorily fine-grained in terms of Kolmogorov complexity when changing from rational to arbitrary real weights [4,18]. In contrast, there is still a gap between integer and rational weights, which results in a jump from regular to recursively enumerable languages in the Chomsky hierarchy. In particular, neural nets with *integer* weights, corresponding to binary-state networks, coincide with finite automata [3,8,9,11,16,20,25]. On the other hand, a neural network that contains *two*

Research of both authors was done with institutional support RVO: 67985807 and partially supported by the grant of the Czech Science Foundation No. P202/12/G061.

F. Drewes et al. (Eds.): LATA 2017, LNCS 10168, pp. 311–322, 2017.
DOI: 10.1007/978-3-319-53733-7_23

analog-state units with *rational* weights, can implement two stacks of pushdown automata, a model equivalent to Turing machines [19]. A natural question arises: what is the computational power of binary-state networks including one extra analog unit with rational weights? Such a model is equivalent to finite automata with a register [21], which accept languages that can be represented by some cut languages combined in a certain way by usual operations (e.g. intersection with a regular language, concatenation, union); see [22] for the exact representation.

In this paper we prove a necessary and sufficient condition when a given cut language is regular (Sect. 3). For this purpose, we introduce and characterize an a-quasi-periodic number within B whose all representations in basis $1/a$ using the digits from B, are eventually quasi-periodic power series (Sect. 2). The concept of quasi-periodicity represents a natural generalization of periodicity, allowing for different quasi-repetends even of unbounded length. There are numbers with uncountably many representations, all of which are eventually quasi-periodic, although only countably many of them can be eventually periodic. For a nonnegative base and digits, we achieve a dichotomy that a cut language is either regular or non-context-free. In addition, we present examples of cut languages that are not context-free and we show that any cut language with a rational threshold is context-sensitive (Sect. 4). Finally, we summarize the results and present some open problems (Sect. 5).

2 Quasi-Periodic Power Series

In this section, we introduce and analyze a notion of a-quasi-periodic numbers within B which will be employed for characterizing the class of regular cut languages in Sect. 3. We say that a power series $\sum_{k=0}^{\infty} b_k a^k$ with coefficients $b_k \in B$ for all $k \geq 0$, is *eventually quasi-periodic* with *period sum* P if there is an increasing infinite sequence of its term indices $0 \leq k_1 < k_2 < \cdots$ such that for every $i \geq 1$,

$$\frac{\sum_{k=0}^{m_i-1} b_{k_i+k}\, a^k}{1-a^{m_i}} = P \tag{2}$$

where $m_i = k_{i+1} - k_i > 0$ is the length of *quasi-repetend* $b_{k_i}, \ldots, b_{k_{i+1}-1}$, while k_1 is the length of *preperiodic part* $b_0, \ldots, b_{k_1-1}$. For $k_1 = 0$, we call such a power series *quasi-periodic.* One can calculate the sum of any eventually quasi-periodic power series as

$$\sum_{k=0}^{\infty} b_k a^k = \sum_{k=0}^{k_1-1} b_k a^k + a^{k_1} P \tag{3}$$

since $\sum_{k=k_1}^{\infty} b_k a^k = \sum_{i=1}^{\infty} a^{k_i} \sum_{k=0}^{m_i-1} b_{k_i+k}\, a^k = P \cdot \sum_{i=1}^{\infty} a^{k_i}(1 - a^{m_i}) = P \cdot \sum_{i=1}^{\infty}(a^{k_i} - a^{k_{i+1}}) = a^{k_1} P$ is an absolutely convergent series. It follows that the sum (3) does not change if any quasi-repetend is removed from associated sequence $(b_k)_{k=0}^{\infty}$ or if it is inserted in between two other quasi-repetends, which means that the quasi-repetends can be permuted arbitrarily.

Example 1. A quasi-periodic power series can be composed of quasi-repetends having unbounded length. For example, for any rational period sum $P \neq 0$, we define three rational digits as $\beta_1 = (1-a^2)P$, $\beta_2 = a(1-a)P$, and $\beta_3 = 0$, that is, $B = \{\beta_1, \beta_2, \beta_3\}$. Then $\beta_1, \beta_2^n, \beta_3$ where β_2^n means β_2 repeated n times, creates a quasi-repetend of length $n+2$ for every integer $n \geq 0$, because $(\beta_1 + \sum_{k=1}^{n} \beta_2 a^k + \beta_3 a^{n+1})/(1-a^{n+2}) = P$ whereas for any integer r such that $0 \leq r < n$, it holds $(\beta_1 + \sum_{k=1}^{r} \beta_2 a^k)/(1-a^{r+1}) \neq P$.

Furthermore, given a power series $\sum_{k=0}^{\infty} b_k a^k$, we define its *tail sequence* $(d_n)_{n=0}^{\infty}$ as $d_n = \sum_{k=0}^{\infty} b_{n+k}\, a^k$ for every $n \geq 0$. Denote by $D(\sum_{k=0}^{\infty} b_k a^k) = \{d_n \mid n \geq 0\}$ the set of tail values.

Lemma 2. *A power series $\sum_{k=0}^{\infty} b_k a^k$ with $b_k \in B$ for all $k \geq 0$, is eventually quasi-periodic with period sum P iff its tail sequence $(d_n)_{n=0}^{\infty}$ contains a constant infinite subsequence $(d_{k_i})_{i=1}^{\infty}$ such that $d_{k_i} = P$ for every $i \geq 1$.*

Proof. Let $\sum_{k=0}^{\infty} b_k a^k$ be an eventually quasi-periodic power series with period sum P, which means there is an increasing infinite sequence of its term indices $0 \leq k_1 < k_2 < \cdots$ such that Eq. (2) holds for every $i \geq 1$. It follows that $a^{k_i}\, d_{k_i} = \sum_{k=k_i}^{\infty} b_k\, a^k = \sum_{j=i}^{\infty} a^{k_j} \sum_{k=0}^{m_j-1} b_{k_j+k}\, a^k = P \cdot \sum_{j=i}^{\infty} a^{k_j}(1-a^{m_j}) = P \cdot \sum_{j=i}^{\infty}(a^{k_j} - a^{k_{j+1}}) = a^{k_i} P$, which implies $d_{k_i} = P$ for every $i \geq 1$.

Conversely, assume that $(d_n)_{n=0}^{\infty}$ contains a constant subsequence $(d_{k_i})_{i=1}^{\infty}$ such that $d_{k_i} = P$ for every $i \geq 1$. We have $\sum_{k=0}^{m_i-1} b_{k_i+k}\, a^k = d_{k_i} - a^{m_i} d_{k_{i+1}} = (1-a^{m_i})\, P$ where $m_i = k_{i+1} - k_i > 0$, which implies (2) for every $i \geq 1$. □

Theorem 3. *A power series $\sum_{k=0}^{\infty} b_k a^k$ with $b_k \in B$ for all $k \geq 0$, is eventually quasi-periodic iff the set of its tail values, $D = D(\sum_{k=0}^{\infty} b_k a^k)$, is finite.*

Proof. Assume that D is a finite set, which means there must be a real number $P \in D$ such that $d_{k_i} = P$ for infinitely many indices $0 \leq k_1 < k_2 < \cdots$, that is, $(d_{k_i})_{i=1}^{\infty}$ creates a constant infinite subsequence of tail sequence $(d_n)_{n=0}^{\infty}$. According to Lemma 2, this ensures that $\sum_{k=0}^{\infty} b_k a^k$ is eventually quasi-periodic.

Conversely, let $\sum_{k=0}^{\infty} b_k a^k$ with $b_k \in B$ for all $k \geq 0$, be an eventually quasi-periodic power series with period sum P. Since $a \in \mathbb{Q}$ and $B \subset \mathbb{Q}$ is finite, P is a rational number by (2) and there exists a natural number $\beta > 0$ such that $B' = \{\beta(b - (1-a)P)/a \mid b \in B\} \subset \mathbb{Z}$ is a finite set of integers. According to Lemma 2, the tail sequence $(d_n)_{n=0}^{\infty}$ of $\sum_{k=0}^{\infty} b_k a^k$ contains a constant infinite subsequence $(d_{k_i})_{i=1}^{\infty}$ such that $d_{k_i} = P$ for every $i \geq 1$. Assume to the contrary that $D = \{d_n \mid n \geq 0\}$ is an infinite set.

We define a modified sequence $(d'_n)_{n=0}^{\infty}$ as $d'_n = \beta(d_{k_1+n} - P)$ for all $n \geq 0$, which satisfies $d'_{k'_i} = 0$ where $k'_i = k_i - k_1$, for every $i \geq 1$, and $D' = \{d'_n \mid n \geq 0\}$ is an infinite set. Furthermore, for each $n \geq 0$,

$$\frac{d'_n}{a} - d'_{n+1} = \frac{\beta(d_{k_1+n} - P)}{a} - \beta(d_{k_1+n+1} - P) = \beta\,\frac{b_{k_1+n} - (1-a)P}{a} \in B' \quad (4)$$

is an integer by the definition of B'. In addition, denote $1/a = \alpha/q \in \mathbb{Q}$ where natural number $\alpha > 0$ and integer $q \neq 0$ are coprime.

Lemma 4. *For every $n \geq 0$, there exists an integer δ and a natural number $p \geq 0$ such that $d'_n = \delta/q^p$.*

Proof. We proceed by induction on n. The assertion is obvious for $n = 0$ when $d'_0 = 0$. Assume that $d'_n = \delta/q^p$ for some $\delta \in \mathbb{Z}$ and $p \geq 0$. Then $d'_{n+1} = d'_n/a - b'$ for some integer $b' \in B' \subset \mathbb{Z}$ according to (4), which can be rewritten as $d'_{n+1} = (\alpha/q) \cdot (\delta/q^p) - b' = (\alpha\delta - b'q^{p+1})/q^{p+1} = \delta_1/q^{p+1}$ where $\delta_1 = \alpha\delta - b'q^{p+1} \in \mathbb{Z}$, completing the proof of Lemma 4. □

Lemma 5. *If $d'_{n+1} \in \mathbb{Z}$, then $d'_n \in \mathbb{Z}$.*

Proof. Let $d'_{n+1} \in \mathbb{Z}$. By (4) there is $b' \in B' \subset \mathbb{Z}$ such that $d'_n/a = d'_{n+1} + b' \in \mathbb{Z}$. According to Lemma 4, $d'_n = \delta/q^p$ for some $\delta \in \mathbb{Z}$ and $p \geq 0$, which gives $d'_n/a = \alpha\delta/q^{p+1} \in \mathbb{Z}$. Since α and q are coprime, q^{p+1} must be a factor of δ, which means $\delta = \delta' q^{p+1}$ for some $\delta' \in \mathbb{Z}$, and hence $d'_n = \delta/q^p = \delta' q \in \mathbb{Z}$, completing the proof of Lemma 5. □

We will show for each $n \geq 0$ that $d'_n \in \mathbb{Z}$. Let $i \geq 1$ be the least index such that $k'_i \geq n$ for which we know $d'_{k'_i} = 0 \in \mathbb{Z}$. By applying Lemma 5 $(k'_i - n)$ times we obtain $d'_{k'_i-1}, d'_{k'_i-2}, \ldots, d'_n \in \mathbb{Z}$.

Thus, $D' \subset \mathbb{Z}$ and since D' is infinite, there exists an index $m \geq 0$ such that $|d'_m| \geq (|a| \cdot M)/(1 - |a|) > 0$ where $M = \max_{b' \in B'} |b'|$. Note that $M > 0$ since for $M = 0$, we would have $B = \{(1-a)P\}$ implying $D = \{P\}$ which contradicts that D is infinite. According to (4), $|d'_{m+1}| \geq |d'_m|/|a| - M$ which implies $|d'_{m+1}| - |d'_m| \geq (1/|a| - 1)|d'_m| - M \geq 0$ by the definition of m. Hence, $|d'_{m+1}| \geq |d'_m|$, and by induction we obtain $|d'_n| \geq (|a| \cdot M)/(1 - |a|) > 0$ for every $n \geq m$. On the other hand, we know that there is an index i such that $k'_i \geq m$ for which $d'_{k'_i} = 0$, which is a contradiction completing the proof of Theorem 3.□

We say that a real number c is *a-quasi-periodic within* B if any power series $\sum_{k=0}^{\infty} b_k a^k = c$ with $b_k \in B$ for all $k \geq 0$, is eventually quasi-periodic. Note that c that cannot be written as a respective power series at all, or can, in addition, be expressed as a finite sum $\sum_{k=0}^{h} b_k a^k = c$ whereas $0 \notin B$, is also considered formally to be a-quasi-periodic. For example, the numbers from the complement of the Cantor set are formally $(1/3)$-quasi-periodic within $\{0, 2\}$.

Example 6. Example 1 can be extended to provide a nontrivial instance of an a-quasi-periodic number that has infinitely many different quasi-periodic representations composed of quasi-repetends of arbitrary length (greater than 1). This includes ordinarily periodic representations composed of one of these quasi-repetends and uncountably many non-periodic ones. Let $a \in \mathbb{Q}$ meet $0 < a < \frac{1}{2}$. We show that any positive rational number c is a-quasi-periodic within B where $B = \{\beta_1, \beta_2, \beta_3\}$ is defined in Example 1 so that $P = c$. Obviously, $\beta_1 > \beta_2 > \beta_3 = 0$. Assume that $c = \sum_{k=0}^{\infty} b_k a^k$ for some sequence $(b_k)_{k=0}^{\infty}$ where $b_k \in B$ for all $k \geq 0$. Observe first that it must be $b_0 = \beta_1$ since otherwise $c = \sum_{k=0}^{\infty} b_k a^k \leq \beta_2 + \sum_{k=1}^{\infty} \beta_1 a^k = a(1-a)c + (1-a^2)c \cdot a/(1-a) = 2ac < c$ due to $a < \frac{1}{2}$. Moreover, for any $n \geq 0$ such that $b_k = \beta_2$ for every $k = 1, \ldots, n$, it holds $b_{n+1} \neq \beta_1$ since otherwise $c = \sum_{k=0}^{\infty} b_k a^k \geq \beta_1 + \sum_{k=1}^{n} \beta_2 a^k + \beta_1 a^{n+1} = (1-a^2)c + a(1-a)c \cdot a(1-a^n)/(1-a) + (1-a^2)c \cdot a^{n+1} = c - a^{n+1}(a^2+a-1)c > c$ due to $a^2 + a - 1 < 0$ for $0 < a < \frac{1}{2}$.

First consider the case when there is $r \geq 1$ such that $b_k = \beta_2$ for all $k \geq r$. Then $b_0, \ldots, b_{r-1}$ is a preperiodic part and $b_k = \beta_2$ for $k \geq r$ represents a repetend of length $m_k = 1$, which proves $\sum_{k=0}^{\infty} b_k a^k$ to be eventually quasi-periodic. Further assume there is no such r, and thus $b_k = \beta_2$ for every $k = 1, \ldots, n_1$ and $b_{n_1+1} = \beta_3$, for some $n_1 \geq 0$. It follows that series $\sum_{k=0}^{\infty} b_k a^k = c$ starts with a quasi-repetend $\beta_1, \beta_2^{n_1}, \beta_3$ of length n_1+2 (cf. Example 1) which can be omitted as $\sum_{k=0}^{\infty} b_{n_1+2+k} a^k = (c - \sum_{k=0}^{n_1+1} b_k a^k)/a^{n_1+2} = c$ due to $\sum_{k=0}^{n_1+1} b_k a^k = c(1-a^{n_1+2})$ by (2), and the argument can be repeated for its tail $\sum_{k=0}^{\infty} b_{n_1+2+k} a^k = c$ to reveal the next quasi-repetend $\beta_1, \beta_2^{n_2}, \beta_3$ for some $n_2 \geq 0$ etc. Hence, $\sum_{k=0}^{\infty} b_k a^k$ is quasi-periodic, which completes the proof that c is a-quasi-periodic within B.

Example 7. On the other hand, we present an example of an eventually quasi-periodic series $\sum_{k=0}^{\infty} b_k a^k = c$ with $b_k \in B$ for all $k \geq 0$, such that c is not a-quasi-periodic within B. Let $a = \frac{2}{3}$, $B = \{0, 1\}$, and define an eventually quasi-periodic series $\sum_{k=0}^{\infty} b_k a^k$ with a preperiodic part $b_0 = b_1 = 0$ and a repetend $b_{2+3k} = 0$, $b_{3+3k} = b_{4+3k} = 1$ for every $k \geq 0$, which sums to $c = ((\frac{2}{3})^3 + (\frac{2}{3})^4) \cdot \sum_{k=0}^{\infty} (\frac{2}{3})^{3k} = \frac{40}{57}$.

Furthermore, we employ a greedy approach to generate a series $\sum_{k=0}^{\infty} b'_k a^k = c$ with $b'_k \in \{0, 1\}$ for all $k \geq 0$, which is not eventually quasi-periodic. In particular, find minimal $k_1 \geq 0$ such that $a^{k_1} < c$ which gives $b'_0 = \cdots = b'_{k_1-1} = 0$, $b'_{k_1} = 1$, and remainder $c_1 = c/a^{k_1} - 1$. For $n > 1$, let $b'_0, \ldots, b'_{k_{n-1}}$ be 0s except for $b'_{k_1} = b'_{k_2} = \cdots = b'_{k_{n-1}} = 1$. Then find minimal $k_n > k_{n-1}$ such that $a^{k_n - k_{n-1}} < c_{n-1}$ which produces $b'_{k_{n-1}+1} = \cdots = b'_{k_n - 1} = 0$, $b'_{k_n} = 1$, and remainder $c_n = c_{n-1}/a^{k_n - k_{n-1}} - 1$. It follows that $c_n = \sum_{k=0}^{\infty} b'_{k_n+k} a^k - 1 = (c - \sum_{i=1}^{n} a^{k_i})/a^{k_n}$ for $n \geq 1$. By plugging $a = \frac{2}{3}$ and $c = \frac{40}{57}$ into this formula, for which $k_1 = 1$ and $k_2 = 9$, we obtain

$$c_n = \frac{20}{19}\left(\frac{3}{2}\right)^{k_n-1} - \sum_{i=1}^{n}\left(\frac{3}{2}\right)^{k_n-k_i} = \frac{3^{k_n-1} - 19 \cdot 2 \cdot \sum_{i=2}^{n} 2^{k_i-2} \cdot 3^{k_n-k_i}}{19 \cdot 2^{k_n-1}} \tag{5}$$

which is an irreducible fraction since both 19 and 2 are not factors of 3^{k_n-1}. Hence, for any natural n_1, n_2 such that $0 < n_1 < n_2$ we know $c_{n_1} \neq c_{n_2}$. It follows that the tail sequence $(d'_n)_{n=0}^{\infty}$ of $\sum_{k=0}^{\infty} b'_k a^k = c$ contains infinitely many different values $d'_{k_n} = c_n + 1$ for $n \geq 1$, which implies that $\sum_{k=0}^{\infty} b'_k a^k$ is not an eventually quasi-periodic series, according to Theorem 3.

Theorem 8. *A real number c is a-quasi-periodic within B iff the tail sequences of all the power series satisfying $\sum_{k=0}^{\infty} b_k a^k = c$ with $b_k \in B$ for all $k \geq 0$, contain altogether only finitely many values, that is,*

$$\mathcal{D} = \bigcup_{\substack{\sum_{k=0}^{\infty} b_k a^k = c \\ forall\, k \geq 0,\, b_k \in B}} D\left(\sum_{k=0}^{\infty} b_k a^k\right) \tag{6}$$

is a finite set. In addition, if c is not a-quasi-periodic within B, then there exists a power series $\sum_{k=0}^{\infty} b_k a^k = c$ with $b_k \in B$ for all $k \geq 0$, whose tail sequence contains pair-wise different values.

Proof. Let $\mathcal{D}$ be a finite set. Then the tail sequence of any power series $\sum_{k=0}^{\infty} b_k a^k = c$ with $b_k \in B$ for all $k \geq 0$, contains only finitely many values and thus includes a constant infinite subsequence. According to Lemma 2, this implies that any $\sum_{k=0}^{\infty} b_k a^k = c$ is eventually quasi-periodic, and hence, c is a-quasi-periodic within B.

Conversely, assume that $\mathcal{D}$ is infinite. Consider a directed tree $T = (V, E)$ with vertex set $V \subseteq B^*$ such that $b_0 \cdots b_{n-1} \in V$ if its tail meets $t(b_0 \cdots b_{n-1}) = (c - \sum_{k=0}^{n-1} b_k a^k)/a^n \in \mathcal{D}$, which includes the empty string ε as a root satisfying $t(\varepsilon) = c$. Define a set of directed edges as

$$E = \{(b_0 \cdots b_{n-1}, b_0 \cdots b_{n-1} b_n) \,|\, b_0 \cdots b_{n-1}, b_0 \cdots b_{n-1} b_n \in V\} \,, \qquad (7)$$

which guarantees the outdegree of T is bounded by $|B|$. Let $T' = (V', E')$ be a subtree of T with a maximal vertex subset $V' \subseteq V$ so that $\varepsilon \in V'$ and $t(v_1) \neq t(v_2)$ for any two different vertices $v_1, v_2 \in V'$.

We show that for any $d \in \mathcal{D}$ there is $v \in V'$ such that $t(v) = d$. On the contrary, suppose $b_0 \cdots b_{n-1} \in V \setminus V'$ is a vertex with minimal n, satisfying $t(v) \neq t(b_0 \cdots b_{n-1}) = d \in \mathcal{D}$ for every $v \in V'$. Clearly, $b_0 \cdots b_{n-2} \in V \setminus V'$ since otherwise vertex $b_0 \cdots b_{n-1}$ could be included into V' which contradicts the maximality of V'. By the minimality of n, we know there is $b'_0 \cdots b'_{m-1} \in V'$ such that $t(b'_0 \cdots b'_{m-1}) = t(b_0 \cdots b_{n-2})$. Thus, we have $t(b'_0 \cdots b'_{m-1} b_{n-1}) = d$ and the maximality of V' implies $b'_0 \cdots b'_{m-1} b_{n-1} \in V'$, which is in contradiction with the definition of $b_0 \cdots b_{n-1}$.

It follows that $\{t(v) \,|\, v \in V'\} = \mathcal{D}$ implying T' is infinite. According to König's lemma, there exists an infinite directed path in T' corresponding to a power series $\sum_{k=0}^{\infty} b_k a^k = c$ whose tail sequence contains pair-wise different values. By Lemma 2, this series is not eventually quasi-periodic and hence, c is not a-quasi-periodic within B. □

3 Regular Cut Languages

In this section we formulate a necessary and sufficient condition for a cut language $L_{<c}$ to be regular (Theorem 11), which is based on a-quasi-periodic thresholds c within B. The following Lemma 9 provides a technical characterization of the regular cut languages, which is proven by Myhill-Nerode theorem, while subsequent Lemma 10 separates the cases when threshold c is represented by a finite sum or when c has no representation in base $1/a$ using the digits from B.

Lemma 9. *Let Σ be a finite alphabet, $b : \Sigma \longrightarrow B$ be a bijection, and c be a real number. Then the cut language $L_{<c} = \{x_1 \cdots x_n \in \Sigma^* \mid \sum_{i=0}^{n-1} b(x_{n-i}) a^i < c\}$ is regular iff the set*

$$C = \left\{ c(b_0, \ldots, b_{\kappa-1}) \;\middle|\; I_\kappa \leq c - \sum_{k=0}^{\kappa-1} b_k a^k \leq S_\kappa \,;\, b_0, \ldots, b_{\kappa-1} \in B \,;\, \kappa \geq 0 \right\} \quad (8)$$

is finite, where

$$I_\kappa = \inf_{\substack{b_\kappa,\ldots,b_{h-1}\in B \\ h\geq\kappa}} \sum_{k=\kappa}^{h-1} b_k a^k \,, \qquad S_\kappa = \sup_{\substack{b_\kappa,\ldots,b_{h-1}\in B \\ h\geq\kappa}} \sum_{k=\kappa}^{h-1} b_k a^k \,, \tag{9}$$

$$c(b_0,\ldots,b_{\kappa-1}) = \begin{cases} \inf C(b_0,\ldots,b_{\kappa-1}) & if\, a^\kappa > 0 \\ \sup C(b_0,\ldots,b_{\kappa-1}) & if\, a^\kappa < 0\,, \end{cases} \tag{10}$$

$$C(b_0,\ldots,b_{\kappa-1}) = \left\{ \sum_{k=0}^{h-\kappa-1} b_{\kappa+k} a^k \;\middle|\; \sum_{k=0}^{h-1} b_k a^k \geq c;\, b_\kappa,\ldots,b_{h-1}\in B\,;\, h\geq\kappa \right\}. \tag{11}$$

Proof. Let $C = \{c_1, \ldots, c_p\}$ in (8) be a finite set such that $c_1 < c_2 < \cdots < c_p$. We introduce an equivalence relation $\sim$ on Σ^* as follows. For any $x, y \in \Sigma^*$ of length $n_x = |x|$ and $n_y = |y|$, respectively, we define $x \sim y$ iff both $z_x = \sum_{i=0}^{n_x-1} b(x_{n_x-i})a^i$ and $z_y = \sum_{i=0}^{n_y-1} b(y_{n_x-i})a^i$ belong either to one of the $p+1$ open intervals $(-\infty, c_1), (c_1, c_2), \ldots, (c_{p-1}, c_p), (c_p, \infty)$, or to one of the p singletons $\{c_1\}, \{c_2\}, \ldots, \{c_p\}$. Obviously, we have $2p+1$ equivalence classes. In order to prove that language $L_{<c}$ is regular we employ Myhill-Nerode theorem by showing that for any $x, y \in \Sigma^*$, if $x \sim y$, then for every $w \in \Sigma^*$, $xw \in L_{<c}$ iff $yw \in L_{<c}$. Thus, consider $x, y \in \Sigma^*$ such that $x \sim y$, and on the contrary, suppose there is $w \in \Sigma^*$ of length $\kappa = |w|$ with $z_w = \sum_{i=0}^{\kappa-1} b(w_{\kappa-i})a^i$, such that $xw \in L_{<c}$ and $yw \notin L_{<c}$. This means $z_w + I_\kappa \leq z_w + a^\kappa z_x < c \leq z_w + a^\kappa z_y \leq z_w + S_\kappa$ by (9), implying $I_\kappa < c - z_w \leq S_\kappa$ which ensures $c_j = c(b(w_\kappa), \ldots, b(w_1)) \in C$ for some $j \in \{1, \ldots, p\}$, according to (8). It follows from (10) and (11) that $z_w + a^\kappa z_x < c \leq z_w + a^\kappa c_j \leq z_w + a^\kappa z_y$ which gives $a^\kappa z_x < a^\kappa c_j \leq a^\kappa z_y$ contradicting $x \sim y$.

Conversely, let $L_{<c}$ be a regular languages. According to Myhill-Nerode theorem, there is an equivalence relation $\sim$ on Σ^* with a finite number p of equivalence classes such that for any $x, y \in \Sigma^*$, if $x \sim y$, then for every $w \in \Sigma^*$, $xw \in L_{<c}$ iff $yw \in L_{<c}$. Assume to the contrary that C in (8) is infinite. Choose $c_0, c_1, \ldots, c_{2p+2} \in C$ so that $c_0 < c_1 < \cdots < c_{2p+2}$, and for each $j \in \{0, \ldots, 2p+2\}$, let $c_j = c(b_{j0}, \ldots, b_{j,\kappa_j-1})$ for some $b_{j0}, \ldots, b_{j,\kappa_j-1} \in B$ and $\kappa_j \geq 0$, according to (8). Definition's (10) and (11) ensure that for each odd $j \in \{1, 3, \ldots, 2p+1\}$, there exists $h_j \geq \kappa_j$ and $b_{j,\kappa_j}, \ldots, b_{j,h_j-1} \in B$ such that $c'_j = \sum_{k=0}^{h_j-\kappa_j-1} b_{j\kappa_j+k}a^k$ is sufficiently close to c_j so that $c_{j-1} < c'_j < c_{j+1}$. Since there are only p equivalence classes, there must be two odd indices $j_x, j_y \in \{1, 3, \ldots, 2p+1\}$, say $j_x < j_y$, determining $x, y \in \Sigma^*$ of length $n_x = |x| = h_{j_x} - \kappa_{j_x}$ and $n_y = |y| = h_{j_y} - \kappa_{j_y}$, respectively, by $b(x_{n_x-i}) = b_{j_x,\kappa_{j_x}+i}$ for $i = 0, \ldots, n_x - 1$ and $b(y_{n_y-i}) = b_{j_y,\kappa_{j_y}+i}$ for $i = 0, \ldots, n_y - 1$, such that $x \sim y$. Thus, $c'_{j_x} = \sum_{i=0}^{n_x-1} b(x_{n_x-i})a^i$ and $c'_{j_y} = \sum_{i=0}^{n_y-1} b(y_{n_y-i})a^i$. For $a^\kappa > 0$, choose $w \in \Sigma^*$ of length $\kappa = |w| = \kappa_{j_x+1}$ so that $c_{j_x+1} = c(b(w_\kappa), \ldots, b(w_1))$, and denote $z_w = \sum_{i=0}^{\kappa-1} b(w_{\kappa-i})a^i$. We know $c'_{j_x} < c_{j_x+1} < c'_{j_y}$. It follows that $z_w + a^\kappa c'_{j_x} < c \leq z_w + a^\kappa c_{j_x+1} < z_w + a^\kappa c'_{j_y}$ since $z_w + a^\kappa c'_{j_x} \geq c$ would contradict that c_{j_x+1} is the infimum according to (10) and (11). Hence, $xw \in L_{<c}$ and

$yw \notin L_{<c}$, which gives the contradiction. Similarly for $a^\kappa < 0$, choose $w \in \Sigma^*$ so that $c_{j_y-1} = c(b(w_\kappa), \ldots, b(w_1))$, which gives $z_w + a^\kappa c'_{j_y} < c \le z_w + a^\kappa c_{j_y-1} < z_w + a^\kappa c'_{j_x}$, leading to the contradiction $xw \notin L_{<c}$ and $yw \in L_{<c}$. □

Lemma 10. *Assume the notation as in Lemma 9. Then the two subsets of* $C, C_1 = \{c(b_0, \ldots, b_{\kappa-1}) \in C \mid \sum_{k=0}^{\kappa-1} b_k a^k + a^\kappa c(b_0, \ldots, b_{\kappa-1}) > c\}$ *and* $C_2 = \{c(b_0, \ldots, b_{\kappa-1}) \in C \mid (\exists\, b_\kappa, \ldots, b_{h-1} \in B\,,\, h \ge \kappa) \sum_{k=0}^{h-1} b_k a^k = c \,\&\, (\forall\, b \in B)$ $c(b_0, \ldots, b_{h-1}, b) \in C_1\}$ *are finite.*

Proof. We define a directed rooted tree $T = (V, E)$ with vertex set $V = \{b_0 \cdots b_{k-1} \in B^* \mid (\exists\, b_k, \ldots, b_{\kappa-1} \in B)\, c(b_0, \ldots, b_{k-1}, b_k \ldots, b_{\kappa-1}) \in C_1\}$, including an empty string as a root, and a set of directed edges (7). Clearly, T covers all the directed paths starting at the root and leading to $b_0 \cdots b_{\kappa-1} \in V$ such that $c(b_0, \ldots, b_{\kappa-1}) \in C_1$. This also guarantees that T includes all $b_0 \cdots b_{\kappa-1} \in V$ such that $c(b_0, \ldots, b_{\kappa-1}) \in C_2$, by the definition of C_2. For each vertex $b_0 \cdots b_{k-1} \in V$ we define a closed interval $I(b_0, \ldots, b_{k-1}) = [\sum_{i=0}^{k-1} b_i a^i + I_k\,, \sum_{i=0}^{k-1} b_i a^i + S_k]$ by using (9). Obviously, $I(b_0, \ldots, b_{k-1}, b_k) \subset I(b_0, \ldots, b_{k-1})$ for any edge $(b_0 \cdots b_{k-1}, b_0 \cdots b_{k-1} b_k) \in E$. Hence, $c \in I(b_0, \ldots, b_{k-1})$ for every vertex $b_0 \cdots b_{k-1} \in V$ since $b_0 \cdots b_{k-1} \cdots b_{\kappa-1} \in V$ such that $c(b_0, \ldots, b_{\kappa-1}) \in C_1$ satisfies $c \in I(b_0, \ldots, b_{\kappa-1}) \subset I(b_0, \ldots, b_{k-1})$ according to (8).

On the contrary, suppose that tree T whose outdegree is bounded by $|B|$, is infinite. According to König's lemma, there exists an infinite directed path corresponding to an infinite sequence $(b_k^*)_{k=0}^\infty$ with $b_k^* \in B$ for all $k \ge 0$, which contains infinitely many vertices $b_0^* \cdots b_{\kappa-1}^* \in V$ such that $c(b_0^*, \ldots, b_{\kappa-1}^*) \in C_1$. On the other hand, interval $I(b_0^*, \ldots, b_{k-1}^*)$ is a nonempty compact set satisfying $c \in I(b_0^*, \ldots, b_{k-1}^*) \supset I(b_0^*, \ldots, b_k^*)$ for every $k \ge 1$, which yields $c \in \bigcap_{k \ge 0} I(b_0^*, \ldots, b_{k-1}^*) \ne \emptyset$ by Cantor's intersection theorem. Hence, $\sum_{k=0}^\infty b_k^* a^k = c$ which implies $\sum_{k=0}^{\kappa-1} b_k^* a^k + a^\kappa c(b_0^*, \ldots, b_{\kappa-1}^*) = c$ for any $b_0^* \cdots b_{\kappa-1}^* \in V$ such that $c(b_0^*, \ldots, b_{\kappa-1}^*) \in C_1$, according to (10) and (11), which contradicts the definition of C_1. It follows that T is finite which implies that C_1, C_2 are finite. □

Theorem 11. *A cut language $L_{<c}$ is regular iff c is a-quasi-periodic within B.*

Proof. According to Lemma 9, language $L_{<c}$ is regular iff set C is finite which is equivalent to the condition that $C \setminus (C_1 \cup C_2)$ is finite, by Lemma 10. It follows from (8)–(11) that for any $b_0, \ldots, b_{\kappa-1} \in B$ and $\kappa \ge 0$, $c(b_0, \ldots, b_{\kappa-1}) \in C \setminus (C_1 \cup C_2)$ iff there exists sequence $(b_k)_{k=\kappa}^\infty$ with $b_k \in B$ for all $k \ge 0$, such that $\sum_{k=0}^{\kappa-1} b_k a^k + a^\kappa c(b_0, \ldots, b_{\kappa-1}) = c$ $(c(b_0, \ldots, b_{\kappa-1}) \notin C_1)$ and $\sum_{k=0}^\infty b_k a^k = c$ $(c(b_0, \ldots, b_{\kappa-1}) \notin C_2)$, which yields $c(b_0, \ldots, b_{\kappa-1}) = \sum_{k=0}^\infty b_{\kappa+k} a^k$. It follows that $C \setminus (C_1 \cup C_2) = \mathcal{D}$ by the definition of $\mathcal{D}$, which is finite iff c is a-quasi-periodic within B, according to Theorem 8. □

4 Non-Context-Free Cut Languages

In this section we show in Theorem 13 that for $0 < a < 1$ and any set of non-negative digits B, a cut language $L_{<c}$ is not context-free if threshold c is not

a-quasi-periodic within B, which is proven by a pumping technique introduced in Lemma 12. According to Theorem 11, we thus achieve a dichotomy that, at least for these parameters, a cut language is either regular or non-context-free. We present explicit instances of rational numbers with no eventually quasi-periodic representations in Example 14. On the other hand, the cut languages with rational thresholds are shown to be context-sensitive in Theorem 15.

We say that an infinite word $x \in \Sigma^\omega$ is *approximable* in a language $L \subseteq \Sigma^*$, if for every finite prefix $u \in \Sigma^*$ of x, there is $y \in \Sigma^*$ such that $uy \in L$.

Lemma 12. *Let $x \in \Sigma^\omega$ be approximable in a context-free language $L \subseteq \Sigma^*$. Then there is a decomposition $x = uvw$ where $u, v \in \Sigma^*$ and $w \in \Sigma^\omega$, such that $|v| > 0$ and for every integer $i \geq 0$, infinite word uv^iw is approximable in L.*

Proof. Consider a context-free grammar G for L in Greibach normal form such that for every nonterminal A of G, there is a derivation of a terminal word from A. Since x is approximable in $L = L(G)$, there is a left derivation $S \Rightarrow \ldots \Rightarrow u_n\alpha_n$ for every n, such that $u_n \in \Sigma^*$ is the prefix of x of length n, and α_n is a sequence of nonterminal symbols. These derivations form an infinite directed rooted tree with the root S, whose vertices are the left sentential forms $u\alpha$ such that u is a prefix of x, and the edges outcoming from $u\alpha$ correspond to an application of one production rule to the left-most nonterminal in α. The degree of each vertex is bounded by the number of production rules. According to König's lemma, there is an infinite left derivation $S \Rightarrow \ldots \Rightarrow u_n\alpha_n \Rightarrow \ldots$ such that for every n, u_n is the prefix of x of length n,and α_n is a non-empty sequence of nonterminal symbols.

Let us call an occurrence of a nonterminal in α_n *temporary*, if it is substituted by a production rule of G in some of the following steps, and *stable* otherwise. We prove that for every n, there is $m \geq n$ such that α_m contains exactly one temporary nonterminal. We know the left-most nonterminal A_1 in $\alpha_n = A_1 \ldots A_i \ldots A_k$ is temporary, and let A_i be the right-most temporary nonterminal in α_n. If $i = 1$, then choose $m = n$. For $i \geq 2$, there is an index m, such that all the temporary nonterminals $A_1, \ldots, A_{i-1}$ in α_n are transformed into terminal words in u_m. If m is the smallest such index, then A_i is the first and the only temporary nonterminal of α_m. It follows that there is an infinite number of indices n such that α_n contains exactly one temporary nonterminal.

Since there are only finitely many nonterminals in G, there exist two indices n_1, n_2 where $n_1 < n_2$, such that $\alpha_{n_1} = A\beta_1$, $\alpha_{n_2} = A\beta_2\beta_1$, and $|u_{n_1}| < |u_{n_2}|$ for some nonterminal A, whereas β_1 and β_2 consist of stable nonterminals in both α_{n_1} and α_{n_2}. Thus, there are two words $u, v \in \Sigma^*$ such that $u_{n_1}\alpha_{n_1} = uA\beta_1$, $u_{n_2}\alpha_{n_2} = uvA\beta_2\beta_1$, and $|v| > 0$, where $A \overset{*}{\Rightarrow} vA\beta_2$. For every $m \geq n_2$, we have $u_m\alpha_m = uv\gamma_m\beta_2\beta_1$ where γ_m is such that $A \overset{*}{\Rightarrow} \gamma_m$. Hence, an infinite word $w \in \Sigma^\omega$ is produced from A, such that $x = uvw$. Clearly, every finite prefix of w is the terminal part of γ_m for some $m \geq n_2$.

For every $i \geq 0$, we can construct an infinite left derivation whose sentential forms contain arbitrarily long prefixes of the sequence uv^iw by combining the above derivations similarly as in the proof of the pumping lemma. The derivation starts as the original derivation until $u_{n_1}\alpha_{n_1} = uA\beta_1$. Then, the derivation $A \stackrel{*}{\Rightarrow} vA\beta_2$ is used i times. Finally, the derivations $A \stackrel{*}{\Rightarrow} \gamma_m$ are used in an infinite sequence for all $m > n_2$. Altogether, we obtain

$$S \stackrel{*}{\Rightarrow} uA\beta_1 \stackrel{*}{\Rightarrow} uv^i A\beta_2^i\beta_1 \Rightarrow \ldots \Rightarrow uv^i\gamma_m\beta_2^i\beta_1 \Rightarrow \ldots \quad \text{for all} m > n_2 \,. \tag{12}$$

We show that for every $i \geq 0$, the infinite sequence uv^iw is approximable in L. For any prefix $u' \in \Sigma^*$ of uv^iw, we employ the derivation (12) until u' is derived. Then, we include any finite derivation of a terminal word from each of the remaining nonterminals. We obtain a word in $L = L(G)$ with prefix u'. □

Theorem 13. *Assume that* $0 < a < 1$, B *contains only nonnegative rationals,* Σ *is a finite alphabet, and* $b : \Sigma \longrightarrow B$ *is a bijection. If* c *is not* a*-quasi-periodic within* B *(see Examples 7 and 14 for instances of such* $c \in \mathbb{Q}$*), then the cut language* $L_{<c}$ *is not context-free.*

Proof. For any string $x = x_1 \ldots x_n \in \Sigma^*$ of length $n = |x|$, denote $z_x = \sum_{k=0}^{n-1} b(x_{k+1})a^k$, whereas $z_x = \sum_{k=0}^{\infty} b(x_{k+1})a^k$ for an infinite word $x \in \Sigma^\omega$. Assume for a contradiction that $L_{<c}$ is a context-free language, and hence the same holds for its reversal $L = L_{<c}^R = \{x \in \Sigma^* \mid z_x < c\}$.

Since c is not eventually a-quasi-periodic within B, Theorem 8 provides an infinite word $x \in \Sigma^\omega$ such that the tail sequence of a power series $z_x = \sum_{k=0}^{\infty} b(x_{k+1})a^k = c$ is composed of pair-wise different values. Moreover, x contains infinitely many non-zero (and thus positive) digits, which ensures that for every prefix u of x, it holds $z_u < z_x = c$, that is, $u \in L$. Hence, x is approximable in L. Let $x = uvw$ where $|v| > 0$, be a decomposition guaranteed by Lemma 12. In particular, uw and $uvvw$ are also approximable in L. We know the tails z_w and z_{vw} are different. If $z_w > z_{vw}$, then define $y = uw$ which meets $z_y = z_{uw} = z_u + a^{|u|}z_w > z_u + a^{|u|}z_{vw} = z_{uvw} = z_x = c$, due to $a > 0$. On the other hand, if $z_{vw} > z_w$, then define $y = uvvw$ which satisfies $z_y = z_{uvvw} = z_{uv} + a^{|uv|}z_{vw} > z_{uv} + a^{|uv|}z_w = z_{uvw} = z_x = c$.

Thus, we have $y \in \Sigma^\omega$ which is approximable in L and $z_y > c$. This means that for every integer $n \geq 0$, there is $y_n \in L$ implying $z_{y_n} < c$, such that y and y_n share the same prefix of length at least n. Hence, $|z_y - z_{y_n}| \leq \beta a^n/(1-a)$ where $\beta = \max\{|b_1 - b_2|\,;\, b_1 \in B,\, b_2 \in B \cup \{0\}\}$. It follows that z_{y_n} converges to z_y as n tends to infinity, which contradicts $z_{y_n} < c < z_y$. □

Example 14. We generalize Example 7 to provide instances of rational numbers c such that any power series $\sum_{k=0}^{\infty} b'_k a^k = c$ with $b'_k \in B$ for all $k \geq 0$, is not eventually quasi-periodic. Let $B = \{0, 1\}$ and $a = \alpha_1/\alpha_2$, $c = \gamma_1/\gamma_2 \in \mathbb{Q}$ be irreducible fractions where $\alpha_1, \gamma_1 \in \mathbb{Z}$ and $\alpha_2, \gamma_2 \in \mathbb{N}$, such that $\alpha_1\gamma_2$ and $\alpha_2\gamma_1$ are coprime. Denote by $0 < k_1 < k_2 < \cdots$ all the indices of a (not necessarily greedy) representation of $c = \sum_{k=0}^{\infty} b'_k a^k$ such that $b'_{k_i} = 1$ for $i \geq 1$. Then formula (5) can be rewritten as

$$c_n = \frac{\gamma_1\alpha_2^{k_n} - \gamma_2\alpha_1 \sum_{i=1}^{n} \alpha_1^{k_i - 1}\alpha_2^{k_n - k_i}}{\gamma_2\alpha_1^{k_n}} \tag{13}$$

which is still an irreducible fraction.

Theorem 15. *Every cut language $L_{<c}$ with threshold $c \in \mathbb{Q}$ is context-sensitive.*

Proof. A corresponding (deterministic) linear bounded automaton M that accepts a given cut language $L_{<c} = L(M)$, evaluates (and stores) the sum $s_n = \sum_{i=0}^{n-1} b(x_{n-i})a^i$ step by step when reading an input word $x_1 \ldots x_n \in \Sigma^*$ from left to right. In particular, M starts with $s_0 = 0$ which updates to $s_i = as_{i-1} + b(x_i)$ every time after M reads the next input symbol $x_i \in \Sigma$, for $i = 1, \ldots, n$. As the numbers $a, b(x_1), \ldots, b(x_n), c \in \mathbb{Q}$ can be represented within constant space, M needs only linear space in terms of input length n, for computing s_n and testing whether $s_n < c$. □

5 Conclusion

In this paper we have introduced the cut languages in rational bases and classified them within the Chomsky hierarchy, among others, by using the quasi-periodic power series. A natural direction for future research is to generalize the results to arbitrary real bases.

We have already strengthened Theorem 8 whose proof is now based on Lemma 2 which does not require rational bases as opposed to stronger Theorem 3 that was used for the proof in a preliminary version [24]. As a consequence of this improvement, the characterization of regular cut languages in Theorem 11 remains valid for arbitrary real bases. For example, for the only real root $a \approx 0.6823278$ of algebraic equation $a^3 + a - 1 = 0$, which is the inverse of a Pisot number, the number $c = 1$ (similarly for $c = 1/a$) is a-quasi-periodic within $B = \{0, 1\}$ and has uncountably many different quasi-periodic representations (including the non-periodic ones) whose tail values form $\mathcal{D} = \{0, a, 1, 1/a, 1+a, a/(1-a), (1+a)/a, 1/(1-a)\}$ (cf. Theorem 8). It is an open question of whether the inverse of the minimal Pisot number (i.e. the inverse of the plastic constant), $a \approx 0.7548777$ which is the unique real solution of the cubic equation $a^3 + a^2 - 1 = 0$, is the greatest such a.

Nevertheless, the generalization of Theorem 3 to arbitrary real bases is still an open problem which can be formulated elementarily as follows. Let a be a real number such that $0 < |a| < 1$, and $(d_n)_{n=0}^{\infty}$ be a sequence of real numbers, containing a constant infinite subsequence (cf. Lemma 2), such that $B = \{d_n - ad_{n+1} \mid n \geq 0\}$ is finite. Is $D = \{d_n \mid n \geq 0\}$ a finite set?

References

1. Adamczewski, B., Frougny, C., Siegel, A., Steiner, W.: Rational numbers with purely periodic β-expansion. Bull. Lond. Math. Soc. **42**(3), 538–552 (2010)
2. Allouche, J.P., Clarke, M., Sidorov, N.: Periodic unique beta-expansions: the Sharkovskiĭ ordering. Ergod. Theory Dyn. Syst. **29**(4), 1055–1074 (2009)
3. Alon, N., Dewdney, A.K., Ott, T.J.: Efficient simulation of finite automata by neural nets. J. ACM **38**(2), 495–514 (1991)

4. Balcázar, J.L., Gavaldà, R., Siegelmann, H.T.: Computational power of neural networks: a characterization in terms of Kolmogorov complexity. IEEE Trans. Inf. Theory **43**(4), 1175–1183 (1997)
5. Chunarom, D., Laohakosol, V.: Expansions of real numbers in non-integer bases. J. Korean Math. Soc. **47**(4), 861–877 (2010)
6. Glendinning, P., Sidorov, N.: Unique representations of real numbers in non-integer bases. Math. Res. Lett. **8**(4), 535–543 (2001)
7. Hare, K.G.: Beta-expansions of Pisot and Salem numbers. In: Proceedings of the Waterloo Workshop in Computer Algebra 2006: Latest Advances in Symbolic Algorithms, pp. 67–84. World Scientic (2007)
8. Horne, B.G., Hush, D.R.: Bounds on the complexity of recurrent neural network implementations of finite state machines. Neural Netw. **9**(2), 243–252 (1996)
9. Indyk, P.: Optimal simulation of automata by neural nets. In: Mayr, E.W., Puech, C. (eds.) STACS 1995. LNCS, vol. 900, pp. 337–348. Springer, Heidelberg (1995). doi:10.1007/3-540-59042-0_85
10. Komornik, V., Loreti, P.: Subexpansions, superexpansions and uniqueness properties in non-integer bases. Periodica Mathematica Hungarica **44**(2), 197–218 (2002)
11. Minsky, M.: Computations: Finite and Infinite Machines. Prentice-Hall, Englewood Cliffs (1967)
12. Parry, W.: On the β-expansions of real numbers. Acta Math. Hung. **11**(3), 401–416 (1960)
13. Rényi, A.: Representations for real numbers and their ergodic properties. Acta Math. Acad. Scientiarum Hung. **8**(3–4), 477–493 (1957)
14. Schmidt, K.: On periodic expansions of Pisot numbers and Salem numbers. Bull. Lond. Math. Soc. **12**(4), 269–278 (1980)
15. Sidorov, N.: Expansions in non-integer bases: Lower, middle and top orders. J. Number Theory **129**(4), 741–754 (2009)
16. Siegelmann, H.T.: Recurrent neural networks and finite automata. J. Comput. Intell. **12**(4), 567–574 (1996)
17. Siegelmann, H.T.: Neural Networks and Analog Computation: Beyond the Turing Limit. Birkhäuser, Boston (1999)
18. Siegelmann, H.T., Sontag, E.D.: Analog computation via neural networks. Theoret. Comput. Sci. **131**(2), 331–360 (1994)
19. Siegelmann, H.T., Sontag, E.D.: On the computational power of neural nets. J. Comput. Syst. Sci. **50**(1), 132–150 (1995)
20. Šíma, J.: Energy complexity of recurrent neural networks. Neural Comput. **26**(5), 953–973 (2014)
21. Šíma, J.: The Power of Extra Analog Neuron. In: Dediu, A.-H., Lozano, M., Martín-Vide, C. (eds.) TPNC 2014. LNCS, vol. 8890, pp. 243–254. Springer, Heidelberg (2014). doi:10.1007/978-3-319-13749-0_21
22. Šíma, J.: Neural networks between integer and rational weights. Technical report, no. V-1237, Institute of Computer Science, The Czech Academy of Sciences, Prague (2016)
23. Šíma, J., Orponen, P.: General-purpose computation with neural networks: A survey of complexity theoretic results. Neural Comput. **15**(12), 2727–2778 (2003)
24. Šíma, J., Savický, P.: Cut languages in rational bases. Technical report, no. V-1236, Institute of Computer Science, The Czech Academy of Sciences, Prague (2016)
25. Šíma, J., Wiedermann, J.: Theory of neuromata. J. ACM **45**(1), 155–178 (1998)

Graphs and Petri Nets

Merging Relations: A Way to Compact Petri Nets' Behaviors Uniformly

Giovanni Casu and G. Michele Pinna(✉)

Dipartimento di Matematica e Informatica, Università di Cagliari, Cagliari, Italy
{giovanni.casu,gmpinna}@unica.it

Abstract. Compacting Petri nets behaviors means to develop a more *succinct* representation of all the possible executions of a net, still giving the capability to *reason* on properties fulfilled by the computations of the net. To do so suitable equivalences on alternative executions have to be engineered. We introduce a general notion of *merging relation* covering the existing approaches to compact behaviors and we discuss how to enforce that the more succinct net is an unravel net, namely a net where dependencies can be identified (almost) syntactically.

Keywords: Petri nets · Data structure compression · Event structures

1 Introduction

The non sequential behavior of a Petri net [2,10] can be described in many ways, *e.g* using *traces* [8], but probably the most popular and used one is the notion of *unfolding* [3,14]. The unfolding of a net N is particularly relevant as it allows to record conflicts and dependencies among the activities modeled with N, and the possibility of finding a finite representation of it (the prefix), has given profitability to the notion, otherwise confined to the purely theoretical modeling realm [4,9]. However the size of a finite unfolding, even of the prefix, can be too large, hence manageable only with big efforts. Several approaches to reduce it have been proposed, based on the idea of identifying suitable conflicting conditions of the unfolding. In the case of *merged process* [6] the criterion is that the conditions must be equally labeled and have the same token occurrence (*i.e.* they represent the same token, in the collective token philosophy of [12]) whereas in the case of *trellis processes* [5] the criterion is the distance of the equally labeled conditions from the initial condition of its component (measuring the *time*). Once conditions have been identified, isomorphic *futures* are identified as well.

The identification of conflicting conditions seems to be a good starting point for compacting nets' behaviors. We pursue this idea further, casting it in a general framework. We first define a notion of incompatibility among places of the behavior that it is not based on the syntax, as in causal nets, but on the semantics; and then we introduce an equivalence relation on places with some

Work partially supported by Aut. Region of Sardinia P.I.A. 2013 "NOMAD".

F. Drewes et al. (Eds.): LATA 2017, LNCS 10168, pp. 325–337, 2017.
DOI: 10.1007/978-3-319-53733-7_24

minimal requirements: it should respect the notion of incompatibility and it should respect the labeling (which is, in the case of the non sequential behavior of a net, the folding morphism). The incompatibility relation should capture the idea that, assuming that a place is identified with a resource, two resources are never *used* together in a computation. This equivalence relation is the basis for compacting behaviours that, following the classic motto, are nets [11,13].

Some of the definable equivalences may give a rather compact net, where executions have to be recovered with some efforts, and causality and conflicts may be deduced only after all the executions have been exploited. To ease the task of finding causality and conflict we propose the notion of *unravel* net which allows to capture easily and syntactically dependencies in each computation, whereas conflict is deduced in a semantic way. Indeed, unravel nets are such that each execution gives an acyclic net, hence causality is easily traceable. Furthermore we believe that this notion is robust enough for representing the non sequential behaviors of nets as it is closely related to a brand of event structures, namely *bundle event structure* [7]. Steps towards this direction have already been done in [1], and here we present this attempt in the more general framework. Our approach is rather flexible. The merging relation may be induced by a *measure* on the places of the net to be compacted and, depending on the kind of measure adopted, the result is an unravel net or there are ways to enrich the net in such a way that the behaviors are preserved and reflected, and the result of the compaction is still an unravel net. Thus the problem of finding the proper merging relation is moved to the search of the useful measure on the places of the net. Clearly a measure which is injective gives the trivial merging relation.

In Sect. 2 we introduce unravel nets and relate them to bundle event structures, then, in Sect. 3, we propose our general framework, which we show adequate in Sect. 4 by casting in it the classic approaches to behaviors compaction. In Sect. 5 we discuss how to ensure that the result of the compaction is still an unravel net.

2 Nets and Bundle Event Structures

With $\mathbb{N}$ we denote the set of natural numbers. Let A be a set, a *multiset* of A is a function $m : A \to \mathbb{N}$. The set of multisets of A is denoted by μA. The usual operations on multisets, like multiset union $+$ or multiset difference $-$, are used. We write $m \subseteq m'$ if $m(a) \leq m'(a)$ for all $a \in A$. If $m \in \mu A$, we denote with $[\![m]\!]$ the multiset defined as $[\![m]\!](a) = 1$ if $m(a) > 0$ and $[\![m]\!](a) = 0$ otherwise; and we use $supp(m)$ as the denotation of the set $\{a \in A \mid m(a) \geq 1\}$. Finally, when a multiset m of A is a set, *i.e.* $m = [\![m]\!]$ (hence $m = supp(m)$), we write $a \in m$ to denote that $m(a) \neq 0$, and often confuse the multiset m with $supp(m)$.

A *Petri net* is a 4-tuple $N = \langle S, T, F, \mathsf{m}\rangle$, where S is a set of *places* and T is a set of *transitions* (with $S \cap T = \emptyset$), $F \subseteq (S \times T) \cup (T \times S)$ is the *flow* relation, and $\mathsf{m} \in \mu S$ is called the *initial marking*. Petri nets are depicted as usual.

Given a net $N = \langle S, T, F, \mathsf{m}\rangle$ and $x \in S \cup T$, we define the following multisets: ${}^{\bullet}x = F(-, x)$ and $x^{\bullet} = F(x, -)$. If $x \in S$ then ${}^{\bullet}x$ ($x^{\bullet}$) is in μT and if $x \in T$

then ${}^\bullet x$ ($x^\bullet$) is in μS A transition $t \in T$ is enabled at a marking $m \in \mu S$, denoted with $m\,[t\rangle$, whenever ${}^\bullet t \subseteq m$. A transition t enabled at a marking m can *fire* and its firing produces the marking $m' = m - {}^\bullet t + t^\bullet$. The firing of a transitions t at a marking m is denoted with $m\,[t\rangle\, m'$. We assume that each transition t of a net N is such that ${}^\bullet t \neq \emptyset$ (which means that no transition may fire *spontaneously*). Given a generic marking m (not necessarily equal to the initial one), the *firing sequence* (fs) starting at m of the net $N = \langle S, T, F, \mathsf{m}\rangle$, is defined as usually: (a) m is a fs, and (b) if $m\,[t_1\rangle\, m_1 \cdots m_{n-1}\,[t_n\rangle\, m_n$ is a fs and $m_n\,[t\rangle\, m'$ then also $m\,[t_1\rangle\, m_1 \cdots m_{n-1}\,[t_n\rangle\, m_n\,[t\rangle\, m'$ is a fs. The set of firing sequences of a net N starting at a marking m is denoted with $\mathbf{\Sigma}_m^N$ and it is ranged over by σ. Given fs $\sigma = m\,[t_1\rangle\, \sigma'\,[t_n\rangle\, m_n$, with $start(\sigma)$ we denote the marking m, with $lead(\sigma)$ the marking m_n and with $tail(\sigma)$ the fs $\sigma'\,[t_n\rangle\, m_n$. Given a net $N = \langle S, T, F, \mathsf{m}\rangle$, a marking m is *reachable* iff there exists a fs $\sigma \in \mathbf{\Sigma}_{\mathsf{m}}^N$ such that $lead(\sigma)$ is m; the set of reachable markings of N is $\mathcal{M}_N = \bigcup_{\sigma \in \mathbf{\Sigma}_{\mathsf{m}}^N} lead(\sigma)$. Given a fs $\sigma = m\,[t_1\rangle\, m_1 \cdots m_{n-1}\,[t_n\rangle\, m'$, with $X_\sigma = \sum_{i=1}^{n} \{t_i\}$ we denote the multiset of transitions associated to this fs. We call this multiset a *state* of the net. The set of states of a Petri net is then $\mathsf{St}(N) = \{X_\sigma \in \mu T \mid \sigma \in \mathbf{\Sigma}_{\mathsf{m}}^N\}$.

Given a set of markings M, with $\mathsf{P}(M)$ we denote the set of places that are marked at some marking in M, namely $\{s \in S \mid \exists m \in M.\ m(s) > 0\}$, and given a fs σ, $\mathsf{M}(\sigma)$ are the markings associated to the fs σ, where $\mathsf{M}(\sigma)$ is $\mathsf{M}(\sigma) = \{m\}$ if $\sigma = m$ and $\mathsf{M}(\sigma) = \{start(\sigma)\} \cup \mathsf{M}(tail(\sigma))$ otherwise.

A net $N = \langle S, T, F, \mathsf{m}\rangle$ is said *safe* if each marking $m \in \mathcal{M}_N$ is such that $m = [\![m]\!]$. In this paper we consider safe nets $N = \langle S, T, F, \mathsf{m}\rangle$ where each transition can be fired, *i.e.* $\forall t \in T\ \exists m \in \mathcal{M}_N.\ m\,[t\rangle$, and each place is marked in a computation, *i.e.* $\forall s \in S\ \exists m \in \mathcal{M}_N.\ m(s) = 1$. A subnet of a net is a net obtained restricting places and transitions, and correspondingly also the relation F and the initial marking. Let $N = \langle S, T, F, \mathsf{m}\rangle$ be a Petri net and let $T' \subseteq T$. Then the subnet generated by T' is the net $N|_{T'} = \langle S', T', F', \mathsf{m}'\rangle$, where $S' = \bigcup_{t \in T'} \left([\![{}^\bullet t]\!] \cup [\![t^\bullet]\!]\right) \cup supp(\mathsf{m})$, F' is the restriction of F to S' and T', and m' is the obvious restriction of m to places in S'. Analogously we can restrict to a subset of places. Let $S' \subseteq S$, then the subnet generated by S' is the net $N|_{S'} = \langle S', T', F', \mathsf{m}'\rangle$, where $T' = \bigcup_{s \in S'} \left([\![{}^\bullet s]\!] \cup [\![s^\bullet]\!]\right)$,$F'$ is the restriction of F to S' and T', and m' is the restriction of m to places in S'.

A net $N = \langle S, T, F, \mathsf{m}\rangle$ is said to be *acyclic with respect to a subset of places* S' whenever, given $N|_{S'} = \langle S', T', F', \mathsf{m}'\rangle$, the transitive and reflexive closure of $[\![F]\!]$ is a partial order on $S' \cup T'$.

An *1-occurrence net* $O = \langle S, T, F, \mathsf{m}\rangle$ is a Petri net where each state is a set, i.e. $\forall X \in \mathsf{St}(O)$ it holds that $X = [\![X]\!]$. The notion of occurrence net we use here is the one called 1-occurrence net in [13] and the intuition behind it is the following: regardless how tokens are produced or consumed, an occurrence net *guarantees* that each transition can *occur* only once.

The notion of occurrence net is a *semantical* one, whereas the one of *causal net* is more syntax oriented. Given a net N, we define $x <_N y$ iff $(x, y) \in F$, and $\leq_N$ is the transitive and reflexive closure of this relation. For denoting places and transitions of a causal net we use B and E (see [14]) and call them conditions and events respectively. A causal net is acyclic, when the whole set of conditions is considered, and equipped with a *conflict* relation. Thus, a *causal net* $C = \langle B, E, F, \mathsf{m}\rangle$ is a safe net satisfying thefollowing restrictions:(1) $\forall b \in [\![\mathsf{m}]\!]$, ${}^\bullet b = \emptyset$, (2)$\forall b \in B.\ \exists b' \in [\![\mathsf{m}]\!]$ such that $b' \leq_C b$, (3) $\forall b \in B.\ {}^\bullet b$ is either empty or a singleton, (4) for all $e \in E$ the set $\{e' \in E \mid e' \leq_C e\}$ is finite, and(5)$\#$ is an irreflexive and symmetric relation defined as follows:(5.a) $e \#_r e'$ iff $e, e' \in E$, $e \neq e'$ and ${}^\bullet e \cap {}^\bullet e' \neq \emptyset$,(5.b)$x \# x'$ iff $\exists y, y' \in E$ such that $y \#_r y'$ and $y \leq_C x$ and $y' \leq_C x'$. The intuition behind this notion is the following: each condition b represents the occurrence of a token, which is produced by the *unique* event in ${}^\bullet b$, unless b belongs to the initial marking, and it is used by only one transition (hence if $e, e' \in b^\bullet$, then $e \# e'$). On causal nets it is natural to define a notion of *causality* among elements of the net: we say that x is *causally dependent* from y iff $y \leq_C x$. Given a causal net $C = \langle B, E, F, \mathsf{m}\rangle$, if $\forall b \in B$ it holds that $b^\bullet$ is at most a singleton, we say that it is a *conflict-free* causal net (the relation $\#$ is empty). Observe that each causal net $C = \langle B, E, F, \mathsf{m}\rangle$ is also an 1-occurrence net. Causal nets capture dependencies (and conflicts) whereas 1-occurrence nets capture the unique occurrence property of each transition. We define a net which will turn out to be, so to say, in between 1-occurrence and causal nets. Like in 1-occurrence nets we assure that each transition happens just once, and we are still able to retrieve dependencies among the firings of transitions, though in a more *semantical* way.

Definition 1. *An* unravel net$R = \langle B, E, F, \mathsf{m}\rangle$ *is a safe occurrence net such that for each state $X \in \mathsf{St}(R)$ the net $R|_{[\![X]\!]}$ is a conflict-free causal net.*

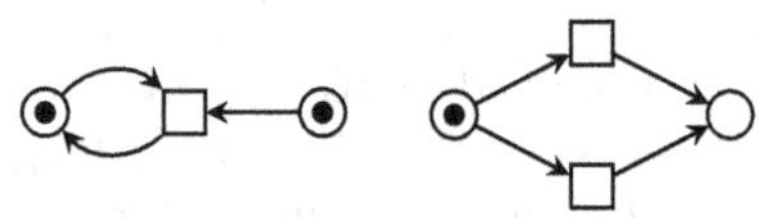

It is straightforward to observe that if $C = \langle B, E, F, \mathsf{m}\rangle$ is a causal net then it is an unravel net as well. The contrary does not hold (see the nets on the side). The net on the right is an unravel net which is not a causal net, whereas the net on the left is a safe 1-occurrence net which is not an unravel one. We state some simple facts on unravel nets. First, as we consider nets where each transition can be executed at some marking, if $s \in \mathsf{m}$ then ${}^\bullet s = \emptyset$. Furthermore if two different transitions t and t' are such that ${}^\bullet t \cap {}^\bullet t' \neq \emptyset$ or $t^\bullet \cap t'^\bullet \neq \emptyset$, then the two transitions cannot appear in the same state of the net.

Unravel nets are closely related to *bundle event structures* [7]. In this brand of event structure causality among events is represented by pairs (X, e), the *bundles*, where X is a non empty set of events and e an event. The meaning of a bundle (X, e) is that if e happens then one (and only one) event of X has to have happened before (events in X are pairwise conflicting). An event e can be caused by several bundles, and for each bundle an event in it should have happened.

Definition 2. *A* bundle event structure *is a triple $\beta = (\mathsf{E}, \mapsto, \#)$, where (a) E is a set of events, (b) $\#$ is an irreflexive and symmetric binary relation on E (the* conflict *relation), (c) $\mapsto \subseteq \mathbf{2}^{\mathsf{E}}_{fin} \times \mathsf{E}$ is the* enabling *relation such that if*

$X \mapsto \mathsf{e}$ *then for all* $\mathsf{e}_1, \mathsf{e}_2 \in X$. $\mathsf{e}_1 \neq \mathsf{e}_2$ *implies* $\mathsf{e}_1 \# \mathsf{e}_2$, *and (d) for each* $\mathsf{e} \in \mathsf{E}$ *the set* $\{X \subseteq \mathsf{E} \mid X \mapsto \mathsf{e}\}$ *is finite.*

The configurations of a BES $\beta = (\mathsf{E}, \mapsto, \#)$ are defined as usual. Let $X \subseteq \mathsf{E}$ be a set of events. Then X is a *configuration* or β iff (a) it is *conflict free*, *i.e.* $\forall \mathsf{e}, \mathsf{e}' \in X.\ \neg(\mathsf{e} \# \mathsf{e}')$, and (b) there exists a linearization $\{\mathsf{e}_1, \ldots, \mathsf{e}_n, \ldots\}$ of the events in X such that $\forall i \in \mathbb{N}$ and for all bundles $X_i \mapsto \mathsf{e}_i$ it holds that $X_i \cap \{\mathsf{e}_1, \ldots, \mathsf{e}_{i-1}\} \neq \emptyset$. With $\mathsf{Conf}(\beta)$ we denote the set of configurations of β.

Given an unravel net $R = \langle B, E, F, \mathsf{m} \rangle$, the associated BES is the triple $\mathcal{E}_{\text{BES}}(R) = (E, \mapsto, \#)$ where $\mapsto$ is defined taking, for each $b \in {}^{\bullet}e$, the set of events ${}^{\bullet}b$ (thus ${}^{\bullet}b \mapsto e$) and the conflict relation $\#$ is defined as $e \# e'$ iff $\forall X \in \mathsf{St}(R).\ \{e, e'\} \not\subseteq [\![X]\!]$. The configurations of the BES associated to an unravel net are precisely the states of the unravel net: $\mathsf{Conf}(\mathcal{E}_{\text{BES}}(R)) = \mathsf{St}(R)$. Furthermore, given a BES $\beta = (\mathsf{E}, \mapsto, \#)$, we can associate an unravel net $\mathcal{N}(\beta) = \langle B, \mathsf{E}, \mathrm{F}, \mathsf{m} \rangle$ where $B = \{(\mathsf{e}, i) \mid \mathsf{e} \in E\} \cup \{(\mathsf{e}, \mathsf{e}') \mid \mathsf{e} \# \mathsf{e}'\} \cup \{(Y, \mathsf{e}) \mid Y \mapsto \mathsf{e}\}$, $(s, \mathsf{e}) \in \mathrm{F}$ if $s = (\mathsf{e}, i)$ or $s = (\mathsf{e}, \mathsf{e}')$ or $s = (\mathsf{e}', \mathsf{e})$ or $s = (Y, \mathsf{e})$; and $(\mathsf{e}, s) \in \mathrm{F}$ if $(s = (Y, \mathsf{e}')$ and $\mathsf{e} \in Y)$ or $s = (\mathsf{e}, o)$, and $\mathsf{m} = \{(\mathsf{e}, i) \mid \mathsf{e} \in E\} \cup \{\{\mathsf{e}, \mathsf{e}' \mid \mathsf{e} \# \mathsf{e}'\}$ and, as before $\mathsf{Conf}(\beta) = \mathsf{St}(\mathcal{N}(\beta))$. Thus among unravel nets andBES there is a similar relationship as the one we have among causal nets and *prime event structure.*

We introduce now labeled nets. Let Λ be a set of labels, a *labeled* net N is the pair (N, l), where $N = \langle S, T, F, \mathsf{m} \rangle$ is a Petri net and $l \colon S \cup T \to \Lambda$ a total mapping such that $l(T) \cap l(S) = \emptyset$. Given a labeled net $\mathsf{N} = (N, l)$ and a fs $\sigma = m\, [t_1\rangle\, m_1\, [t_2\rangle\, m_2 \cdots m_{n-1}\, [t_n\rangle\, m_n$, with $run(\sigma)$ we denote the word on $l(T)^*$ defined as $l(t_1 t_2 \cdots t_n)$, and we call it *trace*. To the fs $\sigma = m$ the empty trace is associated, *i.e.* $run(\sigma) = \epsilon$. The length of a fs σ is the length of $run(\sigma)$.

Let $\mathsf{N} = (N, l)$ be a labeled net where $N = \langle S, T, F, \mathsf{m} \rangle$ and let $t, t' \in T$ be two transitions. We say that t and t' are *identifiable* whenever ${}^{\bullet}t = {}^{\bullet}t'$, $t^{\bullet} = t'^{\bullet}$ and $l(t) = l(t')$. Thus on T it is possible to define an equivalence relation $\simeq$ such that $t \simeq t'$ iff t and t' are identifiable. The set of transitions can be quotiented through this equivalence relation obtaining the set $\{[t]_{\simeq} \mid t \in T\}$. Observe that the transitions in $[t]_{\simeq}$ are pairwise conflicting.

Definition 3. *Let* $(N, l) = (\langle S, T, F, \mathsf{m} \rangle, l)$ *be a labeled net and let* $\simeq$ *be the equivalence relation induced by transitions identifiability. Then we can construct the labeled net* $\widehat{\mathsf{N}} = (\widehat{N}, \hat{l})$ *where* $\widehat{N}$ *is the Petri net* $\langle S, \widehat{T}, \widehat{F}, \mathsf{m} \rangle$ *with* $\widehat{T} = \{[t]_{\simeq} \mid t \in T\}$, $\widehat{F}(s, [t]_{\simeq}) = F(s, t)$ *and* $\widehat{F}([t]_{\simeq}, s) = F(t, s)$, *and* $\hat{l}$ *is the mapping defined as* $\hat{l}(s) = l(s)$ *and* $\hat{l}([t]_{\simeq}) = l(t)$.

Let $\sigma \in \mathbf{\Sigma}^{N}_{\mathsf{m}}$, then $\widehat{\sigma}$ is constructed as follows: $\widehat{\sigma} = \mathsf{m}$ if $\sigma = m$ and $\widehat{\sigma} = \widehat{\sigma'}\, [[t]_{\simeq}\rangle\, m$ if $\sigma = \sigma'\, [t\rangle\, m$. The firing sequences of N and of $\widehat{N}$ are clearly related, as the following proposition shows. Observe that $run(\widehat{\sigma}) = l([t_1]_{\simeq} \cdots [t_n]_{\simeq}) = run(\sigma)$.

Proposition 4. *Let* $(N, l) = (\langle S, T, F, \mathsf{m} \rangle, l)$ *be a labeled net, and let* $\simeq$ *be the equivalence relation induced by transitions identifiability. Let* $\sigma \in \mathbf{\Sigma}^{N}_{\mathsf{m}}$ *be a* fs, *then* $\widehat{\sigma} \in \mathbf{\Sigma}^{\widehat{N}}_{\mathsf{m}}$.

3 Merging Relation

In this section we propose a simple and general framework to compact labeled nets. We first introduce a *semantical* notion of incompatibility on places, capturing the idea that, if a place is akin to a *resource*, two resources are incompatible if they never appear in the same computation, even at different stages. Then we show that, given a suitable equivalence relation, related to places incompatibility, a more succinct version of the net we started with can be obtained, whose behaviors are still related to the original one.

Given a net $N = \langle S, T, F, \mathsf{m}\rangle$, we say that two different places $s, s' \in S$ are *incompatible* iff for each firing sequence $\sigma \in \mathbf{\Sigma}^N_{\mathsf{m}}$ it holds that $\{s, s'\} \not\subseteq \mathsf{P}(\mathsf{M}(\sigma))$, and we denote it with $s \bowtie s'$ (observe that this notion is quite similar to the one of conflict we introduced on unravel nets). Clearly $\bowtie$ is a symmetric and irreflexive relation and if $s \in [\![m]\!]$ and $s \bowtie s'$ then $\forall \sigma \in \mathbf{\Sigma}^N_m.\ s' \notin \mathsf{P}(\mathsf{M}(\sigma))$.

Example 5. Consider the labeled net $\mathsf{N} = (N, l)$ in Fig. 1(a), with initial marking $\mathsf{m} = \{c_0\}$. The relation $\bowtie$ contains the pairs (c_i, c_j) such that $i, j > 0$ and if i is odd then j is even and vice versa as well. Thus $c_4 \bowtie c_7$ and $c_9 \bowtie c_6$ but $c_6 \not\bowtie c_4$.

We introduce now the notion of *merging relation.*

Definition 6. *Let* $\mathsf{N} = (N, l)$ *be a labeled net where* $N = \langle S, T, F, \mathsf{m}\rangle$, *let* $\circledast \subseteq \bowtie$, *and let* $\sim$ *be an equivalence relation such that* $s \sim s' \Leftrightarrow (s \circledast s' \vee s = s') \wedge l(s) = l(s')$. *Then* $\sim$ *is a* merging relation *for* N.

A merging relation is any equivalence relation respecting labeling and incompatibility (better, a relation included into the one of incompatibility). Observe that the identity on places is a trivial merging relation. Furthermore if s is initially marked then $[s]_\sim = \{s\}$.

The *merging* relation is used to *compact* the net. Similarly to what is done in [6], we first merge places by identifying equivalent ones, thus the merged places will be $S' = \{[s]_\sim \mid s \in S\}$. Then, when needed, we may identify also transitions.

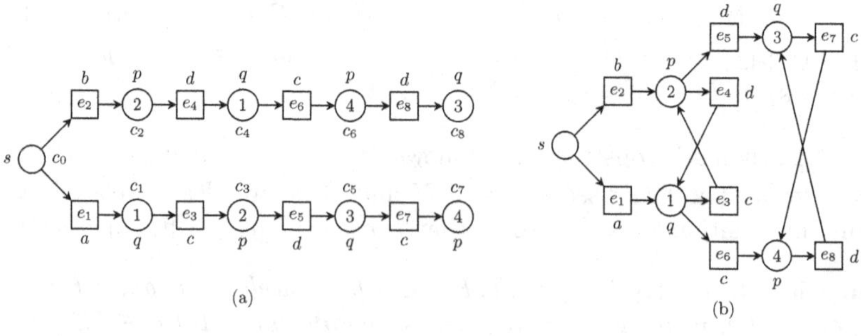

Fig. 1. A labeled net N (a) and its compact representation (b)

Definition 7. *Let* $\mathsf{N} = (N, l)$ *be a labeled unravel net where* $N = \langle S, T, F, \mathsf{m}\rangle$, *and let* $\sim$ *be a merging relation. Then we construct the labeled net* $\widetilde{\mathsf{N}} = (\widetilde{N}, \widetilde{l})$, *where* $\widetilde{N}$ *is the Petri net* $\langle \widetilde{S}, T, \widetilde{F}, \widetilde{\mathsf{m}}\rangle$ *defined as* $\widetilde{S} = \{[s]_\sim \mid s \in S\}$, $\widetilde{F}([s]_\sim, t) = F(s,t)$, $\widetilde{F}(t, [s]_\sim) = F(t, s)$ *and* $\widetilde{\mathsf{m}}([s]_\sim) = \sum_{s \in [s]_\sim} \mathsf{m}(s)$, *and* $\widetilde{l}$ *is the labeling mapping defined as* $\widetilde{l}([s]_\sim) = l(s)$ *and* $\widetilde{l}(t) = l(t)$.

The flow relation is well defined, as $\forall t \in T.\ |[\![{}^\bullet t]\!] \cap [s]_\sim| \leq 1$ and $\forall t \in T.\ |[\![t^\bullet]\!] \cap [s]_\sim| \leq 1$ as well, and the same for the initial marking, as the equivalence class of each place in the initial marking contains just that place.

Example 8. Consider the net of the Example 5. A suitable merging relation can be $c_1 \sim c_4$, $c_2 \sim c_3$, $c_6 \sim c_7$ and $c_5 \sim c_8$ and the result of the merging of these places is the net in Fig. 1(b). Another merging relations could be $c_1 \sim' c_8$, $c_2 \sim' c_3$, $c_6 \sim' c_7$ and $c_5 \sim' c_4$, or simply $c_1 \sim'' c_4$.

The construction can be lifted to the reachable markings and firing sequence. Let $m \in \mathcal{M}_N$, then $\widetilde{m} \in \mu\widetilde{S}$ is defined as $\widetilde{m}([s]_\sim) = \sum_{s \in [s]_\sim} m(s)$. Observe that, as places in $[s]_\sim$ are in conflict, at most one may contain tokens. Consider then $\sigma \in \mathbf{\Sigma}^N_{\mathsf{m}}$, then $\widetilde{\sigma}$ is obtained as follows: if $\sigma = \mathsf{m}$ then $\widetilde{\sigma} = \widetilde{\mathsf{m}}$, if $\sigma = \sigma' [t\rangle\, m$ then $\widetilde{\sigma} = \widetilde{\sigma'} [t\rangle\, \widetilde{m}$. The following proposition points out the obvious relation among the firing sequences of both nets.

Proposition 9. *Let* $\mathsf{N} = (N, l)$ *be a labeled net, let* $\sim$ *be a merging relation and* $(\widetilde{N}, \widetilde{l})$ *be the labeled net of Definition 7. Then* $\forall \sigma \in \mathbf{\Sigma}^N_{\mathsf{m}}\ \exists \sigma' \in \mathbf{\Sigma}^{\widetilde{N}}_{\widetilde{\mathsf{m}}}.\ \widetilde{\sigma} = \sigma'$.

By merging places it may happen that two equally labeled transitions have the same preset and the same postset. Hence the equivalence relation $\simeq$ induced by transition identifiability may be non trivial, *i.e.* different from the identity. We can then apply the construction of Definition 3.

Proposition 10. *Let* $\mathsf{N} = (N, l)$ *be a labeled net and let* $\sim$ *be a merging relation. Let* $(\overline{N}, \overline{l})$ *be the labeled net obtained applying first the construction of Definition 7 and then the one of Definition 3. Then* $\forall \sigma \in \mathbf{\Sigma}^N_{\mathsf{m}}\ \exists \sigma' \in \mathbf{\Sigma}^{\overline{N}}_{\overline{\mathsf{m}}}.\ run(\sigma) = run(\sigma')$.

By merging places and transitions we do not lose any behavior, but the obtained net may have more behaviors with respect to the one we started with, as the net in Fig. 1(b) shows.

4 Compacting Causal Behaviors of Safe Nets

The framework we have devised in the previous section can be applied to any kind of labeled net representing the behavior of a Petri net. Here we test it by focussing on the causal behaviors of *safe* nets, represented as branching processes.

Given a Petri net $N = \langle S, T, F, \mathsf{m}\rangle$, a *branching process* of N (see [3,14]) is a labeled causal net $\mathsf{C} = (C, p)$ with $C = \langle B, E, F, \mathsf{m}_0\rangle$ and $p\colon B \cup E \to S \cup T$ is such that (a) $p(B) = S$, $p(E) = T$, (b) the initial markings m_0 and m are bijectively related and (c) there are bijections between $p({}^\bullet e)$ and ${}^\bullet p(e)$, and between $p(e^\bullet)$ and $p(e)^\bullet$. Such kind of labeling mapping is called *folding* morphism. We apply our framework to merged processes (see [6] for details). The idea behind merged processes is the following: the conditions representing the *same* occurrence of a token in the original net can be identified. The consequence of this identification is that all the computations producing the same set of *tokens* can be considered as equivalent with respect to their possible futures, *i.e.* all these computations share equivalent futures that can be identified. A conflict relation is easily and structurally identifiable on causal nets, without resorting to the semantics, thus we do need some more information to identify conditions in the causal net. Let $\mathsf{C} = (C, p)$ be a branching process of N. Given a condition $b \in B$, the *occurrence depth* of b is $|\{b' \in B \mid b' \leq_C b \text{ and } p(b) = p(b')\}|$ and it is denoted with $\mathsf{tok}(b)$. We are now ready to introduce the merging relation for merged processes: two conditions b and b' are equivalent if (a) they are in conflict, (b) they have the same labeling, and (c) they have the same occurrence depth. The fact that our unifying framework covers the notion of merged process is summarized by the following theorem.

Theorem 11. *Let $\mathsf{C} = (C, p)$ be branching process of N, and let $\sim_{tok}$ be the merging relation defined as follows: $b \sim_{tok} b'$ iff $b \sharp b'$, $p(b) = p(b')$ and $\mathsf{tok}(b) = \mathsf{tok}(b')$, where $\sharp$ is the reflexive closure of the conflict relation $\#$ of the causal net C restricted to conditions only. Then $\overline{\mathsf{C}} = (\overline{C}, \overline{p})$ is a merged process of N.*

Example 12. Consider the net N in Fig. 2(a). A branching process for N is the labeled net $\mathsf{C} = (C, p)$ in Fig. 2(b) and the merging relation is $c_4 \sim c_7$ (both conditions have token occurrence equal to 1 and they are labeled with p_4) and $c_5 \sim c_6$ (both conditions have token occurrence equal to 1 and they are labeled with p_5). The result of the identification of these conditions gives the net $\overline{\mathsf{C}} = (\overline{C}, \overline{p})$ (c), depicted in Fig. 2. Observe that the last step is irrelevant in this case as no transitions have to be identified. The net C is acyclic whereas the $\overline{C}$ is not. Furthermore $\overline{C}$ is not an unravel net.

Instead of the token occurrence, the *time* can be taken into account. We identify conditions when they have been produced at the same time, still provided

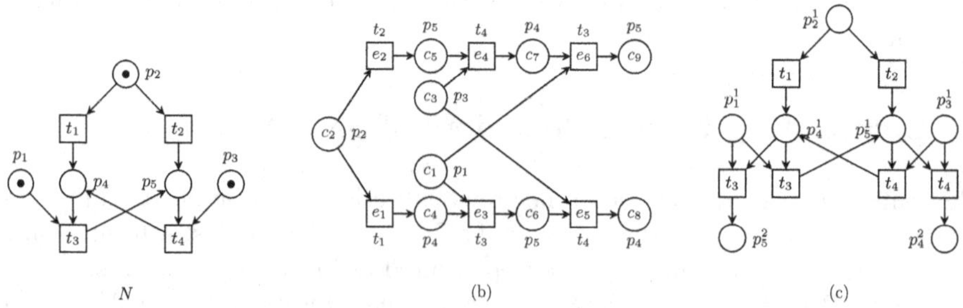

Fig. 2. A net N (a), one of its branching process (b) and the merged process (c)

that they bear the same label. To formalize this idea, on which the notion of *trellis* process is based (see [5]), we do need to guarantee that the proper time can be identified for each condition. To do so we resort to *multi-clock* nets. A multi-clock net is a safe net $N = \langle S, T, F, \mathsf{m}\rangle$ equipped with a *partition* mapping $\nu\colon S \to [\![\mathsf{m}]\!]$ such that $\nu([\![\mathsf{m}]\!])$ is the identity and $\forall s, s' \in [\![\mathsf{m}]\!]\ \nu^{-1}(s) \cap \nu^{-1}(s') \neq \emptyset \Rightarrow s = s'$. Thus a net can be partitioned in a number of components (which are identified using the partition mapping) which synchronize on some common transitions, and each component is a finite state automata which has just a place initially marked. A *trellis* process of the multi-clock net $N = \langle S, T, F, \mathsf{m}\rangle$ with ν as partition mapping, is a labeled net $\mathsf{R} = (R, p)$, where (a) $R = \langle B, E, F', \mathsf{m}'\rangle$ is an unravel net, (b) p is a folding morphism, and (c) R is a multi-clock net under the partition mapping ν_R defined as $\nu_R(b) = \nu(p(b))$; furthermore for each $s \in [\![\mathsf{m}]\!]$ any subnet $R|_{[p^{-1}(s)]_\nu}$ is acyclic, where $[p^{-1}(s)]_{\nu_R} = \{b \in B \mid \nu_R(b) = \nu(s)\}$. For further details on trellises and multi-clock nets we refer to [5].

Let $\mathsf{C} = (C, p)$ be a branching process of the multi-clock N, with ν as partition mapping. Given a condition b of C, the *height* of b, denoted with $\mathsf{height}(b)$, is $|\{b' \in B \mid b' \leq_C b \text{ and } \nu(p(b)) = \nu(p(b'))\}|$, where B are the conditions of C. The height of a condition is well defined in a casual net which is a multi-clock as well, as in the case of branching processes arising from multi-clock nets.

Theorem 13. *Let $\mathsf{C} = (C, p)$ be branching process of N, and let $\sim_{tr}$ be the merging relation defined as follows: $b \sim_{tr} b'$ iff $b \natural b'$, $p(b) = p(b')$ and $\mathsf{height}(b) = \mathsf{height}(b')$, where $\natural$ is the reflexive closure of the conflict relation $\#$ of the causal net C restricted to conditions only. Then $\overline{\mathsf{C}} = (\overline{C}, \overline{p})$ is a trellis process of N.*

Example 14. Consider the net N in Fig. 3(a). It is a multi-clock net considering $\nu(p_3) = p_1$ and $\nu(p_4) = p_2$. The equivalence induced by the height of the conditions in the branching process in Fig. 3(b) is $b_7 \sim b_8$ and $b_9 \sim b_{10}$, whereas $b_5 \not\sim b_8$ as they have a different height though they have the same label. The merging can be applied and the result, which is depicted in Fig. 3(c), is the trellis process associated to this specific branching process. This is an unravel net.

We conclude this section observing that the merging relation is induced assigning to each place a *measure*, and stipulating that two equally labeled and incompatible places are *equivalent* whenever they have the same measure.

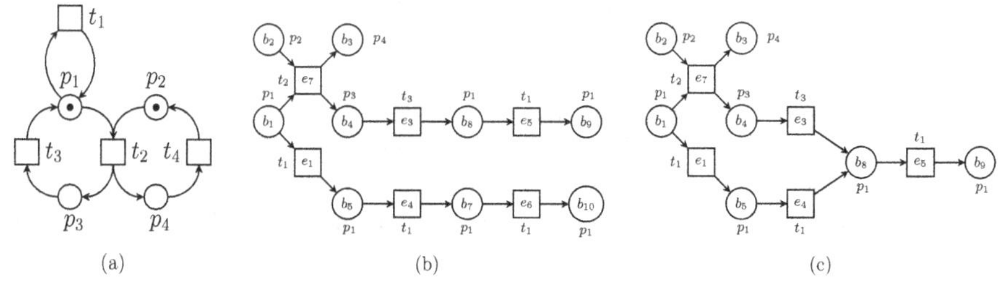

Fig. 3. A multi-clock net (a), one of its branching processes (b) and the corresponding trellis process (c)

5 Enriching to Obtain Unravel Nets

When compacting behaviors we usually start from a labeled unravel net, but the produced net is not necessarily an unravel one, and in the compaction we may lose the tight correspondence among nets and event structures. In fact cycles may be introduced when merging places and transitions, and in some case the cycles may be executable (thus the associated event structure would have a configuration where dependencies are not a partial order).

The possibility of obtaining an unravel net is connected with the measure, associated to places, the merging relation is based upon. Consider a labeled unravel net $\mathsf{R} = (R, l)$, with $R = \langle S, T, F, \mathsf{m}\rangle$, and a *locality* mapping $loc : S \to \mathsf{Loc}$, where Loc is a finite set of *localities*, and take any *measure* $\delta : S \to \mathbb{N}$ such that $\delta(s) = \delta(s')$ implies $s \bowtie s'$. We say that δ is *strictly increasing* if for each state $X \in \mathsf{St}(R)$, and each pair of places s, s' of the net $R|_{[\![X]\!]}$, it holds that $s \leq s' \ \wedge \ loc(s) = loc(s') \ \Rightarrow \ \delta(s) < \delta(s')$.

We can prove the following theorem, stating that the property of being an unravel net is preserved when strictly increasing measure are considered.

Theorem 15. *Let* $\mathsf{R} = (R, l)$ *where* $R = \langle S, T, F, \mathsf{m}\rangle$ *be a labeled unravel net and* $loc : S \to \mathsf{Loc}$ *a locality mapping, let* $\delta : S \to \mathbb{N}$ *be* strictly increasing *and let* $\sim$ *be the equivalence relation induced by* δ, i.e. $s \sim s'$ *iff* $(\delta(s) = \delta(s')$ *and* $l(s) = l(s'))$ *or* $s = s'$. *Then the resulting compact labeled net* $\overline{\mathsf{R}} = (\overline{R}, \overline{l})$ *is a labeled unravel net.*

The measure defined for trellis processes is a strictly increasing one, the locality mapping being the one induced by the partition mapping. Hence we can consider Theorem 13 as a special case of the Theorem 15 above. When the measure is not of this kind we may still obtain an unravel net, but sometimes at the price of *enriching* it in order to forbid certain unwanted executions in the compact version.

Given a labeled unravel net $\mathsf{R} = (R, l)$ with $R = \langle S, T, F, \mathsf{m}\rangle$, we say that a measure $\delta : S \to \mathbb{N}$ is *homogeneous* iff for each $X \in \mathsf{St}(R)$ and each subset of places $\hat{S}$ of $R|_{[\![X]\!]} = \langle S', [\![X]\!], F', \mathsf{m}\rangle$ such that there exists a label a such that $l^{-1}(\mathsf{a}) \cap S' = \hat{S}$, it holds that $\hat{S}'$ can be totally ordered with respect to the reflexive and transitive closure of F', $\delta(\hat{S}') = \{1, \ldots, |\hat{S}'|\}$ and $s \leq s' \ \Rightarrow \ \delta(s) \leq \delta(s')$. An homogeneous measure on causal nets is the token count of merged process. Again, as done before, we may introduce an equivalence relation which is based on an homogeneous measure δ by stipulating that $s \sim s'$ iff either $s = s'$ or $(l(s) = l(s') \ \wedge \ \delta(s) = \delta(s'))$. As the measure is an homogenous one, we do not have to require that the two places are incompatible as it is implied by the definition of the measure itself. When compacting using this merging relation the result may be not an unravel net. However this net may be turned into an unravel one without losing behaviors of the original net by adding some places which solely purpose is to forbid unwanted executions.

Take an unravel net $\mathsf{R} = (\langle S, T, F, \mathsf{m}\rangle, l)$ and an homogeneous measure δ on S. We can add to the net $R = \langle S, T, F, \mathsf{m}\rangle$ a set of places $S_{ng} = \{(l(s), \delta(s), ng) \mid s \in S\} \cup \{(l(s), 0, ng) \mid s \in S \setminus [\![\mathsf{m}]\!]\}$, and connect them to the transitions in T as follows: $F_{ng}((l(s), n, ng), t) = 1$ whenever $\exists s' \in t^{\bullet}.\ l(s) = l(s')$ and $\delta(s') = n+1$, and $F_{ng}(t, (l(s), n, ng)) = 1$ whenever $\exists s' \in t^{\bullet}.\ l(s) = l(s')$ and $\delta(s') = n$; finally the places $(l(s), 0, ng)$ are initially marked as well as $(l(s), 1, ng)$ if $b \in \mathsf{m}$ (and are the multiset m_{ng}). We call these places *no-gap* as in the case that the δ is precisely the token count and $\mathsf{R} = (R, l)$ is a branching process of a safe net N, they assure that the tokens in a place of the original net N are *produced* in the proper sequence.

The net obtained adding these new places S_{ng}, namely $\mathsf{Ng}(R) = \langle S \cup S_{ng}, T, F \cup F_{ng}, \mathsf{m} + \mathsf{m}_{ng}\rangle$, is an unravel net such that to each fs σ of $\mathsf{Ng}(R)$ a fs σ' of R corresponds and they are such that $run(\sigma) = run(\sigma')$ but also the *vice versa* holds, thus to each fs $\hat{\sigma} \in \mathbf{\Sigma}^{R}_{\mathsf{m}}$ a fs $\hat{\sigma}' \in \mathbf{\Sigma}^{\mathsf{Ng}(R)}_{\mathsf{m}+\mathsf{m}_{ng}}$ corresponds such that $run(\hat{\sigma}) = run(\hat{\sigma}')$, hence both unravel nets have exactly the same states, which means that this enriching does not change the behaviors of the net.

Theorem 16. *Let $\mathsf{R} = (R, l)$ be a labeled unravel net, where $R = \langle S, T, F, \mathsf{m}\rangle$. Let $\mathsf{Ng}(\mathsf{R}) = (\mathsf{Ng}(R), \mathsf{Ng}(l))$ where $\mathsf{Ng}(l)(s) = l(s)$ if $s \in S$ and $l((s, n, ng)) = l(n)$ obtained with respect to an homogeneous measure δ. Let $\sim$ be the equivalence relation induced by this measure on the places in S. Then $\overline{\mathsf{Ng}(\mathsf{R})} = (\overline{\mathsf{Ng}(R)}, \overline{\mathsf{Ng}(l)})$ is an unravel net.*

As a corollary of this theorem we have the following.

Corollary 17. *Let $\mathsf{C} = (C, p)$ be a branching process of the safe net N, where $C = \langle B, E, F, \mathsf{m}\rangle$. Let $\mathsf{Ng}(\mathsf{C}) = (\mathsf{Ng}(C), \mathsf{Ng}(p))$ be the unravel net obtained applying Ng to C and p and consider the equivalence relation $\sim$ induced by $\sim_{tok}$, where $\sim_{tok}$ is defined on conditions in B. $\overline{\mathsf{Ng}(\mathsf{C})} = (\overline{\mathsf{Ng}(C)}, \overline{\mathsf{Ng}(p)})$ in a labeled unravel net and furthermore $\mathsf{Ng}(\mathsf{C})|_{B_{\sim_{tok}}}$ is a merging process of N, where $B_{\sim_{tok}}$ are the merged resource conditions.*

Example 18. The causal net in Fig. 1(a), with the appropriate labeling, is a branching process of the net N in Fig. 4. The net $\mathsf{Ng}(C)$ in Fig. 4 is the result of enriching this causal net with no-gap conditions (the black ones). For instance,

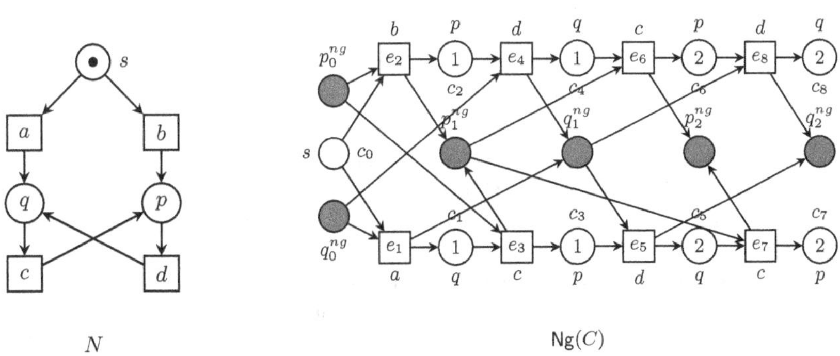

Fig. 4. A labeled net N and one of its enriched branching process $\mathsf{Ng}(C)$

the no-gap condition p_1^{ng} is $(p, 1, ng)$ and the transitions (events) putting a token in it are e_2 and e_3, whereas the events e_6 and e_7 consume the token in it. Clearly $e_2 \# e_3$ and $e_6 \# e_7$ The conditions with the same color have the same token count (the number depicted in the conditions) and are equally labeled. The result of its compaction is the unravel net in Fig. 5.

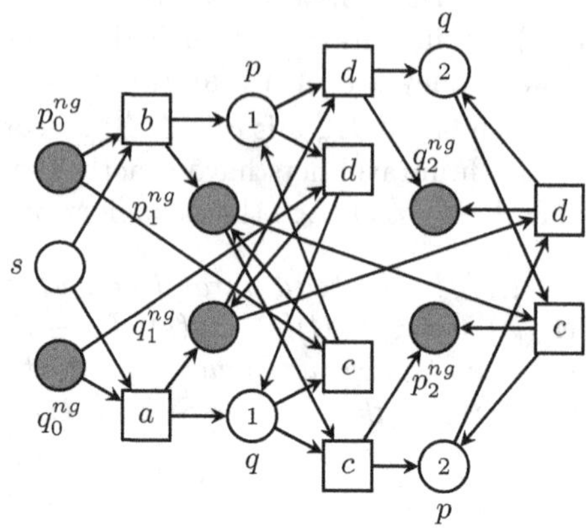

Fig. 5. The resulting unravel net of the compaction of $\mathsf{Ng}(C)$ in Fig. 4

References

1. Casu, G., Pinna, G.M.: Flow unfolding of multi-clock nets. In: Ciardo, G., Kindler, E. (eds.) PETRI NETS 2014. LNCS, vol. 8489, pp. 170–189. Springer, Heidelberg (2014). doi:10.1007/978-3-319-07734-5_10
2. Desel, J., Reisig, W.: The concepts of Petri nets. Softw. Syst. Model. **14**(2), 669–683 (2015)
3. Engelfriet, J.: Branching processes of Petri nets. Acta Informatica **28**(6), 575–591 (1991)
4. Esparza, J., Römer, S., Vogler, W.: An improvement of McMillan's unfolding algorithm. Formal Methods Syst. Des. **20**(3), 285–310 (2002)
5. Fabre, E.: Trellis processes: a compact representation for runs of concurrent systems. Discrete Event Dyn. Syst. **17**(3), 267–306 (2007)
6. Khomenko, V., Kondratyev, A., Koutny, M., Vogler, W.: Merged processes: a new condensed representation of Petri net behaviour. Acta Informatica **43**(5), 307–330 (2006)
7. Langerak, R.: Bundle event structures: a non-interleaving semantics for LOTOS. In: FORTE 1992. IFIP Transactions, vol. C-10, pp. 331–346 (1993)
8. Mazurkiewicz, A.: Basic notions of trace theory. In: Bakker, J.W., Roever, W.-P., Rozenberg, G. (eds.) REX 1988. LNCS, vol. 354, pp. 285–363. Springer, Heidelberg (1989). doi:10.1007/BFb0013025

9. McMillan, K.L.: Using unfoldings to avoid the state explosion problem in the verification of asynchronous circuits. In: Bochmann, G., Probst, D.K. (eds.) CAV 1992. LNCS, vol. 663, pp. 164–177. Springer, Heidelberg (1993). doi:10.1007/3-540-56496-9_14
10. Reisig, W.: Understanding Petri Nets - Modeling Techniques, Analysis Methods, Case Studies. Springer, Heidelberg (2013)
11. Smith, E., Reisig, W.: The semantics of a net is a net: an exercise in general net theory. In: Voss, K., Genrich, H.J., Rozenberg, G. (eds.) Concurrency and Nets: Advances in Petri Nets, pp. 461–479. Springer, Heidelberg (1987)
12. Glabbeek, R.J.: The individual and collective token interpretations of Petri nets. In: Abadi, M., Alfaro, L. (eds.) CONCUR 2005. LNCS, vol. 3653, pp. 323–337. Springer, Heidelberg (2005). doi:10.1007/11539452_26
13. van Glabbeek, R.J., Plotkin, G.D.: Configuration structures, event structures and Petri nets. Theor. Comput. Sci. **410**(41), 4111–4159 (2009)
14. Winskel, G.: Event structures. In: Brauer, W., Reisig, W., Rozenberg, G. (eds.) ACPN 1986. LNCS, vol. 255, pp. 325–392. Springer, Heidelberg (1987). doi:10.1007/3-540-17906-2_31

Partitioning Graphs into Induced Subgraphs

Dušan Knop(✉)

Department of Applied Mathematics, Charles University, Prague, Czech Republic
knop@kam.mff.cuni.cz

Abstract. We study the PARTITION INTO H problem from the parametrized complexity point of view. In the PARTITION INTO H problem the task is to partition the vertices of a graph G into sets $V_1, \dots, V_r$ such that the graph H is isomorphic to the subgraph of G induced by each set V_i for $i = 1, \dots, r$. The pattern graph H is fixed.

For the parametrization we consider three distinct structural parameters of the graph G – namely the tree-width, the neighborhood diversity, and the modular-width. For the parametrization by the neighborhood diversity we obtain an FPT algorithm for every graph H. For the parametrization by the tree-width we obtain an FPT algorithm for every connected graph H. Thus resolving an open question of Gajarský et al. from IPEC 2013 [9]. Finally, for the parametrization by the modular-width we derive an FPT algorithm for every prime graph H.

Keywords: Generalized matching · Parametrized complexity

1 Introduction

We begin with the definition of the PARTITION INTO H problem. We will then present the problem in the light of some well-known problems from computational complexity – for example PERFECT MATCHING or EQUITABLE COLORING – thus demonstrating it as a natural generalization of these and other problems. Finally, we give the summary of our results presented in this paper.

The Partition into H Problem. For graphs $G = (V, E), H = (W, F)$ with $|V| = |W| \cdot r$, we say that it is possible to *partition G into copies of H* if there exist disjoint sets $V_1, V_2, \dots, V_r$ such that

- $\bigcup_{i=1}^{r} V_i = V$, and
- $G[V_i] \simeq H$ for every $i = 1, 2, \dots, r$,

where by $G[V_i]$ we mean the subgraph of G induced by the set of vertices V_i.

Research supported by the CE-ITI grant project P202/12/G061 of GA ČR, by GAUK project 1784214 and by the project SVV–2016–260332.

F. Drewes et al. (Eds.): LATA 2017, LNCS 10168, pp. 338–350, 2017.
DOI: 10.1007/978-3-319-53733-7_25

Problem 1 (PARTITION INTO H).

FIXED: Pattern graph $H = (W, F)$.
INPUT: Graph $G = (V, E)$ with $|V| = r \cdot |W|$ for an integer r.
QUESTION: Is there a partition of G into copies of H?

The complexity of the PARTITION INTO H problem has been studied by Hell and Kirkpatrick [15] and has been proven to be NP-complete for any fixed graph H with at least 3 vertices – they have studied the problem under a different name as the GENERALIZED MATCHING problem. There are applications in the printed wiring board design [12] and code optimization [3].

Some variants of this problem are studied extensively in graph theory. For example when $H \simeq K_2$ the problem PARTITION INTO K_2 is the well known PERFECT MATCHING problem, which can be solved in polynomial time due to Edmonds [7] – the algorithm works even for the optimization version, when one tries to maximize the number of copies of K_2 in G. The characterization theorem for $H \simeq K_2$, that is a characterization of graphs admitting a perfect matching is known due to Tutte [20].

Another frequently studied case of our problem is the PARTITION INTO K_3 problem – also known as the TRIANGLE PARTITION problem. The TRIANGLE PARTITION problem arises as a special case of the SET PARTITION problem (also known to be NP-complete [10]). Gajarský et al. [9] pointed out that the parametrized complexity of the TRIANGLE PARTITION problem parametrized by the tree-width of the input graph was not resolved so far.

The last, but not least, example of a well known problem which can be viewed as a special case of the PARTITION INTO H problem is the EQUITABLE COLORING problem. The task is to color the vertices of an n vertex graph with exactly k colors such that vertices connected by an edge receive different colors and the resulting color classes have equal sizes. It is easy to see that the EQUITABLE COLORING problem is the PARTITION INTO H problem with the edgeless graph on n/k vertices (it is possible to add a clique of appropriate size so that n becomes a multiple of k as it is demanded in our setting).

Very similar application can be found as the so called ℓ-BOUNDED VERTEX COLORINGS, where the task is to find a coloring of a graph G with prescribed number of colors such that each color is used at most ℓ-times. This problem allows a straightforward reduction to the EQUITABLE COLORING by inserting a suitable number of isolated vertices. The connection between these two problems was also studied from the parametrized complexity point of view [2] – an XP algorithm is obtained for parametrization by the tree-width of graph G. Here a special case of this problem is again equivalent to the PARTITION INTO H problem with H being the edgeless graph on ℓ vertices. For this problem a polynomial time algorithm is known for trees [13]. Upper and lower bounds on the number of colors are known for general graphs [11].

Very recently van Bevern et al. [21] studied computational complexity of related problem, where for a fixed graph $H = (W, F)$ the task is to partition the set of vertices of an input graph $G = (V, E)$ into sets $V_1, V_2, \ldots, V_r$ such that $|V_i| = |W|$ and $G[V_i]$ contains subgraph isomorphic to H.

Parametrized Complexity Results. When dealing with an NP-hard problem it is usual to study the problem in the framework of parametrized complexity. While in the previous section we have introduced several problems of the classical complexity, here we give references to parametrized results for these problems.

A similar but more general problem (called the MSOL PARTITIONING problem) was studied by Rao [18]. Here the task is to partition the vertices of the graph G into several sets $A_1, A_2, \ldots, A_r$ such that $\varphi(A_i)$ holds for every $i = 1, 2, \ldots, r$, where $\varphi(\cdot)$ is an MSO_1 formula with one free set variable. If the number r and the clique-width $\mathrm{cw}(G)$ are fixed then the algorithm runs in polynomial time and hence the problem is in XP parametrized by clique-width.

Our Contribution. Our first algorithm is based on the celebrated theorem of Courcelle [4] – a usual starting point for parametrized algorithm design. We would like to point out, that even though the result follows easily, the application is not straightforward.

Theorem 2. *For any fixed connected graph H the* PARTITION INTO H *problem is expressible by an MSO_2 formula.*

As the first algorithm is for graphs with bounded tree-width and thus a sparse class of graphs, we also analyse some variants of the PARTITION INTO H problem for a particular class of dense graphs. Many parameters are suitable for dense graph classes, such as neighborhood diversity and modular-width (we give formal definitions in Sect. 3).

Definition 3 (Prime Graph). *We say that a graph $G = (V, E)$ is* prime graph *if for every subset of vertices $U \subsetneq V$ with at least two vertices there exist $v \in V \setminus U$ such that v is adjacent to at least one vertex in U and v is not adjacent to at least one vertex in U.*

Theorem 4. *For any fixed prime graph H and a graph G the* PARTITION INTO H *problem belongs to the* FPT *class when parametrized by modular width of graph G.*

We derive the result using integer linear programming in a fixed dimension, which can be solved by a parametrized routine [8,14]. It is worth to mention that even though the condition on prime graphs may seem very restrictive this class of graphs contains for example paths P_k on $k \geq 4$ vertices and cycles C_k on $k \geq 5$ vertices. Applications of the PARTITION INTO H problem with H being a path may be found in code optimization [3].

When it is shown that there is an FPT-algorithm for some problem, it is natural to ask, whether the problem admits a polynomial kernel – that is a preprocessing routine running in polynomial time which outputs an equivalent instance of size polynomially bounded in the assumed parameter. We prove that the PARTITION INTO H problem does not have polynomial kernel parametrized by modular-width for any reasonable graph H, that is when H has at least 3 vertices and thus the PARTITION INTO H problem is NP-hard. More precisely, we prove the following.

Theorem 5. *For any fixed graph H with at least 3 vertices. There is no polynomial kernel routine for the* Partition into H *problem when parametrized by modular width of graph G unless* NP$\subseteq$ coNP/poly.

Using techniques similar to those of proof of Theorem 4 we can prove that for every fixed H the Partition into H problem can be solved efficiently on graphs with bounded neighborhood diversity.

Theorem 6. *For any fixed graph H there is an* FPT*-algorithm for the* Partition into H *problem parametrized by neighborhood diversity of graph G.*

2 Preliminaries

For a graph $G = (V, E)$ we denote by $|G|$ the number of vertices of G. For a set U we denote by $\binom{U}{2}$ the set of all two element subsets of U, that is $\binom{U}{2} = \{\{u, v\}: u, v \in U, u \neq v\}$. Let $G = (V, E)$ be a graph and let $U \subseteq V$ the graph induced by U is denoted by $G[U]$ and it is the graph $(U, E \cap \binom{U}{2})$. Let $G = (V, E), H = (W, F)$ be graphs, we say that G is *isomorphic* to H, we denote this by $G \simeq H$, if there exists a bijective mapping $f : V \to W$ such that $\{u, v\} \in E$ if and only if $\{f(u), f(v)\} \in F$. For a set of vertices U we denote the set of incident edges as $\delta(U)$ that is the set of edges $\{\{u, v\}: u \in U, v \in V \setminus U\}$. Finally a complement of a graph $G = (V, E)$ is denoted by $\bar{G}$ is a graph on the same vertex set V with edge set $\binom{V}{2} \setminus E$. We say that a graph G is *connected* if there is a uv path in G for every two distinct vertices of G. For more notation on graphs, we refer reader to a monograph by Diestel [5].

We say that a relation R is an *equivalence relation* on a set X if R is reflexive, symmetric and transitive. An equivalence class determined by an element $x \in X$ is the set $\{y \in X : x \equiv_R y\}$.

2.1 Preliminaries on Refuting Polynomial Kernels

In the following we denote by Σ a finite alphabet, by Σ^* we denote the set of all words over Σ and by $\Sigma^{\leq n}$ we denote the set of all words over Σ and length at most n.

Definition 7 (Polynomial Equivalence Relation). *An equivalence relation $\mathcal{R}$ on the set Σ^* is called* polynomial equivalence relation *if the following conditions are satisfied:*

1. *There exists an algorithm such that, given strings $x, y \in \Sigma^*$, resolves whether $x \equiv_{\mathcal{R}} y$ in time polynomial in $|x| + |y|$.*
2. *Relation $\mathcal{R}$ restricted to the set $\Sigma^{\leq n}$ has at most $p(n)$ equivalence classes for some polynomial $p(\cdot)$.*

Definition 8 (AND-Cross-Composition). *Let $L \subseteq \Sigma^*$ be an unparametrized language and $Q \subseteq \Sigma^* \times \mathbb{N}$ be a parametrized language. We say that L* cross-composes *into Q if there exists a polynomial equivalence relation $\mathcal{R}$ and an* *algorithm $\mathcal{A}$, called the AND-cross-composition, satisfying the following conditions. The algorithm $\mathcal{A}$ takes on input a sequence of strings $x_1, x_2, \dots, x_r \in \Sigma^*$ that are equivalent with respect to $\mathcal{R}$, runs in polynomial time in $\sum_{i=1}^{r} |x_i|$, and outputs one instance $(y, k) \in \Sigma^* \times \mathbb{N}$ such that:*

1. *$k \leq p(\max_{i=1}^{r} |x_i|, \log r)$ for some polynomial $p(\cdot, \cdot)$, and*
2. *$(y, k) \in Q$ if and only if $x_i \in L$ for all i.*

We say that language L has a *polynomial kernel* if there is a kernelization algorithm that takes on input an instance $(x, k) \in \Sigma^* \times \mathbb{N}$, runs in polynomial time in $|x|$ and k, and outputs an equivalent instance $(x', k') \in \Sigma^* \times \mathbb{N}$ with $|x'| \leq p(k')$ and $k' \leq q(k)$, where $p(\cdot), q(\cdot)$ are polynomials. With this framework, it is possible to refute even stronger data reduction techniques.

Definition 9 (Polynomial Compression). *A* polynomial compression *of a parametrized language $Q \subseteq \Sigma^* \times \mathbb{N}$ into an unparametrized language $R \subseteq \Sigma^*$ is an algorithm that takes as input an instance $(x, k) \in \Sigma^* \times \mathbb{N}$, works in polynomial time in $|x| + k$, and returns a string y such that:*

1. *$|y| \leq p(k)$ for some polynomial $p(\cdot)$, and*
2. *$y \in R$ if and only if $(x, k) \in Q$.*

It is easy to see that the polynomial kernelization is a special case of the polynomial compression. It is possible to refute existence of polynomial compression (and polynomial kernel) using AND-cross-composition with the help of use of the following theorem and a complexity assumption that is unlikely to hold.

Theorem 10 ([1,6]). *Assume that an* NP*-hard language L AND-cross-composes to a parametrized language Q. Then Q does not admit a polynomial compression, unless* $\mathsf{NP} \subseteq \mathsf{coNP/poly}$.

3 Preliminaries on Structural Graph Parameters

We give a formal definition of several graph parameters used in this work. For a better acquaint with these parameters, we provide a map of assumed parameters in Fig. 1.

We say that two (distinct) vertices u, v are of the same *neighborhood type* if they share their respective neighborhoods, that is when $N(u) \setminus \{v\} = N(v) \setminus \{u\}$.

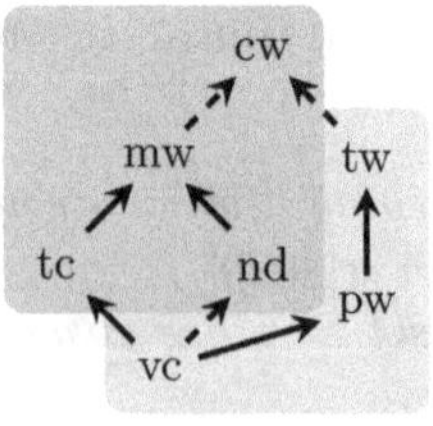

Fig. 1. A map of assumed parameters. A full arrow stands for a linear upper bound, while a dashed arrow stands for an exponential upper bound. For example if a graph G has $\mathrm{vc}(G) \leq k$ then $\mathrm{nd}(G) \leq 2^k + k$.

Definition 11 (Neighborhood Diversity [16]**).** *A graph $G = (V, E)$ has* neighborhood diversity *at most w ($\mathrm{nd}(G) \leq w$), if there exists a partition of V into at most w sets (we call these sets* types*) such that all the vertices in each set have the same neighborhood type.*

Note that every type induces either a clique or an independent set in G and two types are either joined by a complete bipartite graph or no edge between vertices of the two types is present in G. Thus, we use the notion of a *type graph* – that is a graph T_G representing the graph G and its neighborhood diversity decomposition in the following way. The vertices of type graph T_G are the neighborhood types of the graph G and two such vertices are joined by an edge if all the vertices of corresponding types are joined by an edge. Note that any optimal type graph is a prime graph. We would like to point out that it is possible to compute the neighborhood diversity of a graph in linear time [16].

Both previous approaches are generalized by a modular-width, defined by Gajarský et al. [9]. Here we deal with graphs created by an algebraic expression that uses four following operations:

1. create an isolated vertex,
2. the disjoint union of two graphs, that is from graphs $G = (V, E), H = (W, F)$ create a graph $(V \cup W, E \cup F)$,
3. the complete join of two graphs, that is from graphs $G = (V, E), H = (W, F)$ create a graph $(V \cup W, E \cup F \cup \{\{v, w\}: v \in V, w \in W\})$, note that the edge set of the resulting graph can be also written as $E \cup F \cup V \times W$.
4. The substitution operation with respect to a template graph T (for an example see Fig. 2) with vertex set $\{v_1, v_2, \ldots, v_k\}$ and graphs $G_1, G_2, \ldots, G_k$ created by algebraic expression. The substitution operation, denoted by $T(G_1, G_2, \ldots, G_k)$, results in the graph on vertex set $V = V_1 \cup V_2 \cup \cdots \cup V_k$ and edge set $E = E_1 \cup E_2 \cup \cdots \cup E_k \cup \bigcup_{\{v_i, v_j\} \in E(T)} \{\{u, v\}: u \in V_i, v \in V_j\}$, where $G_i = (V_i, E_i)$ for all $i = 1, 2, \ldots, k$.

Definition 12 (Modular-Width [9]**).** *Let A be an algebraic expression that uses only operations* 1–4*. The* width of expression *A is the maximum number of operands used by any occurrence of operation* 4 *in A.*

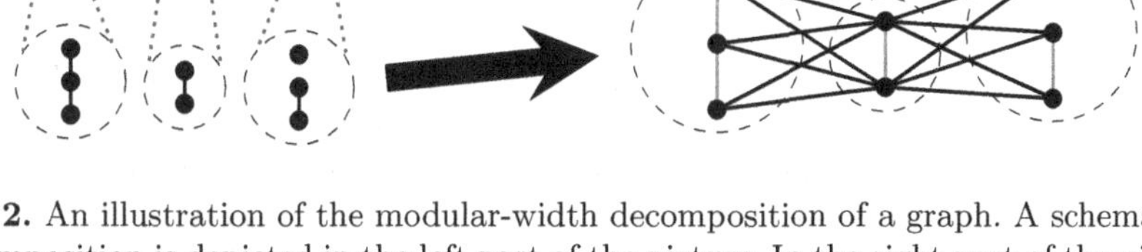

Fig. 2. An illustration of the modular-width decomposition of a graph. A schema of a decomposition is depicted in the left part of the picture. In the right part of the picture there is the resulting graph – gray edges represent edges from the previous step of the decomposition (with template graph T).

The modular-width *of a graph G, denoted as* mw(G)*, is the least positive integer k such that G can be obtained from such an algebraic expression of width at most k.*

When a graph H is constructed by the fourth operation, that is $G = T(G_1, G_2, \ldots, G_k)$, we call the graph T the *template graph*. An algebraic expression of width mw(G) can be computed in linear time [19].

4 Graphs with Bounded Modular-Width

In this section we give a proof of the Theorem 4. We begin with a technical Lemma 13 that demonstrates the limited possibilities of embedding the (fixed) prime graph H into the input graph G with bounded modular-width. This exploits a close connection of the parameters neighborhood diversity and modular-width.

We then formulate the problem as a mixed integer linear problem, where we can bound the number of integer variables by a function in the modular-width mw(G) of the input graph and thus proving the theorem.

By an *embedding* of graph $H = (W, F)$ in graph $G = (V, E)$ we mean a function $h : W \to V$ such that $G[h(W)] \simeq H$, to which we refer as an *induced copy* of H in G.

Recall that by Definition 3 for a prime graph $H = (W, F)$ it holds that $\forall U \subsetneq W$ with at least two vertices there exists vertex $w \in W \setminus U$ such that it is adjacent and non-adjacent to at least one vertex in U.

Embedding of H inside G. The following lemma shows that restricting H to be prime graph leads to only two possibilities of an embedding of H on a particular level of a modular decomposition of the graph G.

Lemma 13. *Let $G = T(G_1, G_2, \ldots, G_k)$ be a graph and let $H = (W, F)$ be a prime graph. For an induced subgraph $G' \simeq H$ of G holds either*

1. *$G' \subseteq G_i$ for some $i \in \{1, 2, \ldots, k\}$, or*
2. *G' contains at most one vertex in every G_i for $i = 1, 2, \ldots, k$.*

Proof. Assume that $G' \nsubseteq G_i$ for any i as otherwise we are done. If there are at least two vertices of G' in some G_i, – we will show (using Definition 3) that this cannot be valid embedding of H inside G.

Let us rearrange vertices of a template graph T (and corresponding graphs G_i) so that G' contains vertices of graphs $G_1, G_2, \ldots, G_\ell$ (with $\ell < |H|$). Let $T' \subseteq T$ be the restriction of T to vertices $v_1, v_2, \ldots, v_\ell$. From our assumption on $\ell < |H|$ it follows that there exists a set $U \subsetneq W$ that is embedded inside one graph G_i. By the definition of prime graphs for this set U there exists vertex $w \in W \setminus U$ and two (different) vertices $u_1, u_2 \in U$ such that $\{u_1, w\} \in F$ and $\{u_2, w\} \notin F$. But this contradicts the fact that G' is an embedding of H inside G as by the definition of modular decomposition for all $v \in G_j$ with $j \neq i$ either v is adjacent to every vertex in U, or v is non-adjacent to all vertices in U. Thus, G' cannot be an embedding of H inside G.

By Lemma 13 for the most complex operation follows that the structure inside graphs $G_1, G_2, \ldots, G_k$ is not important when we try to find graphs of the partition that contains vertices from more than one graph G_i.

Note that when deciding the PARTITION INTO H problem on graph G with $\mathrm{mw}(G) < |H|$, it follows from Lemma 13 that the answer is clearly No – thus this case is trivial. So the task is to design an algorithm when $|H| = \mathrm{nd}(H) \le \mathrm{mw}(G)$.

4.1 Mixed Integer Linear Program Routine

We solve the PARTITION INTO H problem by a recursive algorithm. For each occurrence of operation 4 in the decomposition we design an integer linear program that computes the optimal solution, that is the solution in which there are as many induced copies of H in G as possible. The integer program uses previous solution thus we proceed (recursively) from leaves of the decomposition tree of G towards the root.

In the following mixed integer linear program for the PARTITION INTO H problem on the graph $G = T(G_1, G_2, \ldots, G_k)$ the set $\mathcal{S}$ is the set of all $|H|$-tuples of vertices of the graph T that form an induced copy of H inside T and thus, inside the graph G. An alternative point of view is that $\mathcal{S}$ is the set of all possible copies of H in T. Let U be the vertex set of the graph T, moreover, as graphs $G_1, G_2, \ldots, G_k$ correspond to vertices of T, we will denote these as G_v for $v \in U$.

The Solution, Constants and Variables. The constants w_v represent the number of vertices of the graph G_v that are not covered by a copies of H found by the previous (recursive) solution. The constants p_v represent the number of copies of H in the recursive solution. Thus, the (recursive) solution is represented by pairs (p_v, w_v) for all $v \in U$. It may be wise to unlink some previously made copies of H's (computed by the recursive procedure) – this is why we introduce the variable y_v, which expresses how many previously constructed copies shall by unlinked. An example of a situation in which this is necessary is show on Fig. 3. The ILP tries to cover as many vertices as possible – this is done by minimizing the number of uncovered vertices expressed by r_v for a graph G_v.

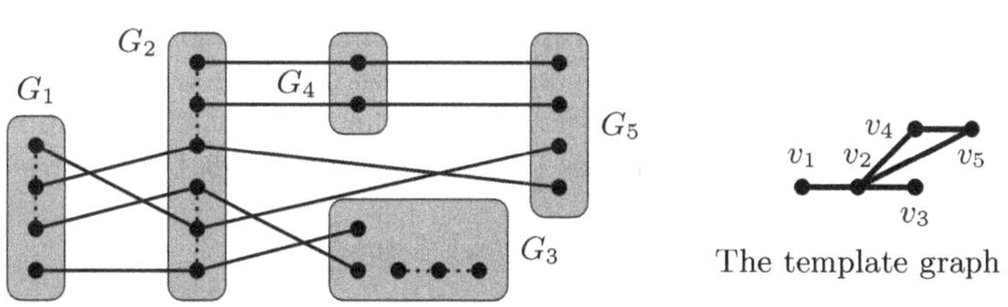

Fig. 3. An example of a graph created by a modular decomposition. Template graph is given on the right. Paths inside blocks (precomputed by an induction) are shown as dotted, while an optimal solution for this graph is drawn with solid edges. The graph shows that it is essential to allow unlinking of previously (recursively) constructed solution.

Mixed Integer Linear Program

$$\text{minimize} \sum_{v \in U} r_i \quad \text{subject to} \quad r_v = w_v + |H| \cdot y_v - \sum_{S \in \mathcal{S} : S \ni v} x_S \qquad \forall v \in U$$

$$y_v \leq p_v \qquad \forall v \in U$$

$$\text{where} \qquad x_S \in \mathbb{N} \qquad \forall S \in \mathcal{S}$$

$$y_v \in \mathbb{N} \qquad \forall v \in U$$

$$r_v \geq 0 \qquad \forall v \in U$$

The total number of integral variables may be upper-bounded by $|T|+|T|^{|H|}$, so if we denote by k the size of the template graph (and thus the modular-width of an input graph) the upper bound can be expressed as $k + k^k$. We can apply the following result of Lenstra [14] (with an enhancement due to Frank and Tardos [8]) to derive Theorem 4.

Proposition 14 ([8,14]). *Let p be the number of integral variables in a Mixed integer linear program and let L be the number of bits needed to encode the program. Then it is possible to find an optimal solution in time $\mathcal{O}(p^{2.5p}\text{poly}(L))$ and a space polynomial in L.*

4.2 Refuting Polynomial Kernels

In this section we prove Theorem 5. First observe that it suffices to prove the theorem only for connected graph H. This is trivial as for every graph G it holds that $\text{mw}(G) = \text{mw}(\bar{G})$ (the complement of graph G) – and thus we can ask the question in complementary setting.

As a polynomial equivalence relation we take the following relation. Two instances $(G_1, H_1), (G_2, H_2)$ are equivalent if $|G_1| = |G_2|$ (that is they have the same number of vertices) and $H_1 \simeq H_2$. As H is fixed this defines a polynomial equivalence relation (together with the class of malformed instances – instances that do not encode a pair of graphs).

Observe that if we take a disjoint union of two graphs G, G' then $\text{mw}(G \dot\cup G') \leq \max\{|G|, |G'|\}$. This is not hard to see as we can take G to be a type graph for G and similarly G' to be a type graph for G'. Then the disjoint union does not change the modular-width as the second operation of modular decomposition is exactly the disjoint union and does not change the width of the decomposition. By an inductive argument for graphs $G_1, G_2, \dots, G_t$ it holds that

$$\text{mw}(G_1 \dot\cup G_2 \dot\cup \cdots \dot\cup G_t) \leq \max_{1 \leq i \leq t} \{|G_i|\}.$$

As the designed polynomial equivalence relation assures that for all i and j the graphs $H_i \simeq H_j$ we write H to be the common graph for all instances. An AND-cross-composition of equivalent instances $(G_1, H), (G_2, H), \dots, (G_t, H)$ we take as instance (G, H) – the disjoint union of all graphs. Because H is connected the new instance (G, H) admits a partition into copies of H if and only if all instances (G_i, H) admit such a partition. The previous paragraph shows that $\mathrm{mw}(G) \leq \max_{1 \leq i \leq t}\{|G_i|\}$. This finishes the design of an AND-distillation and the proof of Theorem 5 for all graphs H for which the PARTITION INTO H problem is NP-hard.

4.3 Graphs with Bounded Neighborhood Diversity

In this section we will present a proof of Theorem 6. The proof is based on a bound of the number of possibilities of embedding a graph H into G.

Note that for the PARTITION INTO H problem parametrized by $\mathrm{nd}(G)$ it is possible that an embedding of a graph H in G does not have to obey the neighborhood diversity decomposition – it is possible that for example a clique type of H may be embedded among several clique (or even independent) types of G. For an example of such a situation see Fig. 4. On the contrary the embedding of H in G has to obey the neighborhood diversity decomposition of graph H. We formalize this in Lemma 15.

The proof of the following lemma is very similar to the proof of Lemma 13. The proof is omitted here (it is possible to find the proof in the Appendix).

Lemma 15. *Let G, H be graphs such that it is possible to partition G into copies of H. Then* $\mathrm{nd}(H) \leq \mathrm{nd}(G)$.

By Lemma 15 the algorithm for the PARTITION INTO H problem we may assume that $\mathrm{nd}(H) \leq \mathrm{nd}(G)$ and that H is a connected graph (we can take the complementary instance of the problem, see Sect. 4.2).

As the graph H is fixed in our setting the number $|H|$ is not a part of the input. Thus an embedding of H in G can be described by specifying a type to which a particular vertex of H is mapped (i.e. by a $\varphi\colon V(H) \to V(T_G)$). There are at most $\mathrm{nd}(G)^{|H|}$ possibilities of embedding H into G. It is not hard to see that it is possible to compactly describe an embedding of H in G by a vector $\mathbf{p} = (p_1, p_2, \ldots, p_{\mathrm{nd}(G)})$ of length $\mathrm{nd}(G)$, where p_i is the number of vertices used for this embedding inside the i-th type in the neighborhood diversity decomposition of graph G. In this case, we say that the embedding corresponds to vector $\mathbf{p}$.

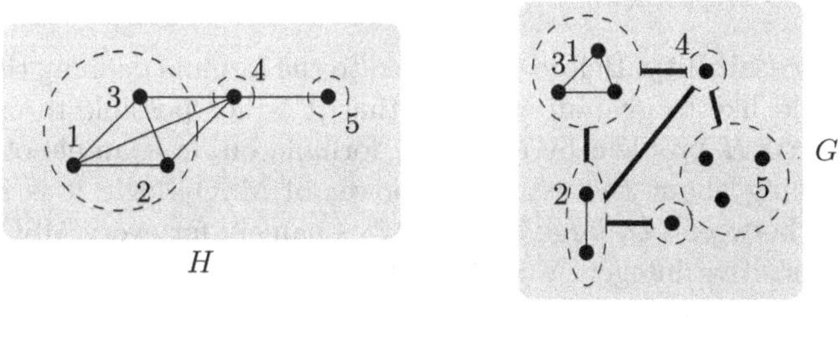

Fig. 4. An example of embedding of a graph H in G – vertices are labeled $1, 2, \ldots, 5$ in both to show the embedding. The types in graphs are indicated by dashed circles around a group of vertices. Bold edges between types represent a complete bipartite graph.

A vector $\mathbf{p} = (p_1, p_2, \ldots, p_{\mathrm{nd}(G)})$ is *admissible* if there exists an embedding of H in G which correspond to vector $\mathbf{p}$. Furthermore, note that it is possible to find the set $\mathcal{P}$ of all admissible vectors in time $\mathcal{O}(\mathrm{nd}(G)^{|H|}|H|^2)$ by searching through all embeddings and checking that edges of graph H are preserved.

The rest is to find a non-negative integral combination of vectors contained in set $\mathcal{P}$ that gives vector $(n_1, n_2, \ldots, n_{\mathrm{nd}(G)})$, where n_i is the number of vertices contained in the i-th type in the neighborhood diversity decomposition of graph G. It is straightforward to do this using integer linear programming (Lenstra's algorithm) as we are asking for non-negative integral combination of vectors in $\mathcal{P}$ of size bounded by $|H|$ and $\mathrm{nd}(G)$. This finishes the proof of Theorem 6.

5 Connected Partition Problem is MSO_2 Definable

In this section we show that for a fixed connected graph H the Partition into H problem can be described by an MSO_2 formula. Even though this is not obvious at the first sight. The straightforward expression by a formula seems to operate with copies of H inside G – but the number of such copies is function of the number of vertices of G and thus cannot be bounded in terms of $\mathrm{tw}(G)$ and $|H|$.

MSO_2 Formula Idea. We will proceed as follows. We will describe the solution to the Partition into H problem as a property of a set of edges which are in the solution. This approach is not expressible in MSO_1. We describe the property of being a solution to the Partition into H problem as "every connected part of the solution is an induced subgraph of G isomorphic to H". We express this by describing that a set of edges S is a solution if

- every vertex of the host graph G is in some connected component of $G[S]$,
- every connected component $G[S]$ is an induced graph (it contains exactly edges present in G between vertices of that particular component) and
- every connected component of $G[S]$ is a graph isomorphic to H (we do this by discovering a copy of H from a particular (fixed in advance) vertex in H).

It is clear that if every vertex of G is in some connected component which form an induced subgraph of G isomorphic to H, then we have the solution to the Partition into H problem.

MSO_1 Inexpressibility. Before we proceed to the formula defining the solution set S, we would like to give an evidence that it is not possible to express the Partition into H problem by an MSO_1 formula on an example of $H \simeq K_3$. Roughly speaking about the expressive power of MSO_1 logic it is impossible to distinguish between two large cliques [17] – namely for every MSO_1 formula φ there is a positive integer N such that it is impossible to distinguish two cliques K_N and K_{N+1}. If we build two graphs G_1, G_2 as $G_1 = K_{N-1} \cup K_{N+1}$ and $G_2 = K_N \cup K_N$ for large enough N that is divisible by 3 the framework of Ehrenfeucht–Frass games [17] graphs G_1 and G_2 give that the Triangle Partition problem is not expressible in MSO_1 logic. It is possible to generalize this idea to other graphs as well.

6 Conclusions

We have studied the Partition into H problem from the parametrized complexity point of view. We would like to enclose the paper with several open problems to which we would like to give a brief description.

We would like to ask a question related to the tree-depth, is there a disconnected graph H such that the Partition into H problem is FPT with respect to the tree-depth (of course, different from the edgeless graph on two vertices)?

We have presented in Sect. 4 an algorithm for a fixed graph H from a certain class of graphs. Is it possible to extend this result to a broader class of graphs H? Most important form this point of view seem graphs on 3 vertices – a path P_3 and a triangle K_3 (the rest of 3 vertex graphs would be resolved using complements).

Another important task in this area is to understand the boundary (viewed from the parametrized complexity perspective) between modular-width and neighborhood diversity, twin-cover and clique-width. We hope that our knowledge in this area can be extended in the highlight of the Partition into H problem – namely we should identify graphs H with the property that on one parameter the problem is fixed parameter tractable while it is W[1]-hard on some other parameter (higher in the parameter hierarchy).

Finally, our techniques from Lemma 15 showed that the Partition into H problem admits an FPT algorithm when the graph H is a prime graph even when the graph H is a part of the input. More generally, there is an FPT algorithm, if we extend the graph class by allowing constant number of vertices inside every type of the graph H. Is it possible to show an FPT algorithm parametrized by neighborhood diversity of graph G that takes the graph H as input?

Our results give possibilities for parametrized algorithms with respect to clique-width – namely for the class of prime graphs. Here we would like to propose a concrete question for the Partition into P_4 (the smallest prime graph) – is there an FPT algorithm for this problem with respect to clique-width?

References

1. Bodlaender, H.L., Downey, R.G., Fellows, M.R., Hermelin, D.: On problems without polynomial kernels. J. Comput. Syst. Sci. **75**(8), 423–434 (2009)
2. Bodlaender, H.L., Fomin, F.V.: Equitable colorings of bounded treewidth graphs. Theoret. Comput. Sci. **349**(1), 22–30 (2005). Graph Colorings 2003
3. Boesch, F.T., Gimpel, J.F.: Covering points of a digraph with point-disjoint paths and its application to code optimization. J. ACM **24**(2), 192–198 (1977)
4. Courcelle, B.: The monadic second-order logic of graphs. I. Recognizable sets of finite graphs. Inf. Comput. **85**(1), 12–75 (1990)
5. Diestel, R.: Graph Theory: Graduate Texts in Mathematics, vol. 173, 4th edn. Springer, Heidelberg (2012)
6. Drucker, A.: New limits to classical and quantum instance compression. In: FOCS, vol. 2012, pp. 609–618 (2012)
7. Edmonds, J.: Paths, trees, and flowers. Can. J. Math. **17**, 449–467 (1965)
8. Frank, A., Tardos, É.: An application of simultaneous diophantine approximation in combinatorial optimization. Combinatorica **7**(1), 49–65 (1987)

9. Gajarský, J., Lampis, M., Ordyniak, S.: Parameterized algorithms for modular-width. In: Gutin, G., Szeider, S. (eds.) IPEC 2013. LNCS, vol. 8246, pp. 163–176. Springer, Heidelberg (2013). doi:10.1007/978-3-319-03898-8_15
10. Garey, M.R., Johnson, D.S.: Computers and Intractability: A Guide to the Theory of NP-Completeness. W.H. Freeman & Co., New York (1979)
11. Hansen, P., Hertz, A., Kuplinsky, J.: Bounded vertex colorings of graphs. Discrete Math. **111**(1–3), 305–312 (1993)
12. Hope, A.K.: Component placement through graph partitioning in computer-aided printed-wiring-board design. Electron. Lett. **8**(4), 87–88 (1972)
13. Jarvis, M., Zhou, B.: Bounded vertex coloring of trees. Discrete Math. **232**(1–3), 145–151 (2001)
14. Lenstra Jr., H.W.: Integer programming with a fixed number of variables. Math. Oper. Res. **8**(4), 538–548 (1983)
15. Kirkpatrick, D.G., Hell, P.: On the completeness of a generalized matching problem. In: STOC 1978, pp. 240–245. ACM, New York (1978)
16. Lampis, M.: Algorithmic meta-theorems for restrictions of treewidth. Algorithmica **64**(1), 19–37 (2012)
17. Libkin, L.: Elements of Finite Model Theory. Texts in Theoretical Computer Science. An EATCS Series. Springer, Heidelberg (2004)
18. Rao, M.: MSOL partitioning problems on graphs of bounded treewidth and clique-width. Theor. Comput. Sci. **377**(1–3), 260–267 (2007)
19. Tedder, M., Corneil, D., Habib, M., Paul, C.: Simpler linear-time modular decomposition via recursive factorizing permutations. In: Aceto, L., Damgård, I., Goldberg, L.A., Halldórsson, M.M., Ingólfsdóttir, A., Walukiewicz, I. (eds.) ICALP 2008. LNCS, vol. 5125, pp. 634–645. Springer, Heidelberg (2008). doi:10.1007/978-3-540-70575-8_52
20. Tutte, W.T.: The factorization of linear graphs. J. Lond. Math. Soc. **s1–22**, 107–111 (1947)
21. van Bevern, R., Bredereck, R., Bulteau, L., Chen, J., Froese, V., Niedermeier, R., Woeginger, G.J.: Star partitions of perfect graphs. In: Esparza, J., Fraigniaud, P., Husfeldt, T., Koutsoupias, E. (eds.) ICALP 2014. LNCS, vol. 8572, pp. 174–185. Springer, Heidelberg (2014). doi:10.1007/978-3-662-43948-7_15

Space Complexity of Reachability Testing in Labelled Graphs

Vidhya Ramaswamy, Jayalal Sarma, and K.S. Sunil(✉)

Indian Institute of Technology Madras, Chennai, India
vidhya0794@gmail.com, jayalal.sarma@gmail.com, sunsks@gmail.com

Abstract. Fix an algebraic structure $(\mathcal{A}, *)$. Given a graph $G = (V, E)$ and the labelling function ϕ ($\phi : E \to \mathcal{A}$) for the edges, two nodes s, $t \in V$, and a subset $F \subseteq \mathcal{A}$, the $\mathcal{A}$-Reach problem asks if there is a path p (need not be simple) from s to t whose yield (result of the operation in the ordered set of the labels of the edges constituting the path) is in F. On the complexity frontier of this problem, we show the following results.

- When $\mathcal{A}$ is a group whose size is polynomially bounded in the size of the graph (hence equivalently presented as a multiplication table at the input), and the graph is undirected, the $\mathcal{A}$-Reach problem is in L. Building on this, using a decomposition in [4], we show that, when $\mathcal{A}$ is a fixed quasi-group, and the graph is undirected, the $\mathcal{A}$-Reach problem is in L. In contrast, we show NL-hardness of the problem over bidirected graphs, when $\mathcal{A}$ is a matrix group over $\mathbb{Q}$. When $\mathcal{A}$ is a fixed aperiodic monoid, we show that the problem is NL-complete.
- As our main theorem, we prove a dichotomy for graphs labelled with fixed aperiodic monoids by showing that for every fixed aperiodic monoid $\mathcal{A}$, $\mathcal{A}$-Reach problem is either in L or is NL-complete.
- We show that there exists a monoid M, such that the reachability problem in general DAGs can be reduced to $\mathcal{A}$-Reach problem for planar non-bipartite DAGs labelled with M. In contrast, we show that if the planar DAGs that we obtain above are bipartite, the problem can be further reduced to reachability testing in planar DAGs and hence is in UL.

1 Introduction

The reachability problem on combinatorial structures has been fundamental and well studied in complexity theory. A most striking example of this is the graph reachability problem which asks, given a directed graph G and two special vertices s and t whether there is a path from s to t in G or not. The problem is known to be NL-complete for directed acyclic graphs. Deterministic logspace algorithms are known for restricted classes of graphs - when each component of the directed graph is Eulerian [19], or the graph has bounded treewidth [10]. Reachability for planar graphs is in unambiguous[1] logspace [7]. See [1] for a survey.

[1] A language is said to be in unambiguous logspace if there exists a non-deterministic logspace Turing machine M such that $\forall x$, M has at most one accepting computation.

F. Drewes et al. (Eds.): LATA 2017, LNCS 10168, pp. 351–363, 2017.
DOI: 10.1007/978-3-319-53733-7_26

Word problems over algebraic structures also play a fundamental role in complexity theoretic characterizations. Fix an algebraic structure $\mathcal{A}$ with an associated binary operation, and a subset $F \subseteq \mathcal{A}$. Given a $w \in \mathcal{A}^*$, test if the sequences of elements and operations among them is in F or not. An important milestone in this direction is the dichotomy result due to Barrington and Thérein [3] classifying the complexity of the word problems over a fixed monoid structure: if the monoid M contains at least one non-solvable group, then the word problem can be shown to be complete for NC^1 (under AC^0 projections) and if all groups are solvable then it characterizes ACC^0. Chandra *et al.* [9] showed that if there are no non-trivial groups then it characterizes the class AC^0. It is also known that word problems over groupoids characterize LogCFL [6]. Beaudry *et al.* [5] showed dichotomy theorem for the complexity of circuit evaluation problem defined over monoids, based on precise algebraic properties of the monoids.

Reachability on labelled graphs is a natural generalization of the graph reachability problem and the word problem on algebraic structures. A graph G is said to be *labelled* if the edges are assigned labels from an underlying set S. When this set also equipped a binary operation $* : S \times S \to S$, the reachability problem asks to test, given the graph G and two vertices s and t and an element $a \in S$, if there is a path (need not be simple) from s to t whose yield (result of the operation in the ordered set of the labels of the edges constituting the path) is a or not. A closely related problem is that of the L-REACH problem where a language L over the alphabet Σ, given a graph $G(V, E)$, two vertices s and t and a labelling function $\phi : E \to \Sigma$, test if there is a path from s to t whose yield (the concatenation of the labels in the ordered set of edges constituting the path) belongs to the language L. In [15], characterizations of the language reachability problem with respect to languages classes and graph classes were obtained.

In this work, we study the problem when the labels come from richer algebraic structures. When the structure $\mathcal{A}$ is a groupoid (equivalently a case of L-REACH problem when the language is restricted to be a context-free language) this problem has been used in inter-procedural slicing and inter-procedural data flow analysis [12,20,21]. On the complexity frontier, it is easy to observe that the $\mathcal{A}$-REACH problem is always harder than the word problem over $\mathcal{A}$, and is harder than the graph reachability problem (under logspace many-one reductions).

Our Results: We start with an observation that the problem of testing reachability on labelled graphs over semigroups can be reduced to testing reachability on an associated directed graph (called product graphs - see Sect. 3). From a complexity-theoretic view point, this motivates the study of the labelled reachability problem. More specifically, in order to show that for a graph class the reachability problem is in L, it is sufficient to reduce it to the reachability problem in a labelled graph such that reachability in the product graph can be solved in L. We prove several properties of this directed graph and explore graph classes and algebraic structures for which the $\mathcal{A}$-REACH problem is in L. In particular, we study this for undirected graphs (for which reachability problem is in L [18]) and show:

Logspace Upper Bounds for Polynomially Growing Groups: We show that when $\mathcal{A}$ is a group, such that $|\mathcal{A}| = O(n^c)$, where n is the size of the graph, and c is a constant (hence equivalently presented as a multiplication table at the input), and the graph is undirected, the $\mathcal{A}$-REACH problem is L-complete.

NL-hardness for Monoids and Matrix Groups: In contrast, we observe that there exists a fixed monoid $\mathcal{A}$ such that $\mathcal{A}$-REACH problem for undirected graphs is NL-complete. Working over a more structured labelling set, we show NL-hardness of the problem over bidirected graphs[2], when $\mathcal{A}$ is a finitely generated subgroup of $\mathsf{GL}_k(\mathbb{Q})$ (for $k \geq 2$)- the group of invertible $k \times k$ matrices with rational entries.

(NL vs L) Dichotomy for Aperiodic Monoids: We show a dichotomy for aperiodic monoids: for any fixed aperiodic monoid $\mathcal{A}$, the $\mathcal{A}$-REACH problem for undirected graphs is either NL-complete or is in L.

Logspace Upper Bounds for Quasigroups: When $\mathcal{A}$ is a fixed quasigroup, the $\mathcal{A}$-REACH problem is L-complete.

Logspace Upper Bounds for Treewidth k Graphs labelled with Monoids: When the graph has bounded treewidth, for any fixed monoid $\mathcal{A}$ the $\mathcal{A}$-REACH problem for undirected graphs is L-complete.

While the general DAGREACH problem is complete for NL, the reachability problem over planar DAGs is known to be in UL [7]. We show that DAGREACH can be reduced to $\mathcal{A}$-REACH over planar DAGs when $\mathcal{A}$ is a specific monoid M. Tightly complementing this, we show that the instances of labelled graph reachability problem obtained in this reduction, with the additional restriction that the graph is bipartite, can be solved in deterministic log-space. Moving towards groups, we show that DAGREACH can be reduced to $\mathcal{A}$-REACH over planar graph when $\mathcal{A}$ is a specific exponentially growing group.

Related Work: Group labelled graphs have been extensively studied in the literature as a generalization of signed graphs (see [11]) with the aim to extend the graph minor theory to group labelled graphs over a fixed finite Abelian group. An important comparison that we make is with the results by Kawase *et al.* [14], where they consider the reachability problem in group labelled graphs: to check if there is a *simple path* from s to t in the given group labelled graph so that the yield of the path is a given element α. It is observed in [14] that the problem is NP-complete over $\mathbb{Z}$, since the undirected Hamiltonian path problem reduces to this problem by replacing each edge with a pair of two arcs of opposite directions with label 1 and letting $\alpha = n - 1$. Huynh [13] showed the problem is polynomial time solvable if the group is a fixed Abelian group.

However, we point out two important differences in our setting. Firstly, in our setting, the problem does not look for simple paths from s to t, and hence

[2] Directed graph $(G(V, E))$ such that $\forall v_i, v_j \in V, (v_i, v_j) \in E \implies (v_j, v_i) \in E$. However, $\phi(v_i, v_j)$ need not be equal to $\phi(v_j, v_i)$. To complement this, we observe (see Corollary 1) that the log-space upper bound for groups whose size is polynomially bounded in terms of input, holds even for bidirected graphs.

the NP-completeness result does not apply. Secondly, for the case of undirected graphs with labelling from a group, the above mentioned results (including [14]) assume that if an edge (u, v) in the graph is labelled with g, the edge (v, u) is labelled with g^{-1}. In our setting, this is not the case - if an edge in the undirected graph is labelled $g \in G$, then the edge contributes to the final product as g itself *irrespective* of the direction that is taken by the path through the edge. Thus, the above results of the problem do not apply in our case.

2 Preliminaries

In this section, we list notations and preliminaries used in the paper. For standard notations and definitions of complexity classes, we refer the reader to the textbook [2]. We now define some graph theoretic terminologies required. A *tree decomposition* of a graph $G = (V, E)$ is a tree $T = (I, F)$ where each vertex $i \in I$ has a label $X_i \subseteq V$ with $\bigcup_{i \in I} X_i = V$ such that: for any edge $(u, v) \in E$, there exists an $i \in I$ with $u, v \in X_i$ and, for any $v \in V$, the vertices containing v in their label form a connected subtree of T. Given a tree decomposition $T = (I, F)$, the *width* of the decomposition is $\max_{i \in I}(|X_i|) - 1$. The *treewidth* of a graph G is the minimum k such that G has a tree decomposition of width k.

We define the algebraic structures that we refer to in the paper. Let $\mathcal{A}$ be an algebraic structure where $*$ is the binary operator. If $*$ has the closure property, $\mathcal{A}$ is said to be a groupoid. Groupoids for which $*$ is associative are called semi-groups. Semi-groups which have an identity element e (that is, $\forall a \in \mathcal{A}, ae = ea = a$)[3] are called monoids. Groups are monoids for which every element has an inverse with respect to *. That is, $\forall a \in \mathcal{A}, \exists\, b \in A$ such that $ab = ba = e$. In general, a monoid M is said to be divided by another monoid N if there exists a surjective morphism from a submonoid of M to N [22]. Quasigroups are a generalization of groups in a different direction; the operation in a quasigroup need not be associative but they are left and right cancellative (that is, $ab = ac \Rightarrow b = c$ and $ab = cb \Rightarrow a = c$).

$\mathcal{A}$-Reach **Problem:** Let $\mathbf{A} = \{(\mathcal{A}, ^*)\}$ be an infinite collection of algebraic structures where each $(\mathcal{A}, ^*)$ is the algebraic structure with set of elements $[k] = \{1, 2, \ldots, k\}$ and the binary operation $*$ defined over $\mathcal{A}$. Let F be a subset of $\mathcal{A}$. Consider a graph $G = (V, E)$ and a function $\phi : E \to \mathcal{A}$. We extend the definition of ϕ to the yield of a path $p = v_0, v_1, \ldots, v_m$, as $\phi(p) = \prod_{i=0}^{m-1} \phi((v_i, v_{i+1}))$ where product is the operation $*$ on the concatenated labels of p.

Definition 1. ($\mathcal{A}$-Reach) *Fix an algebraic structure $\mathcal{A}$. The $\mathcal{A}$-Reach problem asks: given a graph G on n vertices and the labelling function ϕ for the edges, two nodes s, t and accepting set*[4] *$F \subseteq \mathcal{A}$, test whether there is a path p (need not be simple) from s to t such that $\phi(p) \in F$.*

[3] We do not use the operator, whenever it is clear from the context. We use 1 and e interchangeably for the identity element.

[4] If the size of $\mathcal{A}$ is fixed (or even polynomially bounded) we will assume that $|F| = 1$. We also assume that the accepting element a is given as a part of the input. All our results except Theorem 7 hold even if a is fixed apriori.

For studying the variants of the problem, we introduce the following notation: A-GREACH refers to the $\mathcal{A}$-REACH problem defined over the algebraic structure A(Monoid, Aperiodic Monoid, Commutative Aperiodic Monoid, Group, Quasigroup and Semigroup) and the input graphs are restricted to the class G(Tree, Planar, DAG, k-Treewidth, Undirected(U) and Bidirected(B)).

Aperiodic Monoids and Quasigroups: The monoid class **DA** is defined as the class of monoids that satisfy $(stu)^n t(stu)^n = (stu)^n$, for some n, for all s, t, u in the monoid. A language $L = A_0^* a_1 A_1^* a_2 \cdots a_k A_k^*$ is said to be unambiguous if for all $w \in L$, there is a unique factorization $w = w_0 a_1 w_1 a_2 \cdots a_k w_k$, such that $w_i \in A_i^*$ for $i = 0, 1, \ldots, k$. Pin *et al.* [16] showed the following characterization:

Proposition 1. [16] *$L \subseteq A^*$ is recognized by a monoid in* **DA** *if and only if L is a disjoint, finite union of unambiguous products $A_0^* a_1 A_1^* \cdots a_k A_k^*$, where $A_i \subseteq A, a_i \in A$, for $i \in [k]$.*

The following was proved by Raymond *et al.* [17,22].

Proposition 2. [17,22] *Let M be a finite, non-commutative monoid. Then M is divided by one of the following aperiodic monoids. (1) BA_2, the syntactic monoid*[5] *of $(c^*ac^*bc^*)^*$. (2) U, the syntactic monoid of $((b+c)^*a(b+c)^*b(b+c)^*)^*$. (3) The syntactic monoid of $A^*aA^*bA^*$. (4) The syntactic monoid of c^*aA^* or A^*ac^*. Moreover, if $M \notin$* **DA**, *M is divided by either BA_2 or U.*

In [4], Beaudry *et al.* define a *comb* as a left to right bracketing over a word, and claim that any bracketing over the word, for a quasigroup, can be viewed as a finite tree with each leaf as a comb. We state this as the following:

Proposition 3. [4] *Let $q_1 q_2 \cdots q_n$ be a word over a quasigroup Q. If there is a bracketing such that $q_1 q_2 \cdots q_n$ evaluates to q under that bracketing, then there is a bracketing with at most $8^{|Q|}$ combs which yields q.*

3 Logspace Upper Bounds

In this section, we explore the algebraic structure of the label set and graphs which enable us to solve the problem in L. As our main tool, we introduce the product graph, which is inspired by that of product graphs defined in the context of L-REACH problem by Yannakakis [23].

Product Graph and Properties: Let $G = (V, E)$ be a labelled graph, with a labelling $\phi : E \to M$, where M is a semigroup. We construct a new directed graph $G' = (V', E')$ as follows. We set $V' = V \times M$, and define the edge set E' as $\{((v_1, m_1), (v_2, m_2)) | (v_1, v_2) \in E \text{ and } m_1\phi(v_1, v_2) = m_2\}$. We show the following proposition. The proof is given in the full version.

Proposition 4. *For $s, t \in V$, $m \in M$, there is a path p from s to t in G such that $\phi(p) = m \iff$ there is a path from (s, e) to (t, m) in G'.*

[5] We denote the elements of this monoid by $\{1, \alpha, \beta, \alpha\beta, \beta\alpha, 0\}$.

Similarly, we can argue that a path from (s, m_1) to (t, m_2) in G' exists if and only if there is a path from s to t in G, yielding m such that $m_1 m = m_2$.

NL Upper Bounds: Since the above proposition holds even if G has cycles in it, this implies that SemiGroupReach is in NL. In later sections, we show more properties of the product graph. The product graph of an undirected graph labelled with a group is Eulerian. See Theorem 2. Also, the product graph of a graph with a bounded treewidth (labelled with a finite monoid) also has bounded treewidth. See Theorem 1.

If the algebraic structure is non-associative, we have to deal with all possible bracketings. Let us denote the set of all elements obtained by different bracketings of a word w by Yield(w). Caussinus and Lemieux [8] showed that languages recognized by finite quasigroups are regular. Hence, there exists a morphism ψ from any quasigroup Q to a monoid M, and subsets $Q' \subseteq Q, M' \subseteq M$ such that for any word $w \in Q^*$, Yield$(w) \cap Q' \neq \phi$ if and only if $\psi(w) \in M'$. Hence, the product graph construction shows that QuasigroupReach can be solved in NL.

Original Graph vs Product Graph While Group Labelling: It is a natural question to ask when the original graph appears as a subgraph in the product graph. We answer this for group labelled graphs.

Let $G = (V, E)$ be a directed acyclic graph, labelled with a group H, via labelling ϕ. Let the product graph be G'. Suppose G is a tree. We show that G' contains a copy of G. Let us start with any vertex v. For any $g \in H$, (v, g) is in G'. Now, consider all neighbors of v in G. If (v, u) is an edge in G, we have a corresponding edge $((v, g), (u, g\phi(v, u)))$ in G'. Similarly, if (u, v) is an edge in G, $((u, g\phi(u, v)^{-1})(v, g))$ is an edge in G'. Continuing in a breadth first search manner, we get a copy of G in G'. Hence, it is easy to see that if G is a tree, G' contains G as a subgraph. To extend this to general DAGs, we need to understand when (undirected) cycles of G appear in G'. If all cycles (undirected) of G appear in the product graph, G also appears in the product graph.

Let $C = v_1, v_2, \ldots v_k$ be an undirected cycle in G. We define $\psi(v_i, v_j)$ as follows: $\psi(v_i, v_j) = \phi(v_i, v_j)$ if $(v_i, v_j) \in E$ and $\phi(v_j, v_i)^{-1}$ if $(v_j, v_i) \in E$. A proof of the following proposition is given in the full version.

Proposition 5. *G appears as a subgraph in G' if and only if for each cycle $C = v_1, v_2, \ldots v_k$ in G, $\prod_{i=1}^{k} \psi(v_i, v_{i+1}) = \psi(v_k v_1)^{-1}$.*

Bounded Treewidth and Monoid Labelling: Das *et al.* [10] showed that reachability in bounded treewidth graphs can be tested in L. We show that, when a bounded treewidth graph G is labelled with a constant sized monoid M, the product graph of G still has constant treewidth, and hence, reachability in the labelled graph is also in L. The full version contains a detailed proof.

Theorem 1. Monoid-*k*-TreewidthReach *is in* L.

Group Labelled Graphs: Now we show that the $\mathcal{A}$-Reach problem can be solved in L, when the graph is undirected, and labelled with elements of a group, when the group size is polynomial in the size of the graph.

Theorem 2. GROUP-UREACH *is* L*-complete.*

Proof. To show that GROUP-UREACH is in L, we reduce the problem to REACH on Eulerian graphs, by showing that the product graph G' is Eulerian. From [19] we know that this problem can be solved in L and hence, this is sufficient. To solve this in L, Reingold *et al.* [19] observed (without proof) that, when each component of the given directed graph is Eulerian, a directed edge can be replaced by an undirected edge, and this does not alter connectivity of the graph. A proof can be found in the full version of this paper.

To show that G' is Eulerian, consider an edge (v_i, v_j) in G. Let $\phi((v_i, v_j)) = g$. Each vertex (v_i, g_k), is hence connected to $(v_j, g_k g)$. We notice that for each k, $g_k g$ defines a different element in H. Similarly, each vertex (v_j, g_ℓ) is adjacent to $(v_i, g_\ell g)$. Hence, the edge (v_i, v_j) in G corresponds to $2|H|$ edges in G', and these edges are such that each vertex of the form (v_i, g_k) and (v_j, g_ℓ) each have an indegree of 1 and an outdegree of 1. Since each edge in G increases the indegree and outdegree of any vertex in G' by the same amount, G' is Eulerian. Using the result from [19] we see that GROUP-UREACH is in L. To show hardness, we see that GROUP-UREACH is the undirected reachability problem when the underlying group is trivial. Hence, GROUP-UREACH is complete for L. □

Observing that, for any $g \in G$, $g_k g$, is a different element for all k, and that each edge (v_i, v_j) in G gives rise to one incoming and one outgoing edge for each (v_i, g_k) holds even when the graph is bidirected. Hence, we conclude the following corollary.

Corollary 1. GROUP-BREACH *is* L*-complete.*

Logspace Algorithm for QUASIGROUP-UREACH**:** We notice from the proof of Theorem 2, that the product graph G' is Eulerian if the H has right cancellation, that is, if $ab = cb \Rightarrow a = c$. Since this holds for quasigroups as well, the constructed graph is Eulerian when H is a quasigroup. However, since evaluation of a word is over all possible bracketings, checking for a path from (s, e) to (t, h) is no longer sufficient (since this would correspond to only checking a left to right bracketing). Proposition 3 is used to prove the following theorem. The full version of this paper contains the proof.

Theorem 3. QUASIGROUP-UREACH *is* L*-complete.*

4 Symmetrizing by Labelling

In this section, we explore the question of whether we can reduce (in logspace) reachability over directed acyclic graphs to labelled reachability over undirected paths. We call this task as *symmetrization by labelling.* We first observe that symmetrization can be done when the algebraic structure is a specific aperiodic monoid or a specific, finitely generated, matrix group over $\mathbb{Q}$.

Labelling with Aperiodic Monoids: We give a labelling with a non-commutative aperiodic monoid, which makes the $\mathcal{A}$-REACH problem NL-hard.

In [15], Komarath *et al.* give a labelling with $(ab)^*$, for all directed acyclic graphs. We show that the syntactic monoid of this language is aperiodic. To see that it is aperiodic, we verify that for all a in the monoid, $a^3 = a^2$. Hence, this monoid is aperiodic with index 2. We also observe that the monoid is non-commutative.

Labelling with a Finitely Presented Group: In this subsection, we show that for matrix groups (even of size 2) with entries from $\mathbb{Q}$, symmetrization can be done. In Sect. 3, we saw that if symmetrization is done when the algebraic structure is either a polynomially growing group or a fixed size quasigroup, it implies that $\mathsf{NL} = \mathsf{L}$.

Theorem 4. *$\mathcal{A}$ is the group of invertible $k \times k$ matrices with rational entries. $\mathcal{A}$-BREACH is NL-hard.*

Proof. We first show this for $k = 2$. We work over the following subgroup, $H = \left\{\begin{bmatrix}1 & \alpha\\ 0 & 1\end{bmatrix} : \alpha \in \mathbb{Z}\right\}$. This group is finitely generated, since $\begin{bmatrix}1 & 1\\ 0 & 1\end{bmatrix}$ and $\begin{bmatrix}1 & -1\\ 0 & 1\end{bmatrix}$ generate H. We define element $a = \begin{bmatrix}1 & 1\\ 0 & 1\end{bmatrix}$. Given an instance $(G(V,E),s,t)$ of REACH we construct an instance $(G'(V',E'),H,s,t,e)$ of GROUP-BREACH as follows. For every edge $(v_i,v_j) \in E$, we add 2 edges (v_i,v_j) and (v_j,v_i) to E'. We label edge (v_i,v_j) with e, and edge (v_j,v_i) with a.

We now argue correctness of this construction. Suppose there was a directed path from s to t in G. Let this path be $v_0 = s, v_1, v_2, \ldots, v_k = t$. Now, in G', we have the same path. Moreover, since each edge within the path is labelled with e, the entire path multiplies out to the identity element. Thus, we have a path from s to t in G' whose yield is identity.

Suppose there is no path from s to t in G, but there is a path from s to t in G' which yields identity. Let this path be $s = v_0, v_1, v_2, \ldots, v_m = t$. Since this path does not exist in G, there must be an i such that $(v_i, v_{i+1}) \notin E$. Hence, the label on this edge must be a. We can have several edges like this in the path. Thus, the yield of the path is a^k, for some $k \geq 1$. Since the path yields identity, we have

$$\begin{bmatrix}1 & 1\\ 0 & 1\end{bmatrix}^k = \begin{bmatrix}1 & 0\\ 0 & 1\end{bmatrix}$$

However, we see that $a^k = \begin{bmatrix}1 & k\\ 0 & 1\end{bmatrix}$. Hence, the yield cannot be identity, and there is no path from s to t in G' yielding identity.

To extend this to $k \times k$ matrices, we notice that we can embed a into a $k \times k$ matrix b by setting

$$b[i,j] = \begin{cases} a[i,j], & \text{if } i \leq 2, j \leq 2\\ 1, & \text{if } i,j > 2, \text{ and } i = j\\ 0, & \text{if } i,j > 2, \text{ and } i \neq j \end{cases}$$

The forward direction of the proof is easy to see. The reverse direction follows from the fact that b^k can never be identity, for $k > 1$. □

5 A Dichotomy Theorem for Aperiodic Labelling

In this section, we prove the main result of the paper, which is the dichotomy theorem for finite aperiodic monoids with respect to the reachability in labelled graphs. We first settle the complexity in the case of commutative monoids. For non-commutative monoids, we show the dichotomy using the classification of aperiodic monoids by [17,22] (see Proposition 2). We show deterministic logspace algorithms when the monoid is in DA and for the other cases (when the monoids are divided by U or BA_2), we show that the reachability is complete for NL.

Logspace Algorithm for COMMUTATIVEAPERIODIC-UREACH**:**
Let $M = \{1, \alpha_1, \alpha_2, \ldots, \alpha_k\}$ be a commutative aperiodic monoid.

Theorem 5. *Let G be an undirected graph labelled with elements from M, a commutative aperiodic monoid. Checking if there is a path from s to t which evaluates to an element α can be done in* L.

Proof. We notice that any element α in M can be thought of as several tuples of integers $(n_1, n_2, \ldots, n_k)$, such that $\alpha = \alpha_1^{n_1}\alpha_2^{n_2}\cdots\alpha_k^{n_k}$. Hence, checking if a path evaluates to particular element is equivalent to checking if the the number of occurrences of each element in each path is one of the tuples associated with the element. We also know that M is aperiodic with index q ($\forall \alpha \in M, \alpha^{q+1} = \alpha^q$). This implies that, if $\alpha = \alpha_1^{n_1}\alpha_2^{n_2}\cdots\alpha_i^{q}\cdots\alpha_k^{n_k}$, then $\alpha = \alpha_1^{n_1}\alpha_2^{n_2}\cdots\alpha_i^{q+1}\cdots\alpha_k^{n_k}$. Hence, checking for tuples where each value is bounded by q is sufficient.

Let $G = (V, E)$ be the given graph, labelled with a commutative aperiodic monoid M, via a mapping ϕ. Let $s, t \in V$ and $(n_1, n_2, \ldots, n_k)$ be a tuple, where $n_i \leq q, \forall i$. Let $N = \sum_i n_i$. The algorithm does the following.

Repeat the following for each $(u_1, v_1), (u_2, v_2), \ldots, (u_N, v_N) \in E^N$, such that the labels of $(u_1, v_1), (u_2, v_2), \ldots, (u_N, v_N)$ form the tuple $(n_1, n_2, \ldots, n_k)$. Set $v_0 = s, u_{N+1} = t$. Let $P = \{e\} \cup \{\alpha_i | \; n_i = q\}$. Let G' be G without edges labelled with any element from $M \backslash P$. We accept if there is a path from v_i to u_{i+1}, in G for all i.

We see that the algorithm uses only logspace, since N is at most qk.

Correctness: The algorithm iterates over all possible edges, such that the labels of the edges give the tuple. For each set of edges, it verifies if there is a path between these edges, which uses only those labels which have crossed the index (captured by set P). This ensures that the resulting path also evaluates to the same element.

For the reverse direction, since every graph accepted by this algorithm has a path whose tuple is of the form $(n'_1, n'_2, \ldots, n'_k)$, where $n'_i = n_i$ if $n_i < q$, and $n'_i \geq n_i$ if $n_i = q$. Hence, the elements that both these tuples evaluate to must be the same. □

Logspace Algorithm for DA-UREACH**:** We give a logspace algorithm to solve DA-UREACH, when the graph is labelled with letters from an unambiguous concatenation $L = A_0^* a_1 A_1^* a_2 \cdots a_k A_k^*$, where A is the alphabet, $A_i \subseteq A, a_i \in A, \forall i$. From Proposition 1, this is sufficient to show that DA-UREACH can be solved in logspace.

Theorem 6. *Let G be an undirected graph labelled with elements from an alphabet A. Let s and t be given vertices in G. Let $L = A_0^* a_1 A_1 a_2 A_2^* \cdots a_k A_k^*$ be an unambiguous concatenation, where $A_i \subseteq A, a_i \in A, \forall i$. Checking if there is a path from s to t, whose yield is in L can be done in logspace.*

Proof. Let $G = (V, E)$ be the given graph, labelled with an alphabet A, via a mapping ϕ. Let $L = A_0^* a_1 A_1^* a_2 \cdots a_k A_k^*$. Let $s, t \in V$. The algorithm does the following: Repeat the following for $(u_1, v_1), (u_2, v_2), \ldots, (u_k, v_k) \in E^k$, such that $\forall i, \phi(u_i, v_i) = a_i$. Set $v_0 = s, u_{k+1} = t$. For each i, let G_i be G without edges labelled with any element from $A \backslash A_i$. We accept if there is a path from v_i to u_{i+1}, in G_i for all i. Since k is finite, we see that the algorithm chooses all possible edges for the a_i's, and check if paths between these edges are in A_i^*. The algorithm uses only logspace. The correctness of this algorithm is easy to see - if there exists a path from s to t in L, the algorithm will eventually find it, since it runs over all possible edges. For the other direction, we notice that the algorithm only accepts paths in L. □

Labelling with Non-commutative Aperiodic Monoids not in DA: We show that labelling an undirected graph with either BA_2 or U makes the $\mathcal{A}$-REACH problem NL-hard. Komarath *et al.* [15] give a labelling with $(ab)^*$, for all directed acyclic graphs. This immediately gives us a labelling with BA_2. We give a similar labelling with U. We know that any non-commutative aperiodic monoid M not in **DA** is divisible by either U or BA_2. Hence, we have a surjective morphism from a submonoid of M to either U or BA_2. We show that labelling an undirected graph with BA_2 or U makes the $\mathcal{A}$-REACH problem NL-hard. By using the morphism, we can get instances of $\mathcal{A}$-REACH problem over undirected graphs, labelled with M, which are NL-hard.

Theorem 7. *$\mathcal{A}$-REACH for undirected graphs is NL-complete when the graph is labelled with U.*

Proof. We give a labelling from $L = (b^*ab^*bb^*)^*$ (whose syntactic monoid is U) similar to that in [15]. Let $G = (V, E)$ be a directed acyclic graph, with vertices s and t. Without loss of generality, we assume that s is a source (that is, it has only outgoing edges). We create a labelled, undirected graph $G' = (V', E')$ as follows. Each vertex in V is copied to V'. Additionally, for each directed edge (v_i, v_j), we add a vertex m_{ij} to V'. Edges and labels are constructed as follows. If (v_i, v_j) is an edge in G, (v_i, m_{ij}), (m_{ij}, v_j) are edges in G', with (v_i, m_{ij}) being labelled with b, and (m_{ij}, v_j) is labelled with a. That is, we split each edge, labelling the first half with b, and the second half with a. We also add a new vertex t', and add an edge (t, t'), labelled with b. We claim that there is a path from s to t in G if and only if there is a path from s to t' in G', whose yield is in L.

The forward direction is easy to see. Suppose there is a path from s to t in G. Let the path be $s = v_{i_1}, v_{i_2}, \ldots, v_{i_m} = t$. We claim that the path $s = v_{i_1}, m_{i_1 i_2}, v_{i_2}, m_{i_2 i_3}, v_{i_3}, \ldots, m_{i_{m-1} i_m}, v_{i_m} = t, t'$ exists in G' and the yield of the path is in L. By our construction, each of these edges exist in G'. To see the yield, we notice that since $(v_{i_\ell}, v_{i_{\ell+1}})$ is in E, $(v_{i_\ell}, m_{i_\ell i_{\ell+1}})$ is labelled with b, whereas $(m_{i_\ell i_{\ell+1}}, v_{i_{\ell+1}})$ is labelled with a, for all ℓ. Hence, the yield is $(ba)^m b$ which is in L.

Suppose we do not have a path from s to t in G, but there is a path from s to t' in G' with a yield in L. Since there is no path in G, the path in G' must have taken some edges incorrectly. Let (u, v) be the first incorrect edge taken. That is, suppose $(v_i, v_j) \in E$. The edge taken is either of the form (v_j, m_{ij}) or (m_{ij}, v_i). For the first, the yield up to this point is $(ba)^\ell$, for some ℓ, and the edge is labelled with a. This results in two consecutive a's, which cannot be in the language, and the path in G' cannot have any edge of this form. For the second, we see that since (m_{ij}, a_i) is the first incorrect edge taken, the edge taken before this is (a_i, m_{ij}), and both these edges can be ignored. Thus, if all incorrect edges taken are of the second form, we can create a path from s to t in G, contradicting our initial assumption. □

6 Planarizing by Labelling

We now present a reduction from the reachability problem to $\mathcal{A}$-REACH over planar DAGs when $\mathcal{A}$ is the fixed monoid BA_2. The same reduction can be achieved with group labelling when the size of the groups is allowed to be exponentially growing. We give a reduction from REACH to MONOID-PLANARREACH and hence it is NL-hard.

Theorem 8. *Let $G = (V, E)$ be a graph. Let $\phi : E \rightarrow BA_2$ be a labelling function. Then* REACH *reduces to* MONOID-PLANARREACH.

A proof of this theorem is present in the full version. We make an observation that the hard instances to MONOID-PLANARREACH have the property that the underlying undirected graph can be bipartite. In a close contrast to the results in the previous section, we show that if the labels are coming from BA_2, and in particular from the set $\{\alpha, \beta\}$ and the graph is bipartite, then NL = UL. That is, if the labelling had preserved bipartiteness of the graph (which we can ensure in the reachability instances by subdividing every edge into two edges by introducing an intermediate vertex), then NL = UL. The proof of the following theorem is present in the full version.

Theorem 9. *Let $G = (V, E)$ be a planar graph whose underlying undirected graph is bipartite, and labelled with BA_2 with $\phi : E \rightarrow \{\alpha, \beta\}$. The $\mathcal{A}$-*REACH *problem (between any two vertices) in G can be reduced (in log-space) to testing reachability in planar DAGs and hence is in* UL.

Following the quest for more structure in the labelling set, we now give a reduction from REACH to GROUP-PLANARREACH, when labelled with a group having size exponential in the size of the graph, thus showing that it is NL-hard. A proof for the following theorem is present in the full version.

Theorem 10. GROUP-PLANARREACH *is* NL*-hard when the group size is $\Omega(2^{n^4})$ where n is the size of the graph.*

References

1. Allender, E.: Reachability problems: an update. In: Cooper, S.B., Löwe, B., Sorbi, A. (eds.) CiE 2007. LNCS, vol. 4497, pp. 25–27. Springer, Heidelberg (2007). doi:10.1007/978-3-540-73001-9_3
2. Arora, S., Barak, B.: Computational Complexity: A Modern Approach. Cambridge University Press, Cambridge (2009)
3. David, A., Barrington, M., Thérien, D.: Finite monoids and the fine structure of NC^1. J. ACM **35**(4), 941–952 (1988)
4. Beaudry, M., Lemieux, F., Thérien, D.: Finite loops recognize exactly the regular open languages. In: Degano, P., Gorrieri, R., Marchetti-Spaccamela, A. (eds.) ICALP 1997. LNCS, vol. 1256, pp. 110–120. Springer, Heidelberg (1997). doi:10.1007/3-540-63165-8_169
5. Beaudry, M., McKenzie, P., Pladeau, P., Thérien, D.: Finite monoids: from word to circuit evaluation. SIAM J. Comput. **26**(1), 138–152 (1997)
6. Bédard, F., Lemieux, F., McKenzie, P.: Extensions to Barrington's M-program model. In: Proceedings Fifth Annual Structure in Complexity Theory Conference, pp. 200–209 (1990)
7. Bourke, C., Tewari, R., Vinodchandran, N.V.: Directed planar reachability is in unambiguous log-space. ACM Trans. Comput. Theory **1**(1), 4 (2009)
8. Caussinus, H., Lemieux, F.: The complexity of computing over quasigroups. In: Thiagarajan, P.S. (ed.) FSTTCS 1994. LNCS, vol. 880, pp. 36–47. Springer, Heidelberg (1994). doi:10.1007/3-540-58715-2_112
9. Chandra, A.K., Fortune, S., Lipton, R.J.: Unbounded fan-in circuits and associative functions. J. Comput. Syst. Sci. **30**(2), 222–234 (1985)
10. Das, B., Datta, S., Nimbhorkar, P.: Log-space algorithms for paths and matchings in k-trees. In: 27th STACS, pp. 215–226 (2010)
11. Geelen, J., Gerards, B.: Excluding a group-labelled graph. J. Comb. Theory Ser. B **99**(1), 247–253 (2009)
12. Horwitz, S., Reps, T.W., Binkley, D.: Interprocedural slicing using dependence graphs. ACM Trans. Program. Lang. Syst. **12**(1), 26–60 (1990)
13. Huynh, T.C.T.: The linkage problem for group-labelled graphs. Ph.D. thesis, University of Waterloo (2009)
14. Kawase, Y., Kobayashi, Y., Yamaguchi, Y.: Finding a path in group-labeled graphs with two labels forbidden. In: Halldórsson, M.M., Iwama, K., Kobayashi, N., Speckmann, B. (eds.) ICALP 2015. LNCS, vol. 9134, pp. 797–809. Springer, Heidelberg (2015). doi:10.1007/978-3-662-47672-7_65
15. Komarath, B., Sarma, J., Sunil, K.S.: On the complexity of L-reachability. Fundam. Inform. **145**(4), 471–483 (2016)
16. Pin, J.-E., Straubing, H., Therien, D.: Locally trivial categories and unambiguous concatenation. J. Pure Appl. Algebra **52**(3), 297–311 (1988)
17. Raymond, J.-F.Ç., Tesson, P., Thérien, D.: An algebraic approach to communication complexity. In: Larsen, K.G., Skyum, S., Winskel, G. (eds.) ICALP 1998. LNCS, vol. 1443, pp. 29–40. Springer, Heidelberg (1998). doi:10.1007/BFb0055038
18. Reingold, O.: Undirected connectivity in log-space. J. ACM **55**(4), 17 (2008)
19. Reingold, O., Trevisan, L., Vadhan, S.: Pseudorandom walks on regular digraphs and the RL vs. L problem. In: Proceedings of STOC, pp. 457–466 (2006)
20. Reps, T.W.: On the sequential nature of interprocedural program-analysis problems. Acta Inform. **33**(8), 739–757 (1996)

21. Reps, T.W.: Program analysis via graph reachability. Inf. Softw. Technol. **40**(11–12), 701–726 (1998)
22. Tesson, P.: An algebraic approach to communication complexity. Masters thesis, McGill University, Montreal (1998)
23. Yannakakis, M.: Graph-theoretic methods in database theory. In: Proceedings of the 9th ACM PODS, pp. 230–242 (1990)

Non-classical Automata

Most General Property-Preserving Updates

Davide Bresolin[1] and Ivan Lanese[2(✉)]

[1] University of Padova, Padua, Italy
davide.bresolin@unipd.it
[2] Focus Team, University of Bologna/Inria, Bologna, Italy
ivan.lanese@gmail.com

Abstract. Systems need to be updated to last for a long time in a dynamic environment, and to cope with changing requirements. It is important for updates to preserve the desirable properties of the system under update, while possibly enforcing new ones.

Here we consider a simple yet general update mechanism, which replaces a component of the system with a new one. The context, i.e., the rest of the system, remains unchanged. We define contexts and components as Constraint Automata interacting via either asynchronous or synchronous communication, and we express properties using Constraint Automata too. Then we build most general updates which preserve specific properties, considering both a single property and all the properties satisfied by the original system, in a given context or in all possible contexts.

1 Introduction

Update is a relevant topic [19], both for automatic updates, as in the context of adaptive systems [17] or autonomic computing [15], and for manual updates. A main reason is that one wants systems to last for a long time in a changing environment and to satisfy changing user requirements. However, a main point, namely correctness of the system after update, has received scarce attention till now, as remarked also in [14].

In this paper we consider a very simple yet general update mechanism, which replaces a part of the system with a new one. Formally, the system is seen as a context $\mathcal{C}$ containing the component to be updated $\mathcal{A}$, i.e., the system has the form $\mathcal{C}[\mathcal{A}]$. An update replaces $\mathcal{A}$ with $\mathcal{B}$, thus the system upon update has the shape $\mathcal{C}[\mathcal{B}]$. A basic question is: how to build a most general $\mathcal{B}$ such that if $\mathcal{C}[\mathcal{A}]$ satisfies a given property Φ, then also $\mathcal{C}[\mathcal{B}]$ satisfies the same property? This question is answered in Sect. 3. Note that $\mathcal{C}[\mathcal{B}]$ may satisfy further properties that $\mathcal{C}[\mathcal{A}]$ does not satisfy. The answer to the question above, which relates $\mathcal{A}$ and $\mathcal{B}$, depends both on the context $\mathcal{C}$ and on the property Φ. From this observation two generalizations emerge naturally. On one side, one may ask how to build a most general $\mathcal{B}$ such that for a given context $\mathcal{C}$, *all the properties* satisfied by $\mathcal{C}[\mathcal{A}]$ are also satisfied by $\mathcal{C}[\mathcal{B}]$ (Sect. 3). We call such an update correct for a

The authors acknowledge the support from the Italian INdAM – GNCS project 2016 *Logic, automata and games for self-adaptive systems*.

F. Drewes et al. (Eds.): LATA 2017, LNCS 10168, pp. 367–379, 2017.
DOI: 10.1007/978-3-319-53733-7_27

given context w.r.t. any property. On the other side, one may ask how to build a most general $\mathcal{B}$ such that *for each context* $\mathcal{C}$ if $\mathcal{C}[\mathcal{A}]$ satisfies property Φ, then $\mathcal{C}[\mathcal{B}]$ satisfies the same property (Sect. 4). We say that this is a correct update (w.r.t. the property Φ) that can be applied in any context. Finally, one may combine the two generalizations asking how to build a most general $\mathcal{B}$ to ensure correctness of update *in any context and w.r.t. any property* (Sect. 4).

The questions above are very general, and the detailed answer depends on the choice of the model for components and contexts, of the composition operators, and of the formalism for expressing properties. We consider here components, contexts and properties represented as Constraint Automata [5,6], which have been used in the literature, e.g., to give a formal semantics to REO connectors [3] and Rebeca actors [20]. We consider both asynchronous and synchronous composition for components and contexts. We leave the systematic exploration of the research space above to future work. We illustrate the results of our approach by means of a simple running example. All the operations on Constraint Automata were computed using the tool GOAL [21], an interactive tool for defining and manipulating automata, which we extended to deal with Constraint Automata. Technical details not included in the paper for space reasons can be found in [9].

2 Constraint Automata

We model components, contexts and properties as Constraint Automata (CAs) [6], defined below. Throughout the paper we assume a finite set Data of *data values* which can be communicated and a finite set of states for the CAs. As in [6], the finiteness assumption is needed for the effectiveness of our constructions.

Definition 1 (Constraint Automata). *A constraint automaton* $\mathcal{A}$ *is a tuple* $\langle Q, N, q_0, \rightarrow\rangle$ *where:*

1. Q *is a finite set of* states*;*
2. N *is a finite set of* node names *representing the interface between the CA and the outside world;*
3. $q_0 \in Q$ *is the* initial state*;*
4. $\rightarrow \subseteq Q \times \mathsf{CIO}(N) \times Q$ *is the* transition relation*, where* $\mathsf{CIO}(N)$ *is the set of* concurrent I/O operations $c : N \mapsto \mathsf{Data} \cup \{\bot\}$ *mapping every node in* N *to an element of* Data*, or to* $\bot$ *if no data is written/read. We assume that* c *is never the constant function with value* $\bot$*.*

Transitions of a CA are of the form $q \xrightarrow{c} p$, where c is a concurrent I/O operation. A *run* of a CA is a finite/infinite sequence $\rho = q_0 \xrightarrow{c_0} q_1 \xrightarrow{c_1} \dots$ such that q_0 is the initial state and, for every i, $q_i \xrightarrow{c_i} q_{i+1}$ is a transition of the CA. In this case, we say that ρ *accepts* the *trace* $w = c_0c_1\dots$. The *language* of a CA $\mathcal{A}$, denoted $\mathscr{L}(\mathcal{A})$, is the set of traces accepted by $\mathcal{A}$. Since a prefix of a run is again a run, languages are closed under prefix.

Given $c \in \mathsf{CIO}(N)$, we define $\mathsf{Nodes}(c)$ as the set of nodes through which data flow, formally $\mathsf{Nodes}(c) = \{n \in N \mid c(n) \neq \bot\}$. The *domain restriction*

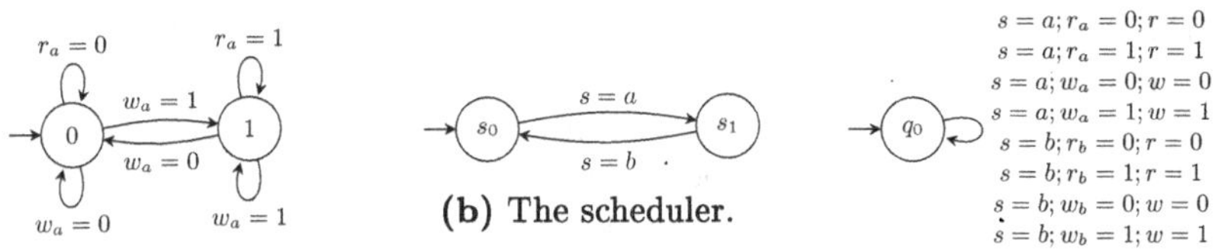

(a) The register a. **(b)** The scheduler. **(c)** The synchronizer.

Fig. 1. The CAs for Example 1.

of a concurrent I/O operation c on a subset of nodes $N' \subseteq N$ is written $c\downarrow_{N'}$. Given two disjoint sets of nodes N_1 and N_2, and two CIOs $c_1 \in \mathsf{CIO}(N_1)$ and $c_2 \in \mathsf{CIO}(N_2)$, we define their *union* as the unique CIO $c_1 \cup c_2 \in \mathsf{CIO}(N_1 \cup N_2)$ such that $(c_1 \cup c_2)\downarrow_{N_1} = c_1$ and $(c_1 \cup c_2)\downarrow_{N_2} = c_2$.

Example 1. We introduce here our running example.

We consider a system which allows one to read and write information from/to two one-bit registers, denoted as a and b. The system is the composition of four components represented in Fig. 1: two registers (only register a is shown, b is analogous), a scheduler that determines which register is active, and a synchronizer that communicates with the registers and the scheduler and proposes to the outside world the nodes r (read) and w (write) to access the active register. Labels on edges represent CIOs, written as semicolon-separated sets of assignments. Each assignment $n = d$ specifies that the data value d is communicated on node n. No communication occurs on nodes that do not appear in the label.

Registers are two-state CAs communicating with the synchronizer on nodes r_a (read a) and w_a (write a) for register a, and on nodes r_b and w_b for register b. The scheduler interacts with the synchronizer on node s. Essentially, the two registers are scheduled in round-robin order a, b. The synchronizer is a one-state CA that forwards the external operations to the currently active register.

We use CAs also to describe properties, which are prefix-closed sets of (finite or infinite) traces. We represent a property as a CA $\varPhi$ accepting the corresponding set of traces. We say that a CA $\mathcal{A}$ satisfies the property $\varPhi$, written $\mathcal{A} \models \varPhi$, iff $\mathscr{L}(\mathcal{A}) \subseteq \mathscr{L}(\varPhi)$. CAs are as expressive as the safety linear μ-calculus [16] and, as a consequence, more expressive of the safety fragment of temporal logics like LTL and CTL.

2.1 Composition of CAs

We consider here a particular type of composition, where a component is embedded in a context. We examine two forms of synchronization between the context and the component: *synchronous* and *asynchronous*. Formally, we assume to have two CAs: $\mathcal{A}$ (the component) and $\mathcal{C}$ (the context). We also assume two disjoint finite sets of node names U and O. Communication between the component and the context goes through U, while communication between the context and the external world goes through O.

In the asynchronous case, at every step the context communicates either with the component via nodes in U, or with the external world via nodes in O, or with both at the same time. In the synchronous case, at every step the context communicates with both the component and the external world.

The embedding of $\mathcal{A}$ in $\mathcal{C}$ is defined by means of two operations on CAs [5]: projection and (synchronous or asynchronous) join.

Definition 2 (Asynchronous Join). *The* asynchronous join *of two CAs* $\mathcal{A} = \langle Q_A, U, q_0^A, \rightarrow_A \rangle$ *and* $\mathcal{C} = \langle Q_C, U \cup O, q_0^C, \rightarrow_C \rangle$ *is defined as the CA* $\mathcal{A} \bowtie_a \mathcal{C} = \langle Q_A \times Q_C, U \cup O, (q_0^A, q_0^C), \rightarrow_a \rangle$ *such that:*

- $(q,p) \xrightarrow{c}_a (q',p')$ *if* $\mathsf{Nodes}(c) \cap U \neq \emptyset$, $q \xrightarrow{c\downarrow_U}_A q'$ *and* $p \xrightarrow{c}_C p'$*;*
- $(q,p) \xrightarrow{c}_a (q,p')$ *if* $\mathsf{Nodes}(c) \cap U = \emptyset$ *and* $p \xrightarrow{c}_C p'$*.*

Definition 3 (Synchronous Join). *The* synchronous join *of two CAs* $\mathcal{A} = \langle Q_A, U, q_0^A, \rightarrow_A \rangle$ *and* $\mathcal{C} = \langle Q_C, U \cup O, q_0^C, \rightarrow_C \rangle$ *is defined as the CA* $\mathcal{A} \bowtie_s \mathcal{C} = \langle Q_A \times Q_C, U \cup O, (q_0^A, q_0^C), \rightarrow_s \rangle$ *such that:*

- $(q,p) \xrightarrow{c}_s (q',p')$ *if* $\mathsf{Nodes}(c) \cap U \neq \emptyset$, $\mathsf{Nodes}(c) \cap O \neq \emptyset$, $q \xrightarrow{c\downarrow_U}_A q'$ *and* $p \xrightarrow{c}_C p'$*.*

Given a CA $\mathcal{B}$ with node names from a set $U \cup O$, the projection on O removes the nodes in U from the interface of $\mathcal{B}$ and hides the communications occurring at those nodes. To define the projection, we need the relation $\rightsquigarrow_O^* \subseteq Q \times Q$, which is the smallest relation such that:

- $q \rightsquigarrow_O^* q$ for each $q \in Q$;
- if $q \rightsquigarrow_O^* p$ and $p \xrightarrow{c} r$ with $\mathsf{Nodes}(c) \cap O = \emptyset$, then $q \rightsquigarrow_O^* r$.

Definition 4 (Projection). *The* projection *of a CA* $\mathcal{B} = \langle Q, U \cup O, q_0, \rightarrow \rangle$ *on* O *is defined as the CA* $\mathcal{B}\downarrow_O = \langle Q, O, q_0, \rightarrow^* \rangle$ *such that* $q \xrightarrow{c}{}^* p$ *iff there exists* $d \in \mathsf{CIO}(U \cup O)$, $r \in Q$ *such that* $d\downarrow_O = c$ *and* $q \rightsquigarrow_O^* r \xrightarrow{d} p$*.*

The *asynchronous embedding* $\mathcal{C}[\mathcal{A}]_a$ and the *synchronous embedding* $\mathcal{C}[\mathcal{A}]_s$ of the component $\mathcal{A} = \langle Q_A, U, q_0^A, \rightarrow_A \rangle$ in the context $\mathcal{C} = \langle Q_C, U \cup O, q_0^C, \rightarrow_C \rangle$ are defined as

$$\mathcal{C}[\mathcal{A}]_a = (\mathcal{A} \bowtie_a \mathcal{C})\downarrow_O \qquad \mathcal{C}[\mathcal{A}]_s = (\mathcal{A} \bowtie_s \mathcal{C})\downarrow_O$$

The above definitions hide all nodes of the component and expose only the nodes from O. We will drop the subscript a or s to refer to both kinds of embedding.

Example 2. We can now build the system outlined in Example 1 by embedding the scheduler into the context, which is obtained by embedding the two registers (in any order) into the synchronizer. All the embeddings are asynchronous.

The states of the whole system, represented in Fig. 2, are tuples (s_i, v_a, v_b) where s_i is the state of the scheduler and v_a and v_b are the values of the registers a and b, respectively.

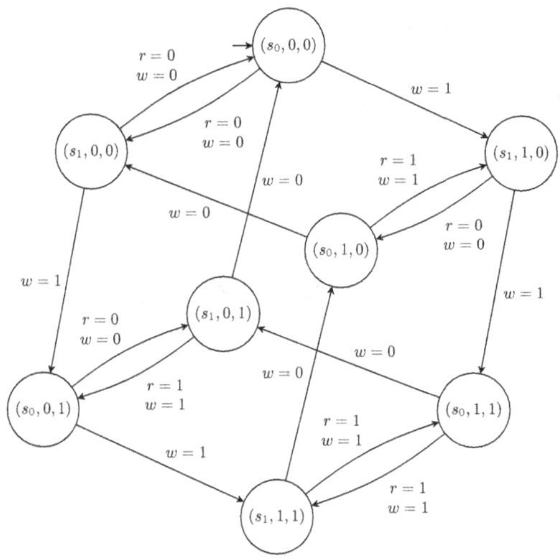

Fig. 2. Embedding of the scheduler in the context.

2.2 Determinization and Complementation of CAs

In the next sections, we will need to complement CAs. Unfortunately, CAs are not closed under complementation. We solve the problem following the approach in [5], reported below.

Given a nondeterministic CA $\mathcal{A}$, by using the standard *subset construction* for finite word automata it is possible to obtain an equivalent deterministic CA $\mathsf{Subset}(\mathcal{A})$ that, in the worst case, is exponentially larger than $\mathcal{A}$.

We can complement $\mathsf{Subset}(\mathcal{A})$ by enriching it with a set of final states $F \subseteq Q$ and a *Büchi acceptance condition*. We say that a finite run is accepting whenever the last state of the run is final, while an infinite run is accepting if the set of final states F is visited infinitely often. Formally, given a deterministic CA $\mathcal{A} = \langle Q, N, q_0, \rightarrow_A \rangle$ we can build a CA with final states $\overline{\mathcal{A}} = \langle Q_\perp, N, q_0, \rightarrow_{\overline{A}}, F \rangle$ accepting the complement language as follows:

- $Q_\perp = Q \cup \{q_\perp\}$ where $q_\perp$ is a distinguished *sink state* not included in Q;
- $F = \{q_\perp\}$ (only the sink state is final);
- $q \xrightarrow{c}_{\overline{A}} q'$ iff $q \xrightarrow{c}_A q'$;
- $q \xrightarrow{c}_{\overline{A}} q_\perp$ for all $q \in Q$ and $c \in \mathsf{CIO}(N)$ such that there is no q' such that $q \xrightarrow{c}_A q'$;
- $q_\perp \xrightarrow{c}_{\overline{A}} q_\perp$ for all $c \in \mathsf{CIO}(N)$.

In the following we will need to compute expressions of the form $\mathcal{C}[\overline{\mathcal{A}}]$. This can be done by using the construction for standard CAs, and by choosing as final states of the result the set $Q_C \times \{q_\perp\}$, where Q_C is the set of states of $\mathcal{C}$ and $q_\perp$ is the sink state of $\overline{\mathcal{A}}$.[1]

[1] This construction is not correct for general CAs with final states, but it is correct in this restricted case [5].

We will also use the following operations on deterministic CAs with final states. $\mathsf{Prefix}(\mathcal{A})$ is the CA obtained by removing all non-final states from $\mathcal{A}$ and taking the connected component including the initial state. Notably, $\mathscr{L}(\mathsf{Prefix}(\mathcal{A}))$ is the maximal prefix-closed language included in $\mathscr{L}(\mathcal{A})$. $\mathsf{Switch}(\mathcal{A})$ is the CA with final states obtained from $\mathcal{A}$ by selecting as final states the non-final states of $\mathcal{A}$, and vice versa.

3 Updates Correct for a Given Context

Given a system $\mathcal{C}[\mathcal{A}]$, an update replacing $\mathcal{A}$ with $\mathcal{B}$ is *correct* w.r.t. a property Φ iff whenever $\mathcal{C}[\mathcal{A}] \models \Phi$ also $\mathcal{C}[\mathcal{B}] \models \Phi$. We assume that $\mathcal{A}$ and $\mathcal{B}$ have the same interface, that is, the same set of node names. This is not restrictive since one can always add node names that are never used.

This section considers both the cases "all properties, given context" and "given property, given context". We show that they can be both reduced to instances of the following problem: given a context $\mathcal{C}$ and a specification $\mathcal{S}$ representing the correct behavior of the whole system, find the $\mathcal{B}$s such that $\mathcal{C}[\mathcal{B}] \models \mathcal{S}$. By definition of $\models$, these are the solutions of the following language inequation:

$$\mathscr{L}(\mathcal{C}[\mathcal{B}]) \subseteq \mathscr{L}(\mathcal{S}) \tag{1}$$

Among all such $\mathcal{B}$s we select one generating the largest language, and we call it a *most general solution* of the inequation. Such a solution is unique up to language equivalence.

Lemma 1. *For each context $\mathcal{C}$ and specification $\mathcal{S}$, Inequation* (1) *has a unique most general solution, up to language equivalence.*

In Inequation (1), when $\mathcal{S}$ is the system before the update $\mathcal{C}[\mathcal{A}]$ we are in the setting "all properties, given context", while when $\mathcal{S}$ is a CA representing a given property Φ we are in the setting "given property, given context".

Inequation (1) has been studied by the logic synthesis and controller design communities, where it is known as the "unknown component problem" [22]. The following result is part of the theory developed in [22].

Theorem 1. *$\mathcal{B}$ is a solution of Inequation* (1) *iff $\mathscr{L}(\mathcal{B}) \subseteq \overline{\mathscr{L}(\mathcal{C}[\overline{\mathcal{S}}])}$.*

The literature does not provide, for our setting, a constructive way of building a most general CA satisfying the constraint above. We propose one below. One would expect that a most general CA is $\overline{\mathcal{C}[\overline{\mathcal{S}}]}$. However, since CAs are not closed under complementation, such a CA in general cannot be built. We show that $\mathsf{Prefix}(\mathsf{Switch}(\mathsf{Subset}(\mathcal{C}[\overline{\mathcal{S}}])))$ is the best possibile approximation which is a CA.

Theorem 2. *$\mathcal{B} = \mathsf{Prefix}(\mathsf{Switch}(\mathsf{Subset}(\mathcal{C}[\overline{\mathcal{S}}])))$ is a most general CA such that $\mathscr{L}(\mathcal{B}) \subseteq \overline{\mathscr{L}(\mathcal{C}[\overline{\mathcal{S}}])}$.*

Theorems 3 and 5 below show that $\mathcal{B}$ is a most general update correct for a given context $\mathcal{C}$. The former considers a given property Φ, the latter any property representable as a CA.

Theorem 3. *Given a system $\mathcal{C}[\mathcal{A}]_x$ with $x \in \{a, s\}$ and a property Φ such that $\mathcal{C}[\mathcal{A}]_x \models \Phi$, $\mathcal{B} = \mathsf{Prefix}(\mathsf{Switch}(\mathsf{Subset}(\mathcal{C}[\overline{\Phi}]_x)))$ is a most general CA such that replacing $\mathcal{A}$ with $\mathcal{B}$ is a correct update w.r.t. Φ.*

Note that the above characterization does not depend on $\mathcal{A}$. However, if $\mathcal{C}[\mathcal{A}]$ does not satisfy the property Φ then every update is correct. Indeed the construction works for any property Φ, which may or may not hold for $\mathcal{C}[\mathcal{A}]$. Thus the approach can also be applied to ensure that new safety properties will hold after the update, e.g., to fix a bug or close a security vulnerability.

Theorem 4. *Given a system $\mathcal{C}[\mathcal{A}]_x$ with $x \in \{a, s\}$ and a property Φ, $\mathcal{B} = \mathsf{Prefix}(\mathsf{Switch}(\mathsf{Subset}(\mathcal{C}[\overline{\Phi}]_x)))$ is a most general CA such that replacing $\mathcal{A}$ with $\mathcal{B}$ ensures that Φ holds in $\mathcal{C}[\mathcal{B}]_x$.*

Theorem 5. *Given a system $\mathcal{C}[\mathcal{A}]_x$ with $x \in \{a, s\}$, $\mathcal{B} = \mathsf{Prefix}(\mathsf{Switch}(\mathsf{Subset}(\mathcal{C}[\overline{\mathcal{C}[\mathcal{A}]_x}]_x)))$ is a most general CA such that replacing $\mathcal{A}$ with $\mathcal{B}$ is a correct update w.r.t. any property.*

Example 3. We can apply Theorem 5 to obtain a most general update for the case "given context, all properties" of the system in Example 1. By minimizing the result (up to language equivalence) we obtain the CA in Fig. 3, where s_0 is the initial state. The solution recognizes the traces where one of the sequences $abababa\ldots$ and $bababab\ldots$ is communicated on node s. This implies that, e.g., replacing the original scheduler with a new one activating the registers in round-robin order b, a is a correct update. This matches the intuition, since the two registers are identical and swapping when they are accessible has no visible effect. Instead, using a scheduler that, e.g., always activates a and never activates b is not. A property falsified by this incorrect update is, for instance, P1 = "if *w=1* is executed at the first step, then at the third step *r=0* cannot be executed".

Example 4. Consider the property P1 above. It can be formalized by the CA Φ in Fig. 4a. There, we use ? to denote 0, 1 or $\perp$, and we assume that at least one node in each constraint has non $\perp$ value. The system of Example 1 satisfies Φ. We want to characterize the updates that preserve Φ.

We can apply Theorem 3 to obtain the most general scheduler depicted in Fig. 4b. Notice that it accepts the following computations:

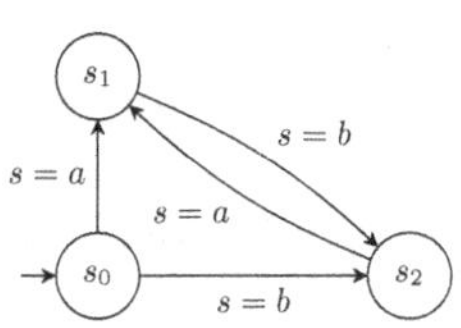

Fig. 3. Most general scheduler of Example 3.

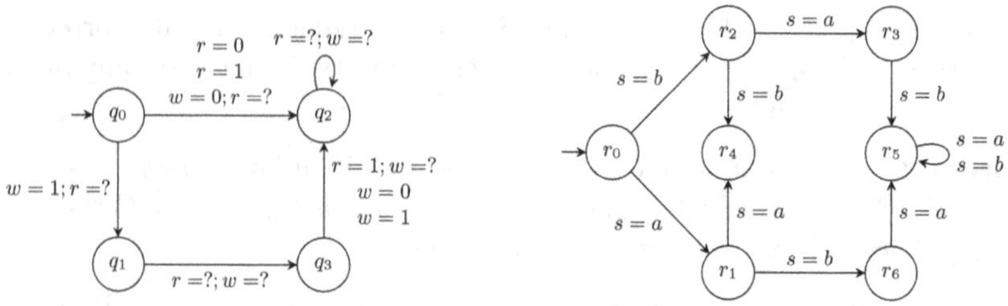

(a) CA Φ for P1.

(b) Most general scheduler.

Fig. 4. CAs of Example 4.

- any computation of length at most 2: in this case the third step is never reached, and the property is trivially satisfied;
- any computation that starts with $s = a, s = b, s = a$ or $s = b, s = a, s = b$: in this case the value 1 written in the register at the first step is not changed in the second step, and made available in the third step.

We now move to the study of the complexity of our construction.

Theorem 6. *Given a system $\mathcal{C}[\mathcal{A}]_x$ with $x \in \{a, s\}$ finding a most general $\mathcal{B}$ such that replacing $\mathcal{A}$ with $\mathcal{B}$ is a correct update for a given property Φ or for any property, or an update that makes Φ hold is in 2-EXPTIME.*

The 2-EXPTIME complexity arises from a double subset construction.

Theorem 7. *Given a system $\mathcal{C}[\mathcal{A}]_x$ with $x \in \{a, s\}$ and a property Φ such that $\mathcal{C}[\mathcal{A}]_x \models \Phi$, finding a most general $\mathcal{B}$ such that replacing $\mathcal{A}$ with $\mathcal{B}$ is a correct update w.r.t. Φ, or that makes Φ hold is EXPSPACE-hard.*

The lower bound is proved by reducing a suitable three-player game to Inequation (1). The game is played on a finite-state graph, with the first player (the component) and the third player (the specification) in a coalition against the second player (the context). At every round of the game, given the current state, the successor state is determined by the choice of moves of the players. A suitable safety condition establishes who wins the game. The reduction shows that a winning strategy for Player 1 corresponds to a correct update of the system, if $\mathcal{C}[\mathcal{A}]_x \models \Phi$, and to an update that makes Φ hold otherwise. The problem of finding a winning strategy in this game is EXPSPACE-complete [10]. The details of the reduction can be found in [9].

Theorem 7 deals with the case "given property, given context". It seems not easy to adapt the reduction to the case "all properties, given context". Finding a lower bound for the latter case is an open problem.

4 Updates Correct for All Contexts

In this section we study both the cases "given property, all contexts" and "all properties, all contexts". Similarly to the previous section, we can assume w.l.o.g.

that $\mathcal{A}$ and $\mathcal{B}$ have the same interface U, and that all the contexts we consider have U as internal interface.

Let us start from the case of a given property. The property defines a minimum set of node names O required for the external interface of the context. For some properties, replacing $\mathcal{A}$ with $\mathcal{B}$ is a correct update iff the traces of $\mathcal{B}$ are included in the traces of $\mathcal{A}$. However, this is not the case for all the properties. For instance, all the updates are correct w.r.t. the properties $\mathbf{tt} = \mathsf{CIO}(O)^* \cup \mathsf{CIO}(O)^\omega$ or $\mathbf{ff} = \emptyset$. Indeed, in the asynchronous case these are the only possibilities.

Theorem 8. *Let Φ be a property and $\mathcal{A}$ a CA. For the asynchronous embedding, the most general CA such that replacing $\mathcal{A}$ with $\mathcal{B}$ is a correct update w.r.t. Φ in all the contexts is* $\mathbf{tt}$ *if Φ is either* $\mathbf{tt}$ *or* $\mathbf{ff}$, *$\mathcal{A}$ otherwise.*

In the synchronous case the context and the component progress in lock-step. Given a property Φ, there are steps i in the computation on which Φ does not pose any restriction: if a trace z of length $i-1$ is in $\mathscr{L}(\Phi)$, then all the traces of length i having z as prefix are also in $\mathscr{L}(\Phi)$. Conversely, there are steps where Φ observes the system and whether a trace of length i is in $\mathscr{L}(\Phi)$ or not depends on the last action of the system. The *observation-point language* contains all the traces whose length identifies an observation point. Since the component $\mathcal{A}$ communicates on the internal interface U, the observation-point language is defined on the alphabet $\mathsf{CIO}(U)$.

Definition 5. *Let Φ be a property. The* observation-point language *of Φ is:*

$$\mathcal{R}(\Phi) = \{u \in \mathsf{CIO}(U)^* \mid \exists z \cdot c' \in \mathsf{CIO}(O)^*. z \in \mathscr{L}(\Phi) \wedge z \cdot c' \notin \mathscr{L}(\Phi) \wedge |u| = |z \cdot c'|\}$$

To compute a CA with final states accepting $\mathcal{R}(\Phi)$ one takes the complement $\overline{\Phi}$ of Φ. The CA $\overline{\Phi}$ has one final state $q_\perp^R$ which is a sink. The CA with final states $\mathcal{R}$ accepting $\mathcal{R}(\Phi)$ is obtained from $\overline{\Phi}$ by removing the self loops in the sink state $q_\perp^R$ and by replacing every transition of $\overline{\Phi}$ with a transition between the same pair of states for every label $c \in \mathsf{CIO}(U)$. Then, to build a most general CA $\mathsf{MGU}(\mathcal{A}, \Phi)$ such that replacing $\mathcal{A}$ with $\mathsf{MGU}(\mathcal{A}, \Phi)$ is a correct update w.r.t. Φ for all contexts, one can proceed as follows.

1. **Determinize** $\mathcal{R}$ using the subset construction.
2. **Complete** $\mathcal{A}$ by adding a sink state $q_\perp^A$ and obtaining $\mathcal{A}_\perp$.
3. **Compute the product of** $\mathcal{A}_\perp$ **with** $\mathsf{Subset}(\mathcal{R})$ using the synchronous join operator to obtain $\mathcal{A}_\perp \bowtie_s \mathsf{Subset}(\mathcal{R})$.
4. **Remove observation states**, that is all states $(q_\perp^A, Q_R)$ such that $q_\perp^R \in Q_R$, and take the connected component including the initial state.
5. **Transform the result into a CA without final states** by dropping the distinction between final and non-final states.

$\mathsf{MGU}(\mathcal{A}, \Phi)$ can be computed in time which is a double exponential in the size of Φ and polynomial in the size of $\mathcal{A}$, where the two exponentials are due to the subset constructions.

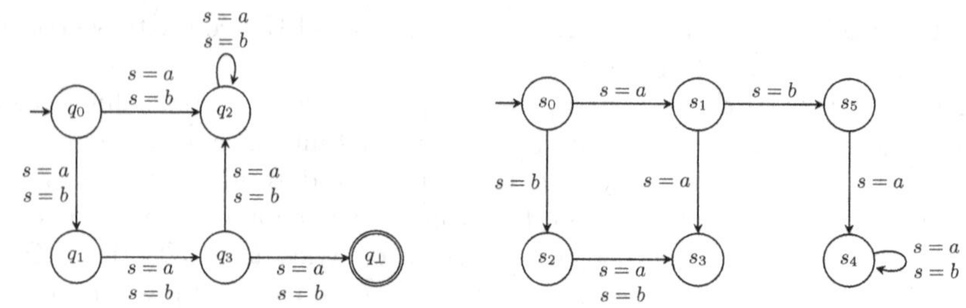

(a) CA with final states for $\mathcal{R}(\varphi)$. **(b)** Most general scheduler.

Fig. 5. CAs of Example 5.

Theorem 9. *Let Φ be a property and $\mathcal{A}$ a CA. For the synchronous embedding, the most general CA such that replacing $\mathcal{A}$ with $\mathcal{B}$ is a correct update w.r.t. Φ and for all contexts is* $\mathsf{MGU}(\mathcal{A}, \Phi)$.

Example 5. Consider the property P1 represented by the CA Φ back in Fig. 4a. By the above procedure we can first obtain the CA with final states for $\mathcal{R}(\Phi)$ in Fig. 5a, and then the most general scheduler $\mathsf{MGU}(\mathcal{A}, \Phi)$ in Fig. 5b, which makes the update correct in the synchronous case for every context and for the property Φ. We are left with two kinds of traces: traces with prefix $r = a, r = b, r = a$ that behave as $\mathcal{A}$ for the first 3 steps, and traces of length less than 3 that behave differently w.r.t. $\mathcal{A}$. This corresponds to the intuition that the property can only reject traces at step 3.

We now characterize the updates correct w.r.t. all the properties and all contexts. In this case there are strong requirements on the updates. To be correct for all contexts, the update needs to be correct for the context that reports every communication to the outside world. Since properties are sets of traces, the new component $\mathcal{B}$ should have at most the traces of $\mathcal{A}$. Indeed, this condition is necessary and sufficient, for both the synchronous and asynchronous embedding.

Theorem 10. *Let $\mathcal{A}$ be a CA. Any $\mathcal{B}$ such that $\mathscr{L}(\mathcal{B}) = \mathscr{L}(\mathcal{A})$ is a most general update such that replacing $\mathcal{A}$ with $\mathcal{B}$ is correct for all properties and all contexts.*

5 Conclusion and Related Work

We studied the problem of finding out whether an update replacing a component $\mathcal{A}$ with a component $\mathcal{B}$ in a given context C is correct w.r.t. a safety property Φ. We also characterized the updates correct in any context (for a given property), for any property (in a given context), and for any property in any context. In all the cases, we considered both synchronous and asynchronous composition.

While many approaches tackle system update [19], the problem of ensuring correctness of a system upon update has received scarce attention till now.

Approaches based on behavioral congruences, such as [8], allow one to prove the correctness of updates when a component is replaced by a syntactically different, but semantically equivalent one. Our approach is more general, allowing one to replace a component with a semantically different one.

Some approaches, such as [13], focus exclusively on type safety, that rules out obviously wrong behaviors, but is insufficient for establishing that given properties are preserved. In [14], instead, a program transformation to combine a program and an update into a new program presenting all the behaviors corresponding to applying the update at any allowed point is presented. The key advantage of our approach is that we can deal with many updates at once by comparing them with the most general one. In [23], a modular model checking approach to verify adaptive programs is proposed. They decompose the model checking problem following the temporal evolution of the system, while we decompose the verification problem following the structure of the system.

A line of work [2,11] uses choreographic descriptions to obtain correctness of the updates by construction. However, this kind of approach can only deal with a few fixed properties such as deadlock freedom, race freedom and orphan-message freedom. Another related approach is presented in [12], where behavioral types are used to ensure that running sessions are not interrupted, and that provided services are preserved. Our approach is much more flexible than the two last approaches since it considers any property expressible as a CA.

The work in [18] categorizes different kinds of reconfigurations in the context of Reo connectors. Our updates correct for any property (in a given context) are called contractive in [18], and a property for which an update is correct (in a given context) is called an invariant for the update. However, in [18], nothing is said about the requirements that an update must satisfy to be contractive or to have a given invariant: these problems have been solved by the present paper.

The work in [22] is related to ours from the technical point of view. In particular, it provides us the framework to solve Inequation (1). However, [22] does not provide a construction for building an actual automaton in our case, namely, for CAs with both finite and infinite traces. Also, [22] has a different aim, since it does not consider update at all. It highlights, however, a connection between update and another challenging problem: the automatic synthesis of systems from logical specifications. Polynomial algorithms for restricted classes of specifications have been identified [1,7]. These results could be exploited both to make our approach more efficient and to extend it to properties that go beyond safety, like liveness and deadlock freedom. Another problem related to ours is supervisory control of discrete event systems (see, e.g., [4]). The main difference is in the composition mechanism, which features a feedback control loop and introduces latency, while this does not happen in our case.

The problem of characterizing correct updates can also be studied in other settings, and indeed we plan to consider some of them in future work. For instance one may consider more complex properties, as hinted at above, or more complex automata, like timed automata or general CAs where the set of data values can be infinite. Finally, we want to apply our technique to more abstract models, starting from the ones based on CAs, such as REO [3] and Rebeca [20].

References

1. Alur, R., La Torre, S.: Deterministic generators and games for LTL fragments. ACM Trans. Comput. Logic **5**(1), 1–25 (2004)
2. Anderson, G., Rathke, J.: Dynamic software update for message passing programs. In: Jhala, R., Igarashi, A. (eds.) APLAS 2012. LNCS, vol. 7705, pp. 207–222. Springer, Heidelberg (2012). doi:10.1007/978-3-642-35182-2_15
3. Arbab, F.: Reo: a channel-based coordination model for component composition. Math. Struct. Comput. Sci. **14**(3), 329–366 (2004)
4. Aziz, A., Balarin, F., Brayton, R.K., Di Benedetto, M.D., Saldanha, A., Sangiovanni-Vincentelli, A.L.: Supervisory control of finite state machines. In: Wolper, P. (ed.) CAV 1995. LNCS, vol. 939, pp. 279–292. Springer, Heidelberg (1995). doi:10.1007/3-540-60045-0_57
5. Baier, C., Sirjani, M., Arbab, F., Rutten, J.: Modeling component connectors in Reo by constraint automata. Sci. Comput. Program. **61**(2), 75–113 (2006)
6. Baier, C., Blechmann, T., Klein, J., Klüppelholz, S.: Formal verification for components and connectors. In: de Boer, F.S., Bonsangue, M.M., Madelaine, E. (eds.) FMCO 2008. LNCS, vol. 5751, pp. 82–101. Springer, Heidelberg (2009). doi:10.1007/978-3-642-04167-9_5
7. Bloem, R., Jobstmann, B., Piterman, N., Pnueli, A., Sa'ar, Y.: Synthesis of reactive(1) designs. J. Comput. Syst. Sci. **78**(3), 911–938 (2012)
8. Bonchi, F., Brogi, A., Corfini, S., Gadducci, F.: A behavioural congruence for web services. In: Arbab, F., Sirjani, M. (eds.) FSEN 2007. LNCS, vol. 4767, pp. 240–256. Springer, Heidelberg (2007). doi:10.1007/978-3-540-75698-9_16
9. Bresolin, D., Lanese, I.: Most general property-preserving updates (TR) (2016). http://www.cs.unibo.it/~lanese/work/lata17-tr.pdf
10. Chatterjee, K., Doyen, L.: Games with a weak adversary. In: Esparza, J., Fraigniaud, P., Husfeldt, T., Koutsoupias, E. (eds.) ICALP 2014. LNCS, vol. 8573, pp. 110–121. Springer, Heidelberg (2014). doi:10.1007/978-3-662-43951-7_10
11. Preda, M., Gabbrielli, M., Giallorenzo, S., Lanese, I., Mauro, J.: Dynamic choreographies. In: Holvoet, T., Viroli, M. (eds.) COORDINATION 2015. LNCS, vol. 9037, pp. 67–82. Springer, Heidelberg (2015). doi:10.1007/978-3-319-19282-6_5
12. Di Giusto, C., Pérez, J.A.: Disciplined structured communications with consistent runtime adaptation. In: SAC, pp. 1913–1918. ACM (2013)
13. Duggan, D.: Type-based hot swapping of running modules. Acta Inf. **41**(4–5), 181–220 (2005)
14. Hayden, C.M., Magill, S., Hicks, M., Foster, N., Foster, J.S.: Specifying and verifying the correctness of dynamic software updates. In: Joshi, R., Müller, P., Podelski, A. (eds.) VSTTE 2012. LNCS, vol. 7152, pp. 278–293. Springer, Heidelberg (2012). doi:10.1007/978-3-642-27705-4_22
15. Huebscher, M.C., McCann, J.A.: A survey of autonomic computing - degrees, models, and applications. ACM Comput. Surv. **40**(3) (2008). Article No. 7
16. Lange, M.: Weak Automata for the Linear Time μ-Calculus. In: Cousot, R. (ed.) VMCAI 2005. LNCS, vol. 3385, pp. 267–281. Springer, Heidelberg (2005). doi:10.1007/978-3-540-30579-8_18
17. Leite, L.A.F., et al.: A systematic literature review of service choreography adaptation. Serv. Oriented Comput. Appl. **7**(3), 199–216 (2013)
18. Oliveira, N., Barbosa, L.S.: On the reconfiguration of software connectors. In: SAC, pp. 1885–1892. ACM (2013)

19. Seifzadeh, H., Abolhassani, H., Moshkenani, M.S.: A survey of dynamic software updating. J. Softw.: Evol. Process **25**(5), 535–568 (2013)
20. Sirjani, M., Jaghoori, M.M., Baier, C., Arbab, F.: Compositional semantics of an actor-based language using constraint automata. In: Ciancarini, P., Wiklicky, H. (eds.) COORDINATION 2006. LNCS, vol. 4038, pp. 281–297. Springer, Heidelberg (2006). doi:10.1007/11767954_18
21. Tsai, M.-H., Tsay, Y.-K., Hwang, Y.-S.: GOAL for games, omega-automata, and logics. In: Sharygina, N., Veith, H. (eds.) CAV 2013. LNCS, vol. 8044, pp. 883–889. Springer, Heidelberg (2013). doi:10.1007/978-3-642-39799-8_62
22. Villa, T., et al.: The Unknown Component Problem - Theory and Application. Springer, Heidelberg (2012)
23. Zhang, J., Goldsby, H., Cheng, B.H.C.: Modular verification of dynamically adaptive systems. In: AOSD, pp. 161–172. ACM (2009)

Over Which Monoids is the Transducer Determinization Procedure Applicable?

Stefan Gerdjikov[1,2] and Stoyan Mihov[2(✉)]

[1] Faculty of Mathematics and Informatics, Sofia University, 5, James Borchier Blvd., 1164 Sofia, Bulgaria
stefangerdzhikov@fmi.uni-sofia.bg

[2] Institute of Information and Communication Technologies, Bulgarian Academy of Sciences, 25A, Acad. G. Bonchev Street, 1113 Sofia, Bulgaria
stoyan@lml.bas.bg

Abstract. The input determinization of a finite-state transducer for constructing an equivalent subsequential transducer is performed by the well-known inductive transducer determinization procedure. This procedure has been shown to complete for rational functions with the bounded variation property. The result has been obtained for functions $f : \Sigma^* \to \mathcal{M}$, where $\mathcal{M}$ is a free monoid, the monoid of non-negative real numbers with addition or a Cartesian product of those monoids. In this paper we generalize this result and define and prove sufficient conditions for a monoid $\mathcal{M}$ and a rational function $f : \Sigma^* \to \mathcal{M}$, under which the transducer determinization procedure is applicable and terminates.

Keywords: Transducers · Rational functions · Twinning property

1 Introduction

Finite-state automata and transducer are widely used in many areas and applications of computer science [4]. Subsequential finite-state transducers are highly computationally efficient for language modelling and text processing tasks, and thus provide a very desirable technique in computational linguistics [6–8].

The transducer determinization procedure [6] is the natural method for constructing subsequential transducer. In [2] Choffrut proved that a rational function $f : \Sigma^* \to \Sigma'^*$ can be represented as a subsequential transducer iff f has the bounded variation property. In [7] Mohri showed that the inductive transducer determinization procedure can be applied to rational functions $f : \Sigma^* \to \mathcal{R}^+$ where $\mathcal{R}^+$ is the monoid of non-negative real numbers with addition (weighted transducers) and proved that the procedure completes iff the target function has the bounded variation property. In [5] an overview of those results is presented. Recently, a generalization for cost register automata was presented in [3].

In this paper we first introduce the sequentiable structures, which characterize the class of monoids over which the inductive transducer determinization procedure is applicable. Further, we prove that any rational function $f : \Sigma^* \to \mathcal{M}$,

F. Drewes et al. (Eds.): LATA 2017, LNCS 10168, pp. 380–392, 2017.
DOI: 10.1007/978-3-319-53733-7_28

where $\mathcal{M}$ is a sequentiable structure, can be represented as a subsequential transducer iff f has the bounded variation property. We prove also the decidability of the functionality and the bounded variation property for functions into sequentiable structures. Finally, we generalize our results for the Cartesian product of sequentiable structures.

2 Formal Preliminaries

Definition 1. *A* semi-group $\mathcal{N}$ *is a pair* $\langle N, \circ \rangle$*, where* N *is a non-empty set of semi-group elements and* $\circ : N \times N \to N$ *is the semi-group operation (used with infix notation), which is associative, i.e.* $\forall a, b, c \in M : a \circ (b \circ c) = (a \circ b) \circ c$.

A semi-group $\mathcal{N} = \langle N, \circ \rangle$ *is* commutative *if* $\forall a, b \in M : a \circ b = b \circ a$.

A monoid $\mathcal{M}$ *is a triple* $\langle M, \circ, e \rangle$*, where* $\langle M, \circ \rangle$ *is a semi-group and* $e \in M$ *is the unit element, i.e.* $\forall a \in M : a \circ e = e \circ a = a$*. With* ab *we denote* $a \circ b$.

The monoid $\mathcal{M}$ *supports* left cancelation *if* $\forall a, b, c \in M : c \circ a = c \circ b \to a = b$.

The Cartesian product *of monoids* $\mathcal{M}_1 = \langle M_1, \circ_1, e_1 \rangle$ *and* $\mathcal{M}_2 = \langle M_2, \circ_2, e_2 \rangle$ *is the monoid* $\mathcal{M}_1 \times \mathcal{M}_2 := \langle M_1 \times M_2, \bar{\circ}, \langle e_1, e_2 \rangle \rangle$*, where* $\bar{\circ} : (M_1 \times M_2) \times (M_1 \times M_2) \to M_1 \times M_2$ *denotes the function* $\langle u_1, u_2 \rangle \bar{\circ} \langle v_1, v_2 \rangle := \langle u_1 \circ_1 v_1, u_2 \circ_2 v_2 \rangle$.

The function $\phi : M_1 \to M_2$ *is a* monoidal homomorphism *between the monoids* $\mathcal{M}_1 = \langle M_1, \circ_1, e_1 \rangle$ *and* $\mathcal{M}_2 = \langle M_2, \circ_2, e_2 \rangle$ *if* $\phi(e_1) = e_2$ *and* $\forall a, b \in M_1 : \phi(a \circ_1 b) = \phi(a) \circ_2 \phi(b)$.

An alphabet Σ *is a set of symbols. Alphabets are assumed to be finite.*

A word w *over an alphabet* Σ *is an* n*-tuple* $w = \langle a_1, \ldots, a_n \rangle$ *where* $n \geq 0$ *and* $a_i \in \Sigma$ *for* $i = 1, \ldots, n$*. The integer* n *is the* length *of* w *and denoted* $|w|$*. We may denote the word* w *as* $w = a_1 a_2 \ldots a_n$.

The (unique) tuple of length 0*, written* ε*, is called the* empty word*.* Σ^* *denotes the set of all words over* Σ.

The concatenation *of two words* $u = \langle a_1, \ldots, a_n \rangle$ *and* $v = \langle b_1, \ldots, b_m \rangle \in \Sigma^*$ *is* $u \cdot v = \langle a_1, \ldots, a_n, b_1, \ldots, b_m \rangle$.

The set Σ^* *with concatenation as monoid operation and the empty word* ε *as unit element is called the* free monoid $\langle \Sigma^*, \cdot, \varepsilon \rangle$ *for alphabet* Σ.

Let $u, v, t \in \Sigma^*$*. The expression* $u^{-1}t$ *denotes the word* v *if* u *is a prefix of* $t = u \cdot v$*, otherwise* $u^{-1}t$ *is undefined.*

The word $w = u \wedge v$ *denotes the* longest common prefix *of* u *and* v.

Definition 2. *A* monoidal finite-state automaton *is a tuple of the form* $\mathcal{A} = \langle \mathcal{M}, Q, I, F, \Delta \rangle$ *where*

- $\mathcal{M} = \langle M, \circ, e \rangle$ *is a monoid,*
- Q *is a finite set called the set of states,*
- $I \subseteq Q$ *is the set of initial states,*
- $F \subseteq Q$ *is the set of final states, and*
- $\Delta \subseteq Q \times M \times Q$ *is a finite set of transitions called the transition relation.*

A proper path *in* $\mathcal{A}$ *is a finite sequence of* $k > 0$ *transitions*

$$\pi = \langle q_0, a_1, q_1 \rangle \langle q_1, a_2, q_2 \rangle \ldots \langle q_{k-1}, a_k, q_k \rangle$$

where $\langle q_{i-1}, a_i, q_i\rangle \in \Delta$ *for* $i = 1 \ldots k$. *The number* k *is called the* length *of* π, *we say that* π *starts in* q_0 *and ends in* q_k. *States* $q_0, \ldots, q_k$ *are* the states on the path π. *The monoid element* $w = a_1 \circ \ldots \circ a_k$ *is called the* label *of* π. *We may denote the path* π *as* $\pi = q_0 \rightarrow^{a_1} q_1 \ldots \rightarrow^{a_k} q_k$. *The* null path *of* $q \in Q$ *is* 0_q *starting and ending in* q *with label* e. *A* successful path *is a path starting in an initial state and ending in a final state.*

The generalized transition relation Δ^* *is defined as the smallest subset of* $Q \times M \times Q$ *with the following closure properties:*

- *for all* $q \in Q$ *we have* $\langle q, e, q\rangle \in \Delta^*$.
- *For all* $q_1, q_2, q_3 \in Q$ *and* $w, a \in M$*: if* $\langle q_1, w, q_2\rangle \in \Delta^*$ *and* $\langle q_2, a, q_3\rangle \in \Delta$, *then also* $\langle q_1, w \circ a, q_3\rangle \in \Delta^*$.

The monoidal language accepted *(or* recognized*) by* $\mathcal{A}$ *is defined as* $L(\mathcal{A}) := \{w \in M \mid \exists p \in I\ \exists q \in F : \langle p, w, q\rangle \in \Delta^*\}$.

A state $q \in Q$ *is* accessible *if* q *is the ending of a path of* $\mathcal{A}$ *starting from an initial state. A state* $q \in Q$ *is* co-accessible *if* q *is the starting of a path of* $\mathcal{A}$ *ending in a final state.*

A monoidal finite-state automaton $\mathcal{A}$ *is* trimmed *iff each state* $q \in Q$ *is accessible and co-accessible.*

A monoidal finite-state automaton $\mathcal{A}$ *is a* monoidal finite-state transducer *iff its underlying monoid* $\mathcal{M}$ *can be represented as the Cartesian product of a free monoid* Σ^* *with another monoid* $\mathcal{M}'$ *i.e.* $\mathcal{M} = \Sigma^* \times \mathcal{M}'$.

A monoidal finite-state transducer $\mathcal{A} = \langle \Sigma^* \times \mathcal{M}', Q, I, F, \Delta\rangle$ *is said to be* real-time *if* $\Delta \subseteq Q \times (\Sigma \times M') \times Q$.

Let $\mathcal{M}$ *be a monoid. A language* $L \subset M$ *is* rational *iff it is accepted by a monoidal finite-state automaton. A* rational function *is a rational language, which is a function.*

Definition 3. *A* monoidal subsequential finite-state transducer *is a tuple* $\mathcal{T} = \langle \Sigma, \mathcal{M}, Q, q_0, F, \delta, \lambda, \Psi\rangle$ *where:*

- Σ *is a finite alphabet,*
- $\mathcal{M} = \langle M, \circ, e\rangle$ *is a monoid,*
- Q *is a finite set of states,*
- $q_0 \in Q$ *is the initial state,*
- $F \subseteq Q$ *is the set of final states,*
- $\delta : Q \times \Sigma \rightarrow Q$ *is (possibly partial) function called transition function,*
- $\lambda : Q \times \Sigma \rightarrow M$ *is a function with domain, dom* $(\lambda) =$ *dom* (δ), *called the transition output function, and*
- $\Psi : F \rightarrow \mathcal{M}$ *is the state output function.*

The generalized transition function δ^* *is defined as the inclusion-wise least function on* $Q \times \Sigma^* \rightarrow Q$ *with the following closure properties:*

- *for all* $q \in Q$ *we have* $\delta^*(q, \varepsilon) = q$.
- *For all* $q \in Q, \alpha \in \Sigma^*$ *and* $a \in \Sigma$*:* $\delta^*(q, \alpha a) = \delta(\delta^*(q, \alpha), a)$.

The generalized transition output function function λ^* *is the inclusion-wise least function on* $Q \times \Sigma^* \to M$ *with the following closure properties:*

- *for all* $q \in Q$ *we have* $\lambda^*(q, \varepsilon) = e$.
- *For all* $q \in Q, \alpha \in \Sigma^*$ *and* $a \in \Sigma$: $\lambda^*(q, \alpha a) = \lambda^*(q, \alpha) \circ \lambda(\delta^*(q, \alpha), a)$.

The output function *represented by the subsequential finite-state transducer* $\mathcal{T}$ *is* $\mathcal{O}_\mathcal{T} : \Sigma^* \to M$ *defined as:* $\mathcal{O}_\mathcal{T}(\alpha) = \lambda^*(q_0, \alpha) \circ \Psi(\delta^*(q_0, \alpha))$ *if* $\delta^*(q_0, \alpha) \in F$.

3 Sequentiable Structures

Definition 4. *A tuple* $\mathcal{M} = \langle M, \circ, e, \sqcap, \|.\| \rangle$ *is a* pre-sequentiable structure *if*

1. $\langle M, \circ, e \rangle$ *is a monoid, which supports left cancelation,*
2. $\langle M, \sqcap \rangle$ *is a commutative semi-group,*
3. *The operations* $\circ$ *and* $\sqcap$ *fulfil the following properties:*
   - $\forall a, b, c \in M : a \circ (b \sqcap c) = (a \circ b) \sqcap (a \circ c)$ *(left distributivity),*
   - $\forall a, b \in M\ \exists c \in M : a = (a \sqcap b) \circ c,$
4. *The function* $\|.\| : M \to \mathbb{R}^+$ *called* norm *is a homomorphism of the monoids* $\langle M, \circ, e \rangle$ *and* $\langle \mathbb{R}^+, +, 0 \rangle$, *which maps only* e *to* 0. *I.e.* $\|a\| = 0 \to a = e$.

Next proposition lists some simple properties of the pre-sequentiable structures.

Proposition 1. *Let* $\mathcal{M} = \langle M, \circ, e, \sqcap, \|.\| \rangle$ *be a pre-sequentiable structure.*

1. *For any* $a, b \in M$, $a \circ b = e \to a = b = e$.
2. *For any* $a \in M$, $e \sqcap a = e$ *and* $a \sqcap a = a$.
3. *For any* $a, b \in M$, $a \sqcap (a \circ b) = a$.
4. *For any* $a, b, c \in M$, $a \sqcap b = c$ *iff there exist* $a', b' \in M$ *such that:* $a = c \circ a'$, $b = c \circ b'$ *and* $a' \sqcap b' = e$.

Definition 5. *A pre-sequentiable structure* $\mathcal{M} = \langle M, \circ, e, \sqcap, \|.\| \rangle$ *is called* sequentiable structure *if it additionally satisfies the condition:*

$$\forall a, b, c, d \in M : a \sqcap b = e \ \&\ a \neq e \ \&\ b \neq e \to (a \circ c) \sqcap (b \circ d) = e \qquad (1)$$

In case of sequentiable structures we additionally get the right cancellation property and Levy-like lemma:

Proposition 2. *Let* $\mathcal{M} = \langle M, \circ, e, \sqcap, \|.\| \rangle$ *be a sequentiable structure.*

1. $\forall a, b, c \in M (a \circ c = b \circ c \to a = b)$ *(right cancellation property),*
2. $\forall a_1, a_2, b_1, b_2 \in M : a_1 \circ a_2 = b_1 \circ b_2 \ \&\ \|b_1\| \geq \|a_1\| \to$ $\exists c \in M : (b_1 = a_1 \circ c \ \&\ a_2 = c \circ b_2)$.

The *product* of structures is a standard technique starting from intuitively simpler structures to obtain more complex ones. Formally, we have:

Definition 6. *For* $\mathcal{M}_i = \langle M_i, \circ_i, e_i, \sqcap_i, \|.\|_i \rangle$ *pre-sequentiable structures for* $i \in \{1, 2\}$ *we define the* Cartesian product *as:* $\mathcal{M} = \langle M_1 \times M_2, \circ, \langle e_1, e_2 \rangle, \sqcap, \|.\| \rangle$, *where*

- *for all* $a_1, b_1 \in M_1$ *and* $a_2, b_2 \in M_2$: $\langle a_1, a_2\rangle \circ \langle b_1, b_2\rangle = \langle a_1 \circ_1 b_1, a_2 \circ_2 b_2\rangle$,
- *for all* $a_1, b_1 \in M_1$ *and* $a_2, b_2 \in M_2$: $\langle a_1, a_2\rangle \sqcap \langle b_1, b_2\rangle = \langle a_1 \sqcap_1 b_1, a_2 \sqcap_2 b_2\rangle$,
- *for all* $a_1 \in M_1$ *and* $a_2 \in M_2$, $\|\langle a_1, a_2\rangle\| = \|a_1\|_1 + \|a_2\|_2$.

Remark 1. The pre-sequentiable structures are closed under Cartesian product. In contrast, the Cartesian product of sequentiable structures is in general not a sequentiable structure.

The following two examples show that the sequentiable structures naturally generalize structures of practical importance, [7]:

Example 1.

1. For any finite alphabet Σ, $\Sigma^* = \langle \Sigma^*, \cdot, \varepsilon, \wedge, |.|\rangle$ is a sequentiable structure.
2. The tuple $\mathcal{R}^+ = \langle \mathbb{R}^+, +, 0, \min, id_{\mathbb{R}^+}\rangle$ is a sequentiable structure.

Next, we present an example for a more complex sequentiable structure construction, which justifies our abstract notion.

The Shuffle Structure. We start with an example. Let us consider Σ^* and $\mathcal{R}^+$. We define a structure consisting of interleaved sequences of nonempty words and positive real numbers, e.g. $m_1 = \langle abc, 0.5, abc, 0.3\rangle$, $m_2 = \langle abc, 0.5, abc, 0.2, ad\rangle$, $m_3 = \langle abc, 0.5, abd\rangle$, $m_4 = \langle 0.24, ab\rangle$. On this structure we can define a monoid operation as concatenation of sequences. For instance:

$$m_1 \circ m_2 = \langle aba, 0.5, abc, 0.3, abc, 0.5, abc, 0.2, ad\rangle \text{ but}$$
$$m_2 \circ m_3 = \langle abc, 0.5, abc, 0.2, adabc, 0.5, abd\rangle \text{ and}$$
$$m_1 \circ m_4 = \langle abc, 0.5, abc, 0.3 + 0.24, ab\rangle = \langle abc, 0.5, abc, 0.54, ab\rangle.$$

Following a similar intuition, we can define a maximal common beginning as:

$$m_1 \sqcap m_2 = \langle abc, 0.5, abc, \min(0.3, 0.2)\rangle = \langle abc, 0.5, abc, 0.2\rangle,$$
$$m_1 \sqcap m_3 = \langle abc, 0.5, abc \wedge abd\rangle = \langle abc, 0.5, ab\rangle.$$

We define a norm on this structure by assigning the sum of lengths of the words plus the sum of the numbers, e.g.: $\|m_1\| = |abc| + 0.5 + |abc| + 0.3 = 6.8$. Below we formalize the general shuffle construction:

Example 2. Let $\mathcal{M}_i = \langle M_i, \circ_i, e_i, \sqcap_i, \|.\|_i\rangle$ for $i = 1, 2$ with $M_1 \cap M_2 = \emptyset$ be sequentiable structures. Let $M_i' = M_i \setminus \{e_i\}$. Then, we define the shuffle of $\mathcal{M}_1$ and $\mathcal{M}_2$ as $\mathcal{M} = \langle M, \circ, \varepsilon, \sqcap, \|.\|\rangle$:

1. $M = \{\langle m_1, m_2, \ldots, m_k\rangle \mid k \geq 0 \text{ and } m_i \in M_1' \leftrightarrow m_{i+1} \in M_2' \text{ for all } i < k\}$.
2. If $m' = \langle m_1', m_2', \ldots, m_k'\rangle \in M$ and $m'' = \langle m_1'', m_2'', \ldots, m_k''\rangle \in M$, then:

$$m' \circ m'' = \begin{cases} \langle m_1', m_2', \ldots, m_k' \circ_j m_1'', m_2'', \ldots, m_l''\rangle \text{ if } m_k', m_1'' \in M_j' \\ \langle m_1', m_2', \ldots, m_k', m_1'', m_2'', \ldots, m_l''\rangle \text{ else.} \end{cases}$$

3. Let i be the largest s.t. $m'_s = m''_s$ for all $s < i$. We set $m' \sqcap m'' = m$ where:

$$m = \begin{cases} \langle m'_1, \ldots, m'_{i-1}, m'_i \sqcap_j m''_i \rangle \text{ if } m'_i, m''_i \in M'_j \text{ and } m'_i \sqcap_j m''_i \neq e_j \\ \langle m'_1, m'_2, \ldots, m'_{i-1} \rangle, \text{else.} \end{cases}$$

4. If $m = \langle m_1, m_2, \ldots, m_k \rangle \in M$, then: $\|m\| = \sum_{j=1}^{2} \sum_{i:m_i \in M_j} \|m_i\|_j$.

Remark 2. The shuffle of sequentiable structures is a sequentiable structure.

Definition 7. *Let $\mathcal{M} = \langle M, \circ, e, \sqcap, \|.\| \rangle$ be a pre-sequentiable structure. Let $u, t \in M$. The expression $u^{-1}t$ denotes the element $v \in M$ if u is a beginning of t i.e. if t can be presented as $t = u \circ v$, otherwise $u^{-1}t$ is undefined.*

Clearly, by the left cancellation property, if $u^{-1}t$ is defined then it is unique.

Definition 8. *Let $\mathcal{M} = \langle M, \circ, e, \sqcap, \|.\| \rangle$ be a pre-sequentiable structure. Then the function $d_{\mathcal{M}} : M \times M \to \mathbb{R}$ defined as $d_{\mathcal{M}}(u, v) := \|u\| + \|v\| - 2\|u \sqcap v\|$ is the* sequential distance[1] *in $\mathcal{M}$.*

The following definitions generalize the bounded variation property in the case of pre-sequentiable structures.

Definition 9. *A function $f : \Sigma^* \to M$, where $\mathcal{M} = \langle M, \circ, e, \sqcap, \|.\| \rangle$ is a pre-sequentiable structure has the* bounded variation property *iff for all $k \geq 0$ there is $K \geq 0$ s.t. for all $u, v \in dom(f)$, $d_{\Sigma^*}(u, v) \leq k$ implies $d_{\mathcal{M}}(f(u), f(v)) \leq K$.*

Definition 10. *A functional monoidal finite-state transducer $\mathcal{T}$ over a pre-sequentiable structure has the* bounded variation property *iff the rational function represented by $\mathcal{T}$ has the bounded variation property.*

4 Sequentialization Procedure

In this section we generalize the input determinization procedure (cf. [6]). Formally, we consider a functional trimmed real-time monoidal finite-state transducer $\mathcal{A} = \langle \Sigma^* \times \mathcal{M}, Q, I, F, \Delta \rangle$ over $\Sigma^* \times \mathcal{M}$, where $\mathcal{M} = \langle M, \circ, e, \sqcap, \|.\| \rangle$ is a pre-sequentiable structure. Moreover, we assume[2] that if $\langle \varepsilon, \alpha \rangle \in L(\mathcal{A})$ then $\alpha = e$. The subsequential transducer $\mathcal{T}' = \langle \Sigma, \mathcal{M}, Q', q'_0, F', \delta', \lambda', \Psi' \rangle$ equivalent to $\mathcal{A}$ is built by induction. At each step we extend the current set of states Q', the set of final states F', the transition function δ' and the output functions λ' and Ψ'. The base of the induction is:

$$\mathcal{T}'^{(0)} = \langle \Sigma, \mathcal{M}, \{q'_0\}, q'_0, \emptyset, \emptyset, \emptyset, \emptyset \rangle, \text{ where } q'_0 = I \times \{e\}.$$

Let us assume that we have constructed $\mathcal{T}'^{(n)} = \langle \Sigma, \mathcal{M}, Q'_n, q'_0, F'_n, \delta'_n, \lambda'_n, \Psi'_n \rangle$. We define $\mathcal{T}'^{(n+1)} = \langle \Sigma, \mathcal{M}, Q'_{n+1}, q'_0, F'_{n+1}, \delta'_{n+1}, \lambda'_{n+1}, \Psi'_{n+1} \rangle$ as follows:

---

[1] It can be easily shown that $d_{\mathcal{M}}$ is a distance.

[2] This assumption is not a significant limitation since if it is not the case we can modify the state output function to output the desired word α for the starting state on the resulting subsequential transducer.

- The transition functions $\lambda'_{n+1}, \delta'_{n+1}$ extend λ'_n, δ'_n s.t. for $S \in Q'_n$ and $\sigma \in \Sigma$

$$\lambda'_{n+1}(S,\sigma) = \bigsqcap_{\langle q,u\rangle \in S} \bigsqcap_{\langle q,\langle \sigma,v\rangle,q'\rangle \in \Delta} u \circ v.$$

$$\delta'_{n+1}(S,\sigma) = \bigcup_{\langle q,u\rangle \in S} \bigcup_{\langle q,\langle \sigma,v\rangle,q'\rangle \in \Delta} \{\langle q', w^{-1}(u \circ v)\rangle\}, \text{ where } w = \lambda'_{n+1}(S,\sigma)$$

- $Q'_{n+1} = Q'_n \cup codom\,(\delta'_{n+1})$,
- $F'_{n+1} = \{S \in Q'_{n+1} \mid \exists \langle q,\beta\rangle \in S \;:\; q \in F\}$,
- $\Psi'_{n+1} = \{\langle S,\beta\rangle \mid S \in F'_{n+1}, \exists\langle q,\beta\rangle \in S \;:\; q \in F\}$.

At each step the transducer is extended with a finite number of states reachable with one symbol from the set of states of the current transducer. Lemma 1 shows that at each step n that Ψ'_n is always a well-defined function. Hence after each step we obtain a proper subsequential transducer.

Lemma 1. *Let $\mathcal{A}$ be as above. Let $\mathcal{T}'^{(n)} = \langle \Sigma, \mathcal{M}, Q', q'_0, F', \delta', \lambda', \Psi'\rangle$ be constructed by the induction given above in n steps. Then:*

1. *for each word $w \in \Sigma^*$ such that $\lambda'^*(q'_0, w)$ and $\delta'^*(q'_0, w)$ are defined it holds:*

$$\lambda'^*(q'_0, w) = \bigsqcap_{q_0 \in I, \langle q_0,\langle w,u\rangle,q\rangle \in \Delta^*} u$$

$$\delta'^*(q'_0, w) = \{\langle q,\gamma\rangle \mid \exists q_0 \in I \; \exists\langle q_0,\langle w,u\rangle,q\rangle \in \Delta^* \;:\; \gamma = \lambda'^*(q'_0,w)^{-1}u\};$$

2. *for each state $S \in Q'$ and $q \in Q$ we have $|\{v \in M \mid \exists\langle q,v\rangle \in S\}| \le 1$;*
3. *for each state $S \in Q'$ and $\langle q_1,v_1\rangle, \langle q_2,v_2\rangle \in S$ we have $q_1 \in F \;\&\; q_2 \in F \rightarrow v_1 = v_2$.*

The following result is also straightforward:

Proposition 3. *Assume that the inductive construction of $\mathcal{T}'$ presented above terminates, i.e. there is $k_0 \in \mathbb{N}$ such that for all $k \ge k_0$, $\mathcal{T}'^{(k)} = \mathcal{T}'^{(k_0)} = \mathcal{T}'$. Then $O_{\mathcal{T}'} = L(\mathcal{A})$ and in this case $\mathcal{A}$ has the bounded variation property.*

5 Sequentialability Conditions

Our proofs of the sequentialability conditions make use of the squaring transducer method presented in [1]. Throughout this section we assume that $\mathcal{A} = \langle \Sigma^* \times \mathcal{M}, Q, I, F, \Delta\rangle$ is a trimmed monoidal transducer over an effective presequentiable structure $\mathcal{M}$.

Proposition 4.

1. *If $\mathcal{A}$ contains a cycle $\langle p, \langle \varepsilon, m\rangle, p\rangle \in \Delta^*$ with $m \neq e$, then $\mathcal{A}$ is not functional.*

2. *If $\mathcal{A}$ does not contain any cycles of the form $\langle p, \langle \varepsilon, m\rangle, p\rangle \in \Delta^*$ with $m \neq e$, then $\mathcal{A}$ can be effectively transformed into a real-time transducer $\mathcal{A}'$ such that $L(\mathcal{A}) \cap (\Sigma^+ \times M) = L(\mathcal{A}') \cap (\Sigma^+ \times M)$. Furthermore, we can effectively compute the set $\{m \mid \langle \varepsilon, m\rangle \in L(\mathcal{A})\}$.*

Theorem 1. *Let $\mathcal{M}$ be a sequentiable structures or Cartesian product of sequentiable structures. Then it is decidable whether a real-time monoidal finite-state transducer $\mathcal{A} = \langle \Sigma^* \times M, Q, I, F, \Delta\rangle$ is functional or not.*

The proof is a generalization of the proof in [5].

From now on we assume that $\mathcal{A} = \langle \Sigma^* \times \mathcal{M}, Q, I, F, \Delta\rangle$ is a trimmed real-time functional monoidal transducer over a pre-sequentiable structure $\mathcal{M}$. The next two theorems are the main results in the paper and will be proved throughout this section.

Theorem 2. *If $\mathcal{M}$ is sequentiable structure and $\mathcal{A}$ has the bounded variation property, then the inductive construction of $\mathcal{T}'$ presented above terminates in the sense that there exists a number $k_0 \in \mathbb{N}$ s. t. for all $k \geq k_0$, $\mathcal{T}'^{(k)} = \mathcal{T}'^{(k_0)} = \mathcal{T}'$.*

Theorem 3. *If $\mathcal{M}$ is sequentiable structure, then it is decidable whether $L(\mathcal{A})$ has the bounded variation property or not.*

Definition 11. *The* square automaton *of $\mathcal{A}$ is $\mathcal{A}^2 = \langle \mathcal{M} \times \mathcal{M}, Q^2, I^2, \Delta_2, F^2\rangle$ where the transition relation is given by:*

$$\Delta_2 = \{\langle\langle p_1, p_2\rangle, \langle m_1, m_2\rangle, \langle q_1, q_2\rangle\rangle \mid \exists a \in \Sigma\ \forall i \in \{1,2\} \langle p_i, a, m_i, q_i\rangle \in \Delta\}.$$

Definition 12. *For $m_1, m_2 \in M$ we define the* reduct *of m_1 w.r.t. m_2 (cf. Proposition 1 p. 4):*

$$\rho(m_1, m_2) = (m_1 \sqcap m_2)^{-1} m_1.$$

Definition 13. *We say that a pair $\langle u_1, u_2\rangle \in M \times M$ is an admissible pair of reducts for a pair of states $p = \langle p_1, p_2\rangle \in Q \times Q$ if there exist a word $w \in \Sigma^*$, initial states $s_1, s_2 \in I$, and elements $m_1, m_2 \in M$ such that:*

$$\forall i \in \{1,2\} (\langle s_i, w, m_i, p_i\rangle \in \Delta^* \text{ and } \langle u_1, u_2\rangle = \langle \rho(m_1, m_2), \rho(m_2, m_1)\rangle), i.e.$$

$$\langle s, \langle m_1, m_2\rangle, p\rangle \in \Delta_2^* \text{ and } \langle u_1, u_2\rangle = \langle \rho(m_1, m_2), \rho(m_2, m_1)\rangle).$$

We denote with $Adm(p) \subseteq M \times M$ the set of admissible reducts for p.
The set of admissible reducts *$Red(\mathcal{A})$ and its first projection $Red_1(\mathcal{A})$ are:*

$$Red(\mathcal{A}) = \bigcup_{p \in Q \times Q} Adm(p) \text{ and } Red_1(\mathcal{A}) = \{u_1 \in M \mid \exists u_2 \langle u_1, u_2\rangle \in Red(\mathcal{A})\}.$$

The imbalance *of $\mathcal{A}$ is the set $Imb(\mathcal{A}) = \{\|u_1\| - \|u_2\| \mid \langle u_1, u_2\rangle \in Red(\mathcal{A})\}$.*

Obviously, if $\langle u_1, u_2\rangle \in Adm(p)$ then $u_1 \sqcap u_2 = e$ and $\langle u_2, u_1\rangle \in Adm(p)$.

Definition 14. *We say that state $p \in Q \times Q$ satisfies the Twinning Property if for any admissible reduct $x = \langle x_1, x_2 \rangle \in Adm(p)$ and any $m = \langle m_1, m_2 \rangle \in M \times M$ such that $m \neq \langle e, e \rangle$ and $\langle p, m, p \rangle \in \Delta_2^*$ the following conditions hold:*

1. *there are $u, v \in M$ such that $m_1 = uv$ and $m_2 = vu$,*
2. *$\rho(x_1 m_1, x_2 m_2) = x_1$ and $\rho(x_2 m_2, x_1 m_1) = x_2$,*
3. *$x_1 = e$ or $x_2 = e$.*

The automaton $\mathcal{A}$ is said to have the Twinning Property if any state $p \in Q \times Q$ with $Adm(p) \neq \emptyset$ has the Twinning Property.

We note that in the special cases where $\mathcal{M} = \Sigma^*$ or $\mathcal{M} = \mathcal{R}^+$ the above definition generalizes the definition of Twinning Property in [5].

We prove the following lemma which extends the results of Choffrut [2] and Mohri [7] to the case of sequentiable structures, and which implies Theorem 2:

Lemma 2. *Let $\mathcal{M}$ be sequentiable structure. Then the following are equivalent:*

1. *$\mathcal{A}$ is of bounded variation.*
2. *$\mathcal{A}$ has the Twinning Property.*
3. *$Red(\mathcal{A})$ is finite.*
4. *The inductive construction of $\mathcal{T}'$ terminates.*

Proof. **3 ⇒ 4)** Since $Red(\mathcal{A})$ is finite, we get that $Red_1(\mathcal{A})$ is finite. Next, each state $q \in Q'_k$ generated by the inductive construction of $\mathcal{T}'$ has the property $q \subseteq Q \times Red_1(\mathcal{A})$. Indeed by Lemma 1 we have that $q = \{\langle q_i, u_i \rangle\}_{i=1}^l$ such that there exist a word $w \in \Sigma^*$, initial states $s_i \in I$, and monoid elements $z, m_i \in M$ with:

$$\forall i \leq l(\langle s_i, w, m_i, q_i \rangle \in \Delta^*) \text{ and } z = \bigsqcap_{i=1}^{l} m_i \text{ and } u_i = \rho(m_i, z).$$

Thus, as it can be shown by induction on l,it follows that for every i there is an appropriate j with $u_i = \rho(m_i, m_j)$. Therefore, $u_i \in Red_1(\mathcal{A})$. Thus, $Q' \subseteq 2^{Q \times Red_1(\mathcal{A})}$ can be extended only finitely many times and the construction will eventually terminate.

4 ⇒ 1) This follows by Proposition 3.

1 ⇒ 2) Assume that $\mathcal{A}$ is of bounded variation. Using similar ideas to the ones in [7] if $p \in Q \times Q$ with $Adm(p) \neq \emptyset$, then for every cycle $\langle p, \langle m_1, m_2 \rangle, p \rangle \in \Delta_2^*$ it holds that $\|m_1\| = \|m_2\|$.

Now, assume that $p = \langle p_1, p_2 \rangle$, $x = \langle x_1, x_2 \rangle \in Adm(p)$, and $m = \langle m_1, m_2 \rangle$ are such that $\langle p, m, p \rangle \in \Delta_2^*$ and $m \neq \langle e, e \rangle$. By the above remark we get that $\|m_1\| = \|m_2\| > 0$. Thus, since $\mathcal{A}$ is of bounded variation and p_1 and p_2 are co-accessible in $\mathcal{A}$ and using Proposition 2 one can show: $x_1 m_1 \sqcap x_2 m_2 \in \{x_1 m_1, x_2 m_2\}$.

First we show that $x_1 = e$ or $x_2 = e$. From the definition of a reduct we have that $x_1 \sqcap x_2 = e$. If we assume that $x_1 \neq e$ and $x_2 \neq e$ by Condition 1 we get that $x_1 m_1 \sqcap x_2 m_2 = e \notin \{x_1 m_1, x_2 m_2\}$. Therefore $x_1 = e$ or $x_2 = e$. Without loss of generality, in the sequel we assume that $x_2 = e$ and therefore $x_1 m_1 \sqcap x_2 m_2 = x_2 m_2 = m_2$.

We now show that there are $u, v \in M$ such that $m_1 = uv$ and $m_2 = vu$. Let $r_1^{(n)} = \rho(x_1 m_1^n, x_2 m_2^n)$ and $r_2^{(n)} = \rho(x_2 m_2^n, x_1 m_1^n)$. Clearly, for every $n \in \mathbb{N}$ we have that $\langle r_1^{(n)}, r_2^{(n)} \rangle \in Adm(p)$ and therefore $r_1^{(n)} = e$ or $r_2^{(n)} = e$. Since

$$x_i m_i^n = (x_1 m_1^n \sqcap x_2 m_2^n) r_i^{(n)} \text{for } i \in \{1,2\}$$

using that $\|m_1\| = \|m_2\|$, we obtain that $\|r_1^{(n)}\| - \|r_2^{(n)}\| = \|x_1\| - \|x_2\|$. Therefore $r_2^{(n)} = e$ and $x_1 m_1^n \sqcap x_2 m_2^n = x_2 m_2^n$. Hence $x_1 m_1^n = (x_1 m_1^n \sqcap x_2 m_2^n) r_1^{(n)} = x_2 m_2^n r_1^{(n)}$. Since $x_2 = e$ we get $x_2 m_2^n r_1^{(n)} = m_2^n r_1^{(n)}$. In this way we obtain:

$$x_1 m_1^n = m_2^n r_1^{(n)}.$$

Let n' be the least integer such that $n'\|m_2\| > \|x_1\| \geq (n'-1)\|m_2\|$. Such an n' exists since $\|m_2\| = \|m_1\| > 0$. From the equality $x_1 m_1^{n'} = m_2^{n'} r_1^{(n')}$ using Proposition 2 Point 2 we get $m_2^{n'} = x_1 u$. On the other hand $x_1 m_1^{n'-1} = m_2^{n'-1} r_1^{(n'-1)}$ and from Proposition 2 we get $x_1 = m_2^{n'-1} v$. Now using the left cancellation property for $\mathcal{M}$ we subsequently get:

$$m_2^{n'} = x_1 u = m_2^{n'-1} vu \Rightarrow m_2 = vu \text{ and}$$
$$x_1 m_1^{n'+1} = m_2^{n'+1} r_1^{(n'+1)} = x_1 u m_2 r_1^{(n'+1)} = x_1 uvu r_1^{(n'+1)}$$

Therefore $m_1 m_1^{n'} = uvu r_1^{(n'+1)}$ and since $\|m_1\| = \|m_2\| = \|u\| + \|v\|$, Proposition 2 Point 2 implies that $m_1 = uv$.

Now we prove that $r_1^{(n)} = x_1$ from which follows that $r_1^{(1)} = x_1$. Using that $x_1 = m_2^{n'-1} v$, $m_1 = uv$, and $m_2 = vu$ we obtain:

$$x_1 m_1^n = m_2^{n'-1} v m_1^n = (vu)^{n'-1} v (uv)^n = (vu)^{n'+n-1} v = m_2^{n'+n-1} v = m_2^n x_1.$$

Now from the equality $x_1 m_1^n = m_2^n x_1 = m_2^n r_1^{(n)}$ by the left cancellation property it follows that $r_1^{(n)} = x_1$ as required.

2⇒ 3) Observe, that by the Twinning Property we have that for every cycle $\langle p, \langle m_1, m_2 \rangle, p \rangle \in \Delta_2^*$ with $Adm(p) \neq \emptyset$ $\|m_1\| = \|m_2\|$. Hence, the set $Imb(\mathcal{A})$ is finite. Let:

1. $Q^c = \{p \in Q \times Q \mid \exists \langle m_1, m_2 \rangle \neq \langle e, e \rangle (\langle p, \langle m_1, m_2 \rangle, p \rangle \in \Delta_2^*)\}$.
2. $Q^r = \{p \in (Q \times Q) \setminus Q^c \mid \exists \langle m_1, m_2 \rangle \exists q \in Q^c (\langle p, \langle m_1, m_2 \rangle, q \rangle \in \Delta_2^*)\}$.
3. $Q^- = (Q \times Q) \setminus (Q^c \cup Q^r)$.

For each state, $p \in Q^c \cup Q^r$ we prove that $|Adm(p)| \leq |Imb(\mathcal{A})|$. To this end, we first consider a state $p \in Q^c \cup Q^r$ and show that for $\langle x_1, x_2 \rangle, \langle y_1, y_2 \rangle \in Adm(p)$:

$$\|x_1\| - \|x_2\| = \|y_1\| - \|y_2\| \Rightarrow \langle x_1, x_2 \rangle = \langle y_1, y_2 \rangle. \quad (2)$$

First consider the case $p \in Q^c$. Let $\langle p, \langle m_1, m_2 \rangle, p \rangle \in \Delta_2^*$ with $\langle m_1, m_2 \rangle \neq \langle e, e \rangle$. Therefore by the Twinning Property we have that $x_1 = e$ or $x_2 = e$ and further for every n:

$$\langle x_1, x_2 \rangle = \langle \rho(x_1 m_1^n, x_2 m_2^n), \rho(x_2 m_2^n, x_1 m_1^n) \rangle.$$

W.l.o.g. we assume $x_2 = e$. Thus $x_2 m_2^n = m_2^n$ and $x_1 m_1^n = m_2^n \rho(x_1 u_1^n, m_2^n)$. Now for n big enough we have that $\|x_1\| \leq n\|m_2\|$ and by Proposition 2 Point 2 we get that $m_2^n = x_1 c$ for some c. Since $\|y_1\| - \|y_2\| = \|x_1\| - \|x_2\|$ and $\|x_2\| = 0$, we get $y_2 = e$ and $\|y_1\| = \|x_1\|$ and as above we get that $m_2^n = y_1 d$ for some d. Hence, $x_1 c = y_1 d$ and by $\|x_1\| = \|y_1\|$ and Proposition 2 Point 2 we get $x_1 = y_1$. Next, let $p \in Q^r$, $q \in Q^c$ and $\langle p, \langle u_1, u_2\rangle, q\rangle \in \Delta_2^*$. By the above discussion:

$$z_1 = \rho(x_1 u_1, x_2 u_2) = \rho(y_1 u_1, y_2 u_2) \text{ and } z_2 = \rho(x_2 u_2, x_1 u_1) = \rho(y_2 u_2, y_1 u_1).$$

Now, since $\langle z_1, z_2\rangle \in Adm(q)$ and $q \in Q^c$ we deduce that $z_1 = e$ or $z_2 = e$. Since $x_1 \sqcap x_2 = e$, by Condition 1 we get $x_1 = e$ or $x_2 = e$ and similarly, $y_1 = e$ or $y_2 = e$. W.l.o.g. assume that $x_2 = e$. Therefore $x_1 u_1 z_1 = u_2 z_2$. $\|y_1\| - \|y_2\| = \|x_1\| - \|x_2\|$ we deduce that $y_2 = e$ and $\|y_1\| = \|x_1\|$. Hence, $x_1 u_1 z_1 = u_2 z_2 = y_1 u_1 z_1$ and by Proposition 2, Point 1 we get that $x_1 = y_1$.

1. If $p \in Q^c \cup Q^r$, since $\|x_1\| - \|x_2\| \in Imb(\mathcal{A})$ for any admissible pair $\langle x_1, x_2\rangle \in Adm(p)$, Eq. 2 we get that $|Adm(p)| \leq |Imb(\mathcal{A})|$.
2. Let $p \in Q^-$. Let $\Pi(p)$ be the set of paths in $\mathcal{A}^2$ that start in $Q \times Q$, use only states from Q^- as inner states, and terminate in p. We prove that:

$$\Lambda(p) = \{label(\pi) \mid \pi \in \Pi(p)\}$$

is finite. Indeed, consider an arbitrary path $\pi \in \Pi(p)$. Clearly, if π contains a cycle $\langle q, \langle m_1, m_2\rangle, q\rangle \in \Delta_2^+$ then $m_1 = e = m_2$. Thus, removing the cycle $\langle q, \langle m_1, m_2\rangle, q\rangle \in \Delta_2^+$ from π would not change the label of π. Therefore, the label of π is the same as the label of some path in $\Pi(p)$ without cycles. We conclude that $\Lambda(p)$ is finite. Now, it is easy to see that:

$$Adm(p) \subseteq \{\langle \rho(u_1, u_2), \rho(u_2, u_1)\rangle \mid \langle u_1, u_2\rangle \in \Lambda(p)\} \cup \bigcup_{\substack{\langle v_1, v_2\rangle \in \Lambda(p) \\ q \in Q^c \cup Q^r}} \{\langle \rho(u_1 v_1, u_2 v_2), \rho(u_2 v_2, u_1 v_1)\rangle \mid \langle u_1, u_2\rangle \in Adm(q)\}$$

Now $\Lambda(p)$ and $Adm(q)$ for $q \in Q^c \cup Q^r$ are finite. Hence $Adm(p)$ is finite.

Since $Red(\mathcal{A}) = \cup_{p \in Q \times Q} Adm(p)$ we obtain that $Red(\mathcal{A})$ is finite. □

Proof (of Theorem 3 (Idea)). We can test the accessible states p in $\mathcal{A}$ for cycles $\langle p, \langle m_1, m_2\rangle, p\rangle$ with $\|m_1\| - \|m_2\| \neq 0$. If some state fails the test, then $\mathcal{A}$ is not of bounded variation. Else we compute $Imb(\mathcal{A})$, Q^c, and Q^r. Now $\mathcal{A}$ is of bounded variation iff $|Adm(p)| \leq |Imb(\mathcal{A})|$ for $p \in Q^c \cup Q^r$ which is decidable.

Theorems 2 and 3 can be extended to the case of Cartesian product of finitely many sequentiable structures. To this end, we use the following technical lemma:

Lemma 3 *Let $\mathcal{M} = \prod_{i=1}^n \mathcal{M}_i$ be the Cartesian product of the sequentiable structures $\mathcal{M}_i$. Let $\mathcal{A}_i$ denote the restriction*[3] *of $\mathcal{A}$ to $\Sigma \times \mathcal{M}_i$. Then:*

[3] That is we ignore the output produced by $\mathcal{M}_j$ for $j \neq i$.

1. *$\mathcal{A}$ is of bounded variation iff each $\mathcal{A}_i$ is of bounded variation.*
2. *$\mathcal{A}$ has the Twinning Property iff each $\mathcal{A}_i$ has the Twinning Property.*
3. *$Red_1(\mathcal{A}) \subseteq \prod_{i=1}^{l} Red_1(\mathcal{A}_i)$.*

Corollary 1. *If $\mathcal{M} = \prod_{i=1}^{n} \mathcal{M}_i$ is Cartesian product of sequentiable structures, then $\mathcal{A}$ has the bounded variation property iff the construction of $\mathcal{T}'$ terminates.*

Proof. The states of $\mathcal{T}'$ are subsets of $Q \times \prod_{i=1}^{n} Red_1(\mathcal{A}_i)$. Now, if $\mathcal{A}$ is of bounded variation, so are $\mathcal{A}_i$ and by Lemma 2 $Red_1(\mathcal{A}_i)$ are finite. Thus, the construction of $\mathcal{T}'$ terminates. The reverse implication follows by Proposition 3.

Corollary 2. *Let $\mathcal{M} = \prod_{i=1}^{n} \mathcal{M}_i$ be a Cartesian product of sequentiable structures. Then, it is decidable whether $\mathcal{A}$ has the bounded variation property.*

Proof. This follows immediately by Corollary 1, Theorem 3 and Lemma 3. □

6 Discussion and Conclusion

In the paper we have introduced the sequentiable and pre-sequentiable structures, for which the transducer determinization procedure is applicable. Furthermore we have generalized and formally proved the results of Choffrut [2] for characterizing the rational functions, which permit input determinization and shown the decidability of this characterization for the general case of functions over sequentiable structures. At the end we have formally proved the statement of Mohri [7] about input determinization for the more general case of rational functions over the Cartesian product of sequentiable structures.

The shuffle structure shown in Example 2 illustrates a non-trivial sequentiable structure for which the results can be used.

Two questions remain: can the results be obtained for a pre-sequentiable structure, which does not satisfy the condition in Definition 5 and how does the presented generalization relates to the one presented in [3]?

References

1. Béal, M.P., Carton, O., Prieur, C., Sakarovitch, J.: Squaring transducers: an efficient procedure for deciding functionality and sequentiality. Theoret. Comput. Sci. **292**(1), 45–63 (2003)
2. Choffrut, C.: Une caractérisation des fonctions séquentielles et des fonctions sous-séquentielles en tant que relations rationelles. Theoret. Comput. Sci. **5**, 325–338 (1977)
3. Daviaud, L., Reynier, P.A., Talbot, J.M.: A generalised twinning property for minimisation of cost register automata. In: Proceedings - Symposium on Logic in Computer Science, pp. 857–866 (2016)
4. Hopcroft, J.E., Motwani, R., Ullman, J.D.: Introduction to Automata Theory, Languages, and Computation, 2nd edn. Addison-Wesley, Reading (2001)
5. Lombardy, S., Sakarovitch, J.: Sequential? Theoret. Comput. Sci. **356**(1–2), 224–244 (2006)

6. Mohri, M.: On some applications of finite-state automata theory to natural language processing. J. Nat. Lang. Eng. **2**, 1–20 (1996)
7. Mohri, M.: Finite-state transducers in language and speech processing. Comput. Linguist. **23**(2), 269–311 (1997)
8. Roche, E., Schabes, Y.: Introduction. In: Roche, E., Schabes, Y. (eds.) Finite-State Language Processing, pp. 1–66. MIT Press, Cambridge (1997)

Color War: Cellular Automata with Majority-Rule

Bernd Gärtner and Ahad N. Zehmakan(✉)

Department of Computer Science, ETH Zurich, Zurich, Switzerland
{gaertner,abdolahad.noori}@inf.ethz.ch

Abstract. Consider a graph $G = (V, E)$ and a random initial vertex-coloring such that each vertex is blue independently with probability $p_b \leq 1/2$, and red otherwise. In each step, all vertices change their current color synchronously to the most frequent color in their neighborhood (in the case of a tie, a vertex conserves its current color). We are interested in the behavior of this very natural process, especially in 2-dimensional grids and tori (cellular automata with majority rule). In the present paper, as a main result we prove that a grid $G_{n,n}$ or a torus $T_{n,n}$ with 4-neighborhood (8-neighborhood) exhibits a threshold behavior: with high probability, it reaches a red monochromatic configuration in a constant number of steps if $p_b \ll n^{-\frac{1}{2}}$ ($p_b \ll n^{-\frac{1}{6}}$), but $p_b \gg n^{-\frac{1}{2}}$ ($p_b \gg n^{-\frac{1}{6}}$) results in a bichromatic period of configurations of length one or two, after at most $2n^2$ ($4n^2$) steps with high probability.

Keywords: Cellular automata · Majority rule · Color war

1 Introduction

Suppose that in a community, people have different opinions on a topic of common interest. Through social interactions, individuals learn about the opinions of others, and as a result may change their own opinion. The goal is to understand and possibly predict how opinions spread in the community. There are numerous mathematical models for such a situation; a very simple deterministic one is the following: the community is modeled as a graph, with edges corresponding to possible interactions between individuals. Opinions spread in rounds, where in each round, each individual adopts the most frequent opinion in its neighborhood, and stays with its opinion in case of a tie. This natural updating rule is called the *majority rule* and has various applications, for example in data redundancy [18], distributed computing [19], modeling biological interactions [3], resource allocation for ensuring mutual exclusion [18], distributed fault-local mending [18], and modeling diffusion of two competing technologies over a social network [5].

Scientists from different fields, from Spitzer [24] to a recent paper by Mitsche et al. [13], have attempted to study the behavior of this natural updating rule, especially on two-dimensional grids and tori where the majority rule can be interpreted

F. Drewes et al. (Eds.): LATA 2017, LNCS 10168, pp. 393–404, 2017.
DOI: 10.1007/978-3-319-53733-7_29

as a cellular automaton. Some theoretical and experimental results concerning its behavior have been obtained (we discuss them in detail in Sect. 1.2); of particular interest is the *consensus time*, the time after which the process reaches a periodic sequence of states (which must eventually happen, as the process is deterministic and has finite state space). Also, one would like to understand how these "final" states looks like, depending on the initial distribution of opinions. For example, what are conditions under which some opinion is eventually taken up by all the individuals?

In this paper, we first present some results in general graphs $G = (V, E)$, regarding consensus time and robust sets (sets of nodes that will never change an opinion that they have in common). Building on them, our main contribution is for the cases where G is an $n \times n$ grid or torus, with 4-neighborhoods, or with 8-neighborhoods.

We study the case of two opinions (modeled by vertex colors blue and red), with an initial coloring that assigns blue (the minority opinion) to every vertex independently with a fixed probability $p_b = p_b(n) \leq 1/2$. We prove that there exists a threshold $p = p(n)$ satisfying the following with high probability: (i) if $p_b \ll p$, all vertices will become red within a constant number of steps; (ii) if $p_b \gg p$, the process becomes periodic (of period one or two) within $O(n^2)$ steps, and with bichromatic colorings. The bound of $O(n^2)$ is best possible, and both periods one or two may occur. We also determine the threshold p and find that it is of the form $p(n) = n^{-2/r}$, where r is the size of the smallest robust set.

We therefore have a classification of the following form (with high probability): If the minority opinion (blue) has initial popularity asymptotically less than p, it will quickly disappear completely. However, if its initial popularity asymptotically exceeds p, then both opinions will survive in the long run. In most cases, the majority rule will therefore not eliminate the minority opinion. However, it does so when the minority opinion is sufficiently unpopular to begin with.

As we discuss in Sect. 1.2, prior empirical research [12,14,16,17,23] suggest that majority cellular automata should show a threshold behavior, and the main contribution of the present paper is proving these empirical observations are true and determining the threshold, periodicity, and consensus time of the process precisely. But, the more surprising part is changing the tie breaking rule can change the behavior of the majority model considerably. As we will discuss later on, Schonmann [22] proved that in biased majority cellular automata (the same as a majority cellular automata except in the case of a tie, a vertex always adopts blue color) in a torus $T_{n,n}$ with 4-neighborhood $p_b \gg 1/\sqrt{\log n}$ results in final complete occupancy by blue color with high probability. Therefore, in majority cellular automata, p_b should be very close to 1 ($p_r \ll n^{-1/2}$) to guarantee a high chance of final complete occupancy by blue, but by just changing the tie breaking rule in favor of blue, the process ends up in a blue monochromatic configuration with high probability even for initial concentration very close to 0 ($p_b \gg 1/\sqrt{\log n}$). Hence, it not only a kind of shows the power and significant impact of tie breaking rule, but also demonstrates how very minor alternations in local behavior can result in considerable changes in global behaviors.

To prove that majority cellular automaton has a threshold behavior, we show there exists a blue and a red robust set (a robust set whose all vertices are blue (red)) in starting configuration with high probability for $p_b \gg n^{-1/2}$ ($p_b \gg n^{-1/6}$ in Moore neighborhood) which result in the survival of both colors, but proving $p_b \ll n^{-1/2}$ (similarly $p_b \ll n^{-1/6}$ in Moore) results in a red monochromatic configuration is more difficult. We show in this situation in one of the first a few generations of the process, the blue cells can be classified such that all blue cells in a cluster behave independently of all other blue cells, and the number of blue cells in none of these cluster is sufficient for survival and they will die eventually (actually, after some constant number of steps). As we will discuss in more detail, this proof technique requires more technical arguments in the case of Moore neighborhood because of switching from 4-neighborhood model to 8-neighborhood model.

The layout of the paper is as follows. In the rest of this section, first we introduce our majority model (which we call color war) formally. Then, in Sect. 1.2 we briefly discuss relevant prior research works. In Sect. 2, we discuss the consensus time and periodicity of color war on an arbitrary graph $G(V, E)$ and present sufficient condition for a graph to reach a cycle of bichromatic generations in color war with high probability. Then, in Sect. 3, we focus on two-dimensional grids and tori (majority cellular automata), and it is proved there is a phase transition.

1.1 Notation, Preliminaries, and Color War Model

Let $G = (V, E)$ be a graph that we keep fixed throughout. For a vertex $v \in V$, $N(v) := \{u \in V : \{v, u\} \in E\}$ is the *neighborhood* of v. We also define $\hat{N}(v) := N(v) \cup \{v\}$. Furthermore, for a set $S \subseteq V$, $N_S(v) := N(v) \cap S$ and $N(S) := \bigcup_{v \in S} N(v)$.

A *generation* is a function $g : V \rightarrow \{b, r\}$ (b and r represent blue and red, respectively). If g is a constant function, g is called a *monochromatic* generation otherwise it is called a *bichromatic* generation. $S \subseteq V$ is a *c-community* in generation g if $\forall v \in S$ $g(v) = c$ for color c. For a generation g, vertex $v \in V$ and color $c \in \{b, r\}$, $N_c^g(v) := \{u \in N(v) : g(u) = c\}$ is the set of neighbors of v of color c in generation g. We also define $\hat{N}_c^g(v) := \{u \in \hat{N}(v) : g(u) = c\}$. For a set $S \subseteq V$, we define $N_c^g(S) := \{v \in N(S) : g(u) = c\}$.

In addition to $g(v) = c$ for a vertex $v \in V$ and $c \in \{b, r\}$, sometimes we also write $g|_S = c$ for a set $S \subseteq V$ which means $\forall v \in S$, $g(v) = c$.

Given an initial generation g_0 such that $\forall v \in V$, $Pr[g_0(v) = b] = p_b$ and $Pr[g_0(v) = r] = p_r$ independently of all other vertices, and $p_b + p_r = 1$. Assume $\forall i \geq 1$ and $v \in V$, $g_i(v)$ is equal to the color that occurs most frequently in v's neighborhood in g_{i-1}, and in the case of a tie, v conserves its current color. More formally:

$$g_i(v) = \begin{cases} g_{i-1}(v), & \text{if } |N_b^{g_{i-1}}(v)| = |N_r^{g_{i-1}}(v)|, \\ argmin_{c \in \{b,r\}} |N_c^{g_{i-1}}(v)|, & \text{otherwise} \end{cases}$$

In the present paper, we discuss the behavior of this deterministic process with a random initial coloring which is called *Color War*.

Remark 1. For a graph $G(V, E)$, we say an event happens with high probability if its probability is at least $1 - o(1)$ as a function of $|V|$.

1.2 Prior Works

As mentioned, Majority-voting rule has been studied in different literatures because of its importance and applications. Therefore, based on different motivations and from a wide spectrum of approaches, various definitions of majority rule have been presented, but in general we may classify them into the three following categories.

The first class is the r-monotone model in which, at each step a vertex becomes blue if at least r of its neighbors are blue, and once blue no cell ever becomes red (in the literature this is also known as *bootstrap percolation*). For example, in [2,7], the authors discussed the case of $r = \frac{d(v)}{2}$ (such that $d(v)$ is the degree of vertex v) on hypercubes and planar graphs, respectively. Recently, Koch and Lengler [11] mathematically analyzed the role of geometry on bootstrap percolation for geometric scale-free networks. Einarsson et al. [4] also showed that tiny changes in the size of the starting blue set can dramatically influence the size of the final blue set.

The second one is the *r-threshold model* in which, at each step, a vertex becomes blue if at least r of its neighbors are blue, otherwise it becomes red. For instance, Schonmann [22] considered the state of $r = \frac{d(v)}{2}$ (tie is in the favor of blue), and he showed that for any initial density of blue vertices in a grid, the probability of final complete occupancy by blue converges to 1 as the grid grows. Fazli et al. [5] also discussed the same model while it seems they were not aware that this model was presented (probably for the first time) in [22]. They presented some thresholds regarding the minimum-cardinality of an initial set of blue nodes which would eventually converge to the steady state where all nodes are blue. In addition, Moore [15] surprisingly showed that in d-dimensional grid for $d \geq 3$ this model can simulate Boolean circuits of AND and OR gates.

Another model is the random r-threshold model such that a vertex takes the value that the r-threshold model would give with probability $1 - p$ and its complement with probability p. For instance, Balister et al. [1] considered the case of $r = \frac{d(v)}{2}$ on 2-dimensional grids. They showed that if p is sufficiently small, then the process spends almost half of its time in each of two generations (all vertices blue or all red).

Color war is a subcategory of *r-threshold model*, and a main idea of that was considered by Gray [10] while similar models were considered much earlier (Spitzer [24] in 1970). Most of the research regarding color war, especially majority cellular automata are by physicists [12,14,16,17,23], and they mostly do computer simulations (i.e., Monte-Carlo methods) and as discussed, their computer simulations show a phase transition behavior characterized by a large connected component of vertices holding the same color appearing when the concentrations of vertices holding the same color (even minority) is above a certain threshold.

It seems the lack of strong mathematical results in this case probably is due to the inherent difficulty of proving anything about them. However, Poljak and Turzik [21] presented an upper bound on the consensus time for a graph $G(V,E)$ and color war W. For instance, this bound implies a 2-dimensional grid $G(V,E)$ needs $O(|V|)$ steps to stabilize. Furthermore, Frischknecht et al. [8] proved there exists graph $G(V,E)$ which needs $\Omega(\frac{|V|^2}{(\log|V|)^2})$ steps to stabilize for some initial colorings in color war.

Different versions of majority updating rule have been discussed in different literatures and from various aspects for diverse aims, but as mentioned there are just few concrete mathematical results regarding the most natural version (color war). In the present paper, we study some essential and interesting aspects of the behavior of this process and present some strong results regarding its stability. More precisely, we focus on asymptotic behavior of a graph (especially a 2-dimensional grid or torus) with a random initial coloring under color war. As a main result we show that color war is a threshold model (as prior experimental research (for instance see [23]) conjecture). Furthermore, we present sufficient condition (see Theorems 1) for a graph $G(V,E)$ to get bichromatic with high probability in color war W. By utilizing the aforementioned results by Poljak and Turizk [21] and results by Poljak and Sura [20], we present tight bounds on the consensus time and periodicity of the process for an arbitrary graph G.

2 Color War

In this section, first we introduce the basic concept of robustness. Then, by using this concept, we present sufficient condition for a graph $G(V,E)$ to stabilize at a bichromatic configuration in color war with high probability. Furthermore, in Sect. 2.2 we discuss the number of steps which a graph $G(V,E)$ needs to stabilize.

2.1 Bichromatic Stability

As we know, if generation g is a constant function, g is called a *monochromatic* generation, and a set $S \subseteq V$ is a c-community in generation g for color c if $g|_S = c$. We are interested in sets of vertices that will keep a common color forever when they create a community, regardless of the colors of the other vertices in color war W.

Definition 1. *Let $S \subseteq V$ in a graph $G(V,E)$. S is called robust in color war W whenever the following holds: if S forms a c-community for a color c and in some generation g_i for $i \geq 0$, then $g_j|_S = g_i|_S = c$ for all generations g_j $\forall j \geq i$ that might arise using the rules of W.*

It follows that once a robust set forms a c-community, it will remain a c-community forever.

Definition 2. *A blue (red) robust set in a generation g means a robust set which is a b-community (r-community) in g.*

Obviously, the definition of a blue (red) robust set S in generation g_i implies that $g_j|_S$ is blue (red) for all generations g_j $\forall j \geq i$ that might arise using the rules of color war W.

Now, we discuss an interesting theorem which present sufficient condition for an arbitrary graph $G(V, E)$ to get bichromatic with high probability in color war W. We exploit this proposition just for grid and torus in this article, but obviously it is applicable to every arbitrary graph.

Definition 3. *For a graph $G(V, E)$, an induced subgraph $G'(V', E')$ is called a robust subgraph in color war if V' is a robust set.*

Assume for a graph $G(V = \{v_i : 1 \leq i \leq n\}, E)$, $G'_j(V'_j, E'_j)$ $\forall$ $1 \leq j \leq k$ are k robust subgraphs; then, we define $s := \max_{1 \leq j \leq k}(|V'_j|)$. Theorem 1 says if there are $k = \omega(p_b^{-s})$ disjoint robust subgraphs in a graph $G(V, E)$, then with high probability color war reaches a cycle of bichromatic generations.

Theorem 1. *For a graph $G(V, E)$, if $G'_j(V'_j, E'_j)$ $\forall$ $1 \leq j \leq k$ are disjoint robust subgraphs, then $Pr[Bichromatic] \geq 1 - 2\exp(-kp_b^s/2)$.*

Proof. We define k random variables x_j such that for $1 \leq j \leq k/2$, x_j is 1 if and only if $g_0|_{V'_j} = b$ and for $\frac{k}{2} + 1 \leq j \leq k$, x_j is 1 if and only if $g_0|_{V'_j} = r$ such that $Pr[x_j = 1] = p_b^{|V'_j|}$ for $1 \leq j \leq \frac{k}{2}$ and $Pr[x_j = 1] = p_r^{|V'_j|}$ for $\frac{k}{2} + 1 \leq j \leq k$. Therefore, if $X_1 \geq 1$ and $X_2 \geq 1$ such that $X_1 = \sum_{i=1}^{\frac{k}{2}} x_i$ and $X_2 = \sum_{j=\frac{k}{2}+1}^{k} x_j$, then color war does not get monochromatic because there is at least a blue robust set and a red robust set in g_0. We show $Pr[X_1 = 0] \leq \exp(-p_b^s k/2)$ and $Pr[X_2 = 0] \leq \exp(-p_r^s k/2)$, then by considering $p_b \leq p_r$, $Pr[\text{Bichromatic}] \geq 1 - 2\exp(-p_b^s k/2)$.

X_1 is the summation of $\frac{k}{2}$ independent Bernoulli random variables, then $Pr[X_1 = 0] \leq (1 - p_b^s)^{\frac{k}{2}} \leq e^{-p_b^s k/2}$, and similarly $Pr[X_2 = 0] \leq (1 - p_r^s)^{\frac{k}{2}} \leq e^{-p_r^s k/2}$. □

2.2 Periodicity and Consensus Time

As we know, for a graph $G(V, E)$ and color war W, the number of possible generations is $2^{|V|}$, and color war is a deterministic process; therefore, the process always reaches a cycle of generations after a finite number of steps and stays there forever, but there are two natural questions which may come up. What is the length of the cycle and how long it takes to reach it?

Goles and Olivos [9], and independently, Poljak and Sura [20] proved that a large class of majority-based models, including color war, always reach a cycle of period one or two. Formally, a specialized version of their result can be presented as Theorem 2.

Theorem 2. *In color war, an arbitrary graph $G(V, E)$ (from any initial coloring) always reaches a cycle of generations of length one or two.*

As mentioned, we are also interested in the consensus time of the process, and it is trivial that it is at most $2^{|V|}$. However, Poljak and Turzik [21] proved a very strong proposition in the literature of cyclically monotonous mappings and symmetric matrices such that a specialized version (restated for our situation) of their result can be presented as Theorem 3.

Theorem 3. *For a graph $G(V, E)$ and color war W, consensus time is at most $\frac{1}{2}(\sum_{v \in V} d(v) + 3s)$ such that s is the number of vertices with odd degree. ($d(v)$ is the degree of vertex $v \in V$)*

Corollary 1. *For a graph $G(V, E)$ with all degrees even, the consensus time is at most $\frac{1}{2} \sum_{v \in V} d(v)$.*

Corollary 2. *For an arbitrary graph $G(V, E)$, the consensus time is at most $\frac{\Delta+3}{2}|V|$. ($\Delta := \max_{v \in V} d(v)$)*

3 Color War in Grid and Torus: Majority Cellular Automaton

In this section, by utilizing some results from Sects. 2.1 and 2.2, it is proved that color war on a torus and a two-dimensional grid is a threshold model.

3.1 Preliminaries

Definition 4. *The* Grid $G_{n,n}$ *is a graph $G(V, E)$ with $V = \{(i,j) : 1 \leq i, j \leq n\}$ and $E = \{((i,j),(i',j')) : |i - i'| + |j - j'| = 1\}$.*

Definition 5. Torus $T_{n,n}$ *is a graph $G(V, E)$ with $V = \{(i,j) : 1 \leq i, j \leq n\}$ and $E = \{((i,j),(i',j')) : |i - i'| + |j - j'| = 1\} \cup \{((1,i),(n,i)),((j,1),(j,n))\}$.*

A *Torus* $T_{n,n}$ is a wrap-around version of a grid $G_{n,n}$ which can be visualized as taping the left and right edges of the rectangle to form a tube, then taping the top and bottom edges of the tube to form a torus (See Fig. 1(b)). The aforementioned definitions of grid and torus follow a neighborhood model which is called Neumann neighborhood or 4-neighborhoods (see Fig. 1(a)). On the other hand, there is another common neighborhood model which is called Moore model (see Fig. 1(a)), and in a torus or grid (by skipping the borders), each cell (we sometimes use the term of *cell* instead of vertex in grids and tori) instead of four neighbors has eight neighbors.

In Fig. 1(c) and (d), you can see a robust set in a torus $T_{n,n}$ respectively with Moore and Neumann neighborhood. Actually, they are the smallest robust sets i.e. the size of the smallest roust set in Moore and Neumann neighborhood are equal to 12 and 4, respectively. One can show in a torus $T_{n,n}$, $p_b = n^{-1/r}$, where r is the size of the smallest robust set, is a threshold for having a constant-size

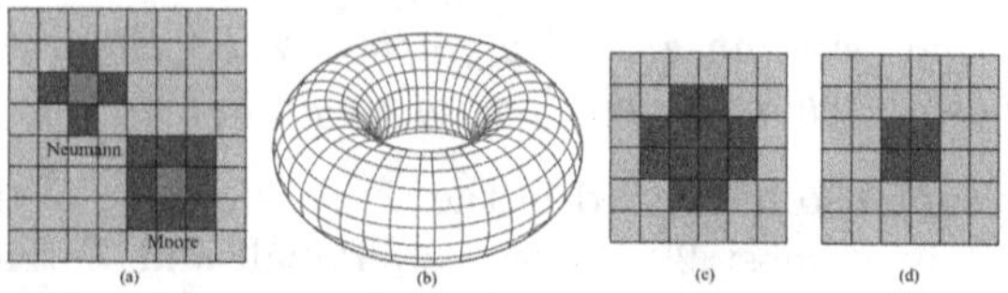

Fig. 1. (a) Neumann and Moore neighborhoods in a grid $G_{8\times 8}$ (b) a torus (c) the smallest robust set: Moore (d) Neumann (Color figure inline)

blue robust set. Surprisingly, in the rest of the paper we prove that it is also a threshold value for getting monochromatic or bichromatic. Therefore, as we discussed briefly before, the size of the smallest robust plays a key role in the behavior of the process.

3.2 Threshold Model

In this section, we prove in color war a torus $T_{n,n}$ with both Moore and Neumann neighborhood shows a threshold behavior.

Definition 6. *For a grid $G_{n,n}$ or torus $T_{n,n}$, $L_{j,b}$ ($L_{j,r}$) is the size of the largest blue (red) cluster in generation g_j for $j \geq 0$ such that a cluster is a connected subgraph by considering Moore neighborhood.*

Notice $L_{j,b}$ ($L_{j,r}$) is defined based on Moore neighborhood even in the case which it is applied to a proposition regarding Neumann neighborhood. In other words, in contrast to Moore neighborhood, in Neumann neighborhood a cluster is not necessarily a connected component.

Lemma 1. *In color war, a torus $T_{n,n}$, Neumann neighborhood, and for a generation g_j $j \geq 0$, if $L_{j,b} \leq 3$, then $L_{j+2,b} = 0$.*

Proof. Assume $L_j := L_{j,b}$ and $L_{j+1} := L_{j+1,b}$ (notice $L_{j,b}$ is defined based on Moore neighborhood). First we prove if $L_j = 1$, then $L_{j+1} = 0$. To prove, assume $L_j = 1$ can result in $L_{j+1} = 1$ i.e. there exists a cell c_1 such that $g_{j+1}(c_1) = b$. We show $L_{j+1} = 1$ contradicts $L_j = 1$. $g_j(c_1) = r$ because a blue cell for staying blue in g_{j+1} needs at least two blue cells in its neighborhood in g_j which contradicts $L_j = 1$. $g_j(c_1) = r$ implies that $|N_b^{g_j}(c_1)| \geq 3$, and $|N_b^{g_j}(c_1)| \geq 3$ results in the existence of at least a blue cluster of size 2 in c_1's neighborhood in g_j which contradicts $L_j = 1$.

Now, it is proved that if $L_j = 2$ or 3, then $L_{j+1} \leq 1$ i.e. blue clusters of size 3 or smaller cannot create a blue cluster of size larger than 1. It is enough to prove $L_{j+1} = 2$ implies $L_j \geq 4$. Assume, there exits a blue cluster S of size 2 in generation g_{j+1}. S can have two different structures which are shown in Fig. 2 (notice a torus is symmetric).

For the first structure $S = \{c_6, c_7\}$, we have three states:

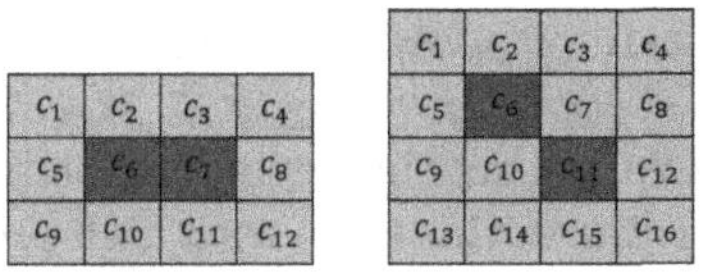

Fig. 2. Two possible structures for a cluster of size 2 (Color figure inline)

(i) if $g_j(c_6) = g_j(c_7) = b$, then c_6 for staying blue in g_{j+1} needs at least a blue cell among $\{c_2, c_5, c_{10}\}$ in g_j and c_7 needs at least a blue cell among $\{c_3, c_8, c_{11}\}$ which result in $L_j \geq 4$.
(ii) if $g_j(c_6) = b$ and $g_j(c_7) = r$ (or similarly $g_j(c_6) = r$ and $g_j(c_7) = b$), then c_7 for getting blue in g_{j+1} needs at least two blue cells among $\{c_3, c_8, c_{11}\}$ in g_j, and c_6 needs at least one blue cell among $\{c_2, c_5, c_{10}\}$ which imply $L_j \geq 4$.
(iii) if $g_j(c_6) = g_j(c_7) = r$, then $g_{j+1}|_{\{c_6,c_7\}} = b$ implies $g_j|_{\{c_2,c_3,c_5,c_8,c_{10},c_{11}\}} = b$ which means $L_j \geq 4$.

For the second structure, also there are three possibilities:

(i) if $g_j(c_6) = g_j(c_{11}) = b$, then c_6, for staying blue in g_{j+1}, needs at least two blue cells among $\{c_2, c_5, c_7, c_{10}\}$ in g_j which implies $L_j \geq 4$.
(ii) if $g_j(c_6) = b$ and $g_j(c_{11}) = r$ (or similarly $g_j(c_6) = r$ and $g_j(c_{11}) = b$), then c_{11}, for getting blue in g_{j+1}, needs at least three blue cells among its neighbors ($\{c_7, c_{10}, c_{12}, c_{15}\}$) in g_j which implies $L_j \geq 4$ again.
(iii) if $g_j(c_6) = g_j(c_{11}) = r$, then $g_{j+1}|_{\{c_6,c_{11}\}} = b$ implies that three cells in $\{c_2, c_5, c_7, c_{10}\}$ and three cells in $\{c_7, c_{10}, c_{12}, c_{15}\}$ are blue in g_j which mean that $L_j \geq 4$.

Therefore, $L_{j+1} = 2$ implies $L_j \geq 4$ which means $L_j \leq 3$ results in $L_{j+1} \leq 1$. Furthermore, we proved $L_j = 1$ outputs $L_{j+1} = 0$. Then, $L_j \leq 3$ provides $L_{j+2} = 0$. □

Corollary 3. *In a torus $T_{n,n}(V, E)$ with Neumann neighborhoods and a generation g_j, if $L_{j,b} \leq 3$, then generation g_{j+2} is red monochromatic.*

Theorem 4. *In color war and a torus $T_{n,n}(V, E)$ with Neumann neighborhood, $p_b \ll n^{-\frac{1}{2}}$ results in a red monochromatic generation in at most 2 steps, but $p_b \gg n^{-\frac{1}{2}}$ outputs a cycle of bichromatic generations of size one or two in at most $2n^2$ steps with high probability.*

Proof. First consider the case of $p_b \ll n^{-\frac{1}{2}}$ in torus $T_{n,n}$ with Neumann neighborhood. Let random variable X be the number of blue clusters of size 4. We claim $E[X] = o(1)$, then by Markov's inequality [6] with the probability of $1 - o(1)$, $L_{0,b} \leq 3$. Based on Corollary 3, $g_2|_V = r$ i.e. g_2 is red monochromatic. Then, it is enough to show that $E[X] = o(1)$. Since the number of clusters of size 4 in T is $\theta(n^2)$, $E[X] = \theta(n^2).p_b^4 = o(1)$.

Now, we discuss the state of $p_b \gg n^{-\frac{1}{2}}$. Consider $\forall 1 \leq i' \leq \lfloor \frac{n}{2} \rfloor$ and $\forall 1 \leq j' \leq \lfloor \frac{n}{2} \rfloor$ we have $S_{i',j'} = \{(i,j)|2i'-1 \leq i \leq 2i' \wedge 2j'-1 \leq j \leq 2j'\}$ (see Fig. 1(d)) as $\lfloor \frac{n}{2} \rfloor^2$ disjoint robust sets in Neumann neighborhood and torus $T_{n,n}$. Based on Theorem 1, color war in this state with high probability reaches a cycle of bichromatic generations. Actually, by utilizing Theorem 2 and Corollary 1, we can say it reaches a cycle of bichromatic generations of size one or two in at most $2n^2$ steps. □

Theorem 5. *In color war and a torus $T_{n,n}(V,E)$ with Moore neighborhood, $p_b \ll n^{-\frac{1}{6}}$ results in a red monochromatic generation in constant number of steps, but $p_b \gg n^{-\frac{1}{6}}$ outputs a cycle of bichromatic generations of size one or two in at most $4n^2$ steps with high probability.*

Proof. First, we discuss the case of $p_b \gg n^{-\frac{1}{6}}$. Consider $\forall 1 \leq i' \leq \lfloor \frac{n}{4} \rfloor$ and $\forall 1 \leq j' \leq \lfloor \frac{n}{4} \rfloor$ we have $S_{i',j'} = \{(i,j)|4(i'-1)+1 \leq i \leq 4i' \wedge 4(j'-1)+1 \leq j \leq 4j'\} \setminus \{(i,j)|i \in \{4i', 4i'-3\} \wedge j \in \{4j', 4j'-3\}\}$ (see Fig. 1(c)) as $\lfloor \frac{n}{4} \rfloor^2$ disjoint robust sets in Moore neighborhood and torus $T_{n,n}$. Based on Theorem 1, color war in this state reaches a cycle of bichromatic generations with high probability. Actually, by utilizing Theorem 2 and Corollary 1, we can say it reaches a cycle of bichromatic generations of size one or two in at most $4n^2$ steps.

Now, we prove $p_b \ll n^{-\frac{1}{6}}$ outputs a red monochromatic generation in constant number of steps with high probability. Assume for $1 \leq i', j', l_1, l_2 \leq n$, set $R(i',j',l_1,l_2) := \{(i,j) : i' \leq i < i'+l_1 \wedge j' \leq j < j'+l_2\}$ is a rectangle of size $l_1 \times l_2$ in torus $T_{n\times n}$ (notice for $i,j \geq n$, we consider i and j mod n). Let random variable X denote the number of squares of size 23×23 (squares $R(i,j,23,23)$ for $1 \leq i,j \leq n$) in torus $T_{n\times n}$ which include more than 11 blue vertices in g_0. Therefore:

$$E[X] \leq \theta(n^2). \sum_{i=12}^{23^2} \binom{23^2}{i} p_b^i = \theta(n^2) p_b^{12} \sum_{i=12}^{23^2} \binom{23^2}{i} p_b^{i-12} = o(1)$$

$E[X] = o(1)$ and Markov's Inequality imply that with high probability $X = 0$ i.e. with high probability there is no square of size 23×23 in $T_{n,n}$ which contains more than 11 blue cells in g_0.

Assume for a set $S \subset V$, $R_s := \{R(i,j,l_1,l_2) : 1 \leq i,j,l_1,l_2 \leq n \wedge S \subseteq R(i,j,l_1,l_2))\}$, then we define that rectangle $R \subset V$ is the smallest covering rectangle of S if R is the smallest rectangle which covers S i.e. $R := argmin_{R'(i,j,l_1,l_2) \in R_s} |l_1 * l_2|$. Based on the definition, obviously the smallest covering rectangle for a set S is not necessarily unique. Furthermore, if for two vertices (cells) $u, v \in V$, $d(u,v)$ is the size of the shortest path between u and v in torus $T_{n,n}(V,E)$ with Moore neighborhood, then for two rectangles $R_1, R_2 \subset V$, $d(R_1, R_2) := \min_{u \in R_1, v \in R_2} d(u,v)$. Consider the following process for torus $T_{n,n}$ with initial generation g_0 ($p_b \ll n^{-\frac{1}{6}}$) such that M is the set of the smallest covering rectangles (as we mentioned, the smallest covering rectangle for a set is not necessarily unique, but in this proof considering any smallest covering rectangle for a set works) for all connected blue components in g_0, and for two rectangles R and R', $Combine(R, R')$ denotes the smallest rectangle which covers all blue cells in both R and R'. Now consider the following process which starts with $M' = M$, and while there exist $R, R' \in M'$ such that $d(R, R') \leq 1$, it sets $M' = M' \setminus \{R, R'\} \cup \{Combine(R, R')\}$.

After the aforementioned process, for every rectangle $R \in M'$ of size $l_1 \times l_2$, we have $l_1, l_2 \leq 23$ with high probability because based on the process, $l_1 > 23$ or $l_2 > 23$ implies that there exists a rectangle of size 23×23 which includes more than 11 blue cells in g_0. More precisely, one can show by induction that every rectangle in M' contains at least a blue cell in every two consecutive columns and a blue cell in every two consecutive rows for rows and columns which intersect the rectangle. On the other hand as we proved, with high probability for $p_b \ll n^{-\frac{1}{6}}$, there is no rectangle of size 23×23 which contains more than 11 blue cells. Therefore, after this process, $\forall R, R' \in M'$, the number of blue cells in R is at most 11 and $d(R, R') \geq 2$ i.e. M' covers blue cells in g_0 with rectangles which have at most 11 blue cells inside and the shortest distance between each pair of rectangles is more than 1. Since the distance between each two rectangles is at least two, all cells out of these rectangles stay red in all upcoming generations. Therefore, if we show that 11 blue cells in a rectangle disappear (rectangle gets completely red) after a constant number of steps, then the proof is complete. Because of the page limitation, we do not present the complete proof of this proposition, but the sketch of the proof is as follows. One can show i blue cells are reduced to at most $i - 1$ blue cells in one or two steps for $5 \leq i \leq 11$, and i blue cells disappear in one step for $i = 1, 2, 3, 4$. Therefore, 11 blue cells disappear in a constant number of steps. The proof of i blue cells disappear in one step for $i = 1, 2, 3, 4$ is straightforward, and for the proof of i blue cells are reduced to at most $i-1$ blue cells in one or two steps for $5 \leq i \leq 11$, we assume i blue cells can create a set S of size more than $i-1$ blue cells in the next step and consider the smallest covering rectangle around this blue set, which implies the leftmost (rightmost) column and highest (lowest) row of the rectangle contain at least one blue cell in S. Now, depending on the size of the rectangle, one can check that always there are some blue cells in S which need at least $i + 1$ blue cells in previous step to become blue which contradicts the assumption. □

We claim that all aforementioned results also can be extended into the case of a grid $G_{n,n}$ instead of a torus $T_{n,n}$ and also the case of $\hat{N}(v)$ neighborhood model instead of $N(v)$.

References

1. Balister, P., Bollobás, B., Johnson, J.R., Walters, M.: Random majority percolation. Random Struct. Algorithms **36**(3), 315–340 (2010)
2. Balogh, J., Bollobás, B., Morris, R.: Majority bootstrap percolation on the hypercube. Comb. Probab. Comput. **18**(1–2), 17–51 (2009)
3. Cardelli, L., Csikász-Nagy, A.: The cell cycle switch computes approximate majority. Sci. Rep. **2** (2012)
4. Einarsson, H., Lengler, J., Panagiotou, K., Mousset, F., Steger, A.: Bootstrap percolation with inhibition. arXiv preprint arXiv:1410.3291 (2014)

5. Fazli, M., Ghodsi, M., Habibi, J., Jalaly, P., Mirrokni, V., Sadeghian, S.: On non-progressive spread of influence through social networks. Theoret. Comput. Sci. **550**, 36–50 (2014)
6. Feller, W.: An Introduction to Probability Theory and its Applications: Volume I, vol. 3. Wiley, London (1968)
7. Flocchini, P., Královič, R., Ružička, P., Roncato, A., Santoro, N.: On time versus size for monotone dynamic monopolies in regular topologies. J. Discret. Algorithms **1**(2), 129–150 (2003)
8. Frischknecht, S., Keller, B., Wattenhofer, R.: Convergence in (social) influence networks. In: Afek, Y. (ed.) DISC 2013. LNCS, vol. 8205, pp. 433–446. Springer, Heidelberg (2013). doi:10.1007/978-3-642-41527-2_30
9. Goles, E., Olivos, J.: Comportement périodique des fonctions à seuil binaires et applications. Discret. Appl. Math. **3**(2), 93–105 (1981)
10. Gray, L.: The behavior of processes with statistical mechanical properties. In: Kesten, H. (ed.) Percolation Theory and Ergodic Theory of Infinite Particle Systems, pp. 131–167. Springer, Heidelberg (1987)
11. Koch, C., Lengler, J.: Bootstrap percolation on geometric inhomogeneous random graphs. arXiv preprint arXiv:1603.02057 (2016)
12. Kozma, R., Puljic, M., Balister, P., Bollobás, B., Freeman, W.J.: Phase transitions in the neuropercolation model of neural populations with mixed local and non-local interactions. Biol. Cybern. **92**(6), 367–379 (2005)
13. Mitsche, D., Pérez-Giménez, X., Prałat, P.: Strong-majority bootstrap percolation on regular graphs with low dissemination threshold. arXiv preprint arXiv:1503.08310 (2015)
14. Molofsky, J., Durrett, R., Dushoff, J., Griffeath, D., Levin, S.: Local frequency dependence and global coexistence. Theoret. Popul. Biol. **55**(3), 270–282 (1999)
15. Moore, C.: Majority-vote cellular automata, ising dynamics, and p-completeness. J. Stat. Phys. **88**(3–4), 795–805 (1997)
16. Oliveira, G.M., Martins, L.G., Carvalho, L.B., Fynn, E.: Some investigations about synchronization and density classification tasks in one-dimensional and two-dimensional cellular automata rule spaces. Electron. Notes Theor. Comput. Sci. **252**, 121–142 (2009)
17. de Oliveira, M.J.: Isotropic majority-vote model on a square lattice. J. Stat. Phys. **66**(1–2), 273–281 (1992)
18. Peleg, D.: Local majorities, coalitions and monopolies in graphs: a review. Theor. Comput. Sci. **282**(2), 231–257 (2002)
19. Perron, E., Vasudevan, D., Vojnovic, M.: Using three states for binary consensus on complete graphs. In: INFOCOM 2009, IEEE, pp. 2527–2535. IEEE (2009)
20. Poljak, S., Sura, M.: On periodical behaviour in societies with symmetric influences. Combinatorica **3**(1), 119–121 (1983)
21. Poljak, S., Turzík, D.: On pre-periods of discrete influence systems. Discret. Appl. Math **13**(1), 33–39 (1986)
22. Schonmann, R.H.: Finite size scaling behavior of a biased majority rule cellular automaton. Phys. A: Stat. Mech. Appl. **167**(3), 619–627 (1990)
23. Shao, J., Havlin, S., Stanley, H.E.: Dynamic opinion model and invasion percolation. Phys. Rev. Lett. **103**(1), 018701 (2009)
24. Spitzer, F.: Interaction of markov processes. Adv. Math. **5**, 246–290 (1970)

On the Computational Power of Affine Automata

Mika Hirvensalo[1,4(✉)], Etienne Moutot[2(✉)], and Abuzer Yakaryılmaz[3(✉)]

[1] Department of Mathematics and Statistics, University of Turku, 20014 Turku, Finland
mikhirve@utu.fi

[2] LIP, ENS de Lyon – CNRS – INRIA – UCBL – Université de Lyon, École Normale Supérieure de Lyon, 69007 Lyon, France
etienne.moutot@ens-lyon.org

[3] Faculty of Computing, University of Latvia, Raina Bulv. 19, Riga 1586, Latvia
abuzer@lu.lv

[4] Turku Centre for Computer Science (TUCS), Turku, Finland

Abstract. We investigate the computational power of affine automata (AfAs) introduced in [4]. In particular, we present a simpler proof for how to change the cutpoint for any affine language and a method how to reduce error in bounded error case. Moreover, we address to the question of [4] by showing that any affine language can be recognized by an AfA with certain limitation on the entries of affine states and transition matrices. Lastly, we present the first languages shown to be not recognized by AfAs with bounded-error.

Keywords: Non-classical models of automata · Affine automata · Cutpoint languages · Bounded error · Compact sets · Error reduction

1 Introduction

Finite automata are interesting computational models because of their simplicity, compared to more complex models like pushdown automata or Turing machines. They also represent a very concrete restriction on computation: they only have a finite memory. A lot of different automata models have been studied during the years, such as deterministic [10], probabilistic [8] and quantum [2] ones. All these models share two common features: the state vector set is compact and the acceptance function can be interpreted as linear. The linearity is desirable because of mathematical simplicity, but on the other hand, it may represent a limitation on the computational power.

M. Hirvensalo—Partially supported by Väisälä Foundation.

E. Moutot—Partially supported by TUCS COM^3-project and ANR project CoCoGro (ANR-16-CE40-0005).

A. Yakaryılmaz—Partially supported by TUCS COM^3-project and ERC Advanced Grant MQC.

F. Drewes et al. (Eds.): LATA 2017, LNCS 10168, pp. 405–417, 2017.
DOI: 10.1007/978-3-319-53733-7_30

Jeandel [5] demonstrated that in the bounded-error acceptance model the finite automata with compact state set accept only regular languages. Hence the compactness property of the state set may be one very important limiting the computational power, but since most known models have a compact state set, it remains open how much the compactness of the state set actually contributes.

Recently, A. Díaz-Caro and A. Yakaryılmaz introduced a new model, called *affine automata* [4], also investigated in [3,13]. It is a purely theoretical model, which means that it cannot be implemented by a physical device like quantum automata. But it allows us to investigate on the power of interference caused by negatives amplitudes in the computation, like in the quantum case. Moreover, this model allows us to study the effect of state set compactness, since unlike quantum automata, affine ones have an unbounded state set. In addition, the final operation corresponding to quantum measurement cannot be interpreted as linear, but it is analogous to renormalization in Kondacs and Watrous [6] and Latvian [1] quantum automata models.

In this paper, we present some stability results (Sect. 3): we show how to obtain a new AfA from two AfAs by tensoring and direct sum. Then, we present a simpler proof for how to change the cutpoint for any affine language and an error reduction method in bounded error case.

Any entry of an affine state or a transition matrix can be arbitrarily away from zero. Here, by addressing to the question of [4], we show that (Sect. 4) any affine language can be recognized by an AfA with the restriction that all the entries of transition matrices are in the interval $[-1,1]$. We also show that by an additional state we can guarantee that any AfA can start its computation from the first deterministic state.

Finally, we present (Sect. 5) the first languages shown not to be recognized by any bounded-error AfA.

2 Preliminaries

We denote the input alphabet Σ and the empty string ε.

Probabilistic automata are a generalization of deterministic finite automata that can make random choices [9]. Formally, a *probabilistic finite automaton* (PFA) P is a 5-tuple $P = (E, \Sigma, \{M_x \mid x \in \Sigma\}, e_s, E_a)$, where $E = \{e_1, \dots, e_k\}$ is the finite set of states of P, $\{M_x \mid x \in \Sigma\}$ is the set of stochastic transition matrices (all their coefficients are real numbers in $[0,1]$ and their columns sums up to 1), v_0 is the initial probabilistic state (the probability distribution on the states), and $E_a \subseteq E$ is the set of accepting states. The computation starts in v_0, and then the given input, say $w = w_1 \cdots w_n \in \Sigma^*$ for some $n > 0$, is read once from left to right symbol by symbol. For each symbol the corresponding transition matrix is applied: $\boldsymbol{v}_f = M_w \boldsymbol{v}_0 = M_{w_n} \cdots M_{w_1} \boldsymbol{v}_0$. Remark that if $w = \varepsilon$, $v_f = v_0$. The *accepting probability* of P on w is given by

$$f_P(w) = \boldsymbol{p} M_w \boldsymbol{v}_0, \tag{1}$$

where $\boldsymbol{p} = \begin{pmatrix}\delta_1 \cdots \delta_k\end{pmatrix}$ and $\delta_i = 1$ if $e_i \in E_a$ and 0 if $e_i \notin E_a$.

Affine automata are a generalization of PFAs allowing negative transition values. Only allowing negative values in the transition matrices does not add any power (generalized probabilistic automata are equivalent to usual ones [11]), but affine automata introduces also a non-linear behaviour. The automaton acts like usual generalized probabilistic automaton until the last operation, a non-linear operation called *weighting*.

A vector $\boldsymbol{v} \in \mathbb{R}^n$ is an affine vector if and only if its coordinates sums up to 1. A matrix M is an affine matrix if and only if all its columns are affine vectors. Remark that if M and N are affine matrices, then MN is also an affine matrix. In particular, if $\boldsymbol{v}$ is an affine vector, then $M\boldsymbol{v}$ is also an affine vector.

Formally, an *affine finite automaton* (AfA) A is a 5-tuple

$$A = (E, \Sigma, \{M_x \mid x \in \Sigma\}, \boldsymbol{v}_0, E_a)$$

where all components exactly the same as for probabilistic automata by replacing stochastic property with affine one in the initial state and transition matrices.

As in PFAs, after reading a word $w = w_1 \cdots w_n$, the final state of A is $\boldsymbol{v}_f = M_w \boldsymbol{v}_0$ like in the probabilistic case, but the function $f_A : \Sigma^* \to [0,1]$ computed by A is defined as

$$f_A(w) = \frac{\sum_{e_i \in E_a} |(v_f)_i|}{\sum_{e_i \in E} |(v_f)_i|}, \tag{2}$$

and referred as the *accepting value* of A on w. Similar to projective measurements, we can rewrite Eq. (2) as given below. First, we define a projection matrix based on E_a: $P_A = P = \begin{pmatrix} \delta_1 & & & \\ & \delta_2 & & \\ & & \ddots & \\ & & & \delta_n \end{pmatrix}$, where $\delta_i = \begin{cases} 1 \text{ if } e_i \in E_a \\ 0 \text{ otherwise} \end{cases}$.

Then, we can denote $f_A(\cdot)$ as

$$f_A(w) = \frac{|PM_w \boldsymbol{v}_0|}{|M_w \boldsymbol{v}_0|}. \tag{3}$$

Notice that the final value for PFA P (1) is defined as matrix product $\boldsymbol{v}_f \mapsto \boldsymbol{p}.\boldsymbol{v}_f$, which is a linear operation on $\boldsymbol{v}_f$. On the other hand, computing final value from $\boldsymbol{v}_f$ as in (3) involves nonlinear operations $\boldsymbol{v}_f \mapsto \dfrac{|P\boldsymbol{v}_f|}{|\boldsymbol{v}_f|}$ due to absolute value and normalization of affine states having length greater than 1.

Given a function $f : \Sigma^* \to [0,1]$ computed by an automaton (stochastic or affine), there are different ways of defining the language of an automaton. The natural one is as follows: A language $L \subseteq \Sigma^*$ is recognized by an automaton A with cutpoint λ if and only if

$$L = \{w \in \Sigma^* \mid f_A(w) > \lambda\}.$$

These languages are called cutpoint languages. In the case of probabilistic (resp. affine automata), the set of cut-point languages are called *stochastic languages* (resp. *affine languages*) and denoted by SL (resp. AfL).

A stronger condition is to impose that accepted and rejected words are separated by a gap: the cutpoint is said to be isolated: A language L is recognized by an automaton A with *isolated cutpoint* λ if and only if there exist $\delta > 0$ such that $\forall w \in L, f_A(w) \geq \lambda + \delta$, and $\forall w \notin L, f_A(w) \leq \lambda - \delta$.

As we shall see, for affine automata it is always possible to shift the cutpoint $\lambda \in (0,1)$ to $\lambda = \frac{1}{2}$, and hence this notion of isolated cutpoint becomes equivalent to the bounded error recognition: Language $L \subseteq \Sigma^*$ is said to be recognized by an automaton A with *bounded error* if and only if there exists $\varepsilon > 0$ such that $\forall w \in L, f_A(w) \geq 1 - \varepsilon$, and $\forall w \notin L, f_A(w) \leq \varepsilon$.

The set of languages recognized with *bounded error* (or isolated cutpoint) affine automata is denoted by BAfL.

A classical result by Rabin [9] shows that isolated cutpoint stochastic languages are regular (denoted REG). Rabin's proof essentially relies on two facts: (1) the function mapping the final vector into $[0,1]$ is a contraction, and (2) the state vector set is bounded.

By modifying Rabin's proof, it is possible to show that also many quantum variants of stochastic automata obey the same principle [7] bounded-error property implies the regularity of the accepted languages. In fact, E. Jeandel generalized Rabin's proof by demonstrating that the compactness of the state vector set together with the continuity of the final function are sufficient to guarantee the regularity of the accepted language if the cutpoint is isolated [5].

In the affine case however, the vector states do not lie in a compact set, we cannot prove that $\mathsf{BAfL} = \mathsf{REG}$ like in the probabilistic (or even quantum) case [5]. In fact, it is even the contrary: $\mathsf{REG} \subsetneq \mathsf{BAfL}$ [4].

We close this section by three basic facts. The following three operations on the state sets will be useful, when constructing new automata from the existing ones:

- $\overline{E} = \{e_i \mid e_i \notin E\}$ the complement of E,
- $E_a \times E_b = \{(e_i, e_j) \mid e_i \in E_a, e_j \in E_b\}$ the Cartesian product of E_a and E_b,
- $E_a \cup E_b = \{e_i \mid e_i \in E_a \text{ or } e_i \in E_b\}$ the union of E_a and E_b.

The following lemma shows how to formulate the above operations by using the formalism of projection matrices.

Lemma 1. *Let E be the set of all states, $E_a, E_b \subseteq E$ and P_a, P_b be the projections associated to them. Then*

- *P is the projection associated to the complement $\overline{E_a}$ if and only if $P = I - P_a$, and,*
- *P is the projection associated to $E_a \times E_b$ if and only if $P = P_a \otimes P_b$.*

Lemma 2. *Let E be the set of all states, $E_a, E_b \subseteq E$, such that $E_a \cap E_b = \emptyset$. Let P_a and P_b be the projections associated to them. Then,*

- *P is the projection associated to $E_a \cup E_b$ if and only if $P = P_a + P_b$, and,*
- *for any matrix M and vector $\boldsymbol{v}$, $|PM\boldsymbol{v}| = |P_a M\boldsymbol{v}| + |P_b M\boldsymbol{v}|$.*

Lemma 3. *If A and B are affine matrices, then $A \otimes B$ is also affine. Moreover, $|A \otimes B| = |A||B|$.*

3 Stability Results

The main results of this section are stability results. The first are about the functions of affine automata. They provide a way to prove an error reduction theorem. We then use this theorem to show the stability of bounded-error affine languages under intersection and union.

Proposition 4. *Let f, g be functions computed by affine automata, then there exists an affine automaton $\mathcal{C}$ such that $f_{\mathcal{C}} = f \times g$.*

Proof. The proof is the same as the stochastic case and essentially relies on the property of tensor product of Lemma 3. □

It is easy to design a 2-state PFA P such that $f_P : \Sigma^* \to \alpha$ for $\alpha \in [0, 1]$. Thus:

Corollary 5. *Let f be a function computed by an AfA and $\alpha \in [0, 1]$, then there exists an AfA $\mathcal{C}$ such that $f_{\mathcal{C}} = \alpha f$.*

Proposition 6. *Let f, g be functions computed by some AfAs and $\alpha, \beta \geq 0$ such that $\alpha + \beta = 1$, then there exists an AfA $\mathcal{C}$ such that $f_{\mathcal{C}} = \alpha f + \beta g$.*

Proof. Let $\mathcal{A} = (E^A, \Sigma, \{A_x\}, \boldsymbol{v}_0^A, E_a^A)$ and $\mathcal{B} = (E^B, \Sigma, \{B_x\}, \boldsymbol{v}_0^B, E_a^B)$ two automata such that $f = f_{\mathcal{A}}$ and $g = f_{\mathcal{B}}$. The idea here is to make two copies of $\mathcal{A} \otimes \mathcal{B}$ working in parallel, one having the final states of $\mathcal{A}$, the other the final states of $\mathcal{B}$. We define $\mathcal{C} = (E^C, \Sigma, \{C_x\}, \boldsymbol{v}_0^C, E_a^C)$ by:

$$C_x = \left(\begin{array}{c|c} A_x \otimes B_x & 0 \\ \hline 0 & A_x \otimes B_x \end{array}\right), \boldsymbol{v}_0^C = \left(\begin{array}{c} \alpha(\boldsymbol{v}_0^A \otimes \boldsymbol{v}_0^B) \\ \hline \beta(\boldsymbol{v}_0^A \otimes \boldsymbol{v}_0^B) \end{array}\right), P^C = \left(\begin{array}{c|c} P^A \otimes I_n & 0 \\ \hline 0 & I_k \otimes P^B \end{array}\right),$$

with P^A, P^B and P^C be the projections on E_a^A, E_a^B and E_a^C. Thus,

$$\begin{aligned} f_{\mathcal{C}}(w) &= \frac{\alpha|(P^A \otimes I_n)(A_x \otimes B_x)(\boldsymbol{v}_0^A \otimes \boldsymbol{v}_0^B)| + \beta|(I_k \otimes P^B)(A_x \otimes B_x)(\boldsymbol{v}_0^A \otimes \boldsymbol{v}_0^B)|}{(\alpha+\beta)|(A_x \otimes B_x)(\boldsymbol{v}_0^A \otimes \boldsymbol{v}_0^B)|} \\ &= \alpha \frac{|P^A A_w \boldsymbol{v}_0^A|}{|A_w \boldsymbol{v}_0^A|} + \beta \frac{|P^B B_w \boldsymbol{v}_0^B|}{|B_w \boldsymbol{v}_0^B|} = \alpha f(w) + \beta g(w). \end{aligned}$$

□

The first consequence of these stability results is a really short proof for shifting the cutpoint of an affine automaton. Although the construction in [4] gives a much more compact automata in term of number of states, our construction is simpler, and does not require as many specific cases.

Proposition 7. *Let $\mathcal{A}$ be an affine automaton and $\lambda_1, \lambda_2 \in [0, 1]$. There exists an affine automaton $\mathcal{B}$ such that*

- $f_{\mathcal{A}}(w) > \lambda_1 \Leftrightarrow f_{\mathcal{B}}(w) > \lambda_2$ *and*
- $f_{\mathcal{A}}(w) = \lambda_1 \Leftrightarrow f_{\mathcal{B}}(w) = \lambda_2$.

Proof. First we suppose $\lambda_1 \neq 1$. Let $\mathcal{B}$ the automaton such that $f_{\mathcal{B}} = \alpha f_{\mathcal{A}} + (1-\alpha)1$, with $\alpha = \frac{1-\lambda_2}{1-\lambda_1}$. Then $f_{\mathcal{A}} > \lambda_1 \Rightarrow f_{\mathcal{B}} > \frac{(1-\lambda_2)\lambda_1+\lambda_2-\lambda_1}{1-\lambda_1} = \lambda_2$. And one has the same with $=$ or $<$.

For $\lambda_1 = 1$ it is even simpler, one has just to "resize" the function by taking $\mathcal{B}$ such that $f_{\mathcal{B}} = \lambda_2 f_{\mathcal{A}}$. And then, $f_{\mathcal{A}} = 1 \Rightarrow f_{\mathcal{B}} = \lambda_2$, and same for $<$. □

Using the same kind of construction we can prove that bounded-error mode, it is always possible to reduce the error. Reducing the error means increasing the gap between accepted and rejected words. The error probability could even be made as close to zero as one wants.

Lemma 8. *Let f be a function computed by affine automaton, then there exists an affine automaton $\mathcal{B}$ such that $f_{\mathcal{B}} = f^2(3-2f)$.*

Proof. Let $\mathcal{A} = (E, \Sigma, \{A_x\}, \boldsymbol{v}_0, E_a)$ such that $f = f_{\mathcal{A}}$. The automaton $\mathcal{B}$ will run 3 copies of $\mathcal{A}$ in parallel, and its final states are made to accept if 2 or 3 copies of $\mathcal{A}$ accept and reject otherwise (i.e. taking the majority answer). Formally, $\mathcal{B} = (E \otimes E \otimes E, \Sigma, \{B_x\}, \boldsymbol{v}_0', E_a')$ with

$$B_x = A_x \otimes A_x \otimes A_x,$$

$$\boldsymbol{v}_0' = \boldsymbol{v}_0 \otimes \boldsymbol{v}_0 \otimes \boldsymbol{v}_0,$$

$$E_a' = (E_a \times E_a \times E_a) \cup \left(\overline{E_a} \times E_a \times E_a\right) \cup \left(E_a \times \overline{E_a} \times E_a\right) \cup \left(E_a \times E_a \times \overline{E_a}\right).$$

Note that the four sets in parenthesis are all pairwise disjoints. Let P and P' be the projections associated to E_a and E_a'. Then,

$$P' = P \otimes P \otimes P + (I-P) \otimes P \otimes P + P \otimes (I-P) \otimes P + P \otimes P \otimes (I-P).$$

And by Lemma 1,

$$\begin{aligned} f_{\mathcal{B}}(w) = \frac{|P' B_w \boldsymbol{v}_0'|}{|B_w \boldsymbol{v}_0'|} &= \frac{|PA_w\boldsymbol{v}_0|^3 + 3|PA_w\boldsymbol{v}_0|\left(|A_w\boldsymbol{v}_0| - |PA_w\boldsymbol{v}_0|\right)}{|A_w\boldsymbol{v}_0|^3} \\ &= f(w)^3 + 3f(w)^2(1-f(w)) \\ &= f(w)^2(3-2f(w)). \end{aligned}$$

□

Proposition 9 (error reduction). *Let $L \in$ BAfL. There exists an affine automaton $\mathcal{A}$ such that:*

- $\forall w \in L, f_{\mathcal{A}}(w) \geq \frac{3}{4}$
- $\forall w \notin L, f_{\mathcal{A}}(w) \leq \frac{1}{4}$

Proof. We do not detail the proof, but the idea is simple: mapping $x \to x^2(3-2x)$ has attracting points at $x = 0$ and $x = 1$. Iterating the mapping, any point $\neq \frac{1}{2}$ will tend to 0 or 1. □

This technique could be applied to get any constant instead of $\frac{1}{4}$, to have an error bound as small as one wants.

This error reduction theorem also applies to probabilistic automata, but is not very interesting because in the probabilistic case it is known that bounded-error languages are exactly regular languages [5], and hence the error probability could always be 0. In our case, bounded-error languages are more complex than regular languages. But thanks to this error reduction, they are stable under union, intersection, and complement, just like regular languages.

Proposition 10. *Let* $L_A, L_B \in \mathsf{BAfL}$. *Then*

- $L_A \cup L_B \in \mathsf{BAfL}$,
- $L_A \cap L_B \in \mathsf{BAfL}$,
- $\overline{L_A} \in \mathsf{BAfL}$.

Proof. Let $\mathcal{A}$ and $\mathcal{B}$ be automata recognizing L_A and L_B with error bound ε at most $\frac{1}{4}$ (thanks to Theorem 9). We define $\mathcal{C}$ and $\mathcal{D}$ such that $f_\mathcal{C} = \frac{1}{2}(f_\mathcal{A} + f_\mathcal{B})$ and $f_\mathcal{D} = f_\mathcal{A} f_\mathcal{B}$. Let $w \in \Sigma^*$. We study the 4 possible options depending on the membership of w to L_A and L_B.

- $w \in L_A, w \in L_B$ (i.e. $w \in L_A \cup L_B, w \in L_A \cap L_B$) $\Rightarrow f_\mathcal{C} \geq \frac{3}{4}$ and $f_\mathcal{D} \geq \frac{9}{16}$,
- $w \in L_A, w \notin L_B$ (i.e. $w \in L_A \cup L_B, w \notin L_A \cap L_B$) $\Rightarrow f_\mathcal{C} \geq \frac{3}{8}$ and $f_\mathcal{D} \leq \frac{1}{4}$,
- $w \notin L_A, w \in L_B$ (i.e. $w \in L_A \cup L_B, w \notin L_A \cap L_B$) $\Rightarrow f_\mathcal{C} \geq \frac{3}{8}$ and $f_\mathcal{D} \leq \frac{1}{4}$,
- $w \notin L_A, w \notin L_B$ (i.e. $w \notin L_A \cup L_B, w \notin L_A \cap L_B$) $\Rightarrow f_\mathcal{C} \leq \frac{1}{4}$ and $f_\mathcal{D} \leq \frac{1}{16}$.

Because $\frac{3}{8} > \frac{1}{4}$ and $\frac{9}{16} > \frac{1}{4}$, $\mathcal{C}$ and $\mathcal{D}$ are deciding $L_A \cup L_B$ and $L_A \cap L_B$ with bounded error.

For the complement one has just to make a copy of $\mathcal{A}$ with accepting states $\overline{E_a}$. The resulting function will be $1 - f_\mathcal{A}$, leading to accept the rejected words of $\mathcal{A}$ and vice-versa. □

4 Equivalent Forms of Affine Automata

General affine automata are hard to study because of the lack of structure of their transition matrices and state vectors. We provide here some equivalent forms which have more restrictive properties. These equivalent forms are useful not only because it provides simpler equivalent models but also because they provide a way understand the power of affine computation.

The first result is that assuming the initial affine (probabilistic) state as the first deterministic state does not change the power of AfAs (PFAs).

Proposition 11. *Let* $\mathcal{A}$ *be an affine automaton with* n *states, there exist* $\mathcal{B}$ *with* $n+1$ *states with the initial state* $(1, 0, \ldots, 0)$ *and such that* $f_\mathcal{A} = f_\mathcal{B}$.

Proof. Let $\mathcal{A} = (E, \Sigma, \{A_x\}, \boldsymbol{v}_0, E_a)$. Then, $\mathcal{B} = (E \cup \{e'\}, \Sigma, \{B_x\}, \boldsymbol{v}'_0, E_a)$, with $\boldsymbol{v}'_0 = (1, 0, \ldots, 0)^T$ and $B_x = \left(\begin{array}{c|c} 0 & 0 \cdots 0 \\ \hline A_x \boldsymbol{v}_0 & A_x \end{array}\right)$. Thus we can deduce $f_\mathcal{B} = f_\mathcal{A}$ from $B_w \boldsymbol{v}'_0 = B_{w_n} \ldots B_{w_2} B_{w_1} \boldsymbol{v}'_0 = \left(\begin{array}{c|c} 0 & 0 \cdots 0 \\ \hline A_w \boldsymbol{v}_0 & A_w \end{array}\right) \begin{pmatrix} 1 \\ 0 \\ \vdots \\ 0 \end{pmatrix} = \begin{pmatrix} 0 \\ A_w \boldsymbol{v}_0 \end{pmatrix}$. □

Then we prove that one could also assume that all state vectors and transition matrices have coefficients only in $[-1, 1]$.

Proposition 12. *Any language in* AfL *can be recognized by a AfA $\mathcal{B}$ with cutpoint $\frac{1}{2}$ such that each entry of affine states during the computation is always in $[-1, 1]$.*

Proof. Let $\mathcal{A} = (E = \{e_1, \ldots, e_k\}, \Sigma, \{A_x\}, v_0 = (1, 0, \ldots, 0)^T, E_a)$ be an AfA such that $w \in L \Leftrightarrow f_\mathcal{A}(w) > \frac{1}{2}$, and $C = \max_{x,i,j} |(A_x)_{i,j}|$. Then, $\mathcal{B}$ is as follows:

$$\mathcal{B} = (E \cup \{e_{n+1}, e_{n+2}\}, \Sigma, \{B_x\}, \boldsymbol{v}'_0, E_a \cup \{e_{n+1}\}) \quad \text{with}$$

$$B_x = \frac{1}{2kC} \left(\begin{array}{ccc|cc} & & & 0 & 0 \\ & 2A_x & & \vdots & \vdots \\ & & & 0 & 0 \\ \hline kC-1 & \ldots & kC-1 & 2kC & 0 \\ kC-1 & \ldots & kC-1 & 0 & 2kC \end{array}\right) \quad \text{and } \boldsymbol{v}'_0 = (1, 0, \ldots, 0)^T.$$

Then, with $w = w_1 \cdots w_n$, we can deduce that

$$B_w = B_{w_n} \cdots B_{w_2} B_{w_1} = \frac{1}{2(kC)^n} \left(\begin{array}{ccc|cc} & & & 0 & 0 \\ & 2A_w & & \vdots & \vdots \\ & & & 0 & 0 \\ \hline (kC)^n - 1 & \ldots & (kC)^n - 1 & 2(kC)^n & 0 \\ (kC)^n - 1 & \ldots & (kC)^n - 1 & 0 & 2(kC)^n \end{array}\right),$$

which gives the final values of the states:

$$\boldsymbol{v}'_f = B_w \boldsymbol{v}'_0 = \frac{1}{(kC)^n} \begin{pmatrix} \vdots \\ \boldsymbol{v}_f \\ \vdots \\ \frac{(kC)^n - 1}{2} \\ \frac{(kC)^n - 1}{2} \end{pmatrix}.$$

Since $|(\boldsymbol{v}_f)_i| \leq k^{n-1} C^n$, it is clear that $|(\boldsymbol{v}'_f)_i| \leq [-1, 1]$: the values of the states are bounded. Now, one has

$$f_\mathcal{B} = \frac{|PA_w \boldsymbol{v}_0| + \frac{(kC)^n - 1}{2}}{|A_w \boldsymbol{v}_0| + (kC)^n - 1},$$

and so,

$$\begin{aligned} w \in L \Leftrightarrow f_{\mathcal{A}} > \frac{1}{2} &\Leftrightarrow |PA_w \boldsymbol{v}_0| > \frac{1}{2}|A_w \boldsymbol{v}_0| \\ &\Leftrightarrow |PA_w \boldsymbol{v}_0| + \frac{(kC)^n - 1}{2} > \frac{1}{2}\left(|A_w \boldsymbol{v}_0| + (kC)^n - 1\right) \\ &\Leftrightarrow f_{\mathcal{B}} > \frac{1}{2}. \end{aligned}$$

□

5 The First Languages Shown to Be Not in BAfL

This part is dedicated to prove that some languages are not recognizable by affine automata. This is an adaptation of the proof of Turakainen [12] for non-stochastic languages. All the difficulty of exhibiting a non-affine language relies in the fact that a large majority of non-stochasticity proof are based on the linearity of the automaton, which is not the case in the affine case. This proof however, is more based on some "regularity" induced by the matrix-based operations, and number theoretic properties of languages like *Prime*. Hence it was possible to adapt it for the affine case, where the only non-linear operation is the final projection.

Let $L \subseteq a^*$ be a unary language. We call **lower density** of L the limit

$$\underline{dens}(L) = \liminf_{n \to \infty} \frac{\left|\{a^k \in L \mid k \leq n\}\right|}{n+1}.$$

Let $(\boldsymbol{x}_n)$ be a sequence of vectors in $\mathbb{R}^k$ and $I = [a_1, b_1) \times \cdots \times [a_k, b_k)$ be an "interval". We define $C(I,n)$ as $C(I,n) = |\{\boldsymbol{x}_i \mod 1 \in I \mid 1 \leq i \leq n\}|$.

We say that $(\boldsymbol{x}_n)$ **is uniformly distributed mod 1** if and only if for any I of such type,

$$\lim_{n \to \infty} \frac{C(I,n)}{n} = (b_1 - a_1) \cdots (b_k - a_k).$$

Proposition 13. *If $L \subseteq a^*$ satisfies the following conditions:*

1. $\underline{dens}(L) = 0$.
2. *For all $Q \in \mathbb{N}^*$, there exist $h \in \mathbb{N}$ and an infinite sequence $(n_i) \in \mathbb{N}^{\mathbb{N}}$ such that $a^{h+n_iQ} \subseteq L$ and for any irrational number α, the sequence $((h + n_iQ)\alpha)_{i \in \mathbb{N}}$ is uniformly distributed mod 1.*

Then L is non-affine ($L \notin$ BAfL).

Proof. Let's assume for contradiction that $L \in$ BAfL. Then there exists an affine automaton A with s states such that

$$f_A(a^n) = \frac{|PM^n \boldsymbol{v}|}{|M^n \boldsymbol{v}|}$$

and there exists $\varepsilon > 0$ such that

- $\forall w \in L, f_A(w) \geq 1 - \varepsilon$,
- $\forall w \notin L, f_A(w) \leq \varepsilon$.

Note that

$$|M^n\boldsymbol{v}| = \sum_{i=1}^{s} |(M^n\boldsymbol{v})_i| \geq \left|\sum_{i=1}^{s}(M^n\boldsymbol{v})_i\right| = 1 \text{ (triangle inequality)}.$$

Hence the denominator of f_A is never 0, and so f_A is continuous.

Using the Jordan decomposition $M = PJP^{-1}$, one has $M^n = PJ^nP^{-1}$. So the coordinates $\boldsymbol{v}_i$ of $M^n\boldsymbol{v}$ have the form

$$\boldsymbol{v}_i = \sum_{k=1}^{s} p_{ik}(n)\lambda_k^n \tag{4}$$

where λ_i are the eigenvalues of M and p_{ik} are polynomials of degree less than the degree of the corresponding eigenvalue. Let $\lambda_i = |\lambda_i|e^{2i\pi\theta_i}$, we assume $|\lambda_1| = \cdots = |\lambda_{s'}| > |\lambda_{s'+1}| \cdots$. Let $\lambda = |\lambda_1|$ be the largest module of all eigenvalues and r be the maximum degree of all polynomials p_{ik}, where $k \leq s'$. Then, one can use (4) to write

$$|M^n\boldsymbol{v}| = \sum_{i\in E} |\boldsymbol{v}_i| = \lambda^n n^r \left(\sum_{i\in E}\left|\sum_{k=1}^{s'} a_{ik}e^{2i\pi n\theta_k}\right| + g_E(n)\right)$$

where a_{ik} is the coefficient of degree r of p_{ik} (note that one can have $a_{ik} = 0$ for some a, k), and g_E a function such that $\lim_{n\to\infty} g_E(n) = 0$. Similarly,

$$|PM^n\boldsymbol{v}| = \sum_{i\in E_a} |\boldsymbol{v}_i| = \lambda^n n^r \left(\sum_{i\in E_a}\left|\sum_{k=1}^{s'} a_{ik}e^{2i\pi n\theta_k}\right| + g_{E_a}(n)\right).$$

Now let $F(n) = f(a^n)$. Using the previous equations, one has

$$\begin{aligned} F(n) &= \frac{|PM^n\boldsymbol{v}|}{|M^n\boldsymbol{v}|} \\ &= \frac{\lambda^n n^r \left(\sum_{i\in E_a}\left|\sum_{k=1}^{s'} a_{ik}e^{2i\pi n\theta_k}\right| + g_{E_a}(n)\right)}{\lambda^n n^r \left(\sum_{i\in E}\left|\sum_{k=1}^{s'} a_{ik}e^{2i\pi n\theta_k}\right| + g_E(n)\right)} \\ &= \frac{\sum_{i\in E_a}\left|\sum_{k=1}^{s'} a_{ik}e^{2i\pi n\theta_k}\right| + g_{E_a}(n)}{\sum_{i\in E}\left|\sum_{k=1}^{s'} a_{ik}e^{2i\pi n\theta_k}\right| + g_E(n)}. \end{aligned}$$

We define

$$G(n) = \frac{\sum_{i\in E_a}\left|\sum_{k=1}^{s'} a_{ik}e^{2i\pi n\theta_k}\right|}{\sum_{i\in E}\left|\sum_{k=1}^{s'} a_{ik}e^{2i\pi n\theta_k}\right|}.$$

As $\lim_{n\to\infty} g_{E_a}(n) = 0$ and $\lim_{n\to\infty} g_E(n) = 0$, one has $G(n) \sim F(n)$, and so,

$$\lim_{n\to\infty} |F(n) - G(n)| = 0. \tag{5}$$

We define $A = \{k \mid 1 \le k \le s', \theta_k \notin \mathbb{Q}\}$ the indices of the "first" eigenvalue angles that are not rational. Let Q, h and the sequence (n_i) be as in the statement. Using the periodic behaviour induced by rational angle of eigenvalues, and by taking a subsequence of the initial one, one can also assume that (n_i) is such that

$$G(h + n_iQ) = \frac{\sum_{i\in E_a} \left|\sum_{k\in A} a_{ik} e^{2i\pi(h+n_iQ)\theta_k} + c\right|}{\sum_{i\in E} \left|\sum_{k\in A} a_{ik} e^{2i\pi(h+n_iQ)\theta_k} + d\right|}$$

with c, d some constants.

By assumption, for all $k \in A$, the sequence $((h + n_iQ)\theta_k)_i$ is uniformly distributed modulo 1. The consequence is that the values $e^{2i\pi(h+n_iQ)\theta_k}$ are dense in the unit circle. If for some n, $G(h + nQ) < \frac{1}{2}$, there exists $\varepsilon > 0$ such that $G(h+nQ) \le \frac{1}{2} - \varepsilon$. Then, thanks to the density argument, there are arbitrarily large values of i for which $G(h + n_iQ) \le \frac{1}{2} - \frac{\varepsilon}{2}$. Since for i sufficiently large, $|F(h + n_iQ) - G(h + n_iQ)| \le \frac{\varepsilon}{2}$ (using (5)), one has $F(h + n_iQ) \le \frac{1}{2}$, and so $a^{h+n_iQ} \notin L$, contradicting condition 2 of the statement.

Therefore, $G(h + nQ) \ge \frac{1}{2}$ for large enough n. Because G is not identically equal to $\frac{1}{2}$ (if it is the case, F would be as close to $\frac{1}{2}$ as one wants, which is impossible since $L \in \mathsf{BAfL}$), again using density, there must be some $\varepsilon > 0$ and k_0 such that $G(h + k_0Q) \ge \frac{1}{2} + \epsilon$.

First if $A = \emptyset$, it means that all the angles of the eigenvalues $\theta_1, \dots, \theta_{s'}$ are rational. We can then write them as $\theta_k = \frac{l_k}{m_k}$. Then $G(n)$ takes a finite number of values, and these values only depend on $(n \mod m_1), \dots, (n \mod m_{s'})$. Let's call $k_1 = h + k_0Q$ the number where G is larger than $\frac{1}{2}$: $G(n_1) > \frac{1}{2}$. G has the same value for all $n \in Z = \{k_1 + km_1 \cdots m_{s'} | k \in \mathbb{N}\}$ (because for n in this set, the values of all $(n \mod m_1), \dots,$ $(n \mod m_{s'})$ are the same). Then, thanks to (5), one has, for $n \in Z$ sufficiently large, $F(n) > \frac{1}{2}$, so $\{a^n \mid n \in Z, n \ge n_1\} \subseteq L$. And because $|\{a^n \mid n \in Z, n \ge n_1\}| \sim \frac{n}{m_1 \cdots m_{s'}}$, one has $\underline{dens}(L) > 0$, which contradicts condition 1 of the statement.

Next, if $A \neq \emptyset$. Let

$$R((x_k)_{k\in A}) = \frac{\sum_{i\in E_a} \left|\sum_{k\in A} a_{ik} x_k + c\right|}{\sum_{i\in E} \left|\sum_{k\in A} a_{ik} x_k + d\right|}.$$

Note that $G(h + n_iQ) = R((e^{2i\pi(h+n_iQ)\theta_k})_{k\in A})$. Then, because the sequences $((h + n_iQ)\theta_k)_i$ are uniformly distributed modulo 1, it follows that any value obtained by the function $R((e^{2i\pi y_k})_{k\in A})$ can be approximated by some $G(h + n_iQ)$ with arbitrary precision. The function R is continuous, therefore there exists an interval $I = (x_1, y_1, \ldots) = ((x_k, y_k))_{k\in A}$ on which $R((x_k)) > \frac{1}{2} + \frac{\varepsilon}{2}$. So, if n_i is large enough and satisfies

$$((h + n_iQ)\theta_1 \mod 1, \dots) = ((h + n_iQ)\theta_k \mod 1)_{k\in A} \in I,$$

then $G(h+n_iQ) > \frac{1}{2}+\frac{\varepsilon}{2}$, which implies $F(h+n_iQ) > \frac{1}{2}$ and hence $a^{h+n_iQ} \in L$. Now we just have to prove that the sequence $(h + n_iQ)$ is "dense enough" to have $\underline{dens}(L) > 0$, contradicting again condition 1.
Because of uniform distribution imposed by condition 2, one has

$$d = \lim_{i\to\infty} \frac{C(I, h+n_iQ)}{h+n_iQ} = \prod_{k\in A} (y_k - x_k)$$

And so for i large enough, $\frac{C(I,h+n_iQ)}{h+n_iQ} \geq \frac{d}{2}$, with $a^{h+n_iQ} \in L$, implying $\underline{dens}(L) > 0$. We have proved that L cannot be affine. □

Turakainen [12] proved that $Prime = \{a^p \mid p \text{ is prime}\}$ and $Poly(q) = \{a^{q(n)} \mid n \in \mathbb{N}, q(n) \geq 0\}$ (where q is any polynomial of degree > 2 with non-negative coefficients) both satisfy the two conditions of Theorem 13. Hence they are not in BAfL .

Corollary 14. *Prime* $\notin$ BAfL *and* $Poly(q) \notin$ BAfL.

6 Conclusion

In this paper we demonstrated that even if they are strictly more powerful, bounded-error languages of affine automata share stability properties with regular languages (which are bounded-error languages of stochastic automata).

We also showed that the computational power of affine automata does not come alone from the unboundedness state vector set: the general model of unbounded state vector set can always be simulated with a bounded state vector set. Hence some of the computational power of affine automata comes from the nonlinear nature of the final projection, at least in the case of unbounded-error computation.

References

1. Ambainis, A., Beaudry, M., Golovkins, M., Kikusts, A., Mercer, M., Thérien, D.: Algebraic results on quantum automata. Theor. Comput. Syst. **39**(1), 165–188 (2006)
2. Ambainis, A., Yakaryılmaz, A.: Automata: from mathematics to applications. Automata Quantum Comput., to appear. arXiv:1507.01988
3. Belovs, A., Montoya, J.A., Yakaryılmaz, A.: Can one quantum bit separate any pair of words with zero-error? Technical report. arXiv:1602.07967 (2016)
4. Díaz-Caro, A., Yakaryılmaz, A.: Affine computation and affine automaton. In: Kulikov, A.S., Woeginger, G.J. (eds.) CSR 2016. LNCS, vol. 9691, pp. 146–160. Springer, Heidelberg (2016). doi:10.1007/978-3-319-34171-2_11. arXiv:1602.04732
5. Jeandel, E.: Topological automata. Theor. Comput. Syst. **40**(4), 397–407 (2007)
6. Kondacs, A., Watrous, J.: On the power of quantum finite state automata. In: FOCS 1997, pp. 66–75 (1997)
7. Li, L., Qiu, D., Zou, X., Li, L., Wu, L., Mateus, P.: Characterizations of one-way general quantum finite automata. Theoret. Comput. Sci. **419**, 73–91 (2012)

8. Paz, A.: Introduction to Probabilistic Automata. Academic Press, New York (1971)
9. Rabin, M.O.: Probabilistic automata. Inf. Control **6**, 230–243 (1963)
10. Sipser, M.: Introduction to the Theory of Computation, 3rd edn. Cengage Learning, Boston (2013)
11. Turakainen, P.: Generalized automata and stochastic languages. Proc. Am. Math. Soc. **21**, 303–309 (1969)
12. Turakainen, P.: On nonstochastic languages and homomorphic images of stochastic languages. Inf. Sci. **24**(3), 229–253 (1981)
13. Villagra, M., Yakaryılmaz, A.: Language recognition power and succinctness of affine automata. In: Amos, M., Condon, A. (eds.) UCNC 2016. LNCS, vol. 9726, pp. 116–129. Springer, Heidelberg (2016). doi:10.1007/978-3-319-41312-9_10

Pushdown Automata and Systems

Detecting Useless Transitions in Pushdown Automata

Dick Grune, Wan Fokkink(✉), Evangelos Chatzikalymnios, Brinio Hond, and Peter Rutgers

Department of Computer Science, Vrije Universiteit Amsterdam, Amsterdam, The Netherlands
w.j.fokkink@vu.nl

Abstract. Pushdown automata may contain transitions that are never used in any accepting run of the automaton. We present an algorithm for detecting such useless transitions. A finite automaton that captures the possible stack content during runs of the pushdown automaton, is first constructed in a forward procedure to determine which transitions are reachable, and then employed in a backward procedure to determine which of these transitions can lead to a final state. An implementation of the algorithm is shown to exhibit a favorable performance.

1 Introduction

Context-free languages are used in language specification, parsing, and code optimization. They are defined by means of a context-free grammar or a pushdown automaton (PDA). Some languages can be specified more efficiently by a PDA than by a context-free grammar, as shown by Goldstine, Price, and Wotschke [6]. PDAs are at the root of deterministic parsers for context-free languages (notably LL, LR), see e.g. [1,10]. We consider PDAs in which any number of symbols can be popped from as well as pushed onto the stack in one transition. Popping zero or multiple symbols is useful in bottom-up parsing, and facilitates the reversal of a PDA.

For context-free grammars, it is rather straightforward to determine whether a production is *useless*, i.e., cannot occur in a derivation from the start variable to a string of terminal symbols; such a method is discussed in many textbooks on formal languages (e.g., [9, Theorem 6.2]). It consists of two parts: detect which variables are reachable from the start variable, and which variables can be transformed into a string of terminal symbols. Productions that contain a useless variable, not satisfying these two properties, can be removed from the grammar without changing the associated language. A grammar generated from a program sometimes consists almost entirely of useless productions, such as in case of "parsing by intersection" [8].

This paper addresses the research question posed in [8] to develop an efficient algorithm for determining the useless transitions in a PDA, meaning that no run of the PDA from the initial configuration to a final state includes this transition.

F. Drewes et al. (Eds.): LATA 2017, LNCS 10168, pp. 421–434, 2017.
DOI: 10.1007/978-3-319-53733-7_31

Such a transition can be removed from the PDA without changing the language accepted by the PDA, and improves the performance of running the PDA. This is especially sensible if the PDA has been generated automatically, because then there tend to be a substantial number of useless transitions. Similar to detecting useless variables in context-free grammars, our algorithm for detecting useless transitions in a PDA consists of two parts. It stays entirely in the realm of automata. The first part finds which transitions are not reachable from the initial configuration. Here we exploit an algorithm by Finkel et al. [5] to construct a finite automaton (NFA) that captures exactly all possible stacks in the reachable configurations of a PDA. Their approach is modified slightly to take into account that multiple symbols may be popped from the stack at once. The second part of our algorithm, which to the best of our knowledge is novel, finds after which transitions it is impossible to reach a final state. Here we use the NFA constructed in the first part to compute in a backward fashion which transitions can lead to a final state in the PDA.

We prove that the algorithm marks exactly the useless transitions. The worst-case time complexity of the algorithm is $O(Q^4 T)$, with Q the number of states and T the number of transitions of the PDA. This worst case actually only occurs in the unlikely case that the NFA is constructed over a large number of iterations, is saturated with ε-transitions, and contains a lot of backward nondeterminism. A prototype implementation of the algorithm exhibits a good performance.

An alternative approach is to use the functions *post*∗ and *pre*∗, to compute the reachable configurations as well as the configurations from which a final state can be reached. This alternative approach was also implemented [3], and it was shown on a large test set of randomly generated PDAs that the algorithm presented in this paper has a much better performance that this alternative approach.

Related Work. Bouajjani et al. [2] employed a method similar to the one in [5] to capture the reachable configurations of a PDA via an NFA, in the context of model checking infinite-state systems. Griffin [7] showed how to detect which transitions are reachable from the initial configuration in a deterministic pushdown automaton (DPDA). For each transition, the algorithm creates a temporary DPDA in which the successive state of the transition is set to a new, final state; all other states in the temporary DPDA are made non-final. Then it is checked whether the language generated by the DPDA is empty; if it is, the transition is unreachable. This algorithm determines which transitions are reachable from the initial configuration, but not which transitions can lead to a final state.

2 Preliminaries

A nondeterministic pushdown automaton (PDA) consists of a finite set of states Q, a finite input alphabet Σ, a finite stack alphabet Γ, a finite transition relation $\delta : Q \times (\Sigma \cup \{\varepsilon\}) \times \Gamma^* \rightarrow 2^{Q \times \Gamma^*}$, an initial state q_0, and a set F of final states.

Here ε denotes the empty string. Note that zero or multiple symbols can be popped from the stack in one transition. It is assumed that the initial stack is empty. (An arbitrary initial stack σ can be constructed by adding a new initial state $\hat{q_0}$ and a transition $\delta(\hat{q_0}, \varepsilon, \varepsilon) = \{(q_0, \sigma)\}$.)

A configuration consists of a state from Q together with a stack from Γ^*. We let a, b, c, d denote elements in Γ, and $\rho, \sigma, \tau, \upsilon, \zeta$ strings in Γ^*, where the left-most element represents the top of the stack. The reverse of a string σ is denoted by σ^R. A transition $(r, \tau) \in \delta(q, \alpha, \sigma)$ with $\alpha \in \Sigma \cup \{\varepsilon\}$ gives rise to moves $(q, \sigma\rho) \xrightarrow{\alpha} (r, \tau\rho)$ between configurations, for any $\rho \in \Gamma^*$. The language accepted by a PDA consists of the strings in Σ^* that give rise to a run of the PDA from the initial configuration (q_0, ε) to a configuration (r, σ) with $r \in F$. A transition of a PDA is *useless* if no run of the PDA from the initial configuration (q_0, ε) to a configuration (r, σ) with $r \in F$, for any input string from Σ^*, includes this transition. To determine the useless transitions, input strings from Σ^* are irrelevant. The point is that, since a run for any input string suffices to make a transition useful, we can assume that any desired terminal symbol from Σ is available as input at any time. Input strings from Σ are therefore disregarded in our algorithm to detect useless transitions. (In the context of model-checking infinite-state systems, PDAs in which input strings are disregarded are called "pushdown systems" or "pushdown processes" [11].) A transition $(r, \tau) \in \delta(q, \sigma)$ is written as $q \xrightarrow{\sigma/\tau} r$. It gives rise to moves $(q, \sigma\rho) \rightarrow (r, \tau\rho)$. We write $(s, \upsilon) \rightarrow^* (t, \zeta)$ if there is a run from (s, υ) to (t, ζ) of the PDA, consisting of zero or more moves.

A nondeterministic finite automaton (NFA) consists of a finite set of states Q, a finite input alphabet Σ, a transition relation $\delta : Q \times (\Sigma \cup \{\varepsilon\}) \rightarrow 2^Q$, an initial state q_0, and a set F of final states. In our application of NFAs, the input alphabet is the stack alphabet Γ from the PDA. A transition $r \in \delta(q, a)$ is written as $q \xrightarrow{a} r$. We write $q \overset{a_1 \ldots a_k}{\rightsquigarrow} r$ if there is a path from q to r in the NFA with consecutive labels $a_1, ..., a_k \in \Gamma$. We write $q \overset{a_1 \ldots a_k}{\Longrightarrow} r$ if there is such a path from q to r, possibly intertwined with transitions labeled by ε. The language accepted by an NFA consists of the strings $a_1 ... a_k$ in Σ^* for which there exists a path $q_0 \overset{a_1 \ldots a_k}{\Longrightarrow} r$ with $r \in F$.

3 Detecting the Useless Transitions in a PDA

Our algorithm for detecting useless transitions in a PDA summarizes all reachable configurations of the PDA in an NFA. As a first step, an NFA is constructed that accepts the stacks that can occur during any run of the PDA. A second step determines which transitions can lead to a configuration from which a final state can be reached. Transitions that cannot be reached from the initial state (as determined in step 1) or that cannot lead to a final state (as determined in step 2) are useless.

3.1 Detecting the Unreachable Transitions

A configuration or transition of a PDA P is reachable if it is employed in a run of P, starting from the initial configuration. The reachable configurations of P are captured by means of an NFA N. The stacks in Γ^* that can occur at a state q in P are accepted at the state q in N, in reverse order. During the construction of N, intermediate non-final states are created when multiple symbols are pushed onto the stack in one transition. They are denoted by n, m, to distinguish them from the states q, r, s, t that are inherited from P and which are taken to be final in N. A state in N that may be either final or non-final is denoted by x, y, z.

Fix a PDA $P = (Q, \Sigma, \Gamma, \delta, q_0, F)$; as said, we will disregard Σ. To achieve a single final state without outgoing transitions that is only reached with an empty stack, we perform a standard transformation on P. A fresh stack symbol b_0 is added to Γ, and the initial stack is b_0 (instead of ε). In each run of the PDA, b_0 is always at the bottom of the stack. Fresh states q_e and q_f are added to Q, and δ is extended with transitions $q \overset{\varepsilon/\varepsilon}{\rightarrow} q_e$ for every $q \in F$, $q_e \overset{a/\varepsilon}{\rightarrow} q_e$ for every $a \in \Gamma \backslash \{b_0\}$, and $q_e \overset{b_0/\varepsilon}{\rightarrow} q_f$. We change F to $\{q_f\}$. The resulting PDA is called P_0.

Initially the NFA N under construction consists only of the transition $m_0 \overset{b_0}{\rightarrow} q_0$; the fresh state m_0 is non-final and q_0 final. Intuitively, this transition builds the initial stack of P_0. The set U_1 of unreachable transitions in P_0 initially, as an overapproximation, contains all transitions in P_0. The NFA N and the set U_1 are constructed as follows.

Algorithm 1. Procedure *forward* to detect the unreachable transitions in a PDA P_0.

For each transition $\theta = q \overset{\sigma/\tau}{\rightarrow} r$ in P_0 do:

1. If q is not a state in N, then stop this iteration step.
2. Determine the set $S_{q,\sigma}$, which either consists only of q, if $\sigma = \varepsilon$, or of the (non-final) states n for which there exists a path $n \overset{a}{\rightarrow} y \overset{\sigma'^R}{\Longrightarrow} q$ in N, if $\sigma = \sigma' a$.
3. If $S_{q,\sigma} = \emptyset$, then stop this iteration step.
4. If $\theta \in U_1$, then delete θ from U_1, and establish a path $\overset{\tau^R}{\rightsquigarrow} r$ in N (see below); the state r in N is final.
5. Let y be the first state in the path $\overset{\tau^R}{\rightsquigarrow} r$. For each state $x \in S_{q,\sigma}$, if the transition $x \overset{\varepsilon}{\rightarrow} y$ is not yet present in N, then add this transition to N.

If N changed during this run, then perform *forward* again, over all transitions in P_0. Else, stop, and return the constructed NFA N and the set U_1 of unreachable transitions in P_0. These transitions are then culled from P_0, producing the PDA P_1.

The sets $S_{q,\sigma}$ need to be recomputed in every run of the *forward* procedure. The sets $S_{q,\sigma}$ computed in the last run of the *forward* procedure are stored, as they will be used in the *backward* procedure in the next section.

The idea behind the construction of N is as follows. Given a transition $\theta = q \overset{\sigma/\tau}{\rightarrow} r$ in P_0, pushing τ onto the stack and moving to state r corresponds to a path $y \overset{\tau^R}{\rightsquigarrow} r$ in N. A state x in N can jump to the first state in this path if there is a path $x \overset{\sigma^R}{\Rightarrow} q$ in N, because then we can reach q from x by pushing σ onto the stack. By executing θ, we pop σ from the stack, leading back to x, then

Algorithm 2. Procedure, called in step 4 of *forward*, which establishes a path $\overset{a_1 \ldots a_k}{\rightsquigarrow} z$ in the NFA N and returns the first state in this path.

4.1 If $k = 0$, then stop and return z.

4.2 If there is a transition $n \overset{a_k}{\rightarrow} z$ in N with n non-final (there is at most one such transition), then establish a path $\overset{a_1 \cdots a_{k-1}}{\rightsquigarrow} n$ in N.

4.3 Else add non-final states $n_1, \ldots, n_k$ and transitions $n_1 \overset{a_1}{\rightarrow} \cdots n_k \overset{a_k}{\rightarrow} z$ to N, stop, and return n_1.

jump to y, and push τ onto the stack via the path $y \overset{\tau^R}{\rightsquigarrow} r$. This jump is captured in N by an ε-transition from (every possible) x to y. To reduce the number of ε-transitions in N, we only consider those x with a path $x \overset{\sigma^R}{\Rightarrow} q$ in N that does not start with an ε-transition.

For each transition of P_0 at most one path is established in N, and for the rest N consists of ε-transitions (between states in such a path), so the construction of N always terminates. The set U_1 returned at the end contains exactly the unreachable transitions in P_0. A proof of this fact is presented at the end of this section.

We give an example construction of NFA N from a PDA. It will serve as running example in the remainder of this paper. As usual, the initial state in PDAs and NFAs is drawn with an incoming arrow, and final states with a double circle.

Example 1. Consider the following PDA P_0.

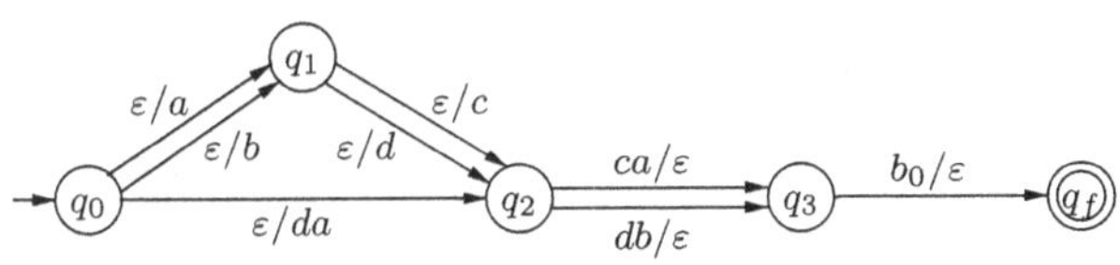

We have taken the liberty to omit the state q_e from P_0, to keep the example small, and since the state q_3 is always reached with the stack b_0.

To determine the reachable transitions in P_0, the following NFA N is constructed.

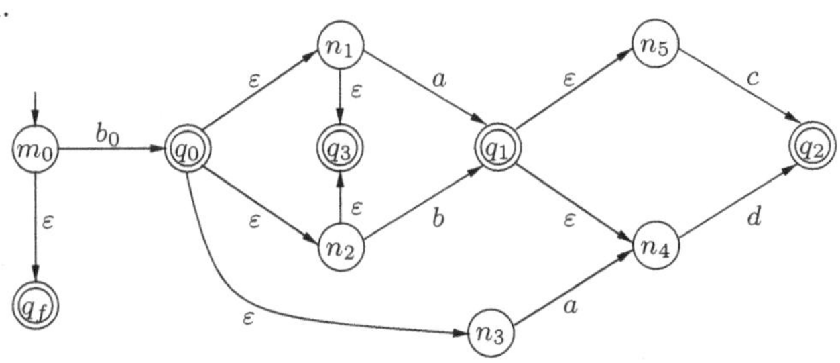

- Initially N consists of $m_0 \xrightarrow{b_0} q_0$.
- First the paths $q_0 \xrightarrow{\varepsilon} n_1 \xrightarrow{a} q_1$ and $q_0 \xrightarrow{\varepsilon} n_2 \xrightarrow{b} q_1$ and $q_0 \xrightarrow{\varepsilon} n_3 \xrightarrow{a} n_4 \xrightarrow{d} q_2$ are added to N, by the transitions $q_0 \xrightarrow{\varepsilon/a} q_1$ and $q_0 \xrightarrow{\varepsilon/b} q_1$ and $q_0 \xrightarrow{\varepsilon/da} q_2$, respectively, in P_0. These transitions are deleted from U_1.
- Next the paths $q_1 \xrightarrow{\varepsilon} n_5 \xrightarrow{c} q_2$ and $q_1 \xrightarrow{\varepsilon} n_4$ are added to N, by the transitions $q_1 \xrightarrow{\varepsilon/c} q_2$ and $q_1 \xrightarrow{\varepsilon/d} q_2$, respectively, in P_0, which are deleted from U_1.
- Next the transitions $n_1 \xrightarrow{\varepsilon} q_3$ and $n_2 \xrightarrow{\varepsilon} q_3$ are added to N, by the transitions $q_2 \xrightarrow{ca/\varepsilon} q_3$ and $q_2 \xrightarrow{db/\varepsilon} q_3$, respectively, in P_0, which are deleted from U_1.
- Finally the transition $m_0 \xrightarrow{\varepsilon} q_f$ is added to N, by the transition $q_3 \xrightarrow{b_0/\varepsilon} q_f$ in P_0, which is deleted from U_1.

Since all transitions in P_0 are applied in the construction of N, they are all reachable. That is, at the end $U_1 = \emptyset$, and P_1 coincides with P_0.

Correctness Proof. The following two properties of N, which follow immediately from its construction, give insight into the structure of N. In particular, Lemma 3 implies that in N, the outgoing transitions of a final state always carry the label ε, while each non-final state has exactly one outgoing transition with a label from Γ.

The following two lemmas can be proved by induction on the construction of N.

Lemma 2. *For each state x in N there is a path $m_0 \overset{\sigma}{\Rightarrow} x$ in N, for some σ.*

Lemma 3. *For each state x in N there is exactly one path $x \overset{\sigma}{\rightsquigarrow} q$ in N, for some σ, q.*

Example 4. Lemma 3 holds for all states in the NFA N from Example 1.

x	m_0	n_1	n_2	n_3	n_4	n_5	q_0	q_1	q_2	q_3	q_f
σ	b_0	a	b	ad	d	c	ε	ε	ε	ε	ε
q	q_0	q_1	q_1	q_2	q_2	q_2	q_0	q_1	q_2	q_3	q_f

Lemma 5. *If there are paths $x \overset{\sigma^R}{\rightsquigarrow} q$ and $x \overset{\tau^R}{\Rightarrow} r$ in N, then there is a run $(q, \sigma) \rightarrow^* (r, \tau)$ of P_1.*

Example 6. $m_0 \overset{b_0}{\rightsquigarrow} q_0$ and $m_0 \overset{b_0ad}{\Rightarrow} q_2$ in the NFA N from Example 1. We have $(q_0, b_0) \rightarrow (q_1, ab_0) \rightarrow (q_2, dab_0)$ in the corresponding PDA $P_1 = P_0$.

The following proposition is a corner stone in the correctness proof.

Proposition 7. *There is a path $m_0 \overset{\sigma^R}{\Rightarrow} r$ in N if, and only if, (r, σ) is reachable in P_0.*

Example 8. In the NFA N from Example 1, the paths from m_0 to a final state are $m_0 \overset{b_0}{\Rightarrow} q_0$, $m_0 \overset{b_0a}{\Rightarrow} q_1$, $m_0 \overset{b_0b}{\Rightarrow} q_1$, $m_0 \overset{b_0ac}{\Rightarrow} q_2$, $m_0 \overset{b_0ad}{\Rightarrow} q_2$, $m_0 \overset{b_0bc}{\Rightarrow} q_2$, $m_0 \overset{b_0bd}{\Rightarrow} q_2$, $m_0 \overset{b_0ad}{\Rightarrow} q_2$, $m_0 \overset{b_0}{\Rightarrow} q_3$, and $m_0 \overset{\varepsilon}{\Rightarrow} q_f$. In the corresponding PDA P_0 the reachable configurations are (q_0, b_0), (q_1, ab_0), (q_1, bb_0), (q_2, cab_0), (q_2, dab_0), (q_2, cbb_0), (q_2, dbb_0), (q_2, dab_0), (q_3, b_0), and (q_f, ε).

Theorem 9. *The returned set U_1 consists of the unreachable transitions in P_0.*

Proof. Suppose $\theta = q \xrightarrow{\sigma/\tau} r$ in P_0 is not in U_1. Then during the construction of N, θ was used in the creation of a path $y \overset{\tau^R}{\rightsquigarrow} r$, together with one or more transitions $x \xrightarrow{\varepsilon} y$. We choose one such x. The construction requires that there is a path $x \overset{\sigma^R}{\Rightarrow} q$ in N. And by Lemma 2, $m_0 \overset{\upsilon^R}{\Rightarrow} x$ for some υ. So by Proposition 7, $(q, \sigma\upsilon)$ is reachable in P_0. In this configuration, θ can be applied, to reach $(r, \tau\upsilon)$. So θ is reachable in P_0.

Vice versa, suppose θ is reachable in P_0. Then a configuration $(q, \sigma\rho)$ is reachable in P_0, for some ρ. So by Proposition 7 there is a path $m_0 \overset{(\sigma\rho)^R}{\Rightarrow} q$ in N. This path splits into $m_0 \overset{\rho^R}{\Rightarrow} x \overset{\sigma^R}{\Rightarrow} q$ in N, where we choose x such that $x \overset{\sigma^R}{\Rightarrow} q$ does not start with an ε-transition. In view of θ, a path $y \overset{\tau^R}{\rightsquigarrow} r$ and a transition $x \xrightarrow{\varepsilon} y$ were added to N. And as a result, θ was deleted from U_1. □

Example 10. In Example 1, the fact that $U_1 = \emptyset$ means that the PDA P_0 does not contain unreachable transitions.

Complexity Analysis. Let Q be the number of states and T the number of transitions in the PDA P_0. For simplicity, in the analysis of the worst-case time complexity of the algorithm we assume that the number of elements popped from and pushed onto the stack in one transition, as well as the size of the stack alphabet, are bounded by some constant. Then the NFA N contains at most $O(Q)$ states.

The worst-case time complexity of the *forward* procedure is $O(Q^4T)$. Firstly, the body of this procedure is run at most $O(Q^2)$ times (because N contains at most $O(Q^2)$ transitions). Secondly, in each run at most T times (once for each transition of P_0), in step 2 a backward scan over ε-transitions is performed, which takes at most $O(Q^2)$ (because there are at most $O(Q^2)$ ε-transitions).

3.2 Detecting Which Transitions Can Lead to the Final State

If the transition $m_0 \xrightarrow{\varepsilon} q_f$ is not in N, then by Proposition 7 the language accepted by P_0 is empty. So then all transitions in P_0 can be reported as useless and we are done.

So we can suppose that the transition $m_0 \xrightarrow{\varepsilon} q_f$ is in N. Recall that the PDA P_1 is obtained by culling the set U_1 of unreachable transitions, computed by the *forward* procedure, from the input PDA P_0. The set U_2 of useless transitions in P_1 is constructed by running the following *backward* procedure over ε-transitions in N that are in a set $E \backslash G$; at the start of such a run an ε-transition from $E \backslash G$ is copied to the set G, while on the other hand during the run ε-transitions from N may be added to E.

Initially U_2, as an overapproximation, contains all transitions in P_1, $E = \{m_0 \xrightarrow{\varepsilon} q_f\}$ and $G = \emptyset$. We recall from step 2 of the *forward* procedure that the set $S_{q,\sigma}$ equals $\{q\}$ if $\sigma = \varepsilon$, or the states n for which there exists a path

$n \xrightarrow{a} y \overset{\sigma'^R}{\Longrightarrow} q$ in N if $\sigma = \sigma' a$. These sets have already been computed in (the last run of) the *forward* procedure.

Algorithm 3. Procedure *backward* to compute the transitions in the PDA P_1 via which the final state cannot be reached.

While $E \backslash G \neq \emptyset$ do:

1. Pick an $x \xrightarrow{\varepsilon} y \in E \backslash G$ and add it to G.
2. Find the path $y \overset{\tau^R}{\rightsquigarrow} r$ in N (for some τ, r); since r denotes a final state, according to Lem. 3, exactly one such path exists.
3. For each transition $\theta = q \overset{\sigma/\tau}{\longrightarrow} r$ in P_1 (for any q, σ) do:

3.1 If $x \notin S_{q,\sigma}$, then stop this iteration step (i.e., return to step 3).

3.2 If $\theta \in U_2$, then delete θ from U_2.

3.3 If $\sigma = \sigma' a$ (i.e., $\sigma \neq \varepsilon$), then add to E the ε-transitions that occur in any path $x \xrightarrow{a} z \overset{\sigma'^R}{\Rightarrow} q$ in N.

Stop, and return the set U_2 of useless transitions in P_1.

The transitions in $U_1 \cup U_2$ that stem from the original PDA P (i.e., not those from the preprocessing step in which q_e and q_f were added) are the useless transitions in P, so can be culled without changing the associated language.

The idea behind the *backward* procedure is that a transition $x \xrightarrow{\varepsilon} y$ in N is added to E when we are certain that, for some ρ, υ and s, there is a path $m_0 \overset{\rho^R}{\Rightarrow} x \xrightarrow{\varepsilon} y \overset{\upsilon^R}{\Rightarrow} s$ in N and a run $(s, \upsilon\rho) \rightarrow^* (q_f, \varepsilon)$ of P_1. Each transition $x \xrightarrow{\varepsilon} y$ in E may in turn give rise to adding ε-transitions in N to E, and removing transitions from U_2. Namely, by Lemma 3 there is exactly one path $y \overset{\tau^R}{\rightsquigarrow} r$ in N (for some τ, r). For each transition $\theta = q \overset{\sigma/\tau}{\longrightarrow} r$ (for any q, σ) in P_1, all ε-transitions in any path $x \overset{\sigma^R}{\Rightarrow} q$ in N can be added to E. The reason is that there is a path $m_0 \overset{\rho^R}{\Rightarrow} x \overset{\sigma^R}{\Rightarrow} q$ in N, as well as a run $(q, \sigma\rho) \rightarrow^* (q_f, \varepsilon)$ of P_1. The transition θ gives rise to the move $(q, \sigma\rho) \rightarrow (r, \tau\rho)$; in view of the paths $y \overset{\tau^R}{\rightsquigarrow} r$ and $y \overset{\upsilon^R}{\Rightarrow} s$ in N, by Lemma 5 there is a run $(r, \tau\rho) \rightarrow^* (s, \upsilon\rho)$ of P_1; and by assumption there is a run $(s, \upsilon\rho) \rightarrow^* (q_f, \varepsilon)$ of P_1. So if there is a path $x \overset{\sigma^R}{\Rightarrow} q$ in N, then θ is useful: in view of the path $m_0 \overset{\rho^R}{\Rightarrow} x \overset{\sigma^R}{\Rightarrow} q$ in N, by Proposition 7, the configuration $(q, \sigma\rho)$ is reachable in P_0; and we argued there is a run $(q, \sigma\rho) \rightarrow^* (q_f, \varepsilon)$ of P_1, which starts with an application of θ. Hence θ can be removed from U_2. To try and avoid adding the same ε-transition to E more than once, we only consider those paths $x \overset{\sigma^R}{\Rightarrow} q$ in N that do not start with an ε-transition.

The *backward* procedure is executed only a finite number of times, as it is performed at most once for each ε-transition of N. The set U_2 returned at the end contains exactly the useless transitions in P_1. The corresponding theorem is presented at the end of this section, together with two propositions needed in its proof.

Example 11. We perform the *backward* procedure on the NFA N from Example 1.

- Initially $E = \{m_0 \xrightarrow{\varepsilon} q_f\}$ and $G = \emptyset$.
- $m_0 \xrightarrow{\varepsilon} q_f$ is added to G; then $\tau = \varepsilon$ and $r = q_f$. Since $S_{q_3,b_0} = \{m_0\}$, the transition $q_3 \xrightarrow{b_0/\varepsilon} q_f$ is deleted from U_2, and the ε-transitions in paths $m_0 \xrightarrow{b_0} z \overset{\varepsilon}{\Rightarrow} q_3$ in N are added to E: $q_0 \xrightarrow{\varepsilon} n_1 \xrightarrow{\varepsilon} q_3$ and $q_0 \xrightarrow{\varepsilon} n_2 \xrightarrow{\varepsilon} q_3$.
- $q_0 \xrightarrow{\varepsilon} n_1$ is added to G; then $\tau = a$ and $r = q_1$. Since $S_{q_0,\varepsilon} = \{q_0\}$, the transition $q_0 \xrightarrow{\varepsilon/a} q_1$ is deleted from U_2.
- $q_0 \xrightarrow{\varepsilon} n_2$ is added to G; then $\tau = b$ and $r = q_1$. Since $S_{q_0,\varepsilon} = \{q_0\}$, the transition $q_0 \xrightarrow{\varepsilon/b} q_1$ is deleted from U_2.
- $n_1 \xrightarrow{\varepsilon} q_3$ is added to G; then $\tau = \varepsilon$ and $r = q_3$. Since $S_{q_2,ca} = \{n_1\}$, the transition $q_2 \xrightarrow{ca/\varepsilon} q_3$ is deleted from U_2, and the ε-transitions in paths $n_1 \xrightarrow{a} z \overset{c}{\Rightarrow} q_2$ in N are added to E: $q_1 \xrightarrow{\varepsilon} n_5$.
- $n_2 \xrightarrow{\varepsilon} q_3$ is added to G; then $\tau = \varepsilon$ and $r = q_3$. Since $S_{q_2,db} = \{n_2\}$, the transition $q_2 \xrightarrow{db/\varepsilon} q_3$ is deleted from U_2, and the ε-transitions in paths $n_2 \xrightarrow{b} z \overset{d}{\Rightarrow} q_2$ in N are added to E: $q_1 \xrightarrow{\varepsilon} n_4$.
- $q_1 \xrightarrow{\varepsilon} n_5$ is added to G; then $\tau = c$ and $r = q_2$. Since $S_{q_1,\varepsilon} = \{q_1\}$, the transition $q_1 \xrightarrow{\varepsilon/c} q_2$ is deleted from U_2.
- $q_1 \xrightarrow{\varepsilon} n_4$ is added to G; then $\tau = d$ and $r = q_2$. Since $S_{q_1,\varepsilon} = \{q_1\}$, the transition $q_1 \xrightarrow{\varepsilon/d} q_2$ is deleted from U_2.

At the end, U_2 consists of $q_0 \xrightarrow{\varepsilon/da} q_2$. So this transition is useless in P_1.

Example 11 shows that in step 2 of the *backward* procedure, the path $y \overset{\tau^R}{\rightsquigarrow} r$ cannot be replaced by all paths $y \overset{\tau^R}{\Rightarrow} r$ in N. Else $q_0 \xrightarrow{\varepsilon/da} q_2$ would be erroneously deleted from U_2, in view of the transition $q_0 \xrightarrow{\varepsilon} n_1$ in E and the path $n_1 \xrightarrow{a} q_1 \xrightarrow{\varepsilon} n_4 \xrightarrow{d} q_2$ in N.

Correctness Proof. The following proposition is needed to show that only useful transitions in P_1 are deleted from U_2 during runs of the *backward* procedure.

Proposition 12. *Let $x \xrightarrow{\varepsilon} y$ be a transition in E, and $y \overset{\tau^R}{\rightsquigarrow} r$ a path in N. Then there is a path $m_0 \overset{\rho^R}{\Rightarrow} x$ in N, for some ρ, such that there is a run $(r, \tau\rho) \rightarrow^* (q_f, \varepsilon)$ of P_1.*

Example 13. We revisit Example 1. According to Example 11, $q_1 \xrightarrow{\varepsilon} n_5 \in E$. Moreover, $n_5 \overset{c}{\rightsquigarrow} q_2$ is a path in N. The only run of P_1 from q_2 with c on the top of the stack to (q_f, ε) is $(q_2, cab_0) \rightarrow^* (q_f, \varepsilon)$. Indeed, as predicted by Proposition 12, there is a path $m_0 \overset{b_0 a}{\Rightarrow} q_1$ in N.

The following proposition is needed to show that all useful transitions in P_1 are eventually deleted from U_2.

Proposition 14. *Let $(r, \tau\rho) \rightarrow^* (q_f, \varepsilon)$ be a run of P_1 and $m_0 \overset{\rho^R}{\Rightarrow} x \overset{\varepsilon}{\rightarrow} y \overset{\tau^R}{\Rightarrow} r$ a path in N. Then $x \overset{\varepsilon}{\rightarrow} y$ is in E when the* backward *procedure terminates.*

Example 15. Again we revisit Example 1. Consider the run $(q_1, ab_0) \rightarrow^* (q_f, \varepsilon)$ of P_1 and the path $m_0 \overset{b_0}{\Rightarrow} q_0 \overset{\varepsilon}{\rightarrow} n_1 \overset{a}{\Rightarrow} q_1$ in N. As predicted by Proposition 14, $q_0 \overset{\varepsilon}{\rightarrow} n_1$ is in E when the *backward* procedure terminates in Example 11.

Theorem 16. *The returned set U_2 consists of the useless transitions in P_1.*

Proof. Suppose the transition $\theta = q \overset{\sigma/\tau}{\rightarrow} r$ in P_1 is not in U_2. Since θ is in P_1, by the *forward* procedure, there is a path $y \overset{\tau^R}{\rightsquigarrow} r$ in N. Since $\theta \notin U_2$, while running the *backward* procedure, for some x, the transition $x \overset{\varepsilon}{\rightarrow} y$ was found to be in E, and a path $x \overset{\sigma^R}{\Rightarrow} q$ was found to be in N. In view of the transition $x \overset{\varepsilon}{\rightarrow} y$ in E and the path $y \overset{\tau^R}{\rightsquigarrow} r$ in N, by Proposition 12, there is a path $m_0 \overset{\rho^R}{\Rightarrow} x$ in N, for some ρ, such that there is a run $(r, \tau\rho) \rightarrow^* (q_f, \varepsilon)$ of P_1. In view of the path $m_0 \overset{\rho^R}{\Rightarrow} x \overset{\sigma^R}{\Rightarrow} q$ in N, by Proposition 7, $(q, \sigma\rho)$ is reachable in P_1. By applying θ to this configuration, $(r, \tau\rho)$ is reached. Since moreover there is a run $(r, \tau\rho) \rightarrow^* (q_f, \varepsilon)$ of P_1, θ is useful in P_1.

Vice versa, suppose θ is useful in P_1. Then there is a run $(q_0, b_0) \rightarrow^* (q, \sigma\rho) \rightarrow (r, \tau\rho) \rightarrow^* (q_f, \varepsilon)$ of P_1. In view of the run $(q_0, b_0) \rightarrow^* (q, \sigma\rho)$, by Proposition 7, there is a path $m_0 \overset{\rho^R}{\Rightarrow} x \overset{\sigma^R}{\Rightarrow} q$ in N, where we choose x such that $x \overset{\sigma^R}{\Rightarrow} q$ does not start with an ε-transition. Since θ is in P_1, by the *forward* procedure, there is a path $x \overset{\varepsilon}{\rightarrow} y \overset{\tau^R}{\rightsquigarrow} r$ in N. In view of the run $(r, \tau\rho) \rightarrow^* (q_f, \varepsilon)$, by Proposition 14, $x \overset{\varepsilon}{\rightarrow} y$ is eventually in E. In view of the paths $y \overset{\tau^R}{\rightsquigarrow} r$ and $x \overset{\sigma^R}{\Rightarrow} q$ in N, during the iteration of the *backward* procedure in which $x \overset{\varepsilon}{\rightarrow} y$ is added to G, θ is deleted from U_2. □

Example 17. In Example 11, the fact that $U_2 = \{q_0 \overset{\varepsilon/da}{\rightarrow} q_2\}$ means that this is the only useless transition of the PDA P_1.

Complexity Analysis. Computing U_2 takes at most $O(Q^4T)$: for each of the at most $O(Q^2)$ ε-transitions in E, and for at most T transitions in P_1, in step 3.3 a forward scan is performed over the ε-transitions in N, which takes at most $O(Q^2)$.

4 Alternative Approaches

We discuss three alternative approaches to detect useless transitions in PDAs.

One approach is to transform the PDA under consideration into an equivalent context-free grammar, and then determine the useless productions. Disadvantage here is that the resulting grammar tends to be much larger than the original PDA.

A second approach is to check for each transition separately whether it is useless: provide the transition with a special input symbol ξ, all other transitions in the PDA with empty input ε, and check whether the language accepted by the resulting PDA intersected with the regular language ξ^+ is empty. Emptiness of a PDA can be checked by getting rid of ε-transitions, determining an upper bound on the length of the shortest string in the language (if any), and checking all strings up to this length. This approach however is much more expensive than the one put forward in the current paper.

The most interesting alternative is to use the algorithms from [2,4] to compute $post*(C)$ and $pre*(C)$, with C a set of configurations of the PDA under consideration: $post*(C)$ contains the configurations reachable in the PDA from a configuration in C, while $pre*(C)$ contains the configurations from which a configuration in C can be reached in the PDA. The idea is as follows. To check whether a transition $\theta = q \overset{\sigma/\tau}{\rightarrow} r$ of the PDA is useless, introduce a fresh state q_θ, and replace θ in the PDA by two transitions: $q \overset{\varepsilon/\varepsilon}{\rightarrow} q_\theta$ and $q_\theta \overset{\sigma/\tau}{\rightarrow} r$. Then θ is useless if and only if

$$post*(\{(q_0, \varepsilon)\}) \ \cap \ (\{q_\theta\} \times \Gamma^*) \ \cap \ pre*(F \times \Gamma^*) \ = \ \emptyset \ .$$

The $post*$ set captures the reachable configurations, while the $pre*$ set captures the configurations from which a final state can be reached. The set $\{q_\theta\} \times \Gamma^*$ checks whether θ is used on a path from initial configuration to final state.

5 Implementation and Performance Comparison

We assessed an implementation of our algorithm with a test suite of randomly generated PDAs. The only real-world PDA, with 294 transitions, was obtained from the grammar of the programming language C. This resulted in an NFA with 339 states and 1030 transitions, of which 695 ε-transitions, and took 3.56 s on a 2 GHz processor.

Achieving this performance required two optimizations, both limiting the influence of ε-transitions. The first concerns determining the set of states leading to q in step 2 of the *forward* procedure. This set is constructed by following paths backwards from q, which may lead through webs of ε-transitions, causing a considerable slow-down. These ε-transitions were created in step 5 of the *forward* procedure. The optimization consists of computing for each state s, in step 5, the set $B(s)$ of states that can reach s through ε-transitions only. If more ε-transitions are added in step 5 during a next iteration, B is updated. The second optimization concerns memoization of ε-transitions as they are encountered on paths to q in step 3.3 of the *backward* procedure.

Furthermore, the third alternative approach described in Sect. 4 was implemented, and its performance was compared with the implementation of our algorithm. Actually four versions of that approach were implemented. In the first version, transitions in the input PDA that pop more than one element from the stack or push more than two elements onto the stack are first broken up into multiple transitions that pop one element from the stack and push at most two elements onto the stack. In the second version, the computations of *pre∗* and *post∗* have been redesigned to avoid this preprocessing step; and unlike the first version, the second version can cope with PDA transitions that pop no elements from the stack. The third and fourth versions make use of the fact that the redesigned *pre∗* and *post∗* procedures are each other's duals and can be defined in terms of each other. The first three versions exhibit a worst-case time complexity of $O(S^3T^4)$ and the fourth version $O(S^2T^4)$, with S the maximum stack string length in the PDA transitions. (We take S into account here because of this small distinction.)

It should be noted that the last three versions of the alternative approach do not terminate for certain input PDAs. This is due to the fact that the redesigned *pre∗* and *post∗* procedures, which eliminate the need for input preprocessing, result in an infinite loop whenever the input PDA contains certain loops. PDAs on which at least one of these algorithms did not terminate have been excluded from the comparison in Table 1.

The prototype implementations of the alternative approach have certain drawbacks, which are described in [3]. The most relevant to the performance comparison is the maximum allowed set size (*L_SIZE*). For each transition in the PDA, the alternative approach computes the intersection of two NFAs in order to determine whether the transition is useless. As a result, the set of states overflows fairly quickly even for small inputs. *L_SIZE* has to be adjusted for each input PDA at compile time. This posed a limit on the size of the PDAs that could be tested. An additional parameter, *M_SIZE*, exists and serves a similar purpose to that of *L_SIZE*. For certain inputs this parameter has to be adjusted as well. To keep the comparison fair, all implementations were tested using the same *M_SIZE* and *L_SIZE* for a particular input. Some indicative results are presented in Table 1. Q denotes the number of states, T the number of transitions, and S the maximum stack string length in the PDA. The PDAs were generated using the *PDAgen* tool. The number of useless transitions they contain, which ranges from none to all transitions, appears to have no impact on the running time of the algorithms.

In Table 1, entries have been sorted on the basis of the S^3T^4 size of the input PDA. This performance analysis shows that the algorithm presented in the current paper clearly outperforms the four implementations based on the third approach in Sect. 4. Our algorithm's running time shows a favorable running time when the size of the input PDA is increased, owing to the fact that its worst-case time complexity $O(Q^4T)$ only occurs in the unlikely case that the NFA is constructed over a large number of iterations, is saturated with ε-transitions, and contains a lot of backward nondeterminism. Rather its efficiency is affected by an increase of *L_SIZE*, while increasing this parameter is actually only needed for the implementation of the alternative approach in the above test cases. To illustrate this and indicate how our algorithm performs when PDA size increases, Table 2 shows the performance of our algorithm on different-sized inputs. For larger input PDAs *M_SIZE* and *L_SIZE* have been adjusted as necessary.

Table 1. Performance of our algorithm against the alternative approach

Input PDA					Algorithm (sec)				
Q	*T*	*S*	*M_SIZE*	*L_SIZE*	Ours	Alt. 1	Alt. 2	Alt. 3	Alt. 4
4	5	5	600	1200	0.38	1.33	1.08	1.29	1.00
6	6	9	600	2000	0.66	3.14	2.16	2.32	2.12
11	10	5	600	1200	0.32	2.82	2.13	2.55	1.89
7	10	7	600	1200	0.38	3.59	2.36	2.56	2.18
8	10	8	600	2000	0.66	4.84	3.36	3.77	3.23
7	10	12	600	2800	1.02	16.86	11.57	6.29	11.17
16	20	6	600	2000	0.65	18.21	12.68	11.58	7.69
6	10	17	600	5000	2.06	34.48	25.56	11.15	26.14
22	31	5	600	3000	1.04	26.35	22.86	26.61	19.20
9	20	10	600	6000	2.50	78.33	159.49	45.00	99.24
8	20	13	600	8000	3.83	156.01	108.35	90.24	116.95
8	20	13	600	10000	5.96	274.46	325.94	141.99	376.41

A detailed account of the implementation of the alternative approach and the performance comparison is presented in [3].

Table 2. Scalability of our algorithm

Input PDA				Algorithm (sec)
Q	T	*M_SIZE*	*L_SIZE*	Our alg.
16	20	600	1200	0.38
26	40	600	1200	0.45
30	50	600	1200	0.47
29	60	600	1200	0.50
33	70	600	1200	0.68
44	80	600	1200	0.68
60	120	600	1200	1.39
86	140	600	1200	1.33
3	294	600	1200	3.56
107	200	1200	2000	5.54
128	300	1200	2000	5.58
155	400	2000	3000	31.02
170	500	2000	3000	39.12
185	600	3000	4000	75.26
250	600	3000	4000	74.77

Acknowledgments. Javier Esparza proposed the alternative approach using *pre*∗ and *post*∗. Jörg Endrullis provided a useful suggestion for the efficient implementation of this alternative approach.

References

1. Bertsch, E., Nederhof, M.-J.: Regular closure of deterministic languages. SIAM J. Comput. **29**(1), 81–102 (1999)
2. Bouajjani, A., Esparza, J., Maler, O.: Reachability analysis of pushdown automata: application to model-checking. In: Mazurkiewicz, A., Winkowski, J. (eds.) CONCUR 1997. LNCS, vol. 1243, pp. 135–150. Springer, Heidelberg (1997). doi:10.1007/3-540-63141-0_10
3. Chatzikalymnios, E.: Comparison of two algorithms for detecting useless transitions in pushdown automata. BSc. thesis, Vrije Universiteit Amsterdam (2016). http://www.cs.vu.nl/~tcs/chatzikalymnios-bscthesis.pdf
4. Esparza, J., Hansel, D., Rossmanith, P., Schwoon, S.: Efficient algorithms for model checking pushdown systems. In: Emerson, E.A., Sistla, A.P. (eds.) CAV 2000. LNCS, vol. 1855, pp. 232–247. Springer, Heidelberg (2000). doi:10.1007/10722167_20
5. Finkel, A., Willems, B., Wolper, P.: A direct symbolic approach to model checking pushdown systems. In: INFINITY 1997. ENTCS, vol. 9, pp. 27–37. Elsevier (1997)
6. Goldstine, J., Price, J.K., Wotschke, D.: A pushdown automaton or a context-free grammar - which is more economical? Theoret. Comput. Sci. **18**, 33–40 (1982)
7. Griffin, C.: A note on deciding controllability in pushdown systems. IEEE Trans. Autom. Control **51**(2), 334–337 (2006)
8. Grune, D., Jacobs, C.: Parsing Techniques - A Practical Guide, 2nd edn. Springer, Heidelberg (2008)
9. Linz, P.: An Introduction to Formal Languages and Automata. Jones & Bartlett, Burlington (2011)
10. Nederhof, M.-J., Bertsch, E.: Linear-time suffix parsing for deterministic languages. J. ACM **43**(3), 524–554 (1996)
11. Walukiewicz, I.: Pushdown processes: games and model checking. In: Alur, R., Henzinger, T.A. (eds.) CAV 1996. LNCS, vol. 1102, pp. 62–74. Springer, Heidelberg (1996). doi:10.1007/3-540-61474-5_58

Hardness Results for Coverability Problem of Well-Structured Pushdown Systems

Chunmiao Li and Xiaojuan Cai(✉)

School of Electronic Information and Electrical Engineering, Shanghai Jiao Tong University, No. 800, Dongchuan Rd, Shanghai 200240, China
{lichunmiao,cxj}@sjtu.edu.cn

Abstract. Well-Structured Pushdown Systems (WSPDSs) are pushdown systems extended with states and stack alphabet to be vectors, for modeling (restricted) recursive concurrent programs. It has been considered to be "very close to the border of undecidability". In this paper, we prove some hardness results for the coverability problem of WSPDSs. We show that for WSPDS with three dimensional vectors as states and WSPDS with three dimensional vectors as stack alphabet, the coverability problem becomes Ackermann-hard.

Keywords: Automata and logic · Coverability · Lower bounds

1 Introduction

A *Well-Structured Pushdown System (WSPDS)* [4] has been proposed to combine *Pushdown Systems (PDS)* [2] and *Well-Structured Transition System (WSTS)* [1], for modeling multi-threaded recursive programs. Simply speaking, WSPDSs are PDSs with well-quasi-ordered (potentially infinite) sets as states or stack alphabet. WSPDSs have powerful expressiveness and are considered as "being close to the border of undecidability" [8], which can be illustrated by the following example.

Example 1. The program in Fig. 1 weakly computes the Ackermann function $A(2, n)$ (see Eq. 1) with only one global variable. Note that since we do not allow *zero-tests*, the expression $*$ nondeterministically evaluates to `true` or `false`. It can not exactly evaluate $A(2, n)$, but the largest value of `x` is $A(2, n)$.

This program can be formalized as the WSPDS on the right of Fig. 1, where states are pairs of current value of global variable `x` and the line number in the codes, and stack symbols correspond to names of procedures. The transitions between states tell how to manipulate the global variable and the stack. For example the cyclic transition -1, *push* A_1 on state 5 means $x = x - 1$ for global x and push symbol A_1 to the stack. The transition *pop* A_0 from state 22 to 20 means (checking and) popping the top element A_0 from the stack.

Recursive nonnegative integer programs can be modeled as WSPDSs where either the states are vectors (global nonnegative integer variables) or the stack

F. Drewes et al. (Eds.): LATA 2017, LNCS 10168, pp. 435–446, 2017.
DOI: 10.1007/978-3-319-53733-7_32

```
x ← n
procedure MAIN
    A2
procedure A2
    if (* ∧ x > 0)
        x ← x - 1
        A2
        A1
    else
        x ← x + 1
        A1
procedure A1
    if (* ∧ x > 0)
        x ← x - 1
        A1
        A0
    else
        x ← x + 1
        A0
procedure A0
    x ← x + 1

```

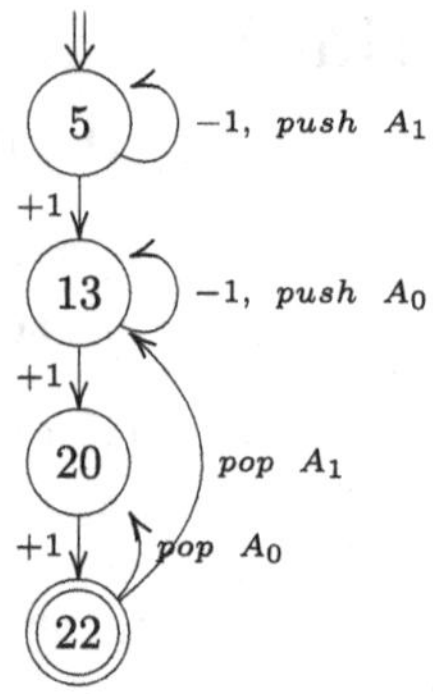

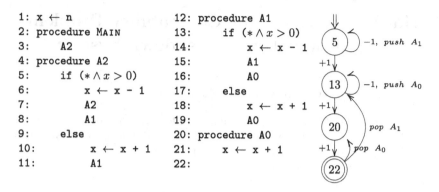

Fig. 1. The program that computes Ackermann function with only one global variable, and its corresponding WSPDS

alphabets are vectors (local nonnegative integer variables). Recursive concurrent programs also can be modeled as WSPDSs where the stack symbols are vectors representing the number of active threads [3]. So the coverability problem of WSPDS can be applied to recursive program analysis. However, the results in this paper indicate these problems are very hard.

In this paper, we investigate the coverability of two subclasses of WSPDSs: one is WSPDS with vectors as states but finite stack alphabet, and another is with finite states but vectors as stack symbols. Our contributions include:

- We show a general framework to prove hardness results of the coverability problem, inspired by the elegant work by Schnoebelen *et al.* [5,11]. We proved that once a model can *weakly compute* and *weakly reversely compute* some function f, then its coverability problem is f-hard.
- We prove that for WSPDSs with 3-dimensional vector as states but finite stack alphabet, and those with finite states but 3-dimensional vectors as stack alphabet, the coverability problems are Ackermann-hard.

Related Work. There are a few hardness results for models such as Vector Addition Systems (VAS), Reset VAS, Pushdown VASS, *ect.*

- The best known lowerbounds for VAS was given by Lipton in his seminal work [9]. He proved that the lowerbounds of coverability and reachability of VAS are EXPSPACE, which has never been improved in the last 40 years.
- With the same technique as Lipton's, Lazíc [6] proved that the lower bound of coverability for pushdown systems with vectors as states is TOWER-hard.
- Schnoebelen *et al.* [5,11] proved that the coverability problem of reset Petri Nets is Ackermann-hard by using another brilliant technique especially worked for models with reset-zeros.

We use techniques proposed by Schnoebelen *et al.*. The main idea is substituting *zero-tests* on bounded counters with resettings. If you reset non-zeros to zeros, then you will get "punished" afterwards. The simulation forces and guarantees a correct run which is similar to real zero-tests.

Reset Petri Nets are special cases of WSPDS. However, in their result, the dimension of Reset Petri Nets is related to m in the value $A(m, n)$. In WSPDSs, with the help of stack, the reductions are independent from the value of either m or n.

Leroux *et al.* [8] proved the decidability of termination problem of Pushdown VASS, and they also give a Hyper-Ackermannian lower bound of the reachability tree algorithm for termination. Note their lower bounds are established for specific algorithms, not for the problem.

2 Preliminary

Throughout the paper, we use p, q to range over states, α, β over stack symbols, and w, v over stack words. We write $\mathbb{N}$ (resp. $\mathbb{Z}$) for the set of natural numbers (resp. integers), and $\mathbb{N}^k$ (resp. $\mathbb{Z}^k$) is the set of k-dimensional vectors over $\mathbb{N}$ (resp. $\mathbb{Z}$). We use $\vec{n}, \vec{m}$ to range over vectors in $\mathbb{N}^k$, and $\vec{a}, \vec{a}'$ for vectors in $\mathbb{Z}^k$. We write $\vec{n}[j]$ to denote the j-th element of $\vec{n}$. ϵ is an empty word.

2.1 Well-Structured Pushdown System

Definition 2. *A* Well-Structured Pushdown System (WSPDS) *is a triplet* $\langle P, \Gamma, \Delta\rangle$ *where*

- *P, the set of states is finite or $P = \mathbb{N}^k$ for some k,*
- *Γ, the stack alphabet is finite, or $\Gamma = \mathbb{N}^d$ for some d, and*
- *Δ is a finite set of monotonic partial functions: $P \times \Gamma^{\leq 2} \to P \times \Gamma^{\leq 2}$.*

Monotonicity means if $f(p, w) = (q, v)$ for $p, q \in P$ and $w, v \in \Gamma^{\leq 2}$, then for any $p' \geq p, w' \gtrsim w$ we have $f(p', w') = (q', v')$ and $q' \geq q, v' \gtrsim v$. Here $\gtrsim$ is an element-wise extension of $\geq$ on Γ^*. The termination problem for WSPDSs is decidable [7]. However, if we remove monotonicity, *Well-Structured Pushdown System* becomes Turing complete.

A *configuration* $\langle p, w\rangle$ is a pair of a state p and a stack content (word) w. One step transition $\hookrightarrow$ between configurations can be seen as the configuration rewriting, and $\hookrightarrow^*$ is the reflexive transitive closure of $\hookrightarrow$.

$$\frac{(p, w \to q, v) \in \Delta}{\langle p, ww'\rangle \hookrightarrow \langle q, vw'\rangle}$$

Given an initial configuration c_0 and final configuration $c_f = \langle q, v\rangle$, the *reachability* problem asks whether $c_0 \hookrightarrow^* c_f$, and the *coverability* problem determines whether there exist $q' \geq q$ and $v' \gtrsim v$ such that $c_0 \hookrightarrow^* \langle q', v'\rangle$.

Example 3. Let $\mathrm{M} = \langle(\mathbb{N}, \leq), (\mathbb{N}, \leq), \Delta\rangle$ be a WSPDS where

$$\Delta = \begin{cases} r_1 : p, \alpha \to p+2, (\alpha-2)(\alpha-2), & if\ \alpha \geq 2 \\ r_2 : p, \epsilon \to p-2, 2, & if\ p \geq 2 \end{cases}$$

The configuration $c_0 = \langle 2, 0\rangle$ can reach $\langle 2, 000\rangle$. It can not reach $\langle 1, 000\rangle$, which can be covered however.

2.2 Two-Counter Machine

Definition 4. *A* counter machine *is a triplet* $M = \langle P, C, \Delta \rangle$*, where* P *is a finite set of states,* C *is a finite set of counters and* $\Delta \subseteq P \times op(C) \times P$ *are finite transition rules. The instruction set* $op(C)$ *is a set of rules which are defined below and* C_i *is the i-th counter of* M*.*

$$op ::= C_i = 0? \mid C_i{+}{+} \mid C_i > 0?C_i{-}{-}$$

A *configuration* is a tuple $(p, \vec{n})$ with $p \in P$ and $\vec{n} \in \mathbb{N}^{|C|}$, representing the current contents of each counter.

The transition between configurations $(p, \vec{n}) \hookrightarrow (q, \vec{m})$ is defined as follows.

- If $(p, C_i = 0?, q) \in \Delta$ and $\vec{n}[i] = 0$, then $\vec{m} = \vec{n}$;
- If $(p, C_i{+}{+}, q) \in \Delta$, then $\vec{m}[i] = \vec{n}[i] + 1$ and $\vec{m}[j] = \vec{n}[j]$ for $j \neq i$;
- If $(p, C_i > 0?C_i{-}{-}, q) \in \Delta$ and $\vec{n}[i] > 0$, then $\vec{m}[i] = \vec{n}[i] - 1$ and $\vec{m}[j] = \vec{n}[j]$ for $j \neq i$;

Given an initial configuration $(p_0, \vec{0})$ and a final configuration $(p_f, \vec{0})$, the *reachability* problem asks whether there exists a run $(p_0, \vec{0}) \hookrightarrow^* (p_f, \vec{0})$.

Two-counter machines (counter machines with $|C| = 2$) are Turing complete [10]. However, we can restrict their computing power by applying a bound for counters. For example, if the bound is 2^{2^n} where n is the input size, then the reachability problem is EXPSPACE-hard. Similarly, if the bound is Ackermann function, then the reachability problem is Ackermann-hard.

We write $(p, \vec{n}) \overset{B}{\hookrightarrow} (q, \vec{m})$ to denote the run bounded by B, i.e., the sum of all counters does not exceed B during the run. We write $\overset{B}{\hookrightarrow}^*$ for the reflexive and transitive closure of $\overset{B}{\hookrightarrow}$.

We recall the definition of Ackermann function here, and note that Ackermann function is strictly monotonic.

$$A(m, n) = \begin{cases} n + 1 & \text{if } m = 0 \\ A(m-1, 1) & \text{if } n = 0 \\ A(m-1, A(m, n-1)) & \text{otherwise} \end{cases} \tag{1}$$

Lemma 5. *Ackermann function is strictly monotonic: For any* $m' > m$*,* $A(m', n) > A(m, n)$*, and for any* $n' > n$*,* $A(m, n') > A(m, n)$*.*

3 General Reduction Framework

We apply techniques proposed by Schnoebelen *et al.* [5,11], in which they reduce the reachability problem of Ackermann-bound two counter machines to the coverability of Reset Petri Nets. In this section, we give a general framework of the reduction from the reachability problem of f-bound two-counter machine to the coverability problem of some model, where f is a strictly monotonic function.

Briefly speaking, the reduction consists of three parts:

1. M_A computes the value $f(\vec{n})$ given the input $\vec{n}$;
2. M^b simulates a two-counter machine with $f(\vec{n})$-bounds;
3. M_A^{-1} reversely computes $f(\vec{n})$.

Given some $\vec{n}$, the first part M_A computes the bound for M^b. This bound is at most $f(\vec{n})$. After the simulation, M^b will decrease (wrong simulation) or keep (correct simulation) the value of the bound. Then this value is passed to the third part M_A^{-1} for reverse computation. The strict monotonicity guarantees that if the passed value is smaller than $f(\vec{n})$, we can not cover $\vec{n}$ in the third part. Only a correct simulation run can lead to the coverability of $\vec{n}$. We depict the idea in Fig. 2.

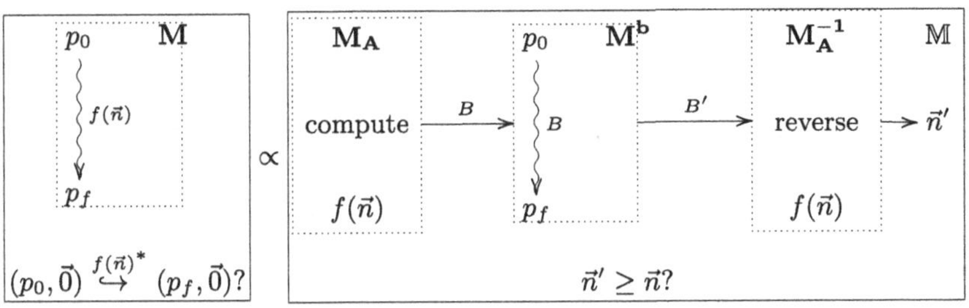

Fig. 2. Reduction from the reachability problem of two-counter machine with $f(\vec{n})$-bounds to the coverability problem of $\mathbb{M}$

3.1 Simulation of Two-Counter Machines with Bounds

In this part, we explain the construction of M^b in Fig. 2. Assume $M = \langle P, C, \Delta \rangle$ be a counter machine. We use $M^b = \langle P', C \cup \{b\}, \Delta' \rangle$ to simulate M under the bound of value b. Starting from $P' = P$ and $\Delta' = \emptyset$, we construct M^b by considering each rule $(p, op(C), q)$ in Δ:

- If $op(C)$ is $C_i{+}{+}$, then $P' = P' \cup \{s\}$ where fresh state $s \notin P'$, and $\Delta' = \Delta' \cup \{(p, b > 0?b{-}{-}, s), (s, C_i{+}{+}, q)\}$;
- If $op(C)$ is $C_i > 0?C_i{-}{-}$, then $P' = P' \cup \{s\}$ where fresh state $s \notin P'$, and $\Delta' = \Delta' \cup \{(p, C_i > 0?C_i{-}{-}, s), (s, b{+}{+}, q)\}$;
- If $op(C)$ is $C_i = 0?$, then $\Delta' = \Delta' \cup \{(p, \texttt{reset}\ C_i, q)\}$

Note that different models might have different syntax for the operation `reset` C_i, which resets counter C_i to 0. The idea is depicted in Fig. 3. It is easy to have the following two observations:

1. During the run of M^b, if `reset` C_i for any i never happens, the summation of counters will keep unchanged.
2. During the run of M^b, if `reset` C_i for some i happens, the summation of counters might decrease. Once we reset $C_i \neq 0$ to 0, we decrease C_i without increasing b, which makes the summation shrink.

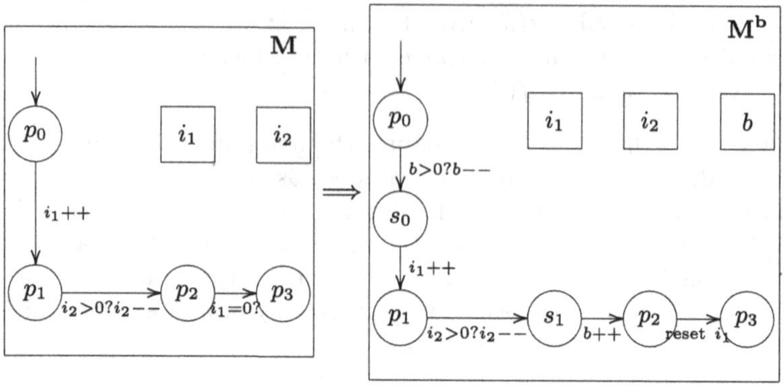

Fig. 3. The construction of M^b

If the summation of counters does not change during the run of M^b, we can conclude that every `reset` exactly simulates *zero-test*. Therefore, we have the following lemma describing the correspondence between M and M^b.

Lemma 6. *Let M be a two-counter machine, and M^b is constructed as above.*

- *If $(p,(i_1,i_2)) \overset{b}{\hookrightarrow}{}^* (q,(i'_1,i'_2))$ in M, then there exists a run $(p,(i_1,i_2,b)) \hookrightarrow^* (q,(i'_1,i'_2,b'))$ in M^b such that $i_1+i_2+b = i'_1+i'_2+b'$.*
- *If $(p,(i_1,i_2,b)) \hookrightarrow^* (q,(i'_1,i'_2,b'))$ in M^b, then $i'_1+i'_2+b' \le i_1+i_2+b$. Moreover, if $i'_1+i'_2+b' = i_1+i_2+b$, then there exists a run $(p,(i_1,i_2)) \overset{b}{\hookrightarrow}{}^* (q,(i'_1,i'_2))$ in M.*

3.2 Computing and Reversely Computing Function $f(\vec{n})$

Let f be a k-ary function on natural numbers and $\vec{n} = (n_1,...,n_k)$. We say f is *strictly monotonic* if for all $i \in [1..k]$ $n'_i > n_i$ implies $f(n_1,...,n'_i,...,n_k) > f(n_1,...,n_i,...,n_k)$.

The computation and reverse computation of $f(\vec{n})$ could not be exact if our model is not Turing complete. But fortunately, we do not need an exact value of $f(\vec{n})$ for the simulation because M^b will not increase this value. Therefore, if the value computed by M_A is no larger than $f(\vec{n})$, then after the simulation of M^b, this value will still be no larger than $f(\vec{n})$. In the third part, M_A^{-1} reversely compute $\vec{n}'$. If the computation is monotonic, it always holds that $\vec{n}' \not> \vec{n}$. We call this kind of non-exact but monotonic computation "weak computation".

Definition 7. *The model M_A* weakly computes *function f if the largest output of M_A is exactly $f(\vec{n})$ given the input $\vec{n}$.*

The model M_A^{-1} weakly reversely computes *function f if given the input b, and let S denote the set of all the outputs of M_A^{-1}. It satisfies: a) If $f(\vec{n}) = b$, then $\vec{n} \in S$; b) If $\vec{n} \in S$, then $f(\vec{n}) \le b$.*

There is still one more detail needed to be clarify: How to connect M_A with M^b and M^b with M_A^{-1}? After M_A finishes the computation, it triggers p_0 in M^b, and only when M^b is in state p_f can it trigger M_A^{-1}. So the final state of M_A connects to p_0, and p_f connects the initial state of M_A^{-1}. Note that M_A, M^b and M_A^{-1} share same counters. We conclude this section by following theorem which will be used in next two sections.

Theorem 8. *Let f be a* strictly monotonic *k-ary function, M_A weakly computes f and M_A^{-1} weakly reversely computes f. Assume M is a two-counter machine, and M^b is the simulation model of bounded M as shown in Fig. 3. Given the input of M_A is $\vec{n}$.*

- *If $(p_0, (0,0)) \overset{f(\vec{n})^*}{\hookrightarrow} (p_f, (0,0))$ in M, then the largest output of M_A^{-1} is $\vec{n}$;*
- *If M_A^{-1} can output $\vec{n}' \geq \vec{n}$, then there exists a run $(p_0, (0,0)) \overset{f(\vec{n})^*}{\hookrightarrow} (p_f, (0,0))$ in M.*

Proof. The proof is mainly by Lemma 6.

- If $(p_0, (0,0)) \overset{f(\vec{n})^*}{\hookrightarrow} (p_f, (0,0))$ in M, then there must exist
$$(p_0, (0,0,f(\vec{n}))) \hookrightarrow^* (p_f, (0,0,f(\vec{n})))$$
in M^b by Lemma 6. Since M_A weakly computes f, the largest value passed to M^b is $f(\vec{n})$. Since M_A^{-1} weakly reversely computes f, hence the largest output of M_A^{-1} is $\vec{n}$.
- If M_A^{-1} outputs $\vec{n}' \geq \vec{n}$, then firstly there exists a run in M^b such that $(p_0, (0,0,b)) \hookrightarrow^* (p_f, (i_1, i_2, b'))$ with $b' \geq f(\vec{n}') \geq f(\vec{n})$. Also by Lemma 6, $b \geq i_1 + i_2 + b' \geq f(\vec{n})$. Since M_A weakly computes f, so the only possibility is $b = i_1 + i_2 + b' = b' = f(\vec{n}') = f(\vec{n})$, i.e., $(p_0, (0,0,f(\vec{n}))) \hookrightarrow^* (p_f, (0,0,f(\vec{n})))$, which implies the run $(p_0, (0,0)) \overset{f(\vec{n})^*}{\hookrightarrow} (p_f, (0,0))$ in M. □

4 Lower Bounds for the Coverability Problem of WSPDS

In this part, we consider two subclasses of WSPDSs, i.e. vectors as states ($P = \mathbb{N}^3, |\Gamma| < \infty$), and vectors as stack symbols ($|P| < \infty, \Gamma = \mathbb{N}^3$). Both can weakly compute and reversely compute the Ackermann function which is strictly monotonic. Therefore by Theorem 8, the coverability problems of both models are Ackermann-hard.

4.1 Vectors as States

For simplicity, we define a WSPDS $M_w = \langle \mathbb{N}^2, \mathbb{N}, \Delta \rangle$ with 2-dimensional vectors as states and 1-dimensional vectors as stack symbols to weakly compute $A(m,n)$, where

$$\Delta = \begin{cases} r_1 : ((m,n),\epsilon) \to ((m,n-1),m-1) \\ r_2 : ((m,0),\epsilon) \to ((m-1,1),\epsilon) \\ r_3 : ((0,n),b) \to ((b,n+1),\epsilon) \end{cases}$$

r_1 changes state from (m,n) to $(m,n-1)$ and push $m-1$ into the stack. r_3 pops an element b from stack and turns the state $(0,n)$ to $(b,n+1)$. Note that each rule denotes a monotonic function, such as $((m,0),\epsilon) \to ((m-1,1),\epsilon)$ means for any $m',n' \geq 0$ we have transitions $((m',n'),\epsilon) \to ((m'-1,1),\epsilon)$. Here we write $(m,0)$ for readability.

Lemma 9. *Ackermann function $A(m,n)$ can be weakly computed by M_w in the sense that:*

$$A(m,n) = max\{\ b+1 \mid \langle (m,n),\epsilon\rangle \hookrightarrow^* \langle (0,b),\epsilon\rangle\}.$$

Proof. The configuration $\langle (m,n),\epsilon\rangle$ is corresponding to $A(m,n)$ defined as

- if $m=0, A(m,n)=n+1$. In M_w, $\langle (m,n),\epsilon\rangle = \langle (0,n),\epsilon\rangle, A(m,n)=n+1$.
- if $m>0, A(m,n) = \underbrace{A(m-1,A(m-1,...,A(m-1,}_{n+1}1)))$. Correspondingly in M_w, the configuration run is $\langle (m,n),\epsilon\rangle \overset{r1}{\hookrightarrow}^* \overset{r2}{\hookrightarrow} \langle (m-1,1),(m-1)^n\rangle$. By induction hypothesis, $A(m-1,1) = max\{b'+1 \mid \langle (m-1,1),\epsilon\rangle \hookrightarrow^* \langle (0,b'),\epsilon\rangle\}$. After that, the configuration is $\langle (0,b'),(m-1)^n\rangle$. Using r_3, we get $\langle (m-1,b'+1),(m-1)^{n-1}\rangle$. Then the state $(m-1,b'+1)$ is treated as (m,n) as before to compute until the configuration becomes $\langle (0,b''),(m-1)^{n-1}\rangle$. Repeat this process until the configuration is $\langle (0,b),\epsilon\rangle$.

However, because of the monotonicity, comparing with the correct transitions there may exist data loss due to some wrong transitions:

- if $m>0, n>0$,use r_2 rather than r_1, i.e. $A(m,n)$ is regarded as $A(m,0)$.
- if $m>0, n>0$,use r_3 rather than r_1, i.e. $A(m,n)$ is seen as $A(0,n)$.
- if $m>0, n=0$,use r_3 rather than r_2, i.e. $A(m,0)$ is taken as $A(0,0)$.

If no wrong transition happens, we are sure that $b+1$ is the right result. □

Construction of M_A. With a careful analysis of M_w, we can put the values in stack into states and weakly compute Ackermann function with finite stack alphabet as follows: $M_p = \langle \mathbb{N}^3, \{\bot,\lambda_0,\lambda_1\},\Delta\rangle$, where

$$\Delta = \begin{cases} r_{11}: ((0,x,y),\bot) \to ((x-1,x,y-1),\lambda_0\bot) \\ r_{12}: ((0,x,y),\lambda_1) \to ((x-1,x,y-1),\lambda_0\lambda_1) \\ r_{13}: ((0,x,y),\lambda_0) \to ((x-1,x,y-1),\lambda_1\lambda_0) \\ r_{14}: ((t,x,y),\lambda_0) \to ((t-1,x,y),\lambda_0\lambda_0) \\ r_{15}: ((t,x,y),\lambda_1) \to ((t-1,x,y),\lambda_1\lambda_1) \\ r_2: ((0,x,0),\epsilon) \to ((0,x-1,1),\epsilon) \\ r_{31}: ((0,0,y),\lambda_0) \to ((1,0,y+1),\epsilon) \\ r_{32}: ((0,0,y),\lambda_1) \to ((1,1,y+1),\epsilon) \\ r_{33}: ((t,0,y),\lambda_1) \to ((0,t-1,y),\lambda_1) \\ r_{34}: ((t,0,y),\lambda_0) \to ((t+1,0,y),\epsilon) \\ r_{35}: ((t,1,y),\lambda_1) \to ((t+1,1,y),\epsilon) \\ r_{36}: ((t,1,y),\lambda_0) \to ((0,t-1,y),\lambda_0) \\ r_{37}: ((t,0,y),\bot) \to ((0,t-1,y),\bot) \\ r_{38}: ((t,1,y),\bot) \to ((0,t-1,y),\bot) \end{cases}$$

Lemma 10. *Ackermann function $A(m,n)$ can be weakly computed by M_p in the sense that:*

$$A(m,n) = max\{\ b+1 \mid \langle(0,m,n),\bot\rangle \hookrightarrow^* \langle(0,0,b),\bot\rangle\}.$$

Proof. The transition rules in M_p have the same effects with those in M_w.

- Rules r_{11} - r_{15} simulate r_1 in M_w.
- Rule r_2 imitates r_2 in M_w.
- Rules r_{31} - r_{38} simulate r_3 in M_w.

Concretely, in rules r_{11} - r_{15}, t control the number of elements which are pushed into the stack. And the run of λ_0 or λ_1 express different numbers, which appear in the stack alternatively. Note that the number t of sequential λ_0 or λ_1 represents the natural number $t-1$. In rule r_{31}, the state $(1,0,y+1)$ stands for the top of the stack is λ_0 before pop. Similarly, in rule r_{32}, the state $(1,1,y+1)$ stands for the top of the stack is λ_1 before pop. Then rule r_{34} and rule r_{35} are used to count the number of sequential λ_0 or λ_1. Rule r_{33},rules r_{36}- r_{38} mean that $t-1$ has been b in r_3 in M_w. So the transitions in M_p is equivalent to the transitions in M_w. We obtain Lemma 10 directly from Lemma 9. □

Construction of M_A^{-1}. Conversely, if given an Ackermann value b, we construct the initial configuration $\langle(0,0,b-1),\bot\rangle$. Because $A(0,b-1)=b$. Then, if all transition rules in M_p are reversed, each time when the configuration is $\langle(0,m,n),\epsilon\rangle$, the pair (m,n) happens to be an argument pair. It will reach every possible pair (m,n) such that $A(m,n)=b$ from the smallest $m=0$ to the largest m.

We define the WSPDS associating to reverse-Ackermann function computation as $M_{p^{-1}}$.

Lemma 11. *M_p^{-1} weakly reversely computes Ackermann function.*

Since *reset* operation is monotonic, 3-dimensional WSPDS $M = \langle P = \mathbb{N}^3, |\Gamma| < \infty, \Delta\rangle$ can easily simulate M^b. By Theorem 8, we obtain one of our main results:

Theorem 12. *For WSPDSs with 3-dimensional well-quasi-ordered states but finite stack alphabet, the lower bounds of coverability problem are Ackermann-hard.*

4.2 Vectors as Stack Symbols

In this section we prove the hardness result for WSPDS $M = \langle |P| < \infty, \Gamma = \mathbb{N}^3, \Delta\rangle$: the coverability of it is Ackermann-hard. We will compute $A(m,n)$ with the model, whose size is independent of the m,n.

Construction of M_A. The idea is just liking program Ackermann function with functional programming languages. We define a 3-dimensional WSPDS $M_r = (\{\bullet\}, (\mathbb{N} \cup *) \times (\mathbb{N} \cup \{*\}) \times (\mathbb{N}), \Delta)$, where

$$\Delta = \begin{cases} r_1: (*, m, n) \to (m-1, m, n-1)(*, m, n) \\ r_2: (*, m, 0) \to (*, m-1, 1)(*, m, 0) \\ r_3: (*, 0, n) \to (*, *, n+1) \\ r_4: (r, m, n) \to (m-1, m, n-1)(r, m, n) \\ r_5: (r, 0, n) \to (*, *, n+1)(r, 0, n) \\ r_6: (r, m, 0) \to (*, m-1, 1)(r, m, 0) \\ r_7: (*, *, n)(r, m, n') \to (*, r, n) \\ r_8: (*, *, n)(*, m, n') \to (*, *, n) \end{cases}$$

Here we just remove states in transitions since there is only one state $\bullet$.

Lemma 13. *For each configuration in the run of M_r, if the stack has two elements at least, the stack must belong to one of these conditions:*

- $(*, m, n)(*, m', n')w$ *or* $(*, m, n)(r', m', n')w$*, then* $A(m, n) = A(m', n')$.
- $(r, m, n)(*, m', n')w$ *or* $(r, m, n)(r', m', n')w$*, then* $A(r, A(m, n)) = A(m', n')$.
- $(*, *, n)(*, m', n')w$ *or* $(*, *, n)(r', m', n')w$*, then* $A(m', n') = n$.

Proof. Firstly, the form of the second element from the top of the stack must be $(*, m', n')$ or (r', m', n') because of five push rules $(r_1, r_2, r_4, r_5, r_6)$.

- If the top element is $(*, m, n)$, which is from r_2, r_6 or r_7. No matter r_2 or r_6, $A(m, n) = A(m' - 1, 1) = A(m', 0) = A(m', n')$.
  Before r_7, the stack is $(*, *, n)(r, m'', n'')(*, m', n')\omega$ or $(*, *, n)(r, m'', n'')(r', m', n')\omega$(by r_1 and r_4).
  By induction hypothesis, we have $A(m'', n'') = n$ and $A(r, A(m'', n'')) = A(m', n')$. So $A(r, n) = A(m', n')$.
- If the top element is (r, m, n), which is from r_1 or r_4.
  $A(r, A(m, n)) = A(m' - 1, A(m', n' - 1)) = A(m', n')$.
- If the top element is $(*, *, n)$, which is from r_3, r_5, r_8. For r_3 and r_5, $A(0, n') = n' + 1 = n$. Before r_8, the stack is $(*, *, n)(*, m'', n'')(*, m', n')\omega$ or $(*, *, n)(*, m'', n'')(r', m', n')\omega$ (by r_2 and r_6). By induction hypothesis, we have $A(m'', n'') = A(m', n')$ and $A(m'', n'') = n$. So $A(m', n') = n$. □

Lemma 14. *Ackermann function $A(m, n)$ can be weakly computed by M_r in the sense that:*

$$A(m, n) = max\{\ b \mid \langle \bullet, (*, m, n) \rangle \hookrightarrow^* \langle \bullet, (*, *, b) \rangle \}.$$

Proof. $A(m, n)$ is computed in M_r like these conditions.

- $m = 0$: to compute $A(0, n)$ and the initial configuration of M_r is $\langle \bullet, (*, 0, n) \rangle$. By r_3 of M_r, we get the ackermann value $b = n + 1 = A(0, n)$.
- $m > 0$: to compute $A(m, n)$. From the analysis of the proof for Lemma 13, we can deduce that in the run, the final configuration must be $\langle \bullet, (*, *, b) \rangle$ after using r_8. So we can get the final ackermann value b.

Similarly to M_w in Sect. 4.1, there may exist data loss in the run because of nondeterminacy. If the stack is $(0,3,3)w$, use r_2 and get $A(2,1)$ rather than the right one $A(2,A(3,2))$. So, the result computed by M_r is $A(m,n)$ at most. □

Construction of M_A^{-1}. Different from the last case, if we just reverse the transition rules in M_r, the transition rules are not monotonic any more. So We define a new 3-dimensional WSPDS $M_{r^{-1}} = \langle\{\bullet\}, (\mathbb{N}^3 \cup \{\bot\}, \leqslant), \Delta\rangle$, where

$$\Delta = \begin{cases} r_1 : \ (1,m,1) \to (1,m+1,0) \\ r_2 : \ (1,m,n)(1,m-1,n') \to (1,m,n+1) \\ r_3 : \ (1,m,n)) \to (1,0,n-1)(1,m,n) \end{cases}$$

Here we just omit states in the transition rules since there is only one state $\bullet$. We can prove that every time we reach the bottom of the stack, we get a pair (m,n) such that $A(m,n) \leq b$.

Lemma 15. *For any value b, let S be the set of all the pairs of (m,n) that can reached from the initial configuration $\langle\bullet,(1,0,b-1)\bot\rangle$, i.e.,*

$$S = \{(m,n) \mid \langle\bullet,(1,0,b-1)\bot\rangle \hookrightarrow^* \langle\bullet,(1,m,n)\bot\rangle\}.$$

For any m,n, if $A(m,n) = b$ then $(m,n) \in S$. For any $(m,n) \in S$, $A(m,n) \leq b$.

Proof. r_1 constructs (m+1, 0) from (m, 1) since their same ackermann value. r_2, r_3 are to search whether n in (m, n) can be the ackermann value relating to the pair $(m+1,n')$. The transition rules above is mapped one-to-one from the reverse Ackermann computation rules. So each time the configuration whose form is $\langle\bullet,(1,m,n)\bot\rangle$, (m,n) must be a proper argument pair corresponding to the Ackermann value b. But our rules are monotonic, we might do wrong computation. Similar to the proof of Lemma 9, we can show that every wrong computation lead to a smaller (m,n) such that $A(m,n) < b$. And we are done. □

Corollary 16. *M_r^{-1} weakly reversely computes Ackermann function.*

Since *reset* operation is monotonic, 3-dimensional WSPDS $M = \langle |P| < \infty, \Gamma = \mathbb{N}^3, \Delta\rangle$ can simulate M^b. By Theorem 8, we obtain our another main result:

Theorem 17. *For WSPDSs with finite states but 3-dimensional well-quasi-ordered stack alphabet, the lower bounds of coverability problem are Ackermann-hard.*

5 Summary

In this paper, we prove Ackermann-hard results for the coverability problems of two subclasses of Well-Structured Pushdown Systems, by reductions from the reachability problem of Ackermann-bounded two-counter machines. Further, because of the close relation between recursive natural numbers programs and these two models, we can conclude that it is very hard to analyze recursive nonnegative integer programs.

The techniques applied in this paper heavily rely on *reset* operations. However, some interesting subclasses of WSPDS do not allow *resets*, such as pushdown VASS. For these models, Lipton's technique will be more suitable, however, we observe that Lipton's methodology works for proving f-hardness results where f is primitively recursive. We still do not know how to get higher lowerbounds for nonprimitive functions without *resets*.

Acknowledgements. This research is partially supported by NSFC project 61472238, 61261130589, and 61511140100. The authors would like to thank Prof. Mizuhito Ogawa and anonymous reviewers for their helpful comments on the earlier version of this work.

References

1. Abdulla, P.A., Čerāns, K., Jonsson, B., Tsay, Y.: Algorithmic analysis of programs with well quasi-ordered domains. Inf. Comput. **160**(1), 109–127 (2000)
2. Autebert, J., Berstel, J., Boasson, L.: Context-free languages and pushdown automata. In: Rozenberg, G., Salomaa, A. (eds.) Handbook of Formal Languages, pp. 111–174. Springer, Heidelberg (1997)
3. Bouajjani, A., Emmi, M.: Analysis of recursively parallel programs. In: Proceedings of Principles of Programming Languages, POPL 2012, pp. 203–214. ACM (2012)
4. Cai, X., Ogawa, M.: Well-Structured Pushdown Systems. In: D'Argenio, P.R., Melgratti, H. (eds.) CONCUR 2013. LNCS, vol. 8052, pp. 121–136. Springer, Heidelberg (2013). doi:10.1007/978-3-642-40184-8_10
5. Haddad, S., Schmitz, S., Schnoebelen, P.: The ordinal-recursive complexity of timed-arc Petri nets, data nets, and other enriched nets. In: Proceedings of Logic in Computer Science, LICS 2012, pp. 355–364. IEEE (2012)
6. Lazic, R.: The reachability problem for vector addition systems with a stack is not elementary. CoRR abs/1310.1767 (2013)
7. Lei, S., Cai, X., Ogawa, M.: Termination and boundedness for well-structured pushdown systems. In: Proceedings of International Symposium on Theoretical Aspects of Software Engineering, TASE 2016, pp. 22–29 (2016)
8. Leroux, J., Praveen, M., Sutre, G.: Hyper-Ackermannian bounds for pushdown vector addition systems. In: Proceedings of Joint Meeting of Computer Science Logic and Logic in Computer Science, CSL-LICS 2014, pp. 1–10 (2014)
9. Lipton, R.J.: The reachability problem requires exponential space. Technical report, Yale University (1976)
10. Minsky, M.L.: Computation: Finite and Infinite Machines. American Mathematical Monthly (1968)
11. Schnoebelen, P.: Revisiting Ackermann-hardness for lossy counter machines and reset Petri nets. In: Hliněný, P., Kučera, A. (eds.) MFCS 2010. LNCS, vol. 6281, pp. 616–628. Springer, Heidelberg (2010). doi:10.1007/978-3-642-15155-2_54

Reachability Analysis of Pushdown Systems with an Upper Stack

Adrien Pommellet[1(✉)], Marcio Diaz[1], and Tayssir Touili[2]

[1] LIPN, Université Paris-Diderot, Paris, France
pommellet@lipn.univ-paris13.fr
[2] LIPN, CNRS, Université Paris 13, Villetaneuse, France

Abstract. Pushdown systems (PDSs) are a natural model for sequential programs, but they can fail to accurately represent the way an assembly stack actually operates. Indeed, one may want to access the part of the memory that is below the current stack or base pointer, hence the need for a model that keeps track of this part of the memory. To this end, we introduce pushdown systems with an upper stack (UPDSs), an extension of PDSs where symbols popped from the stack are not destroyed but instead remain just above its top, and may be overwritten by later push rules. We prove that the sets of successors $post^*$ and predecessors pre^* of a regular set of configurations of such a system are not always regular, but that $post^*$ is context-sensitive, so that we can decide whether a single configuration is forward reachable or not. In order to underapproximate pre^* in a regular fashion, we consider a bounded-phase analysis of UPDSs, where a phase is a part of a run during which either push or pop rules are forbidden. We then present a method to overapproximate $post^*$ that relies on regular abstractions of runs of UPDSs. Finally, we show how these approximations can be used to detect stack overflows and stack pointer manipulations with malicious intent.

Keywords: Pushdown systems · Reachability analysis · Stack pointer · Finite automata

1 Introduction

Pushdown systems (PDSs) were introduced to accurately model the *call stack* of a program. A *call stack* is a stack data structure that stores information about the active procedures of a program such as return addresses, passed parameters and local variables. It is usually implemented using a *stack pointer (sp)* register that indicates the head of the stack. Thus, assuming the stack grows downwards, when data is *pushed* onto the stack, *sp* is decremented before the item is placed on the stack. For instance, in $x86$ architecture *sp* is decremented by 4 (pushing 4 bytes). When data is *popped* from the stack, *sp* is incremented. For instance, in $x86$ architecture *sp* is incremented by 4 (popping 4 bytes).

This work was partially funded by the FUI project Freenivi.

F. Drewes et al. (Eds.): LATA 2017, LNCS 10168, pp. 447–459, 2017.
DOI: 10.1007/978-3-319-53733-7_33

However, in a PDS, neither push nor pop rules are truthful to the assembly stack. During an actual pop operation on the stack, the item remains in memory and the stack pointer is increased, as shown in Figs. 1 and 2, whereas a PDS deletes the item on the top of the stack, as shown in Figs. 3 and 4.

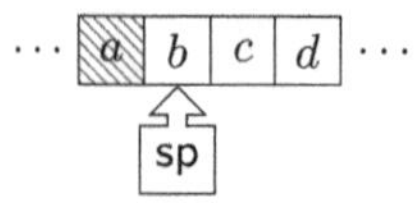

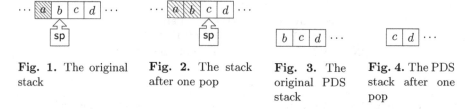

Fig. 1. The original stack

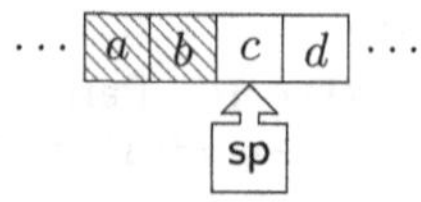

Fig. 2. The stack after one pop

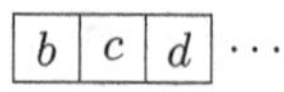

Fig. 3. The original PDS stack

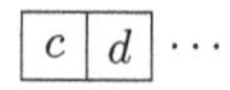

Fig. 4. The PDS stack after one pop

This subtle difference becomes important when we want to analyze programs that directly manipulate the stack pointer and use assembly code. Indeed, in most assembly languages, *sp* can be used like any other register. As an example, the instruction mov eax [sp − 4] will put the value pointed to at address sp − 4 in the register eax (one of the general registers). Since sp − 4 is an address above the stack pointer, we do not know what is being copied into the register eax, unless we have a way to record the elements that had previously been popped from the stack and not overwritten yet. Such instructions may happen in malicious assembly programs: malware writers tend to do unusual things in order to obfuscate their payload and thwart static analysis.

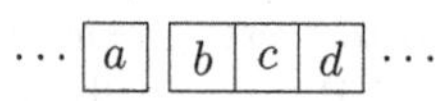

Fig. 5. The original UPDS stacks

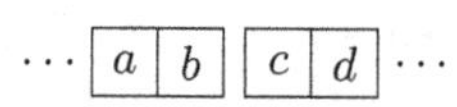

Fig. 6. The UPDS stacks after one pop

Thus, it is important to record the part of the memory that is just above the stack pointer. To this end, we extend PDSs in order to keep track of this *upper stack*: we introduce in this paper a new model called *pushdown system with an upper stack (UPDS)* that extends the semantics of PDSs. In a UPDS, when a letter is popped from the top of the stack (*lower stack* from now on), it is added to the bottom of a write-only *upper stack*, effectively simulating the decrement of the stack pointer. This is shown in Figs. 5 and 6, where after being popped, b is removed from the lower stack (on the right) and added to the upper stack (on the left) instead of being destroyed. The top of the lower stack and the bottom of the upper stack meet at the stack pointer.

Paper Outline. The first contribution of this paper is a more precise model of the stack of a program as outlined above and defined in Sect. 2.

We then investigate the sets of predecessors and successors of a regular set of regular configurations of an UPDS. Unfortunately, in Sect. 3 we prove that neither of them are regular. However, we show that the set of successors is context-sensitive. As a consequence, we can decide whether a single configuration is forward reachable or not in an UPDS.

Then, in Sect. 4, we prove that the set of predecessors of an UPDS is regular given a limit of k phases, where a phase is a part of a run during which either pop or push rules are forbidden. Bounded phase reachability is an underapproximation of the actual reachability relation on UPDSs that we can use to detect some incorrect behaviours.

In Sect. 5, we give an algorithm to compute an overapproximation of the set of successors. Overapproximation algorithms are often used while proving safety properties since a set of bad configurations not reachable in the overapproximation is not reachable in the original model either. Our idea is to first overapproximate the runs of the UPDS, then compute an overapproximation of the reachable upper stack configuration from this abstraction of runs and consider its product with the regular, accurate and computable set of lower stack configurations.

Finally, in Sect. 6, we use these approximations on programs to detect stack overflow errors and malicious attacks that rely on stack pointer manipulations.

Related Work. In [2,5,6], the *pre** and *post** of a regular set of configurations on a pushdown system are shown to be regular. UPDSs are more expressive than PDSs, since they feature both an upper stack and a lower stack, the latter being equivalent to the single stack of PDSs.

One way to improve the expressiveness of pushdown automata is to change the way transition rules interact with the stack. Ginsburg et al. introduced in [7] *stack automata* that can read the inside of their own stack using a moving stack pointer but can only modify the top. As shown in [8], stack automata are equivalent to linear bounded automata (LBA). A LBA is a non-deterministic Turing machine whose tape is bounded between two end markers that cannot be overwritten. This model cannot simulate a UPDS whose lower stack is of unbounded height.

Uezato et al. defined in [13] *pushdown systems with transductions*: in such a model, a finite transducer is applied to the whole stack after each transition. However, this model is Turing powerful unless the transducers used have a finite closure, in which case it is equivalent to a simple pushdown system. When the set of transducers has a finite closure, this class cannot be used to simulate UPDSs.

Multi-stack automata have two or more stacks that can be read and modified, but are unfortunately Turing powerful. Following the work of Qadeer et al. in [10], La Torre et al. introduced in [12] *multi-stack pushdown systems with bounded phases*: in each phase of a run, there is at most one stack that is popped from. Anil Seth later proved in [11] that the *pre** of a regular set of configurations of a multi-pushdown system with bounded phases is regular; we use this result to perform a bounded phase analysis of our model.

2-visibly pushdown automata (2-VPDA) were defined by Carotenuto et all. in [4] as a variant of two-stack automata where the stack operations are driven by the input word. Reachability is decidable for a subclass of 2-VPDA with an ordering constraint on stack operations. However, these ordered 2-VPDA cannot simulate UPDSs.

2 Pushdown Systems with an Upper Stack

Definition 1 (Pushdown system with an upper stack). *A* pushdown system with an upper stack *(UPDS) is a triplet $\mathcal{P} = (P, \Gamma, \Delta)$ where P is a finite set of control states, Γ is a finite stack alphabet, and $\Delta \subseteq P \times \Gamma \times P \times (\{\varepsilon\} \cup \Gamma \cup \Gamma^2)$ a finite set of transition rules.*

We further note $\Delta_{pop} = \Delta \cap P \times \Gamma \times P \times \{\varepsilon\}$, $\Delta_{switch} = \Delta \cap P \times \Gamma \times P \times \Gamma$, and $\Delta_{push} = \Delta \cap P \times \Gamma \times P \times \Gamma^2$. If $\delta = (p, w, p', w') \in \Delta$, we write $\delta = (p, w) \to (p', w')$. In a UPDS, a write-only *upper stack* is maintained above the stack used for computations (from then on called the *lower stack*), and modified accordingly during a transition.

For $x \in \Gamma$ and $w \in \Gamma^*$, $|w|_x$ stands for the number of times the letter x appears in the word w, and w^R for the mirror image of w. Let $\bar{\Gamma}$ be a disjoint copy (bijection) of the stack alphabet Γ. If $x \in \Gamma$ (resp. Γ^*), then its associated letter (resp. word) in $\bar{\Gamma}$ (resp. $\bar{\Gamma}^*$) is written $\bar{x}$.

A *configuration* of $\mathcal{P}$ is a triplet $\langle p, w_u, w_l \rangle$ where $p \in P$ is a control state, $w_u \in \Gamma^*$ an upper stack content, and $w_l \in \Gamma^*$ a lower stack content. A set of configurations $\mathcal{C}$ of a UPDS $\mathcal{P}$ is said to be *regular* if for all $p \in P$, there exists a finite-state automaton $\mathcal{A}_p$ on the alphabet $\bar{\Gamma} \cup \Gamma$ such that $\mathcal{L}(\mathcal{A}_p) = \{\bar{w_u} w_l \mid \langle p, w_u, w_l \rangle \in \mathcal{C}\}$, where $\mathcal{L}(\mathcal{A})$ stands for the language recognized by an automaton $\mathcal{A}$.

From the set of transition rules Δ, we can infer an *immediate successor relation* $\Rightarrow_{\mathcal{P}} = \left(\bigcup_{\delta \in \Delta} \overset{\delta}{\Rightarrow} \right)$ on configurations of $\mathcal{P}$, which is defined as follows:

Switch rules: if $\delta = (p, a) \to (p', b) \in \Delta_{switch}$, then $\forall w_u \in \Gamma^*$ and $\forall w_l \in \Gamma^*$, $\langle p, w_u, a w_l \rangle \overset{\delta}{\Rightarrow} \langle p', w_u, b w_l \rangle$. The top letter a of the lower stack is replaced by b, but the upper stack is left untouched (the stack pointer doesn't move).

Pop rules: if $\delta = (p, a) \to (p', \varepsilon) \in \Delta_{pop}$, then $\forall w_u \in \Gamma^*$ and $\forall w_l \in \Gamma^*$, $\langle p, w_u, a w_l \rangle \overset{\delta}{\Rightarrow} \langle p', w_u a, w_l \rangle$. The top letter a popped from the lower stack is added to the bottom of the upper stack (the stack pointer moves to the right).

Push rules: if $\delta = (p, a) \to (p', bc) \in \Delta_{push}$, then $\forall w_l \in \Gamma^*$, $\langle p, \varepsilon, a w_l \rangle \overset{\delta}{\Rightarrow} \langle p', \varepsilon, bc w_l \rangle$ and $\forall w_u \in \Gamma^*$, $\forall x \in \Gamma$, $\langle p, w_u x, a w_l \rangle \overset{\delta}{\Rightarrow} \langle p', w_u, bc w_l \rangle$. A new letter b is pushed on the lower stack, and a single letter is deleted from the bottom of the upper stack in order to make room for it, unless the upper stack was empty (the stack pointer moves to the left).

The *reachability* relation $\Rightarrow^*_{\mathcal{P}}$ is the reflexive and transitive closure of the immediate successor relation $\Rightarrow_{\mathcal{P}}$. If $\mathcal{C}$ is a set of configurations, we introduce its set of *successors* $post^*(\mathcal{P}, \mathcal{C}) = \{c \in P \times \Gamma^* \times \Gamma^* \mid \exists c' \in \mathcal{C}, c' \Rightarrow^*_{\mathcal{P}} c\}$ and its set of *predecessors* $pre^*(\mathcal{P}, \mathcal{C}) = \{c \in P \times \Gamma^* \times \Gamma^* \mid \exists c' \in \mathcal{C}, c \Rightarrow^*_{\mathcal{P}} c'\}$. We may omit the variable $\mathcal{P}$ when only a single UPDS is being considered.

For a set of configurations $\mathcal{C}$, let $\mathcal{C}_{low} = \{\langle p, w_l \rangle \mid \exists w_u \in \Gamma^*, \langle p, w_u, w_l \rangle \in \mathcal{C}\}$, $\mathcal{C}_{up} = \{\langle p, w_u \rangle \mid \exists w_l \in \Gamma^*, \langle p, w_u, w_l \rangle \in \mathcal{C}\}$, and $post^*_{up}(\mathcal{P}, \mathcal{C}) = (post^*(\mathcal{P}, \mathcal{C}))_{up}$. We define $post^*_{low}(\mathcal{P}, \mathcal{C})$, $pre^*_{up}(\mathcal{P}, \mathcal{C})$ and $pre^*_{low}(\mathcal{P}, \mathcal{C})$ in a similar fashion.

A *run* r of $\mathcal{P}$ from a configuration c_0 is a sequence $r = (\delta_i)_{i=1,\ldots,n} \in \Delta^*$ such that $c_0 \overset{\delta_1}{\Rightarrow} c_1 \overset{\delta_2}{\Rightarrow} c_2 \ldots \overset{\delta_n}{\Rightarrow} c_n$, where $(c_i)_{i=1,\ldots,n}$ is a sequence of configurations of $\mathcal{P}$. We then write $c_0 \overset{r}{\Rightarrow} c_n$. We say that r is a run of $\mathcal{P}$ from a set of configurations $\mathcal{C}$ if and only if $\exists c \in \mathcal{C}$ such that r is a run of $\mathcal{P}$ from c.

These definitions are related to similar concepts on simple PDSs detailed in [2,6]. A UPDS and a PDS indeed share the same definition, but the semantics of the former expand the latter's. For a set $\mathcal{C} \subseteq P \times \Gamma^*$ of lower stack configurations (the upper stack is ignored) and a UPDS $\mathcal{P}$, let $post^*_{PDS}(\mathcal{P}, \mathcal{C})$ and $pre^*_{PDS}(\mathcal{P}, \mathcal{C})$ be the set of forward and backward reachable configurations from $\mathcal{C}$ using the PDS semantics. The following lemmas hold:

Lemma 2. *For a UPDS $\mathcal{P} = (P, \Gamma, \Delta)$, r in Δ^*, and a set of configurations $\mathcal{C}$, r is a run from $\mathcal{C}$ with respect to the UPDS semantics if and only if r is a run from $\mathcal{C}_{low}$ with respect to the standard PDS semantics.*

Lemma 3. $post^*_{low}(\mathcal{P}, \mathcal{C}) = post^*_{PDS}(\mathcal{P}, \mathcal{C}_{low})$, $pre^*_{low}(\mathcal{P}, \mathcal{C}) = pre^*_{PDS}(\mathcal{P}, \mathcal{C}_{low})$.

3 Reachability Properties

As shown in [2,5,6], we know that pre^*_{PDS} and $post^*_{PDS}$ are regular for a regular set of starting configurations. We prove that these results cannot be extended to UPDSs, but that $post^*$ is still context-sensitive. This implies that reachability of a single configuration is decidable for UPDSs.

3.1 *post** Is Not Regular

The following counterexample proves that, unfortunately, $post^*(\mathcal{P}, \mathcal{C})$ is not always regular for a given regular set of configurations $\mathcal{C}$ and a UPDS $\mathcal{P}$. The intuition behind this statement is that the upper stack can be used to store symbols in a non-regular fashion. The counter-example should be carefully designed in order to prevent later push operations from overwriting these symbols.

Let $\mathcal{P} = (P, \Gamma, \Delta)$ be a UPDS with $P = \{p, p'\}$, $\Gamma = \{a, b, x, y, \bot\}$, and Δ the following set of pushdown transitions:

$$\begin{array}{llll} (S_x) & (p, x) \to (p, a) & (R_a) & (p, a) \to (p, \varepsilon) \\ (S_y) & (p, y) \to (p, b) & (R_b) & (p, b) \to (p, \varepsilon) \\ (C) & (p, a) \to (p, ab) & (E) & (p, \bot) \to (p', \bot) \end{array}$$

Let $\mathcal{C} = \{p\} \times \{\varepsilon\} \times x\,(yx)^* \bot$ be a regular set of configurations. We can compute a relevant subset L of $post^*(\mathcal{C})$:

Lemma 4. $L = \left\{\langle p', a^{n+1} b^n, \bot \rangle, n \in \mathbb{N}\right\} \subseteq post^*(\mathcal{C})$.

Then, we prove an inequality that holds for any configuration in *post**:

Lemma 5. $\forall \langle p, w_u, w_l \rangle \in post^* (\mathcal{C})$, $w = \bar{w_u} w_l$, $|w|_b + |w|_{\bar{b}} + 1 \geq |w|_a + |w|_{\bar{a}}$.

If we suppose that $post^* (\mathcal{C})$ is regular, then so is the language $L^{p'}$, where $L^{p'} = \{\bar{w_u} w_l \mid \langle p', w_u, w_l \rangle \in post^* (\mathcal{C})\}$, and by the pumping lemma, it admits a pumping length k. We want to apply the pumping lemma to an element of L in order to generate a configuration that should be in *post** but does not comply with the previous inequality.

According to Lemma 4, $L \subseteq post^* (\mathcal{C})$ and as a consequence $w = \overline{a^{k+1} b^k} \bot \in L^{p'}$. Hence, if we apply the pumping lemma to w, there exist $x, y, z \in (\Gamma \cup \bar{\Gamma})^*$ such that $w = xyz$, $|xy| \leq k$ and $xy^i z \in post^* (\mathcal{C})$, $\forall i \geq 1$. As a consequence of w's definition, $x, y \in \bar{a}^*$, $|y| \geq 1$, and $z \in (\bar{a} + \bar{b})^*$.

Hence, for i large enough, $w_i = xy^i z \in L^{p'}$ and $|w_i|_{\bar{a}} > |w_i|_{\bar{b}} + 1$. By Lemma 5, this cannot happen and therefore neither $L^{p'}$ nor $post^* (\mathcal{C})$ are regular.

It should be noted that $L^{p'}_{up}$ is not regular either. Indeed, from the definition of $\mathcal{P}$ and $\mathcal{C}$, it is clear that $\forall \langle p', w_u, w_l \rangle \in post^* (\mathcal{C}), w_l = \bot$, so $L^{p'}_{up}$ and $L^{p'}$ are in bijection. We have therefore proven the following theorem:

Theorem 6. *There exist a UPDS $\mathcal{P}$ and a regular set of configurations $\mathcal{C}$ for which neither $post^* (\mathcal{C})$ nor $post^*_{up} (\mathcal{C})$ are regular.*

3.2 *pre** Is Not Regular

We now prove that *pre** is not regular either. Let $\mathcal{P} = (P, \Gamma, \Delta)$ be a UPDS with $P = \{p\}, \Gamma = \{a, b, c\}$, and Δ the following set of pushdown transitions:

$$(C_0)\ (p, c) \rightarrow (p, ab)\ (R_a)\ (p, a) \rightarrow (p, \varepsilon)$$
$$(C_1)\ (p, c) \rightarrow (p, cb)\ (R_b)\ (p, b) \rightarrow (p, \varepsilon)$$

We define the regular set of configurations $\mathcal{C} = \{p\} \times (ab)^* \times \{c\}$ and again, compute a relevant subset of $pre^* (\mathcal{C})$:

Lemma 7. $L = \{\langle p, b^n, c^n c \rangle, n \in \mathbb{N}\} \subseteq pre^* (\mathcal{C})$.

Given the rules of $\mathcal{P}$, the following lemma is verified:

Lemma 8. *If $\langle p, b^m, c^n \rangle \Rightarrow^* \langle p, w_u, w_l \rangle$, then $|w_u|_a + |w_l|_a \leq n$.*

If $pre^* (\mathcal{C})$ is regular, then so is $L^p = \{\bar{w_u} w_l \mid \langle p, w_u, w_l \rangle \in pre^* (\mathcal{C})\}$, and by the pumping lemma, it admits a pumping length k. Moreover, by Lemma 7, $w = \bar{b}^k c^k c \in L^p$.

If we apply the pumping lemma to w, there exist $x, y, z \in (\Gamma \cup \bar{\Gamma})^*$ such that $w = xyz$, $|xy| \leq k$ and $w_i = xy^i z \in pre^* (\mathcal{C})$, $\forall i \geq 1$. As a consequence of w's definition, $x, y \in \bar{b}^*$ and $z \in \bar{b}^* c^k c$.

Since $w_i \in L^p$, $\forall i \geq 1$, there exists an integer n_i such that $w_i \Rightarrow^* c_i = (ab)^{n_i} c$. Moreover, the size of the stack must grow or remain constant during a computation, hence $|c_i| \geq |w_i|$ and $n_i \geq \frac{|w_i|-1}{2}$. Since words in the sequence $(w_i)_i$ are unbounded in length, the sequence $(n_i)_i$ must be unbounded as well. However, by Lemma 8, $n_i = |c_i|_{\bar{a}} \leq |w_i|_c = k+1$.

Hence, there is a contradiction and $pre^* (\mathcal{C})$ is not regular.

Theorem 9. *There exist a UPDS $\mathcal{P}$ and a regular set of configurations $\mathcal{C}$ for which $pre^* (\mathcal{C})$ is not regular.*

3.3 *post** Is Context-Sensitive

We prove that, if $\mathcal{C}$ is a regular set of configurations of a UPDS $\mathcal{P}$, then $post^* (\mathcal{P}, \mathcal{C})$ is context-sensitive. This implies that we can decide whether a single configuration is reachable from $\mathcal{C}$ or not.

We first show that the problem of computing $post^* (\mathcal{P}, \mathcal{C})$ can be reduced w.l.o.g. to the case where $\mathcal{C}$ contains a single configuration. To do so, we define a new UPDS $\mathcal{P}'$ by adding new states and rules to $\mathcal{P}$ such that any configuration c in $\mathcal{C}$ can be reached from a single configuration $c_\$ = \langle p_\$, \varepsilon, \$ \rangle$. Once a configuration in $\mathcal{C}$ is reached, $\mathcal{P}'$ follow the same behaviour as $\mathcal{P}$.

Theorem 10. *For each UPDS $\mathcal{P} = (P, \Gamma, \Delta)$ and each regular set of configurations $\mathcal{C}$ on $\mathcal{P}$, there exists a UPDS $\mathcal{P}' = \left(P', \Gamma \cup \bar{\Gamma} \cup \{\$\}, \Delta'\right)$, $P \subseteq P'$, and $p_\$ \in P' \setminus P$ such that $post^* (\mathcal{P}, \mathcal{C}) = post^* (\mathcal{P}', \{\langle p_\$, \varepsilon, \$ \rangle\}) \cap (P \times \Gamma^* \times \Gamma^*)$.*

We can compute a context-sensitive grammar recognizing $post^*$. Our intuition is to represent a configuration $\langle p, w_u, w_l \rangle$ of $\mathcal{P}$ by a word $\top w_u p w_l \bot$ of a grammar $\mathcal{G}$. We use Theorem 10 so that the single start symbol of $\mathcal{G}$ can be matched to a single configuration $c_\$$. The context-sensitive rules of $\mathcal{G}$ mimic the transitions of the UPDS. As an example, a rule $\delta = (p, a) \rightarrow (p', \varepsilon) \in \Delta_{pop}$ can be modelled by three rules $pa \dashrightarrow_{\mathcal{G}} p g_\delta$, $p g_\delta \dashrightarrow_{\mathcal{G}} a g_\delta$, and $a g_\delta \dashrightarrow_{\mathcal{G}} a p'$ such that $pa \dashrightarrow^*_{\mathcal{G}} a p'$, where $\dashrightarrow_{\mathcal{G}}$ stands for the one-step derivation relation and g_δ is a nonterminal symbol of $\mathcal{G}$.

Theorem 11. *Given a UPDS $\mathcal{P}$ and a regular set of configurations $\mathcal{C}$, we can compute a context-sensitive grammar $\mathcal{G}$ such that $\langle p, w_u, w_l \rangle \in post^* (\mathcal{P}, \mathcal{C})$ if and only if $\top w_u p w_l \bot \in \mathcal{L}(\mathcal{G})$*

Since the membership problem is decidable for context-sensitive grammars, the following theorem holds:

Theorem 12. *Given a UPDS $\mathcal{P}$, a regular set of configurations $\mathcal{C}$, and a configuration c of $\mathcal{P}$, we can decide whether $c \in post^* (\mathcal{P}, \mathcal{C})$ or not.*

Unfortunately, this method cannot be extended to pre^*, as the backward reachability relation does not comply with the monotony condition of context-sensitive grammars (a word can only grow or keep the same length during a computation).

4 Underapproximating *pre**

Underapproximations of reachability sets can be used to discover errors in programs: if $\mathcal{X}$ is a regular set of forbidden configurations of a UPDS $\mathcal{P}$, $\mathcal{C}$ a regular set of starting configurations, and $U \subseteq pre^* (\mathcal{X})$ a regular underapproximation, then $U \cap \mathcal{C} \neq \emptyset$ implies that a forbidden configuration can be reached from the starting set. The emptiness of the above intersection has to be decidable, hence, the need for a regular approximation.

In this section, we use results on *multi-stack pushdown automata* to define an underapproximation of pre^* for UPDSs. Multi-stack pushdown systems (MPDSs) are pushdown systems with multiple stacks where, for a given transition, in a given control state, only one stack is read and modified: a rule of the form $(p, w, n) \to (p', w')$ is applied to the n-th stack with semantics similar to those of common pushdown systems.

Multi-stack automata are unfortunately Turing powerful even with only two stacks. Thus, La Torre et al. introduced in [12] a restriction called *phase-bounding*: runs are divided into phases during which only a single stack can be popped from, and only the runs that have a number of phases lower than a chosen bound k are allowed. Let $pre^*_{\text{MPDS}} (\mathcal{M}, \mathcal{C}, k)$ be the set of backward reachable configurations from $\mathcal{C}$ using only runs with k phases. A theorem has been proven in [11]:

Theorem 13. *Given a MPDS $\mathcal{M}$ and a regular set of configurations $\mathcal{C}$, the set $pre^*_{MPDS} (\mathcal{M}, \mathcal{C}, k)$ is regular and effectively computable.*

The notion of bounded-phase computations can be extended to UPDSs. A run r of $\mathcal{P}$ is said to be *k-phased* if it is of the form: $r = r_1 \cdot r_2 \ldots r_k$ where $\forall i \in \{1, \ldots, k\}$, $r_i \in (\Delta_{Push} \cup \Delta_{Switch})^* \cup (\Delta_{Pop} \cup \Delta_{Switch})^*$. During a phase, one can either push or pop, but can't do both. Such a run has therefore at most k alternations between push and pop rules.

The *k-bounded* reachability relation $\Rightarrow^*_k$ is defined as follows: $c_0 \Rightarrow^*_k c_1$ if there exists a k-phased run r on $\mathcal{P}$ such that $c_0 \overset{r}{\Rightarrow} c_1$. Using this new reachability relation, given a set of configurations $\mathcal{C}$, we can define $pre^* (\mathcal{P}, \mathcal{C}, k)$.

We can show that a UPDS $\mathcal{P}$ can be simulated by a MPDS $\mathcal{M}$ with two stacks, the second stack of $\mathcal{M}$ being equivalent to the lower stack, and the first one, to a mirrored upper stack followed by a symbol $\perp$ that can't be popped and is used to know when the end of the stack has been reached. Elements of $P \times \Gamma^* \times \Gamma^*$ can equally be considered as configurations of $\mathcal{P}$ or $\mathcal{M}$, assuming in the latter case that we consider the mirror of the first stack and add a $\perp$ symbol to its bottom. Thus:

Lemma 14. *For a given UPDS $\mathcal{P} = (P, \Gamma, \Delta)$ and a regular set of configurations $\mathcal{C}$, there exists a MPDS $\mathcal{M}$, a regular set of configurations $\mathcal{C}'$, and $\perp \notin \Gamma$ such that $\langle p, w_u^R \perp, w_l \rangle \in pre^*_{MPDS} (\mathcal{M}, \mathcal{C}', k) \cap (P \times \Gamma^* \times \Gamma^*)$ if and only if $\langle p, w_u, w_l \rangle \in pre^* (\mathcal{P}, \mathcal{C}, k)$.*

From Theorem 13, we get:

Theorem 15. *Given a UPDS $\mathcal{P}$ and a regular set of configurations $\mathcal{C}$, the set $pre^*(\mathcal{P}, \mathcal{C}, k)$ is regular and effectively computable.*

$pre^*(\mathcal{P}, \mathcal{C}, k)$ is obviously an underapproximation of $pre^*(\mathcal{P}, \mathcal{C})$.

5 Overapproximating *post**

While underapproximations of reachability sets can be used to show that an error can occur, *overapproximations* can, on the other hand, prove that a program is safe from a particular error. If $\mathcal{X}$ is a regular set of forbidden configurations on an UPDS $\mathcal{P}$, $\mathcal{C}$ a regular set of starting configurations, and $O \supseteq post^*(\mathcal{C})$ a regular overapproximation, then $O \cap \mathcal{X} = \emptyset$ implies that no forbidden configuration can be reached from the starting set and that the program is therefore safe. The emptiness of the above intersection has to be decidable, hence, the need for a regular approximation.

5.1 A Relationship Between Runs and the Upper Stack

We prove here that from a regular set of runs of a given UPDS, a regular set of corresponding upper stacks can be computed. A subclass of programs whose UPDS model has a regular set of runs are programs with finite recursion (hence, with a stack of finite height).

Theorem 16. *For a UPDS $\mathcal{P} = (P, \Gamma, \Delta)$, a regular set of configurations $\mathcal{C}$, and a regular set of runs R of $\mathcal{P}$ from $\mathcal{C}$, the set of upper stack configurations reachable using runs in R, $\mathcal{T}(R) = \left\{ \langle p, w_u \rangle \mid \exists c \in \mathcal{C}, \exists r \in R, c \overset{r}{\Rightarrow} \langle p, w_u, w_l \rangle \right\}$, is regular and effectively computable.*

Thanks to Theorem 10, we consider the single configuration case where $\mathcal{C} = \{c_\$\}$ w.l.o.g. Let $\mathcal{A}_R = (\Delta, Q, E, I, F)$ be a finite state automaton such that $\mathcal{L}(\mathcal{A}_R) = R$. We can assume that $Q = \bigcup_{p \in P} Q_p$ where $\forall q \in Q_p$, if there is an edge $q' \xrightarrow{\delta}_E q$, then the pushdown rule δ is of the form $(p', a) \to (p, w)$. We write $F_p = Q_p \cap F$.

We introduce the finite automaton $\mathcal{A}_\mathcal{T} = (\Gamma, Q, E', I, F)$ whose set of transitions E' is defined by applying the following rules until saturation:

(S_{pop}) if there is an edge $q_0 \xrightarrow{\delta}_E q_1$ in $\mathcal{A}_R$ and δ is of the form $(p, a) \to (p', \varepsilon)$, then we add the edge $q_0 \xrightarrow{a} q_1$ to E'.

(S_{switch}) if there is an edge $q_0 \xrightarrow{\delta}_E q_1$ in $\mathcal{A}_R$ and δ is of the form $(p, a) \to (p', b)$, then we add the edge $q_0 \xrightarrow{\varepsilon} q_1$ to E'.

(S_{push}) if there is an edge $q_0 \xrightarrow{\delta}_E q_1$ in $\mathcal{A}_R$ and δ is of the form $(p, a) \to (p', bc)$, then for each state q such that either $q \in Q$ and $q \xrightarrow{x}{}^*_{E'} q_0$ for $x \in \Gamma$ or $q \in I$ and $q \xrightarrow{\varepsilon}{}^*_{E'} q_0$, we add an edge $q \xrightarrow{\varepsilon} q_1$ to E'.

Our intuition behind the above construction is to create a new automaton that follows the structure of the run automaton but accepts upper stack words instead: an upper stack word w is accepted by $\mathcal{A}_T$ with the path $q_i \xrightarrow{w}^*_{E'} q_f$, $q_i \in I$, $q_f \in F_p$, if $\mathcal{A}_R$ accepts a run r with the path $q_i \xrightarrow{r}^*_E q_f$ and r starts from $c_\$$, ends in state p and produces the upper stack word w. This property is preserved at every step of the saturation procedure.

Consider a run r and its associated upper stack word w. Suppose that r and w satisfy the property above: there is a path $q_i \xrightarrow{r}^*_E q_0$ in $\mathcal{A}_R$ and a path $q_i \xrightarrow{w}^*_{E'} q_0$ in $\mathcal{A}_T$. Let $q_0 \xrightarrow{\delta}_E q_1$ be a transition of $\mathcal{A}_R$, $q_1 \in Q$ and $\delta \in \Delta$. $r\delta$ is also a run of $\mathcal{P}$ with a labelled path $q_i \xrightarrow{r\delta}^*_E q_1$ in $\mathcal{A}_R$, and in order to satisfy the above property, a path $q_i \xrightarrow{w'}^*_{E'} q_1$ labelled by its associated upper stack word w' should exist in $\mathcal{A}_T$ as well.

We show that the saturation rules above ensure such a path exists. If $\delta \in \Delta_{pop}$, the run $r\delta$ produces an upper stack word of the form $w' = wa$, $a \in \Gamma$. Rule (S_{pop}) creates an edge $q_0 \xrightarrow{a} q_1$ to $\mathcal{A}_T$ such that there is a path $q_i \xrightarrow{w}^*_{E'} q_0 \xrightarrow{a}_{E'} q_1$ labelled by w'. Rules (S_{switch}) and (S_{push}) follow in a similar fashion.

Following this intuition, we can prove that $\mathcal{A}_T$ only accepts reachable upper stack configurations:

Lemma 17. *At any step of the saturation procedure, if $q_i \xrightarrow{w_u}^*_{E'} q'$, $q_i \in I$, $q' \in Q_p$, then there exists a run r of $\mathcal{P}$ and $w_l \in \Gamma^*$ such that $q_i \xrightarrow{r}^*_E q'$ and $c_\$ \overset{r}{\Rightarrow} \langle p, w_u, w_l \rangle$. Moreover, if $q' \in F_p$, then $r \in R$.*

On the other hand, $\mathcal{A}_T$ accepts every reachable upper stack configuration:

Lemma 18. *For every run r such that $\exists q_i \in I$, $\exists q \in Q_p$, $q_i \xrightarrow{r}^*_E q$, then there exists a path $q_i \xrightarrow{w_u}^*_{E'} q$ in $\mathcal{A}_T$ and $w_l \in \Gamma^*$ such that $c_\$ \overset{r}{\Rightarrow} \langle p, w_u, w_l \rangle$. Moreover, if $q' \in F_p$, then $\mathcal{A}_T$ accepts w_u.*

Let $\mathcal{L}_p(\mathcal{A}_T) = \left\{ w \mid \exists i \in I, \exists f \in F_p, i \xrightarrow{w}^*_{E'} f \right\}$ be the set of paths in $\mathcal{A}_T$ ending in a final node related to a state p of $\mathcal{P}$. By Lemmas 18 and 17, $\mathcal{T}(R) = \{\langle p, w_u \rangle \mid w_u \in \mathcal{L}_p(\mathcal{A}_T)\}$. Since the languages $\mathcal{L}_p$ are regular and there is a finite number of them, $\mathcal{T}(R)$ is regular as well and can be computed using $\mathcal{A}_T$.

5.2 Computing an Overapproximation

The set of runs of a UPDS $\mathcal{P} = (P, \Gamma, \Delta)$ from a regular set of configurations $\mathcal{C}$ is not always regular. By Lemma 2, runs of $\mathcal{P}$ are the same for the UPDS and PDS semantics. Thus, we can apply methods originally designed for PDSs to overapproximate runs of a UPDS in a regular fashion, such as [1,3,9].

With one of these methods, we can compute a regular overapproximation $\mathcal{R}(\mathcal{P},\mathcal{C})$ of the set of runs of $\mathcal{P}$ from $\mathcal{C}$. Using the saturation procedure underlying Theorem 16, we can then compute the set $\mathcal{T}(\mathcal{R}(\mathcal{P},\mathcal{C}))$ of upper stack configurations reachable using overapproximated runs of $\mathcal{P}$, hence, an overapproximation of the actual set of reachable upper stack configurations. However, we still lack the lower stack component of the reachability set. As shown in [6], $post^*_{\mathrm{PDS}}(\mathcal{P},\mathcal{C})$ is regular and computable, and we can determine the exact set of reachable lower stack configurations.

With $O = \{\langle p, w_u, w_t\rangle \mid \langle p, w_u\rangle \in \mathcal{T}(\mathcal{R}(\mathcal{P},\mathcal{C})), \langle p, w_t\rangle \in post^*_{\mathrm{PDS}}(\mathcal{P},\mathcal{C})\}$, we get a regular overapproximation of $post^*(\mathcal{P},\mathcal{C})$.

6 Applications

The UPDS model can be used to detect stack behaviours that cannot be found using a simple pushdown system. In this section, we present three such examples.

6.1 Stack Overflow Detection

A stack overflow is a programming malfunction occurring when the call stack pointer exceeds the stack bound. In order to analyze a program's vulnerability to stack overflow errors, we compute its representation as a UPDS $\mathcal{P} = (P, \Gamma, \Delta)$, using the control flow model outlined in [6].

Let $\mathcal{C} = P \times \top\#^m \times L$ be the set of starting configurations, where $\top \in \Gamma$ is a top stack symbol that does not appear in any rule in Δ, $\# \in \Gamma$ a filler symbol, m an integer depending on the maximal size of the stack, and L a regular language of lower stack initial words. Overwriting the top symbol would represent a stack overflow malfunction. Since there is no such thing as an upper stack in a simple pushdown automaton, we need a UPDS to detect this error.

Let $\mathcal{X} = P \times (\Gamma \setminus \{\top\})^* \times \Gamma^*$ be the set of forbidden configurations where the top stack symbol has been overwritten. If the intersection of the underapproximation $\mathcal{U}$ of $pre^*(\mathcal{X})$ with $\mathcal{C}$ is not empty, then a stack overflow does happen in the program. On the other hand, if the intersection of the overapproximation $\mathcal{O}$ of $post^*(\mathcal{C})$ with the set $\mathcal{X}$ of forbidden configurations is empty, then we are sure that a stack overflow will not happen in the program

6.2 Reading the Upper Stack

Let us consider the piece of code 1.1. In line 1, the bottom symbol of the upper stack sp − 4, just above the stack pointer, is copied into the register eax. In line 2, the content of eax is compared to a given value a. In line 3, if the two values are equal, the program jumps to an error state err.

Listing 1.1. Reading the upper stack

```
1   mov eax, [sp - 4]
2   cmp eax, a
3   je err
```

Using a simple PDS model, it is not possible to know what is being read. However, our UPDS model and the previous algorithms provide us with reasonable approximations which can be used to examine possible values stored in eax.

To check whether this program reaches the error state *err* or not, we define the regular set $\mathcal{X} = P \times \Gamma^* a \times \Gamma^*$ of forbidden configurations where a is present on the upper stack just above the stack pointer. If the intersection of the underapproximation of $pre^*(\mathcal{X})$ with the set of starting configurations $\mathcal{C}$ of the program is not empty, then eax can contain a critical value, and the program is unsafe. On the other hand, if the intersection of the overapproximation of $post^*(\mathcal{C})$ with the set $\mathcal{X}$ is empty, then the program can be considered safe.

6.3 Changing the Stack Pointer

Another malicious use of the stack pointer sp would be to change the starting point of the stack. As an example, the instruction mov sp, sp - 12 changes the stack pointer in such a manner that, from the configuration of Fig. 7, the top three elements above it now belong to the stack, as shown in Fig. 8.

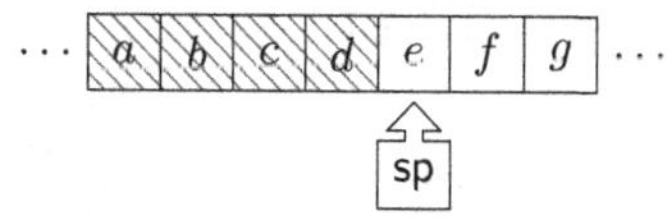

Fig. 7. Original stack

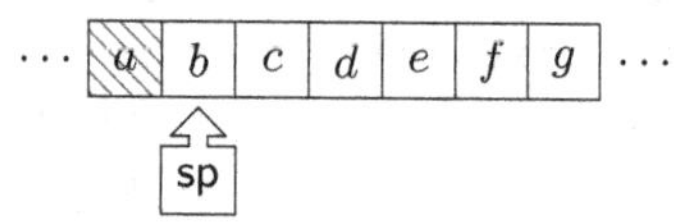

Fig. 8. After changing sp

If we model a program as a UPDS, then using our previous algorithms to compute approximations of the reachability set would allow us to have an approximation of the content of the new stack after the stack pointer change.

References

1. Bermudez, M.E., Schimpf, K.M.: Practical arbitrary lookahead LR parsing. J. Comput. Syst. Sci. **41**, 230–250 (1990)
2. Bouajjani, A., Esparza, J., Maler, O.: Reachability analysis of pushdown automata: application to model-checking. In: Mazurkiewicz, A., Winkowski, J. (eds.) CONCUR 1997. LNCS, vol. 1243, pp. 135–150. Springer, Heidelberg (1997). doi:10.1007/3-540-63141-0_10
3. Bouajjani, A., Esparza, J., Touili, T.: A generic approach to the static analysis of concurrent programs with procedures. In: POPL 2003 (2003)
4. Carotenuto, D., Murano, A., Peron, A.: 2-visibly pushdown automata. In: Harju, T., Karhumäki, J., Lepistö, A. (eds.) DLT 2007. LNCS, vol. 4588, pp. 132–144. Springer, Heidelberg (2007). doi:10.1007/978-3-540-73208-2_15
5. Caucal, D.: On the regular structure of prefix rewriting. Theor. Comput. Sci. **106**, 61–86 (1992)

6. Esparza, J., Hansel, D., Rossmanith, P., Schwoon, S.: Efficient algorithms for model checking pushdown systems. In: Emerson, E.A., Sistla, A.P. (eds.) CAV 2000. LNCS, vol. 1855, pp. 232–247. Springer, Heidelberg (2000). doi:10.1007/10722167_20
7. Ginsburg, S., Greibach, S.A., Harrison, M.A.: Stack automata and compiling. J. ACM **14**, 172–201 (1967)
8. Hopcroft, J., Ullman, J.: Sets accepted by one-way stack automata are context sensitive. Inf. Control **13**, 114–133 (1968)
9. Pereira, F.C.N., Wright, R.N.: Finite-state approximation of phrase structure grammars. In: ACL 1991 (1991)
10. Qadeer, S., Rehof, J.: Context-bounded model checking of concurrent software. In: Halbwachs, N., Zuck, L.D. (eds.) TACAS 2005. LNCS, vol. 3440, pp. 93–107. Springer, Heidelberg (2005). doi:10.1007/978-3-540-31980-1_7
11. Seth, A.: Global reachability in bounded phase multi-stack pushdown systems. In: Touili, T., Cook, B., Jackson, P. (eds.) CAV 2010. LNCS, vol. 6174, pp. 615–628. Springer, Heidelberg (2010). doi:10.1007/978-3-642-14295-6_53
12. Torre, S.L., Madhusudan, P., Parlato, G.: A robust class of context-sensitive languages. In: LICS 2007 (2007)
13. Uezato, Y., Minamide, Y.: Pushdown systems with stack manipulation. In: Hung, D., Ogawa, M. (eds.) ATVA 2013. LNCS, vol. 8172, pp. 412–426. Springer, Heidelberg (2013). doi:10.1007/978-3-319-02444-8_29

Author Index

Printed in the United States
By Bookmasters